A Federal History of the Habsburg Empire, 1815–1918

A Federal History of the Habsburg Empire, 1815–1918

JANA OSTERKAMP

OXFORD
UNIVERSITY PRESS

OXFORD
UNIVERSITY PRESS

Great Clarendon Street, Oxford, OX2 6DP,
United Kingdom

Oxford University Press is a department of the University of Oxford.
It furthers the University's objective of excellence in research, scholarship,
and education by publishing worldwide. Oxford is a registered trade mark of
Oxford University Press in the UK and in certain other countries.

The original edition appeared under the title
Jana Osterkamp: Vielfalt ordnen. Das föderale Europa der
Habsburgermonarchie (Vormärz bis 1918)

Published in the United States of America by Oxford University Press
546 Fifth Avenue, New York, NY 10036, United States of America

British Library Cataloguing in Publication Data
Data available

Library of Congress Control Number: 2026943783

ISBN 9780198943600

DOI: 10.1093/9780198943631.001.0001

Contents

Acknowledgments

Any interdisciplinary research is bound to depart from well-trodden paths. As far as my work is concerned, the route to a federal history of the Habsburg Monarchy was a circuitous one. It first led me away from law—the discipline I had trained in—to history and then once again to state and constitutional theory. My interest in the nineteenth century as a source of contemporary federal culture was encouraged by my two late academic mentors, Hasso Hofmann (Humboldt University of Berlin) and Michael Stolleis (Max Planck Institute for European Legal History, Frankfurt), who both modelled cross-disciplinary approaches themselves. I am grateful that they were able to witness the book's original publication.

The generous Emmy Noether Program of the German Research Foundation (DFG) afforded me the great freedom to conduct intensive research, teach, and write for nearly ten years. I was engaged in a lively exchange with the members of my junior research group, 'Ordering Diversity: Conceptions of Federalism in the Habsburg Monarchy and Its Successor States.' Further important impulses came from our collaboration with colleagues from Siegen in the DFG research group 'Integrating through Governing' on federalism in the German Empire. I greatly valued, moreover, the exchange in the study group 'Empires' at the Graduate School for East and Southeast European Studies at LMU Munich and the University of Regensburg.

The Feodor Lynen Program of the Alexander von Humboldt Foundation supported research at the archives in Vienna in 2014. Peer Vries, Peter Eigner, and the late Markus Cerman were my congenial hosts at the Vienna Institute for Economic and Social History. Conversations with colleagues from the University of Vienna and the Austrian Academy of Sciences were formative and have fostered academic friendships to this day. Peter Becker and the members of our research group 'The Emperor's Desk: The Imperial Cabinet Chancellery of Franz Joseph' (Vienna/Munich), jointly funded by the DFG and the Austrian Science Foundation, shared with me the rare enthusiasm for administrative history.

Further support for my endeavour to write the federal history of the Habsburg Monarchy in the long nineteenth century across disciplinary boundaries and as readably as possible came from colleagues and friends. In the early phase, these included Gerald Stourzh, Dieter Langewiesche, and Robert Luft. At their colloquia and at joint conferences, I received crucial intellectual stimuli on empires from Pieter Judson, Martin Aust, and Benjamin Schenk; on statehood from Arndt Brendecke, Ulrich Pfister, and Laurence Cole; on federations from Christoph Möllers, Dietmar Willoweit, Volker Depkat, Stefan Oeter, Christoph Schönberger, and Martin Schennach. I also thank Wolfram Siemann and Milan Hlavačka for their suggestions, as well as my Munich university colleagues Marie-Janine Calic, Christoph Neumann, and Roland Wenzlhuemer. Philipp Ther, Kerstin S. Jobst, Helmut Rumpler, Ulrike Harmat, Krisztián Csaplár-Degovics, Frank Hadler, Börries Kuzmany, Yvonne Kleinmann, and Luboš Velek also offered me, in some cases repeatedly, the opportunity to share my ideas with them.

During my research in archives and libraries, I received valuable assistance. Special thanks go to the Austrian State Archives and the Moravian Regional Archive. Georg von Hohenberg graciously permitted me to use the fascinating papers of his grandfather, the Heir to the Throne Franz Ferdinand. The collections of the Austrian National Library and the Bavarian State Library left little to be desired and what is more, enabled me to work digitally.

On my path to publication with Oxford University Press, Wolfram Siemann and Joachim Whaley supported me with their generous and selfless advice. Marion Wullschleger, Thomas Ditt, and Timm Krägenow, as well as Bianca Hoenig and Martina Niedhammer, helped greatly with making the German manuscript more accessible and less technical. During the translation's editing, Jonathan Triffith, Oliver Ranner, Lori Frey Ranner, and Isabel Frey Ribeiro took on this role to create a book of interest to non-jurists and non-historians as well. The University of Augsburg generously contributed to the editing costs. For locating the illustrations, I would like to thank once again the staff of the Austrian National Library, the Czech National Gallery, the Czech Literary Archive, as well as Rudolf Jaworski, Tobias Heinzelmann, and Herta Rohringer. My great thanks are due to Oxford University Press for accepting the book for publication and to the editors Tom Stottor and Jo Spillane for their patient and expert support.

Since the publication of the German and later the Czech edition, I have had the good fortune to continue debating and developing my ideas, arguments, and interpretations with academic friends and outstanding scholars. Within the field of Habsburg studies and Central European History, I would particularly like to thank Peter Becker, Pieter Judson, Mark Cornwall, Alison Frank Johnson, and Dominique Reill for their congenial support. I am likewise indebted to several other friends and colleagues for their advice and inspiration, including Clemens Ableidinger, Marion Averbeck-Dotter, Birgitta Bader-Zaar, John Deak, Andreas Enderlin-Mahr, Gábor Egry, Johannes Feichtinger, Mareike zum Felde, Franz Fillafer, Peter Haslinger, Andreas Gottsmann, Martin Klečacký, Günther Kronenbitter, Sevan Pearson, Joachim von Puttkamer, Oliver Jens Schmitt, Reinhard Stauber, Peter Urbanitsch, Natasha Wheatley, and Thomas Winkelbauer.

With some luck, departing from well-trodden paths opens up new routes and vistas. More difficult territories must be bridged though. For the personal encouragement without which this book would not have been written, I thank my family. Due to her untimely death, my mother Regina Lachmund did not live to see the book's publication. My Prague parents Václav Soukup and Zuzana Soukupová (who translated the book into Czech), my parents-in-law Barbara Osterkamp as well as Ernst Osterkamp and Ulrike Bosse, have been attentive interlocutors, each supporting me in their own way. My daughters Charlotte and Luise awaited the end of this seemingly never-ending book project with patience. In the meantime, they have outgrown their wish for a children's book version 'Habsburg for Everyone'. My husband Thomas Osterkamp had to bear the greatest burden of all and yet never failed in engaging me in joyful discussion and lending me encouragement, confidence, and strength. This book is dedicated to him, with love.

List of Figures

Figure 0.1 'Barke mit der Austria, Kaiser Franz Joseph I. und den Allegorien der Kronländer' [Barque with Austria, Emperor Franz Joseph I and allegories of the crown lands]. Lithograph by August Strixner. Vienna, c.1848.

Introduction

Habsburg Europe

The Habsburg Monarchy has often been called a 'Europe in miniature' because of the diversity of its peoples, languages, landscapes, denominations, and cultures. The comparison was made as early as the *Vormärz* period, the decades before the March Revolution of 1848, in a prominent German state encyclopedia.[1] Later, in 1915, shortly before the final collapse of Austria-Hungary, it is found in the writings of Hugo von Hofmannsthal who surmises that his 'fatherland' needs 'Europe more than any other country—after all, it is itself a Europe in miniature'.[2] The diversity of Europe, both in miniature and at large, needed—and still needs—an organizing political principle that can do justice to diversity. Federalism offers one such possibility. Whereas 'nation states' (based on cultural or ethnic unity of society) and 'unitary states' (based on centralized governance) seek to homogenize society and state institutions, federalism is designed to organize diversity and to integrate differences.

With its principle of unity in diversity, federalism has become a guiding idea worldwide. After two world wars, the fall of the Iron Curtain and other crises and upheavals in different regions of the world, federalism offers an alternative to the unitary state.[3] Indeed, many books on federal theories follow the same assumption, introducing federalism as a promise for the future.[4] At the same time, this political principle is subject to criticism, both old and new: federalism promotes inequality, slows down progress, and prevents unified development and rapid crisis management.

Federalism is indeed conservative: it preserves social, cultural, ethnic, religious, economic, and regional diversity as well as existing structures, traditions, and

[1] 'Lemma Oestreich'. In Carl von Rotteck and Carl Welcker (eds), *Staats-Lexikon oder Encyklopädie der Staatswissenschaften*. Vol. 12. Altona, 1841, 143.

[2] Hugo von Hofmannsthal, 'Krieg und Kultur' [1915]. In Hofmannsthal, *Gesammelte Werke in zehn Bänden: Reden und Aufsätze*. Vol. 2: *1914–1924*, ed. Bernd Schoeller. Frankfurt am Main, 1979, 417.

[3] The more recent federalized states include Somalia, Iraq, and the United Arab Emirates. In current debates, federalism plays a role for Spain, Myanmar, the Philippines, Sri Lanka, or a reunified Cyprus.

[4] The classic work is Rudolf Schlesinger, *Federalism in Central and Eastern Europe*. New York, 2001 (reprint of the 1945 edition), p. ix. Arising from the complex current debate Eva Marlene Hausteiner, 'Föderalismus als internationale politische Theorie'. In Hausteiner (ed.), *Föderalismus in Deutschland*. Baden-Baden, 2016, 11; Dietmar Willoweit, 'Einführung'. In Willoweit (ed.), *Föderalismus in Deutschland: Zur seiner wechselvollen Geschichte vom ostfränkischen Königtum bis zur Bundesrepublik*. Vienna, 2019, 17–18.

differences. At the same time, however, federalism derives its dynamism from these very differences and from a division of power over several planes of governance. How these differences are balanced, and what kind of diversity is recognized as fundamental, are part of a constant process of negotiation and underlie historical change. The political balancing of diversity cannot be determined and made permanent solely 'from above'; it also requires social recognition 'from below'. This leads to a typical federal tension between integration on the one hand and demarcation (even to the point of separation) on the other; the aim is to secure a balance in which diversity is not absorbed into unity and unity does not collapse because of diversity. The willingness of states and societies to endure this tension is based not least on the idea of federal parity, the almost utopian and rarely realized ideal of equality of regions, individuals, cultures, and communities. According to this federal ideal, diversity should not be organized arbitrarily, but on an equal footing. It is precisely against this idealistic background of a voluntary association of equal members that today's united Europe is described as a federation.

In Europe's past, however, federalism was more widespread than is often assumed. Frequently, it existed in plain sight, but under other political labels. Thanks to recent historiography and historically informed political theories which apply the idea of federalism to historical governance, drawing on our contemporary understanding of governance structures such as the European Union, we can include the concept of multi-level governance in the history of the federal.[5] This book shows how different principles of federalism were reflected in the history of the Habsburg Monarchy.

A federal history of the Habsburg Monarchy in the nineteenth century, a century often seen as the archetypal era of modernity, builds bridges between traditions of pre-modern times and the disillusioned postmodernity of today. The Italian writer and literary historian Claudio Magris contrasts the Habsburg polity with the 'modernity' of Napoleon. Since the eighteenth century, the French state had pursued a policy of complex unification. The nation-building was accompanied by granting abstract individual rights to all citizens and by a simultaneous territorialization, that is a state administration reaching out equally to every corner of the country. The Habsburg Monarchy, on the other hand, was permeated to the very end by a political culture of difference and disparity intended or at least accepted. According to Magris, the 'Danube Empire' breathes an 'Austrian

[5] For a comparative overview, see Olivier Beaud, *Théorie de la Fédération*. 2nd edn. Paris, 2009; Christoph Schönberger, 'Die Europäische Union als Bund: Zugleich ein Beitrag zur Verabschiedung des Staatenbund-Bundesstaat-Schemas', *Archiv des öffentlichen Rechts*, 129 (2004), 81–120; Stefan Oeter, '"Föderation" oder "Bund" als Oberbegriff: Erscheinungsformen des Föderalen jenseits von Bundesstaat und Staatenbund'. In Hausteiner, *Föderalismen*, 235–66; Anna Katharina Mangold, *Gemeinschaftsrecht und deutsches Recht: Die Europäisierung der deutschen Rechtsordnung in historisch-empirischer Sicht*. Tübingen, 2011. Cf. Willoweit, *Föderalismus in Deutschland*, as well as Gerold Ambrosius, Christian Henrich-Franke, and Cornelius Neutsch (eds), *Föderalismus in historisch vergleichender Perspektive*. Vol. 2: *Federal Systems: Föderale Systeme: Kaiserreich—Donaumonarchie—Europäische Union*. Baden-Baden, 2015, and vol. 6: *Integrieren durch Regieren*. Baden-Baden, 2018.

spirit, at once pre-modern and postmodern'.[6] If one disregards the Theresian-Josephinian and neo-absolutist reforms of state-building, Habsburg politics subverted the enlightened, rational-abstract ideal of a unified state in favour of a rule that was subtly differentiated by regions. Such a complex interweaving of levels of governance characterizes not only the 'pre-modern era' but also the European 'postmodern era' with its supranational order that transcends the idea of the nation state with one people and the unitary state with one administration.

This new federal history of the Habsburg Empire is told from two complementary perspectives—political *ideas* and political *practices*. The Habsburg Monarchy was one of the world's most innovative laboratories for federal concepts. Its complex, multi-layered system of governance was repeatedly rejected by contemporaries as dysfunctional and in need of reform. Manifold political reform proposals outlined a wide range of federal possibilities. Around 1848, political thinkers developed five basic federal models that would ultimately retain lasting influence to this day. The federal 'nationality state' creates new territories to all peoples, each nationality enjoys equally a territory of its own (today we speak of ethno-federalism or multinational federalism). 'Historical crown land federalism' draws on the given monarchical hereditary lands. Federal 'dualism' and 'trialism' divides the Empire into two or three large territorial blocks. The ideas of 'non-territorial autonomy' develop a federal composition, based on national or confessional communities, not territories. There is also the 'administrative' or 'executive federalism', which relies on administrative territories governed according to different principles. This concept isn't found in the sources though—it passed under different names at the time. Habsburg federal thinking experienced peaks around 1818, 1848, 1867, and 1900 as well as a final upsurge in 1918. Far from being a relic of the monarchical past, federalism remained an option for future state-building after the end of the Habsburg Monarchy.[7] Federal models were still discussed when it came to reforming the newly created states of 1918, founding new states or—as in the case of the 'Danube Federation'—creating supranational ties to bind them together.

[6] Claudio Magris, *Donau: Biographie eines Flusses*. 11th edn. Munich, 2018, 89. Cf. Steven Beller, *The Habsburg Monarchy 1815–1918*. Cambridge, 2018, 5.

[7] Cf. Schlesinger, *Federalism in Central and Eastern Europe*, p. ix; Jana Osterkamp, 'Ein Reich ohne Eigenschaften? Das Erbe föderaler Ideen in den "Nachfolgestaaten" der Habsburgermonarchie'. In Helmut Rumpler and Ulrike Harmat (eds), *Die Habsburgermonarchie 1848–1918*. Vol. 12: *Bewältigte Vergangenheit? Die nationale und internationale Historiographie zum Untergang der Habsburgermonarchie als ideelle Grundlage für die Neuordnung Europas*. Vienna, 2018, 431–57; Holly Case, 'The Strange Politics of Federative Ideas in East-Central Europe', *Journal of Modern History*, 85 (2013), 833–66; Marcela Rossová (ed.), *Integration und Desintegration in Mitteleuropa: Pläne und Realität*. Munich, 2009; Richard Georg Plaschka (ed.), *Mitteleuropa-Konzeptionen in der ersten Hälfte des 20. Jahrhunderts*. Vienna, 1995. For more recent debates, see Włodzimierz Borodziej (ed.), *Option Europa: Deutsche, polnische und ungarische Europapläne des 19. und 20. Jahrhunderts*. 3 vols. Göttingen, 2005; Hausteiner, *Föderalismus*; see also Börries Kuzmany, *A History of Non-Territorial Autonomy: Accommodating National Diversity in Modern Europe*, 1848-1939. Oxford, 2027.

This study is the first to examine the Habsburg Monarchy as a *living* federation, moving beyond the history of federal ideas and entering new academic territory. The focus is on the political practices of federal governance in the Austrian Empire. Aside from a brief interlude in 1849, federalism was not embedded in a typically 'modern' constitution with a clear-cut structure of federal and provincial competences. Bound to the terminology of the time, contemporaries would not have thought of coining Austrian governance as federal. In our contemporary understanding of federalism, however, we can best analyse the institutions and practices that emerge from the mid-nineteenth century onwards as federal. In order to make this overall history of the federal visible, this study adapts concepts of federalism theory developed for multi-level governance regimes such as the European Union. This broad conception of federation allows for a common narrative of federal ideas and the living federation of the Habsburg Monarchy—the inspiration for these very ideas in modern Europe.

0.1. Federal Iconography

For contemporaries, there was *one* federal moment in the history of the Habsburg Empire. It is illustrated by the cover picture of this book (Figure 0.1). August Strixner's 1849 lithograph 'Barque with Austria, Emperor Franz Joseph I and the Crown lands'[8] is a rare iconographic representation of Habsburg federalism. The way the picture was received later reveals a yearning for federal equality that persisted long after its publication. Fifty years after it had first appeared in print, it was reissued in the special volume *Unser Kaiser* (Our Emperor) in 1898 and made known to a wider public.[9] By this time, the political practice of federalism was far removed from the ideals of March 1849.

This graphic depicts the fluidity between federation, empire, and nation state, which will be central to my federal history of the Habsburg Monarchy. On the one hand, it shows the Habsburg Monarchy as a monarchical *federation*. The crowned Emperor Franz Joseph I and the personification of 'Austria' sit in the same barque (a class of sailing ship) with seventeen young women representing the crown lands. In this symbolic 'ship of state',[10] all passengers are placed on an equal footing, including the female figure of 'Hungary'. This equality amongst the *Länder* refers to the short-lived March Constitution of

[8] It originates from a drawing by the historical painter Joseph Hasslwander; both artists belonged to a liberal circle. Selma Krasa-Florian, *Allegorie der Austria: Die Entstehung des Gesamtstaatsgedankens in der österreichisch-ungarischen Monarchie und die bildende Kunst*. Vienna, 2007, 78; Werner Telesko, *Geschichtsraum Österreich: Die Habsburger und ihre Geschichte in der bildenden Kunst des 19. Jahrhunderts*. Vienna, 2006, 216.

[9] Carl Klopfer (ed.), *Unser Kaiser: Ein Gedenkbuch der fünfzigjährigen Regierung, zugleich ein Lebens- u. Characterbild Kaiser Franz Josef I*. Vienna, 1898.

[10] Krasa-Florian, *Allegorie der Austria*, 53.

1849, which was the first (and last) attempt to federalize the relationship between the whole *Reich* and the *Länder*, including the Hungarian lands, and guarantee them freedom, independence, and inviolability. By 1850, this constitution was overthrown by the restorative policies of neo-absolutism. In 1898, when the lithograph was reissued, the constitutional situation had changed once again. After the Compromise Acts of 1867 and the dualistic division of the Habsburg Monarchy, Hungary, Croatia-Slavonia, and Transylvania travelled no longer in the same class as the other crown lands. The parity symbolized in the lithograph thus now refers only to the crown lands of the Austrian part of the empire, whose legal equality went back to the unified *Landesordnungen* (provincial ordinances) of 1861.

The graphic provides not only a pictorial programme of the Habsburg federation, but also testifies to Austria's self-image as an *empire*. The male figure, the emperor, is depicted as a Roman Augustus, outfitted with a cloak and sceptre, and crowned with a laurel wreath. These attributes allude to the Habsburgs' past dignity as emperors of the Holy Roman Empire, but also to their present and future claim to imperial rule.[11] The stylized figure represents the young Franz Joseph I, as is indicated by a banner draped over the tree of life in the centre of the vessel bearing a double-headed eagle and his motto *Viribus Unitis* (With United Forces). Closer inspection reveals an imperial hierarchy among the female figures representing the crown lands. One group forms an outwardly closed circle facing the emperor. This proximity to the emperor did not reflect the federal programme of crown land equality, but rather the asymmetrical reality of the empire: the Austrian and Bohemian crown lands, which formed the economic, political, and social core of the Habsburg Monarchy, were part of this elite circle. It was no coincidence that Dalmatia and Serbian Vojvodina were left out and positioned at the bow of the ship.

The iconography of the 'Barque with Austria' also presents the Habsburg Monarchy as a *state*. The barque is steered by a female personification of 'Austria'. She looks down at the 'Constitution' lying in her lap, she determines the direction of travel, and she is protected from toppling overboard by a railing with the inscription of 'Ministry'. The lithograph thus sets the scene for a constitutional understanding of governance: the state, symbolized by the ship, protects its inhabitants against dangers from outside and grants constitutional rights inside. This pictorial symbolism of the 'ship of state', in which the monarch and the crown lands are united, thus alludes to a widespread 'master narrative' of constitutional law at the time, the idea of the Austrian *Gesamtstaat* (comprehensive state). According to this idea, the Austrian Empire was an indivisible dominion that had developed over the centuries from the core dynastic lands of the Habsburgs into a

[11] Telesko, *Geschichtsraum Österreich*, 217.

unified administrative state.[12] As we shall see in this study, the depiction in the 1849 lithograph 'Barque with Austria' never corresponded to the political reality of the Habsburg Monarchy.

0.2. Conceptual Approaches: Federation, Empire, Nation State

Anyone seeking to apply a new concept to the history of the Habsburg Monarchy is confronted with the verdict of contemporaries that the empire was unique in its complexity, could not be reduced to general principles, and was a 'land of improbabilities, intangibilities and absurdities' that remained 'incomprehensible to any non-Austrian.'[13] As a protagonist of 'Viennese Modernism', the poet Hugo von Hofmannsthal felt an abiding discomfort with general concepts. In 1902, he published an autobiographically tinged piece of prose known as the 'Chandos letter'. Here, the lyrical self laments its inability to describe reality: 'The abstract words, which the tongue must naturally use to express any kind of judgement, fell apart in my mouth like mouldy mushrooms.... Everything fell into pieces, the pieces into pieces again, and nothing could be grasped as a concept.'[14] It is no historical accident that Hofmannsthal identified this conceptual fatigue with politics. In his eyes, it was, among other things, 'the affairs of the court, the events in parliament', that could no longer be summed up in a single term. With his essay, Hofmannsthal anticipated the end of the 'grand narratives' that Jean-François Lyotard would call for many decades later.[15] In historiography, scepticism about unambiguous concepts also led to doubts about older 'master narratives' that attempted to capture the diversity of rule and society in the Habsburg Monarchy in a *single* concept.

Federalism, which is used here as a new perspective for our historical understanding of the Habsburg Monarchy, is not an attempt to create an entirely new master narrative. It is simply one guiding historical idea among others. Federal categories clarify certain historical phenomena of territorial governance, institutional interdependence, political interaction, and social participation. In many cases, the federal approach makes them visible for the first time. A federal history of the monarchy does not negate previous histories of empire statehood.[16] On the

[12] Martin Schennach, 'Die "österreichische Gesamtstaatsidee": Das Verhältnis zwischen "Gesamtstaat" und Ländern als Gegenstand rechtshistorischer Forschung'. In Schennach (ed.), *Rechtshistorische Aspekte des Österreichischen Föderalismus: Beiträge zur Tagung an der Universität Innsbruck am 28. und 29. November 2013*. Vienna, 2015, 1–29.

[13] On the much-cited 'land of improbabilities', see Ferdinand Kürnberger, *Siegelringe: Eine ausgewählte Sammlung politischer und kirchlicher Feuilletons*. Hamburg, 1874, 219. On the 'legal' uniqueness Schennach, 'Österreichische Gesamtstaatsidee', 1–3.

[14] Hugo von Hofmannsthal, 'Brief des Lord Chandos an Francis Bacon (1902)'. <https://www.projekt-gutenberg.org/hofmanns/prosa/chandos.html>

[15] Jean François Lyotard, *Das postmoderne Wissen: Ein Bericht*. Vienna, 1999.

[16] On the imperial history-inspired New Habsburg Studies, see Pieter M. Judson, *The Habsburg Empire: A New History*. Cambridge, MA, and London, 2016. On the history of state and statehood

contrary, it complements them by offering a third, hitherto unjustly neglected perspective: the Habsburg Monarchy oscillated between empire, federation, and state. This interweaving of three different concepts calls for a clarification.

The Concept of Federation

While the history of federal ideas is well researched, a history of the Habsburg Monarchy as a *living* federation requires new methods and bridges to be built between disciplines. Two trends have emerged in the study of Habsburg federalism. One group of authors is interested in the history of federal *ideas* and comes from fields like political history, political science, and sociology.[17] Their research will be systematically processed into our typology of 'Habsburg' federal thought. Regarding the history of 'living' governance, other authors, especially experts on state law and constitutional historians, are often anxious to show that the political reality of the Habsburg Monarchy could *not* be encompassed by federal concepts. Instead, they prefer terms such as 'composite state', 'decentralised unitary state', or 'composite monarchy'.[18] The reason for this frequent scepticism towards the federal concept lies in an outdated understanding of federation and statehood, which we should not adopt uncritically.

This conceptualization of federalism as power relation is rooted in a political theory focused primarily on statehood and sovereignty. Its subjects are the historical constitutions of the United States of America after 1787, the Swiss Confederation of 1848, and the German Empire after 1871.[19] Insofar as politicians, constitutional scholars, and historians of constitutionalism deal with the

John Deak, *Forging a Multinational State: State Making in Imperial Austria from the Enlightenment to the First World War*. Stanford, CA, 2015. Peter Becker, 'Der Staat: Eine österreichische Geschichte?', *Mitteilungen des Instituts für Österreichische Geschichtsforschung* (hereafter *MIÖG*), 126 (2018), 317–40. On the afterlive of the plurality of Habsburg statehood Natasha Wheatley, *The Life and Death of States: Central Europe and the Transformation of Modern Sovereignty*. Princeton, 2023.

[17] There are just a few historical works. Classics include Robert A. Kann, *Das Nationalitätenproblem der Habsburgermonarchie: Geschichte und Ideengehalt der nationalen Bestrebungen vom Vormärz bis zur Auflösung des Reichs im Jahre 1918*. Vol. 2: *Ideen und Pläne zur Reichsreform*. 2nd edn. Graz and Cologne, 1964; Rudolf Wierer, *Der Föderalismus in Donauraum*. Graz, 1960; Schlesinger, *Federalism in Central and Eastern Europe*; Joachim Kühl, *Föderationspläne im Donauraum und in Ostmitteleuropa*. Munich, 1958. Alina Teslaru-Born, *Ideen und Projekte zur Föderalisierung des Habsburgischen Reiches mit besonderer Berücksichtigung Siebenbürgens 1848–1918*. University dissertation, Frankfurt am Main, 2006 relies heavily on the previously mentioned works. Holly Case focuses on the interwar period and the link between federalism and nationalism, Case, 'Strange Politics'.

[18] Cf. Wilhelm Brauneder, 'Die Habsburgermonarchie als zusammengesetzter Staat'. In Hans-Jürgen Becker (ed.), *Zusammengesetzte Staatlichkeit in der europäischen Verfassungsgeschichte: Tagung der Vereinigung für Verfassungsgeschichte in Hofgeismar vom 19.3.–21.3.2001*. Berlin, 2006, 197–236; John H. Elliott, 'A Europe of Composite Monarchies', *Past and Present*, 137 (1992), 48–71. On the contemporary debate, Chapters 7 and 8.

[19] Cf. Reinhart Koselleck, 'Bund (Bündnis, Föderalismus, Bundestaat)'. In Otto Brunner et al. (eds), *Geschichtliche Grundbegriffe*. Subvol. 1: *Historisches Lexikon zur politisch-sozialen Sprache in Deutschland*. Stuttgart, 2004, 582–671.

legal structures and political practices of the Habsburg Monarchy, they apply the dichotomy of *Staatenbund* (confederation) on the one hand and *Bundesstaat* (federation, federal state) on the other. Since the Monarchy did not fit this dichotomy, they claim the Habsburg Monarchy cannot be characterized as federal at all.[20]

A *confederation* is considered to be an association of sovereign states that have joined together for a specific purpose, such as a common defence. Legally, such an arrangement can be terminated at any time. Joint decisions are taken unanimously, and the citizens of the member states are not subject to any common legislation of the confederation.

In a *federation,* the constituent states are not considered to be sovereign. They cede their final decision-making rights to the highest level on a permanent basis. A federation also has a vertical division of powers. Administration, legislation, and jurisdiction are found at both the federal level and at the level of the member states. A bicameral parliament is typical, consisting of a House of States or *Länderkammer* (representing the constituent states) and a *Volkshaus* (representing the people). Federations pursue common external objectives, such as common defence, foreign affairs, and economic policy, as well as internal objectives such as welfare policy.

Reinhard Koselleck rightly observes that 'the terms "federation" and "confederation" remain in constant need of definition, without a unanimous opinion having ever been reached. Behind the legal positions, political forces and constellations become apparent.'[21] Koselleck is alluding to the conflict between liberal and conservative legal theorists of the German Empire after 1871. Those who used the term 'federation' in theory wanted to achieve greater unity in the political practice of Germany. Those who instead spoke of a 'confederation' wished to strengthen the diversity, but also the particularism, of the member states. For the Habsburg Monarchy, these legal terms, which date from the time of the 'modern' state, are deficient. The use of 'confederation' or 'federation' goes back to the imaginary world of German classical state theory in the late nineteenth century. Both concepts presuppose the ideal of a constitutionally anchored sovereignty and a clear division of powers. This ideal barely applied to the reality of the two-tiered federation of *Reich* and *Länder* in the German Empire. For the 'pre- and postmodern' conglomerate of the Habsburg Monarchy after 1867, which comprised (at least) three levels of governance—the empire as a whole, the imperial parts of Austria and Hungary, and the crown lands—it proved all the more unsuitable.

A history of the Habsburg Monarchy written today has to analyse the terminology of the nineteenth century, but it cannot stop there. It can and must go

[20] Cf. Chapter 7. [21] Koselleck, 'Bund', 649.

beyond the views of the time, especially when other approaches prove to be more appropriate. The international theory of federalism underwent a fundamental shift in the twentieth century. New concepts followed the advent of multi-level systems of governance such as the European Union. Legal and political scientists now abandon sovereignty and statehood as the distinguishing features between 'confederation' and 'federation'. Complex constructions of governance are studied as a federal order, even if they are not necessarily sovereign states. The federalism theorist Olivier Beaud succinctly encourages us to 'sortir la fédération de l'orbite de l'état' (remove the federation from the orbit of the state) and 'oublier la souveraineté pour penser le fédéralisme' (put sovereignty aside to consider federalism).[22] German federalism theorists such as Christoph Schönberger, Stefan Oeter, Katharina Mangold, and Eva Hausteiner propose *Bund* (union) as a new term, which is however synonymous with federation.[23] Such new concepts of 'federation' in political theory fit the 'concurrently pre-modern and postmodern' Habsburg Empire much better than a 'modern' nineteenth-century theory of state and federalism, which is inclined to the ideal of nation state and constitutional sovereignty.

In the following, federalism will be understood as a condition for solidarity. Federalism characterizes 'what unites, not what divides', for federations are 'not orders of hierarchy, but orders of coordination'.[24] From a socio-historical point of view, federations open spaces of different loyalties.[25] In the Habsburg Monarchy, political loyalties aligned with larger imperial units such as Austria or Hungary, the crown lands, and linguistic and religious communities. However, for most people belonging to the entire monarchy was inconceivable without reference to the person of the emperor. This lack of emotional and institutional bonds in the society as a whole is typical of empires.[26] To show the difference, but also the fluidity between federations and empires, my study will repeatedly refer to the concept of empire.[27]

22 Beaud, *Théorie de la Fédération*, 37 and 58.

23 Schönberger, 'Die Europäische Union als Bund'; Beaud, *Théorie de la Fédération*; Oeter, '"Föderation" oder "Bund"'; Hausteiner, *Föderalismus*; Mangold, *Gemeinschaftsrecht und deutsches Recht*. On the Habsburg idea of Europe, see Moritz Csáky, *Das Gedächtnis Zentraleuropas: Kulturelle und literarische Projektionen auf eine Region*. Vienna, 2019.

24 Arthur Benz, 'Demokratisches Regieren im Föderalismus: Neue Literatur zu einem alten Thema', *Neue Politische Literatur*, 64 (2019), 517; Schönberger, 'Die Europäische Union als Bund', 98.

25 Dieter Langewiesche, 'Historische Reflexionen zum Föderalismus in Deutschland: Wandel und Kontinuität seit dem 19. Jahrhundert'. In Ines Härtel (ed.), *Handbuch des Föderalismus*, vol. 1: *Grundlagen des Föderalismus und der deutsche Bundesstaat*. Berlin, 2012, 135.

26 Jürgen Osterhammel, *The Transformation of the World: A Global History of the Nineteenth Century*. Princeton, 2014.

27 On the fluid transitions, see only Stefan Berger and Alexey Miller, *Nationalizing Empires*. Budapest, 2015; Jörg Leonhard and Ulrike von Hirschhausen, *Empires and Nation States in the 19th Century*. Göttingen, 2009; Ann Laura Stoler, 'Imperial Formations and the Opacities of Rule'. In Craig Calhoun, Frederick Cooper, and Kevin W. Moore (eds), *Lessons of Empire: Imperial Histories and American Power*. New York, 2006, 48–60. For conceptual history, see also Franz Bosbach, and

The Concept of Empire

Throughout Habsburg history, imperial cultures, policies, and legal frameworks of difference endured. The monarchy's multi-ethnic and multi-religious diversity was subject to imperial hegemony, violence, and asymmetrical centre–periphery relations. As the picture 'Barque with Austria' shows, the Austrian and Bohemian provinces are distinguished as belonging to an 'inner circle' around the emperor and thus highlighted as imperial cores over distant peripheries. In the living political reality, further imperial distinctions emerged. Some peoples, such as Germans and Magyars, enjoyed advantages over others. Catholicism benefited from a de facto privilege by comparison to other religions. Social groups, such as the nobility and the upper middle classes, enjoyed privilege over other classes.

In recent Habsburg scholarship, the concept of empire has become a popular field of research.[28] Recent studies, often with a culturalist approach, go beyond the story of imperialism and its emphases on hegemonic greatness, territorial expansion, and the use of force both at home and abroad. The traditionalist history of empires and imperialism treats the Habsburg Monarchy of the nineteenth century as marginal after the loss of its hegemonic position in the German Confederation, its defeat in wars, and its forfeiture of territories in Italy.[29] Nevertheless, the imperial mindset of the Habsburg elites continued to play an important role up to its end. In the Balkans, Bosnia was partly seen as a 'colony' and a merchant fleet expanded as part of an 'informal empire'.[30] According to the self-image of the Habsburg elites, the monarchy was an almost classical empire.

The culturalist 'new history of empire' builds on this traditionalist picture of power and hegemony but simultaneously expands its aperture. The capacity of imperial rule to sustain and maintain social diversity is emphasized.[31] Therefore, these historians no longer consider the decline of empires as inevitable, caused by the emerging idea of the nation state in the eighteenth century. Their key categories are multi-ethnicity, a pluralism of religions, and a culture of fine distinctions.[32]

Hermann Hiery, 'Einleitung'. In Bosbach and Hermann (eds), *Imperium/Empire/Reich: Ein Konzept politischer Herrschaft im deutsch-britischen Vergleich*. Munich, 1999, 11–16.

[28] In more detail Jana Osterkamp, 'Kooperatives Imperium: Eine neue Perspektive auf Anspruch und Wirklichkeit imperialer Herrschaft'. In Osterkamp (ed.), *Kooperatives Imperium: Politische Zusammenarbeit in der späten Habsburgermonarchie*. Göttingen, 2018, 1–21.

[29] Judson, *Habsburg Empire*, 10.

[30] Alison Frank, 'Continental and Maritime Empires in an Age of Global Commerce', *East European Politics and Societies*, 25/4 (2011), 779–84.

[31] Gary B. Cohen, 'Neither Absolutism nor Anarchy: New Narratives on Society and Government in Late Imperial Austria', *Austrian History Yearbook*, 29 (1998), 37–61.

[32] See Kathleen Wilson, 'Introduction: Histories, Empires, Modernities'. In Wilson (ed.), *A New Imperial History: Culture, Identity, and Modernity in Britain and the Empire 1660–1840*. Cambridge and New York, 2004, 1–26; Ulrike von Hirschhausen and Jörn Leonhard, 'Zwischen Historisierung

The Habsburg Monarchy, with its diversity of peoples, languages, and religions, is an ideal object of study in this respect. 'Empire' was thus not only a topos of contemporary self-description but once again becomes a category of historical analysis for the Habsburg Monarchy.[33]

Nonetheless, many attributes of empire also apply to non-imperial states. Striving for great power and size, multi-ethnicity and a pluralism of religions, cultures of fine distinctions, and asymmetries of centres, peripheries, and colonies can also be found in huge nation states. This is a major criticism of the concept of empire. There is, however, one distinguishing feature that will be important for the argument of this book. An empire typically concentrates, controls, and separates political communication and cooperation. Jürgen Osterhammel has characterized this practice of governance as 'radial rule'.[34] A federation is essentially based on political cooperation.[35]

This history of political cooperation shows the extent to which imperial and federal aspects were intertwined. In the Habsburg Monarchy, numerous institutions—the pre-1848 provincial estates or, later, the provincial diets, associations, political parties, chambers of commerce and trade, as well as regional road-building authorities—were legally prohibited to exchange any political ideas with each other. At the end of the nineteenth century, this ban on cooperation within a framework of 'radial' rule was undermined in a federal sense. The ruling elites of the state, the crown lands, and the society cooperated to answer the challenges of 'modernity'. Political cooperation had to be informal, but increasingly took place with 'top-down' approval. This study therefore applies the category of 'cooperative empire' to the Habsburg Monarchy.[36]

The Concept of the State

A history of federal ideas and governance is incomplete without a history of statehood. The political reality of European federations was conceptualized at the time in terms of the modern idea of the state. Legal experts perceived the state as the collective unity of a territory, its sovereign governance, and its people. Political thinkers referred to these 'ideas of the state' when formulating ideas of federal reform. The 'state', moreover, serves as a critical yardstick for analysing the

und Globalisierung: Titel, Themen und Trends der neueren Empire-Forschung', *Neue Politische Literatur*, 56 (2011), 389–404.

[33] Prominently Judson, *Habsburg Empire*.

[34] Osterhammel, *Transformation of the World*, 555. Alexander Motyl speaks of the 'wagon wheel with spokes without rims'. Motyl, *Imperial Ends: The Decay, Collapse and Revival of Empires*. New York, 2001, 16.

[35] Benz, 'Demokratisches Regieren', here 517.

[36] Jana Osterkamp, 'Cooperative Empires: Provincial Initiatives in Imperial Austria', *Austrian History Yearbook*, 47 (2016), 128–46.

federal relation of the Habsburg and Hohenzollern monarchies, and of the German Confederation. Back then, this complex co-dependence and independence of governance was regarded as anachronistic.

But a federal history of the Habsburg Monarchy cannot deal with 'the state' in the abstract. It is true that 'the state' is a common research framework for historians of the nineteenth century as a period of rapid political change. The 'functions of the state' increased at the expense of the social sphere. The 'public' and the 'private' became more distinct. The manorial system and other noble and clerical privileges were replaced by the idea of a (propertied) 'civic society'. 'State activity' reached previously unimaginable dimensions in fields like infrastructure development, the economy, education, and welfare, and swallowed up vast sums of public money. A federal history is concerned with how this 'state' was divided across various levels, institutions, and actors.

I therefore embrace research that contextualizes *legal* concepts of the state and understands them in terms of their *historical* manifestations.[37] Like the terms 'confederation' and 'federation', the holistic concept of the state as commonly used today is a product of nineteenth-century state theory. Going back to Georg Jellinek and Max Weber, it is characterized by the triad *one* rule, *one* territory, and *one* people; in the parlance of the time, the state had advanced to become a 'legal person' capable of legal action.[38] Historians of the early modern period in particular, however, have warned against the pitfalls of a 'Weberian trap'. The Weberian or 'Jellinek' trap also exists for historians of the nineteenth century. We will not apply normative categories of an ideal modern state to the history of statehood.[39] Whereas the normative legal concept of the state developed in the nineteenth century was conceived for a future unitary state, usually a nation state, it does not respond to the reality of empires at the time.[40]

Moreover, from the perspective of the history of federalism, the classical concept of the state is too narrow to explain which territories and spaces contemporaries considered to be 'states' and thus form potential parts of the Habsburg federation. Within the Habsburg crown lands, for example, key features of the separation of powers were not fully developed until the very end. There were provincial diets and a rudimentary provincial administration, but no provincial governments, ministries, or courts. Nevertheless, crown lands such as Bohemia, Tyrol, or Croatia were described and perceived as states on the basis of their

[37] On the etatism of German historians Gabriele Metzler, *Der Staat der Historiker: Staatsvorstellungen deutscher Historiker seit 1945*. Berlin 2018.

[38] On the concept of the legal person, Michael Stolleis, *Geschichte des öffentlichen Rechts in Deutschland*. Vol. 2: *Staatsrechtslehre und Verwaltungswissenschaft 1800–1914*. Munich, 1992, 368–70.

[39] André Holenstein, 'Introduction: Empowering Interactions. Looking at Statebuilding from Below'. In Wim Blockmans, André Holenstein, and Jon Mathieu (eds), *Empowering Interactions: Political Cultures and the Emergence of the State in Europe 1300–1900*. Farnham, 2009, 7.

[40] On the state as a legal master narrative, Becker, 'Staat', 317–18. On Jellinek Jens Kersten, *Georg Jellinek und die klassische Staatslehre*. Tübingen, 2000.

'historic state law'. For the history of federal ideas, it is therefore important to illustrate the whole spectrum of concepts of the state insofar as they played a role in the respective federal concepts.

According to the broad understanding of federalism adopted here, the constituent parts of a federation do not necessarily have to be states. This understanding follows the recent history of the state, which modifies the *concept* of the state. Patrick Joyce is a prominent representative of this trend. He criticizes historians for reifying 'the state' and conceiving of it as a substantial entity, a kind of transpersonal subject or agent capable of action.[41] By contrast, Joyce and others describe the history of statehood as the history of a multiplicity of human, institutional, and material components, networks, interactions, and communications that are, or can be, attributed to the state.[42] These views represent a historiography of the state 'from below'. They have not gone unchallenged. The German historian Wolfgang Reinhard writes in a polemic titled 'No Statebuilding from Below' that the formation of statehood is, by definition, a 'top-down process' based on the interests of the ruling elites and the needs of the society.[43]

The perspective proposed here mediates between these two views. Ideas of the state and state formation are examined in their interactions 'from above' and 'from below'.[44] For the history of federal ideas, as well as of the living federal reality, this book will ask how the attributes and tasks of 'the state' were distributed across the different levels of governance, both in theoretical discussions and in practice. For this purpose, 'the state' is broken down into fields of 'state activity'. For the interpretation of the Compromise of 1867 as the federal basis of the relationship between the empire (Austria-Hungary) and its components (Austria and Hungary), for example, the concept of the state thus appears, on the one hand, as a contemporary category of state theory and, on the other, as a contemporary category of analysis for various policy fields. The 'state' as an analytical concept will also become important in determining the federal character of the Austrian crown lands. This study shows that the crown lands acted like states in the central policy areas of welfare, education, infrastructure building, and finance, even if they weren't classified as states in legal terms.

[41] Patrick Joyce, *The State of Freedom: A Social History of the British State since 1800*. Cambridge, 2013, 1.

[42] Joyce, *State of Freedom*, 15–17; Stefan Nellen and Thomas Stockinger, 'Staat, Verwaltung und Raum im langen 19. Jahrhundert: Introduction', *Administory*, 2/1 (2017), 5.

[43] Wolfgang Reinhard, 'No Statebuilding from Below! A Critical Commentary'. In Blockmans et al., *Empowering Interactions*, 299–304. See also the reply by Jon Mathieu, 'Statebuilding from Below: Towards a Balanced View'. In Blockmans et al., *Empowering Interactions*, 305–11.

[44] On the history of long-term processes of state transition instead of a teleology of politics or state Barbara Stollberg-Rilinger, 'The Impact of Communication Theory on the Analysis of the Early Modern Statebuilding Processes'. In Blockmans et al., *Empowering Interactions*, 317.

0.3. Thematic Horizons

The federal history of the Habsburg Monarchy is narrated in twelve chapters combining thematic and chronological approaches. It begins with the collapse of the Habsburg Monarchy in October 1918. The first chapter scrutinizes the federal thinking of the highest government circles in 1917/1918. The second chapter takes the reader back a hundred years. The pre-March period between 1817 and 1848 lacked an important pre-condition for federalism, namely the territoriality of the federal units. However, this pre-modern diversity of Habsburg governance, which was exceptional even for the Europe of the time, became an important condition for federalism. From 1817 to 1867, the federal idea took off, with four types of federalism: executive federalism, the federal nationality state, crown land federalism, and dualism or trialism. Each type of federalism is examined in its own context and in a separate chapter.

The executive federalism proposed by Klemens Metternich reorganized the empire for the purposes of defence, security, and effective control. In the neo-absolutist era, the executive federalism then practised served to bring statehood down to the local level within a very short time, albeit with great regional disparities (Chapter 3). In contrast, the idea of the federal nationality state, which was prominent in the March Revolution of 1848, adapted the modern idea of nationhood. The mobilizing effect of 'nation' and the fluidity of this concept are illustrated by the blueprints for multinational federalism drawn up for the Austrian Diet, the Slavic Congress, and, finally, the Frankfurt Parliament, the *Paulskirche* (Chapter 4). A case study of the petition movement for the partition of Galicia takes a closer look at the expectations of the population of one of the poorest Habsburg lands with regard to multi-ethnic federalism (Chapter 5). In political practice, crown land federalism that structured the monarchy historically and led to the strengthening of crown land patriotism was of the utmost importance for the empire and later for its Austrian territories (Chapter 6).

The second half of the book is devoted to the living federalism after 1867. First, it illustrates the continuing imperial features of the monarchy, especially the crown land privileges accorded to Croatia, Galicia, and Tyrol (Chapter 7). By contrast, the Austro-Hungarian Compromise and a common foreign, customs, defence, and economic policy can be conceived as a (con)federation (Chapter 8). Simultaneously, the Austrian crown lands began to act like states in the domains of modern beneficiary governance, such as infrastructure, welfare, and education. They interacted both with the Viennese central authorities and regional civic institutions (Chapter 9). This vertical interdependence also led to a horizontal interdependence between the empire, its two halves, and the crown lands when a new system of fiscal compensation was negotiated between 1905 and 1914 (Chapter 10).

In the last decade of Austria-Hungary, federalism regained momentum (Chapter 11). The partial introduction of universal suffrage in 1907, the annexation of Bosnia and Herzegovina in 1908, the increase in national and social conflicts, and the indecisiveness of the emperor plunged the empire into a crisis of legitimacy. Earlier federal ideas were adapted to new problems. Reformist discussions found their way into the highest circles. The book concludes with Archduke Franz Ferdinand's final programme for his accession to the throne in 1914, which had hitherto been considered lost (Chapter 12). This important source has been reconstructed from Franz Ferdinand's papers. The plans of the heir to the throne also played an important role in the federalist ideas of Emperor Karl and his advisers. By 1918, however, they were no longer creating cohesion, but in fact initiating the final disintegration of the Habsburg Monarchy.

Nevertheless, federal ideas and a living federation contributed to long-lasting cohesion of the Monarchy in the nineteenth century. The book follows the federal history of this cohesion along three threads of change that run throughout the nineteenth century. First, the redistribution of power and governance: how did policy fields, public functions, and resources change after the pre-March period and how were they distributed between the monarch, the empire, the intermediary levels, and the crown lands? Second, political loyalties: in the Habsburg Monarchy, as with everywhere in Europe, national and social loyalties gained political importance over confessional ones. This shift in allegiances also shaped the history of federalism. Third, territoriality: it was not until the last third of the nineteenth century that the empire (Austria-Hungary), the parts of the empire (Austria and Hungary), and the crown lands emerged as political territories and thus as separate units.

Finally, this book searches for new answers to the old question of what held Habsburg polity together and why it ultimately fell apart. By looking back to this 'Europe in miniature', its history both of cohesion and disintegration forces us to think about our present and future, about what unites and divides the 'Europe en gros'. In the *federal* history of the Habsburg Monarchy, we are reading the prequel to today's Europe.

A Federal History of the Habsburg Empire, 1815–1918. Jana Osterkamp, Oxford University Press.
 DOI: 10.1093/9780198943631.003.0001

Figure 1.1 Karl I, Emperor of Austria, Empress Zita, and Crown Prince Otto participating in the funeral procession for Emperor Franz Joseph I, Photograph, Vienna 1916.

1
The Young Emperor and the Old Empire

On 16 October 1918, in a 'Manifesto to his Peoples', Emperor Karl promised to transform the Habsburg Monarchy into a federation. In light of the military defeat of the Central Powers in the First World War, his primary goal was to 'secure an honourable peace'.[1] The public had been restlessly awaiting his proposals since 1916 when the 'old' emperor, Franz Joseph I, had been buried and Karl ascended the throne (Figure 1.1). The 'Peoples' Manifesto', however, was published late. It was finally issued, not coincidentally, at the same time as reports of the American President Woodrow Wilson's negative response to the German peace offer appeared in the press. During this period, the public had been eagerly expecting the Allies' response to Austria.

As a signal of both his domestic and, more significantly, his foreign policy, Karl saw his promise of a federation as a means to obtain the national freedom of his peoples. He and his advisers sought to meet the peoples' aspirations for greater independence as well as Wilson's Fourteen Points of January 1918. Wilson had demanded that 'the peoples of Austria-Hungary, whose place among the nations we wish to see safeguarded and assured, should be accorded the freest opportunity for autonomous development'. At the time, the American president had no intention of guaranteeing any form of state autonomy for the peoples of the monarchy. Instead, he wanted to preserve the Habsburg state for the sake of the balance of power in Europe and as a bulwark against the threat of 'Bolshevism'.[2] As the social democratic *Arbeiterzeitung* (Worker's Newspaper) noted sarcastically, the 'Peoples' Manifesto' was 'only the decree of implementation' of Wilson's programme.[3]

[1] The manifesto was first published in a special issue of the pro-imperial and pro-government *Wiener Zeitung* on 17 Oct. 1918. In detail Helmut Rumpler, *Das Völkermanifest Kaiser Karls vom 16. Oktober 1918: Letzter Versuch zur Rettung des Habsburgerreiches*. Munich, 1966; Christopher Brennan, 'Reforming Austria-Hungary: Beyond his Control or beyond his Capacity? The Domestic Policies of Emperor Charles I November 1916–May 1917'. Dissertation, London School of Economics and Political Science, 2012.

[2] Ulrike Harmat, 'Untergang, Auflösung, Zerstörung der Habsburgermonarchie? Zeitgenössische Bedingungen der Erinnerung und Historiographie'. In Harmat and Helmut Rumpler (eds), *Die Habsburgermonarchie 1848–1918*. Vol. 12: *Bewältigte Vergangenheit? Die nationale und internationale Historiographie zum Untergang der Habsburgermonarchie als ideelle Grundlage für die Neuordnung Europas*. Vienna, 2018, 68–9.

[3] 'Der Bundesstaat', *Arbeiterzeitung* (Morgenblatt), 18 Oct. 1918, 1.

It is more than a mere irony of Habsburg federal history that the final federalization programme launched by an emperor coincided with the end of the monarchy. It was only under the mounting pressure of wartime circumstances that Karl grasped at this final straw, but despite his endeavours, he still failed to preserve the empire for the post-war era. Only three days after its publication, on 19 October, the press reported that Wilson would not respond to Austria's peace offer. Washington declared that it no longer felt bound by the Fourteen Points, that it recognized the Czechs and the South Slavs as belligerents against Austria, and that it supported their aspirations for a free nation state of their own.[4]

All signs pointed to separation. Within a few days, Austria-Hungary ceased to exist. Despite his hopes, the nationalities did not use the 'Peoples' Manifesto' to unite in a federation under Karl's sceptre. Indeed, the Hungarian government under Sándor Wekerle had already dissolved the union with Austria on 16 October 1918.[5] The Czechs meanwhile had demonstratively stayed away from preliminary talks with the Viennese government over a possible multinational federation.[6] They now invoked the 'Washington Declaration', which called for an independent state together with the Slovaks of Upper Hungary. The declaration had been submitted to the American State Department by the government-in-exile under Tomáš G. Masaryk on 18 October and was published the next day. The Southern Slavs also rejected the manifesto. Ten days later, on 29 October, the Croatian-Slavonian Diet, the Sabor, severed all legal ties with Austria-Hungary. On 24 November 1918, the Croatian government declared itself in favour of union with the Kingdom of Serbia. To the east, the Romanians also hoped for a separate state, proposing a 'Danubian Confederation' which would grant the Hungarian-speaking Szeklers and the Transylvanian Saxons 'the greatest possible autonomy'.[7] Elsewhere, in Lemberg (Lwów, Lviv), Yevhen Petrushevych, a member of the Austrian House of Representatives, proclaimed the 'creation of a Ukrainian state on all ethnographically Ukrainian territories of Austria and Hungary'.[8] Eastern Galicia was not to be part of the new 'independent state of Poland' guaranteed by the Allies, but of 'the new Ukrainian federal member state in Austria'.[9] To the south, some Italians demanded the 'independence of Friuli within the framework of the Austrian federation' and wanted to make its continued association with Austria dependent on a referendum; others had already begun to seek their futures outside the Habsburg Monarchy.[10]

[4] Robert Lansing to Ekenberg. In: *Foreign Relations of the United States* (hereafter *FRUS*) *Supplement*, 1 (1918), 368.

[5] *Neues Wiener Tagblatt*, 17 Oct. 1918.

[6] *Neues Wiener Tagblatt*, 17 Oct. 1918.

[7] *Az Est*, 26 Oct. 1918, German translation in Österreichisches Staatsarchiv Wien, Abteilung Haus-, Hof- und Staatsarchiv (hereafter ÖStA, HHStA), Ministerium des Äußern (hereafter MdÄ), Zeitungsarchiv, Box 113-3 'Manifest des Kaiser Karl zur Neugestaltung Österreichs'.

[8] *Neues Wiener Tagblatt*, 22 and 24 Oct. 1918.

[9] *Zeit*, 25 Oct. 1918.

[10] *Der Morgen*, 24 Oct. 1918.

Amidst this building maelstrom, the cohesion of even the German-speaking crown lands began to unravel. Politicians from Styria, Carinthia, and Tyrol discussed joining the German Empire;[11] Vorarlberg flirted with a federal future in Switzerland.[12]

1.1. Federalists in the Vienna Chamber of Deputies, 1917

In the 'Peoples' Manifesto' of 16 October 1918, Karl sought to respond to the 'wishes of the Austrian peoples' for national autonomy. On the occasion of his first speech from the throne to the Austrian Parliament in May 1917, these wishes had been prominently expressed by Slavic nationalists. To better understand the Peoples' Manifesto, we must therefore step back a year.

On 30 May 1917, Austria's bicameral parliament, the Reichsrat, which had not met for more than three years, was reconvened. During the first years of the war, under Franz Joseph, mistrust between the governments and peoples of Austria and Hungary was deepened by orchestrated treason trials, waves of arrests, a rigid military administration, and a severe censorship regime. The harshest measures were reserved for high-ranking Czech, Croatian, and Romanian nationalist activists, who were sentenced to death, though not ultimately executed.[13] After his accession to the throne, Karl relaxed this authoritarian regime and continued to rely, as late as 1917, on amnesties to regain lost confidence.

At the reopening of the Imperial Diet at the end of May 1917, representatives of the nationalities expressed their expectations for a reformed empire.[14] Both the Czech and South Slav parliamentary clubs were in favour of federalization. Their point of reference was no longer a deepened crown land federalism that adhered to the existing historical-political borders of, for example, the Kingdom of Bohemia or the Duchy of Carinthia. Both sides instead demanded a territorial reorganization along ethnic-national-linguistic lines. They wanted to break with Austrian-Hungarian dualism and the privileged position of Hungary.

These so-called May Declarations became a fixed baseline for the national movements in these crown lands.[15] They created an unprecedented degree of unity which spanned the divides between Czech and South Slavic political parties. Further support came from a nationalized Catholic clergy. In August, for instance, the Prince-Bishop of Laibach (Ljubljana), Anton Jeglic, urged his diocese to 'stand

[11] *Fremdenblatt*, 20 Oct. 1918.

[12] Ulrich Nachbaur, '1918: Selbständiges Land Vorarlberg'. In Peter Bußjäger (ed.), *3. November 1918: Die Länder und der neue Staat*. Vienna, 2019, 57–139.

[13] Mark Cornwall, 'Treason in an Era of Regime Change: The Case of the Habsburg Monarchy', *Austrian History Yearbook*, 50 (2019), 124–49.

[14] Some of the declarations were made spontaneously; see Minutes of the Chamber of Deputies, Opening Session of the XXII Session on 30 May 1917, 34–7.

[15] Cf. Brennan, 'Reforming Austria-Hungary', 299–300.

up for the proclamation of a South Slavic state law'.[16] Bohemia's minor clergy, meanwhile, advocated the state's historic rights and preached celebratory sermons to the Czech nation on St Wenceslas's Day.[17]

Against this background of feverishly high hopes, Karl's speech from the throne, delivered just one day later on 31 May 1917, was a striking disappointment. The emperor spoke only vaguely of constitutional and administrative reforms and of the freedom of national and cultural development for all the peoples of the monarchy. Expectations of a constitutional rejuvenation by the young ruler, who was not yet 30, were not fulfilled. To many of those involved, Karl's speech seemed like an empty ceremony: 'The emperor is looking very fresh and young—even younger than he is—and read the very long speech from the throne very nicely.'[18] Many felt that this was too little. An important opportunity for a new beginning had been lost.

In reality, Karl's room for manoeuvre was limited, as he had already committed to a particular course regarding federal reform. Six months earlier, on his accession to the throne in November 1916, he formally recognized the Austro-Hungarian dualist confederal constitution. By allowing himself to be crowned king of Hungary, moreover, he had given dualism a powerful symbolic sanction. This move did not go uncontested. Indeed, his closest advisers had sought to dissuade Karl from agreeing to a coronation, which they foresaw as an obstacle to fundamental constitutional reform after the end of the war. The dualistic confederation was nonetheless consolidated and confirmed. In 1917, it was augmented further when Karl concluded a new economic compromise between Austria and Hungary. In the eyes of the other peoples and nationalities of his empire, this recognition of the existing order signalled preferential treatment for Hungary and the Magyars.

In the months following the 'May Declarations' in the Chamber of Deputies and the speech from the throne, the emperor squandered much of his credibility by failing to push for a reorganization that would meet the needs of the time. In day-to-day politics, Vienna was reluctant to deviate from rule by emergency decree under Article 14. By adhering to these rules of 'war dictatorship',[19] the

[16] 'Eine neue Herausforderung des Fürstbischofs Jeglic', *Deutsches Volksblatt*, 24 Sept. 1918, 1; *Neue Freie Presse* (Morgenblatt), 27 Aug. 1918, 6; 'Das Gleichgewicht der Beschwerden', *Reichspost* (Morgenblatt), 6 Sept. 1918, 6.

[17] 'Ein Beschluss, über den die Kirchenfeinde sich freuen', *Reichspost* (Nachmittagsausgabe), 6 Sept. 1918, 2; 'Nicht einmal die Geistlichen folgen den Bischöfen', *Arbeiterzeitung*, 12 Sept. 1918, 5; 'Die Bischöfe Böhmens gegen die staatsrechtliche Agitation der Geistlichkeit', *Neue Freie Presse*, 21 Sept. 1918, 3; 'Die Bischöfe Böhmens gegen die staatsrechtliche Agitation der Geistlichen', *Österreichische Landzeitung*, 28 Sept. 1918, 1. On the split between church hierarchy and clergy: Martin Schulze Wessel, *Revolution und religiöser Dissens: Der römisch-katholische und russisch-orthodoxe Klerus als Träger religiösen Wandels in den böhmischen Ländern und in Russland 1848–1922*. Munich, 2011.

[18] Josef Redlich, *Schicksalsjahre Österreichs: Die Erinnerungen und Tagebücher Josef Redlichs 1869–1936*. Vol. 2: *Tagebücher 1915–1936*. Vienna, 2011, 301.

[19] Josef Redlich, *Österreichische Regierung und Verwaltung im Weltkriege*. Vienna, 1929, 268–70.

government and the emperor were forced into a confrontation with a strong anti-war Social Democratic majority in the House of Representatives. The two sides sought to take the *Reich* in opposite directions. As they faced off, social conflicts intensified, with the often brutal suppression of 'hunger riots' and strikes.[20] Hunger, disease, and impoverishment increasingly burdened the daily lives of large sections of the population, but plans for a new social policy drawn up by the Austrian minister Joseph Maria Baernreither during these turbulent years were not implemented until after the war.[21] In south-eastern Europe, more than anywhere else, religious lines of conflict added to widening national and social divides.[22]

1.2. Nationalization of Politics

On the 'national question', Austria-Hungary acted indecisively; neither the emperor nor the government was able to pacify conflicts between the nationalities. From July 1917 onwards, Vienna aligned itself more strongly than before with German nationalist interests. Under his prime ministers Heinrich Clam-Martinic and Ernst Seidler von Feuchtenegg, Karl pursued a 'German course' in the Austrian part of the empire, which extended the privileges of the German-speaking population. For the Kingdom of Bohemia, he planned a new constitution imposed 'from above' and issued a decree on the division of districts.[23] These plans, together with the establishment of a new district court in German-speaking Trautenau (Trutnov), were a political gift to the Germans in Bohemia, but sharply exacerbated national tensions with the Czechs.[24]

At the same time, foreign and domestic policy became inextricably intertwined. This is evidenced by the 'Bread Peace' of February 1918 between the Central Powers and Ukraine which had seceded from the Russian Empire. The separate peace preceded further peace treaties with Romania and Soviet Russia (both in March 1918) and was intended, in part, to alleviate famine in Austria and Germany. At Brest-Litovsk, German Foreign Minister Richard Kühlmann and Austro-Hungarian Foreign Minister Ottokar Czernin negotiated with the

[20] Peter Heumos, '"Kartoffeln her oder es gibt eine Revolution": Hungerkrawalle, Streiks und Massenproteste in den böhmischen Ländern 1914–1918', *Mitteilungsblatt des Instituts für soziale Bewegungen*, 3 (2000), 158–76.

[21] Carl Gutheil-Knopp-Kirchwald, *Vom K. K. Ministerium für Soziale Fürsorge zum Bundesministerium für Soziale Verwaltung: Die Errichtung des Österreichischen Sozialministeriums*. Vienna, 1998.

[22] Peter Techet, 'Gewaltmomente unter ländlichen Katholiken in der späten Habsburgermonarchie: Kirchenstreit in Ricmanje bei Triest'. In Evelyn Bouwers (ed.), *Glaubenskämpfe. Katholiken und Gewalt im 19. Jahrhundert*. Göttingen, 2019, 117–40. Cf. Chapter 9.4.

[23] Decree of the Minister of the Interior of 19 May 1918, concerning the delegation of the duties of governor to district governors to be appointed permanently in Bohemia, No. 175/1918 RGBl.

[24] Arthur Polzer-Hoditz, *Kaiser Karl: Aus der Geheimmappe seines Kabinettschefs*. Zurich, 1929, 551.

Ukrainian socialists.[25] Their final agreement recognized the principle of national self-determination. Formally speaking at least, the Central Powers were thus among the first states in the world to endorse this concept. It soon became clear, however, that the recognition of a Ukrainian state on the basis of the right of peoples to self-determination was a rather ambivalent strategy to make the desired hegemony of the Central Powers in the East palatable to weaker and dependent states.[26] The violent regime of occupation soon established in Ukraine quickly belied the idea that negotiations and treaties were conducted on an equal footing.[27] Both the recognition of Ukraine by the two foreign ministers and the promise made during the negotiations to grant the Habsburg Ruthenians (now Ukrainians) their own crown land—so that they could separate territorially from the Habsburg crown land of Galicia—contradicted other wartime promises. A future Kingdom of Poland, for example, over which the Hohenzollerns and Habsburgs fought bitterly at the end of the war, supposedly also had a claim to the Ruthenian part of Galicia.

Vienna's diplomatic recognition of Ukraine as a nation state had the effect of further strengthening the national and ethnic strand of politics throughout the monarchy.[28] Foreign policy and promises made to the 'Habsburg' Poles and Ruthenians came into conflict with the domestic nationality policy towards the Czechs and the South Slavs. As a response to the May declarations of the South Slavs and Czechs, the recognition of national self-determination for all could not have been further from the minds of the emperor or his governments. The Christian Socialist Ignaz Seipel, who enjoyed the confidence of the court, was defending a policy of *divide and rule* as late as 1 October 1918. He quoted the Austrian prime minister: 'One could and should come to an agreement with the South Slavs [and] separate them from the Czechs.'[29]

Against this foreign and domestic political backdrop of 1917–1918, the nation, 'national self-determination', and the nation state became the most important baselines against which Karl's rule and planned reforms were measured. However, in the disputes between Prague, Laibach (Ljubljana), and Vienna, as well as in Washington, 'national self-determination' took on very different meanings. For Wilson, 'national' was closely linked to 'democratic' self-determination. As his Fourteen Points show, he was initially and primarily concerned with

[25] Mark von Hagen, 'The Entangled Eastern Front and the Making of the Ukrainian State: A Forgotten Peace—A Forgotten War and Nation-Building'. In Rumpler and Harmat, *Die Habsburgermonarchie 1848–1918*, 283–319.

[26] Eckart Conze, *Die große Illusion: Versailles 1919 and the New Order of the World.* Munich, 2018, 105.

[27] Von Hagen, 'Entangled Eastern Front'.

[28] Tara Zahra, 'Imagined Noncommunities: National Indifference as a Category of Analysis', *Slavic Review*, 69/1 (2010), 93–119; Gerald Stourzh, 'The Ethnicizing of Politics and "National Indifference" in Late Imperial Austria'. In Stourzh, *Der Umfang der österreichischen Geschichte: Ausgewählte Studien*, 283–323.

[29] Diary entry of 2 Oct. 1918, Redlich, *Schicksalsjahre Österreichs*, 2. 437.

democratization, not the creation of new nation states.[30] This, however, was precisely what the exiled governments of the Czechs, South Slavs, and Romanians demanded under the banner of 'national self-determination': autonomy within independent nation states. Wilson accepted these demands in the summer of 1917. The national politicians who had remained in the Habsburg Monarchy and who had been advocating for a multinational federation since May 1917 understood 'self-determination' to mean autonomy in a reconstituted empire.

Nationalists at home and in exile were well aware that the realities of the Habsburg Empire permitted only limited organization into nation states. In the crown lands, nationalities lived side by side with other nationalities. In the territories they claimed for their future nation states, they rarely formed a majority of the population.[31] They were nationalities without clearly defined territories.

To assess contemporary debates on the future, one must also bear in mind the impressive reality of 'national self-government' before 1914.[32] The nationalities were legally recognized linguistic and cultural communities and, at least in the Austrian half of the empire, had their own powers and means for political action. In the political fields of education, culture, and language, the Austrian nationalities enjoyed freedom, equality, and participation through so-called 'councils' (school councils, provincial agricultural councils, and others). Nationalities in some 'western' empires, not to mention non-Magyar ethnic groups in the Hungarian half of the Habsburg Empire, could only dream of such rights. The equality of nationalities was guaranteed by the rule of law but the war, which did so much to push European nations apart, also widened the gap between the nationalities within the empires.

1.3. 'Propaganda Campaign' in August 1918

In the summer of 1918, rumours of federalization began to circulate once more in the daily press. It is difficult to assess what the general public thought about possible federal reforms. After all, freedom of expression was strictly curtailed by press censorship, treason trials, and bans on associations. One particular press campaign in August 1918, therefore, offers a rare cross-section of public opinion.

This 'propaganda campaign' provides a lesson in the political culture of the late Habsburg Empire. On 7 August, the editor of the *Österreichische Rundschau* (Austrian Review), Leopold Chlumecký, revealed to an acquaintance, Josef

[30] Margaret Macmillan, *Peacemakers: The Paris Conference of 1919 and its Attempt to End War* . London, 2001, 11–24; Jörn Leonhard, *Pandora's Box: A History of the First World War*. Cambridge, 2018, 649.

[31] On the character of the successor states as 'new empires' Pieter Judson, *The Habsburg Empire: A New History*. Cambridge, MA, 2016, 442–52.

[32] Gerald Stourzh, *Die Gleichberechtigung der Nationalitäten in der Verfassung und Verwaltung Österreichs 1848–1918*. Vienna, 1985.

Redlich, his plans to instigate 'a propaganda [campaign] in favour of Austria' in the press.[33] At the time, Redlich was considered a likely contender for the post of Austrian prime minister. Chlumecký had also coordinated his plans with the then-head of the Austrian government, Hussarek. Through this campaign, Chlumecký floated plans for federalization. Although the Austrian government mostly remained on the side-lines, a comparison of press reports and private conversation notes shows how skilfully the coverage was orchestrated, apparently with the knowledge and approval of the authorities. Indeed, while the government initially denied the federalization rumours, several newspapers questioned the denials.[34]

The filing of press reports in a separate archival collection of the Austro-Hungarian Foreign Ministry suggests that the 'propaganda campaign' had indeed been authorized 'from above' and possibly even directed from its seat at the Ballhausplatz or from the Imperial Cabinet Chancellery, i.e. the emperor's office.[35] The highest decision-makers of the empire and the Austrian government had a great interest in sounding out public opinion on federalization in its various regional and social facets. The Swiss press, considered the mouthpiece of the Allies, reported with almost one voice that the Entente could 'impose federalization' on Austria-Hungary 'by a European decision'.[36] As early as 1917, France had signalled that it considered the 'idea of a federation worth discussing'.[37] In the spring of 1918, the Viennese expert on international law Heinrich Lammasch had travelled to Switzerland on a secret mission on behalf of the emperor to speak with the American and British middleman George Herron about Habsburg ideas for a federation.[38]

The collection of the press reports at the Ballhausplatz nevertheless demonstrate the explosive power federalist ideas had for society. Mere rumours of federalization efforts by the Austrian government under Prime Minister Hussarek provoked contentious and sometimes hostile reactions. On 11 August 1918, federalist rumours appeared in a Catholic Sunday paper in Prague. The 'exclusive news of the *Čech* (The Czech)' stated that Hussarek would soon 'emerge from the fog of

[33] Diary entry of 8 Aug. 1918, Redlich, *Schicksalsjahre Österreichs*, 2. 425.

[34] 'Die angebliche Verfassungsreform in Österreich: Ungarische Blätterstimmen', *Neues Wiener Journal*, 16 Aug. 1918, 2. Cf. also 'Dementi der Hussarekschen Verfassungspläne', *Gemeinsame Kriegsausgabe der Czernowitzer Allgemeinen Zeitung und des Czernowitzer Tagblatts*, 17 Aug. 1918, 1.

[35] Cf. the extensive archive of newspaper articles in ÖStA, HHStA, MdÄ, Zeitungsarchiv, carton 113-3 'Manifest des Kaiser Karl zur Neugestaltung Österreichs in einen Bundesstaat, Forderung und Frage der Verfassungsreform, Föderalisierungsgerüchte' [Manifesto of Emperor Karl on the Reorganization of Austria into a Federal State, Demand and Question of Constitutional Reform, Rumors of Federalization 1917–1918].

[36] 'Hafer und Peitsche für die österreichisch-ungarische Monarchie: Lockungen und Drohungen in der Entente', *Neue Freie Presse*, 24 Aug. 1918, 17.

[37] Diary entry of 20 Aug. 1917, Redlich, *Schicksalsjahre Österreichs*, 2. 334.

[38] George D. Herron, 'Heinrich Lammasch's Suggestion for Peace in Bern 1918'. In Marga Lammasch (ed.), *Heinrich Lammasch: Seine Aufzeichnungen, sein Wirken und seine Politik*. Vienna, 1922, 186–97. See also Heinrich Benedikt, *Die Friedensaktion der Meinlgruppe 1917/18: Die Bemühungen um einen Verständigungsfrieden nach Dokumenten, Aktenstücken und Briefen*. Graz and Cologne, 1962, 230–45.

general platitudes' and that he planned the constitutional transformation of the Habsburg Empire into a 'confederation of nation states'. His constitutional reform envisaged a 'German, Bohemian, Polish, South Slavic and Hungarian state (i.e., the crown lands of St. Stephen)'.[39] He enjoyed the confidence of the crown and was advised by 'trusted men from the right in the upper house' and 'eminent men of all nations'. 'Leading military circles' also looked on him favourably, 'not out of love for the non-German nationalities, but from the realization that domestic policy has been weakening Austria more and more in foreign affairs'.[40] Hussarek's Constitutional Commission was to include 'not only proven parliamentarians but also the first men of science, industry, trade, [and] agriculture, and national experts from the administration'.[41]

A government that enjoyed the confidence of all nationalities was to draft and implement the constitution. Lammasch was mentioned as a possible leading figure, to whom 'the lion's share of the new plan' was due.[42] After its initial publication in Czech-language newspapers, this information was rapidly taken up and disseminated by the leading press in Vienna and Budapest.[43] The matter of personnel, namely the controversy about Lammasch, was now often omitted. In fact, the plan was similar to the ideas Lammasch had conveyed to the Allies in Geneva in preparation for a federal peace order. Only a few newspapers outside Vienna, such as the social democratic *Arbeiterwille* (Workers' Will) in Graz, referred specifically to Lammasch, remarking that this proposal sounded 'so reasonable as to be unbelievable'.[44] Behind the scenes in Vienna, meanwhile, newspaper editors such as Ernst Benedikt of the *Neue Freie Presse* (The New Free Press) and bystanders such as Hermann Bahr, then dramaturge at the Burgtheater, puzzled over who was behind the news and what it meant.[45] At the beginning of September 1918, Bahr reported to Redlich that Lammasch was being assisted on the draft constitution by the theologian and Christian Social politician Ignaz Seipel and Bahr's friend, the political writer Benno Karpeles.[46] The trio of Lammasch, Seipel, and Karpeles stood for the Christian character of any future reform.[47]

[39] The original message was published as 'Situační zpráva politická (Pův. zpráva "Čecha")', *Čech*, 11 Aug. 1918, 1; paraphrased in *Neues Wiener Tagblatt*, 15 Aug. 1918; 'Reforma ústavy', *Čech*, 15 Aug. 1918, 6. Unless otherwise noted, this and all subsequent translations are by the author.

[40] 'Situační zpráva politická (Pův. zpráva "Čecha")', *Čech*, 11 Aug. 1918, 1; abridged paraphrase in *Neues Wiener Tagblatt*, 15 Aug. 1918.

[41] 'Situační zpráva politická (Pův. zpráva "Čecha")', *Čech*, 11 Aug. 1918, 1.

[42] 'Situační zpráva politická (Pův. zpráva "Čecha")', *Čech*, 11 Aug. 1918, 1.

[43] *Mír*, 26 Aug. 1918; *Čech*, 26 Aug. 1918.

[44] 'Eine Ente?', *Arbeiterwille*, 17 Aug. 1918, 1. Cf. also 'Die Pläne des Freih. V. Hussarek: Eine Vereinigung nationaler Staaten?—Lammasch der Urheber der Verfassungsreform?', *Grazer Tagblatt*, 17 Aug. 1918, 6.

[45] On 27 Aug. 1918, Ernst Benedikt of the *Neue Freie Presse* called on Josef Redlich to obtain more information. Diary entry of 27 Aug. 1918, Redlich, *Schicksalsjahre Österreichs*, 2. 428.

[46] Redlich, *Schicksalsjahre Österreichs*, 2. 430.

[47] Cf. Klemens von Klemperer, *Ignaz Seipel: Staatsmann einer Krisenzeit*. Graz, 1976.

The federalist rumours received a negative reception in many crown lands. The positive attitude towards a federal reorganization that had been expressed in parliament in May 1917 had clearly weakened. This development was particularly evident in Bohemia, where it formed part of a wider reaction against the German nationalist course of the Austrian prime ministers. Demands for an independent Czechoslovak state had replaced the federalist demands of May 1917.[48] In August 1918, the Brno newspaper *Lidové Noviny* (People's Newspaper) therefore asked, with ironic astonishment, why nothing was known about the 'confidants' of the Czech people who were advising Hussarek on federalization.[49] The Catholic-nationalist newspaper *Hlas* (Voice) spoke of intrigues.[50] Summing up the distrust of many Czechs, the agrarian *Venkov* (Countryside) recalled the decreed district division of Bohemia and predicted that old sins against the constitution and parliament would now be followed by new ones.[51] The social democratic *Právo Lidu* (The People's Law) argued that one could not speak of a constitutional reform, but only of a 'constitutional war substitute'.[52] Václav Klofáč, vice-president of the Czechoslovak National Council, meanwhile, flatly rejected negotiations with the Austrian government unless they were based on the Czech declaration of 30 May 1917, in particular the territorial union with the Slovaks.[53] The South Slavs took a similarly uncompromising approach.[54]

From the apparently safe haven of dualism, reactions in Hungary to rumours of federalization were casual and nonchalant. Through a mixture of threats and wait-and-see irony, Hungarian politicians formulated the stance that they would no longer feel bound by dualism and the common federation if Austria were to give itself a new constitution. The newspaper *Pester Lloyd* wrote pointedly:[55]

> They would have us believe that the spectre of federalism stalks the other side of the Leitha in broad daylight and that dualism is threatened.... But we do not believe in the federalist danger. Mr. von Hussarek may be up to plotting something like that; in any case, the semi-official denials of rumours to that effect in the Czech press do not rule it out.

[48] Cf. Luboš Velek, 'Die tschechischen bürgerlichen Parteien im Weltkrieg 1914–1918'. In Heeresgeschichtliches Museum (ed.), *Der Erste Weltkrieg und der Vielvölkerstaat*. Vienna, 2012, 165–78.

[49] *Lidové Noviny*, 27 Aug. 1918.

[50] *Hlas*, 26 Aug. 1918.

[51] See the press reports in *Neue Freie Presse*, 28 and 29 Aug. 1918. Similarly, *Národní Politika*, 29 Aug. 1918; *Čech*, 29 Aug. 1918.

[52] *Právo Lidu*, 29 Aug. 1918.

[53] *Vídenský denník*, 1 Sept. 1918; *Český socialista*, 5 Sept. 1918; also *Neues Wiener Tagblatt*, 24 Sept. 1918.

[54] Cf. Janko Pleterski, 'Trialismus bei den Slowenen und die jugoslawische Einigung'. In Richard G. Plaschka and Karlheinz Mack (eds), *Die Auflösung des Habsburgerreiches: Zusammenbruch und Neuorientierung im Donauraum*. Vienna, 1970, 195–202.

[55] Cf. *Neue Freie Presse*, 30 Aug. 1918; 'Die Gerüchte über eine neue Staatsform in Österreich—Die Stimme eines ungarischen Staatsmannes', *Neue Freie Presse*, 31 Aug. 1918; cf. *Neues Pester Journal*, 29 Aug. 1918.

The article concludes that the Hungarian government would examine the compatibility of proposals with the Compromise of 1867 and draw the appropriate conclusions.[56] Only the social democratic newspaper *Népszava* (Voice of the People) welcomed a constitutional reform with more rights for nationalities, even in Hungary.[57] The vanguard of the so-called German Radicals in Austria, Oskar Teufel and Ferdinand Pantz, cautiously demanded the right of the Hungarian Germans to opt for an '*Anschluss* to German Austria' in the event of federalization.[58]

1.4. Karl's 'Manifesto to his Peoples'

Following the government's denial of federalization rumours in August, Karl made his plans public. On 17 October 1918, the morning edition of the *Wiener Allgemeine Zeitung* (Vienna General Newspaper) announced the 'Manifesto to his Peoples' under the headline 'Austria as a Federal State. The Manifesto Will Be Published this Evening. Fierce Fighting in the West.'[59] Karl published his programme for reform in the midst of an atmosphere of crisis, replete with foreign policy and military uncertainties, the threat of defeat in the war, and continuing food supply and public health emergencies. Nonetheless, as on the occasion of his accession in 1916 and his speech from the throne at the reopening of parliament in 1917, the imperial media described his message in October 1918 as 'long awaited' and 'longed for'.[60] On the day of the proclamation, the *Wiener Allgemeine* commented that 'sooner or later, Old Austria will have to make way for a rejuvenated state and that the entire monarchy... cannot possibly be satisfied in the future with those foundations of state law on which it had been rebuilt half a century ago'. This allusion to the dualistic constitution of the empire of 1867 ended with the words: 'What was new then has now become old.'

The *Wiener Allgemeine* was in favour of a federalization of the monarchy based on the 'principle of the self-determination of the nations'. Furthermore, it justified a federation with the 'irrefutable belief' that the peoples of the monarchy 'must remain together despite the transformation of state forms, because they are bound by indissoluble historical, cultural and economic realities ties'. The

[56] *Pester Lloyd*, 31 Aug. 1918.
[57] *Nepszava*, 9 Mar. 1918, German translation in ÖStA, HHStA, MdÄ, Zeitungsarchiv, carton 113-3 'Manifesto of Emperor Karl for the Reorganization of Austria'.
[58] *Fremdenblatt*, 12 Oct. 1918. On the German Radicals Lothar Höbelt, *'Stehen oder Fallen?' Österreichische Politik im Ersten Weltkrieg*. Vienna, 2015, 247–8.
[59] *Wiener Allgemeine Zeitung*, 17 Oct. 1918, 1. See here for the following quotations, unless otherwise noted.
[60] 'Ein Bund freier Völker', *Wiener Allgemeine Zeitung*, 18 Oct. 1918, 1.

future federation was thus legitimized by the diversity of the nations *and* a unity established by history, culture, and economics. Moreover, the future federal state had to be built on cooperation and the common interest of all: 'centuries of coexistence' had shown that 'these peoples cannot simply live side by side, but only together'.[61]

The central passage of the Peoples' Manifesto read: 'According to the will of her peoples, Austria shall become a federal state, in which each nationality (*Volksstamm*) on its territory of settlement shall form its own polity.'[62] Restrictions to this principle were to follow: 'The unification of the Polish territories of Austria with the independent Polish state is not hereby anticipated. The city of Trieste, together with its territory, will receive a special status according to the wishes of its population.' The application was limited to Austria, since the proposed 'reshaping...shall in no way affect the integrity of the lands of the Holy Hungarian Crown'. In Austria, on the other hand, the reorganization was to 'guarantee the independence of each individual national state'. However, preserving a degree of unity among the states would serve the common interest, especially with regard to the fallout of the imminent capitulation.

1.5. Typology of Habsburg Federalism

Karl's promise of federalization in 1918 has all but been sanctified as a missed opportunity for saving the Habsburg Monarchy. This glorification process began during the interwar period and gained a new momentum in the wake of Karl's beatification in 2010.[63] Some saw the Manifesto as the greatest possible concession to the nationalities. From this point of view, the Czechs' and South Slavs' unwavering insistence on national statehood was to be branded as utterly self-serving.[64] For others, the political bridge-building from the imperial house to the nationalities came too late to bring the dissolution of the empire to a halt. The historian Helmut Rumpler, in the most important scholarly publication on Karl's 'Manifesto to his Peoples', dismissed the idea that federalizing the Danube region in the autumn of 1918 would ultimately have appeased the nationalities as a 'myth'.[65]

[61] 'Ein Bund freier Völker', *Wiener Allgemeine Zeitung*, 18 Oct. 1918, 1.

[62] The following quotations are from the first publication, 'An meine getreuen österreichischen Völker' [To my Faithful Austrian Peoples]. Special edition of the *Wiener Zeitung*, 17 Oct. 1918.

[63] Brennan, 'Reforming Austria-Hungary'; Elisabeth Kovács, *Untergang oder Rettung der Donaumonarchie?* Vol. 1: *Die österreichische Frage. Kaiser und König Karl I./IV. und die Neuordnung Mitteleuropas (1916–1922)*. Vienna, 2004; Eva Demmerle, *Kaiser Karl I.: 'Selig, die Frieden stiften…' Die Biographie*. Vienna, 2005.

[64] Cf. the former adviser to Franz Ferdinand and collaborator on Karl's Manifesto of Nations Johann Andreas Eichhoff, 'Die geplante Gründung der "Vereinigten Staaten von Großösterreich": Das vorbereitete Thronmanifest des Erzherzogs Franz Ferdinand—ein tragisches, geschichtliches Dokument', *Reichspost*, 28 Mar. 1926, 1–3.

[65] Rumpler, *Das Völkermanifest Kaiser Karls*, 5.

Regardless of such historical assessments, however, the federation promised in the 'Manifesto to his Peoples' of 16 October 1918 becomes harder to pin down the closer one tries to get to it. Contrary to what is often claimed, the Manifesto did not proclaim an exclusively 'federal state of nationalities'. Such a polity could hardly have been implemented given the monarchy's unique multinational form. It was for this reason that Karl and his advisers opted for a federal hybrid.

Karl's Manifesto, and the accompanying government declarations, reveal the typology of Habsburg federalism. This typology includes the federal nationality state, dualism and trialism, non-territorial personal autonomy, and historical crown land federalism. These four types had already been formed by the nineteenth century. They later shaped the living constitution. During the controversy following the Manifesto, the advantages and disadvantages of each type came up for critical discussion against the background of past experiences. It is precisely the Manifesto's references and allusions to these variations of federalism that make it so instructive for a federal history of the Habsburg Monarchy.

Federal Nationality State

The Peoples' Manifesto's promise of an Austrian 'federal state, in which each nationality (*Volksstamm*) shall form its own polity on its territory of settlement' is that of a federal nationality state. This type is characterized by a federal state structure in which political and ethno-linguistic borders coincide. A division of the Habsburg Monarchy along ethno-linguistic lines was first proposed by František Palacký in 1848 and subsequently attracted strange bedfellows. After 1899, it was advocated by both the Austrian Social Democrats in their party programme and advisers around the heir to the throne, Franz Ferdinand.[66]

A federal state of nationalities is typically a guarantor of national equality. In the Habsburg Monarchy, it would have had to consider all peoples equally: German Austrians; Czechs in Bohemia, Moravia, and Silesia; Italians in South Tyrol; Slovenes in southern Styria, the Littoral, Gorizia-Gradisca, and Carinthia; the Croats in Dalmatia; Ruthenians in eastern Galicia and Bukovina; Romanians in Bukovina; Germans in western Bohemia and northern Silesia; and the Silesian Poles.

Such far-reaching national equality, however, was by no means Karl's intention. On 17 October 1918, one of the most widely read newspapers in the monarchy, the *Neues Wiener Tagblatt* (New Vienna Daily), reported on a meeting between Austrian Prime Minister Hussarek and representatives of the parliamentary clubs. At the gathering, Hussarek explained the planned constitutional reform; significantly, he left open which nationalities could hope for a separate

[66] Cf. Chapter 12.

constituent state. He hinted at 'a German-Austrian, a Czecho-Slavic, a South Slavic (Illyrian), and a Ukrainian state'.[67] The social democratic *Arbeiterzeitung* also reported on the 'transformation of the state into a union of four nation states'.[68] Hussarek was further quoted as saying that 'a national representation of the Italians and Romanians living in Austria is also being considered'.[69] On the same day, Hussarek made clear to the leaders of the German-Austrian Independence Party that he was only concerned with the 'right of self-determination for "mature" peoples'. In its report, the *Neue Freie Presse* printed Hussarek's insulting statement in quotation marks. Notwithstanding the prime minister's choice of words, the planned federal state of all nations had surreptitiously become a 'quadralistic' federation.[70] Indeed, Hussarek's ideas were similar to those which sparked the 'federalization rumours' of August 1918 and, albeit without the inclusion of Hungary, the corresponding plans of the so-called Meinl group.[71]

Dualism and Trialism

Karl's federal nationality state encompassed only the Austrian part of the empire. The 'Manifesto to his Peoples' thus cemented the Austro-Hungarian dualism of 1867, declaring that it 'shall in no way infringe on the integrity of the lands of the Holy Hungarian Crown'. Karl had exempted Hungary from his plans at the instigation of the Hungarian prime minister, Sándor Wekerle, who had threatened to halt Hungarian grain shipments. Since the Hungarian part of the empire was as multinational as its Austrian counterpart, the monarch thus denied his 'Hungarian peoples'—Croats, Slavonians, Slovaks, Serbs, Romanians, Ruthenians, and Germans—the right to federal national self-determination. On 16 October 1918, however, the Hungarian prime minister dissolved the *Realunion* with Austria based on the Compromise Acts of 1867 and the confederal union in matters of defence, security, finances, and economy. From then on, Hungary wanted to be linked to Austria only through the monarch and a *Personalunion*. To achieve this independence, Hungary hoped for help from the Allied powers.

[67] 'Bevorstehender Staatsakt über die Umgestaltung der österreichischen Verfassung', *Neues Wiener Tagblatt,* 17 Oct. 1918.

[68] 'Das Ende eines Reiches', *Arbeiterzeitung* (Morgenblatt), 19 Oct. 1918, 1.

[69] Upcoming State Act on the Transformation of the Austrian Constitution. *Neues Wiener Tagblatt,* 17 Oct. 1918.

[70] 'Mitteilungen in der Deutschösterreichischen Unabhängigkeitspartei über die Pläne zur Bildung eines Bundesstaates', *Neue Freie Presse,* 17 Oct. 1918.

[71] The 'peace campaign' of the 'Meinl group', named after its initiator, the food magnate Julius Meinl, also included the lawyers Heinrich Lammasch and Josef Redlich. It sought informal understanding with foreign countries in order to achieve peace for Austria-Hungary by renouncing territorial expansions. Benedikt, *Friedensaktion der Meinlgruppe 1917/18,* 267–77.

In nineteenth-century Europe, the federal type of dualism—either as a real or personal union—had predominantly emerged in composite states consisting of several dynastic territories. European dualism, often referred to by scholars as 'dual statehood', included the unions of Norway-Sweden, Denmark-Iceland, Russia-Finland, but also the British unions of England-Scotland, England-Ireland, and England-Wales.[72] In the Habsburg Monarchy, the mid-nineteenth-century idea of dualism had initially been related to the relationship between the monarchy and the German Confederation. Later, it was applied to the association between the Hungarian and non-Hungarian crown lands.

The 'Manifesto to his Peoples' maintained the dualism of 1867. At the same time, it showed an openness to constitutional restructuring in the direction of trialism. The references to 'uniting the Polish territories of Austria with the independent Polish State' alluded both to the recognition by the Central Powers of a new Kingdom of Poland in 1916 and to Austrian efforts to beat the Hohenzollerns to its crown.[73] One possible scenario entailed 'independent' Poland receiving the 'Polish' part of Galicia in exchange for submitting to the Habsburg sceptre. With the changing fortunes of the war, Karl had repeatedly sought this so-called Austro-Polish solution, including in 1918. Polish statehood under Habsburg hegemony pointed towards trialism.[74]

Non-Territorial Personal Autonomy

Karl's 'Manifesto to his Peoples', which promised the primacy of the national principle, created conundrums in the multinational empire. Many of its nationalities were not settled in clearly demarcated territories, but were scattered throughout the empire. Moreover, not all political communities were 'nations' according to Wilson's and Karl's definitions. The Austrian Jewry, for example, was in danger of falling through the national grid, even though many of its members identified strongly with Austria as a supranational state.[75] In the negotiations between

[72] From recent scholarship see: Alvin Jackson, *The Two Unions: Ireland, Scotland, and the Survival of the United Kingdom 1707–2007*. Oxford, 2012. On the practical, not legal, preservation of Finnish constitutional laws in Russia, Frank Nesemann, *Ein Staat, kein Gouvernement: Die Entstehung und Entwicklung der Autonomie Finnlands im russischen Zarenreich*. Frankfurt am Main, 2003; Arnold H. Barton, *Sweden and Visions of Norway: Politics and Culture 1814–1905*. Carbondale, IL, 2003.

[73] Damian Szymczak, *Między Habsburgami a Hohenzollernami. Rywalizacja niemiecko-austro-węgierska w okresie I wojny światowej a odbudowa państwa polskiego*. Kraków, 2009.

[74] Cf. Lothar Höbelt, 'Die austro-polnische Lösung—eine unendliche Geschichte'. In Heeresgeschichtliches Museum (ed.), *Der Erste Weltkrieg und der Vielvölkerstaat*. Vienna, 2012, 35–54. As mentioned, this had not prevented the Austrian foreign minister, Czernin, from granting parts of Western Galicia to the Ukrainians in the 'Bread Peace' of Brest-Litovsk, Feb. 1918. Cf. Von Hagen, 'Entangled Eastern Front', 306–7.

[75] Marsha L. Rozenblit, 'The Dilemma of Identity: The Impact of the First World War on Habsburg Jewry'. In: Ritchie Robertson and Edward Timms (eds), *The Habsburg Legacy: National Identity in*

Jewish representatives, the emperor, and his government before the publication of the Manifesto, the vital issue was whether the Austrian Jews should, would, or even could form a nation. The second pressing question was how Austrian Jews—who constituted significant minorities in several crown lands—should be integrated into a 'federal union of nation states'.

In an audience with the emperor two weeks before the declaration of the Manifesto, the new Chief Rabbi of Vienna, Zvi Perez Chajes, expressed a desire for Jewish-national personal autonomy.[76] This idea of personal autonomy can be traced back to Transylvania's early modern union. While a comparatively small territory, Transylvania was nonetheless home to a number of different religions and linguistic communities.[77] Its constitution gave individual communities rights of self-determination in regard to worship, education, and culture. The communities voted separately on these matters in the joint diet. In the late Habsburg Monarchy, Austro-Marxists (and later advisers of Franz Ferdinand's) referred to this type of self-determination by the cumbersome labels 'non-territorial personal autonomy' and 'national personal autonomy',[78] which consequently found their way into the provincial constitutions of the Austrian crown lands of Moravia (1905), Bukovina (1910), and Galicia (1914), as well as into the constitution of Bosnia-Herzegovina (1910). Although Jews formed a significant part of the population in these crown lands, they were not included in these reforms.

From the beginning of 1918, negotiations between Jewish representatives and the Austrian government over political recognition intensified, albeit with little progress at first.[79] In allusion to the so-called Balfour Declaration a year earlier, in which the British government favourably mooted the establishment of 'a national home for the Jewish people', Prime Minister Hussarek suggested in the autumn of 1918 that a kingdom of Palestine should be reserved for the Austrian Jews.[80] In early October, according to the newspapers, he was thinking about recognizing the Jews as a nationality.[81] In response, Zionists and Jewish nationalists began to

Historical Perspective. Edinburgh, 1994, 144–57, 148–9; Armin A. Wallas, 'Mythen der Übernationalität und revolutionäre Gegenmodelle: Österreich-Konzeptionen jüdischer Schriftsteller zwischen Monarchie und Exil. In Wallas, *Deutschsprachige jüdische Literatur im 20. Jahrhundert*. Vol. 1. Wuppertal, 2008, 205–36.

[76] 'Oberrabbiner Dr. Chajes beim Kaiser', *Jüdische Zeitung*, 4 Oct. 1918, 1; 'Dr. Chajes beim Kaiser', *Jüdische Zeitung*, 11 Oct. 1918, 2; 'Die Judenfrage vor Kaiser Karl', *Jüdische Korrespondenz*, 22 Oct. 1918, 2–3. 'Audienz des Wiener Oberrabbiners bei Kaiser Karl', *Dr. Bloch's Österreichische Wochenschrift*, 11 Oct. 1918, 650; 'Hussarek und die Judenfrage', *Dr. Bloch's Österreichische Wochenschrift*, 42, 25 Oct. 1918, 677.

[77] Cf. Chapter 2.5. [78] Cf. Chapters 11 and 12.

[79] On these negotiations, 'Die Jüdisch-Nationalen und die österreichische Regierung', *Jüdische Zeitung*, 22 Mar. 1918, 1; 'Denkschrift der national organisierten Judenschaft an die österr. Regierung', *Jüdische Zeitung*, 22 Mar. 1918, 1.

[80] 'Hussarek und die Judenfrage', *Dr. Bloch's Österreichische Wochenschrift*, 42, 25 Oct. 1918, 677.

[81] 'Der neue Wiener Oberrabbiner über die Judenfrage', *Reichspost* (Morgenblatt), 6 Oct. 1918, 6. Cf. 'Die nationalen Gemeinwesen im künftigen Bundesstaate Österreich'. *Reichspost* (Morgenblatt), 18 Oct. 1918. Similar reports also in the *Pilsener Tagblatt*, 18 Oct. 1918, 2; *Dělnické Listy*, 18 Oct. 1918, 3.

mobilize their supporters. Mass demonstrations took place across Austrian cities; on one day, 14 October 1918, more than 5,000 people gathered at the Vienna Konzerthaus.[82] Chajes, the Chief Rabbi, was repeatedly celebrated for his success in persuading the emperor to grant Jewish national autonomy.[83]

The core question of how, or even if, Jews should organize themselves politically in a future Austrian federal state remained the subject of fierce internal conflicts. This was keenly observed by an editorial in the official organ of the Viennese Jewish community, *Dr. Bloch's Österreichische Wochenschrift* (Dr Bloch's Austrian Weekly). It said,

> [the Jews] who even amidst their fiercest internal conflicts and centripetal aspirations, found themselves in affirmation of the Austrian state idea, are through this commonality on the whole, the most sincere, secure and unconditional support for the state and the dynasty: these nearly two and a half million Jews, who together could form an independent force, are to be torn apart according to the new plans for reorganization, divided up like the spoils of war.[84]

A glance at contemporary Jewish periodicals gives an idea of these 'fiercest internal conflicts.'[85] The *Österreichische Wochenschrift*,[86] edited by Rabbi Joseph Samuel Bloch, was warmly disposed towards Emperor Karl and distanced itself from both Zionism and the orthodox tradition of Eastern Jewry. This paper stood for the 'Western' self-image refined by liberal, culturally assimilated Jews in Vienna, but it increasingly sympathized with diaspora nationalism. Orthodox Judaism was represented by the *Jüdische Korrespondenz* (Jewish Correspondence), which rejected non-religious (and therefore national) understandings of Judaism. Between these liberal and orthodox poles, the *Jüdische Zeitung* (Jewish Newspaper) acted as the mouthpiece of Jewish nationalists. It

[82] Cf. 'Exekutivkomitee der Zionisten Österreichs: An das jüdische Volk in Österreich!', *Jüdische Zeitung*, 11 Oct. 1918, 1. See also: 'Der Wille des Volkes und Die Wiener Massenversammlung', *Jüdische Zeitung*, 42, 18 Oct. 1918, 1–2. 'Kundgebungen der Provinz', *Jüdische Zeitung*, 25 Oct. 1918, 2–3. 'Eine Versammlung wegen des "Selbstbestimmungsrechts der Juden"', *Bloch's Österreichische Wochenschrift*, 18 Oct. 1918, 864–5. These meetings were also reported in the journal of the Imperial and Royal Foreign Ministry: 'Das Selbstbestimmungsrecht der Juden', *Fremden-Blatt* (Morgenausgabe), 12 Oct. 1918, 3.

[83] 'Der Wille des Volkes', *Jüdische Zeitung*, 18 Oct. 1918, 2; B., 'Der Kampf um den Zionismus in Ungarn', *Jüdische Zeitung*, 1 Nov. 1918, 4; 'Rabb. Dr. P. H. Chajes-Hain', *Der jüdische Nationalfonds, Beilage zur Jüdischen Zeitung*, 1 Nov. 1918, 1; 'Ein Dank des Oberrabbiner Chajes', *Der jüdische Nationalfonds, Beilage zur Jüdischen Zeitung*, 1 Nov. 1918, 6.

[84] 'An die Arbeit', *Bloch's Österreichische Wochenschrift*, 4 Oct. 1918, 625.

[85] Cf. Walter R. Weitzmann, 'The Politics of the Viennese Jewish Community 1890–1914'. In Ivar Oxaal, Michael Pollak, Michael, and Gerhard Botz (eds), *Jews, Antisemitism, and Culture in Vienna*. New York, 1987, 121–51.

[86] On Bloch, see Ian Reifowitz, *Imagining an Austrian Nation: Joseph Samuel Bloch and the Search for a Supraethnic Austrian Identity 1846–1918*. New York, 2003.

supported both the establishment of Palestine as a Jewish homeland and a form of diaspora nationalism based on *Landespolitik* ('homeland politics') and *Gegenwartsarbeit* ('work in the present'). More than any other publication, it advocated strongly for the recognition of Jews as a nationality in Austria-Hungary.[87] Even in Austria, the Jews were to 'stand in unity'.[88] In October 1918, writers with *Bloch's Wochenblatt* deduced from the national right to self-determination a Jewish '*duty* of self-determination'.[89] In view of this nationalization of politics, concerns grew among orthodox and liberal Jews that the freedom to determine their own religious, national, and cultural affiliation was slipping from their grasp.

These concerns were heightened by an increasingly exclusionary confessionalization of politics. The rumours of federalization in August 1918 had been accompanied by press articles that testified to the government's desire to impose a Catholic stamp on the planned federal state of nationalities. The empire's Catholic self-image could be traced to a baroque culture of piety—the proverbial 'pietas austriaca'.[90] A pastoral letter from the archbishops and bishops of Austria of 4 August 1918 defended religion as a core element of a new state order. Alluding to monarchical divine grace, it read:

> Our Empire has hitherto enjoyed the special protection of Divine Providence.... Austria has a providential task to fulfil as the supreme Catholic power at the heart of Europe and as the fatherland for the league of nations which it protects. Austria's strength rests in the unity of its peoples which itself rests in the Catholic faith.... If our enemies should succeed in depriving the peoples of this empire of their Catholic faith, then the rivers of blood which have been shed for a new and strong Austria would have flowed in vain.[91]

[87] On the distinction between diaspora nationalism and Zionism, see Robert M. Seltzer, *Simon Dubnow's 'New Judaism': Diaspora Nationalism and the World History of Jews*. Leiden, 2014, 155–63, 202–4; Robert S. Wistrich, *The Jews of Vienna in the Age of Franz Joseph*. Oxford, 2006. After the autonomy movement had initially been rejected by the Zionists as a distraction from the founding of the state in Palestine, a change took place with the congress of Russian Zionists in Helsingfors (Helsinki) in 1906. Henry Abramson, *A Prayer for the Government: Ukrainians and Jews in Revolutionary Times 1917–1920*. Cambridge, MA, 1999, 25. In the Czech lands, the line between Zionism and diaspora nationalism was unclear anyway: Kateřina Čapková, *Czechs, Germans, Jews? National Identity and the Jews of Bohemia*. New York and Oxford, 2012.

[88] 'Entscheidende Stunden', *Jüdische Zeitung*, 4 Oct. 1918, 2.

[89] 'Selbstbestimmungsrecht—Selbstbestimmungspflicht', *Bloch's Österreichische Wochenschrift*, 11 Oct. 1918, 641.

[90] Cf. Daniel L. Unowsky, 'Reasserting Empire: Habsburg Imperial Celebrations after the Revolutions of 1848–1849'. In Maria Bucur and Nancy M. Wingfield (eds), *Staging the Past: The Politics of Commemoration in Habsburg Central Europe 1848 to the Present*. West Lafayette, IN, 2001, 12–45; Alfred J. Rieber, *The Struggle for the Eurasian Borderlands: From the Rise of Early Modern Empires to the End of the First World War*. Cambridge, 2015, 93–4. On the Jewish communities, Wistrich, *Jews of Vienna*, 181. On the baroque roots of this dynastic piety, see the classic work by Anna Coreth, *Pietas Austriaca*. West Lafayette, IN, 2004.

[91] 'Die Erzbischöfe und Bischöfe Österreichs: Hirtenbrief', *Wiener Diözesanblatt*, 24 Aug. 1918, 105.

The pastoral letter was to be read out in instalments 'on the following Sundays' and explained 'in a colloquial way', with particular reference to the religious origin of the monarch's power.[92] Its echo in the press multiplied the text's effect.[93] Religion thus took on an increasingly exclusionary tone. When the archbishops referred, in graphic terms, to the 'well-known secret societies whose share in this war has repeatedly been made public',[94] their words could easily be read as anti-socialist and anti-Semitic in the context of other statements in the press.[95] Criticism of the letter therefore appeared predominantly in socialist newspapers. Seeking to anchor *political* support for the empire in the Catholic faith, to which 80 per cent of the population adhered, went hand in hand with discrimination against other religious communities in this multi-religious empire.

Historic Crown Land Federalism

In the debates on the 'Manifesto to his Peoples', historic crown land federalism appears as a fourth type of federalism and as a negative foil of the reform. Of the variants, it was the one that had most strongly shaped the federal history of the nineteenth century. Crown land federalism, as impressively symbolized by the 1849 lithograph 'Barque with Austria', is characterized by the emergence of constituent states from the crown lands. As political-historical 'nations', they were home to different linguistic and cultural communities. During the era of political nationalization, historic crown land federalism typified the 'old' order, in stark contrast to the 'new' federal state of the nationalities.

[92] 'Die Erzbischöfe und Bischöfe Österreichs: Hirtenbrief', *Wiener Diözesanblatt*, 24 Aug. 1918, 105. Emperor Karl had lost popularity after the so-called Sixtus Affair, when he lost face regarding domestic and foreign policy due to the revelation of secret negotiations of his foreign minister, Ottokar Czernin, with France.

[93] Cf. 'Hirtenbrief der Erzbischöfe und Bischöfe von Österreich: Über den politischen Treubruch und über die Fehler der Nahrungspolitik', *Neue Freie Presse* (Abendblatt), 29 Aug. 1918, 1; 'Der Hirtenbrief des österreichischen Episkopats: Über Krieg und Frieden und die Ernährungsfrage', *Neue Freie Presse* (Abendblatt), 29 Aug. 1918, 2; 'Österreichs Bischöfe über ernste Fragen der Kriegszeit', *Reichspost*, 29 Aug. 1918, 3–4; 'Hirtenbrief', *Wiener Zeitung*, 29 Aug. 1918, 3; 'Das Recht auf Ernte: Der Hirtenbrief des österreichischen Episkopats', *Neues Wiener Journal*, 30 Aug. 1918, 2; 'Hirtenbrief des österreichischen Episkopats', *Prager Tagblatt* (evening edition), 29 Aug. 1918, 1; 'Ein Hirtenbrief der Bischöfe Österreichs', *Pilsener Tagblatt*, 30 Aug. 1918, 3; 'Ein gemeinsamer Hirtenbrief', *Vorarlberger Volksblatt*, 31 Aug. 1918, 1; 'Der Hirtenbrief der Bischöfe Österreichs', *Der Tiroler*, 31 Aug. 1918, 1; 'Ein Hirtenbrief der Erzbischöfe und Bischöfe Österreichs', *Linzer Volksblatt*, 31 Aug. 1918, 1; 'Hirtenbrief des österreichischen Episkopats', *Fremdenblatt*, 30 Aug. 1918, 5; 'Hirtenbrief des österreichischen Episkopats', *Salzburger Chronik*, 30 Sept. 1918, 3–4; 'Das Hirtenschreiben der österreichischen Bischöfe', *Linzer Volksblatt*, 1 Sept. 1918, 6.

[94] 'Die Erzbischöfe und Bischöfe Österreichs: Hirtenbrief gegeben am 4.8.1918', *Wiener Diözesanblatt*, 24 Aug. 1918, 99.

[95] Cf. the anti-Semitic cartoon on the pastoral letter: 'Der Hirtenbrief der Bischöfe', *Kikeriki*, 8 Sept. 1918, 7. On anti-Semitism in the Austrian press, Jens Malte Fischer, *Karl Kraus: Der Widersprecher*. Vienna, 2020.

The importance of the crown lands in the day-to-day politics of war-ravaged Austria was, however, far greater than Karl's abandonment of the historic crown lands in favour of a federation of the nationalities would have us believe. During the First World War, it was often the institutions of the crown lands that felt responsible for remedying supply crises. In tackling these challenges, they drew on informal networks of cooperation that had existed before the war. Indeed, during this period of crisis, exchanges between the crown lands intensified. They were suddenly confronted with collapsing food and housing supplies and the loss of welfare and other basic infrastructures. Vienna was particularly hard hit.[96] Crown land institutions had to fill the gaps left by an imperial government that was increasingly incapable of dealing with such matters. Already in the first year of the war, the crown land governors of Gorizia-Gradisca, Istria, Trieste, Dalmatia, Carniola, Carinthia, Styria, Tyrol, and Vorarlberg met in Gorizia to find a solution to the food crisis.[97]

At the last meeting of the crown lands (*Länderkonferenzen*) in 1918, held in the Lower Austrian *Landhaus* in Vienna's Herrengasse, the delegates discussed very specific provincial powers that were to be defended against encroachments by the empire.[98] Collectively, the various governors drew up a communiqué 'against the efforts of the government to curtail the rights of the crown lands laid out in the constitution and to significantly restrict their powers of action'.[99] In this communiqué, they objected to restrictions on the 'autonomy of the provinces' in the areas of agriculture, water rights, electricity use, social welfare, public health, finances, and teachers' salaries.[100]

In this last year of war, the crown lands also faced competition from local non-state organizations, most notably the 'people's councils' and 'welfare' and 'economic' committees.[101] During the strike of January 1918, this rivalry intensified as workers' (and later soldiers') councils based on the Russian model sprang up throughout Austria under the aegis of the Social Democrats.[102] Faced with a catastrophic supply situation, newly established 'National People's Councils' assumed public functions in the mixed-language crown lands.[103] At both the imperial level

[96] See Maureen Healy, *Vienna and the Fall of the Habsburg Empire: Total War and Everyday Life in World War.* Cambridge, 2004, and Pieter Judson and Tara Zahra, The Great War and the Transformation of Habsburg Central Europe. New York, 2025.

[97] Nachbaur, '1918. Selbständiges Land Vorarlberg', 68.

[98] On meetings of the *Länder* and government representatives, detailed Nachbaur, '1918. Selbständiges Land Vorarlberg', 76.

[99] 'Kundgebung gegen die Eingriffe in die Länderautonomie', *Salzburger Chronik,* 15 Mar. 1918, 1.

[100] 'Kundgebung gegen die Eingriffe in die Länderautonomie', *Salzburger Chronik,* 15 Mar. 1918, 1.

[101] Alfred Ableitinger, 'Demokratisierung und Landesverfassung 1918–1920: Versuch einer Bilanz'. In Ableitinger (ed.), *Demokratisierung und Verfassung in den Ländern 1918–1920.* Vienna, 1983, 186.

[102] Erika Weinzierl, 'Revolution und Demokratisierung in Österreich'. In: Ableitinger, *Demokratisierung und Verfassung,* 19.

[103] Nachbaur, '1918. Selbständiges Land Vorarlberg', 68.

in the Vienna Reichsrat and at the regional and local level in the crown lands, a 'socialization' of politics ran in parallel with 'nationalization'.

Apart from this practical importance of the *Länder*, German-speaking politicians wanted to preserve the historic crown land federalism out of fear that a future federal state of nationalities would erode de facto German supremacy in the *Länder*. As the *Deutsche Volksblatt für Galizien* (German People's Gazette for Galicia) put it bluntly in May 1918: the purpose and direction of constitutional reform could only be 'to finally and with all available means secure the long-threatened *Deutschtum* (German identity), surrounded on all sides, either where it is necessary, through the autonomy of the *Länder*, or where it proves more expedient, through the autonomy of the peoples.'[104] In October, the former Austrian minister of justice, the scholar and later member of the Paris peace delegation Frank Klein, wrote in the *Neue Freie Presse* that reform should not restrict the present position of the individual nations. He remarked: 'Federalism must not become a pretext or a cover for national conquests or oppression, and as things stand, it must certainly not be abused to strike at the heart of Austrian *Deutschtum*.'[105]

1.6. Dissolution and Cohesion

Unravelling the federal history from its end reveals that federalism remained one of the most important political guiding principles until the last days of the Habsburg Monarchy. It was meant to create both order and unity in diversity. Unlike in May 1917, however, by the autumn of 1918, federalism had lost much of its appeal.

The *Pester Lloyd*, published in Budapest, observed of a nationally based federalism that:

> the neglected geography poses almost intractable problems. A Ruthenian state in eastern Galicia, or even a Romanian dwarf state in Bukovina, would only be able to communicate with the other federal states via foreign territory. German Bohemia and German Silesia are also geographically separated from the rest of German Austria. If the Czech state closed itself off from them, only lengthy detours would allow the parts of German Austria to remain in contact with each other.[106]

The important point here, however, is the author's insight into the need for cohesion, which is also evident in the newspaper articles and private notes of others.

[104] 'Selbstregierung der Völker oder der Länder', *Deutsches Volksblatt für Galizien*, 23 May 1918, 1.
[105] 'Die Grenzen des Föderalismus', *Neue Freie Presse*, 1 Oct. 1918.
[106] 'Das kaiserliche Manifest über die Neugestaltung Österreichs', *Pester Lloyd*, 18 Oct. 1918, 1–2.

He goes on to say: 'Even in a federal state, the hearts of the citizens must beat in the same rhythm; even in a federal state, the state exists through the will of its citizens; even in a federal state, the federal feeling is the supreme condition of common life.'[107]

It was precisely this cohesion of peoples and nationalities that was eroded by the radiance of the nation-state idea. After the collapse of the Habsburg Monarchy, a 'federalism paradox' arose in the state and constitution building of its successor states.[108] The democratic federal state of Austria emerged from the German-speaking lands, whose elites had been considered 'centralist' during the monarchy. The 'federalist' crown lands and communities, by contrast, above all the Bohemian, South Slavic, and Romanian, established centralized states.

A Federal History of the Habsburg Empire, 1815–1918. Jana Osterkamp, Oxford University Press.
 DOI: 10.1093/9780198943631.003.0002

[107] 'Das kaiserliche Manifest über die Neugestaltung Österreichs', *Pester Lloyd*, 18 Oct. 1918, 1–2.

[108] Jana Osterkamp, 'Ein Reich ohne Eigenschaften? Das Erbe föderaler Ideen in den "Nachfolgestaaten" der Habsburgermonarchie'. In Rumpler and Harmat, *Die Habsburgermonarchie 1848–1918*, 431–57.

Figure 2.1 Railway viaduct over the lagoons to Venice. Steel engraving, 1847.

2
Multiplicity of Governance Before 1848

A century before Karl's 'Manifesto to his Peoples', Central Europe was a patchwork of territories under various forms of governance. The innovations of the *Vormärz* period, in particular the railroad and telegraph, created new networks between these territories. Spectacular construction projects were received with enthusiasm: contemporaries hailed the Austrian railway line across the lagoons to Venice (Figure 2.1), as the 'longest bridge in the world'. Despite this ever-increasing interconnectedness, the Enlightenment model of a centrally controlled *Verwaltungsstaat* (administrative state), developed under Maria Theresa and Joseph II, now seemed antiquated and ill-suited to modernity.[1] The organization of diversity became the mantra of the pre-1848 period. In 1840, Johann Springer, a leading statistician, political scientist, and university professor wrote:

> Considering the diversity of nations and organic institutions which characterises our Monarchy, the same laws could never be applied to every one of its subjects... For this reason, it has become the system of Austrian legislation to regulate and guide the unique circumstances of the provinces by means of special provisions.[2]

The way in which territories and regions overlapped in the Habsburg Monarchy is without parallel in European history.[3] Since the early modern period, complex 'entanglements'[4] had developed with the Holy Roman Empire, whose imperial crown the Habsburgs wore for centuries. This constellation was one of the most important foundations of the later Habsburg laboratory of federalist ideas. The multinational and multi-religious diversity of the imperial territories and regions

[1] Barbara Stollberg-Rilinger, *Der Staat als Maschine: Zur politischen Metaphorik des absoluten Fürstenstaats*. Berlin, 1986.

[2] Johann Springer, *Statistik des österreichischen Kaiserstaates*. Vol. 2. Vienna, 1840, 5–6. On Metternich's turn towards a culturally based nationalities policy in the 1840s, Wolfram Siemann, *Metternich: Strategist and Visionary*. Cambridge, MA, 2019, 665–7. Similar on the ruling principle of diversity, Johann Philipp Weber, 'Über die Gränzen des Landes Österreich unter der Enns', *Beiträge zur Landeskunde Oesterreichs unter der Enns*, 1 (1832), 169.

[3] On the characteristics of European statehood cf. Wolfgang Reinhard, *Geschichte der Staatsgewalt: Eine vergleichende Verfassungsgeschichte Europas von den Anfängen bis zur Gegenwart*. 2nd edn. Munich, 2000, 16.

[4] Petr Maťa, 'Die Habsburgermonarchie'. In Maťa Michael Hochedlinger, and Thomas Winkelbauer (eds), *Verwaltungsgeschichte der Habsburgermonarchie in der Frühen Neuzeit*. Vol. 1/1: *Hof und Dynastie, Kaiser und Reich, Zentralverwaltungen, Kriegswesen und landesfürstliches Finanzwesen*. Vienna, 2019, 30.

set the monarchy apart from the *Kleinstaaterei* of the principalities in the German Confederation. In order to understand the distinctive features of the Habsburg *Vormärz*, we must distinguish territories and spaces from one another.

Political *territories* have geographical demarcations (borders) within which control over public life, or a part of it, is exercised. In the pre-1848 period, this control was rarely vested in a single sovereign—a monarch, a state, an authority, the estates, or landed authorities—but was shared among different actors.[5] For this reason, federal ideas referred to different overlapping territories—the dynastic territories of the monarchy, the territories of the estates, the historical *Länder*, the administrative territories of the central and gubernatorial authorities, or the German federal territories.

Political *spaces*, by contrast, delineate existing and imagined differences between nations, linguistic groups, religions, or economic systems. Their delineations are often unclear and characterized by vague and blurred boundaries.[6] By including linguistic, cultural, religious, and economic areas as future constituent states of a federation, federalist thinkers sought to capture a diversity that might be at odds with territorial borders.

2.1. Territorialization in the Heart of Europe

During the *Vormärz*, the government structures of both the Habsburg Monarchy and the German Confederation were closely interwoven. Over several centuries, the Habsburgs had attained their 'ultimate dynastic goal', namely the imperial crown of the Holy Roman Empire, without merging the two orders of power into one.[7] The territories with a dual affiliation to the monarchy and the Deutscher Bund (German Confederation) were the Kingdom of Bohemia,[8] the Archduchies Above and Below the Enns (Upper and Lower Austria), the Duchies of Styria, Carinthia and Carniola, the Margraviate of Moravia, the County of Tyrol, and Austrian Silesia.[9] The Archdiocese of Salzburg and the Diocese of Trento also fell

[5] Charles S. Maier, 'Transformations of Territoriality 1600–2000' In Gunilla Budde, Sebastian Conrad, and Oliver Janz (eds), *Transnationale Geschichte: Themen, Tendenzen und Theorien*. Göttingen, 2006, 34.

[6] Matthias Middell and Katja Naumann, 'Global History and the Spatial Turn: From the Impact of Area Studies to the Study of Critical Junctures of Globalization', *Journal of Global History*, 5/1 (2010), 159.

[7] Maťa, 'Habsburgermonarchie', 30. Cf. Axel Gotthard, 'Die habsburgischen Länder und das Alte Reich'. In Maťa et al., *Verwaltungsgeschichte der Frühen Neuzeit*, 1/1. 372.

[8] Bohemia was not eligible for fiefdom in the Old Empire, but only lent its electoral dignity (*Kurwürde*), which meant that it was not included in the imperial institutions until the beginning of the eighteenth century. See below and Barbara Stollberg-Rilinger, *Das Heilige Römische Reich Deutscher Nation. Vom Ende des Mittelalters bis 1806*. Munich, 2006, 22.

[9] On the formation of the Inner Austrian Lands and a corresponding regional consciousness see Ernst Bruckmüller, *Nation Österreich: Kulturelles Bewusstsein und gesellschaftlich-politische Prozesse*. 2nd edn. Vienna, 1996, 159–99.

into this category. Before reverting to the Habsburgs after the Napoleonic Wars, they had been ecclesiastical state territories in the Holy Roman Empire and thus reinforced the monarchy's character as the supreme Catholic power in Central Europe.[10] The Kingdoms of Galicia-Lodomeria and Lombardy-Venetia, as well as Dalmatia and the Lands of the St Stephen's Crown, lay outside the German Confederation.

However, neither the German Confederation nor the Habsburg Monarchy was 'sovereign' in a modern sense. The Habsburg rulers, for instance, had ceded some sovereign rights to the German federal institutions. Conversely, given Vienna's hegemonic aspirations, no long-term 'federal policy' could be pursued in Germany without considering Austria and its Hungarian, Italian, and Galician interests. The political, legal, and social consequences of this arrangement have recently been described as a diversity 'forgotten' by the historiography.[11] Although many state law experts and politicians at the time did not consider this conglomerate of diverse forms of governance to be sustainable in the long run, it remained an open question as to whether the German Confederation, the federal states, or the 'empires' of Austria and Prussia would one day develop into states, federations, or empires.

What Kind of State?

Contemporary legal scholars, when describing this multiplicity of governance, often articulated their political aspirations for the future only in an implied way. In the German state theory of the time, however, the German Confederation played a major role both as a constitutional state and a *nationally* consolidated federal state.[12] Johann Ludwig Klüber, a Frankfurt legal theorist, is a prime example. His major work, *Öffentliches Recht des Teutschen Bundes und der Bundesstaaten* (Public Law of the German Confederation and the Federal States), contained a hidden paean of praise for future German unity.[13] Klüber treated Austrian state law—as well as the state law of the other monarchical federal states—as part of a wider German imperial law. He compared governmental structures in the various German federal states, labelling their collective commonalities 'a general German state law'. Behind these scholarly and legal machinations, Klüber masked his political and 'patriotic' motivation to replace 'the

[10] Gotthard, 'Die habsburgischen Länder', 360.

[11] Steffi Marung and Katja Naumann, 'Einleitung'. In Marung and Naumann (eds), *Vergessene Vielfalt: Territorialität und Internationalisierung in Ostmitteleuropa seit der Mitte des 19. Jahrhunderts*. Göttingen, 2014, 9–44.

[12] Michael Stolleis, *Geschichte des öffentlichen Rechts in Deutschland*. Vol. 2: *Staatsrechtslehre und Verwaltungswissenschaft 1800–1914*. Munich, 1992, 85.

[13] Johann Ludwig Klüber, *Öffentliches Recht des Teutschen Bundes und der Bundesstaaten*. 3rd edn. 2 vols. Frankfurt am Main, 1831.

missing unity, at least in part'.[14] Klüber's approach met with positive responses in Austria, not least from Johann Springer. In his aforementioned *Statistik*, Springer had defended the multiform character of Austrian dynastic rule, but now gave Klüber an extremely favourable review.[15]

Despite this determination to find unity, state theory in the Habsburg Monarchy could not simply adopt the idea of a nation state. In its place, Austrian legal theorists had been cultivating what was called *Gesamtstaatsidee* (comprehensive state idea) since the eighteenth century. Based in the Enlightenment ideals of common welfare and efficiency, it was eagerly advanced by the Austrian government which sought to reinvent the dynasty as a modern state. The 'comprehensive state idea' has rightly been described as a 'legal master narrative' (Martin Schennach) or as a 'state mythology' (Barbara Stollberg-Rilinger), which skilfully combined the dynastic familial and hereditary rights of the Habsburgs with their actual exercise of power.[16] The glue holding the state together was to be the Pragmatic Sanction of 1713. Establishing uniform rules of succession for all Habsburg dominions, it declared that the Habsburg inheritance, namely the provinces, were to be 'indivisible and inseparable'.[17] This was augmented by an unequivocal and politically symbolic religious claim to dominion as the supreme Catholic power of the 'Christian West'.[18]

Habsburg enthusiasm for making the 'comprehensive state idea' a practical reality waned during the *Vormärz* period. Activist policies to establish a comprehensive state and a polity governed according to *uniform* principles had predominantly been the concern of Maria Theresa and her son Joseph II who continued her modernization of the government. Joseph wanted to replace the monarchy's traditional division into hereditary provinces (and, concurrently, the influence of the provincial estates, especially the noble elites) with a centralized and unified state administration.[19] Since the end of the eighteenth century, the expansion of

[14] Stolleis, *Geschichte des öffentlichen Rechts*, 2. 84.

[15] Johann, Springer, 'Oeffentliches Recht des deutschen Bundes und der Bundesstaaten, von Johann Ludwig Klüber', *Zeitschrift für österreichische Rechtsgelehrsamkeit und politische Gesetzkunde*, 3 (1831), 421–3.

[16] Martin P. Schennach, 'Die "österreichische Gesamtstaatsidee": Das Verhältnis von Gesamtstaat und Ländern als Gegenstand rechtshistorischer Forschung'. In Schennach (ed.), *Rechtshistorische Aspekte des österreichischen Föderalismus: Beiträge zur Tagung an der Universität Innsbruck am 28. und 29. November 2013*. Vienna, 2015, 1–29; Barbara Stollberg-Rilinger, *Maria Theresia: The Habsburg Empress in her Time*. Princeton, 2021, 250–2; Reinhard, *Geschichte der Staatsgewalt*, 58. Representative for this master narrative Hermann Ignaz Bidermann, *Geschichte der österreichischen Gesamt-Staats-Idee 1526–1804*. Vol. 1: *1526–1705*. Innsbruck, 1867; vol. 2: *1705–1740*. Innsbruck, 1889.

[17] Wilhelm Brauneder, *Die Pragmatische Sanktion*. In Brauneder (ed.), *Studien I: Entwicklung des Öffentlichen Rechts I*. Frankfurt am Main, 1994, 85–116. In comparative state history, dynastic indivisibility is also considered a criterion for the transition from provincial dominion to the territorial state. Reinhard, *Geschichte der Staatsgewalt*, 56.

[18] Gotthard, 'Die habsburgischen Länder', 364–5.

[19] Irmgard Plattner, *Josephinismus und Bürokratie*. In Helmut Reinalter (ed.), *Josephinismus als aufgeklärter Absolutismus*. Vienna, 2008, 53–96.

the Austrian central administration proceeded like a creeping *frontier*[20] to the north, west, and south, with each step the Habsburg rulers took towards centralization.[21] Despite the new institution of the *Vereinigte Hofkanzlei* (United Court Chancellery), however, growth of the Austrian central administration did not extend beyond the inner border with Hungary.

In the *Vormärz*, the emperors Franz and Ferdinand ultimately abandoned Maria Theresa's and Joseph's idea of a 'comprehensive state'. Klemens von Metternich and other imperial advisers were no longer able to implement governance according to uniform principles and laws emanating from *one* central authority for the entire territory; Emperor Franz lacked the conviction to help, Emperor Ferdinand the capacity.[22] Interpretations of this volte-face away from the 'comprehensive state' either label it a serious error, or frame it positively as an imperial 'policy of discernment'.[23] In addition to the United Court Chancellery for the Austrian, Bohemian, Italian, Galician, and Dalmatian territories, there existed a Hungarian Chancellery and a Transylvanian Chancellery.[24] The statistician Springer commented: 'Hungary and Transylvania are excluded from the common legislation; their laws differ markedly, both in system and content, from those of the other lands of the monarchy.'[25] The insistence on three central chancelleries both reinforced the boundaries between the Hungarian and non-Hungarian lands delineated by the German Confederation and anticipated later borders under dualism after 1867.[26]

The asymmetry between these central authorities is evidenced by the way in which their subordinate offices were organized. The United Court Chancellery for the Austrian, Bohemian, Italian, Galician, and Dalmatian territories oversaw twelve government or governorate districts with twelve provincial capitals.[27] Below these provincial governorates, *Kreisämter* (county offices) emerged as a further level of centralization. These offices were intended to monitor the local administration (district authorities, feudal dominions, and municipalities) and to act as a liaison between the central administration and the estates and feudal dominions.[28] The Hungarian and Transylvanian chancelleries, on the other hand,

[20] For frontiers as a concept see below.

[21] Georg Seiderer, *Österreichs Neugestaltung: Verfassungspolitik und Verwaltungsreform im österreichischen Neoabsolutismus unter Alexander Bach 1849–1859*. Vienna, 2015, 55. See also Marco Bellabarba, *Das Habsburgerreich 1765–1918*. Berlin and Boston, 2020.

[22] John Deak, *Forging a Multinational State: State Making in Imperial Austria from the Enlightenment to the First World War*. Stanford, CA, 2015, 34–49.

[23] Maťa, 'Habsburgermonarchie', 48.

[24] Springer, *Statistik des Kaiserstaates*, 2. 19.

[25] Springer, *Statistik des Kaiserstaates*, 2. 6.

[26] Maťa, 'Habsburgermonarchie', 48.

[27] This involved the provincial gubernias of Lower Austria (Vienna), Upper Austria and Salzburg (Linz), Styria (Graz), Tyrol and Vorarlberg (Innsbruck), Carinthia and Carniola (Laibach, Ljubljana), Littoral (Trieste), Bohemia (Prague), Moravia and Silesia (Brno), Galicia and Bukovina (Lemberg, Lviv, Lwów), Venice, Lombardy (Mailand, Milan) and Dalmatia (Zara, Zadar). Springer, *Statistik des Kaiserstaates*, 2. 20–1.

[28] There were eighty-five county offices and seventeen delegations, as the counties in Lombardy-Venetia were called. Springer, *Statistik des Kaiserstaates*, 2. 27. See also Seiderer, *Österreichs Neugestaltung*,

had no intermediate state authorities under their control, even though the comitats (equivalents of the counties) of Hungary and Transylvania formed mid-sized administrative units. In addition, the heads of the comitat offices were not trained civil servants; instead these positions were seen as the hereditary property of local noble families.[29]

What Kind of Empire?

The creation of a new Central European state under Austrian leadership was the concern not only of liberal thinkers; conservative theorists had a significant impact as well. Just as liberal thinkers applied the idea of the state, oscillating between the nation state and the administrative state, to various possible territories—the monarchy as a whole, its administrative units, or even the German Confederation—for conservatives, there were also several ideas of the *Reich* (empire).

Ideas of the *Reich* were, for a start, linked to the emperorship. In 1804, Franz II, Holy Roman Emperor, proclaimed himself Franz I, the hereditary Emperor of Austria. Emperor Franz thus extracted the imperial dignity from the declining Holy Roman Empire and 'demonstratively placed the dynastic Habsburg identity above the traditional imperial dignity'.[30] Unlike the imperial dignity of the 'old' empire, the 'new' Austrian empire initially included the Hungarian, Galician, and Italian lands. In this *translatio imperii*, the Austrian imperial title took on a symbolic rather than dynastic meaning. Its assumption did not directly alter existing relations of historical and hereditary rule. Instead, the Austrian emperorship was based (like that of Napoleon) on an act of self-empowerment that needed to be sanctioned by external recognition.[31] Franz successfully removed the mantle of Europe-wide prestige and ceremonial prerogatives that had been borne by the old imperial title and placed it around himself and his empire.[32] To reinforce this illusion, the government commissioned new panegyrics, monuments, and regional descriptions.[33] Artists heralded the emperor in a genealogy stretching back to Rome, portraying him as a 'Roman Imperator'.[34]

56; Jiří Klabouch, 'Die Lokalverwaltung in Cisleithanien'. In Adam Wandruszka and Peter Urbanitsch (eds), *Die Habsburgermonarchie 1848–1918*. Vol. 2: *Verwaltung und Rechtswesen*. Vienna, 1975, 270–305.

[29] Springer, *Statistik des Kaiserstaates*, 2. 36.

[30] Stollberg-Rilinger, *Das Heilige Römische Reich*, 115.

[31] Dieter Langewiesche, *Die Monarchie im Jahrhundert Europas: Selbstbehauptung durch Wandel im 19. Jahrhundert*. Heidelberg, 2013.

[32] Gotthard, 'Die habsburgischen Länder', 365.

[33] For the art-historical discussion see Werner Telesko, *Geschichtsraum Österreich: Die Habsburger und ihre Geschichte in der bildenden Kunst des 19. Jahrhunderts*. Vienna, 2006; Selma Krasa-Florian, *Die Allegorie der Austria: Die Entstehung des Gesamtstaatsgedankens in der österreichisch-ungarischen Monarchie und die bildende Kunst*. Vienna, 2007.

[34] Telesko, *Geschichtsraum Österreich*, 217.

The spatial scope of the new imperial title varied, precisely because this new empire was dependent on recognition from outside. What Europe granted the emperor during the *Vormärz* was denied to him by the Hungarian provinces after 1848. Hungarian legal scholars refused to recognize the ruler as 'emperor' and thus his territories as a unified empire. In their view, the Habsburgs were emperors in Austria, but in Hungary only kings.[35]

Moreover, the new concept of empire was challenged by its predecessor. The old Holy Roman Empire had created deep-rooted attachments, especially among the German-speaking population. Habsburg policy towards Germany had kept these ties alive. When the old empire fell in 1806, Vienna's ambitions to dominate Germany remained unchanged. Leading politicians such as Metternich, as well as many politically literate observers in the German-speaking population, continued to see the German Confederation and the Habsburg Monarchy as parts of a composite, yet common empire dominated by Austria.[36]

The older, traditional imperial title contained a list of all the territories to which the Habsburgs had had historical claims. This list expressed a different idea of unity. According to their 'lesser title of sovereignty', the Habsburg ruler was concurrently 'Emperor of Austria, King of Hungary, Bohemia, Lombardy and Venice, of Galicia, Lodomeria and Illyria, [and] Archduke of Austria'. The place of each crown in the hierarchy was historically informed. The Hungarian St Stephen's Crown, the Bohemian Wenceslas Crown, and the Lombard Iron Crown each had centuries-old histories. Even in the pre-1848 period, they continued to be celebrated in pompous and elaborate coronation ceremonies. As a young man, the historian František Palacký had composed the Czech-language speeches given as the new king was paid homage by the estates and welcomed at a reception by Prague's governor Karl von Chotek in 1836.[37] These celebrations created a sense of belonging to the 'crown', rather than to the empire as a whole. The Kingdom of Galicia (1772) and the Kingdom of Illyria (1814) were artefacts of more recent provenance that did not merit such costly coronation ceremonies.[38]

According to the so-called 'intermediate title of sovereignty', the kingdoms of 'Dalmatia, Croatia, Slavonia' still existed within Hungary, as the archduchies of Carinthia and Carniola did within Illyria.[39] The epithet 'King of Jerusalem', which was also included, was to be understood more as a symbolic 'commemorative title',[40] a kind of appellative *lieu de mémoire*. For state reformers, federal thinkers,

[35] Friedrich Tezner, *Der österreichische Kaisertitel, das ungarische Staatsrecht und die ungarische Publicistik*. Vienna, 1899.

[36] Siemann, *Metternich*, 680.

[37] Jiří Kořalka, *František Palacký (1798–1876): Der Historiker der Tschechen im österreichischen Vielvölkerstaat*. Vienna, 2007, 171.

[38] Deak, *Forging a Multinational State*, 37. See also Langewiesche, *Monarchie*, 11.

[39] The 'great title of rule' was even more elaborate and provided each individual territory with a respective dominion predicate.

[40] Springer, *Statistik des Kaiserstaates*, 2. 11.

and nationalist politicians, titles of sovereignty such as these were crucial when it came to claiming historical regions as constitutional territories. The importance of the title as an instrument for empowering territorial expansion can be seen in the naming of the 'Kingdom of Rama'.[41] In 1878, it justified occupation of Bosnia-Herzegovina 'under international law'. The idea of the imperial territories inherent in sovereign titles thus extended beyond the territories actually ruled.

Which Kind of Participation?

The new definition of the Austrian Empire did not change anything about the fact that the Austrian monarch ruled the respective hereditary territories in his capacity as *Landesfürst* (duke of the state), not as 'emperor'. His sovereignty was founded on the *Landesverfassungen* (state charters) and he had to share this power with the provincial estates, where they still existed. The multiplicity of governance in the territories consisted of both the lands administered by the estates (the hereditary lands) and the 'territories' of their individual members (the landed dominions).

Throughout the monarchy, the landed estates varied in composition, social stratification, and sovereignty. The Hungarian and Transylvanian diets maintained extensive legislative and judicial powers. In the non-Hungarian territories, taxation and legislative competence rested with the emperor. The purview of the estates had been significantly curtailed. They were entitled to make requests or to table suggestions and criticisms.[42] Recent research describes the interaction between the emperor and the estates as a mixture of cooperation and competition.[43]

Nevertheless, the political weight of the provincial diets was such as to make them central to the plans for federal reform after 1848. By the 1860s they had established themselves as an integral part of the new federal empire. Napoleon's dissolution of the Old Empire was the wellspring of this development. The *Reichsdeputationshauptschluss* (Imperial Recess) of 1803, which had secularized extensive territories across the Holy Roman Empire, had laid the 'intellectual

[41] On this ancient designation for Bosnia and Herzegovina, cf. Ludwig Albrecht Gebhardi, *Geschichte der Königreiche Dalmatien, Kroatien, Szlavonien, Servien, Raszien, Bosnien, Rama und des Freystaats Ragusa*. Pest, 1808.

[42] Springer, *Statistik des Kaiserstaates*, 1. 255.

[43] Volker Press, 'Landstände des 18. und Parlamente des 19. Jahrhunderts'. In Helmut Berding and Hans-Peter Ullmann (eds), *Deutschland zwischen Revolution und Restauration*. Königstein im Taunus, 1981, 145. The history of the estates is still under-researched, cf. Gerhard Ammerer, William D. Godsey Jr, Martin Scheutz, Peter Urbanitsch, and Alfred Stefan Weiss, 'Die Stände in der Habsburgermonarchie: Eine Einleitung'. In Ammerer, Godsey, Scheutz, Urbanitsch, and Weiss (eds), *Bündnispartner und Konkurrenten des Landesfürsten? Die Stände in der Habsburgermonarchie*. Vienna and Munich, 2007, 14–15.

foundations for the development of modern statehood' in the provinces.[44] The Treaties of Teplitz (Teplice) of 1813, meanwhile, affirmed the 'absolute independence of the individual states'.[45] In 1819, the Austrian Emperor signed the declaration of accession to the *Deutsche Bund* (German Confederation) on behalf of individual provinces, rather than Austria as a whole.[46] Later still, the Federal Act of 1820 guaranteed the territorial integrity of the hereditary lands and promised them estate-based constitutions. Because the Viennese government did not universally abide by these guarantees the diets and estates in Styria, Lower Austria, or Bohemia took many political matters into their own hands during the *Vormärz*. These activities helped to keep the provinces politically relevant.

At the same time, the elements of the Holy Roman Empire feudalism remained prominent. Local administration and jurisdiction were often exercised by the landed gentry and manorial lords, who were monitored, but not directed, by the county offices of the state.[47] Regional variation was considerable.[48] In Lombardy-Venetia, Dalmatia, Salzburg, or Tyrol, which had been under Bavarian or Franco-Italian rule during the Napoleonic period, the patrimonial dominions were not permanently re-established after 1815. Instead, political administration was centralized. The aristocratic and ecclesiastical elites, however, managed to retain their influence, in practice if not in law.[49]

After 1848, the landed dominions ceased to exist as political entities. For political liberals, the exercise of public authority by private individuals had become outdated. The transfer of patrimonial rights to the central government in exchange for compensation had already been advocated by some landlords in Lower Austria during the pre-1848 period, particularly those who owned small, costly, and thus unviable estates. Vienna, however, showed no interest in assuming these responsibilities and costs.[50] One responsibility the estates tried to shed and the central government refused to pick up was the so-called 'Schubwesen', the

[44] Ingo Knecht, *Der Reichsdeputationshauptschluß vom 25. Februar 1803*. Berlin, 2007, 238; Bernd Grzeszick, *Vom Reich zur Bundesstaatsidee: Zur Herausbildung der Föderalismusidee als Element des modernen deutschen Staatsrechts*. Berlin, 1996, 136–7.

[45] Reinhard Stauber, 'Föderative Staatlichkeit in der Mitte Europas: Zur Entstehung des Deutschen Bundes'. In Dietmar Willoweit (ed.), *Föderalismus in Deutschland: Zu seiner wechselvollen Geschichte vom ostfränkischen Königtum bis zur Bundesrepublik*. Vienna, 2019, 215.

[46] 'Österreichische Erklärung über die zum Deutschen Bund gehörenden Provinzen und Gebiete der österreichischen Monarchie vom 6.4.1818'. In Eckhardt Treichel (ed.), *Quellen zur Geschichte des Deutschen Bundes*. Vol. 2: *Organisation und innere Ausgestaltung des Deutschen Bundes 1815–1819*. Munich, 2016, No. 51, 200–1.

[47] See Seiderer, *Österreichs Neugestaltung*, 53–71.

[48] Ralph Melville, *Adel und Revolution in Böhmen: Strukturwandel von Herrschaft und Gesellschaft in Österreich um die Mitte des 19. Jahrhunderts*. Mainz, 1998, 15–60. On the German Confederation see Monika Wienfort, 'Ländliche Rechtsverfassung und bürgerliche Gesellschaft: Patrimonialgerichtsbarkeit in den deutschen Staaten 1800–1855', *Der Staat*, 33/2 (1994), 207–39.

[49] Seiderer, *Österreichs Neugestaltung*, 59–60.

[50] Helmut Feigl, 'Der Adel in Niederösterreich 1780–. In Armgard von Reden-Dohna (ed.), *Der Adel an der Schwelle des bürgerlichen Zeitalters 1780–1860*. Stuttgart, 1988, 196. The state only took over criminal jurisdiction, cf. Melville, *Adel und Revolution*, 66.

repatriation of beggars and the socially needy[51] who found themselves stranded at the gates of Vienna.

Liberal doubt over patrimonial rule paved the way for greater participation. The diets' traditional role as representative bodies for the *interests* of the nobility and the clergy was gradually transformed under the enlightened ideal of universal *representation* and service of the common good for the entire population and province.[52] The diets of Vorarlberg and Tyrol already counted burghers and peasants in their ranks.[53] Lower Austria and Styria likewise began to include burghers, town representatives, and peasants in the diet.[54] In 1843, the highly popular pamphlet 'Österreich und dessen Zukunft' (Austria and its Future), written by the aristocrat Viktor von Andrian-Werburg, called for a constitutionally guaranteed representation of the people as the foundation of a new federally structured monarchy.[55] His aim was not only to make the diets fully representative, but also to weaken the central authorities. Within the somewhat disparate and scattered estates movement, Andrian became an important and visible leader.[56]

Territorialization at Varying Paces

The expansion of governance in the political territories unfolded at varying speeds. There was a tension, typical of empires, between the imperial centre and the peripheries. If one superimposes the territories of the Monarchy, the German Confederation, the United Court Chancellery, and the politically active estates, a small area emerges in the Bohemian and Austrian lands where they overlap—the imperial centre. This heartland between Vienna, Linz, Graz, Prague, Brno, and Ostrava flourished economically, politically, culturally, and socially and was closely interwoven with both the German Confederation and the Habsburg Monarchy as a whole.

Proximity to the capital was decisive. With a population of 476,000 inhabitants in 1849, Vienna was the largest metropolis in the German Confederation and one of the largest in Europe. In addition to its political, cultural, and social importance

[51] Waltraud Heindl-Langer and Edith Saurer (eds), *Grenze und Staat: Paßwesen, Staatsbürgerschaft, Heimatrecht und Fremdengesetzgebung in der österreichischen Monarchie 1750–1867*. Vienna, 2000.

[52] On the idea of representation Hasso Hofmann, *Repräsentation: Studien zur Wort- und Begriffsgeschichte von der Antike bis ins 19. Jahrhundert*. Berlin, 1974.

[53] Hans Heiss, 'Ein neues Land: Tirol in Restauration und Vormärz'. In Ellen Hastaba and Siegfried de Rachewiltz (eds), *'For Freedom, Truth and Justice!' Joseph Ennemoser and Jakob Philipp Fallmerayer. Tyrol from 1809 to 1848/49*. Innsbruck, 2009, 37.

[54] Christine Mueller, *The Styrian Estates 1740–1848. A Century of Transition*. New York, 1987, 296–8, 352.

[55] Madelaine Rietra (eds), *Wirkungsgeschichte als Kulturgeschichte. Viktor von Andrian-Werburgs Rezeption im Vormärz. Eine Dokumentation, mit Einleitung, Kommentar und einer Neuausgabe von 'Österreich und dessen Zukunft' (1843)*. Amsterdam, 2000.

[56] Rietra, *Wirkungsgeschichte als Kulturgeschichte*, 55–61.

as a residence city, Vienna—and Lower Austria more generally—was the economic hub at which domestic and foreign trade routes crossed. Here, a large proportion of goods, supplies, and wares were cleared through customs, including those destined for Hungary. Per capita revenues from direct taxes and indirect levies were also at their highest here.[57] The empire's web-like infrastructure of roads, railways, and telegraphy radiated out from the Viennese nucleus.[58] Beyond this Austro-Bohemian core, however, consolidation was uneven; this was a 'Habsburg monarchy of two or more speeds'.[59]

In examining the history of territories, regions, and political spaces in the *Vormärz*, this book takes a regional approach, focusing on seven major regions. These are Habsburg Inner Austria, Bohemia, Italy, Hungary, Galicia, Illyria, and the frontiers. These major regions were part of even larger political territories, but also comprised smaller territorial elements. Additional attention is given to the linguistic, religious, cultural, and economic spaces that extended beyond the territorial borders and became important for later federal history.

2.2. Habsburg Inner Austria

The Inner Austrian cluster of lands comprised Lower and Upper Austria, Salzburg, Styria, Tyrol, and Vorarlberg and formed the core of the Habsburg Empire. Within, Lower Austria, together with Vienna, formed the imperial centre. State law textbooks described Lower and Upper Austria in flowery terms as the 'true mother state' and 'the ancestral homeland' around which the other lands were grouped.[60] In contemporary lithographic depictions of the Habsburg lands, the allegorical figure of Lower Austria was always front and centre.[61] In the lithograph 'Barque with Austria', it will be recalled, the allegories of the Inner Austrian lands formed the elite circle around the emperor. Its predominantly German-speaking population distinguished Inner Austria from other multilingual and multi-religious Habsburg territories. Its inhabitants felt a closer bond with the neighbouring German states than with Habsburg provinces like Galicia or Croatia, notwithstanding their common dynastic links. The constitutional progress of southern Germany was admired and followed by liberal nobles, upwardly

[57] Lombardy-Venetia ranked second, Upper Austria third, cf. *Tafeln zur Statistik der österreichischen Monarchie für die Jahre 1847 und 1848*. Vienna, 1853. Erster Teil, erste Abteilung, Tafel 26. On economic setbacks Roman Sandgruber, *Ökonomie und Politik: Österreichische Wirtschaftsgeschichte vom Mittelalter bis zur Gegenwart*. Vienna, 1995, 181.

[58] For economic statistics, see the appendices at Rudolf Sieghart, *Zolltrennung und Zolleinheit: Die Geschichte der österreichisch-ungarischen Zwischenzoll-Linie*. Vienna, 1915.

[59] Maťa, 'Habsburgermonarchie', 48.

[60] E.g. Ignaz de Luca, *Vorlesungen über die Oestreichische Staatsverfassung*. Vol. 1. Vienna, 1791, 98; Springer, *Statistik des Kaiserstaates*, 1. 3.

[61] Krasa-Florian, *Allegorie der Austria*, 79.

mobile burghers, and the minor clergy.[62] Through a common German-speaking cultural space, they felt a sense of belonging to the German states, as was typified by the celebrations to mark the completion of Cologne Cathedral. In Styria, these proceeded in 1842 with an imperial stamp of approval under the patronage of Archduke Johann.[63]

Economic ties were equally important for Inner Austria's relations with the German Confederation. As competition with France for hegemony in Europe grew, so did the perception of a specifically 'German' cohesion. When access to Mediterranean markets was expanded and Graz was connected to Trieste by rail, many saw this as a success for the 'German' market.[64] But cracks soon began to appear. In view of Hungary's economic backwardness, the Habsburg Monarchy did not participate in the *Zollverein* (German Customs Union). This was despite the fact that Inner Austria's population would have benefited economically; high expectations were ultimately followed by acute disappointment.[65] What had once been a common economic market with the German states was now divided by new customs barriers.[66] Defence policy was another divisive issue. After the Napoleonic Wars and the advent of alliances against Austria, Vienna strengthened its borders to the west, fortifying Salzburg and Linz in defence against Bavaria.[67]

The creation of fortifications and economic borders marked a new territorial divide at the heart of the German Confederation. In the *Vormärz*, this boundary had symbolized Vienna's efforts at internal consolidation of the Habsburg Empire. After 1866, it was solidified as the formal 'state border' between Germany and Austria. Nevertheless, the *Vormärz* territorial stabilization of the Habsburg Monarchy was not intended to sever ties with the German Confederation, as Metternich's efforts made clear. Metternich presented plans for greater integration with the German Confederation to the emperor, but they were never made public.[68] Within Inner Austrian society, faith in a common German language and culture nevertheless thrived. During the March Revolution, this sense of social and cultural belonging gave rise to calls for a common state.[69] Thus, all but one of the twenty-six Styrian delegates to the Paulskirche assembly in Frankfurt supported the creation of a federal Greater Germany, including the Habsburg Monarchy.[70]

[62] Hans Spatzenegger, 'Die Katholische Kirche von der Säkularisation (1803) bis zur Gegenwart'. In Heinz Dopsch and Hans Spatzenegger (eds), *Geschichte Salzburgs: Stadt und Land*. Vol. 2–3. Salzburg, 1991, 1444.

[63] Mueller, *Styrian Estates*, 300 and 344.

[64] Mueller, *Styrian Estates*, 345.

[65] Mueller, *Styrian Estates*, 345.

[66] Sieghart, *Zolltrennung und Zolleinheit*, 111.

[67] Hanns Haas, 'Salzburg in der Habsburgermonarchie: Vormärz, Revolution und Neoabsolutismus'. In Dopsch and Spatzenegger, *Geschichte Salzburgs*, 2–2. 665.

[68] Siemann, *Metternich*, 677–81 and 710.

[69] For more detail F. A. Gatti, *Die Ereignisse des Jahres 1848 in der Steiermark: Auf Grundlage authentischer Quellen zusammengestellt*. Graz, 1850, 11–99.

[70] Mueller, *Styrian Estates*, 384.

While cultural affinities and a common language inspired visions of a collective political space for the German states, religion created a sense of cohesion within Inner Austria itself. The Habsburgs, with their political culture of Catholicity, played the decisive role. Simply put, Catholicism was a foundational pillar of their rule.[71] Far from a purely private matter, religious affiliation was an element of political control. The Inner Austrian lands passed rigid laws restraining non-Catholics on where they could stay, settle, and own property.[72] The enforcement of this Catholic unity and cohesion rested largely with the Salzburg Cathedral chapter, which reported to Vienna and administered large parts of Inner Austria up to the borders of Italy, Hungary and Croatia.[73] As late as 1837, more than 400 Tyrolean Protestants were expelled from the Zillertal by an imperial order initiated by the Archbishop of Salzburg.[74] In the border triangle between Switzerland, Bavaria, and Vorarlberg, the Jewish community of Hohenems represents one of the few instances of the toleration of non-Catholics.[75]

As elsewhere in the Monarchy, the consolidation of central power in Vienna provoked conflict with the estates in Inner Austria. The territories of the provincial estates, meanwhile, developed at different rates across Inner Austria. In Lower Austria and Styria, the estates took the reins on important initiatives to develop the land in the 1840s.[76] They focused on public education, infrastructure, and, above all, agriculture. These fields would later align with the crown lands' federal competences outlined in the March Constitution of 1849 and the

[71] Concise on this Stollberg-Rilinger, *Maria Theresia*, 565.

[72] The Tolerance Patent of 1781 had formally tolerated the Protestants. However, the Graz community was not granted a priest and prayer house until 1821. Since the expulsions of the Jews under Emperor Maximilian I, the Jewish population had been subject to a rigid ban on settlement, residence, and property. Cf. Franz Ilwof, *Der Protestantismus in Steiermark, Kärnten und Krain vom 16. Jahrhundert bis in die Gegenwart*. Graz, 1900; Stephan Laux, 'Dem König eine "ergetzlichkhait": Die Vertreibung der Juden aus der Steiermark (1496/1497)'. In Gerald Lamprecht (ed.), *Jüdisches Leben in der Steiermark: Marginalisierung—Auslöschung—Annäherung*. Innsbruck, 2004, 33–57; Astrid von Schlachta, 'Die "Verfassung" des Landes: Ein Erinnerungsort in der politischen Kommunikation in Tirol'. In Brigitte Mazohl and Bernhard Mertelseder (eds), *Abschied vom Freiheitskampf? Tirol und '1809' zwischen politischer Realität und Verklärung*. Innsbruck, 2009, 149–50. In Innsbruck seven Jewish families were tolerated until the 1860s, in Bolzano two. Cf. Thomas Albrich, 'Einleitung'. In Albrich (ed.), *Von Salomon Sulzer bis 'Bauer & Schwarz': Jüdische Vorreiter der Moderne in Tirol und Vorarlberg*. Innsbruck, 2009, 8.

[73] Haas, 'Salzburg in der Habsburgermonarchie', 671; Spatzenegger, 'Die Katholische Kirche', 1434.

[74] Martin Schulze Wessel, 'Frühneuzeitliche Glaubensflucht: Grenzüberschreitende Zugehörigkeiten und die Mythen von Toleranz und Vertreibung'. In Rudolf von Thadden, Steffen Kaudelka, and Thomas Serrier (eds), *Europa der Zugehörigkeiten: Integrationswege zwischen Ein- und Auswanderung*. Göttingen, 2007, 17–32.

[75] On Hohenems, based on a wide range of sources, first Aron Tänzer, *Die Geschichte der Juden in Tirol und Vorarlberg*. Vols. 1–2: *Geschichte der Juden in Hohenems und im übrigen Vorarlberg*. Meran, 1905. On the 'unity of faith', Florian Huber, *Grenzkatholizismen: Religion, Raum und Nation in Tirol. 1830–1848*. Göttingen, 2016, 346–53. On piety cultures already [Joseph Hörmann von Hörbach], *Tirol unter der baierischen Regierung: Mit Aktenstücken*. Vol. 1. Aarau, 1816, 63.

[76] Still helpful, Viktor Bibl, *Die niederösterreichischen Stände im Vormärz: Ein Beitrag zur Vorgeschichte der Revolution des Jahres 1848*. Vienna, 1911. On the prehistory of the estates in the eighteenth century now William D. Godsey, *The Sinews of Habsburg Power: Lower Austria in a Fiscal-Military State 1650–1820*. Oxford, 2018.

Provincial Ordinances of 1861.[77] In Salzburg, on the other hand, the *Größerer Ständeausschuss* (Grand Committee of the Provincial Estates), which the emperor had only begrudgingly established following persistent petitions and deputations, convened once in January 1825 and never met again.[78]

The activities of the provincial estates led to struggles over finances. To resurrect the political effectiveness of their diet, the Lower Austrian estates invoked the right to consult with the sovereign on the budget, a provision which was guaranteed in their provincial constitution, but had long since fallen into disuse.[79] The Styrian estates similarly insisted on having a say on taxes, bonds, and loans. At the beginning of the nineteenth century, according to the historian Christine Mueller, they permanently had 'a finger on the fluttering pulse of the monarchy's finances'.[80] In Salzburg, by contrast, provincial assets had been confiscated during the transfer of sovereignty to the Habsburgs. It was only in the last third of the nineteenth century that a partial restitution was achieved and financial agency restored.[81] Until the end of the empire, conflicts over provincial finances remained an indicator of the power and potential of the crown lands.[82]

Salzburg is also an important example of how a historic territory could remain anchored in the public consciousness despite possessing impotent provincial estates and even ceasing to exist after incorporation into the administrative territory of Upper Austria. In May 1848, the bourgeois politician Franz Peitler called for the 'restoration of the former provincial government' of Salzburg, since 'the great problems: federal state or confederation of states, centralization or autonomy etc., etc., are all up in the air'.[83] He launched a well-organized petition campaign.[84] The son of a brewery owner, he had studied law in Padua, Pavia, Prague, and Vienna, and from 1831 was employed at various administrative district courts in Upper Austria-Salzburg. In this role he defended the peasantry against the interests of the landed gentry with such zeal that he was disciplined in 1848.[85] Because he attended both the *Paulskirche* Revolutionary Assembly and the Austrian Reichstag as a delegate in 1848, he was punitively transferred and did

[77] Bibl, *Die niederösterreichischen Stände*, 209, 240, 286–90.

[78] Haas, 'Salzburg in der Habsburgermonarchie', 673.

[79] Hanns Schlitter, *Aus Österreichs Vormärz*. Vol. 4: *Lower Austria*. Vienna, 1920, 15, 53 ff. On the development in the German states, Rainer Wahl, 'Die Entwicklung des deutschen Verfassungsstaats bis 1866'. In Wahl, *Verfassungsstaat, Europäisierung, Internationalisierung*. Frankfurt am Main, 2003, 289–90; Reinhart Koselleck, *Preußen zwischen Reform und Revolution: Allgemeines Landrecht, Verwaltung und soziale Bewegung von 1791 bis 1848*. Munich, 1989, 284–397; Bibl, *Die niederösterreichischen Stände*, 251 and 260.

[80] Mueller, *Styrian Estates*, 200.

[81] Adolf Ritter von Steinhauser, 'Franz Peitler', *Salzburger Zeitung*, 28 Mar. 1877, 1.

[82] See Chapter 10. [83] Steinhauser, 'Franz Peitler'.

[84] Pre-printed petition forms from Salzburg parishes to the 'High Austrian Chamber of Deputies' of the 30 May 1848, e.g. Az. 4392/RT 1848–49. Österreichisches Staatsarchiv Wien, Abteilung Haus-, Hof- und Staatsarchiv, Landesangelegenheiten Österreichischer Reichstag 1848/49 (further ÖStA, HHStA, LA ÖRT 1848/49), Box 86, fol. 169.

[85] Cf. the obituary by Steinhauser, 'Franz Peitler', *Salzburger Zeitung*, 26–30 Mar. 1877, always 1–2.

not return to the provincial diet and provincial committee until 1861. As it was, Peitler's efforts were not for naught; in 1849, Salzburg once again became a state in its own right.

Despite its close cultural and economic ties with the German Confederation, Inner Austria was anything but homogeneous, especially in terms of national ambitions and linguistic dispositions. In southern Styria, there remained a large Slovenian-speaking population, in southern Tyrol a large Italian-speaking one.[86] It was in these non-German-speaking regions that federal ideas of national spheres emerged that transcended existing territorial borders. In 1848, the Styrian Slovenes demanded 'the unification of the politically fragmented Slovenian tribe in the governorates of Laibach (Ljubljana), Graz and Trieste into a kingdom of "Slovenia" with its own provincial diet'.[87] Tyrolean Italians demanded a separate political territory within the monarchy, greater rights of self-government, or, in isolated cases, the permission to affiliate with a soon to be united Italy.[88]

2.3. Habsburg Bohemia

More than any other region, the Bohemian lands reflected the 'diversity of Central Europe [and its] permanent overlapping of linguistic and national boundaries'.[89] The three lands of the Bohemian Crown—Bohemia, Moravia, and Silesia—had long been honoured members of the Holy Roman Empire, the German Confederation, and the Habsburg Empire. As their sole territory possessing the *Kurwürde* (dignity to elect the Holy Roman Emperor), Bohemia had contributed significantly to the hegemonic position of the Habsburgs in the Holy Roman Empire. This cachet was reflected both at the imperial court and in the bureaucracy where Bohemian nobles formed a large part of the empire's service aristocracy. In the *Vormärz* period, their influence even increased during the regency of Franz Anton von Kolowrat-Liebsteinsky.[90] A symbolic detail bears witness to this: while the representatives of the Bohemian Diet were admitted to court as a

[86] Reinhard Stauber, *Der Zentralstaat an seinen Grenzen. Administrative Integration, Herrschaftswechsel und politische Kultur im südlichen Alpenraum 1750–1820*. Göttingen, 2001.

[87] Petition of the Slovenes to the Emperor (submitted to the Petitions Committee of the Kremsier Reichstag) of 21 June 1848, Az. 5013/RT 1848–49. In: ÖStA, HHStA, LA ÖRT 1848/49, Box 86, fol. 194. Cf. Gatti, *Die Ereignisse*, 146 and 153.

[88] Thomas Götz, *Bürgertum und Liberalismus in Tirol 1840–1873: Zwischen Stadt und 'Region', Staat und Nation*. Cologne, 2001, 34–41; Brigitte Mazohl-Wallnig and Marco Meriggi, *Österreichisches Italien—Italienisches Österreich? Interkulturelle Gemeinsamkeiten und nationale Differenzen vom 18. Jahrhundert bis zum Ende des Ersten Weltkriegs*. Vienna, 1999; Brigitte Mazohl, *Österreichischer Verwaltungsstaat und administrative Eliten im Königreich Lombardo-Venetien 1815–1859*. Mainz, 1993; Sergio Benvenuti, *L'autonomia trentina al Landtag di Innsbruck e al Reichsrat di Vienna: Proposte e progetti. 1848–1914*. Trento, 1978.

[89] Martin C. Putna, *Obrazy z kulturních dějin Střední Evropy*. Prague, 2018, 21.

[90] Using Kolowrat as an example, Siemann speaks of lobbying on behalf of the Bohemian nobility infiltrating the entire empire, Siemann, *Metternich*, 705-6.

deputation, the provincial representatives of Lower Austria were not.[91] In April 1848, Emperor Ferdinand acquiesced to the demands of the Bohemian estates for even greater influence and power, promising the Kingdom of Bohemia important attributes of statehood in his 'Bohemian Charter'.

Symbolically, socially, economically, and culturally, the Kingdom of Bohemia was an important imperial heartland.[92] The population of the Bohemian lands was equally German- and Czech-speaking, with a Polish-speaking community in Silesia. Thanks to privileges granted to Silesian Protestants and the all-but-continuous settlement of Jewish families in Bohemia and Moravia, the different denominations were more integrated in Bohemia than in predominantly Catholic Inner Austria.[93] Bohemia's diversity with regard to its political territories, nationalities, and layered identities inspired federalist thinking. In the March Revolution, both the Kingdom of Bohemia and all three Bohemian lands were variously imagined as becoming part of a federal Slavic union, a Habsburg federation of nationalities, a reformed German Confederation, or a federation of the historic crown lands.

The Bohemian lands, like Inner Austria, markedly differed from one another. The territorialization of the western part, the Kingdom of Bohemia, owed much to the initiatives of the central authorities in Vienna as well as to the *Oberstburggraf* (the provincial governor in Bohemia), Karl von Chotek. Even though he was extremely unpopular with the provincial estates, the economy boomed during his tenure between 1825 and 1843. Interaction between public and private initiatives intensified.[94] The economy was highly diversified, including the textile and cotton industry, brewing, milling, the production of sugar, coal, ironworks, glass, building materials, and machines. Chotek also initiated the secularization of health and social services after 1828.[95] Like Vienna, however, Prague suffered from the negative consequences of industrialization; riots by the city's workers in 1844 foreshadowed the social conflicts of the coming March Revolution.[96]

Bohemia was developed not only through the efforts of the central and regional state authorities, but also through the policies of the provincial estates.[97] Large-scale

[91] Bibl, *Die niederösterreichischen Stände*, 264.

[92] Pieter M. Judson, 'L'Autriche-Hongrie était-elle un empire?', *Annales. Histoire, Sciences Sociales*, 63/3 (2008), 563–96; Robert Luft, 'Machtansprüche und kulturelle Muster nichtperipherer Regionen: Die Kernlande Böhmen, Mähren und Schlesien in der späten Habsburgermonarchie'. In Johannes Feichtinger, Moritz Csáky, and Ursula Prutsch (eds), *Habsburg Postcolonial: Machtstrukturen und kollektives Gedächtnis*. Innsbruck, 2003, 165–88; Andrea Komlosy, *Grenze und ungleiche regionale Entwicklung: Binnenmarkt und Migration in der Habsburgermonarchie*. Vienna, 2003.

[93] Kateřina Čapková and Hillel J. Kieval (eds), *Prague and Beyond: Jews in the Bohemian Lands*. Philadelphia, 2021.

[94] Zdeněk Jindra, *Hospodářský vzestup českých zemí od poloviny 18. století do konce monarchie*. Prague, 2015, 259–78.

[95] Milan Hlavačka, Pavel Cibulka, Jiří Pokorný, Olga Fejtová, and Pavel Bek, *Sociální myšlení a sociální praxe v českých zemích 1781–1939: Ideje, legislativa, instituce*. Prague, 2015, 238–9.

[96] Otto Urban, *Die tschechische Gesellschaft 1848–1918*. Vol. 1. Vienna, 1994, 34–5.

[97] See Antonin Okáč, *Český sněm a vláda před březnem 1848: Kapitoly o jejich ústavních sporech*. Prague, 1947, 84–5, 125, 188.

investments by the estates, however, were acutely hampered by a paucity of strong financial institutions.[98] Instead, money from the provincial estates' comparatively robust budgets flowed into infrastructure, education, culture, and agriculture. In the field of education, the focus was predominantly on primary schools, which also employed Czech-speaking teachers (though, as a disappointed František Palacký reported to the governor, the teaching of the Czech language left much to be desired),[99] as well as technical and agricultural education.[100] The establishment of the Royal Bohemian Society of Sciences, the Bohemian National Museum, the Prague Estates Theatre (which staged performances in both German and Czech), and the planned construction of the Prague National Theatre became the flagship initiatives of the Bohemian estates.[101]

Moravia and Silesia, by contrast, were subject to a more *imperial* policy of territorialization. After a sizeable swathe of Silesia had been lost to Prussia in 1742, Austrian Silesia had become the administrative laboratory of a centralizing fiscal-military state complete with a direct state tax administration.[102] This was followed by its fusion with Moravia into one administrative unit. The development of roads, railways, and telegraphy was encouraged by Vienna and prepared the ground for an industrial boom.[103] In the nineteenth century, east–west and north–south railway connections allowed Moravia to emerge as an economically prosperous transit space between Prussia (and overseas ports via the Baltic), Russia, Galicia, Hungary, and the thriving Mediterranean entrepôt at Trieste.[104] From the beginning of the nineteenth century, a new coal-mining district in the north-east of Moravia and Silesia provided the necessary raw materials.[105] In the south, Brno became the 'Manchester' of the empire's wool industry.[106]

[98] The only active empire-wide credit institution, the Vienna National Bank, did not open its Prague branch until 1847; there were only savings banks and a network of smaller banking families. Jindra, *Hospodářský vzestup českých zemí*, 393–405.

[99] Kořalka, *František Palacký*, 162.

[100] Luft, 'Machtansprüche und kulturelle Muster', 170–1.

[101] Kořalka, *František Palacký*, 244.

[102] Dan Gawrecki, 'Schlesien als Randgebiet der Habsburgermonarchie nach 1742'. In Christoph Maner (ed.), *Grenzregionen der Habsburgermonarchie im 18. und 19. Jahrhundert*. Münster, 2005, 134. See Adolf Beer, 'Die Finanzverwaltung Oesterreichs 1749–1816', *MIÖG* 15 (1894), 237–366; Karl Vocelka, *Glanz und Untergang der höfischen Welt: Repräsentation, Reform und Reaktion im habsburgischen Vielvölkerstaat*. Vienna, 2001, 356–7.

[103] Dan Gawrecki (ed.), *Dějiny Českého Slezska: 1740–2000*. Vol. 1. Opava, 2003, 85–7; Roland Wenzlhuemer, 'The Development of Telegraphy: 1870–1900. A European Perspective on a World History Challenge', *History Compass*, 5 (2007), 1720–42.

[104] The tariffs on goods between the Hungarian and the non-Hungarian lands can be read as an indicator of the long-term success of these imperial efforts: In 1843, Moravia and Silesia ranked third in absolute terms after Lower Austria and Styria. Cf. *Tafeln zur Statistik der österreichischen Monarchie für das Jahr 1843*. Vienna, 1847, Tafel 10.

[105] Although Moravia-Silesia only comprised 4 per cent of the Habsburg territories with a population share of 6 per cent, the iron industry with 118 factories was able to compete with its rivals in Styria (176 factories), Carinthia and Carniola (139 factories), and Bohemia (131 factories). *Tafeln zur Statistik*, Tafel 41; Gawrecki, *Dějiny Českého Slezska*, 1. 78.

[106] Sandgruber, *Ökonomie und Politik*, 181.

One reason why the development of Moravia and Silesia remained a Viennese imperial project was the weakness of the provincial institutions. Unlike their counterparts in Bohemia, the estates did not pursue their own agenda of territorialization. Indeed, Silesia was not even a unified estate territory.[107] Even in the twilight years of the medieval era, the land had been regarded as a 'unique conglomerate of about one and a half dozen independent, differently consolidated principalities and autonomous dominions'.[108] In the pre-1848 period, only two of the four existing Silesian principalities still possessed estate assemblies.[109] Day-to-day affairs were managed by a common committee, which was controlled by the state authorities.[110] The Moravian estates, however, did have more substantial formal rights, including the right to legislate.[111] Nevertheless, they did not see themselves as a counterweight to Vienna. Their main concerns were charitable provincial institutions, elementary schools, the provincial museum, and other cultural institutions, as well as the construction of roads and waterworks.[112] Resistance arose only in 1847, when the Viennese government urged the estates to agree on peasants' *robot* obligations (compulsory labour) under private law, with the intention of abolishing patrimonial rights in the long run.[113] This imperial demand was also rejected in Bohemia.[114]

Against this background, federalist ideas came mainly from the scattered estates movement in Bohemia. Liberal aristocrats opposed Viennese centralism and called for local self-government based on the English model.[115] The estates were to be given more power and were to bring in wealthy burghers from the 'aristocracy of money', alongside the traditional nobility and clergy.[116] Other demands included a voice in the provincial legislature and in provincial finances.[117] Following a scandal involving the financial dealings of the governor burgrave Karl von Chotek, who for his large-scale projects had embezzled funds from the estates' coffers, the Bohemian elites expected concessions from Vienna.[118]

[107] Christian D'Elvert, *Die Verfassung und Verwaltung von Österreichisch-Schlesien in ihrer historischen Ausbildung*. Brno, 1854, 244.

[108] Maťa, 'Habsburgermonarchie', 36.

[109] D'Elvert, *Verfassung und Verwaltung*, 251–2.

[110] D'Elvert, *Verfassung und Verwaltung*, 208.

[111] See Gotthold Rhode, 'Stände und Königtum in Polen/Litauen und Böhmen/Mähren: Bemerkungen zur Entwicklung ihres Verhältnisses vom 16. bis ins 18. Jahrhundert', *Jahrbücher für Geschichte Osteuropas*, 12/2 (1964), 221–46.

[112] For a survey see Rudolf Dvořák, *Jednání sněmů moravských v letech 1792–1835*. Brno, 1904; Rudolf Dvořák, *Jednání sněmů moravských v letech 1835–1848*. Brno, 1906.

[113] Dvořák, *Jednání sněmů moravských 1835–1848*, 229–30.

[114] Melville, *Adel und Revolution*, 66–7 and 70.

[115] Tatjana Tönsmeyer, *Adelige Moderne: Großgrundbesitz und ländliche Gesellschaft in England und Böhmen 1848–1918*. Vienna, 2012; Jiří Georgiev, *Až do těch hrdel a statků? Konzervativní myšlení a otázka samosprávy v politických strategiích české stá-toprávní šlechty po roce 1848*. Prague, 2011.

[116] Urban, *Die tschechische Gesellschaft*, 1. 35–6.

[117] Schlitter, *Österreichs Vormärz*, 2. 3, 5, 15, 22, 42, 52, 55.

[118] For a meticulous list of details, including the salary and the right of indigenate of the provincial president, co-financing of the military academy in Wiener Neustadt, rules of procedure and proceedings of the provincial diet and provincial committee, see Okáč, *Český sněm*; Schlitter, *Österreichs Vormärz*, vol. 2, *Böhmen*.

Compared with Lower Austria or Styria, the Bohemian opposition and its landowning and bourgeois leadership found themselves in a peculiar position. To legitimize their demands for more political say, they had to invoke their *historic* rights.[119] After the Battle of White Mountain in 1620, the Bohemian Provincial Ordinance had considerably curtailed the estates' rights and, unlike in the Inner Austrian provinces, no longer covered their claims.[120] The historiographical basis of Bohemian state law was provided by the 'historiographer of the Bohemian state', František Palacký.[121] In his monumental *History of Bohemia*, published first in German and then in Czech, Palacký presented his views to a wider audience. He argued that Bohemia had never ceased to be a sovereign state despite its association with the Holy Roman Empire.[122]

This idea of continuous and undiminished Bohemian sovereignty remained a central theme in Czech national historiography well into the twentieth century.[123] Palacký's thinking echoed the 'historical school' of German state law. Just as the German legal scholar Klüber invoked 'universal German principles' in his studies of the German federal states, Palacký sought to synthesize a 'purely Slavic basis' for the older Bohemian law, making cross-references to Serbian, Russian, and Polish legislation.[124] The personal background of the Protestant Palacký, who had spent his early years tutoring noble pupils in Upper Hungary, now Slovakia, corresponded to a broad linguistic and cultural understanding of a Bohemian-Slavic nation.

Bohemian state law later became the legal-political argument par excellence and left a unique and indelible mark on Habsburg federal history. It could produce territories of very different dimensions. Similarly, Palacký's own work availed itself of diverging arguments in state law. He was not only a historian employed by the Bohemian estates, but the historiographer of a Bohemian nation and the 'historian of the Czechs'.[125] His visions of a Bohemian nation corresponded with

[119] Originally, the estates saw themselves as the actual sovereigns of the country, since they elected their king, see Alexander Begert, *Böhmen, die böhmische Kur und das Reich vom Hochmittelalter bis zum Ende des Alten Reiches. Studien zur Kurwürde und zur staatsrechtlichen Stellung Böhmens.* Husum, 2003, 582–4.

[120] Until the beginning of the nineteenth century, however, the monarchy had repeatedly deviated from the Renewed Land Ordinance in favour of the estates. On the reassessment of the actions of the absolutist rulers now Patr Mat'a and Thomas Winkelbauer (eds), *Die Habsburgermonarchie 1620 bis 1740: Leistungen und Grenzen des Absolutismusparadigmas.* Stuttgart, 2006; Jaroslav Pánek, 'Ferdinand I: Der Schöpfer des politischen Programms der österreichischen Habsburger?' In Mat'a and Winkelbauer, *Die Habsburgermonarchie*, 63–72. Already Rhode, 'Stände und Königtum', 221–46; Ernest Denis, *La Bohème depuis la Montagne Blanche.* Vol. 1. Paris 1903, 113; Eila Hassenpflug, 'Die böhmische Adelsnation als Repräsentantin des Königreichs Böhmen: Von der Inkraftsetzung der Verneuerten Landesordnung bis zum Regierungsantritt Maria Theresias', *Bohemia*, 15/1 (1974), 71–91.

[121] Okáč, *Český sněm*, 78.

[122] Kořalka, *František Palacký*, 197.

[123] Among the most prominent representatives was Josef Pekař, *Z duchovních dějin českých.* Prague, 1941, 110.

[124] Kořalka, *František Palacký*, 196–7.

[125] Kořalka, *František Palacký*, 196–7, for a comparative frame Monika Baár, Historians and Nationalism: East-Central Europe in the Nineteenth Century. New York, 2010.

both the concept of a *národ československý* (Czech-Slavic people) or a *národ český* (peoples of Bohemia).[126] Bohemia, as a political territory based on state law, overlapped—though never perfectly—with the Czech linguistic area.[127]

By looking back to its historical past and its relations with Moravia and Silesia, it was possible to create the narrative of a Bohemian 'empire'. Expressions such as 'lands of the Wenceslas Crown', or the narrative of the 'main land' Bohemia and its 'secondary lands' Moravia and Silesia, indicated this implicit claim to superiority.[128] In the 'secondary lands', such narratives, intended to create a transnational unity, led to accusations of a Bohemian hegemony and 'imperial aspirations'.[129] Moravia promoted the legend that it was older than both Bohemia and Austria and that it had been founded on the spiritual unity of Christians and Slavs.[130] Silesia likewise created its own expansionist, 'imperial' narrative based on historic state law. In 1848, it claimed the duchies of Auschwitz (Oświęcim) and Zator, which were located near Krakow and had belonged to Silesia until the beginning of the sixteenth century.[131] When the Prague Diet called on the emperor in the 1840s to unite the three lands of the Bohemian Crown—Bohemia, Moravia, and Silesia—into a single political territory, the Moravian and Silesian estates firmly rejected the proposal.[132] The vision of a single state uniting not only Czechs but also Slovaks was not realized until after 1918.

Bohemian state law placed the history of territories, spaces, affiliations, and identities in a new context. Dual membership of the German Confederation and the Monarchy caused much deeper divisions in the Bohemian lands than in Inner Austria. The pre-1848 conflicts between 'Czechomans' and 'Teutomans' in Bohemia, for example, dwarfed those that unfolded between German- and Slovene-speaking Styrians.[133] In academic writings, newspaper articles, memoranda, and petitions to the highest imperial court authorities, the belligerents' opposing views clashed unfiltered.[134] Many German-speaking Bohemians insisted on belonging to the German Confederation.[135] Indeed, Palacký's German-speaking academic colleagues in Prague were convinced of an inherent Austrian determination to stifle the rise of the Czech language and an independent Czech 'mentality'.[136] The Czechs, on the other hand, viewed nation-building

[126] This distinction was already to be found in the 1820s. Cf. Kořalka, *František Palacký*, 136.

[127] Peter Haslinger, *Nation und Territorium im tschechischen politischen Diskurs 1880–1938*. Munich, 2010; Putna, *Obrazy z kulturních dějin*, 25.

[128] Maťa, 'Habsburgermonarchie', 39.

[129] Maťa, 'Habsburgermonarchie', 38.

[130] Putna, *Obrazy z kulturních dějin*, 43.

[131] This had been rejected several times in the eighteenth and nineteenth centuries. Cf. D'Elvert, *Verfassung und Verwaltung*, 191.

[132] *Gednánj pánů stawů Morawských*. Tr. Alois W. Šembera. Brno, 1849, 31.

[133] Urban, *Die tschechische Gesellschaft*, 1. 38–9.

[134] Cf. the numerous examples in Kořalka, *František Palacký*. See also Gatti, *Die Ereignisse*, 147.

[135] Otto Urban, 'Der böhmische Landtag'. In Peter Urbanitsch and Helmut Rumpler (eds), *Die Habsburgermonarchie 1848–1918*. Vol. 7/2: *Verfassung und Parlamentarismus: Die regionalen Repräsentativkörperschaften*. Vienna, 2000, 1993.

[136] Kořalka, *František Palacký*, 176.

in the German Confederation with acute scepticism, fearing it as a future threat to the Habsburg pluralism.

2.4. Habsburg Italy

In the pre-1848 period, federalist ideas also found fertile ground in the petty states of Italy. Although a federal Italy ultimately never materialized, federal models prevailed among those who developed ideas for a united peninsula.[137] Intellectuals such as Vincenzo Gioberti advocated an Italian confederation under the leadership of the Pope. In 1847, the newly elected Pope Pius IX fuelled these hopes when he broke with the servile attitude of his predecessor Gregory XVI and defied Vienna's constant interference.[138] In Lombardy-Venetia, still part of Austria, some strived for autonomy. For others, the idea of a united Italy was more attractive. Nationalist aspirations found far less support in the aristocracy-dominated institutions than national ideas within the bourgeois-liberal strata of society.[139]

Lombardy-Venetia had come to Austria after the Napoleonic Wars. In both territories, this was a return to the past. Lombardy had previously experienced Austrian rule between 1706 and 1796 (as well as in 1799/1800), and Venetia between 1797 and 1805. These preludes gave important impetus for economic and administrative modernization. On the one hand, Austria had carefully extracted tax revenues but, on the other, it also sought to engineer Lombardy into a 'model province of the Enlightenment'.[140] After 1815, many hoped for the resurrection of these reforms, but they were to be disappointed.[141] Instead, the inhabitants found themselves neglected and cut off from developments elsewhere. Time seemed to have come to a standstill. They watched as neighbouring states—Sardinia-Piedmont, Tuscany, and the Papal States—began to reform in earnest between 1847 and 1848.[142]

[137] Cf. Daniel Ziblatt, *Structuring the State: The Formation of Italy and Germany and the Puzzle of Federalism*. Princeton, 2006; Alexander Grasse, *Italiens langer Weg in den Regionalstaat: Die Entstehung einer Staatsform im Spannungsfeld von Zentralismus und Föderalismus*. Opladen, 2000, 48–9; Pierangelo Schiera, 'Zentralismus und Föderalismus: Strukturen und Kulturen im deutsch-italienischen Vergleich. Einleitende Bemerkungen'. In Schiera, Oliver Janz, and Hannes Siegrist (eds), *Zentralismus und Föderalismus im 19. und 20. Jahrhundert: Deutschland und Italien im Vergleich*. Berlin, 2000, 29.

[138] Grasse, *Italiens langer Weg*, 54–5.

[139] Marco Meriggi, 'Der lombardo-venezianische Adel im Vormärz'. In Armgard von Reden-Dohna and Ralph Melville (eds), *Der Adel an der Schwelle des bürgerlichen Zeitalters*. Stuttgart, 1988, 230.

[140] Brigitte Mazohl, 'Vom Tod Karls VI. bis zum Wiener Kongress 1740–1815'. In Thomas Winkelbauer (ed.), *Geschichte Österreichs*. Stuttgart, 2015, 351; Carlo Capra, 'Die Zentralbehörden für die italienischen Provinzen 1713–1796'. In Maťa et al., *Verwaltungsgeschichte in der Frühen Neuzeit*, 1/1. 522–33.

[141] *Worte eines Lombarden an die Deutschen*. Frankfurt am Main, 1848, 11 (author unknown). See John Rath, *The Provisional Austrian Regime in Lombardo-Venetia. 1814–1815*. Austin, TX, and London 1969; Bellabarba, *Das Habsburgerreich*, 16–17, 49–59.

[142] See c. Italia, 1847, 1–2; *Worte eines Lombarden*, 20.

The Austrian administrative state provoked popular discontent. Critics took aim at a sluggish bureaucracy, a backlog of administrative and judicial reforms, and a general sense of political stagnation.[143] Austrian officials were considered *stranieri* and *barbari*, foreigners and barbarians.[144] The provincial administration rested in the hands of a Milanese and a Venetian government, whose power reached the lowest political levels.[145] Although the patrimonial system had ceased to exist, Austrian rule continued to depend after 1815 on a narrow class of the old patrician aristocracy.[146] Their alliance with the crown guaranteed the high nobility a majority in the consultative bodies of the governorates and provinces, the so-called central and provincial congregations.[147] Elsewhere, however, noble participation in the administration declined drastically.[148]

Vienna's financial and tax administration became a symbol of foreign domination and was widely discussed in the press. Since 1817 Vienna had levied a tax surcharge which was higher than in other regions.[149] This provoked passionate debate in the European press as to whether the Austrian state was actually investing in Lombardy-Venetia or plundering it like a colony with 'bayonet in hand'.[150] Vienna did in fact invest considerable sums in the development of the region, as the bridge over the Venetian lagoons attests. Infrastructural expansion of the railways, however, was directed squarely towards Vienna, in accordance with an imperial logic that had already been tested in Galicia and Silesia.[151]

This centralist policy outraged the Italians, who felt cut off from the Italian economic and cultural mainland and their traditional markets.[152] Moreover, Lombardy, with its leading silk manufacturers, was strongly oriented towards Western Europe, while agricultural Venetia looked towards the Mediterranean

143 Meriggi, 'Der lombardo-venezianische Adel', 234.

144 Franz de Paula von Hartig, *Das kaiserliche Manifest vom 20.9.1848. Oder, Freimüthige Bemerkungen über die österreichische Herrschaft im lombardisch-venetianischen Königreiche*. Prague, 1848, 9. Pointedly Mazohl-Wallnig, *Österreichischer Verwaltungsstaat*, 276 ff.

145 Cf. Andreas Gottsmann and Stefan Malfèr, 'Die Vertretungskörperschaften und die Verwaltung in Lombardo-Venetien'. In Rumpler and Urbanitsch, *Die Habsburgermonarchie*, 7/2. 1592–1632; Mazohl-Wahlnigg, *Österreichischer Verwaltungsstaat*; Mazohl-Wallnig and Meriggi, *Österreichisches Italien—Italienisches Österreich?*; Augusto Sandonà, *Il Regno Lombardo-Veneto 1814–1859. La costituzione e l'amministrazione*. Milan, 1912; Marco Meriggi, *Il Regno Lombardo-Veneto*. Turin, 1986.

146 Franz Kübeck had discouraged the restoration of a special position for the nobility, but the emperor was willing to compromise, Meriggi, *Il Regno Lombardo-Veneto*, 227.

147 Gottsmann and Malfèr, 'Vertretungskörperschaften und Verwaltung', 1596 and 1599.

148 Gottsmann and Malfèr, 'Vertretungskörperschaften und Verwaltung', 1595–7, 1616; Meriggi, 'Der lombardo-venezianische Adel', 230.

149 Gottsmann, and Malfèr, 'Vertretungskörperschaften und Verwaltung', 1610–13.

150 Quoted from *Worte eines Lombarden*, 14. Cf. Correnti, *L'Austria e la Lombardia*. See also Rupert Pichler, *Die Wirtschaft der Lombardei als Teil Österreichs: Wirtschaftspolitik, Außenhandel und industrielle Interessen 1815–1859*. Berlin, 1997, 44.

151 Venice was connected to the Austrian railway network via Padua, and railway lines led from Milan to Graz and Vienna. Andreas Helmedach, 'Integration durch Verkehr: Das Habsburger Reich', *Osteuropa*, 3 (2005), 18–32; Adolfo Bernadello, *Veneti sotto l'Austria: Ceti popolari e tensioni sociali 1840–1866*. Verona, 1997, 43–58.

152 Sandgruber, *Ökonomie und Politik*, 192; Correnti, *L'Austria e la Lombardia*, 29.

entrepôts. Local critics accused Vienna of only caring for the Bohemian-Austrian economy.[153] The Italians had learned from Friedrich List to see the railways as not only a means of economic expansion, but as an instrument of national-political spatial organization.[154] As a result, market and trade relations were no longer seen as purely economic issues in the pre-1848 period. Europe's various customs unions were instead understood as a prelude to political (and often federal) unions.[155] List's book, *The National System of Political Economy*, argued that the development of a national economy was a requirement for the creation of a nation state. It became an important reference point in the national-political debate in Lombardy-Venetia, as it had been in Hungary.

The common front of the two Italian provinces against Vienna should not, however, make us forget their internal differences.[156] The densely populated Lombardy, with its fertile Po Valley, was one of the most important agricultural regions of the Habsburg Monarchy. The modernization and capitalization of land and soil meant that agriculture took off here much earlier than in Venetia, where similar reforming impulses were notably lacking.[157] Venice's hinterland, the *terra ferma*, was characterized by agricultural subsistence farming.[158] The lagoon city, meanwhile, saw its Mediterranean trade in steady decline; only in 1831 was it belatedly granted limited free port status. In the face of its rival Trieste, it resembled 'an aged lung afflicted with laboured breathing'.[159]

2.5. Habsburg Hungary

Initially, the Hungarian lands played only a peripheral role in the federal history of the monarchy. Vienna's relationship with Habsburg Hungary was driven by imperial politics. The monarchy's status as a great European power, after all, was due in no small part to the vast territories of the fertile Pannonian Plain. Hungary, Croatia-Slavonia, and Transylvania stood out from the other provinces by their sheer size, accounting for more than one-third of the total area of the Monarchy. Their geographical location further symbolized the Monarchy's status in the European balance of power as a 'Christian' bulwark against the Ottomans and a

[153] *Worte eines Lombarden*, 16; Correnti, *L'Austria e la Lombardia*, 29.

[154] Correnti, *L'Austria e la Lombardia*, 17. Cf. Maier, 'Transformations of Territoriality', 45.

[155] Sieghart, *Zolltrennung und Zolleinheit*.

[156] Gernert, 'Italien 1848: Revolution auf italienisch'. In Heiner Timmermann (ed.), *1848: Revolution in Europa*. Berlin, 1999, 270.

[157] Carl Czoernig, *Die lombardische Gemeindeverfassung nach ihrer Entstehung und Ausbildung, ihrem Verfalle und ihrer Wiederherstellung*. Heidelberg, 1843, 82; Pichler, *Wirtschaft der Lombardei*, 145–6.

[158] To this and the following Bernadello, *Veneti sotto l'Austria*, 53.

[159] Bernadello, *Veneti sotto l'Austria*, 56.

latent 'Turkish danger' that was still existent in contemporary perception.[160] The history of Hungary, Croatia-Slavonia, and Transylvania is far from an atypical example of how, in the nineteenth century, Habsburg administrative and estate territories could be elevated to the status of 'sovereign' lands (Croatia), on the one hand, and, on the other, how early modern constitutional states could become mere administrative territories (Transylvania).

Vienna's neglect of Hungary resulted in a lack of territorial development 'from above'. The respective Hungarian and Transylvanian court chancelleries were responsible not only for internal administration, justice, and finance, but also for the so-called 'peasant question', army supplies, religion, welfare, education, and public health.[161] In terms of implementation, however, they rarely made inroads at the intermediate level of government, the comitats (counties).[162] To people of time, the fifty-two comitats were akin to 'republics' because of their far-reaching autonomy.[163] Each comitat was presided over by a king's representative in the county sent by Vienna, called the *Obergespan*, who did not exercise much effective political control and was rarely even personally present in the province. More important were the *Vizegespane* (second-in-command assistant gespans), recruited from the local nobility.[164] The comitats were thus not administrative units within a bureaucratic territorial state, but they were remnants of a state based on the personal association of the ruler and the nobles—the personal dependency state.

The failure of centralization owed much to the strong estates. The Hungarian Diet (including the Croatian estates) shared with the monarch the right to legislate, to levy taxes, and to authorize recruitment.[165] Furthermore, the strength of the Hungarian estates vis-à-vis Vienna was based on their ability to cooperate. Deputies were beholden to the comitats that sent them, and which coordinated through extensive correspondence and consultative meetings in advance.[166] If deputies failed to follow their instructions, they could be recalled from the diet. This degree of cooperation between the noble comitats was unique and would have been unthinkable in the non-Hungarian provinces. There, under the supervision of Vienna, provinces and estates were legally prohibited from collaborating

[160] Johannes Feichtinger and Johann Heiss (eds), *Kritische Studien zur 'Türkenbelagerung'*. Vol. 2: *Der erinnerte Feind*. Vienna, 2013.

[161] Robert J. W. Evans, 'The Habsburgs and the Hungarian Problem. 1790–1848', *Transactions of the Royal Historical Society—Essays in Modern History*, 39 (1989), 46.

[162] Péter Lászlo, 'Die Verfassungsentwicklung in Ungarn'. In Peter Urbanitsch and Helmut Rumpler (eds), *Die Habsburgermonarchie 1848–1918*. Vol. 7/1: *Verfassungsrecht, Verfassungswirklichkeit, zentrale Repräsentativkörperschaften*. Vienna, 2000, 252.

[163] Evans, 'Hungarian Problem', 51.

[164] Hanns Schlitter, *Aus Österreichs Vormärz*. Vol. 3: *Ungarn*. Zurich, 1920, 30.

[165] See Lászlo, 'Verfassungsentwicklung in Ungarn', 245 und 253–5.

[166] Evans, 'Hungarian Problem', 54.

like this. In Hungary, by contrast, the coordination among the comitats effectively amounted to a takeover of the legislative power of the provinces.[167]

Transylvania paints a different picture. The chain of decision-making ran directly between Vienna and Cluj (Kolozsvár, Klausenburg). The Court Chancellery ran the Transylvanian administration while the state treasury monitored the finances as the province had no budget of its own.[168] This centralization of governance was underpinned by the Transylvanian estates' lack of representation in the Hungarian Diet.[169] The authorities in Vienna focused on the expansion of military infrastructures; in terms of typical development projects such as road and water construction, the province lagged far behind.[170] Transylvania was part of an eastern defence area and thus shared similarities with the other Habsburg frontiers.

In formal terms, the Croatian Diet (Sabor) possessed greater scope for action.[171] The Croatian-Slavonian estates convened both at their own diet in Agram (Zagreb) and at the joint Hungarian Diet in Pressburg (Bratislava). However, the Sabor in Agram served only as a symbol of a sovereignty that, in fact, it did not have the power to act on. Only the joint diet at Pressburg could pass meaningful legislation. A feudal mentality hindered agrarian reform, and, even more so, an agrarian revolution. The Croatian landed gentry did not live off the economic output of their estates, but off the dues of their subjects. Consequently, they showed little interest in increasing yields. Even more than in Hungary, the conditions for the development of the bourgeoisie and industry were lacking. The Sabor had surrendered important sovereign rights, such as the right to approve taxes, to the joint diet of the Hungarian Lands in Pressburg.

Viewed as a prequel to federalism, pre-1848 political thought, especially in the form of 'Hungarian State Law', highlights the totally contradictory ideas of Hungarian, Croatian, and Transylvanian jurists and put them into focus. This plurality of voices was not solely the result of power struggles. It was owed to the fact that the Hungarian, Croatian-Slavonian, and Transylvanian constitutions—like the British constitution—were based on ancient customary law and thus unwritten, uncodified, and subject to interpretation.[172]

167 Schlitter, *Österreichs Vormärz*, 3. 20; Franz de Paula von Hartig, *Genesis der Revolution in Oesterreich im Jahre 1848*. Leipzig, 1850, 87.

168 Joseph Bedeus von Scharberg, *Die Verfassung des Großfürstenthums Siebenbürgens aus dem Gesichtspunkte der Geschichte, der Landesgesetze und des bestehenden öffentlichen Rechtes*. Vienna, 1844, 98.

169 Bedeus von Scharberg, *Die Verfassung*, 8–43.

170 *Tafeln zur Statistik für das Jahr 1843*, Tafel 44.

171 Mirjana Gross, *Die Anfänge des modernen Kroatien: Gesellschaft, Politik und Kultur in Zivil-Kroatien und -Slawonien in den ersten dreißig Jahren nach 1848*. Vienna, 1993, 7–16.

172 Lászlo, *Verfassungsentwicklung in Ungarn*, 242; Bedeus von Scharberg, *Verfassung Siebenbürgens*; Mirjana Stefanovski, *Ideja hrvatskog državnog prava i stvaranje Jugoslavije*. 2nd edn. Belgrade, 2008; Simion Retegan, Die Siebenbürgischen Landtage 1848–1865'. In Urbanitsch and

The Hungarian state law doctrine at the time reveals an imperial tendency for the historic constitution and could be used to claim territories that did not form part of the existing dominion. Hungarian scholars, for example, expansively interpreted the coronation oath to the Crown of St Stephen by which every Habsburg ruler promised to 'regain and incorporate lost territories'.[173] In his classic *State Law* of 1791, Josef von Ürményi had thus counted among Hungary's crown territories 'the kingdoms of Dalmatia, Croatia, Slavonia, Rama or Bosnia, Servia, Galicia, Lodomeria, Romania and Bulgaria, the Grand Duchy of Transylvania, the despotate of Wallachia, Moldavia, and Bessarabia'.[174] In the pre-1848 period, Hungarian state law experts, such as Anton Viroszil, continued this approach.[175] In Croatia-Slavonia, too, historic state law was used to legitimize expansion beyond the provincial borders. Croatian representatives of 'Illyrianism' claimed an area from the 'Military Border' as far as Dalmatia, the Serbian Voivodeship, Banat, Bosnia, or Fiume.[176]

Another objective of Hungarian state law scholarship was the expansion of statehood.[177] State law could be used to provide a historical justification for the 'sovereignty' of the provinces and their diets—a concept of sovereignty, which, however, was modified by elements of modern state theory. As the 'lawful revolution' led by the liberal Lájos Kossuth impressively demonstrated in 1848, the issue was not some kind of medieval statehood, but the nation state.[178] In this respect, state law scholars across the Leitha proceeded in the same way as Palacký, who anchored Bohemia's sovereignty in history to tackle political problems of his time. Palacký had close relations with Hungarian jurists. Since his youth, he had been friends with Anton Viroszil,[179] author of the six-volume treatise *Jus publicum regni Hungariae a primordiis hujus regni*.[180] Both came from Slavic families, but unlike the Czech-minded Palacký, Viroszil was from central Slovakia

Rumpler, *Die Habsburgermonarchie. 1848–1918. 7/2: Die regionalen Repräsentativkörperschaften*, 2317–43.

[173] Quoted through Stephan Rosenmann at Heinrich Marczali, *Ungarisches Verfassungsrecht*. Tübingen, 1911, 25.

[174] Stephan Rosenmann [pseudonym of Josef von Ürményi], *Staatsrecht des Königreichs Ungarn. Nach der heutigen Verfassung dieses Reichs bearbeitet*. Vienna, 1791, 19. See Lászlo, *Verfassungsentwicklung in Ungarn* 2000, 264; Marczali, *Ungarisches Verfassungsrecht*; Anton Viroszil, *Das Staats-Recht des Königreichs Ungarn, vom Standpunkte der Geschichte, und der vom Beginn des Reiches bis zum Jahre 1848 bestandenen Landes-Verfassung*. Vol. 1. Pest, 1865, 63–79.

[175] Viroszil, *Das Staats-Recht des Königreichs Ungarn*, 166.

[176] See Chapter 8.2.

[177] A weakening of the power of the comitats and a strengthening of the central, estates-based provincial administration was particularly advocated by Joseph Eötvös, *Die Reform in Ungarn*. Leipzig, 1846.

[178] István Deák, *The Lawful Revolution: Louis Kossuth and the Hungarians 1848–1849*. New York, 1979.

[179] Kořalka, *František Palacký*, 49.

[180] Anton Viroszil, *Jus publicum regni Hungariae a primordiis hujus regni usque ad recentissima tempora ordine scientifico deductum*. 6 vols. Buda, 1850–4. The later German version was considered a classic of Hungarian constitutional law in the Habsburg Monarchy, cf. Viroszil, *Das Staatsrecht des Königreichs Ungarn*.

(historically and politically speaking from Upper Hungary) and thus identified as a pro-Austrian Hungarian and not as a Slav.[181]

The nationalist turn amongst the Hungarian ruling elites created tensions with the other peoples of Hungary. The concept of a Hungarian 'nation' oscillated between a political nation of citizens and a linguistic nation. Traditionally, 'nation' had referred to the aristocracy of the Hungarian estates, which saw itself as supranational and non-denominational.[182] A significant proportion of the Hungarian nobility was Protestant and had studied in Germany, where they had been exposed to modern ideas of nationhood.[183] In the pre-1848 period, the concept of a political nation was combined with that of a linguistic nation.[184] All the peoples of Hungary were to belong to a 'Hungarian nation', united by a common language.[185] Between 1836 and 1845, a nationalist language policy saw Latin replaced with Hungarian as the common language of legislation, parliament, and education.[186] This Magyarization policy copied the Germanization policy of enlightened absolutism under Joseph II, and was directed more against Slavs than Germans and Romanians.[187] It provoked fierce criticism from Slovak, Croatian, and Transylvanian nationalist politicians, but also from leading Austrian nobles such as Leo Thun-Hohenstein. In correspondence published in Prague in 1843, Thun-Hohenstein and Francis (Ferenc) von Pulszky exchanged strikingly frank arguments for and against linguistic assimilation of the Slavs.[188]

Rejecting the idea of a single Hungarian nation state, Slavic politicians emphasized the autonomy of existing territories (Croatia-Slavonia) or reinforced the political relevance of national spheres that were not yet territories (such as Upper Hungary, later Slovakia).[189] To this end, the Sabor in Agram demanded greater powers for the Banus, i.e. the royal administrator, a government of its own, its own fiscal powers, and unification with Dalmatia. Remarkably, ties with Hungary were not to be severed. Instead, they were placed within a confederative framework, using arguments from Croatian state law. Croatian scholars argued that their merger with Hungary in the twelfth century was not forced by the sword, but was a voluntary association reached through a treaty of union.[190] By this logic, Hungary and Croatia were cast as legal equals and historical confederates.

In Transylvania, federalist ideas divided the province. The Magyar elites of Transylvania increasingly looked to Pressburg and in 1848 formed a new union with Hungary. By contrast, the other nationalities pointed to the historic union

[181] Kořalka, *František Palacký*, 49. [182] Critically Eötvös, *Reform in Ungarn*, 2–5.

[183] Katalin Gönczi, *Die europäischen Fundamente der ungarischen Rechtskultur: Juristischer Wissenstransfer und nationale Rechtswissenschaft in Ungarn zur Zeit der Aufklärung und im Vormärz*. Frankfurt am Main, 2008.

[184] On the language dispute Deák, *Lawful Revolution*, 16, 28–30.

[185] Deák, *Lawful Revolution*, 45. [186] Evans, 'Hungarian Problem', 44.

[187] Deák, *Lawful Revolution*, 45.

[188] Printed in Leo Thun-Hohenstein, *Die Stellung der Slowaken in Ungarn*. Prague, 1843.

[189] See Chapter 4. [190] Stefanovski, *Ideja hrvatskog državnog prava*, 14.

constitution in order to defend their representation. The Transylvanian constitution had institutionalized the balance of interests between three nations (Hungarian-speaking Szeklers and Magyars as well as German-speaking Saxons) and the corresponding religious antagonisms between Catholics, Protestants, and Uniates. According to a contemporary state law expert, it was because of the 'union (*Verbrüderung*) existing between the three nations, that one nation was obliged to maintain the others in their rights, privileges and confirmed statutes, regardless of religion or person'.[191] No group was allowed to interfere in the internal affairs of another nation, language, or church.[192] Nonetheless, the Romanians were noticeably excluded from the diet and from political participation, and thus from the utopia of federal equality among the Transylvanian inhabitants. They constituted the peasant, Orthodox majority of the population and, like the Jews, had been striving in vain for recognition as a political nation since the eighteenth century.[193] The Transylvanian model of national-denominational curiae nevertheless became formative and was translated into the model of national personal autonomy after 1900.[194]

2.6. Habsburg Galicia

The Kingdom of Galicia-Lodomeria was an imperial artefact and, in the words of the American historian Larry Wolff, 'a fantasy'.[195] Galicia's borders appeared arbitrary as they did not correspond with any known historic territory. Nonetheless, as the largest and one of the most populous provinces of the Monarchy, Galicia, like Hungary, underpinned Austria's position as a European great power. In the pre-March period, Bukovina was still part of the kingdom. The great size of Galicia posed a constant challenge to federalist thinkers who sought equality and equilibrium between the possible federal territories. Partition was already considered in the pre-March period and in 1848 it was the subject of one of the most sweeping petition campaigns in the Monarchy.[196]

For some years, Vienna's rule in Galicia had borne the hallmarks of a *fiscal-military state*. Fiscal exploitation of the province reflected the detached imperial view that Galicia was merely 'compensation' for the Silesian territories lost in 1742.[197] Negative perceptions of Galicia as a 'colony of the Austrian provinces'

191 Bedeus von Scharberg, *Verfassung Siebenbürgens*, 60.
192 Bedeus von Scharberg, *Verfassung Siebenbürgens*, 60.
193 Retegan, 'Die Siebenbürgischen Landtage', 2317. 194 See Chapter 11.2.
195 Larry Wolff, *The Idea of Galicia: History and Fantasy in Habsburg Political Culture*. Stanford, CA, 2010.
196 See Chapter 5.
197 Of the central civil authorities, the tax authorities employed the most officials, almost 1,500 in 1843, cf. *Tafeln zur Statistik für das Jahr 1843*, 41, Tafel 5, 'Anzahl u. persönl. Bezüge aller in activer Dienstleistung stehenden'. Concisely, Hans-Christian Maner, 'Zwischen "Kompensationsobjekt",

became entrenched among the local elite.[198] In terms of military policy, meanwhile, Galicia was developed as a 'glacis', i.e. an 'area of deployment and retreat'.[199] This policy was inextricably linked to an imperial concept of territory. Galicia was assigned two roles: as an eastern military frontier and as a civilizational bulwark or 'rampart' of European culture against encroachments by the Ottoman Empire and Russia.[200]

Vienna started the economic integration of Galicia in the pre-1848 period by expanding and consolidating its local infrastructure, most notably the railway. The economy, which had been oriented north- and eastwards since the time of the *Rzeczpospolita*, was to be redirected towards the interior.[201] The north–south railway linked the commercial centre of Trieste with the coal pits and rock salt mines of western Galicia and the economic heartland of the monarchy in Bohemia, Moravia, Silesia, and Austria. However, there was little interest on the part of Vienna in a more far-reaching development of the territory as demonstrated by its limited efforts at bureaucratization. Unlike the geographically much smaller crown lands of Lombardy-Venetia and Illyria, which each comprised two provincial governorates, the administration in Galicia was not further subdivided. The provincial and county authorities that did exist were notoriously under-resourced and renowned for their lack of ambition or cooperation. As the Galician governor, Franz von Stadion, damningly surmised, 'there was no guiding principle, no collaboration'.[202] According to Stadion, the Habsburg state in Galicia gave the impression of being torn apart by disunity and opposition.[203] Here, the local gentry exercised patrimonial rights for far longer than elsewhere. The state county offices, meanwhile, exercised only partial control over the lower administration and judiciary, which remained part of the patrimonial dominion.[204] Nevertheless, the county authorities did provide at least rudimentary protection to the serfs.

In 1846, the Austrian annexation of Krakow, the only independent territory to survive the partitions of Poland, allowed Metternich to pursue earlier plans to reform the empire.[205] He proposed the partition of Galicia into two parts and a

"Musterland" und "Glacis": Wiener politische und militärische Vorstellungen von Galizien von 1772 bis zur Autonomieära'. In Maner, *Grenzregionen der Habsburgermonarchie*, 103–22.

[198] This colonialism debate was recently continued in historiography with post-colonial studies, cf. Klemens Kaps, *Ungleiche Entwicklung in Zentraleuropa: Galizien zwischen überregionaler Verflechtung und imperialer Politik. 1772–1914*. Vienna, 2015, 303.

[199] Maner, 'Kompensationsobjekt', 116.

[200] Wolff, *Idea of Galicia*, 102–3.

[201] Günter Dinhobl, '...die Cultur wird gehoben und verbreitet'. In Endre Hárs (ed.), *Zentren, Peripherien und kollektive Identitäten*. Tübingen, 2006, 81, 84. See Kaps, *Ungleiche Entwicklung*.

[202] Report of 5 Oct. 1846, quoted in Hanns Schlitter, *Aus Österreichs Vormärz*. Vol. 1: *Galicia and Krakow*. Vienna, 1920, 123.

[203] Hanns Schlitter, *Aus Österreichs Vormärz*, 1. 77.

[204] This limited control was based on a compromise between the state bureaucracy and the nobility, practised until the *Vormärz*, not to turn subject suits against the latter, cf. Roman Rosdolsky, *Untertan und Staat in Galizien: Die Reformen unter Maria Theresia und Joseph II*. Mainz, 1992, 249.

[205] Schlitter, *Österreichs Vormärz*, 1. 28.

new central authority for Krakow based in Vienna. In February 1847, Metternich received the emperor's approval to bisect Galicia and construct administrative centres in Lemberg and Krakow. The Free State of Krakow would belong to Western Galicia and Bukovina to Eastern Galicia. Stadion, however, delayed the project so as not to break the political, cultural, and economic ties between the two halves.[206]

Bukovina had its own peculiarities, not least linguistically, as it housed Polish-, Ukrainian-, Romanian-, and Yiddish-speaking populations. Since the Bukovina was once part of the Moldavian territories of the Ottoman Empire,[207] Vienna decided to waive taxes in Bukovina in an attempt to win the loyalty of the elites and population.[208] More than half of the provincial territory fell within the domain of the 'Greek-Oriental Non-Uniated Religious Fund', whose assets, following secularization, were jointly administered by the Orthodox Church and the state authorities.[209] Due to its ambiguous nature as both the province's largest 'private' landowner and an estates institution oriented towards the common good, the Religious Fund became a driving force for modernization, economic initiatives, and nation-building projects in favour of the Romanian Orthodox population.[210] At the same time, the ruling elite upheld the idea of autonomy and, as the representatives of the estates, refused continuously to participate in the Galician Diet in Lemberg.[211] For this reason, a 'pan-Galician' identity failed to materialize.[212] Shortly before the outbreak of the March Revolution, plans for Bukovina's independence remained hopeless. Change was on the horizon, however; in 1849, Bukovina was granted crown land status in a scheme to reduce Galicia's political weight in the empire.

[206] In the first revolutionary months of 1848, the administrative division of Galicia was confirmed by the Council of Ministers. Cf. Schlitter, *Österreichs Vormärz*, 1. 61–71; Jan Kozik, *Ukrainian National Movement*. Edmonton, 1986, 266–85; Hans-Christian Maner, *Galizien: Eine Grenzregion im Kalkül der Donaumonarchie im 18. und 19. Jahrhundert*. Munich, 2007, 90.

[207] Kurt Scharr, *'Die Landschaft Bukowina': Das Werden einer Region an der Peripherie*. Vienna, 2010, 147. Cf. Cristina Florea, *Bukovina: The Life and Death of an East European Borderland*. Princeton, 2025.

[208] Scharr, *Die Landschaft Bukowina*, 133, 144. There also on alternative administrative ideas.

[209] Kurt Scharr, 'Der griechisch-orientalische Bukowinaer Religionsfonds 1783–1949: Einfluss und Bedeutung einer Institution'. In Markus Winkler (ed.), *Partizipation und Exklusion: Zur Habsburger Prägung von Sprache und Bildung in der Bukowina. 1848–1918–1940*. Regensburg, 2015, 229–48.

[210] Scharr, 'Der griechisch-orientalische Bukowinaer Religionsfonds', 233.

[211] Mihai-Ştefan Ceauşu, 'Zur sozioökonomischen Gesamtsituation der Bukowina im Vormärz vom Josephinischen Kataster 1786 bis 1848'. In Helmut Rumpler, Kurt Scharr, and Constantin Ungureanu (eds), *Der Franziszeische Kataster im Kronland Bukowina/Czernowitzer Kreis: 1817–1865. Statistik und Katastralmappen*. Vienna, 2015, 22.

[212] Scharr, *Die Landschaft Bukowina*, 161.

2.7. Habsburg Illyria

Illyria was also seen an 'artificial state',[213] an image that, unlike newly autonomous Galicia, it was never able to shed entirely. It remained a political construct, never attaining elevation to an imperial territory. The name 'Illyria' was derived from the 'Illyrian Provinces', a Napoleonic creation which existed between 1809 and 1814. Its successor, Habsburg Illyria, was somewhat smaller, comprising Carinthia, Carniola, Istria (including the entrepôt of Trieste), and Gorizia-Gradisca.[214] The border of the German Confederation ran straight through the 'kingdom'. Responsibility for territorial development 'from above' rested with the administrative centres of Trieste (for Istria, the Littoral, and Gorizia-Gradisca) and Laibach (for Carniola and Carinthia).[215] In contrast to Inner Austria, the centralization efforts did not affect the hereditary lands at the intermediate level. Patrimonial privileges as well as the rights of the estates had been abolished under Napoleon and were not revived by Austria.[216]

The lack of integration into the central state was due to the absence of clear administrative structures. For instance, the administrative territories of Trieste and Laibach did not coincide with the jurisdiction of the respective administrative authorities. In key areas, Carinthia and Carniola were more closely linked to Styria than to Illyria.[217] Contemporary statistics and civics handbooks were awash with confusing and contradictory information caused by this territorial melange.[218] Even a symbolic-political embodiment of the 'Kingdom of Illyria', such as a viceroy as in Lombardy-Venetia, was conspicuous by its absence.[219]

[213] Cf. Reinhard Stauber, 'Politische und soziale Integration in "Illyrien" in der ersten Hälfte des 19. Jahrhunderts'. In Marco Bellabarba, Ellinor Forstner, Hans Heiss, Andrea Leonardi, and Brigitte Mazohl (eds), *Eliten in Tirol zwischen Ancien Régime und Vormärz*. Innsbruck, 2010, 62. On Carinthia in the eighteenth century Armin A. Wallas, *Stände und Staat in Innerösterreich im 18. Jahrhundert: Die Auseinandersetzung um die Gerichts- und Verwaltungsorganisation zwischen den Kärntner Landständen und der zentralistischen Reformpolitik Wiens*. Klagenfurt, 1989.

[214] Arnold Suppan, 'Die Untersteiermark, Krain und das Küstenland zwischen Maria Theresia und Franz Joseph: 1740–1918'. In Suppan (ed.), *Zwischen Adria und Karawanken*. Berlin, 1998, 282. At the end of the eighteenth century, the 'Illyrica' were synonymous with Serbian affairs in Croatia-Slavonia, see János Kalmár and Michael Hochedlinger, 'Die Hofkommission (Hofdeputation) in Transylvanicis, Banaticis et Illyricis und die Illyrische Hofkanzlei'. In Maťa et al., *Verwaltungsgeschichte in der Frühen Neuzeit*, 1/1. 519–20.

[215] The term 'Küstenland', 'Küstenlande', or 'Litorale' refers to the Habsburg domains on the upper Adriatic, which became a crown land in 1849. Joachim Hösler, *Von Krain zu Slowenien: Die Anfänge der nationalen Differenzierungsprozesse in Krain und der Untersteiermark von der Aufklärung bis zur Revolution 1768 bis 1848*. Munich, 2006, 51.

[216] Stauber, 'Integration', 71; Janez Šumrada, 'Les principaux traits de la politique napoléonienne dans les Provinces illyriennes'. In Šumrada (ed.), *Napoleon na Jadranu. Napoléon dans l'Adriatique*. Koper and Zadar 2006, 43–58, 308–11.

[217] For example, in customs, levies, the military, and appellate jurisdiction. Cf. Werner Drobesch, *Grundherrschaft und Bauer auf dem Weg zur Grundentlastung: Die 'Agrarrevolution' in den innerösterreichischen Ländern*. Klagenfurt, 2003, 19.

[218] Stauber, 'Integration', 66. [219] Stauber, 'Integration', 66.

In part, the territorial consolidation of Illyria failed to materialize because a potential 'all-Illyrian' identity was overshadowed by competing affiliations. In each of the provinces concerned—Carinthia, Carniola, and the Littoral—historical societies were founded in order to preserve the memory of former estate-run territories and fostered a regional consciousness. In Carinthia, the historical society corresponded with the newly founded Austrian Academy of Sciences.[220] In Carniola, its counterpart cultivated an identity that was not yet national (in this case Slovenian), but regional.[221] In Trieste, the journal *L'Istria*, edited by the historian Pietro Kandler, was mainly devoted to municipal history.[222] The *Landesvereine* (provincial societies) that sprang up all over the Habsburg Monarchy at this time had a resounding effect in Illyria. During the March Revolution, this regional patriotism turned into crown land patriotism. In Carinthia in 1848, the 'Reinforced Carinthian Estates Provisional Committee' united formerly separate social demographics by calling for the establishment of Carinthia as a separate crown land.[223] Calls for provincial autonomy were also heard in Gorizia-Gradisca and Istria.[224]

Imperialism and provincialism went hand in hand in Illyria. Home to modern capital and insurance institutions such as the *Assicurazioni Generali* (Generali Insurance, founded in 1831 and still operating globally today), the free port of Trieste was a window display which advertised Habsburg power and economic prowess across the oceans to the wider world. It is hard to overestimate the importance of Trieste as a vibrant hub of globally connected wholesalers. By itself, it was akin to an 'informal empire', possessing more than three times as many major trading offices as Vienna and four times as many international ships as Venice.[225] But while Carniola and the Littoral surged ahead economically, Carinthia was increasingly behind.[226]

Neither the economic elites of Trieste nor the rural landowners showed any interest in a possible federal development of the Monarchy. A mercantile city like Trieste was primarily interested in its own privileges; when it looked to its 'hinterland', it had economic, rather than political-federal integration, in mind. With

[220] 'Wirken des historischen Vereins für Kärnten', *Carinthia*, 38/5 (29 Jan. 1848), 1.

[221] Hösler, *Von Krain zu Slowenien*, 57.

[222] See vol. 3 of 1848, e.g. 'Pensieri su Trieste dettati nel 1785', *L'Istria*, 3/39 (15 July 1848), 154–156; 'Consiglio Municipale di Trieste nel 1749', *L'Istria*, 3/41–42 (29 July 1848), 165–6; and many more.

[223] Iris Binder, 'Der Kärntner Landtag'. In Urbanitsch and Rumpler, *Die Habsburgermonarchie*, 7/2. 1719.

[224] Harald Krahwinkler, 'Die Landtage von Görz-Gradisca und Istrien'. In Rumpler and Urbanitsch, *Die Habsburgermonarchie*, 7/2. 1874–5.

[225] On the 'informal Empire' and the following cf. Alison Frank, 'Continental and Maritime Empires in an Age of Global Commerce', *East European Politics and Societies*, 25/4 (2011), 779–84. See also *Tafeln zur Statistik für das Jahr 1843*, Tafel 41, 'Industrie, Fabriken und Gewerbe', and Tafel 43, 'Seehandel und Seeschiffahrt'.

[226] Werner Drobesch, 'Kärnten-Böhmen: Annotationen zum Strukturwandel von Gesellschaft und Wirtschaft während des Vormärz'. In Claudia Fräss-Ehrfeld (ed.), *Kärnten und Böhmen, Mähren, Schlesien*. Klagenfurt, 2004, 257–76; Sandgruber, *Ökonomie und Politik*, 229.

the disappearance of its estates institutions, the province of 'Illyria' lacked an important political arena for the articulation of federal ideas. Instead, it was the linguistic areas that extended farther than Illyria's political and historical territories that became central to federalism. The term 'Illyrian' was alternatively used to refer to an indigenous Slavic population in the region (the Serbs, the inhabitants of Bosnia and Dalmatia), or to all Southern Slavs.[227] From the 1830s, 'Illyrianism' referred to the South Slavic unification movement formulated by the Croatian nationalists Ludovít Gaj and Janko Drašković. Drašković in particular wanted to make Civilian Croatia, the Military Border, Dalmatia and Carniola the starting point for a unification of all Balkan Slavs. Although both Metternich and the emperor initially considered this Illyrian programme as a vehicle for organizing the Monarchy, it was ultimately banned in 1843. Illyrianism, in the judgement of European diplomats, had been to blame for the uprisings in Bosnia.[228]

Visions of the South Slavic area as a 'state' met with fierce resistance from Germans and Italians in the region. For the Carinthian magazine *Carinthia*, the mere founding of a Slovene society in Klagenfurt was enough to prompt an alarmed editorial: 'Germans, take heed!'[229] Trieste's *L'Istria* pursued an 'Italian linguistic chauvinism'[230] and wrote that the Slavic language was a 'lingua da trivio, incapace ad essere scritta'—trivial and impossible to write down.[231] The Kingdom of Illyria was dissolved after 1848. In its place, the historic provinces, including Carniola, the Littoral, Carinthia, and Gorizia-Gradisca, were re-established. National linguistic spaces continued to overlap with the old-new crown land borders. Until the end of the Monarchy, a federal unity of the Southern Slavs remained an open question and an unfulfilled utopia.

2.8. Habsburg Frontiers

The European continental empires were traditionally separated by military buffers. The remnants of these Habsburg frontiers on the borders with Tsarist Russia and the Ottoman Empire included parts of Galicia and Transylvania, as well as the Military Border.[232] The territory of the Military Border was carved from Civilian Croatia and Slavonia in the eighteenth century. In later years, it

[227] Peter Vodopiviec, 'Sympathisanten und Gegner der französischen Regierung in Krain'. In Claudia Fräss-Ehrfeld (ed.), *Napoleon und seine Zeit*. Klagenfurt, 2009, 209–24.

[228] Helmut Rumpler, *1804–1914: Eine Chance für Mitteleuropa. Bürgerliche Emanzipation und Staatsverfall in der Habsburgermonarchie*. Vienna, 1997, 196–200.

[229] 'Deutsche, habt Acht!', *Carinthia*, 38/47 (12 Dec. 1848), 1.

[230] Krahwinkler, 'Landtage von Görz-Gradisca'.

[231] 'Sulla nazionalità del popolo di Trieste', *L'Istria*, 3/43–44 (5 Aug. 1848), 176 and 3/45–46, 178. Only Serbian was excluded from this.

[232] Michael Hochedlinger, 'The Habsburg Monarchy: From "Military-Fiscal State" to "Militarization"'. In Christopher Storrs (ed.), *The Fiscal-Military State in Eighteenth-Century Europe*. Farnham, 2009, 62.

was repeatedly enlarged in order to supply the regiments with a sufficient number of men fit for military service.[233] The 'military population' was directly subordinated to the Court War Council or Ministry of War.[234] Legal experts, therefore, considered the Military Border a 'component of the imperial army'.[235] Demographically speaking, the sparsely populated Military Border was very rural, albeit without the usual distinctions between local lords and subjects. Socio-political conflicts, which elsewhere had disrupted agrarian society, were absent.[236] Various religious groups lived in harmony with each other. A multilingual elementary school system served the Orthodox, Catholics, Protestants, and Jews.[237] It was not until 1882 that the Military Border was reincorporated into Croatia-Slavonia.

Dalmatia showed some parallels with the Military Border, but ultimately developed into an independent crown land.[238] A civil administration was not established, however, until the late nineteenth century.[239] What elsewhere would be considered the basic characteristics of rule, namely, infrastructure, education, a rudimentary administration, or even a police force to guarantee security, were underdeveloped. Vienna invested instead in fortifications and its military presence.[240] Traditional economic land routes to the Ottoman Empire were cut off,[241] and with few alternative markets, the Dalmatian ports stagnated.[242] While neighbouring Trieste became a global economic hub, Vienna did not grant Dalmatia 'the means to turn the periphery into a non-periphery'.[243] The locals were noticeably detached from regional and imperial structures: they were exempt from military conscription, lacked a tradition of estate participation, and were largely excluded from the Austrian civil service.[244] As a result, an insular sense of identity

[233] Karl Kaser, *Freier Bauer und Soldat: Die Militarisierung der agrarischen Gesellschaft an der kroatisch-slawonischen Militärgrenze 1535–1881*. Vienna, 1997, 386–91.

[234] Of the 1.2 million inhabitants of the military frontier, approx. 57,000 men served; in Hungary, with a total population of 10.5 million, there were only slightly more, approx. 63,000 men. Cf. *Tafeln zur Statistik für das Jahr 1843*, Tafel 2.

[235] Comprehensively Kaser, *Freier Bauer und Soldat*, 624.

[236] Kaser, *Freier Bauer und Soldat*, 387.

[237] While in the inner-Austrian provinces there was a privileged Catholicism, here a rich denominational landscape developed with Greek Orthodox believers (49%), Roman and Greek Catholics (47%), Protestants (4%), and Jews (0.03%); unlike in many other hereditary provinces, separate state primary schools as well as Orthodox schools were financed for Jews, *Tafeln zur Statistik für das Jahr 1843*, Tafel 2 and Tafel 47.

[238] Konrad Clewing, 'Der begrenzte Wert strategischen Wertes: Dalmatia als habsburgische Randprovinz'. In Maner, *Grenzregionen der Habsburgermonarchie*, 220.

[239] Anton Orosz, *Worte eines eifrigen und uneigennützigen Staatsdieners, die bei Regulierung der neuen Verhältnisse des Constitutionellen Dalmatien beachtet werden mögen*. Zara, 1848, 36.

[240] On the costs of fortresses and the military presence Orosz, *Worte eines Staatsdieners*.

[241] Clewing, 'Dalmatien als habsburgische Randprovinz', 230.

[242] Clewing, 'Dalmatien als habsburgische Randprovinz', 222.

[243] Clewing, 'Dalmatien als habsburgische Randprovinz', 233.

[244] Orosz, *Worte eines Staatsdieners*, 44. On loyalty-building Martin Schulze Wessel, 'Identitäten und Loyalitäten im Zeitalter (neo-) imperialer Politik: Die Tschechoslowakei 1938 und die Ukraine heute im Vergleich'. In Yvonne Kleinmann, Jürgen Heyde, Karsten Holste, Dietlind Hüchtker, and

developed.[245] Due to its strategic significance and geographically central location, however, Dalmatia was repeatedly a bone of contention in the history of federalism. Despite belonging to the Austrian part of the empire after 1867, it was nonetheless claimed by Hungary as well as Croatia-Slavonia and Bosnia-Herzegovina.

2.9. Malleability of the Habsburg Territories

The Habsburg Monarchy of the pre-1848 period was not yet a federation. Only the German Confederation, which included the Austrian and Bohemian lands, was inherently federal, at least in principle. Nonetheless, the pre-1 multiplicity of governance did shape later federal thinking. Advocates of crown land federalism took inspiration from the estates in Bohemia, Vorarlberg, or Carinthia, and their call for more political participation. Champions of dualism, trialism, or administrative federalism, meanwhile, looked to the administrative territories of the three central authorities (the United Court Chancellery, the Hungarian Chancellery, and the Transylvanian Chancellery) and the administrative provinces (the twelve provincial gubernias). National and ethno-linguistic spaces that extended beyond existing territories served as inspiration for believers in a federal state of nationalities. Others dreamt on a grander scale, including the German Confederation in their federal visions for a 'Greater Germany-Greater Austria'. Therefore, a federal history must provide an outline of the political relevance that actors attached to certain territories and regions.

A special feature of Habsburg territories and regions was their malleability. At the stroke of a pen, Salzburg or Bukovina could become an independent crown land, or, conversely, Transylvania became a province of the past. Neither the Federal Act of 1820, which safeguarded the provinces' existence, nor earlier guarantees of indivisibility in the Pragmatic Sanction prevented territorial reorganization 'from above'. Each province had its 'own' sovereign—the Bohemians, Hungarians, Italians, Galicians, and Illyrians had their king; the Moravians their margrave; and the Lower Austrians their archduke. Despite his many hats, this was always the same man—the Habsburg emperor. In the German Confederation, on the other hand, the multiplicity of monarchs served to preserve the territories and made the principalities 'guarantors of the federal foundation'.[246]

The extension of the central authority to the regions unfolded in a complex interplay between state and estate institutions. In Silesia, Moravia, Salzburg, the Kingdom of Illyria, Dalmatia, or Bukovina, the estates played little or no role at

Katrin Steffen (eds), *Dekonstruieren und doch erzählen: Polnische und andere Geschichten*. Göttingen, 2015, 39–45.

[245] Konrad Clewing, *Staatlichkeit und nationale Identitätsbildung: Dalmatien in Vormärz und Revolution*. Munich, 2001, 51.

[246] Langewiesche, *Monarchie*, 14.

all. In Lower Austria, Bohemia and Styria in particular, some public tasks were facilitated by productive cooperation, and others inhibited by competition between the state, the estates, and nobles.[247] The same was true of Hungary and Transylvania. On the one hand, the central administration of each was located in Vienna. On the other, their estates' privileges included participation in the legislative process. At the frontiers, military control brought the 'state' closer to the people.

The unsystematic, disorganized, and anachronistic nature of the *Vormärz* governance order was condemned by contemporaries as the 'Metternich system'.[248] They showered contempt on the confused conglomerate of overlapping spheres of authority and influence created by the German Confederation, the Viennese central authorities, the estate institutions, and the landed gentry. The system was muddled, outdated, and lacked societal participation. In 1848, it was stuck to the drawing board and fundamentally revised by a cadre of revolutionaries and reformers. They were not as novel and innovative as they may have believed, however. Plans for a Habsburg federation had long sat on the desks of pre-1848 reformists—including State Chancellor Metternich himself.[249]

A Federal History of the Habsburg Empire, 1815–1918. Jana Osterkamp, Oxford University Press.
 DOI: 10.1093/9780198943631.003.0003

[247] On the research desiderata regarding the *Vormärz* and the provincial administrations Ammerer et al., 'Die Stände in der Habsburgermonarchie'.

[248] On a reassessment of Metternich, who promoted the supranational, cultural character of the empire and at the same time was interested in a 'national perspective for Germany' and federal reform, now Siemann, *Metternich*, 677–81, 710.

[249] See Chapter 3.

Figure 3.1 Vessel with the inscription 'Wůle národa' (Will of the People). Cartoon with the subtitle 'The Ministry does not want to stand back in the effort for a liberal and popular system, but deems it its duty to be in this endeavour first'. Šotek, 11 Feb. 1849.

3
Ordering Diversity
Administrative Federalism (from the Pre-March Period to 1867)

Before 1867, rule by the Habsburgs was rule without parliament. During the pre-March period, many of the provincial diets no longer had the right to legislate; of those that did, few exercised that right. After the revolutionary dust had settled in 1849, all provincial diets were legally suspended, and the following decade would see only ineffective separation and division of powers. Modern parliamentary constitutionalism, as dreamt and fashioned by the 1848 Revolution, had failed. Prague's *Národní nowiny* (National Newspapers) made clear who was to blame. In a cartoon published in February 1849, the liberal central government is depicted blocking the ship of state, bearing the inscription 'People's Will', from docking on the island of 'Freedom' (Figure 3.1).[1]

In practice, Habsburg rule in the nineteenth century was essentially administrative.[2] It was divided into a regulatory, gubernatorial branch under the control of the emperor, his advisers, and the governors, and an executive branch that implemented the decisions.[3] Administration in this latter sense was carried out by the central authorities of the court chancelleries, the provincial governorates, and the intermediate district, county, and comitat authorities.[4] This division of rule between government and administration was common to both the pre-March period and 'post-March' neo-absolutism. Before and after 1848, the political system

[1] Cartoon 'Ilustrace k liberálnímu programu [Illustration of the liberal programme]' with the subtitle 'Ministerstwo nehodlá při snaze po swobodomyslném a lidumilowném zřízení po zadu zůstati, anobrž to spíše za swou powinnost uznáwá, se tomuto dychtění w čelo postawiti [The Ministry does not want to stand back in the effort for a liberal and popular system, but deems it its duty to be in this endeavour first]'. *Šotek*, 11 Feb. 1849, 23 (supplement to the *Národní nowiny*). With courtesy of the Ústav pro českou literaturu Akademie věd České republiky.

[2] Lutz Raphael, *Recht und Ordnung: Herrschaft durch Verwaltung im 19. Jahrhundert*. Frankfurt am Main, 2000. See also Marco Bellabarba, *Das Habsburgerreich 1765–1918*. Berlin and Boston, 2020, 59–63.

[3] On the political and legal distinction between gubernative and administrative powers, which is helpful for an analysis of the non-parliamentary period in the Habsburg Monarchy, see Christoph Möllers, *Gewaltengliederung: Legitimation und Dogmatik im nationalen und internationalen Rechtsvergleich*. Tübingen, 2005, 219–20; Philipp Dann, 'The Gubernative in Presidential and Parliamentary Systems: Comparing Organizational Structures of Federal Governments in the USA and Germany', *Zeitschrift für ausländisches öffentliches Recht und Völkerrecht*, 66 (2006), 1–40.

[4] In the pre-March period, there were still three independent central authorities for Hungary, Transylvania, and the 'rest', which were merged into one central administration in 1849.

was designed to marginalize parliaments and their participation in the political decision-making processes. By the late 1850s, the March Revolution of 1848/1849, with its trumpeting of civic participation and call for representative assemblies, was seen by many as little more than a short-lived aberration.

Against this background, a federal history of the Habsburg Monarchy is essentially a history of executive federalism. Executive federalism—in contrast to historic crown land federalism, the federal state of nationalities, dualism, or personal autonomy—is not a term one will find in historical sources. Its use here derives instead from the analytical category of present-day executive federalism in Germany, Austria, and the European Union.[5] From a historical perspective, we can speak of executive federalism as an idea or as a practice when three conditions are met: first, where the central, regional, and provincial institutions have political autonomy independent of each other; second, where the different provinces are considered equal to each other; and third, where there are central, regional, and provincial governmental and administrative bodies, but no parliaments.

As a conceptual framework, executive federalism allows us to compare and study very different reform ideas. This chapter examines on the one hand the reform ideas of State Chancellor Klemens von Metternich in 1817, the *Ständischer Zentralausschuss* (Central Committee of the Estates) in April 1848, and on the other, the neo-absolutist restructuring of the state and its administration of Minister of the Interior Alexander von Bach in the 1850s. The common political platform was the rejection of parliamentary institutions. Despite their reformist intentions, this rendered the various forms of executive federalism *conservative* in character.

3.1. The 'Composite Monarchy' and Metternich's 1817 Reform Plan

After the Congress of Vienna established a new order for Europe-at-large, it made sense to many that a new order for the Habsburg 'Europe in miniature' should naturally follow. Interestingly, one of the most innovative minds behind the reform of the 'Metternich system' was State Chancellor Klemens von Metternich himself. His thinking was not oriented towards the liberal ideas of the nation state and the constitutional state but revolved around ways to legitimize monarchical

[5] Despite the legislative primacy of the present-day federal government and the European Union, the responsibility for national administration lies with the *Länder*. On Germany Gerhard Lehmbruch, 'Der unitarische Bundesstaat in Deutschland: Pfadabhängigkeit und Wandel'. In Lehmbruch and Arthur Benz (eds), *Föderalismus: Analysen in entwicklungsgeschichtlicher und vergleichender Perspektive*. Wiesbaden, 2002, 103. On Austria Peter Bußjäger, 'Föderalismus durch Macht im Schatten? Österreich und die Landeshauptmännerkonferenz', *Jahrbuch des Föderalismus* (2003), 79–99. On Europe Philipp Dann, *Parlamente im Exekutivföderalismus: Eine Studie zum Verhältnis von föderaler Ordnung und parlamentarischer Demokratie in der Europäischen Union*. Berlin, 2004.

rule in Europe. These included great-power status, security, defence, and effective governance for the common good. When Emperors Franz I (until 1835) and Ferdinand I (r. 1835–48) and their cabinets wanted to dissolve, reorganize, reduce, or enlarge the territorial units of the empire, they referred in justification to tangible concerns like the defence capabilities of the Military Border or Lombardy-Venetia, or to the unwieldy and ponderous size of Galicia. Where it seemed more expedient, they also included historical arguments (or excuses) to legitimize the reorganization of the dynasty.

But even considering this monarchy's claim to power, in the view of Metternich and many of his contemporaries the empire was still 'administered, but not governed'.[6] The central authorities in Vienna, especially the State Conference which advised the emperor, did not provide clear policies for the administration to implement.[7] Even if the administration managed to carry out its day-to-day business, the political question of how the empire was to be constituted in principle remained unresolved.[8] In a memorandum to Franz I, Metternich wrote: 'Fortunately, the machinery of the state is already constituted on such clear terms that…the machinery itself cannot really be reproached. Everything I have to suggest concerns the basic driving force behind it all.'[9] But if these impulses did not work, and the state machine was only able to run autonomously because 'its internal driving mechanisms are solidly built and well maintained',[10] then this was a damning verdict on the quality of political governance from above. Metternich himself drew up proposals for improving the governance of the Habsburg Monarchy in the period of revival following the Congress of Vienna. Biographers have presented contradictory descriptions of Metternich as both visionary[11] and reactionary,[12] federalist[13] and centralist.[14]

Metternich tried his hand as an engineer of imperial territories and a unifier of imperial rule. He wanted to subject the administration of the Habsburg Empire to central, but not centralist, principles. This is illustrated by his idea in 1817 to

[6] Franz de Paula Hartig, *Genesis der Revolution in Österreich im Jahre 1848*. Leipzig, 1850, 45 and 49.

[7] See for context and research desiderata Wolfram Siemann, *Metternich. Staatsmann zwischen Restauration und Moderne*. Munich, 2010, 93–103.

[8] Josef Redlich, *Das österreichische Staats- und Reichsproblem: Geschichtliche Darstellung der inneren Politik der habsburgischen Monarchie von 1848 bis zum Untergang des Reiches*. Vol. 1: *Der dynastische Reichsgedanke und die Entfaltung des Problems bis zur Verkündigung der Reichsverfassung von 1861*. Subvol. 1: *History*. Leipzig, 1920, 41.

[9] Clemens Metternich, 'Organisation der Central-Verwaltung in Österreich: Alleruntertänigster Vortrag vom 27.10.1817'. In Richard Metternich-Winneburg (ed.), *Aus Metternich's nachgelassenen Papieren*. Vol. 3. Vienna, 1880–4, 64.

[10] Metternich, 'Organisation der Central-Verwaltung', 65.

[11] Wolfram Siemann, *Metternich: Strategist and Visionary*. Cambridge, MA, 2019; Arthur G. Haas, *Metternich, Reorganization and Nationality 1813–1818: A Story of Foresight and Frustration in the Rebuilding of the Austrian Empire*. Wiesbaden, 1963.

[12] Alan Sked, 'Metternich and the Ficquelmont Mission of 1847–1848: The Decision against Reform in Lombardy-Venetia', *Central Europe*, 2/1 (2004), 24.

[13] Egon Radvany, *Metternich's Projects for Reform in Austria*. The Hague, 1971.

[14] Alan Sked, *Metternich and Austria: An Evaluation*. Basingstoke, 2008, 113.

reorganize the empire by creating sub-regions of equal legal standing. According to the wording of the resultant Imperial Patent, the administration of the individual territories was to take into account regional and historical peculiarities, 'either with regard to their historical origins or... kinship of language, customs, or previous constitution'.[15] Linguistic-cultural affiliation thus became a factor, albeit not the decisive one, in the state organization of the Habsburg Monarchy.

Metternich's proposal divided the empire into Bohemia-Moravia-Galicia, Inner Austria, Illyria, Lombardy-Venetia, Hungary, and Transylvania.[16] Each territory would be equal in the eyes of the imperial centre. In this way, Metternich applied to the internal order of the Habsburg Monarchy a structural principle laid down in the *Deutsche Bundesakte* (German Federal Act), which he himself had initiated. According to this principle, the states of the German Confederation were recognized as equal, with 'respected parity'.[17] His proposal reflects a general tendency in the Habsburg pre-March period to think in terms of large territories and to consider, in broad terms, linguistic differences within the population. Comparable drafts by the Hungarian Transylvanian nobleman Nikolaus (Miklós) Wesselényi in 1844 illustrate this. Under national auspices, Wesselényi advocated a constitutional 'confederation' of the German, Bohemian, Galician, Lombardo-Venetian, and Hungarian lands. Despite its geographical remoteness, Silesia, as a 'predominantly German province', was to be part of the German constituent state.[18]

Metternich's idea was distinct in advocating for the creation of administrative units of equal legal standing and independence vis-a-vis the emperor and, at the same time, a strong central administration as a guarantor of unity between them. For the German Confederation, Metternich had thus created a peace-keeping system based on a balance of powers.[19] By transferring this idea of parity to the Monarchy, Metternich aimed to curb the 'prerogatives of Hungary and Transylvania in particular, which were sufficient to paralyse the great state machine'.[20] In the case of the Austrian and Bohemian lands, he sought to reverse

[15] Metternich, 'Organisation der Central-Verwaltung', 73–4.

[16] Metternich, 'Organisation der Central-Verwaltung', 62–74. He then wanted to establish, in addition to the existing court chancellery for Hungary and Transylvania, a Bohemian-Moravian-Galician, an Austrian (with Lower and Upper Austria, Styria, Innviertel, Salzburg and Tyrol), an Illyrian (with Illyria and Dalmatia), and an Italian (Lombardy and Venice) court chancellery.

[17] Siemann, *Metternich Strategist*, 370–1.

[18] The five regional groups were formed along national-ethnic principles. Nicolaus Wesselényi, *Eine Stimme über die ungarische und slavische Nationalität*. Leipzig, 1844, 165. See Robert A. Kann, *The Multinational Empire: Nationalism and National Reform in the Habsburg Monarchy 1848–1918*. Vol. 1: *Empire and Nationalities*. New York, 1950, 119–21; Ágnes Deák, 'Miklós Wesselényi on the Future of the Habsburg Empire and Hungary'. In Ignác Romsics and Béla K. Király (eds), *Geopolitics in the Danube Region: Hungarian Reconciliation Efforts 1848–1998*. Budapest, 1999, 33–4.

[19] Siemann, *Metternich Strategist*, 370.

[20] Metternich, 'Organisation der Central-Verwaltung', 69. For this reason, Hungarian historiography disputes the image of Metternich as a federalist, Erzsébet Andics, *Metternich und die Frage Ungarns*. Budapest, 1973, 32.

the pre-existing 'system of fusion' through the United Court Chancellery. The central administration from Vienna had hitherto ignored the peculiar circumstances of each province and their respective 'local idiosyncrasies' and had thus blurred the differences between them.[21] In a *symbolic* sense, Metternich's state concept preserved the various 'names and constitutions'.[22] The redistribution of administrative powers between the empire and the provinces was based on the idea neither to increase the asymmetry between central and provincial administration nor to impose United Court Chancellery's administration on all provinces alike. In the spirit of executive federalism, Metternich was instead concerned with provincial administrative autonomy that, nevertheless, was under the control of the centre. This regional autonomy was to be supervised by court chancelleries, each of which in charge of one specific province. Conversely, the authority of the regional estates was to be diminished, not least by withholding their right to a common representative body.

The emperor approved only parts of Metternich's ambitions project. As a result, it was only implemented in a piecemeal fashion. The Court Chancelleries for Hungary and Transylvania, for example, whose exceptional status Metternich wanted to curtail, continued to exist unchanged. The emperor did appoint a Bohemian-Moravian-Silesian Chancellor, but there was no longer any mention of merging Bohemia with Galicia.[23] The latter continued to exist as an administrative and patrimonial estates territory, albeit without a chancellor of its own.[24] A vice-chancellor was appointed for Austrian Illyria, but by 1825 Vienna had abandoned the idea of a 'Kingdom of Illyria'.[25] Lombardy and Venetia benefited from Metternich's initiative by acquiring their own chancellor in addition to the viceroy, even though the latter had only 'administrative pseudo-functions' or 'the mandate of 'mere' representation'.[26]

In the remaining decades of Metternich's tenure as state chancellor, the planned administrative units were not further consolidated, and he himself, as a foreign politician, lost interest in them.[27] It was the Galician unrest of 1846 that prompted Metternich to take a fresh approach. He now proposed a division into Eastern and Western Galicia, the former being '*Russniak*' and the latter '*Mazurian*', i.e.

[21] Metternich, 'Organisation der Central-Verwaltung', 69.

[22] John Elliott, 'A Europe of Composite Monarchies', *Past and Present*, 137 (1992), 48–71.

[23] Haas, *Metternich: Reorganization and Nationality*, 120–23.

[24] Larry Wolff, *The Idea of Galicia. History and Fantasy in Habsburg Political Culture*. Stanford, CA, 2010. Cf. Chapter 2.6.

[25] Joachim Hösler, *Von Krain zu Slowenien*. Munich, 2006, 51. Cf. Chapter 2.7.

[26] Brigitte Mazohl, *Österreichischer Verwaltungsstaat und administrative Eliten im Königreich Lombardo-Venetien 1815–1859*. Mainz, 1993, 319–20; Joseph Alexander Helfert, *Zur Geschichte des lombardo-venezianischen Königreichs*. Vienna, 1908, 14–17.

[27] Emperor Franz's adviser on domestic policy, Anton von Kolowrat-Liebsteinsky, Metternich's main rival in Vienna, pursued a different administrative reform. Isabella Schüler, *Franz Anton Graf von Kolowrat-Liebsteinsky (1778–1861): Der Prager Oberstburggraf und Wiener Staats- und Konferenzminister*. Munich, 2016, 224–30.

Ukrainian and Polish.[28] The corresponding Imperial Decree of 29 March 1847 was implemented only with hesitation.[29]

Metternich's proposals were motivated by the crises of the empire. His reform plans, both for the empire's large-scale administrative units and for the partition of Galicia, were primarily driven by the pragmatics of power. Above all, a new territorial order had to guarantee the defence and security of the empire. The key prerequisite for this goal, as Metternich explicitly noted, was an effective administration.[30] His position was that the central decision-makers in Vienna should only have to trouble themselves with basic aspects of politics—a reflection of their gubernative role. It was at the provincial level, meanwhile, where an implementing administration would really be effective and relieve Vienna of the burden and tedium of trivial, day-to-day administrative work.[31] In his advice to Pope Pius IX, he summarized this idea more generally: 'Le gouvernement doit être exercé dans le centre; l'administration doit être reservée aux parties.'[32]

Can Metternich's proposals be described as forward-looking, federalist thinking? In order to answer this question in the affirmative, however cautiously, one must bear in mind the practical implications of Metternich's ideas. In a system of governance that, first, did not contain a pan-imperial legislative body besides the emperor; that, second, did not have a pan-imperial constitution, but only provincial constitutions; and in which, third, there was only an ineffective separation of the imperial government and the imperial administration (a *ceterum censeo* of Metternich's), the decentralization of administrative tasks would undoubtedly have increased the power of the administrative units that Metternich wanted to establish on an equal footing. Given the very limited control of the imperial centre, the top officials in the provinces had relative autonomy in implementing government policies.[33] The scope for action by regional political elites would

[28] Clemens Metternich, 'Aphoristische Betrachtungen über die dermaligen Zustände in Galizien'. In Metternich-Winneburg, *Metternich's nachgelassene Papieren VII*, 208.

[29] Delays resulted from the unsettled status of Krakow. Hanns Schlitter, *Aus Österreichs Vormärz*. Vol. 1: *Galicia and Krakow*. Zürich, 1920, 64. See also Hans-Christian Maner, *Galizien: Eine Grenzregion im Kalkül der Donaumonarchie im 18. und 19. Jahrhundert*. Munich, 2007, 90. On reorganizing Galicia's administration, carl Brockhausen, *Verwaltungsrechtliche und verwaltungspolitische Essays*. Vienna and Leipzig, 1908, 56.

[30] Explicitly Metternich, 'Organisation der Central-Verwaltung', 67.

[31] Radvany, *Metternich's Projects*, 135.

[32] Clemens Metternich, 'Rathschläge für Pius IX'. In Metternich-Winneburg: *Metternich's nachgelassene Papiere VII*, 248. Austria acted as a protective power for the Vatican territories in the pre-March period, see Alan Reinerman, *Austria and the Papacy in the Age of Metternich*. 2 vols. Washington, 1979, 1989. Since 1847, this was seen as a hostile act by the Italian national movement, see Simonetta Soldani, 'Annäherung an Europa im Namen der Nation: Die italienische Revolution 1846–1849'. In Dieter Dowe, Heinz-Gerhard Haupt, and Dieter Langewiesche (eds), *Europa 1848: Revolution und Reform*. Bonn, 1998, 139–40 and 147.

[33] Metternich, however, shied away from a legal extension of provincial competence. Sked lists alternative plans for the order of the governors in Lombardy-Venetia, Peter Goess and Karl Inzaghi. Sked, 'Ficquelmont Mission', 18, 20, 22.

have increased, even if social participation as a whole would not have been strengthened.[34]

Metternich himself repeatedly used the term federalism. In 1817, he said that 'in political-administrative terms...the Austrian Empire, through the diversity of its constituent parts, forms, as it were, a federal state'.[35] The verdict of the Metternich biographer Alan Sked, on the other hand, is unequivocal: 'Metternich was no federalist.'[36] Sked's central argument concerns the fact that Metternich did not plan a common parliament of the imperial provinces and regions.[37] Indeed, the state chancellor categorically rejected representative bodies at both the imperial and provincial level.[38] Although delegates from the entire monarchy were to attend the Council of State or the State Conference, this body was to exercise only an advisory function.[39] However, Metternich's negative attitude towards parliamentary legislation was not fuelled by scepticism towards federalism, but by a distrust of parliamentarism and its consequences for the status quo.

Metternich's ideas did not align with the nascent kind of federalism beginning to emerge in Switzerland and the United States, with its emphasis on the decentralization of the legislature.[40] In this, Sked is right. Instead, Metternich's focus rested on a few large administrative units which, despite their internal differences, were to be treated equally by the imperial centre. Metternich can therefore be seen as a pioneer of executive federalism.

Metternich's concern with administrative units was informed by his interest in preserving the state and its elites. He was less concerned with society at large. Aside from a fundamental allegiance to the emperor, any other loyalties the people may have had—to their region, denomination, or social class—were of

[34] Around the same time, Mikhail Speransky, as secretary to the Russian Tsar Alexander I, similarly considered reorganizing Russian administrative territories with regard to historical traditions and population structure. Mark von Hagen, 'Federalisms and Pan-Movements: Re-Imagining Empire'. In Von Hagen, Jane Burbank, andAnatolij V. Remnev (eds), *Russian Empire: Space, People, Power 1700–1930*. Bloomington, IN: 2007, 494–510; Marc Raeff, *Michael Speransky: Statesman of Imperial Russia 1772–1839*. 2nd edn. The Hague, 1969, 151–53, 242.

[35] Metternich, 'Organisation der Central-Verwaltung', 66. Even later he still calls the Austrian Empire a 'confederation of states', letter from Metternich to Kübeck of 14 Feb. 1851. In Metternich-Winneburg, *Metternich's nachgelassene Papiere VIII*, 512.

[36] Sked, 'Ficquelmont Mission', 15.

[37] Sked, *Metternich and Austria*, 108 and 113. In fact, Metternich could imagine the coexistence of parliaments with equal rights for the German Confederation, cf. letter to Kübeck of 20 Feb. 1850, 'Hingeworfene Betrachtungen über die deutschen Zustände, am Ende Februar 1850'. In Max von Kübeck (ed.), *Metternich und Kübeck: Ein Briefwechsel*. Vienna, 1910, 215.

[38] Radvany, *Metternich's Projects*, 37. Only later did Metternich consider abolishing the estates in favour of broader representation, Hanns Schlitter, *Aus Österreichs Vormärz*. Vol. 2: *Böhmen*. Zürich, 1920, 63.

[39] Siemann, on the other hand, speaks of Metternich as a statesman who thought that 'the principle of political participation was the foundation for political action'. This is too far-reaching in my opinion, Siemann, *Metternich Strategist*, 534.

[40] On this model Reinhart Koselleck, 'Bund (Bündnis, Föderalismus, Bundesstaat)'. In Otto Brunner et al. (eds), *Geschichtliche Grundbegriffe*. Subvol. 1: *Historisches Lexikon zur politisch-sozialen Sprache in Deutschland*. Stuttgart, 2004, 665.

secondary importance. Therein lay the crucial difference with the coming revolution of 1848. But how important were populations, societies, and nationalities in Metternich's thinking? On several occasions he emphasized the 'just protection' provided to the nationalities by the Austrian state which 'cared for the coexistence of its different peoples (*Volksstämme*)'.[41] At the same time, however, he called for the 'German element' to be strengthened because it 'educated' other nations. Its would-be pupils included provinces in crisis such as Galicia after 1846.[42] Thus Metternich attributed *a political function* to the German ethnic group. Its loyalties could be mobilized for the emperor and the imperial state. In Bohemia, Galicia, Hungary, Croatia, and Lombardy-Venetia,[43] the emperor and the government also supported the establishment of professorships in the provincial languages, provincial libraries, museums, and academies, as well as vernacular newspapers and 'national monuments'.[44] Insofar as the imperial elites regarded the nationalities of the non-German population primarily as *cultural* entities, they denied that these nationalities and their respective loyalties had any *political* significance.[45]

For Metternich, nationality was a concept comprising 'linguistic, cultural, and geographical peculiarities due to settlement'. Consequently, he rejected it as a 'guiding principle for state-building',[46] as Wolfram Siemann aptly put it. Metternich's conceptual use of nation and nationality was ambiguous. On the one hand, he referred to linguistic groups with their own culture and history. He referred to all 'Slavs' as a nationality, but also to individual groups such as '*Mazurians*' (Poles), '*Russniaks*' (Ukrainians), Southern Slavs, or Czechs.[47] On the other hand, he also spoke of the German inhabitants of the various historical and administrative territories of the Holy Roman Empire as separate 'nationalities',[48] but rejected the

[41] Metternich, 'Aphoristische Betrachtungen', 207 and 209.

[42] Metternich, 'Aphoristische Betrachtungen', 207 and 209. See Hans-Christian Maner, 'Zwischen "Kompensationsobjekt", "Musterland" und "Glacis"'. In Maner (ed.), *Grenzregionen der Habsburgermonarchie im 18. und 19. Jahrhundert*. Münster, 2005, 113–14.

[43] David Laven and Laura Parker, 'Foreign Rule? Transnational, National, and Local Perspectives on Venice and Venetia within the "Multinational" Empire', *Modern Italy*, 19/1 (2014), 5–19.

[44] Siemann, *Metternich Staatsmann*, 106–8; Schlitter, *Aus Österreichs Vormärz*, 2. 74.

[45] Polish intellectuals like Adam Mickiewicz reproached the Czechs for this difference; they were satisfied with museums, libraries, and poems, without wanting to fight for national independence. Václav Žáček, *Čechové a poláci roku 1848: Studie k novodobým politickým stykům česko-polským*. Vol. 1. Prague, 1947, 287. On the embeddedness of this idea in rural areas, cf. Alice Velková and Luboš Velek, 'Vnímání národnostní identity u venkovského obyvatelstva v Čechách na začátku 19. století'. In Velková and Jiří Pokorný (eds), *Nacionalismus, společnost a kultura ve střední Evropě 19. a 20. století*. Prague, 2007, 39–51.

[46] Siemann, *Metternich Staatsmann*, 105. Cf. also Metternich himself: 'The generalization of concepts through catchwords is a means from which the revolutionary sense knows how to draw benefit in the current period, and nationality is one of these words'. Letter to Kübeck, 20 Feb. 1850, 'Hingeworfene Betrachtungen über die deutschen Zustände, am Ende Februar 1850'. In Kübeck, *Briefwechsel*, 211.

[47] Metternich, 'Aphoristische Betrachtungen', 207.

[48] 'Alleruntertänigster Vortrag Metternichs am 24.5.1816', printed in Haas, *Metternich: Reorganization and Nationality*, 175.

concept of a single 'German nation' as ahistorical.[49] This understanding, that multiple German nations existed within the German Confederation was typical for the time. Contemporary thinking revolved, first and foremost, around the role of the various 'German' and 'Germanic' tribes (with different political loyalties to the territories), but hardly recognized the possibility of an all-German nation (with one political loyalty to the nation).[50]

Metternich's idea of reform was therefore not motivated by the question of how to organize diverse nationalities. He was primarily interested in European and Austrian power politics, defence, security, and efficient administration. Indeed, in his ideas about territorial reorganization, he hardly acknowledged the concerns of the population or the nationalities, nor the constitutional-historical structure of the monarchy.[51] Only context-specific power-political calculations can explain, for example, why Galicia was earmarked for union with Bohemia in 1817, then permitted to remain independent, and then designated for partition in 1846. Elsewhere, Metternich concluded that Carniola 'might as well be a province of Illyria as of Inner Austria'.[52] These calculations did not prevent him from promoting, both in existing and new territories, locally limited forms of national patriotism. Such loyalties were to be solely cultural, not political. They could not be allowed to endanger the unity of the empire, as, for instance, the Polish elite did by its demands for national autonomy.[53]

In the final analysis, Metternich's aim was to overcome the *Vormärz* disparity within a composite monarchy that had three central authorities, the Habsburg court chancelleries, acting separately from one another. To that end, he designed a system of administrative federalism. From his office in the Ballhausplatz, it seemed as though the Habsburg territories could never be governed by a purely centralized administration.

3.2. The Central Committee of the Estates in 1848

In the late pre-1848 period, the estates elite, whose political influence had often been the target of Metternich's policies, also adopted elements of administrative federalism into their reformist thinking. But their conception was quite different

[49] Letter to Kübeck, 4 Apr. 1850. In Kübeck, *Briefwechsel*, 102. Letter to Kübeck, 20 Feb. 1850, 'Hingeworfene Betrachtungen über die deutschen Zustände, am Ende Februar 1850'. In Kübeck, *Briefwechsel*, 211.

[50] The lexicons of the pre-1848 period do not yet contain the lemma 'nation' or 'nationality', Wolf D. Gruner, *Der Deutsche Bund 1815–1866*. Munich, 2012, 34.

[51] In contrast, Siemann emphasizes more strongly for Metternich the importance of a 'national identity' in the sense of an invention of tradition, e.g. for Illyria, and the 'idea of equality between the nations', Siemann, *Metternich Strategist*, 536, 749.

[52] 'Alleruntertänigster Vortrag Metternichs am 24.5.1816', printed in Haas, *Metternich: Reorganization and Nationality*, 175. On the composition of the population Hösler, *Von Krain zu Slowenien*, 67–74.

[53] This also applied to the German Confederation, Gruner, *Der Deutsche Bund*, 36–7.

from that of the Austrian State Chancellor. State-building and territorialization of the whole state were to be pushed back in favour of state-building and territorialization of the provinces. The estates had formed a regionally unequal counterweight to the emperor, the government, and Metternich.[54] In the short interim between the outbreak of the revolution in March 1848 and April 1848, a reform of the empire by the estates based on interprovincial cooperation seemed possible.[55] However, the constitutions and privileges of the estates, where they still existed, were soon to fall victim to the revolution.[56]

The transitional nature of the intense period between Metternich's dismissal, the abolition of the old estates order, and the establishment of a provisional, clearly bourgeois constitution by Pillersdorf is further illustrated by the fluctuation in the estates' expressions of loyalty. Even in the pre-March period, different notions of belonging coexisted. These included loyalties to a social class, to the local province, to the dynasty, and, in a few cases, to the empire. As the idea of the unitary nation state began to emerge, these points of reference multiplied even further. According to the composite monarchy theorist J. H. Elliott: 'The relationship of component regions and provinces both to each other and to the state itself would involve complex and constantly changing shifts in the balance of loyalties—shifts based on political calculation, economic realities and changing cultural attitudes.'[57] Thus, in the days of the revolution, a new strand was added to the existing patchwork of loyalties among the estates: they identified with state-building in the German Confederation as an expression of German nation-building.

The Central Committee of the Estates played an important part in articulating these allegiances. Modelled on the Prussian *Vereinigter Landtag* (United Provincial Diet), it convened in Vienna from 10 to 17 April 1848,[58] breaking with the imperial tradition which was to prevent any political communication between the Austrian estates. Austria had not seen such a 'central representation' of the provincial estates since the early seventeenth century. The reason for this was that the emperor and his government were deeply suspicious of any 'movement towards a unified state built on the participation of the estates', which they viewed as a potential rival for power.[59] The early modern understanding of the idea of a 'confederation' of the estates was twofold. On the one hand, confederation denoted an association

[54] Cf. Chapter 2.

[55] The first imperial constitutional promise of 15 Mar. 1848 had announced the convening of the deputies of all provincial estates.

[56] § 70 Reichsverfassung, No. 150/1849 RGBl. On the estates constitutions of the pre-March period, Ignaz Beidtel, *Geschichte der österreichischen Staatsverwaltung 1740–1848*. Vol. 2: *1792–1848*. Innsbruck, 1898, 399–434. He overemphasizes their opposition to the state, Gerhard Ammerer et al., 'Die Stände in der Habsburgermonarchie: Eine Einleitung'. In: Ammerer et al. (eds), *Bündnispartner und Konkurrenten der Landesfürsten? Die Stände in der Habsburgermonarchie*. Vienna, 2007, 15.

[57] Elliott, 'Europe of Composite Monarchies', 70.

[58] On Prussia Klaus Herdepe, *Die Preußische Verfassungsfrage*. Neuried, 2003.

[59] Redlich, *Staats- und Reichsproblem*, 1/1, 17–24.

forbidden by imperial law for the purpose of revolt, insurrection, and rebellion against the emperor; on the other, it designated an accepted alliance for securing peace.[60]

According to this imperial logic, there could not be such a thing as an interprovincial alliance of the estates. By contrast with their Hungarian counterparts, Austrian police in the pre-March period keenly monitored any signs of suspicious cooperation.[61] For their part, the estates gave little reason to suspect cross-border conspiracies. They observed each other carefully, keeping close tabs on who was being listened to and favoured in Vienna, on what they demanded and with what consequence. The mouthpiece of the estates' opposition was the Leipzig *Grenzboten* (Border Courier), edited by the Bohemian Ignaz Kuranda, which published minutes of meetings and debates in individual provinces.[62] Although banned in the Habsburg Monarchy, the *Grenzboten*, like many other similar periodicals, was displayed and read in Viennese coffee houses.[63] In other respects, however, the provincial estates complied with the communication barriers imposed on them. The flow of information was channelled through the 'eye of the imperial needle' which permitted little contact between the provinces.[64]

These imperial structures influenced the reformist ideas of the provincial estates. In line with the 'radial structure' of governance (Osterhammel), the estates referred exclusively to their respective provinces when, in the face of embezzlement or financial mismanagement, they demanded a say in provincial finances, budgets, and legislation;[65] or when they belatedly demanded the expansion of provincial diets to include burghers and peasants;[66] or when they demanded the abolition of the patrimonial system and serfdom, the *robot*,[67] in favour of municipal

[60] Thomas Fröschl, 'Confoederationes, uniones, ligae, Bünde'. In Fröschl (ed.), *Föderationsmodelle und Unionsstrukturen: Über Staatenverbindungen in der frühen Neuzeit vom 15. zum 18. Jahrhundert*. Vienna, 1994, 36.

[61] Viktor Bibl, *Die niederösterreichischen Stände im Vormärz: Ein Beitrag zur Vorgeschichte der Revolution des Jahres 1848*. Vienna, 1911, 320–1.

[62] Hartig, *Genesis der Revolution*, 51. One issue of the *Grenzboten* (1846, vol. 3), for example, contained reports on the 'estates' situation' in Bohemia, Lower Austria, and Tyrol and printed a memorandum from the Lower Austrian estates to the emperor.

[63] For an instructive and comprehensive statistical evaluation of the censorship practice Norbert Bachleitner, *Die literarische Zensur in Österreich von 1751 bis 1848*. Vienna, 2017.

[64] On this 'radial structure', typical of empires, Jürgen Osterhammel, *The Transformation of the World: A Global History of the Nineteenth Century*. Princeton, 2014, 427. See also Ivo Cerman, 'Opposition oder Kooperation? Der Staat und die Stände in Böhmen 1749–1789'. In Ammerer et al., *Bündnispartner und Konkurrenten der Landesfürsten?* Vienna, 2007, 376–7; William D. Godsey, *The Sinews of Habsburg Power: Lower Austria in a Fiscal-Military State 1650–1820*. Oxford, 2018.

[65] 'Denkschrift der drei oberen Stände Niederösterreichs an den Kaiser' [July 1846] (so-called 'Magna Carta' of the Austrian estates), *Grenzboten*, 5/3 (1846), 472–86. On Bohemia, Bruska, 'Die jüngsten Kämpfe der böhmischen Stände', *Grenzboten*, 7/1 (1848), 251–62.

[66] Despite the references to the 'welfare' of the province, the Lower Austrian Diet of Estates only hesitantly approached the other population groups, documented at Bibl, *Die niederösterreichischen Stände*, 299–329.

[67] 'Zur Robotabolitionsfrage in Böhmen', *Grenzboten*, 7/1 (1848), 81–83.

self-government.[68] In their dealings with the emperor and the government, the estates traditionally functioned as a body representing a privileged elite. Only towards the end of the pre-March period, did they come nearer to representing the respective province in its entirety. The general public was, therefore, often left in doubt as to the true purpose of the estates' demands; whether they were to benefit primarily the estates or the 'provincial nation' as a whole.[69] The former was the view of many bourgeois liberals who saw the provincial estates as self-serving conservative institutions, supported by the imperial centre and blind to the needs of their province.[70] They mocked the obsequious appearance of the '"bureaucratized" estates' in their anachronistic gala uniforms.[71]

By the outbreak of the March Revolution in Vienna at the latest, the Lower Austrian Estates had proved that provincial estates could stand up, on a case to case basis, for issues concerning the entire society.[72] By delivering the 'Petition of the People' to the monarch, they took on the role of mediator between the emperor and then insurrectionists, contributing to a de-escalation and the historic fall of Metternich within the first days of the revolution.[73] This mediation facilitated the subsequent convening of the Central Committee of the Estates in April 1848. In just a few days, the committee outlined common ideas for a reorganization of the Monarchy. Among its most important figures were Karl von Kleyle and Alexander von Bach, who would become minister of the interior during the neo-absolutist era. The committee was hampered, however, by the absence of important provinces such as Hungary, Lombardy-Venetia, and Bohemia. The latter's absence was due to the 'Bohemian Charter' of 8 April, which had already promised an independent administration, legislature, and judiciary, and the equality of its provincial languages.

In April 1848, the Central Committee drafted plans for a loose constitutional confederation united by a common monarch. The four major territories proposed were Austria, Hungary, Galicia, and Lombardy-Venetia. Having forced Metternich from office, the estates could not openly adopt his territorial ideas, but the

[68] On the reform requests of the estates Bibl, *Die niederösterreichischen Stände*; instructively Christine Mueller, *The Styrian Estates 1740–1848*. New York, 1987.

[69] Redlich, *Staats- und Reichsproblem*, 1/1, 122.

[70] Speech by Dr Alexander Bach in support of his motion for reforming the provincial-state institute of 27 Mar. 1848, printed as supplement XI in Karl Hugelmann, 'Die Landtagsbewegung des Jahres 1848 in Österreich unter der Enns', *Jahrbuch für Landeskunde in Niederösterreich*, 14–15 (1914–15), 524–6.

[71] See Franz Xaver von Pillersdorf, *Handschriftlicher Nachlaß des Freiherrn von Pillersdorff*. Vienna, 1863, 265–70. Against this Bibl, *Die niederösterreichischen Stände*, 331. Quoted in Gerald Stourzh, 'Länderautonomie und Gesamtstaat in Österreich 1848–1918'. In Stourzh, *Der Umfang der österreichischen Geschichte: Ausgewählte Studien 1990–2010*. Vienna, 2011, 41. On the significance of uniforms as symbolic distinction, cf. also William D. Godsey, *The Sinews of Habsburg Power*. Oxford, 2018, 379.

[72] Immediately before this, the Lower Austrian estates negotiated a petition to the emperor, as they wanted to convene a conference of all estates due to the financial situation of the provinces. Hugelmann, 'Landtagsbewegung', 495–6.

[73] Bibl, *Die niederösterreichischen Stände*, 327.

similarities between the two proposals are striking. Within the pre-March tradition of multi-level governance in the German Confederation and the Habsburg Monarchy, these four territories were to fit into further federations within Europe. The Kingdom of Lombardy-Venetia, with its 'Iron Crown', was to remain dynastically attached to the Habsburgs.[74] It was assumed, however, that it would 'naturally have to join the great confederation of Italy'.[75] Voluntary admission to this planned confederation of the estates was left open to Hungary and Galicia once 'they felt the need for a closer union'.[76]

Political unification with Germany was at the centre of all considerations. The states of the German Confederation were to unite in a German-Austrian Confederation. To that end, Austria was to be internally centralized. Habsburg lands which also belonged to the German Confederation were to form 'a state and not a confederation of states' and be part of a strengthened 'German National Empire'.[77] The 'centralism' of the Central Committee of Estates, which historians regularly cite, thus referred only to 'Austria'. What can be seen at work here is the overpowering force of the nation-state idea that had seized the Austrian estates. When they looked to other Habsburg territories, they were satisfied with a loose personal union. But with regard to their relationship with a future 'Germany', they yearned for the closer and stronger bond of federation.

After only a few weeks, the Central Committee of the Estates lost its position as the leading voice for a reform in Austria. New constitutional ideas were beginning to emerge from the bourgeois-liberal government formed during the revolution under Franz Xaver von Pillersdorf.[78] In the early stages of the revolution, Pillersdorf's government had sought cooperation with the Central Committee. It quickly became clear, however, that the government preferred the future legislative to be made up by a body of parliamentary representation rather than the provincial estates.[79] Concurrent debates in the German National Assembly on universal suffrage influenced this decision.[80] In the case of the estates, the government feared the dominance of aristocratic interests; reorganization of the

[74] On plans for a mere personal union between Lombardy-Venetia and Austria on the part of the later head of the civil administration Albert Graf von Montecuccoli, Brigitte Mazohl-Wallnig, 'Il governo austriaco durante il biennio rivoluzionario'. In Alba Lazzaretto Zanolo (ed.), *La 'primavera liberale' nella terraferma veneta 1848–1849*. Venice, 2000, 25.

[75] The Viennese government also expected the loss of at least Lombardy in Upper Italy. The Court Commissioner Franz Count Hartig was appointed for reforms or a cession, cf. Thomas Kletečka, 'Einleitung'. In *Die Protokolle des österreichischen Ministerrates* (hereafter *ÖMR*). Vol. 1/1: *Die Ministerien des Revolutionsjahres 1848 (20. März 1848–21. November 1848)*. Vienna, 1996, pp. xxxviii–xli. As a slippery slope towards the dissolution of the state, this is sensationalized by Matthias Koch, *Pillersdorf und die Wahrheit*. Vienna, 1849, 23.

[76] Redlich, *Staats- und Reichsproblem*, 1/1, 127.

[77] Redlich, *Staats- und Reichsproblem*, 1/1, 129.

[78] Kletečka, 'Einleitung'. In *ÖMR* 1/1, p. xviii.

[79] Karl Hugelmann, 'Der ständische Zentralausschuss in Österreich in April 1848', *Jahrbuch für Landeskunde von Niederösterreich*, 12 (1913), 247 ff.

[80] Thomas Stockinger, *Dörfer und Deputierte: Die Wahlen zu den konstituierenden Parlamenten von 1848 in Niederösterreich und im Pariser Umland (Seine-et-Oise)*. Vienna, 2012, 379.

empire should involve more than just the old elite.[81] At the provincial level by contrast, the government refrained from anything 'that might inhibit or disrupt the independent functioning of the provincial estates and national institutions'.[82] Initially then, interference with the estates' interests was off the table. The long-term goal of the Pillersdorf administration was to establish popular participation at the imperial level.

Having been put in their place by the liberal government, the estates argued for greater administrative powers for the provinces. The similarities with Metternich's ideas of executive federalism are obvious, although the motives were different. In view of their previous function, the estates demanded reforms in future provincial constitutions. 'Instead of a legislative competence, which is not merely insufficient, but necessarily confusing, they should be assigned the principal tasks of administration.'[83] To that end, the Central Committee applied the idea of municipal self-government, which had spread from England to early constitutional thinking in Germany and Austria, to the Habsburg territories, designating them the 'pillars of administration'.[84] The keyword was autonomy.[85] If the empire had a unifying legislative power, the implementation of the laws should be left to the provinces.

Even in April 1848, as under Metternich, the administration was still regarded as the true form of governance. When the provincial estates newly sought to make administration their main purview and simultaneously renounced legislative work, they were drawing on their political experience. In provinces such as Bohemia, Lower Austria, and Styria, the estates had already begun to develop their own policies in areas such as welfare, education, and agriculture before March 1848. As a result, they had come to appreciate their administrative independence.[86] Simply implementing imperial laws did not satisfy the Central Committee, which insisted on the greatest possible administrative autonomy for the provinces. Among the responsibilities demanded by the estates were 'the allocation and collection of approved taxes, the management of the provincial credit, welfare and educational institutions, the provincial road system, and the gendarmerie…They should also advise and supervise the head of the provincial government'.[87] This enumeration in 1848 of policy fields like provincial finance, welfare, education, roads, and gendarmerie looked to the future. In the second half of the nineteenth century, it was precisely these provincial agendas that became decisive for the independence and autonomy of the crown lands.

81 Thus, in retrospect, the then prime minister, cf. Pillersdorf, *Nachlaß*, 265–70.
82 Council of Ministers of 22 Apr. 1848. In Kletečka, *ÖMR* 1/1, No. 18, 101–3.
83 Hugelmann, 'Zentralausschuss', 247 ff.
84 Redlich, *Staats- und Reichsproblem*, 1/1, 261. The Franco-Belgian influence of the 'pouvoir municipal' is emphasized by Stourzh, 'Länderautonomie und Gesamtstaat', 44.
85 On contemporary language use Stourzh, 'Länderautonomie und Gesamtstaat', 43.
86 Redlich, *Staats- und Reichsproblem*, 1/1, 248.
87 Hugelmann, 'Zentralausschuss', 247 ff.

Fundamental differences emerge when one compares the administrative federalism envisaged by the estates in April 1848 with that proposed by Metternich thirty years earlier. The main contrast concerned the personnel who were to execute these policies. In Metternich's plan, this was a professional staff of civil servants under state control, starting with the governor and ending with the administrative apparatus of the counties. As a 'conservative innovator', Metternich relied on a meritocratic bureaucracy for effecting a territorialization that took account of regional differences. The provincial estates, meanwhile, ascribed this decisive role to themselves, thus preserving their status and privileges. The spokesman for Lower Austria in the Central Committee, Karl von Kleyle, rejected 'provincial parliaments', 'because the provinces should not become semi-sovereign cantons'.[88] The provincial estates should administer provincial affairs.

Against this background, executive federalism appears as a strategy oriented towards the self-interest of the estates. It allowed regional territorialization to be pursued in a decentralized manner without broadening popular participation. By contrast, representative provincial institutions, as demanded by revolutionaries on the streets, would not only have increased the number of burghers and peasants in the diets, but also the number of non-German-speaking representatives. The supremacy of the German-speaking elite would have been undermined and threatened by delegations of hitherto underrepresented 'Slavs' in the Bohemian lands and Styria, or of Italians in Tyrol.[89]

3.3. Administrative Reorganization and Executive Federalism in the Post-March Period, 1851–1861

While the idea of administrative federalism flourished in the pre-March period, its heyday as active form of rule fell in the era of neo-absolutism. An observer of the monarchy in late 1851 could have been forgiven for assuming that nothing particularly notable had happened since the pre-March period. For the powers-that-be, the long revolutionary year of 1848/49 and the imposition of the March Constitution of 1849 were to be relegated to the past as two fundamentally misguided developments. The president of the Imperial Council, Karl Friedrich von Kübeck, who initiated the process of deconstitutionalization, virtually described the political system of 1849 as a 'lie'.[90] Through the Sylvester Patent of 31 December 1851, the emperor repealed both the imposed March Constitution and the provincial constitutions enacted since its passing.

[88] Hugelmann, 'Zentralausschuss', 247 ff.

[89] Peter Burian, *Die Nationalitäten in 'Cisleithanien' und das Wahlrecht der Märzrevolution 1848/49*. Graz and Cologne, 1962, 48–51.

[90] Kübeck in a letter of 27 Aug. 1851 to his daughter, quoted in Thomas Kletečka and Anatol Schmied-Kowarzik, 'Einleitung'. In *ÖMR* 2/5: *Das Ministerium Schwarzenberg (4. Juni 1851–5. April 1852)*. Vienna, 2013, p. xv.

Both before and after 1848/49, decision-makers in the emperor's entourage were concerned with transforming the Habsburg Monarchy into a strong administrative state with regional subdivisions while also suppressing, so far as was possible, any social participation.[91] Neo-absolutism had clear features of executive federalism: both popular participation and the separation of powers were missing. The neo-absolutist monarchy was not a unitary state, however. Even though the emperor and his government, as sole legislators, issued general guidelines of governance, the provincial administrations, headed by the governorates, retained significant discretion in their implementation. They issued general, not just executive, regulations for their administrative territories.

By suspending the constitution in 1851, the emperor returned the reins of legislative, judicial, and administrative powers to himself.[92] The Sylvester Patent abandoned the provincial parliaments—announced in the imposed March Constitution but not yet established—as neither 'appropriate' nor 'practicable'. The same applied to the strict separation of administrative and judicial powers.[93] New provincial constitutions which *had* been enacted were repealed without the old estates constitutions being reinstated.[94] Elsewhere, the Imperial Council was downgraded to a merely advisory body to 'the crown', rather than to the Council of Ministers.[95] Similarly, ministers swore a revised oath to the emperor, rather than to the constitution.[96] Highest administrative officials swore their allegiance also personally to the emperor, not to the state or the constitution.[97] One liberal minister who did not support this development, Anton von Schmerling, had already packed his bags.[98]

This was the 'absolute' in neo-absolutism: now the emperor alone stood at the summit of the empire.[99] By wiping the 1849 Constitution from the slate, the Sylvester Patent unreservedly reactivated the 'monarchical principle' of the Vienna Final Act. During the revolution, this principle had featured prominently and

[91] Georg Seiderer, *Österreichs Neugestaltung: Verfassungspolitik und Verwaltungsreform im österreichischen Neoabsolutismus unter Alexander Bach 1849–1859*. Vienna, 2015; John Deak, *Forging a Multinational State. State Making in Imperial Austria from the Enlightenment to the First World War*. Stanford, CA, 2015, 99–135; Waltraud Heindl, *Josephinische Mandarine: Bürokratie und Beamte* in Österreich. Vol. 2: *1848–1914*. Vienna, 2013.

[92] Pointedly on the following Deak, *Forging a Multinational State*, 101–6.

[93] Imperial Patent of 31 Dec. 1851, para. 2, No. 2/1852 RGBl.

[94] Kletečka and Schmied-Kowarzik, 'Einleitung'. In *ÖMR* 2/5, pp. xxv and xxviii.

[95] Ah. Kabinettsschreiben vom 20.8.1851, No. 196/1851 RGBl.

[96] Ah. Kabinettsschreiben vom 20.8.1851, No. 194/1851 RGBl. On this Kletečka and Schmied-Kowarzik, 'Einleitung'. In *ÖMR* 2/5, xv–xvi.

[97] On the tie to the emperor Karl Megner, *Civil Servants: Economic and Socio-Historical Aspects of the Imperial-Royal Civil Service*. Vienna, 1985, 334–6.

[98] Kletečka, 'Einleitung'. In: *ÖMR* 2/4: *Das Ministerium Schwarzenberg (14. Oktober 1850–30. Mai 1851)*. Vienna, 2011, p. xxxv.

[99] On the conservative turn see Helmut Rumpler, '"Dass neu und kräftig möge Österreichs Ruhm erstehen!": Der Thronwechsel vom 2. Dezember 1848 und die Wende zur Reaktion'. In Ernst Bruckmüller and Wolfgang Häusler (eds), *1848: Revolution in Österreich*. Vienna, 1999, 139–54.

repeatedly as a guiding principle in the correspondence of European monarchs.[100] Nonetheless, the monarchical programme of the neo-absolutist era was based on an understanding of rule that could not be described as 'absolute' in the eighteenth-century sense. The monarch stood 'in the state, not above the state', even if he held the power in his hands.[101] Monarchical sovereignty was no longer derived from dynastic hereditary and property rights but was linked to one territorial entity. In terms of international law, this corresponded to a 'structural change of monarchical rule' in Europe. Monarchical rule was no longer understood as the coexistence of princely houses but of states.[102]

The 'neo' in neo-absolutism in 1851 thus denoted new ideas of the state, which now was finally conceived of as a territorial entity. Metternich alluded to this crucial point in one of his letters of 1850 to the architect of neo-absolutism, Karl von Kübeck. He sought to trace the transition from princely to state sovereignty within the Holy Roman Empire and the German Confederation:

> I grew up in a German household, I have been part of it since the days of the *Confederation of Princes*;...I have attended its dissolution and been the architect of the *Confederation of States*, the only possible means for uniting the German tribes into one political body after the demise of the Old Empire.[103]

The thinking of Metternich and his disciple Kübeck belonged to a tradition that no longer attributed territorial sovereignty to a specific person, but to the state as an organism in its own right. Territorial sovereignty became state sovereignty.[104]

[100] Kübeck's memorandum 'Skizzierung einiger Ideen über den künftigen politischen Organismus des österreichischen Kaiserstaats' [Sketch of Some Ideas about the Future Political Organism of the Austrian Imperial State], Point 2. Österreichisches Staatsarchiv, Abteilung Allgemeines Verwaltungsarchiv, Nachlass Bach, Box 40, File Verfassung II. Printed at Adolf Beer (ed.), *Kübeck und Metternich: Denkschriften und Briefe*. Vienna, 1897, 47–8. For both a constitutional and historical perspective, Ernst-Wolfgang Böckenförde, 'Der deutsche Typ der konstitutionellen Monarchie im 19. Jahrhundert'. In Böckenförde, *Recht, Staat, Freiheit*. Frankfurt am Main, 1991, here 278. On divergent interpretations Michael Stolleis, *Geschichte des öffentlichen Rechts in Deutschland*. Vol. 2: *Staatsrechtslehre und Verwaltungswissenschaft 1800–1914*. Munich, 1992, 102–5. On the revolution see Johannes Paulmann, 'Europäische Monarchen in der Revolution von 1848/49' In Dieter Langewiesche (ed.), *Demokratiebewegung und Revolution 1847–1849*. Karlsruhe, 1998, 118 and 124.

[101] Böckenförde, 'Konstitutionelle Monarchie', 278.

[102] Dieter Langewiesche, *Die Monarchie im Jahrhundert Europas*. Heidelberg, 2013; Johannes Paulmann, *Pomp und Politik: Monarchenbegegnungen in Europa zwischen Ancien Régime und Erstem Weltkrieg*. Paderborn, 2000, 68; Böckenförde, 'Konstitutionelle Monarchie', 278. On international law in Europe, cf. Matthias Schulz, 'Macht, internationale Politik und Normenwandel im Staatensystem des 19. Jahrhunderts'. In Ulrich Lappenküper and ReinerMarcowitz (eds), *Macht und Recht: Völkerrecht in den internationalen Beziehungen*. Paderborn, 2010, 113–34.

[103] Letter to Kübeck, 4 Apr. 1850. In Kübeck, *Briefwechsel*, 102 (emphasis in the original).

[104] Ernst-Wolfgang Böckenförde, 'Der Staat als Organismus: Zur staatstheoretisch-verfassungspolitischen Diskussion im frühen Konstitutionalismus'. Böckenförde, *Recht, Staat, Freiheit*. Frankfurt am Main, 1991, 265.

Neo-Absolutism and Organic State Theory

The state-philosophical cue for the new legitimation of neo-absolutism was provided by an accompanying text to the Sylvester Patent, the 'Principles for Organic Institutions'.[105] The term 'organic' had a dual meaning. First, it referred to planned 'organs' in the sense of institutions and organizations. Second, it referred to the 'organic doctrine of the state' as a contemporary type of conservative thinking. The idea of the 'state as an organism'[106] had been popular at the Viennese court since 1809. Adam Müller, a university friend of Friedrich Gentz, had inspired Emperor Franz I with his political romanticism. Later, the historical school of law of Karl von Savigny and the patrimonialism of Carl Ludwig von Haller also caught on in Vienna.[107]

This organic doctrine of the state represented a polemical break with the rational individualist state doctrine of the Enlightenment.[108] The Enlightenment had, to put it bluntly, constructed the state as an order of equality. It had carved out a protected domain of individual and collective freedoms from the state's sphere of influence. This had created a logical opposition between the state, society, and the individual. The 'order of equality' in the Kremsier draft constitution (March 1849), and to a lesser extent in the Olomouc constitution (4 March 1849), had taken up this approach.[109]

The organic theory contrasted the 'wilfully made and deliberately regulated' state of Enlightenment thinking with the 'wholeness' and 'totality' and the 'grown' and 'living' character of *historical* structures.[110] The national economist Georg von Buquoy, for example, compared the 'lithobiotic', 'phytobiotic', or 'zoobiotic' life of crystals, plants, and animals with the 'anthropobiotic' forms of state philosophy. The latter were alive in the variety of state constitutions as 'polibiotic entities that have become historical'.[111] In the subtitle of his work 'Restoration', which gave its name to the entire epoch, Carl Ludwig von Haller spoke of 'macrobiotics' of

[105] Appendix 'Grundsätze für organische Einrichtungen in den Kronländern des österreichischen Kaiserstaates' to the Imperial Patent of 31.12.1851, No. 2/1852 RGBl., so-called Sylvester Patent.

[106] Böckenförde, 'Staat als Organismus', 263–272.

[107] Helmut Rumpler, *1804–1914: Eine Chance für Mitteleuropa. Bürgerliche Emanzipation und Staatsverfall in der Habsburgermonarchie*. Vienna, 1997, 93–4. Still worth reading Karl Mannheim, *Konservatismus: Ein Beitrag zur Soziologie des Wissens*. Frankfurt am Main, 1984, 149–58.

[108] For organic thought in Bohemia and Moravia see Jiří Georgiev, *Až do těch hrdel a statků? Konzervativní myšlení a otázka samosprávy v politických strategiích české státoprávní šlechty po roce 1848*. Prague, 2011; Christoph Stölzl, Die Ära Bach in Böhmen: Sozialgeschichtliche Studien zum Neoabsolutismus 1849–1859. Munich, 1971, 40. On academic state theory in German-speaking Austria see Friedrich Engel-Janósi, 'Die Theorie vom Staat im deutschen Österreich 1815–, *Zeitschrift für öffentliches Recht*, 2 (1921), 360–94.

[109] Cf. Chapter 6.

[110] Böckenförde, 'Staat als Organismus', 268–9. See Adam H. Müller, *Elemente der Staatskunst*. 2 vols. Ed.Jakob Baxa. Jena, 1922.

[111] Georg von Buquoy, *Einige der wesentlichen Punkte, die jeder Theorie des Debattirens in den Kammern einer echten Volks-Repräsentativ-Verfassung entsprechen müssen, gleichsam als eine Vorschule zu den Kammer-Debatten im Oesterreichischen Staate*. Prague, 1848, 31–2 and 36.

governance.[112] Enlightenment constitutions were meant to be universal; they could be (and were) adopted almost word-for-word in different countries. In organic state theory, this would not pass; an organic state organization was particular and had to be shaped by the prevailing historical circumstances.[113]

The conservatives drew the foundations of their programme from the fact that what had historically grown could prove unequal. Karl Graf Wolkenstein, president of the Moravian Diet in 1848 and a member of the *Verstärkter Reichstag* (Reinforced Imperial Council) in 1860, wrote in a memorandum of February 1849 that there were two possible future paths for European 'humanity'. Either it 'returns to the principles of an organic construction of society, or it continues on the path of negation and disorganization. In the first case, it must recognize the principle of inequality, because there is no organization without higher and lower people, without dependence'.[114] Kübeck, the author of the implementing rules for the Sylvester Patent, the 'Principles for Organic Institutions', was also sympathetic to this point of view.[115]

The Sylvester Patent of 1851 abolished the separation of powers of the imposed March Constitution of 1849. It was inspired by the idea of an organic state whose power could not be divided into separate state functions. The doctrine of the separation of powers had prescribed a functional and thus controllable structure of government.[116] By contrast, the variety implied by the organic state idea appears chaotic. The internal structures of the state were not only determined by public institutions. Of equal importance were special 'life circles' and 'organic intermediate members' of society.[117] These included estates bodies, occupational interest corporations (such as the chambers of commerce and trade), autonomous ecclesiastical institutions, and, above all, the municipalities.[118]

For the history of neo-absolutism as executive federalism, it is worth taking a look at the discussions behind state philosophy. From here, the 'organic' state structure after 1851 becomes visible as a deliberate construction. When interpreting the organic state system in the age of neo-absolutism, it would be a misunderstanding to equate a rejection of the separation of powers with a refusal to differentiate between separate spheres of governance. The 'Organic Principles' provided for a subtle gradation of rule, not in terms of legislation, but in terms of

[112] Carl Ludwig von Haller, *Restauration der Staatswissenschaft oder Theorie des natürlich-geselligen Zustands, der Chimäre des künstlich-bürgerlichen entgegengesetzt*. 6 vols. Aalen, 1964 (repr.).

[113] Buquoy, *Volks-Repräsentativ-Verfassung*, 22 and 28.

[114] Letter from Karl Graf Wolkenstein to Leo Graf Thun on the future of the Bohemian nobility, 1 Feb. 1849, reprinted in Stölzl, *Ära Bach*, 317.

[115] Kübeck, 'Organismus des österreichischen Kaiserstaates', Point 4.

[116] Christoph Möllers, *Die drei Gewalten: Legitimation der Gewaltengliederung in Verfassungsstaat, Europäischer Integration und Internationalisierung*. 2nd edn. Weilerswist, 2015.

[117] Böckenförde, 'Staat als Organismus', 271.

[118] Georgiev, *Až do těch hrdel a statků?*, 168–75; Thomas Götz, *Bürgertum und Liberalismus in Tirol, 1840–1873: Zwischen Stadt und 'Region', Staat und Nation*. Cologne, 2001, 239–317.

administration.[119] As in Metternich's *Vormärz* plans, the administrative-federal arrangement served to push back parliamentary participation and institutions. An 'organic' doctrine of the state legitimized these conservative structures.

The details of this administrative multi-level governance were set out in ministerial decrees and accompanying legislation.[120] The four planned administrative levels had already been laid down by Franz von Stadion in the imposed March Constitution. In order of scale, these were the crown lands, counties, districts, and municipalities. The new minister of the interior, Alexander von Bach, reconfigured their relationships. Stadion had been sceptical about increasing the power of the crown lands, placing his trust in the intermediate administrative authorities and forging 'the most liberal of all self-administration laws' for the municipalities.[121] Bach, by contrast, adopted one of Metternich's basic ideas: he strengthened the crown lands at the expense of the counties.

The Crown Lands

The crown lands nominally became administrative territories. The regional administrations, however, did not only have executive functions, but enjoyed a broader remit for general regulation. After the estates' participatory rights had been put on hold, the governors, as powerful provincial administrators, took over all provincial affairs 'in a leading capacity', as well as the business 'personally' assigned to them by the central authorities in Vienna.[122] According to their explicit mandate, the governors were to 'remedy the apparent defects in the administration of the province'.[123] They undoubtedly played a key role as conduits between their local administration and the central bureaucracy in Vienna. This was true even after 1852, when they lost their original role as provincial viceroys and were more closely integrated into the governorates, which were no longer

[119] Historians have therefore recently discussed a modification of the term 'neo-absolutism', Harm-Hinrich Brandt (ed.), *Der österreichische Neoabsolutismus als Verfassungs- und Verwaltungsproblem: Diskussionen über einen strittigen Epochenbegriff*. Vienna, 2014; Helmut Rumpler, 'Der österreichische Neoabsolutismus als Herrschafts- und Modernisierungssystem'. In Dušan Kováč, Arnold Suppan, and Emilia Hrabovec (eds), *Die Habsburgermonarchie und die Slowaken 1849–1867*. Bratislava, 2001, 9–21; Seiderer, *Österreichs Neugestaltung*, 31–35.

[120] Ordinance of the Ministers of Interior, Justice and Finance of 23 Jan. 1853, No. 10/1853 RGBl.

[121] Stadion's state ideas were not conveyable to the Schwarzenberg cabinet, Kletečka, 'Einleitung'. In *ÖMR* 2/1: *Das Ministerium Schwarzenberg (5. Dezember 1848–7. Jänner 1850)*. Vienna, 2002, p. xiv (quote). See Heinrich Heffter, *Die deutsche Selbstverwaltung im 19. Jahrhundert*. 2nd edn. Stuttgart, 1969, 313.

[122] The governors were instructed about such 'personal' assignments by imperial handwritten letters, cf. Andreas Gottsmann, *Venetien 1859–1866: Österreichische Verwaltung und nationale Opposition*. Vienna, 2005, 26.

[123] § 14 of the Ordinance of the Ministers of Interior, Justice and Finance of 19 Jan. 1853, No. 9/1853 RGBl. and the Ordinance of the Ministers of Interior, Justice and Finance of 19 Jan. 1853, Supplement C, No. 10/1853 RGBl.

monocratic but collegial.[124] In the broad field of provincial policing, the governors retained an arsenal, if needed, for 'a repressive pre-emptive strike against revolution'.[125]

Occasionally, the governors were further delegated province-specific tasks. In Hungary, for example, they were obliged by law to settle the 'fundamental question concerning the relationship of church and state, or of the faith traditions among themselves'.[126] In Venetia, meanwhile, the governor Georg Otto von Toggenburg was instructed by handwritten letter in 1859 to replace the pre-existing military regime with a tough approach by the civilian authorities and to concurrently prevent future interference by the military in provincial administration.[127] The exceptional position of governors like Toggenburg is further underlined by their loyalty frameworks: their oath was to the 'Imperial-Royal-Apostolic Majesty'. Heads of the counties and comitats, by contrast, pledged their loyalty to the governor.[128] In Hungary, this loyalty could be further cultivated through the patronage of honours. Governors were trusted to apply to the supreme authority 'for the granting of noble ranks, decorations, titles and awards' to their subjects.[129] Regional diversity was both a condition and consequence of this executive federalism, which in itself came to be seen as a symbol of this unique symbiosis between central and provincial administration in the Habsburg Empire.

Counties

The counties, on the other hand, as the 'leading supervisory and executive intermediate authorities' below the governor's office, were tasked with administration and implementation rather than the creation of policies of their own. They existed only in the larger crown lands, having been dispensed with in Carinthia,

[124] For plans from 1849 cf. Seiderer, *Österreichs Neugestaltung*, 200–1; Heindl, *Josephinische Mandarine*, 51–2. See also Mazohl, *Österreichischer Verwaltungsstaat*, chapter 4, 281–382.

[125] There was controversy over the reintroduction of the collegial constitution in the governorates, cf. Seiderer, *Österreichs Neugestaltung*, 190–216.

[126] § 22 of the Ordinance of the Ministers of Interior, Justice and Finance of 19 Jan. 1853, No. 9/1853 RGBl. Hungary had been exempted from the reorganization of the relationship between the state and Protestants at the beginning of the 1850s, Kletečka and Schmied-Kowarzik, 'Einleitung'. In *ÖMR* 2/2: *Das Ministerium Schwarzenberg (8. Jänner 1850–30. April 1850)*. Vienna, 2005, p. xxv.

[127] Gottsmann, *Venetien*, 26–9. Cf. Antonio Schmidt-Brentano, *Die Armee in Österreich: Militär, Staat und Gesellschaft 1848–1867*. Boppard am Rhein, 1975, 335–51.

[128] § 8 of the Ordinance of the Ministers of the Interior, Justice and Finance of 19 Jan. 1853, No. 9/1853 RGBl. and of the Ordinance of the Ministers of Interior, Justice and Finance of 23 Jan. 1853, Supplement C, No. 10/1853 RGBl.

[129] § 20 of the Ordinance of the Ministers of the Interior, Justice and Finance of 19 Jan. 1853, No. 9/1853 RGBl. The background to this may have been the severely disturbed loyalty of the Hungarian elite after the March Revolution, as lamented by the governor Archduke Albrecht, see Zsolt K. Lengyel, 'Zum Problem der Landesvertretung im neoabsolutistischen Ungarn'. In Harm-Hinrich Brandt (ed.), *Der österreichische Neoabsolutismus als Verfassungs- und Verwaltungsproblem: Diskussionen über einen strittigen Epochenbegriff*. Vienna, 2014, 383–412.

Carniola, Salzburg, Silesia, and Bukovina.[130] Their responsibilities included, amongst other things, coordinating the recent empire-wide proliferation of infrastructure projects (such as bridges, roads, and waterways) between the municipalities and districts.[131] Compared with the crown lands and the territorially subordinate districts, the counties were one of the weaker pillars of the imperial administration. After the lost Italian war in 1859, they fell victim to austerity measures and were ultimately abolished.[132]

Districts

Despite being smaller than counties, the districts were the second most important administrative unit after the crown lands. With their administrative and judicial functions, districts adopted the functional legacy of the abolished patrimonial dominions. Spatially, however, they did not coincide with the former landed estates, as had once been the intention with the so-called *Gaugemeinden*, especially in Bohemia.[133] Law enforcement, jurisdiction, and taxation were now concentrated in a single first-level authority.[134] Districts also received additional responsibilities for a wide range of matters including policing, 'the promotion of the common good', the care of the poor, and the building of bridges and roads.[135] Previously, the care of the poor, welfare, and health care had been the purview of ecclesiastical and aristocratic charities. In a sense, this had been the paternalistic flipside of the authoritarian relationship between patrimonial landlords and peasant subjects.[136] The landlords had long regarded the peasants as 'about as capable of action as immature children'.[137] From their latifundia, aristocratic magnates such as the south Bohemian Johann Adolph zu Schwarzenberg resented the fact that

[130] In Hungary the counties were called comitats, in Lombardy-Venetia delegations; § 5 of the Ordinance of the Ministers of Interior, Justice and Finance of 19 Jan. 1853, No. 10/1853 RGBl.

[131] § 1 of the Ordinance of the Ministers of Interior, Justice and Finance of 23 Jan. 1853, Supplement B, No. 10/1853 RGBl. For details Carl Czoernig, *Österreichs Neugestaltung 1848–1858.* Stuttgart and Augsburg 1858, 328–34.

[132] Initially, the county authorities in Lower and Upper Austria, in Styria, in Tyrol with Vorarlberg, in Dalmatia, Moravia, and the Littoral were suspended and finally abolished in 1868. Seiderer, *Österreichs Neugestaltung*, 247.

[133] On the mixed district offices, their perception and exercise of procedure cf. Seiderer, *Österreichs Neugestaltung*, 216–47. On the nobility's claim to dominion in the districts, see Ralph Melville, Ralph, *Adel und Revolution in Böhmen.* Mainz, 1998, 272–3.

[134] Rule of law standards of the March Constitution were thus withdrawn, Seiderer, *Österreichs Neugestaltung*, 220–39.

[135] §§ 23, 28, 39 of the Ordinance of the Ministers of Interior, Justice and Finance of 23 Jan. 1853, Supplement A, No. 10/1853 RGBl.

[136] Tatjana Tönsmeyer, *Adelige Moderne: Großgrundbesitz und ländliche Gesellschaft in England und Böhmen 1848–1918.* Vienna, 2012, 194–225, 231.

[137] Ernst Bruckmüller, '"Kein Robot! Kein Zehent mehr!" Die Bauern, der Reichstag und die Grundentlastung'. In Bruckmüller and Wolfgang Häusler (eds), *1848: Revolution in Österreich.* Vienna, 1999, 89.

what they had hitherto done voluntarily was now demanded of them as a compulsory contribution to an abstract common good.[138] After 1848, the everyday life of the rural population was no longer regulated by patrimonial officials, but those from state districts. Almost 1,500 districts were established in the empire, each with approximately 10,000 to 20,000 inhabitants.[139] In the process, the administration and the state were brought closer to the people,[140] who were suddenly confronted with an army of district officials dressed in standard-issue dark green uniforms. District personnel represented the state and the ruler; they 'were to be the emperor's feet on the ground'.[141] The territorialization and étatisation of the Habsburg Monarchy had thus reached an extent which would not have been enforceable under Metternich. As a consequence, albeit with some regional variations, this administrative expansion into the territories reduced privileges and differences between the various crown lands.

Municipalities and Estates

For the municipalities, neither territorialization nor *étatisation* were a given in the 1850s. Among historian, there is a common assumption that, beginning in the late eighteenth century, 'the municipalities have been overwhelmed by the state'. However, in many cases the state had yet to arrive in the regions.[142] Since the reforms of neo-absolutism, municipal legislation in Austria, unlike that in Prussia, no longer distinguished between rural and urban municipalities. Some industrial towns were nonetheless particularly well represented in the provincial diets.[143] The incorporation of the municipality as the smallest building block in the state structure brought about the greatest distortions.[144] The patrimonial landlords were interested in exempting the manorial area from public administration as a 'state-free' space. They wished to carry on exercising state functions themselves. The bureaucratic territorial state, for its part, was aiming for comprehensive control. Municipalities thus became the battleground on which these fronts were formed. On the one side were liberal representatives of local self-government,

[138] Raimund Paleczek, *Die Modernisierung des Großgrundbesitzes des Fürsten Johann Adolph II. zu Schwarzenberg.*. Marburg, 2009, 121 and 273.

[139] Deak, *Forging a Multinational State*, 121.

[140] Heindl, *Josephinische Mandarine*, 52.

[141] Deak, *Forging a Multinational State*, 125. Under Bach, it once again became mandatory to wear the uniform, Megner, *Beamte*, 241.

[142] Martin P. Schennach, 'Das Provisorische Gemeindegesetz 1849 und das Reichsgemeindegesetz 1862 als Zäsur? Reflexionen zum österreichischen Gemeindebegriff im 19. Jahrhundert', *MIÖG* 120 (2012), 378.

[143] City statutes were only enacted for selected towns, cf. Josef Redlich, *Das Wesen der österreichischen Kommunalverfassung.* Leipzig, 1910, 17, 24–5, 38–51.

[144] Lothar Gall, 'Gemeinde und Staat in der politischen Theorie des frühen 19. Jahrhunderts', In Peter Blickle (ed.), *Theorien kommunaler Ordnung in Europa*. Munich, 1996, 63–74; Redlich, *Das Wesen der österreichischen Kommunalverfassung*, 17.

personified by Franz von Stadion, who had already experimented with self-government in the Littoral.[145] On the other side, Stadion and his allies faced aristocratic opponents who equated 'self-government' with local seigneurial rule and resisted any curtailment of their prerogatives.[146]

Aristocratic rule achieved an overwhelming dominance in provinces such as Bohemia, Moravia, and Galicia. Unlike in Inner Austria, landed property here meant large-scale property.[147] More than 35 per cent of the taxed provincial territory in Moravia, almost 42 per cent in Bohemia, and around 50 per cent in Galicia belonged to landed estates.[148] They could also be found in Silesia, but in the Teschen region some villages were administered by several landlords.[149] In 1844, the largest latifundium in South Bohemia, located around Krummau (Český Krumlov), only comprised a part of the Schwarzenberg estate yet still included over 50,000 inhabitants, several towns, almost 300 villages, twenty-four parishes, and forty schools.[150]

Many landlords had hoped that the Sylvester Patent would exempt them from the neo-absolutist administrative pyramid. Even Kübeck had argued that the undivided manor property should be treated as an independent level in the state structure and thus be spared integration into the district system.[151] This tedious dispute was finally resolved in favour of the bureaucratic state with the Imperial Municipalities Act of 1859 and the Land Municipalities Ordinances of the 1860s. Only in exceptional cases was special treatment to be provided for noble estates, unlike other municipalities. Locally, however, aristocratic landowners continued to lord over others in matters of public administration. For some time, they claimed the final word in the municipalities, not only in matters of policing, but also in issues relating to schools, roads, endowments, and care of the poor.[152]

145 Apollonio, Almerigo, 'Gli esperimenti d'autogoverno comunale del governatore Francesco Stadion in Istria e nel Gorizano 1844–1847', *Quaderni Giuliani di Storia*, 17/2 (1996), 31–98.

146 On the 'state-free' or 'state-hostile' community cf. Heffter, *Selbstverwaltung*, 372–403 (on Gneist), 445–52 (on von Stein); Redlich, *Das Wesen der österreichischen Kommunalverfassung*, 52, 56, 59. The strong position of the nobility made the example of England attractive in the Habsburg Monarchy, Tönsmeyer, *Adelige Moderne*, 278.

147 Ralph Melville, 'Von der Patrimonialverwaltung zur Gemeindeselbstverwaltung in Böhmen und Österreich um 1848', *Documenta Pragensia*, 14 (1997), 56.

148 Melville, 'Patrimonialverwaltung', 62.

149 Clerical property, on the other hand, was atypical in East Silesia, Dan Gawrecki et al. (eds), *Dějiny Českého Slezska 1740–2000*. Vol. 1. Opava, 2003, 71 and 77.

150 Paleczek, *Modernisierung des Großgrundbesitzes*, 82 and 306.

151 Kübeck, 'Organismus des österreichischen Kaiserstaates', point 4.

152 Jiří Klabouch, *Die Gemeindeselbstverwaltung in Österreich 1848–1918*. Vienna, 1968, 51; Milan Hlavačka, *Zlatý věk české samosprávy: Samospráva a její vliv na hospodářský, sociální a intelektuální rozvoj Čech 1862–1913*. Prague, 2006, 13–14. Conversely, the municipalities repeatedly tried to pass on financial burdens to the landowners alone, Tönsmeyer, *Adelige Moderne*, 262–78; Stölzl, *Ära Bach*, 39–40.

Territorialization through Bureaucratization

In the neo-absolutist era, the political territory was successfully subjugated to the authority of the public state. As civil servants, the bourgeois-liberal classes participated in the bureaucratization, territorialization, and modernization of the Habsburg Monarchy. They also set the tone in the chambers of commerce and trade established in 1850. With enormous effort and high investment in administration, infrastructure, and, most notably, the army, Austria tried to close the development gap with other European states, especially Prussia and members of the Customs Union. Ten years later, high-ranking officials such as Karl Czoernig looked back with pride on what had been achieved. In their eyes, 'no public affair has been left untouched by Austria's reorganization.'[153]

Political participation was further marginalized. At the behest of the state leaders, the reforms were carried out in direct denial of the revolutionary demands for a greater say in legislation. In many cases, the separation of powers initiated in 1848 was simply reversed. Without doubt, the central instrument of territorialization and *étatisation* was the administration. It was regionally differentiated vis-à-vis its subjects and included many bourgeois liberals in its ranks. Below the highest level—the government in Vienna—the governors and governorates enjoyed particular leeway for action. They passed general, quasi-legislative regulations in the form of 'decrees', which differed from province to province. This regional divergence becomes evident when the neo-absolutist era is understood in administrative-federalist rather than centralist terms. By the 1850s, executive federalism had already created a basic system of multi-level governance—an administrative scaffolding that often outlasted the Habsburg Monarchy in its successor states.[154]

A Federal History of the Habsburg Empire, 1815–1918. Jana Osterkamp, Oxford University Press.
 DOI: 10.1093/9780198943631.003.0004

[153] Czoernig, *Österreichs Neugestaltung*, p. v.

[154] Waltraud Heindl, 'Verwaltungseliten im Neoabsolutismus. Professionelles und politisches Profil vor dem Horizont der Modernisierung.' In Harm-Hinrich Brandt (ed.), *Der österreichische Neoabsolutismus als Verfassungs- und Verwaltungsproblem. Diskussionen über einen strittigen Epochenbegriff.* Vienna, 2014, 146.

Figure 4.1 'Amazonka na barikádě na malém rynečku/Die Amazone auf der Barrikade am kleinen Ring' [Amazon on the Barricade in the Lower Square]. Lithograph, Prague 1848.

4

Multi-Ethnic Federalism

Federation of Nationalities and Nation-Building, 1848

1848 in Europe was the year of the nation and constitutions. The mantra of the March Revolution read 'one nation, one state', but such political algebra did not produce a neat solution—a single constitutional nation state for the conundrum of pre-March Habsburg rule. Instead, this 'Europe in miniature' gave rise to myriad complex and contradictory opinions as to which nations, and how many, should have the right of political self-determination. Seeking to meet the demands of demonstrators in the streets for a 'constitution', and to create an 'empire of the peoples', politicians at the Frankfurt National Assembly, in the Austrian *Reichstag*, and at the Prague Slav Congress set off a veritable firestorm of ideas about 'national self-determination'.[1] Indeed, so heated was the atmosphere that Hungarian and Italian aspirations for autonomy led to violent secessionist wars in the Habsburg south and east.

The movement towards nation- and constitution-building was supported by novel forms of social participation. In the March Revolution of 1848, the first 'European revolution',[2] reformist thinking swept through all social circles. Along with aristocrats, the bourgeois, and civil servants, priests, peasants, and workers participated in the reorganization of their homelands and empires. Political mobilization of the population unfolded on an unprecedented scale.[3] Women also fought on the front line for revolutionary rights, such as the iconic 'Amazon on the Barricade in the Lower Square' in the Pentecostal Storm of Prague, or otherwise acted as petitioners or 'flag mothers' in the National Guard (Figure 4.1).[4]

[1] Marco Bellabarba, *Das Habsburgerreich 1765–1918*. Berlin and Boston, 2020, 86.

[2] On the European nature of the revolution and its common trends, Dieter Dowe, Heinz-Gerhard Haupt, and Dieter Langewiesche (eds), *Europa 1848: Revolution und Reform*. Bonn, 1998. Jonathan Sperber, *The European Revolutions.1848–1851*. 2nd edn. Cambridge, 2005, here 258–83.

[3] Heinz-Gerhard Haupt and Dieter Langewiesche, 'Die Revolution in Europa 1848: Reform der Herrschafts- und Gesellschaftsordnung—Nationalrevolution—Wirkungen'. In Dowe et al., *Europa 1848*, 11–41, here 18–21; Jonathan Sperber, 'Kirchen, Gläubige und Religionspolitik in der Revolution von 1848'. In Dowe et al., *Europa 1848*, 933–59. On political mobilization in rural areas Thomas Stockinger, *Dörfer und Deputierte: Die Wahlen zu den konstituierenden Parlamenten von 1848 in Niederösterreich und im Pariser Umland (Seine-et-Oise)*. Vienna, 2012, 49–52, 74–7.

[4] Pieter M. Judson, *The Habsburg Empire: A New History*. Cambridge, MA, and London, 2016, 181; Mark Traugott, *The Insurgent Barricade*. Berkeley, CA, 2010, 194.

The revolutionaries' ambition to encourage greater political participation democratized federal thinking and led to new ideas of federal reorganization. In contrast with the tendency towards 'federative nationalism' (Dieter Langewiesche), which became visible in the future Germany, the spectrum of federal ideas in the Habsburg Monarchy was noticeably broader. In addition to the ideas of estates or executive federalism, covered in the previous chapter, there now emerged the concepts of a federation of nationalities and of historic crown land federalism.

In contrast to crown land federalism, which was based on the crown lands' historically inherited borders, the federation of nationalities was a real innovation: Newly drawn national boundaries were to guarantee the equal status of all nations. Thus, the idea of the nation state was adjusted to fit a multi-ethnic society. In particular, the ideal of statehood was widened to encompass not only the level of central government, but also those of the member states, regional, and local institutions. The idea of a federation of nationalities was neither monolithic nor clear-cut, however. Its interpretations were as varied and diverse as those of 'the nation' within any given epoch. On the table in 1848 were ideas as contrasting as the federal organizations of Greater Germany-Greater Austria or the Habsburg Monarchy, a union of the Slavs, or a national partition of Galicia and Tyrol.[5] By grafting the powerful new idea of the nation onto the traditional concept of the federal union, the federation of nationalities retained an enigmatic, yet alluring character which continued to fascinate until the end of the Monarchy. Known as ethno-federalism or multinational federalism, this line of thinking remains an integral part of international federalism theory to this day.[6]

For federal history, these varying interpretations of the federation of nationalities can be used as a litmus test of social affiliations and loyalties. The way in which the architects of federal ideas related nations to territories reveals which communities they regarded as nations and, at the same time, as politically significant. In contrast to the idea of executive federalism and its underlying ideal of an efficient, public-spirited, and well-run administration, the ideal of the nation appealed to emotions, encompassed broader social strata, and was far more politicized. Reinhart Koselleck has diagnosed an 'emphasis on emotional moments' with regard to the historical terms 'union' or 'federalism'.[7] This is particularly true of the national type of federalism.

[5] The partition of Galicia will be analysed in more detail below (cf. Chapter 5); for Tyrol, cf. Chapter 8.4.

[6] See Alain-G. Gagnon, *The Case for Multinational Federalism: Beyond the All-Encompassing Nation*. London, 2010; Michael Burgess and John Pinder, *Multinational Federations*. London, 2007.

[7] Koselleck, however, does not elaborate on this thought. Reinhart Koselleck, 'Bund (Bündnis, Föderalismus, Bundestaat)'. In Otto Brunner et al. (eds), *Geschichtliche Grundbegriffe*, 1. *Historisches Lexikon zur politisch-sozialen Sprache in Deutschland*. Stuttgart, 2004, 582–671, here 582.

4.1. One Revolution, Many Constitutional Assemblies, and Many 'Nations'

At the very beginning of the revolution, the question of what constituted the territory of a nation produced a scandal. On 11 April 1848, the Czech nationalist and historian František Palacký turned down an invitation to the Frankfurt National Assembly. As 'a Bohemian of Slavic origin', he could not participate in the drafting of a constitution for a new Germany, 'a German people's union'.[8] As for the calls for a 'Greater Germany' expressed in the revolutionary streets of Prague, Vienna, Graz, or Linz, he wrote, 'if there are people in Vienna itself who want their (sic) Frankfurt to be the capital, then one must cry out to them "Lord! forgive them, for they do not know what they want"'.[9] In his famous statement, Palacký emphasized the existential necessity of the Austrian Empire for the nationalities living within it. The empire's supranational basis excluded any subordination to an all-German government and a German nation state. As a result, inhabitants of the Bohemian lands (including many Germans from Prague)[10] and the Slovene-populated areas of Styria,[11] as well as Poles from the Posen region of Prussia,[12] boycotted the German election. In the end, only one Polish delegate attended the *Paulskirche*, the German Revolutionary Parliament.[13]

[8] This was preceded by his historical state law studies on whether Bohemia formed a jurisdiction of the German Confederation or not. Jiří Kořalka, *František Palacký (1798–1876): Der Historiker der Tschechen im österreichischen Vielvölkerstaat*. Vienna, 2007, 269–76. The rejection letter is printed in František Palacký, *Oesterreichs Staatsidee*. Prague, 1866, 79–86 (quote p. 80). On the negative image of Palacký in Germany, Jiří Štaif, 'Palacký, der Slavenkongress und die Zeitung "Die Grenzboten": Bilder des "Anderen" in der revolutionären Gesellschaft'. In Andreas Moritsch (ed.), *Der Prager Slavenkongress 1848*. Vienna, 2000, 47–61.

[9] Palacký, *Oesterreichs Staatsidee*, 84. On the consequences of manoeuvring between the 'free German people' and the 'Bohemian state federation' and the exchange of insults on the streets of Prague, cf. 'Erklärung des Ausschusses der Deutschen an das National-Comité' of 12 Apr. 1848 and 'Antwort des Nationalausschusses auf die Erklärung des Comité der Deutschen' of 14 Apr. 1848, printed in Franz Joseph Schopf, *Wahre und ausführliche Darstellung der am 11. März 1848 zur Erlangung einer constitutionellen Regierungs-Verfassung in der königlichen Hauptstadt Prag begonnenen Volks-Bewegung*. Leitmeritz, 1848, 81–2 and 86–9.

[10] On the conflict over the German population of Prague in the German-liberal camp cf. Peter Burian, *Die Nationalitäten in 'Cisleithanien' und das Wahlrecht der Märzrevolution 1848/49*. Graz and Cologne, 1962, 79–80.

[11] Ljubov' A. Kirilina, *Slovency i revoljucija 1848–1849 gg*. Moscow, 2000, 54–7. The Slovenes later petitioned against incorporation into the German Confederation. Otto Hoerhan, *Die Petitionen an den Kremsierer Reichstag 1848/49* (university diss.). Vienna, 1965, 262.

[12] In forty-eight of sixty-eight electoral districts in Bohemia and Moravia, no deputies were elected to the Frankfurt National Assembly. Burian, *Nationalitäten in 'Cisleithanien'*, 73. The election boycott also came from the German-speaking population, such as the conservative, state-law-minded inhabitants of Prague. Cf. Jiří Štaif, *Revoluční léta 1848–1849 a české země*. Prague, 1990, 118. See Krzysztof Makowski, 'Das Großherzogtum Posen im Revolutionsjahr 1848'. In Rudolf Jaworski and Robert Luft (eds), *1848/49 Revolutionen in Ostmitteleuropa*. Munich, 1996, 149–72, here 160. For the Slovenian boycott call cf. Joachim Hösler, *Von Krain zu Slowenien: Die Anfänge der nationalen Differenzierungsprozesse in Krain und der Untersteiermark von der Aufklärung bis zur Revolution 1768–1848*. Munich, 2006, 281.

[13] Hans Henning Hahn, 'Die polnische Nation in den Revolutionen von 1846–49'. In Dowe et al., *Europa 1848*, 231–52, here 231–2.

On the issue of a future 'German' nation state, the Austrian government held back and clung to the pluralist structure of governance that had existed during the pre-1848 period. The existence of parallel spheres of governance was symbolized by the appointment of the Habsburg Archduke Johann as *Reichsverweser* (Imperial Governor) in June 1848. In this role, he became the de facto representative of the Habsburg monarch in a future Germany.[14] Johann appointed a German government in which the most important Austrian politician was the conservative liberal Anton von Schmerling.[15] Facing Prussia's growing power, many Austrian politicians hoped to regain the Habsburgs' former hegemonic position in the German Confederation.[16]

This pre-modern multiplicity of rule, combined with an ambiguous framing of the nation, prompted several constitutional assemblies during the revolution. The *Paulskirche*, the Austrian Reichstag, and the Slav Congress all competed for the political mandate to represent the nations. Many deputies were sent by their electoral districts to both the Frankfurt *Paulskirche* and the Austrian Reichstag.[17] Austrian voices were in danger of being lost in Frankfurt, as many of these delegates preferred to concentrate on their duties at home. In December 1848, Schmerling went so far as to propose that the Austrian deputies to the *Paulskirche* be instructed to 'go to their posts' to fight proposals for Prussian hegemony.[18] However, the simmering conflicts between Frankfurt and Vienna over the political authority of each assembly were never resolved. Many deputies in the *Paulskirche* wanted to settle questions pertaining to *all* territories in the German Confederation. The Viennese government, on the other hand, withheld consent on all matters coming before the *Paulskirche* concerning Austria.[19]

Prime Minister Pillersdorf, therefore, allowed the elections to the Frankfurt Parliament,[20] but imposed, on 25 April, a separate constitution for the Austrian Empire (the Pillersdorf Constitution). His initiative failed to calm the revolutionary

[14] Thomas Kletečka, 'Einleitung'. In Kletečka (ed.), *Protokolle des Österreichischen Ministerrates* (hereafter *ÖMR*) 1/1. *Die Ministerien des Revolutionsjahres 1848 (20. März 1848–21. November 1848)*. Vienna, 1996, pp. ix–xlviii, here xliii.

[15] Anton von Schmerling, *Der Vater der Verfassung: Aus der Sicht des Staatsministers Anton v. Schmerlings*. Ed. Lothar Höbelt. Frankfurt am Main, 1994, 13–19.

[16] Hans Günter Telle, *Das österreichische Problem im Frankfurter Parlament im Sommer und Herbst 1848*. Marburg, 1933, 56–62; Wolfgang J. Mommsen, *1848. Die ungewollte Revolution. Die revolutionären Bewegungen in Europa 1830–1849*. Frankfurt am Main, 1998, 154–5.

[17] Wilhelm Schüßler, *Die nationale Politik der österreichischen Abgeordneten im Frankfurter Parlament*. Berlin and Leipzig, 1913, 10. The number of deputies was distributed among the provinces as follows: Lower Austria 24, Upper Austria 17, Styria 16, Tyrol 17, Illyria 12, Littoral 5, Moravia and Silesia 27, Bohemia 7, giving a total of 125. Cf. Council of Ministers of 12 June 1848. In Kletečka, *ÖMR* 1/1. *Die Ministerien des Revolutionsjahres 1848*, no. 69, 411–16.

[18] Council of Ministers of 26 Dec. 1848. In Kletečka, *ÖMR* 2/1. *Das Ministerium Schwarzenberg (5. Dezember 1848—7. Jänner 1850)*. Vienna, 2002, no. 8, 50–6.

[19] Günter Wollstein, *Das 'Großdeutschland' der Paulskirche. Nationale Ziele in der bürgerlichen Revolution 1848/49*]. Düsseldorf, 1977, 268.

[20] The electoral mode followed the guidelines of the Federal Parliament on the basis of parish districts. Council of Ministers from 14 Apr. 1848. In Kletečka, *ÖMR* 1/1. *Die Ministerien des Revolutionsjahres 1848 (20. März 1848–21. November 1848)*. Vienna, 1996, no. 12, 63–71.

mood, however. With unrest persisting in the streets of Vienna, Pillersdorf was forced to compromise and the constitution was declared provisional on 16 May.[21] The government promised a 'constitutional Reichstag' and conceded 'to elect only one chamber; thus, there would be no census at all for the elections and any doubt of an imperfect representation of the people would cease to exist'.[22] The social diversity of the constitutional assemblies in Frankfurt and Vienna was thus very different. In the Austrian Reichstag, the bourgeoisie and the peasantry were strongly represented and the aristocracy poorly so.[23] Its counterpart in Frankfurt was, by contrast, considered a 'parliament of dignitaries', of the 'patricians of education, money and title', with only a single peasant amongst a surplus of lawyers,[24] academics, and aristocrats.[25]

The social composition of the constitutional assemblies had a direct impact on how they perceived federalism. As the nationalities of the Monarchy were more strongly represented in the Austrian Imperial Diet (but for the Hungarian and Italian provinces), the constitutional debate at Kremsier (Kroměříž) sought to accommodate and reconcile different national affiliations more so than the Constitutional Assembly at Frankfurt. There, on the other hand, the revolutionary idea called for 'the unification of the states of the German Confederation into a common nation state'. 'Parts of the Confederation at its borders [were] to be separated from the nation state'.[26] The federal form was determined by the coexistence of *Teutschland* (Germany) as an all-German cultural nation, on the one hand and small-scale, regional affiliations to one's own province, on the other.[27] In the Habsburg Monarchy, national, regional, and linguistic affiliations were reflected in the plans for federal organization, even if they could not be integrated into an overarching idea of a single nation.

The sense of nation was too fluid in the Habsburg Monarchy to result in an unambiguous concept of nationhood. For a German-speaking Tyrolean, it was not certain whether he felt a 'national' affiliation primarily to his province of Tyrol, to the German-Austrian group of provinces, to the Austrian Empire, or

[21] Stockinger, *Dörfer und Deputierte*, 381–92.

[22] Imperial-August Patent of 25 Apr. 1848 'Verfassungs-Urkunde des österreichischen Kaiserstaates' (Pillersdorf's Constitution); Proclamation of 16 May 1848 'Erklärung des ersten Reichstages als einen constituirenden nur mit einer Kammer und angeordnete Abänderung der früheren Wahlordnung'. See Stockinger, *Dörfer und Deputierte*, 378–92.

[23] A quarter were peasants and the aristocracy was barely represented, apart from the Polish nobility. Jiří Kořalka, 'Revolutionen in der Habsburgermonarchie'. In Dowe et al., *Europa 1848*, 197–230, here 208. Details for Lower Austria, Stockinger: *Dörfer und Deputierte*, 747–71.

[24] Wolfram Siemann, *Die Frankfurter Nationalversammlung 1848/49 zwischen demokratischem Liberalismus und konservativer Reform: Die Bedeutung der Juristendominanz in den Verfassungsverhandlungen des Paulskirchenparlaments*. Bern, 1976.

[25] Veit Valentin, *Geschichte der deutschen Revolution von 1848–49*. 2 vols. Berlin, 1930, here vol. 2, 11-13.

[26] Haupt and Langewiesche, 'Revolution in Europa', 23.

[27] Wolf D. Gruner, *Der Deutsche Bund 1815–1866*. Munich, 2012, 35. On the lasting effect of this regional patriotism Alon Confino, 'Federalism and the "Heimat" Idea in Imperial Germany'. In Maiken Umbach (ed.), *German Federalism: Past, Present, Future*. Basingstoke, 2002, 70–90.

even to the German Confederation. Italian-speaking South Tyroleans, meanwhile, wanted to disentangle Trentino from the province and Confederation altogether.[28] Similar national conflicts flared up in the German-Polish-Czech region of Teschen in Austrian Silesia, where national affiliations to 'Prussia', 'Poland', and 'Austria' competed fiercely with one another.[29] Even a Transylvanian Saxon might see himself culturally as part of the German nation, while politically as part of the 'Saxon royal soil' or Transylvania or Austria (but only rarely as part of the Hungarian provinces).[30] For the Slovene-speaking rural inhabitants of Carniola, Styria, and Carinthia, 'nation' meant something vaguely 'Slavic', a nebulous patriotic connection to their territory. Visions of a common Slovenia remained anaemic and only found supporters in 'Klagenfurt, Graz and above all Vienna'.[31] Even in the Adriatic region, where the idea of a 'multinational Adriatic'[32] was on the decline due to the Risorgimento, graded national affiliations remained typical. It was unthinkable that one would cease 'to feel Venetian or Milanese, Sicilian and Tuscan, Roman and Bolognese', and become just Italian.[33] In the *Paulskirche*, the puzzle of Germany's diverse national and provincial affiliations had been answered with a federal form of nationalism. For the Habsburg Monarchy, the solution appeared to be a multi-ethnic federalism.

4.2. Prague in Summer: The Slav Congress and the 'League of Equal Nations'

The intellectual forerunner of the idea of a state constructed as a federation of nationalities was the 'Slav Congress'. For two weeks between 2 and 12 June 1848,

[28] Laurence Cole and Hans Heiss, '"Unity vs. Difference": The Politics of Region-Building and National Identities in Tyrol 1830–1867'. In Laurence Cole (ed.), *Different Paths to the Nation. Regional and National Identities in Central Europe and Italy 1830–70*. Basingstoke, 2007, 37–59, here 42–3; Hans Heiss and Thomas Götz, *Am Rand der Revolution: Tirol 1848/49*. Vienna, 1998, 122–3.

[29] Czech national allegiances were rudimentary. Dan Gawrecki, 'Schlesien als Randgebiet der Habsburgermonarchie nach 1742'. In Hans-Christian Maner (ed.), *Grenzregionen der Habsburgermonarchie im 18. und 19. Jahrhundert: Ihre Bedeutung und Funktion aus der Perspektive Wiens*. Münster, 2005, 133–43; Dan Gawrecki et al. (eds), *Dějiny Českého Slezska 1740–2000*, vol. 1. Opava, 2003, 127–9, 142–5, 176.

[30] On their difficult negotiating position in Frankfurt, András Gergely, 'Das Bündnis zwischen Frankfurt und Pest-Buda und die österreichische Frage'. In Jaworski and Luft, *1848/49 Revolutionen in Ostmitteleuropa*, 257–78, here 264–5. On the protest of the Transylvanian Saxons against a union with Hungary, cf. Council of Ministers of 1 June 1848. In Kletečka, *ÖMR* 1/1. *Die Ministerien des Revolutionsjahres 1848*, no. 58, 357–61.

[31] Hösler, *Von Krain zu Slowenien*, 340; Vasilij Melik, 'Das Jahr 1848'. In Harald Krahwinkler (ed.), *Staat—Land—Nation—Region: Gesellschaftliches Bewußtsein in den österreichischen Ländern Kärnten, Krain, Steiermark und Küstenland 1740–1918*. Klagenfurt, 2002, 229–37, here 232–6.

[32] Dominique K. Reill, *Nationalists Who Feared the Nation: Adriatic Multi-Nationalism in Habsburg Dalmatia, Trieste, and Venice*. Stanford, CA, 2012, 201.

[33] Simonetta Soldani, 'Annäherung an Europa im Namen der Nation: Die italienische Revolution 1846–1849'. In Dowe et al., *Europa 1848*, 125–65, here 128. On federal ideas of Italy Daniel Ziblatt, *Structuring the State: The Formation of Italy and Germany and the Puzzle of Federalism*. Princeton, 2006.

this informal constitutional assembly met in Prague, allowing the 'Slavs', who had been underrepresented in Frankfurt, to make their voices heard in the debate on the new organization of Europe.[34] The participants proudly described their meeting as an 'unusual event, as much in Europe, as among us Slavs ourselves'.[35] Together, delegates sketched a counter-programme to the German-national idea of a federal state. The Viennese government feared, not without reason, that 'a sort of Slavic parliament would be formed by the deputies of all Slavic nations'.[36] In vain it urged the Bohemian Gubernial President Leo von Thun-Hohenstein to forbid the meeting. However, he rejected such a move outright since a significant number of his peers in the Bohemian nobility were involved in the preparations for the congress.[37]

In its call to convene, the Slav Congress put a 'Slav Confederation' on the agenda and set out five points for negotiation.[38] More than 340 political and religious representatives of various Slavic nationalities met in Prague. The majority were Czechs, Moravians, and Slovaks, followed by Poles and Ruthenians as well as Croats, Serbs, and Slovenes.[39] Although the Russian revolutionary and pan-Slavist Michael A. Bakunin was also present in Prague, the Congress advocated Austro-Slavism and addressed itself primarily to the Slavic population of the Austrian Empire.[40] The invitation to meet in Prague contained a foreboding prediction: if the German Confederation were to be turned into a nation state with the help of the *Paulskirche* deputies, it could 'destroy not only the unity of Austria, but also

[34] Democraticly minded exiled Poles refused to participate, being 'not Slavs, but only Poles'. Václav Žáček, *Čechové a Poláci roku 1848: Studie k novodobým politickým stykům česko-polským*, vol. 2. Prague, 1948, 96.

[35] 'Proklamation der ersten Slavenversammlung in Prag an die Völker Europas', 12 June 1848, printed in Jan Peter Jordan, *Aktenmäßiger Bericht über die Verhandlungen des ersten Slawenkongresses in Prag*. Prague, 1848, 34–9, here 34. The Manifesto goes back to a Polish initiative. Antoni Cetnarowicz, 'Die Polen und der Prager Slavenkongress'. In Moritsch, *Prager Slavenkongress*, 103–14, here 110. On plans for a union, Włodzimierz Borodziej, Błażej Brzostek, and Maciej Górny, 'Polnische Europa-Pläne des 19. und 20. Jahrhunderts'. In Włodzimierz Borodziej (ed.), *Option Europa: Deutsche, polnische und ungarische Europapläne des 19. und 20. Jahrhunderts, 1. Essays*. Göttingen, 2005, 43–134, here 56.

[36] Council of Ministers of 12 May 1848. In Kletečka, *ÖMR* 1/1. *Die Ministerien des Revolutionsjahres 1848*, no. 35, 207–14.

[37] Council of Ministers of 10 May 1848. In Kletečka, *ÖMR* 1/1. *Die Ministerien des Revolutionsjahres 1848*, no. 33, 191–8.

[38] The negotiating prompts were: 'Brothers, are you in favour of the creation of a Slavic federation for mutual protection and in what way?', 'Under what conditions do we demand the establishment of an Austrian federal state?', 'What are your wishes for the non-Austrian Slavs and in what way can Slavic science and art be elevated?', 'Should the decisions of the Frankfurt Parliament have legal validity and if so, for which parts of Slavic Austria? And in what way should we protest against them?', cf. 'Program Sjezdu slovanského' of the Provisional Committee of 27 May 1848, printed in Jan M. Černý, *Boj za právo: Sborník aktů politických u věcech státu a národa českého od roku 1848*. Vol. 1. Prague, 1893, 256–62.

[39] For the membership, cf. the list by name and origin in Václav Žáček, *Slovanský sjezd v Praze roku 1848: Sbírka dokumentů*. Prague, 1958, 544–61.

[40] Žáček, *Čechové a Poláci roku 1848 II*, 61. The first signatories included Josef Mathias Count von Thun, Albert Count Deym, and Johann Ritter von Neuberg, as well as Georg Prince von Lubomirski, who came from Galicia. On Palacký and the Slav Congress cf. Kořalka, *František Palacký*, 285–90.

the present association and independence of the Slavic tribes... whose nationality would thereby be endangered.'[41]

When plans for a federation of the Slavic peoples became public, pre-existing fears amongst the German population in the Habsburg Monarchy and German Confederation over Slavic political empowerment were sharply exacerbated.[42] For many Germans, the fear of a 'Slavic danger' obscured their view of the Prague meeting.[43] The alleged national antagonism between 'Slavs' and 'Germans' played a major role both at the Slav Congress and in its perception by the European public. At the European level, French diplomats assessed the centripetal tendencies of the Prague assembly as a threat to Austria's existence.[44] Europe's security system, headed by the five Great Powers, had been effective since 1815 but was now called into question by the Congress's conception of the entire Slavic community as a 'nationality' and as a federally organized nation state. To the Great Powers, such a union simply was tantamount to greater power for Russia.

The repression of the Pentecostal Storm of Prague brought the congress to a premature conclusion. Amidst the upheaval, the delegates hastily adopted a manifesto, the 'Proclamation of the First Slav Assembly in Prague to the Peoples of Europe'. In lofty imagery, the document invoked the Slavs' yearning for freedom and peace, their role as victims of the 'Germanic and Romanic peoples', and the need to overcome their oppression.[45] The demand for equality between the Slavs and other peoples was a signpost to a peaceful coexistence in Europe. It was Palacký who incorporated this profoundly federal ideal into the manifesto. Political equality was to be granted not only to individuals, but also to peoples, including those who had no territory of their own.[46] Austria was to become a

[41] Call for the Slav Congress 'Slované, bratři!' resp. 'Slawenbrüder!' of 1 May 1848, printed in Žáček, *Slovanský sjezd*, 48–9, here 49.

[42] Because of Austria's hegemonic position in the German Confederation, Franz Schuselka disapproved of the high number of Slavs and fuelled the public debate by overstating the figures for the Slav population. Franz Schuselka, *Ist Österreich deutsch?*. Leipzig, 1843. See Jiří Štaif, *Obezřetná elita: Česká společnost mezi tradicí a revolucí 1830–1851*. Prague, 2005, 123–5. From the many contemporary pamphlets see Friedrich Nork [pseudonym for Friedrich Korn], *Die Ansprüche der Slawen in den österreichischen und preußischen Staaten, namentlich in Galizien, Posen und Prag*. Weimar, 1848; Andreas Moritsch, 'Revolution 1848—Österreichs Slawen wohin?'. In Moritsch, *Prager Slavenkongress*, 5–18, here 5–6.

[43] On the emotional history and survival of the fear of the 'Slavic danger' or 'Pan-Slavism' in German politics, cf. Patrick Bormann, 'Furcht und Angst als Faktoren deutscher Weltpolitik 1897–1914'. In Patrick Bormann, Thomas Freiberger, and Judith Michel (eds), *Angst in den Internationalen Beziehungen*. Göttingen, 2010, 71–90, here 75–9. This rhetoric is still found later. See Schüßler, *Politik der österreichischen Abgeordneten*, 5.

[44] De la Cour wrote to Lamartine on 12 May 1848: 'La poursuite de ce rêve ne peut qu'exposer la Monarchie Autrichienne à des dangers de toute nature.' Printed in Žáček, *Slovanský sjezd*, 192; Catherine Horel, 'La France et l'Empire d'Autriche 1815–1918', *Bulletin de l'Institut Pierre Renouvin*, 32/2 (2010), 57–79, here 64–5.

[45] This self-description is traceable to Herder's characterization of the Slavs, cf. Holm Sundhaussen, *Der Einfluß der Herderschen Ideen auf die Nationsbildung bei den Völkern der Habsburger Monarchie*. Munich, 1973, 50–8, 179–80.

[46] Palacký used natural law as a justification. Kořalka, *František Palacký*, 289. Michael Bakunin's slogan of 'liberty, equality and fraternity of all nations' was linked to this postulate. Bakunin, *Aufruf an die Slaven*. Koethen, 1848, 10.

'federation of equal nations' and the state was to grant the Slavs 'full recognition and status'.[47] In view of the pre-existing Great Power system, this Europe of amicable, liberally constituted, and federally united peoples was a veritable utopia.

Not all participants of the Congress approved of the manifesto's message. The Russian pan-Slavist, revolutionary, and anarchist Michael Bakunin considered an Austro-Slavic solution, equal rights for Slavic political interests within the Habsburg Monarchy, to be unrealistic. Instead, he wanted to unite all Slavic peoples, including those of Prussia and Russia, into a 'Slav Council' of politically independent Slavic 'nations'.[48] He envisioned this federation of Slavs within the framework of a federal Europe.[49] Success, however, ultimately eluded both Bakunin and other pan-Slavic thinkers who dreamt of pushing the borders of the Austrian Empire further into Russia or Poland.[50]

The example of the Poles can serve as a prism through which the differences between pan-Slavic and Austro-Slavic ideas, as well as alternative nation state formations, may be seen. At the time of the Prague Congress, the 'Polish question' did not yet evoke the same negative backlash in Germany and Europe as it would in the autumn of 1848, when the foreign-policy interests of Prussia, Austria, and Russia once again prevented Poland from becoming a nation state.[51] In particular, non-Galician Poles who hoped for Polish independence objected to an Austro-Slavic solution and to Galicia remaining part of Austria.[52] Jędrzej Moraczewski, a nationalist politician and historian from Poznan, warned against a continued German and Hungarian hegemony in an Austro-Slavic federation. He advocated for a democratic Poland within its 1772 borders, which would include all of Galicia and possibly the Ruthenian part of Hungary.[53] Only later did he advocate for a federative buffer state of the 'Western Slavs', 'a barrier between Russia and

[47] 'Proklamation der ersten Slavenversammlung in Prag an die Völker Europas' of 12 June 1848, printed in Jordan, *Aktenmäßiger Bericht*, 37.

[48] He referred to thoughts by Joachim Lelewel. Martin Schulze Wessel, *Russlands Blick auf Preußen: Die polnische Frage in der Diplomatie und der politischen Öffentlichkeit des Zarenreiches und des Sowjetstaates 1697–1947*. Stuttgart, 1995, 185. See Bakunin's Polish draft 'Podstawy zasadnicze nowej polityki słowiańskiej', printed in Žáček, *Slovanský sjezd*, 383–6.

[49] Bakunin repeated his pan-Slavic thoughts in a German-language pamphlet, which was later also translated into Czech. See Bakunin, *Aufruf an die Slaven*. On this Alfred Fischel, *Der Panslawismus bis zum Weltkrieg*. Stuttgart and Berlin, 1919, 290–2; Vladislav Šťastný (ed.), *Slovanství v národním životě Čechů a Slováků*. Prague, 1968, 181, 189–92. Palacký later turned away from Bakunin. František Palacký, *Nothgedrungene Erklärung (über Bakunin)*, 26 Jan. 1849, printed in Palacký, *Gedenkblätter. Auswahl von Denkschriften, Aufsätzen und Briefen aus den letzten fünfzig Jahren. Als Beitrag zur Zeitgeschichte*. Prague, 1874, 181–4.

[50] In the Polish-Russian section it was disputed whether a new Poland should join the Empire of Austria or, conversely, whether Galicia should become part of the new Poland. Cf. Žáček, *Čechové a Poláci roku 1848 II*, 158–66; Olga V. Pavlenko, 'Die "slavische Frage": Im Kontext der russisch-österreichischen Beziehungen während der Revolution 1848/49'. In Moritsch, *Prager Slavenkongress*, 19–38, here 28–9 and 33–5.

[51] On the persistence of the security rationale during the Revolution, Schulze Wessel, *Russlands Blick auf Preußen*, 115–20.

[52] Borodziej et al., *Polnische Europa-Pläne*, 60–1.

[53] Jędrzej Moraczewski, 'O Kongresie słowiańskim w Pradze zebranym 31. Maja 1848', printed in Žáček, *Slovanský sjezd*, 513–33. See Žáček, *Čechové a Poláci roku 1848 II*, 213.

the rest of Europe'.[54] While Moraczewski argued for a republic, Walerjan Krasiński, an exiled Pole and historian of religion living in England, doubted that Eastern Europeans were ready for republicanism. To that end, he proposed a monarchical confederation under the umbrella of the House of Habsburg.[55] The idea of Poland as a 'barrier', 'buffer', or 'rampart' between East and West tapped into a centuries-old diplomatic argument in favour of a European balance of power.[56]

While the Habsburg authorities viewed it with considerable distrust, support for the Slavs' demand to have their own territory came from French initiatives such as the Parisian 'Société de l'émancipation des peuples slaves', led by the Slavist Cyprien Robert.[57] Other Parisian action plans went even further, moving beyond the idea of a Slavic federation. The 'Hôtel Lambert', led by the exiled Pole and former Russian foreign minister Adam Jerzy Czartoryski, promoted a 'Danube federation' of Poles, Hungarians, Romanians, Croats, Serbs, and Slovaks. A congress was held in Paris, producing a 'Slav-Hungarian Treaty'.[58]

Notwithstanding these variations, the majority of the Slav Congress thought in Austro-Slavic terms.[59] Federal spaces were conceived in less strikingly ethnic or national terms than a glance at the manifesto, heady with revolutionary pathos and hastily drafted, would suggest. Within it, one finds demands for freedom, equality, and fraternity for the '80 million Slavs', not to mention independent statehood.[60] On closer inspection, however, many of the Prague protagonists were moving along the familiar lines of historic state law. They were reluctant to

[54] Valerian Krasinski, *Panslavism and Germanism*. London, 1848, 315; Maciej Górny, 'Das ethnographische Motiv in den polnischen Föderationsplänen des 19. Jahrhunderts'. In Borodziej, *Option Europa I*, 187–203, here 189.

[55] Krasiński proposed an equal union between Russia and Poland but preferred a union of Poland and the Habsburg Monarchy (without Italy): Krasiński, *Panslavism and Germanism*, 312–38. This last aspect is overlooked by Alexander Maxwell, 'Walerjan Krasiński's Panslavism and Germanism (1848). Polish Goals in a Panslav Context', *New Zealand Slavonic Journal*, 42/1 (2008), 101–20. Krasiński's federation was multi-religious, otherwise Rudolf Wierer, *Der Föderalismus in Donauraum*. Graz, 1960, 33.

[56] Schulze Wessel, *Russlands Blick auf Preußen*, 133–6.

[57] The Sorbonne professor was still advocating a Polish-dominated, pan-Slavic federation in 1852. Cyprien Robert, *Le monde slave: Son passé, son état présent et son avenir*. Paris, 1852, 116. On the connection with the Polish emigration around Czartoryski and the 'Hôtel Lambert' cf. Leszek Kuk, *Wielka emigracja a powstanie słowianofilstwa francuskiego. W kręgu działalności Cypriana Roberta*. Toruń, 1991, 125–44, 222–6; Kořalka, *František Palacký*, 297.

[58] Ferenc Pulczky and František Ladislav Rieger were also present at the conference in Paris. Joanna Nowak, *Władysław Zamoyski: O sprawę polską w Europie 1848–1868*. Poznan, 2002, 105–6. On the 'Hôtel Lambert' as a place of Polish conservative politics cf. Hans Henning Hahn, *Außenpolitik in der Emigration. Die Exildiplomatie Adam Jerzy Czartoryskis 1830–1840*. Munich and Vienna, 1978.

[59] Slavs from Austria were therefore invited to the Congress as members, while Slavs from outside Austria were invited as guests, cf. Žáček, *Čechové a Poláci roku 1848 II*, 58–71. A Czech Austro-Slavism unfolded in the 1840s (Štaif, *Obezřetná elita*, 126–43). In Croatia it was an effect of 1848. Iskra Iveljić, 'Die Kroaten und der Prager Slavenkongress'. In Moritsch, *Prager Slavenkongress*, 171–81, here 176. See Andreas Moritsch (ed.), *Der Austroslavismus: Ein verfrühtes Konzept zur politischen Neugestaltung Mitteleuropas*. Vienna, 1996.

[60] 'Proklamation der ersten Slavenversammlung in Prag an die Völker Europas' of 12 June 1848, printed in Jordan, *Aktenmäßiger Bericht*, 34.

radically reorganize the territories of (Central) Europe into a federation of nationalities based *solely* on ethnic-national loyalties. Startling conflicts of interest further complicated matters.

An important reference point at the Slav Congress, in addition to the postulated 'nationality of the Slavs', was the privileges of Bohemia based on the 'Bohemian Charter'.[61] This was a handwritten imperial letter dated 8 April 1848 which promised Bohemia greater independence.[62] The province would acquire its own institutions for legislation, administration, and justice, and a 'responsible central authority'. It granted the 'complete equality of the Bohemian language with German' in administration and education, while Catholics, Protestants, and Jews could all practise their religion freely.[63] Bohemia's wish to unite with Moravia and Silesia was turned down by the emperor, however, after loud protests from these lands.[64] This 'Bohemian Charter' was also to be the first in a series of imperial promises of autonomy that were subsequently withdrawn.[65]

This historic basis, on which this autonomy was promised, hindered the Czechs at the Slav Congress from rallying behind a purely ethno-federal programme that would have united the Czech settlements into one political territory and left historic state laws and privileges behind. The Czech nationalist Karel Havlíček had already emphasized in the pre-March period that they were Czechs, not Slavs.[66] Similarly, the 'Polish state', which seemed imminent in the spring of 1848, prevented the Slavs from speaking with one voice in Prague.[67] Moreover, phrases such as 'Bohemians of Slavic origin' or 'Galicians of Polish and Ruthenian origin' demonstrate that 'nation' referred not only to a Slavic cultural and linguistic community, but also to historical affiliations. Arguments about territories and privileges inspired by this historical awareness moved the Slavic Congress away from the federal idea of Slavic solidarity and equality. For the Moravians and Galicians

[61] Some Czech deputies were convinced that Bohemia was 'the only Slavic power in Austria'. See Jiří Pokorný, 'Der Prager Slavenkongress und die Tschechen', In Moritsch, *Prager Slavenkongress*, 63–70, here 67.

[62] 'Allerhöchstes Kabinettsschreiben an Pillersdorf vom 8.4.1848', interpreted and printed with Karl Hugelmann, 'Das kaiserliche Kabinettschreiben vom 8. April 1848 und das Ministerium Pillersdorf', *Jahrbuch für Landeskunde von Niederösterreich*, 15–16 (1916–17), 492–512. On the pre-March prehistory, Hanns Schlitter, *Aus Österreichs Vormärz*, vol. 2. *Böhmen*. Zürich, 1920.

[63] This was followed by anti-Jewish riots (Štaif, *Obezřetná elita*, 202), which lasted for several weeks. Cf. the report on Prague May Day in Schopf, *Volks-Bewegung*, 37–40.

[64] Burian, *Nationalitäten in 'Cisleithanien'*, 81.

[65] On the later commitments cf. Anton Ottokar Zeithammer, *Zur Geschichte der böhmischen Ausgleichsversuche 1865–1871*, vol. 1. *Von Belcredi zu Hohenwart*. Prague, 1912; Thomas Kletečka, *Der Ausgleichsversuch des Ministeriums Hohenwart-Schäffle mit Böhmen im Jahre 1871: Mit besonderer Berücksichtigung des reichsdeutschen Einflusses* (university diss.). Vienna, 1984. See Luboš Velek, 'Böhmisches Staatsrecht auf "weichem Papier": Tatsache, Mythos und ihre symbolische Bedeutung in der tschechischen politischen Kultur', *Bohemia*, 47/1 (2007), 103–18. As the examples of Galicia, Transylvania, and Croatia discussed below show, the Bohemians and Czechs were not alone in receiving these empty promises.

[66] Quoted in Burian, *Nationalitäten in 'Cisleithanien'*, 19.

[67] Žáček, *Čechové a Poláci roku 1848 II*, 96.

present at the Slav Congress, a 'privilegium' won from the emperor by negotiation was a more practical goal than an imaginary Austro-Slavic community.[68] When the congress participants outlined their wishes in a final petition to the Austrian Emperor, the Moravians[69] and 'Galicians of Polish and Ruthenian origin' demanded 'the same rights' in Austria as 'their fellow tribesmen, the Bohemians'.[70]

The innovative potential of the idea of a federation of nationalities, beyond the confines of thought along historical borders, is most strikingly demonstrated by the Slovaks. The Slovaks inhabited a part of the Hungarian hereditary lands. Initially, the Hungarian government attempted to limit attendance at the Slav Congress to Czechs. This was intended to prevent the Galician Slavs from uniting with the Hungarian Slavs in a federal state.[71] Slovak federalist ideas had previously respected the borders of the Hungarian Crown, which nationalists such as Ludovít Štúr, Jozef M. Hruban, and Michal M. Hodža referred to as their homeland.[72] The Hungarian government, however, responded with military force and denied the Slovak claims for autonomy.[73] This repressive Magyar reaction led to a change in Slovak political thinking. Leading politicians such as Štúr had initially tended to adhere to Bakunin's pan-Slavic programme.[74] In their petition to the emperor, they now called for a Slovak grand principality directly under the emperor, with a provincial diet and representation in the Imperial Diet in Vienna. Lajos Kossuth, the leading Hungarian liberal and nationalist, was willing to compromise with the Slovaks only after the failure of his own Hungarian nation-state project in 1849. In a draft constitution for a 'Danube Confederation',

[68] Miroslav Šesták, 'Jihoslovanské slovanství v habsburské monarchii v letech revoluce 1848–1849'. In Václav Veber, *150 let Slovanského sjezdu (1848): Historie a současnost* [150 Years of the Slav Congress (1848): History and Present]. Prague, 2000, 127–43, here 136–7.

[69] A few weeks earlier, the Moravian Diet had refused to agree to a union of Moravia with Bohemia. Jindřich Dvořák, *Moravské sněmování roku 1848–49: Na padesátiletou památku novodobého sněmu a zrušení roboty na Moravě, jakož i nastoupení císaře a krále Františka Josefa I. na trůn*. Telč, 1898, 24. Compared to other provincial assemblies, it was considerably active. See 'Darstellung der dem Ministerium des Innern offiziell bekanntgewordenen Verhandlungen der Provinziallandtage'. Österreichisches Staatsarchiv Wien, Abteilung Haus-, Hof- und Staatsarchiv, Landesangelegenheiten Österreichischer Reichstag 1848/49, Box 85 'Anträge, Beschlüsse', here fol. 62.

[70] On the following 'Petition des Slaven-Congresses in Prag an Seine k. k. Majestät' of 12 June 1848, printed in Žáček, *Slovanský sjezd*, 370–5.

[71] 'Ministerstvo uherské proti sjezdu slovanskému', May 1848, printed in Černý, *Boj za právo I*, 262. Cf. the discussion in the Council of Ministers on the note of the Hungarian Ministry of 19 May 1848, Kletečka, *ÖMR* 1/1. *Die Ministerien des Revolutionsjahres 1848*, no. 43, 254–64.

[72] Šťastný, *Slovanství v národním životě*, 197 and 200.

[73] Šťastný, *Slovanství v národním životě*, 200. The Hungarian elite rejected the pan-Slavic idea. György Szabad, 'Lajos Kossuth's Role in the Conceptualization of a Danubian Federation'. In Ignác Romsics and Béla K. Király (eds), *Geopolitics in the Danube Region: Hungarian Reconciliation Efforts 1848–1998*. Budapest, 1999, 61–97, here 63; Ágnes Deák, 'Miklós Wesselényi on the Future of the Habsburg Empire and Hungary'. In: Romsics and Király, *Geopolitics*, 21–40, here 22–3; István Deák, *The Lawful Revolution: Louis Kossuth and the Hungarians 1848–1849*. New York, 1979, 45.

[74] Šťastný, *Slovanství v národním životě*, 199–206; Dušan Škvarna, 'Die Slovaken und der Prager Slavenkongress' [The Slovaks and the Prague Slav Congress]. In Moritsch, *Prager Slavenkongress*, 71–80, here 71; Tatiana Ivantyšynová, 'Die slovakische Politik und der Austroföderalismus'. In Moritsch, *Austroslavismus*, 44–54, here 49. Cf. Deák, *Lawful Revolution*, 122–4.

sketched out in exile in 1863, he made concessions to the non-Magyar nationalities. Within the framework of a confederation of Hungary, Croatia, Transylvania, Romania, and Serbia, they were to be granted free choice of language in the municipalities as well as national associations for cultural and educational matters.[75]

The Croats went one step further in their demands at the Slav Congress. They had left the union with Hungary on 25 April under Banus Jellačić and now sought a union with a future Serbian voivodeship and a united Slovenia within a confederated Habsburg Monarchy.[76] With the creation of a Serbian voivodeship and a 'united Slovenia', Serbs and Slovenes also hoped for a territorial reorganization that would transcend existing borders.[77] Mirroring the tensions between Poles and Czechs in the north, however, Croats and Serbs in the south accused each other of seeking control. The Serbs in particular were increasingly sceptical of Croatian 'Illyrianism'. Their co-nationals in the Ottoman Empire, meanwhile, strove for a nation state separate from the Sublime Porte. In their endeavours, they were influenced by the Polish diaspora in Paris under Adam Jerzy Czartoryski, who wanted to bring down the empires through an alliance of Slavic nation states.[78] Both domestic and foreign policy considerations probably facilitated the Viennese government's subsequent decision to establish a new political territory, the Serbian Voivodeship, in November 1849.[79] The Slovenes, by contrast, lacked similar popular support, but also any concerted action by their deputies to achieve comparable success.[80]

One diplomatic success of the Slav Congress was its mediation in the dispute between the Poles and the Ruthenians. For the first time on the international stage, the Slav Congress recognized the independence of a Ruthenian people—an

[75] Lajos Kossuth, 'Der Donaubund' (1862). In Borodziej, *Option Europa III. Texte*. Göttingen, 2005, 111–16, 114–15.

[76] Iveljić, 'Die Kroaten und der Prager Slavenkongress', 176 and 181.

[77] For the different conceptions see Kirilina, *Slovency i revoljucija*.

[78] Adam Jerzy Czartoryski sent emissaries to the region as early as the pre-1848 period. Marie-Janine Calic, *The Great Cauldron. A History of Southeastern Europe*. Cambridge, MA, 2019, 263 and 288–9; Steffi Marung, Matthias Middell, and Uwe Müller, 'Territorialisierung in Ostmitteleuropa bis zum Ersten Weltkrieg'. In Frank Hadler and Matthias Middell (eds), *Handbuch einer transnationalen Geschichte Ostmitteleuropas*, 1. *Von der Mitte des 19. Jahrhunders bis zum Ersten Weltkrieg*. Göttingen, 2017, 37–130, here 49. Details in Vasa Čubrilovič, *Istorija političke misli u Srbiji XIX veka*. Belgrade, 1958, 162–77.

[79] The establishment of the Serbian Voivodeship by the Viennese Court was meant to weaken Hungary. Drago Roksandić, 'Austroslavische Tendenzen bei den Serben'. In Moritsch, *Austroslavismus*, 138–46, here 143–4. See Naum Kajčev, *Ilirija. Ot Varna do Vilach. Chărvatskoto nacionalno văzraždane, sărbite i bălgarite (do 1848 g.)*. Sofia, 2015, 252–3; Dušan T. Batakovič, *The Foreign Policy of Serbia 1844–1867: Ilija Garašanin's Načertanije*. Belgrade, 2014.

[80] Hösler diagnoses a political-organizational weakness. Hösler, *Von Krain zu Slowenien*, 352; also Melik, *Jahr 1848*, 231–6. According to their address to the Slav Congress, the Slovenes wanted to unite the 'Carniolan, Styrian, Carinthian and Littoral Slovenes into one land with the name Slovenija'. In Prague, they constituted the numerically smallest group. Cf. Janez Cvirn, 'Die Slovenen und der Prager Slavenkongress'. In Moritsch, *Prager Slavenkongress*, 127–35, here 131 and 133.

important basis for the statehood of today's Ukraine.[81] The existence of an independent Ukrainian-speaking nation had long been denied—and would continue to be thereafter—especially by the Polish and Russian sides.[82] The subsequent treaty between the Poles and the Ruthenians of Galicia concerned 'the mutual guarantees of their nationalities'. It divided public sectors such as administration, education, and the national guard into two categories: those on whose developments the nationalities in Galicia were to cooperate and those which were to be developed separately.[83]

The consensus at the Slavic Congress was mediated by Czech politicians.[84] The treaty they helped to produce was emblematic of the basic idea of a federation of equals and could have served as a model for other rivals. It explicitly guaranteed both communities 'equality of humanistic, political, and religious rights', allowing them to overcome national as well as religious rifts.[85] However, the agreement did not withstand the events that followed. Poles and Ruthenians simultaneously and independently courted the Vienna Council of Ministers to safeguard their respective demands. The respective minor clergies, meanwhile, which had enjoyed close dialogue at the beginning of the revolution, now began to cooperate less and less with each other.[86] Galicia's future affiliation to a restored Poland or to Austria remained as controversial as the distribution of power within the province itself.[87]

The Slav Congress, which had begun with high hopes and great political fervour, came to an abrupt end at the hands of General Alfred zu Windischgrätz and his military intervention against the Prague Pentecostal Storm. Some delegates were arrested; Palacký was unsuccessfully indicted by a military committee of investigation on the basis of fictitious accusations.[88] Instinctively reactionist, both Windischgrätz and the Bohemian gubernial president Thun disapproved of the liberal course taken by the Vienna Council of Ministers and founded a conservative

[81] Vasyl' Botušans'kyj, 'Die Ukrainer und der Prager Slavenkongress'. In Moritsch, *Prager Slavenkongress*, 115–22, here 118.

[82] Borodziej et al., *Polnische Europa-Pläne*, 61; Górny, 'Das ethnographische Motiv', 190–1.

[83] On the Ruthenian National Guard see Hoerhan, *Petitionen*, 254.

[84] 'Vertrag zwischen den am Slavenkongress anwesenden galizischen Polen und Ruthenen über die Art und Weise der welchselseitigen Garantirung ihrer Nationalitäten', printed in Žáček, *Slovanský sjezd*, 373–4; Jan Kozik, *The Ukrainian National Movement in Galicia 1815–1849*. Edmonton, 1986, 229.

[85] On the confessional formation of parties at the Slav Congress Christian Hannick, 'Das Problem der Konfession am Prager Slavenkongress'. In Moritsch (ed.), *Prager Slavenkongress*, 39–46, here 42–3.

[86] Marian Stolarczyk, *Działalność Lwowskiej Centralnej Rady Narodowej. W świetle źródeł polskich*. Rzeszów, 1994, 153. Cf. Oleh Turij, 'Ukraińsko-polskie pograniczе i problem podziału Galicji w połowie XIX wieku'. In Józef Półćwiartek (ed.), *Sąsiedstwo: Osadnictwo na pograniczu etnicznym polsko-ukraińskim w czasach nowożytnych*. Rzeszów, 1997, 111–20, here 114. The concept of a 'partition of Galicia into two gubernias, one Russian and one Mazurian' dates from 2 June 1848 and was adopted on 9 June 1848. Oleh Turij, *Holovna Rus'ka Rada 1848–1851. Protokoly zasidan' i knyha korespondencii*. Lviv, 2002, 26, 30, 32.

[87] Detailed Kozik, *Ukrainian National Movement*, 215–36, here 232.

[88] Kořalka, *František Palacký*, 293.

'Prague Provisional Government'.[89] The military suppression of the uprising in Prague and the course of appeasement chosen by the Viennese government eventually prompted Czech nationalists to support the federalists in the Austrian Reichstag.[90] Nonetheless, the idea of an Austro-Slavic and pan-Slavic confederation retained its power long into the future.[91]

4.3. Kremsier in Winter: Palacký's Federation of Nationalities in the Reichstag

After their failure in Prague, the Austro-Slavic federalists brought their ideas of political organization to the Austrian constitutional assembly in Kremsier; there they further radicalized their plans.[92] František Palacký proposed a federation of nationalities without regard to historic borders. He was an influential figure at the Imperial Diet, being both a member of the Constitutional Committee and part of its five-man Subcommittee for the Constitutional Organization of the Empire. His concept of a federation of nationalities emerged only gradually but represented a turning point for the federal reorganization of the empire and attracted widespread attention.

Palacký's first draft constitution of September 1848 had adopted the *Vormärz* way of thinking in terms of large administrative spaces. With the exception of Hungary and Lombardy-Venetia,[93] which were absent from the diet, Palacký divided the empire into four groups of provinces: Polish (Krakow, Galicia, Bukovina), Bohemian (Bohemia, Moravia, Silesia), German-Austrian (Lower and Upper Austria, Salzburg, Tyrol with Vorarlberg, Styria) and Illyrian (Carinthia, Carniola, Littoral, Dalmatia).[94] The decisive parameter for this classification was the linguistic group or linguistic nation. In addition, he used historic state law and traditions for the territorial delimitation of the provincial groups.[95]

89 This was not approved by the emperor, but no action was taken against Thun and Windischgrätz. Cf. the Council of Ministers of 1, 2, and 25 June 1848. In Kletečka, *ÖMR* 1/1. *Die Ministerien des Revolutionsjahres 1848*, nos. 58, 59, and 83, 357–66 and 477–82.

90 Kletečka, 'Einleitung'. In *ÖMR* 1/1. *Die Ministerien des Revolutionsjahres 1848*, here p. xxviii.

91 Slav solidarity was later taken up and the Slav Congress was 'repeated' in 1908. Cf. the contributions, especially Frank Hadler, '"Nevertheless, a Great Theatrical Exhibition of Slav Solidarity": Der Prager Slawen-Kongress von 1908 als Hauptaktion des Neoslawismus'. In Frank Hadler and Krzysztof A. Makowski (eds), *Approaches to Slavic Unity. Austro-Slavism, Pan-Slavism, Neo-Slavism, and Solidarity among the Slavs Today*. Poznan, 2013, 131–52.

92 However, the 'Slavs' did not form a unified faction in Kremsier. Cf. Šťastný, *Slovanství v národním životě*, 182.

93 Palacký gave parliament the competence to decide on the 'admission and exchange of individual parts of the lands'. František Palacký, 'Erster Entwurf einer Constitution von Oesterreich (Monat September 1848)', printed in Palacký, *Gedenkblätter. Auswahl von Denkschriften*, 169–76, here 174.

94 Palacký, *Gedenkblätter. Auswahl von Denkschriften*, 170.

95 Here, Palacký was still relying on the Bohemian historic state law. Cf. Andreas Gottsmann, *Der Reichstag von Kremsier und die Regierung Schwarzenberg: Die Verfassungsdiskussion des Jahres 1848 im Spannungsfeld zwischen Reaktion und nationaler Frage*. Munich, 1995, 51.

The creation of large provincial groups was to facilitate effective administration. It was believed that certain policy fields could not be dealt with efficiently in territorial units that were too small.[96] The historical provinces with the capitals Vienna, Lemberg (Lwów, Lviv), Brünn (Brno), Prague, Linz, Innsbruck, Grätz, Laibach (Ljubljana), Trieste, Zadar (Zara) were to be integrated into the four larger provincial groups. Each was to have a responsible provincial government and a representative provincial diet.[97] The internal organization of the provinces was three-tiered, with counties, districts, and municipalities. Each province was to have its own provincial laws.[98] Palacký's first draft did not yet clarify the relationship between the provincial groups as large administrative units and the medium-sized provinces. The latter were to enjoy self-legislation and self-administration in the areas of political administration, justice, education, religion, and industry.[99]

Subsidiarity was to be the organizing principle of the empire's relationship with the *Länder*. Accordingly, the provinces were to cede to the central power 'only that part of their independence and autonomy which is indispensable for the existence of an internally strong and externally powerful comprehensive state or empire'.[100] At the same time, sovereignty derived from the 'totality of the empire', not the individual provinces.[101] Imperial law was paramount to provincial law.[102] Given the classical distinction between a federation and a confederation based on the criterion of sovereignty, Palacký thus tended towards the federal state. He nonetheless declared the hotly debated legal question of the ultimate source of federal power—the empire or the states—to be irrelevant. Instead,

[96] František Palacký on 25 and 30 Jan. 1849 in the Constitutional Committee. Anton Springer, *Protokolle des Verfassungsausschusses im Österreichischen Reichstage 1848–1849*. Leipzig, 1885, 37 and 72–3. See Bohuš Rieger, 'Ústava dle Frant. Palackého v l. 1848–49'. In *Památník na oslavu stých narozenin Františka Palackého*. Prague, 1898, 602–45, here 612.

[97] Privileged representation of estates, corporations, and interests was prohibited under section 64. In line with the controversial debate in the Bohemian Diet, urban residents were given disproportionate representation. Palacký, 'Erster Entwurf einer Constitution von Oesterreich', 175.

[98] Palacký, 'Erster Entwurf einer Constitution von Oesterreich', 170 (§5).

[99] Gottsmann, *Der Reichstag von Kremsier*, 51. Another interpretation with Rieger, 'Ústava dle Frant. Palackého', 614.

[100] In particular, he included foreign policy, finance, defence, trade, and public works. Cf. Palacký: 'Erster Entwurf einer Constitution von Oesterreich', 170–1.

[101] §37, Palacký: 'Erster Entwurf einer Constitution von Oesterreich', 170. See also 'Denkschrift der böhmischen Abgeordneten über die von ihnen auf dem constituierenden Reichstage zu Vienna und Kremsier befolgten politischen Grundsätze', 21 Mar. 1849, printed in Palacký, *Gedenkblätter: Auswahl von Denkschriften*, 189–205, here 193.

[102] Palacký 'Erster Entwurf einer Constitution von Oesterreich', 176. This clarity was lost in the later Austrian constitution, which treated federal and provincial law as of equal rank. See Ewald Wiederin, *Bundesrecht und Landesrecht: Zugleich ein Beitrag zu Strukturproblemen der bundesstaatlichen Kompetenzverteilung in Österreich und in Deutschland*. Vienna, 1995; Gerald Stourzh, 'Länderautonomie und Gesamtstaat in Österreich 1848–1918'. In Stourzh, *Der Umfang der österreichischen Geschichte: Ausgewählte Studien 1990–2010*. Vienna, 2011, 37–67, 51.

'discretion and good will...on both sides are indispensable'.[103] Palacký thus recognized the central role of loyalty as a constitutional principle in the federal state. Today, it is enshrined in the German Constitution as *Bundestreue* (federal loyalty) and framed for the European Union as *Unionstreue* (union loyalty).[104]

Palacký's thinking can be understood as 'centralized federalism'.[105] Later, the constitutional historian Bohuš Rieger, Palacký's grandson, was justly outraged by attacks that denigrated Palacký as an alleged 'German-eater', a 'traitor of the state', or a narrow-minded, biased pro-Czech politician who, as a representative of 'the loosest federal constitution imaginable', could not be taken seriously.[106] The fact that Palacký was genuinely concerned with creating an organization that would do justice to the multi-ethnic state[107] was particularly evident in his legal safeguarding of the equality of all provinces and nationalities. To this end, the Reichstag was to be drawn from the provincial diets in proportion to the number of inhabitants. It would initiate and discuss legislative projects and control the state administration, with the authority to appeal to a court of arbitration in federal conflicts.[108] With regard to the nationalities, the Imperial Diet had to ensure that their 'equal rights' within the state were protected and that 'individual provinces were not favoured or preferred over others'.[109] However, Palacký's first draft failed to convince the Kremsier Subcommittee on the Constitutional Organization of the Empire. For many deputies, the democratization of the state was more important than its federalization. They aimed at greater representation in a future Reichstag of the people and the political 'nation', not of the provinces and nationalities.[110]

[103] Instead of 'federation' he wanted to speak of 'union'. Cf. František Palacký, 'Union—Nicht Centralisation, noch Föderation' [1849]. In Palacký, *Gedenkblätter: Auswahl von Denkschriften*, 206–14, here 210. Against a categorical distinction between a federal state and a confederation of states today: Christoph Schönberger, 'Die Europäische Union als Bund: Zugleich ein Beitrag zur Verabschiedung des Staatenbund—Bundesstaat-Schemas', *Archiv des öffentlichen Rechts*, 129 (2004), 81–120.

[104] The idea of federal integration through 'federally loyal behaviour' was formulated by Rudolf Smend in a pioneering way for constitutional interpretation. Cf. Stefan Korioth, *Integration und Bundesstaat: Ein Beitrag zur Staats- und Verfassungslehre Rudolf Smends*. Berlin, 1990, 85–91; Hartmut Bauer, *Die Bundestreue: Zugleich ein Beitrag zur Dogmatik des Bundesstaatsrechts und zur Rechtsverhältnislehre*. Tübingen, 1992; Armin Hatje, *Loyalität als Rechtsprinzip in der Europäischen Union*. Baden-Baden, 2001.

[105] Rieger, 'Ústava dle Frant. Palackého', 641.

[106] Rieger, 'Ústava dle Frant. Palackého', 629; Springer, *Protokolle des Verfassungsausschusses*, 6.

[107] Gottsmann, *Der Reichstag von Kremsier*, 55.

[108] Palacký, 'Erster Entwurf einer Constitution von Oesterreich', 172–3. The federal Austrägal or arbitration jurisdiction was an institution of the Holy Roman Empire and was discussed for the German Confederation but blocked by Bavaria. Eckhardt Treichel,' Einleitung'. In *Quellen zur Geschichte des Deutschen Bundes, 2. Organisation und innere Ausgestaltung des Deutschen Bundes 1815–1819*. Munich, 2016, pp. lxv–lxxv.

[109] Palacký, 'Erster Entwurf einer Constitution von Oesterreich', 174.

[110] Springer, *Protokolle des Verfassungsausschusses*, 6. Against Palacký's emphasis on the powers of the provinces cf. Joseph Alexander Helfert, *Oesterreich und die Nationalitäten: Ein offenes Wort an Herrn Frz. Palacky*. Vienna, 1850.

In January 1849, Palacký presented a second draft constitution. His radical model of a federation of nationalities, he later noted, was 'inseparably linked with the revolution and was only made possible by the enormous storms that had preceded it'. He had tried to 'to make good use of them and exploit them for the common good'.[111] Palacký turned his back on the historic state law in favour of a federation along ethnic lines. Background consultations outside the Reichstag with the Croatian Banus Jellačić prompted this radical rethinking.[112] In the meantime, the return of Hungary and Lombardy-Venetia into the Habsburg Empire had become likely. The Hungarian state law, as the all-encompassing umbrella for the Hungarian lands including Croatia-Slavonia and Transylvania, however, no longer offered a locus of common allegiance acceptable to the non-Magyar elite. After the civil war and the Hungarian government's violent repression of national ambitions amongst the Croats, Slavonians, Serbs, Slovaks, and Romanians, Palacký's original idea of large provincial groups could no longer be applied to the Hungarian lands.[113] It was therefore appropriate to federalize Hungary—and thus also Austria—according to the national principle. From Jellačić's circle of advisers, Ognjeslav Ostrožinski had already presented a draft constitution of this kind. He intended it to be a building block of a European, conservative, and estates-based federation.[114]

Palacký defined the Austrian state not nationally, but dynastically and historically. He resorted to the Pragmatic Sanction of 1713, which had postulated that the dynastic heritage of the Habsburgs was 'indivisible and inseparable'. Palacký thus found himself in the camp of the Austrian conservatives in Frankfurt's Paulskirche. They, too, availed themselves of the Pragmatic Sanction to argue for the preservation of the Habsburg Monarchy.[115] Fighting for their independence, Hungary and Lombardy-Venetia did not send their representatives to the Imperial Diet at Kremsier. Nevertheless, Palacký and his colleagues included Hungary and Lombardy-Venetia in their constitutional draft.[116] This contradicted the idea of the people as the *pouvoir constituant* and the fundamentally voluntary nature of a confederation.

Nevertheless, Palacký's second draft constitution aimed at a carefully balanced federation with comparatively strong constituent states. The privileges of the estates were to be abolished and a separation of powers introduced at the imperial

[111] Národ of 20 Apr. 1865, translated and printed in Palacký, *Oesterreichs Staatsidee*, 36.

[112] Rieger, 'Ústava dle Frant. Palackého', 615–16.

[113] Matija Kavčič of 22 Jan. 1849. In Springer, *Protokolle des Verfassungsausschusses*, 12–13.

[114] The draft was in favour of the conservative estates and was not intended to stand in the way of Austria's union with Germany. Cf. Ognjeslav Ostrožinski, 'Programm zur Konstituierung des österreichischen Kaiserstaates nach dem Prinzipe der konstitutionellen Freiheit und der nationalen Gleichberechtigung'. In Stjepan Pejaković (ed.), *Aktenstücke zur Geschichte des kroatisch-slavonischen Landtages und der nationalen Bewegung vom Jahre 1848*. Vienna, 1861, supplement II, 13–24.

[115] Telle, *Das österreichische Problem im Frankfurter Parlament*, 21.

[116] This earned Palacký reproaches, cf. Gottsmann, *Der Reichstag von Kremsier*, 49.

and provincial levels. Matters of nationwide interest were assigned to the empire, in particular foreign affairs, the military, finance, pan-imperial infrastructure, trade, and the economy, as well as civil and criminal law. For their part, the lands were responsible for provincial policing, jurisdiction and administration of justice, education, the arts and sciences, social welfare, agriculture, and industry, as well as provincial finance, infrastructure, and local government.[117]

In this second draft, Palacký explicitly legitimized the idea of subsidiarity between the empire and the provinces with a natural-law concept of self-government.[118] He reiterated his idea, incorporated in the manifesto of the Slav Congress, that not only individuals, but also peoples—represented through their provinces—were entitled to self-government. Newly created courts were to enforce the rights of individuals, nationalities, and provinces. Palacký's terminology repeatedly revealed elements of conservative thought: in the 'former kingdoms', the provincial governor was to be appointed by the emperor and called a viceroy.[119] Like his other colleagues on the Constitutional Committee, Palacký advocated for a constitutional monarchy[120] and not for a republic and democracy.

Palacký left the beaten track when it came to the internal organization of the federation, proving to be an 'independent political mind, a new constructor' (as Bohuš Rieger aptly put it).[121] He presented his design for a federation of nationalities to the five-man constitutional reform committee.[122] While his first sketch had been based on historical provinces and large administrative units such as the provincial groups, Palacký now assigned political territories to eight national population groups: German Austrians, Bohemians, Poles, Illyrians, Italians, South Slavs, Magyars, and Wallachians. The eight associated territories cut across historic borders in Bohemia, Moravia, Silesia, Hungary, Transylvania, and Tyrol.[123] The provincial groups of the first and second drafts thus dealt with affiliations in different ways. The provincial groups of the first draft were based on larger linguistic families, historical tradition, and administrative efficiency.

[117] František Palacký, 'Druhý návrh říšské ústavy (leden 1849)'. In *Spisy drobné*. Vol. 1. *Spisy a řeči z oboru politiky*. Ed. Bohuš Rieger. Prague, 1898, 69–74, here 70.

[118] He defined the provincial government power in §2b as a 'consequence of the right to self-government'. Cf. Palacký, 'Druhý návrh (leden 1849)', 69.

[119] Palacký, 'Druhý návrh (leden 1849)', 74. [120] Rieger, 'Ústava dle Frant. Palackého', 606.

[121] Rieger, 'Ústava dle Frant. Palackého', 611.

[122] This draft is available in print in Czech. Palacký, 'Druhý návrh (leden 1849) I'. It is based on the lithographed draft in Palacký's papers titled 'Eigentlich vereinbarter Entwurf der Fünfer-Commission Gobbi-Mayer-Palacký-Goldmark und Smolka', Palacký, *Spisy a řeči z oboru politiky*, 68.

[123] The eight territories were formed, first, from the German-speaking parts of Bohemia, Moravia, Silesia, Lower and Upper Austria, Styria, Carinthia, Salzburg, German Tyrol, and Vorarlberg; second, from the Czech parts of Bohemia, Moravia, and Silesia as well as Slovakia; third, from Galicia, Cracow, and Hungarian Ruthenia; fourth, from the Slovene parts of Lower Styria, Southern Carinthia, Carniola, and the Littoral; fifth, from Trentino and Lombardy-Venetia; sixth, from Dalmatia, Croatia, Slavonia, and Serbian Vojvodina; seventh, from the Magyar parts of Hungary and Transylvania; eighth, from the Romanian parts of Hungary, Transylvania, and Bukovina.

For the provincial territories of the second draft, imagined nationalities were the dominant determining factor.

This federation of nationalities upended the hierarchy of provincial patriotic loyalties on the one hand and national loyalties on the other. The 'Bohemians' of the first draft, which included all inhabitants of the lands of the Bohemian Crown, i.e. Czechs, Germans, Poles, and Jews, became a provincial group (reduced in the west, enlarged in the east) nominally of Czechs and Slovaks. The German-speaking parts of the Bohemian lands were to be united with Lower and Upper Austria, Styria, Carinthia, Salzburg, German Tyrol, and Vorarlberg. Poles and Ruthenians, who had just pledged mutual respect for each other's nationality at the Slav Congress, became a purely 'Polish' group once again. The Transylvanian Saxons, meanwhile, belonged to the 'Wallachians', or Romanians. Elsewhere, the Slovenes now found themselves in the 'Illyrian' group in a separate territory consisting of parts of Lower Styria, Southern Carinthia, Carniola, and the Littoral. A 'South Slavic group' was formed from Dalmatia, Croatia, Slavonia, and the Serbian Voivodeship, despite the presence of many Hungarians, Germans, and Italians in these regions. Finally, the *Welschtiroler*, i.e. the Italian-speaking Tyroleans, were granted their wish to unite with Lombardy-Venetia. Thus, the eight 'provincial nations' did not represent the full spectrum of linguistic and national diversity in the monarchy; the Ruthenians and Slovaks, for example, are notable for their absence. For these groups, Palacký contemplated supplementary national counties below the provincial level, though this was obviously a downgrade compared to the federal 'national territories' granted to other groups.

Palacký sought to provide the revolution's idea of a nation state with a federal foundation. Similar proposals were made by the German-Austrian member of the Reichstag Ludwig von Löhner from Saaz (Žatec)[124] and the Slovenian member of the Constitutional Committee in Kremsier, Matija Kavčič (or Kautschitsch).[125] Löhner, who founded the Association of Germans in Austria, had originally propagated a centralized comprehensive state with nationally demarcated counties and municipalities. He wanted to abolish the crown lands and to separate the provinces that belonged to the German Confederation from the rest.[126] At the meeting of the democratic German-Bohemian constitutional associations in Teplitz (Teplice), a one-day Slav Congress in miniature, the 'delegates [who] gathered in the name of the German cities, municipalities and constitutional associations of Bohemia' supported Löhner's plan. Austria was to be divided 'into imperial counties according to linguistic boundaries', and the 'provincial borders' were to be

[124] 'Programm einiger Reichstagsdeputierter zur Konstitution des österreichischen Staats', *Brünner Zeitung*, 28 Nov. 1848, supplement.

[125] On Kavčič cf. Gottsmann, *Der Reichstag von Kremsier*, 5, 52; Springer, *Protokolle des Verfassungsausschusses*, 12.

[126] Burian, *Nationalitäten in 'Cisleithanien'*, 76–80; Ernst Karl Sieber, *Ludwig von Löhner: Ein Vorkämpfer des Deutschtums in Böhmen, Mähren und Schlesien im Jahre 1848/1849*. Munich, 1965, 133–9.

abolished.[127] National federalization appeared to offer a means for detaching the predominantly German-speaking West Bohemia from the historic province of Bohemia and for linking it, together with the other German-Austrian provinces, more closely to a future German federation.[128] The need for equality and cooperation between the nationalities was repeatedly emphasized in Teplitz.[129] After the failure of ambitions for a Greater Germany in the Frankfurt Parliament, Löhner converted to federalism. His reorganization of Austria was to include '5 nation states: Polish Austria, Czech Austria, Slavonic Austria, German Austria, Italian Austria'. The Left in the Austrian Reichstag included this partition in its political programme in early 1849.[130]

The federation of nationalities proposed by Palacký, Löhner, and Kavčič reversed pre-existing principles of political organization. Traditionally, a person's nationality had been defined by the provincial territory in which they resided. Now the process was inverted: ethnolinguistic nationalities would divide the imperial space into federal provincial territories. Such innovations did not find favour with the majority of the Kremsier Constitutional Committee, however. The deputies were all too aware that 'nationality' was not a sharply defined concept in ethnically and religiously diverse regions such as Bukovina, Transylvania, and the Serbian Voivodeship, or in the mixed and multilingual areas of Bohemia and Moravia.[131] They denounced the planned abolition of the historic crown lands as a legacy of Metternich, who had 'suppressed all provincial, all national life'.[132] Some warned of the danger of national segregation through ethnic federalism.[133] Palacký's critic, Joseph Alexander Helfert, feared a 'general migration of peoples...until all tribal kinsmen have settled side-by-side in closed areas and without mixing with other

[127] *Stenographischer Bericht über die Verhandlungen der am 28. August 1848 in Teplitz im Namen deutscher Städte, Gemeinden und konstitutioneller Vereine Böhmens zusammengekommenen Vertrauensmänner*. Leitmeritz, 1848, here 8 (greater German-democratic principle) and 23 (centralization). On the later rejection of this plan cf. Burian, *Nationalitäten in 'Cisleithanien'*, 82; Karl F. Bahm, 'Demokratie, Nationalismus und das Schicksals eines "nationalen Zwitters": Uffo Horn und die 1848er Revolution in Böhmen'. In Alice Velková, Luboš Velek, and Jiří Pokorný (eds), *Nacionalismus, společnost a kultura ve střední Evropě 19. a 20. století. Pocta Jiřímu Kořalkovi k 75. narozeninám/Nationalismus, Gesellschaft und Kultur in Mitteleuropa im 19. und 20. Jahrhundert: Festschrift für Jiří Kořalka zum 75. Geburtstag*. Prague, 2007, 53–69, here 66.

[128] Sieber, *Löhner*, 139. Cf. *Stenographischer Bericht über die Verhandlungen in Teplitz*, 8–9.

[129] *Stenographischer Bericht über die Verhandlungen in Teplitz*, 12, 23, 43–4.

[130] Quoted in Sieber, *Löhner*, 145. The administrative languages were Polish and Ruthenian in the Polish part, but only Ruthenian in the rest. Croatia was to be able to join the Slavonian part. Cf. Paula Geist-Lányi, *Das Nationalitätenproblem auf dem Reichstag zu Kremsier 1848/1849: Ein Beitrag zur Geschichte der Nationalitäten in Österreich*. Munich, 1920, 71–2.

[131] At the Imperial Diet, a failed attempt was made to draw a map of national borders, Helfert, *Oesterreich und die Nationalitäten*, 18 and 21. Even Palacký himself admitted that 'nationality' as a concept had not yet taken root in the people's consciousness. Cf. Palacký, 'Union—Nicht Centralisation, noch Föderation', 212.

[132] Kajetan Mayer of 25 Jan. 1849. In Springer, *Protokolle des Verfassungsausschusses*, 42.

[133] On segregation through ethno-federalism today Andreas Heinemann-Grüder, *Föderalismus als Konfliktregelung. Indien, Russland, Spanien und Nigeria im Vergleich*. Opladen, 2011.

nationalities'.[134] The judicial official Eduard Cavalcabo argued similarly in the Constitutional Committee: 'If one believes that one must separate the nations from one another in the provinces, one proves that even in the monarchy the different nations cannot live next to one another.'[135]

4.4. Frankfurt in Winter: Sommaruga's 'Empire of Seventy Millions'

The idea of a federation of nationalities was meant to offer an alternative to the nation state not only within the Habsburg Monarchy as such, but also insofar as its relationship with the German Confederation was concerned. At the turn of 1848/1849, the Viennese government and the emperor had succeeded in consolidating the state militarily. In the *Paulskirche*, meanwhile, debates escalated over Austria's complete exclusion from a future federal German state. In November 1848, the German-Austrian delegate, Franz Seraph von Sommaruga, published a leaflet containing a draft constitution based on the 'only redemptive principle of the true equality of nationalities'. The pamphlet is of historical interest not least because of the esteem in which Sommaruga was held by the Austrian government under Schwarzenberg.

Sommaruga was one of a number of possible candidates whom the Austrian government considered for the task of drafting a constitution to unite the German Confederation, Prussia, and Austria into an 'Empire of Seventy Millions'.[136] He qualified for the role as a high-ranking Viennese lawyer and politician who had been involved in important liberal legislative projects in the pre-1848 period. He was also a founding member and president of the unofficial political centre of the Liberals, the *Juridisch-Politischer Leseverein* (Juridico-political Book Club). In May 1848, he was finally appointed Austrian minister of education and justice in the reformist cabinet under Pillersdorf.[137]

Sommaruga, in his own words, had initially 'flirted with the idea of a German empire'. It was not until the winter of 1848, however, that he turned away from this 'cherished desire' for a German nation state.[138] Many former supporters of a 'Greater Germany' made a similar about-turn at the end of the revolutionary year. Faced with secessionist Hungary and Lombardy-Venetia, they became

[134] Helfert, *Oesterreich und die Nationalitäten*, 19.

[135] Cavalcabo of 25 Jan. 1849. In Springer, *Protokolle des Verfassungsausschusses*, 37.

[136] Council of Ministers of 12 Dec. 1848. In Kletečka, *ÖMR* 2/1. *Das Ministerium Schwarzenberg*, no. 2, 12–18.

[137] Hans Peter Hye, 'Sommaruga Franz Ser. Vincenz Emanuel Frh. Von'. In *Österreichisches Biographisches Lexikon 1815–1950*, vol. 12. Vienna, 2005, 411–12; Wilhelm Brauneder, *Leseverein und Rechtskultur: Der Juridisch-politische Leseverein zu Wien 1840–1990*. Vienna, 1992.

[138] Franz von Sommaruga, *Österreichs Zukunft und dessen Stellung in Deutschland*. Stuttgart, 1848, 39.

increasingly worried about the potential political consequences of the nation-state idea for polyglot Central Europe.[139] Faced with the threat of the empire's disintegration, all-Austrian loyalties prevailed over Greater German loyalties.[140] Sommaruga's essay 'Austria's Future and its Position in Germany' attempted to do justice to both sides.

As a response to the 'October Debate', Sommaruga's federal house of states offered space for the 'German nation' and the Habsburg nationalities. Articles 2 and 3 of the constitution then under discussion in Frankfurt had prohibited a federal union between the German Empire and non-German-speaking territories.[141] This prohibition would have affected Austria with its Galician, Hungarian, and Italian possessions, and Prussia with East and West Prussia and Posen (Poznan). Many members of the *Paulskirche* were in favour of a German nation state with a linguistically homogeneous population.[142]

Sommaruga's federal project, on the other hand, involved several levels. The Habsburg Monarchy and the German Confederation were to be united in a new confederation. Internal organization of the Habsburg Monarchy itself was also to be federal, for which Sommaruga proposed five linguistic-national territories. These five groups of lands comprised, first, all the lands of the German Confederation in Austria (Inner Austria and Bohemia); second, Galicia; third, Lombardy-Venetia; fourth, Hungary with the 'Slovaks'; and fifth, 'Illyria' with Croatia-Slavonia, Dalmatia, the Military Border, and the Serbian Voivodeship.[143] In territorial terms, his sketch bore similarities to Metternich's provincial groups.

A further innovation was the introduction of a bicameral legislative system based on the North American and Swiss models.[144] Sommaruga's state administration was highly centralized with five imperial ministries for foreign affairs, defence, finance, trade, and infrastructure. They were responsible to the legislature—a clear departure from the pre-March administrative state. Sommaruga sought cohesion through a common administration, rejecting separate administrations for Hungary, Lombardy-Venetia, or Galicia and thus the stance taken by spokesmen of the 'October debate'.[145] Civil and criminal law, administrative organization, education,

[139] Sommaruga, *Österreichs Zukunft*, 30.

[140] This is exemplified by the influential pamphlet by Ignaz Beidtel, *Die politischen Zustände der österreichischen Staaten nach dem Zustande vom 16. April 1848*. Vienna, 1848, 27.

[141] This stipulation was weakened in the final constitution, where §2 of the Constitution of the German Empire of 28 Mar. 1849 (Paulskirchenverfassung) still states: 'If a German Land has the same head of state as a non-German Land, the German Land shall have its own constitution, government and administration separate from the non-German Land. Only German citizens may be appointed to the government and administration of the German Land.'

[142] Wolfgang Wippermann, '"Gesunder Volksegoismus": Vorgeschichte, Verlauf und Folgen der Polendebatte in der Paulskirche'. In Heiner Timmermann (ed.), *1848. Revolution in Europa. Verlauf, politische Programme, Folgen und Wirkungen*. Berlin, 1999, 351–65. The German–Polish antagonism also divided individual regions' on Poznan, see Makowski, 'Posen im Revolutionsjahr', 172.

[143] Sommaruga, *Österreichs Zukunft*, 4. [144] Sommaruga, *Österreichs Zukunft*, 12–13.

[145] Gergely, 'Bündnis zwischen Frankfurt und Pest-Buda'. Cf. Telle, *Das österreichische Problem im Frankfurter Parlament*, 92, 109–11.

and public services were to be uniform throughout the empire.[146] In all other matters, the provincial groups were autonomous. Below the five provincial groups with so-called united provincial diets, Sommaruga envisaged further parliaments that would reflect the national composition of each province. For the provincial group Galicia, for example, he advocated a 'legislative and administrative separation' between Poles and Ruthenians.[147] For the Hungarian group of provinces, meanwhile, he wanted to separate Hungarians, Slovaks, and Ruthenians.[148] A People's Congress with 'representatives from all parts of the monarchy' was to negotiate this future Austrian federal state.[149]

Sommaruga took a lone position by arguing for an emotional bond between the population and the Austrian Empire. Prompted by the Hungarian and Italian civil wars, the peoples of Austria, 'contrary to the desire for separation that had not infrequently arisen among them in the past, had in a short time matured into such a remarkable sense of unity'.[150] The constitutionalization of Austria in 1848 had virtually 'chained the peoples to Austria'. Sommaruga vouched for the fact that 'Austria's peoples are serious about preserving the commonwealth that has united them for centuries, to which they owe everything they possess, and from which alone they can expect strong and sufficient protection of their political and national interests'.[151] With a remarkable singlemindedness, Sommaruga tied such affiliations into a multi-level federalist framework. All federal levels—the national provinces, the groups of provinces grouped according to linguistic communities, the Austrian federation as a whole, and the German-Austrian 'Empire of Seventy Millions'—were based on a specific conception of nation with different ethnic, linguistic, political, and cultural nuances.

Sommaruga did not want to jeopardize the 'great work of Germany's political reorganization' with the internal federalization of the Habsburg Monarchy. Instead, he sought to complement it.[152] A modernized, reformed Germany was just as important to him as 'Austria's German vocation'.[153] Rather than being divided up, all of Austria was to be united with all of Germany.[154] He also wanted the German-Austrian Union to have a common defence, economic, trade, and infrastructure policy. A common imperial citizenship with freedom of movement

[146] Sommaruga, *Österreichs Zukunft*, 11–12.

[147] Sommaruga was alluding to a statement made in the Frankfurt pre-parliament that 'the injustice committed against Poland by the partition… must be atoned for'. In the 'Polish question', however, the Prussian interest in maintaining the partition of Poland ultimately prevailed. Using almost the same wording, the Slav Congress also called on the 'cabinets' to 'atone for the sin' committed against the Poles. Cf. Wollstein: *Das 'Großdeutschland' der Paulskirche*, 98–188, 132; 'Proklamation der ersten Slavenversammlung in Prag an die Völker Europas' of 12 June 1848, printed in Jordan, *Aktenmäßiger Bericht*, 38.

[148] Sommaruga, *Österreichs Zukunft*, 7–8, 11 (quote p. 8).

[149] Sommaruga, *Österreichs Zukunft*, 7 and 16–17.

[150] Sommaruga, *Österreichs Zukunft*, 20.

[151] Sommaruga, *Österreichs Zukunft*, 21.

[152] Sommaruga, *Österreichs Zukunft*, 21.

[153] Sommaruga, *Österreichs Zukunft*, 19.

[154] The intellectual origins of a 'double alliance' or 'dualism' reached back to the time of the Liberation Wars. Wollstein, *Das 'Großdeutschland' der Paulskirche*, 290 n. 133.

and settlement was a further demand. These 'popular freedoms' would be protected by an Imperial Court which would also arbitrate 'differences between the united German states and the non-German state complex of Austria.'[155] Sommaruga showed a keen sense of the tasks that lay ahead in the German Confederation. After 1848, federal policy was indeed shaped by the very agenda of a common economic, trade, legal, customs, and infrastructure space which he envisaged.[156] The common citizenship law of the German Confederation, which existed only in an 'embryonic' form, did not become a reality in Germany until 1871.[157]

Sommaruga saw his federal semi-detached house as an 'audacity'.[158] Although his grand ideas were basically in line with those of other thinkers and tone-setting newspapers,[159] Sommaruga was more outspoken in his rejection of a merely loose confederation between the German Confederation and the Habsburg Monarchy.[160] *Paulskirche* deputies such as Karl Moering, Friedrich List, Paul Pfizer, Viktor von Andrian-Werburg, and Franz Schuselka justified the inclusion of Hungary or Transylvania in such a loose confederation on the basis of economic considerations, such as the 'great connecting route between the North Sea and the Black Sea, between America and Asia' or the colonization opportunities for German settlers.[161] Such an emphasis on politico-economic interests, however, relegated questions of social cohesion, which played an essential role for Sommaruga, to the background.

In January 1849, the antagonisms between 'Greater German' and 'Lesser German' thinking came to a head.[162] Prussia talked aloud of excluding Austria from the new Germany.[163] In this struggle between Prussia and Austria, between the Houses of Hohenzollern and Habsburg, for hegemony over Central Europe, the Viennese government under Bruck-Schwarzenberg made a final push for an 'Empire of Seventy Millions' under Austrian auspices. The *Paulskirche* rejected the proposal with a formulaic compromise.[164] According to Heinrich von Gagern,

[155] Sommaruga, *Österreichs Zukunft*, 34 and 38.

[156] According to Vienna's wishes, these agendas were to include Hungary; the actual unification of commercial, exchange, and other private law was only achieved decades later. Cf. Stephan Buchholz, 'Zur Rechtsvereinheitlichung in Deutschland in der zweiten Hälfte des 19. Jahrhunderts', *Rabels Zeitschrift für ausländisches und internationales Privatrecht*, 50 (1986), 77–110.

[157] Christoph Schönberger, *Unionsbürger: Europas föderales Bürgerrecht in vergleichender Sicht*. Tübingen, 2005, 97.

[158] Sommaruga, *Österreichs Zukunft*, 38.

[159] Wollstein, *Das 'Großdeutschland' der Paulskirche*, 275–7. As 'utopia' see Telle, *Das österreichische Problem im Frankfurter Parlament*, 103.

[160] Krauß and Stadion represented this idea in the Council of Ministers. Council of Ministers from 26 Dec. 1848. In Kletečka, *ÖMR 2/1. Das Ministerium Schwarzenberg*, no. 8, 50–6.

[161] Wollstein, *Das 'Großdeutschland' der Paulskirche*, 268–71, 290. The topos of Hungary as a colony did indeed find its way into discussions in the Vienna Council of Ministers. Cf. Council of Ministers of 9 Sept. 1850. In Thomas Kletečka and Anatol Schmied-Kowarzik, *ÖMR 2/2. Das Ministerium Schwarzenberg (8. Jänner 1850–30. April 1850)*. Vienna, 2005, no. 392.

[162] Günter Wollstein, 'Die Oktoberdebatte der Paulskirche'. In Jaworski and Luft, *1848/49 Revolutionen in Ostmitteleuropa*, 279–302, here 299.

[163] Wollstein, *Das 'Großdeutschland' der Paulskirche*, 281.

[164] Wolfram Siemann, *Vom Staatenbund zum Nationalstaat. Deutschland 1806–1871*. Frankfurt am Main and Vienna, 1995, 386.

an empire of seventy million people would violate the 'development of freedom on a national basis'. Only later did he add that the 'national right of unification with German Austria...would by no means be renounced'.[165]

At the same time, Vienna was pursuing a secret plan to draw up a constitution for a great empire with Prussia, behind the backs of the *Paulskirche* deputies.[166] The men proposed for the drafting of such a constitution for the Schwarzenberg government were 'Camphausen, Closen, Gagern, the Austrian minister of trade v. Bruck, or if he does not take on this task, Dr. Würth or Baron Sommaruga'.[167] These machinations rapidly hit the rails when Prussia replied uncompromisingly that an empire of seventy millions was unacceptable; only an 'independent status Austria' would be considered.[168] Many delegates on both sides hoped that a 'national' unification of Germany and Austria could still be negotiated later. After 1848, however, such a union, which contemporaries called 'dualism', failed to materialize.[169]

4.5. The Opacity of Nationality

The various visions of a federation of nationalities outlined here illustrate one important point: the nature of this idea was as ambiguous as the revolutionary paradigm of nation and nation state. The Prague Slav Confederation was based on the idea of a nation of all Slavs. However, it also treated Czechs, Slovaks, Poles, Serbs, and, for the first time, Ukrainians (known then as Ruthenians) as linguistic nations and also recognized Bohemian, Moravian, or Galician provincial nations. Palacký's later constitutional drafts contained a comparable linguistic, ethnic, and historical-political understanding of nationhood. Sommaruga's federalism, meanwhile, formulated national affiliations for the German Confederation, the Habsburg Empire, and individual nationalities.

A multi-layered concept of nation was also typical of the *Paulskirche*, the Frankfurt Parliament. In Frankfurt, the 'German nation' was composed of many 'fatherlands'.[170] Given these competing affiliations, the question in 1848 was whether the unity of Germany (with a tendency towards a federal state) or the

[165] Franz Wigard (ed.), *Stenographischer Bericht über die Verhandlungen der Deutschen Constituirenden Nationalversammlung zu Frankfurt am Main*, vol. 6. Frankfurt am Main, 1849, 4648. See also Wigard (ed.), *Stenographischer Bericht über die Verhandlungen der Deutschen Constituirenden Nationalversammlung zu Frankfurt am Main*, vol. 8. Frankfurt am Main, 1849, 5901.

[166] Council of Ministers of 12 Dec. 1848. In Kletečka, *ÖMR* 2/1. *Das Ministerium Schwarzenberg*, no. 2, 12–18.

[167] Kletečka, *ÖMR* 2/1. *Das Ministerium Schwarzenberg*, no. 2, 12–18.

[168] Read at the Council of Ministers of 25 Dec. 1848. In Kletečka, *ÖMR* 2/1. *Das Ministerium Schwarzenberg*, no. 7, 45–9.

[169] Wollstein, *Das 'Großdeutschland' der Paulskirche*, 293–8; Brian E. Vick, *Defining Germany: The 1848 Frankfurt Parliamentarians and National Identity*. Cambridge, MA, 2002, 161–71.

[170] Abigail Green, *Fatherlands: State-Building and Nationhood in Nineteenth-Century Germany*. Cambridge, 2001.

autonomy of the particular states (with a tendency towards a confederation of states) should take precedence in the federal future.[171] Dieter Langewiesche speaks of the 'fundamental federative feature of German history' and a 'federal national consciousness' amongst the Germans. This contrasts, for example, with the French idea of the nation, which brought together the nation of citizens and the linguistic and cultural nation, to the detriment of smaller linguistic groups.[172] In the Habsburg Monarchy, the organization of peoples and 'nations' was added to the federal balance between the territorial whole and its parts. This led to the guiding idea of the federation of nationalities or multinational federalism.

Palacký's federation of nationalities did not succeed in the Constitutional Committee at Kremsier. Negotiations concluded with an agreement on a form of centralized historic crown land federalism based on Kajetan Mayer's draft.[173] His plan provided for the division of the empire into the historic crown lands, but also considered the national composition of the respective provincial populations when reassigning the counties. The planned dismantling of the provincial diets strengthened the central power while the ethnic-national division of the counties protected the minorities. This compromise combined the federal integrative power of the historical regions with that of national communities. It is therefore considered by the Habsburg historian Helmut Rumpler to be the 'finest hour of Austrian nationality policy and Austrian parliamentarism'.[174]

Nevertheless, the politicization of the idea of the nation had a long-lasting effect. The revolutionary year triggered a nationalization of communities that had previously seen themselves as purely social or confessional. The elites of formerly underrepresented groups sought to make the national character of their communities credible in order to amplify their voices in Europe. They observed each other's demands and national rhetoric and learned from them.[175] The petition campaign in 1848 for and against the partition of Galicia, for example, enabled the Ruthenians of Galicia to see themselves no longer as a religious community, but as an independent nation.

A Federal History of the Habsburg Empire, 1815–1918. Jana Osterkamp, Oxford University Press.
 DOI: 10.1093/9780198943631.003.0005

171 Koselleck, 'Bund (Bündnis, Föderalismus, Bundestaat)', 582–671.

172 Dieter Langewiesche, *Reich, Nation, Föderation: Deutschland und Europa*. Munich, 2008, 230.

173 National counties, at least, were envisaged. On the debate on this Springer, *Protokolle des Verfassungsausschusses*, 124–6. According to these ideas, Galicia was to be divided into ten, Bohemia into nine, Moravia into four, Lower Austria and Tyrol-Vorarlberg into three each, and Styria into two counties. Wierer, *Föderalismus in Donauraum*, 41.

174 Helmut Rumpler, *Eine Chance für Mitteleuropa: Bürgerliche Emanzipation und Staatsverfall in der Habsburgermonarchie*. Vienna, 1997, 315.

175 The Ruthenian Central Council in particular perceived the Polish national movement not only as a threat but also as a model for its own nationalization. Turij, *Holovna Rus'ka Rada*, p. xviii. The German Bohemians also referred to the Czech National Associations as a model worthy of imitation; in one debate it was said: 'Let us learn from the Czechs, let us learn from them to be eager, determined and obedient, we can confidently take their associations as a model for ourselves.' Cf. *Stenographischer Bericht über die Verhandlungen in Teplitz*, 11.

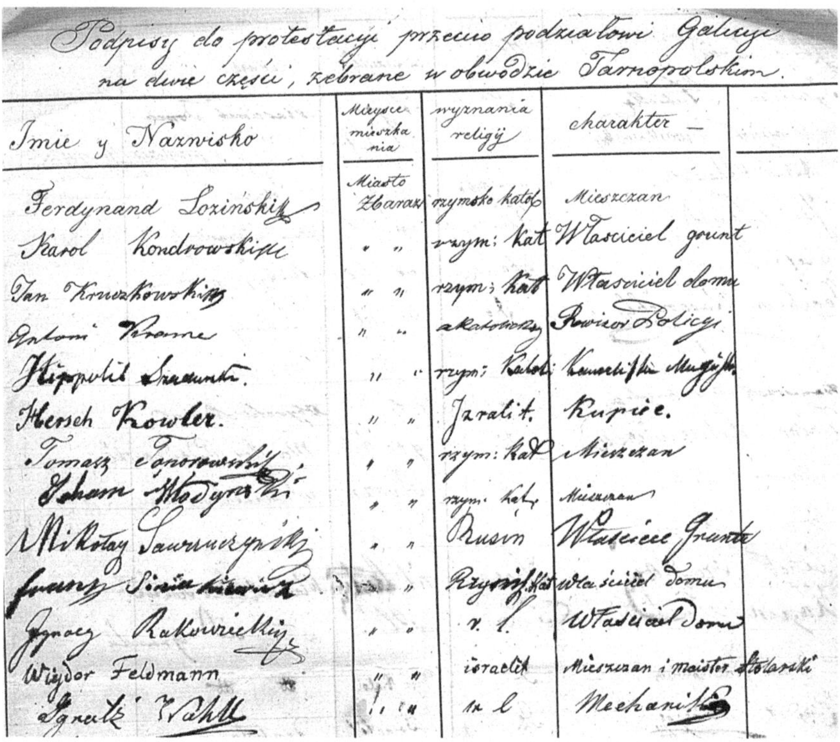

Podpisy do protestacyi przeciw podziałowi Galicyi na dwie części, zebrane w obwodzie Tarnopolskim.

Imie y Nazwisko	Miejsce mieszkania	wyznania religij	charakter
Ferdynand Łoziński	Miasto Zbaraz	rzymsko katol.	Mieszczan
Karol Kondrowski	" "	rzym: Kat	Właściciel grunt
Jan Kruszkowski	" "	rzym: Kat	Właściciel domu
Antoni [illegible]	" "	a katolicky	Rewizor Policyi
Hippolit [illegible]	" "	rzym: Kat.	[illegible]
Hersch Kowler	" "	Izralit	Kupiec
Tomasz [illegible]	" "	rzym: Kat	Mieszczan
Johann Młodyński	" "	rzym. kat.	Mieszczan
Mikołay Ławruczyński	" "	Rusin	Właściciel Gruntu
Franz Siniakiewicz	" "	Rzym. Kat	Właściciel domu
Ignacy Rakowiecki	" "	r. k.	Właściciel domu
Isydor Feldmann	" "	israelit	Mieszczan i maister stolarski
Ignatz Wahl	" "	r. k.	Mechanik

Figure 5.1 Detail from a petition sheet to the Austrian Parliament in1849, petition from Zbaraz against a division of Galicia.

5

Small Town Federalism

The Galician Campaigns of Petitions, 1848/49

At the three constitutional assemblies in Vienna, Frankfurt, and Prague, delegates balanced demands for national independence against the need for federal, peaceful cohesion in both the Habsburg 'Europe in miniature' and Europe at large. At the same time, the inhabitants of the Monarchy, in countless petitions and memoranda, demanded the 'national' partition of their territories or radical new compositions on the basis of exclusive 'national' loyalties. They countered the universalist ideas of a new Europe with particularist sentiments, questioning the historical-regional ties that had hitherto held the European order together. This was the flipside of the Revolution's dream of the 'nation state'.

Reading between the lines of the petitions of 1848/49, one encounters a paradox. While they emphasize separating factors such as language, denomination, ethnicity, or 'nation'—often placed front and centre by the authors—they also reveal traces of a long-standing peaceful coexistence in the villages, small towns, and cities that had little in common with their divisive rhetoric. Thus the petition movements not only shed light on contemporary political thinking 'from below' but also illustrate a social history of federalism marked by distinctions and commonalities.

Petition campaigns were hardly uncommon in the European Revolution; indeed, they served as a mouthpiece of political opinion.[1] Already in the era of early southern German constitutionalism, petition campaigns had been used to mobilize the rural population for political and public causes. In the Habsburg Monarchy, during the revolutionary year of 1848, the majority of petitions received by the Reichstag were sent by peasants, even though they were normally assisted in drafting them by clergymen and civil servants.[2] Such petitions were primarily addressed to the emperor or the government, but during the revolutionary phase they were generally passed on to the Constitutional Committee of the Austrian Diet.[3]

[1] Heinz-Gerhard Haupt and Dieter Langewiesche, 'Die Revolution in Europa 1848: Reform der Herrschafts- und Gesellschaftsordnung—Nationalrevolution—Wirkungen'. In: Dieter Dowe, Heinz-Gerhard Haupt, and Dieter Langewiesche (eds), *Europa 1848: Revolution und Reform*. Bonn, 1998, 20–1. On the example of Baden Niels Grüne, *Dorfgesellschaft—Konflikterfahrung—Partizipationskultur. Sozialer Wandel und politische Kommunikation in Landgemeinden der badischen Rheinpfalz 1720–1850*. Stuttgart, 2011, 401–13.

[2] Otto Hoerhan, *Die Petitionen an den Kremsierer Reichstag 1848/49* (university diss.). Vienna, 1965, 16–17.

[3] The 'Verzeichnis der dem Constitutions-Ausschuss zugekommenen Acten. Registratur' comprises several booklets. ÖStA, HHStA, LA ÖRT 1848/49, Box 81, fols. 178–90.

The largest petition campaign in the Habsburg Monarchy, attracting more than 250,000 signatures, concerned the federal reorganization of Galicia. A similarly impressive number of petitioners in Tyrol supported the preservation of 'Catholic religious unity', a scheme to deny non-Catholics the right to settle there.[4] Also from Tyrol came a petition for the independence of South Tyrol, which attracted tens of thousands of signatories from almost every town in the Rovereto and Trento regions.[5] In addition, the Italian Tyroleans spoke out in favour of a separate province of Welschtirol in the Constitutional Committee of the Revolutionary Assembly. They argued that 'the climate, the products, the way of life, the aspirations, and the sympathies of the southern and northern Tyroleans' were diametrically opposed.[6] Other petitions were less successful. The initiative for a united Slovenia as a separate crown land received only about 6,000 signatures. Not wishing to be part of a reformed German Confederation, the Slovenes presented a map on which they had drawn their plans for a separate crown land territory.[7] Dalmatian deputies, for their part, petitioned the government because they did not want to be incorporated into either Hungary or Croatia and instead demanded the 'requisite separate administration and autonomy'.[8] To the north, parishes around Salzburg petitioned for the separation of the crown lands of Salzburg and Upper Austria.[9] In Bohemia, even the largest rural petition only accumulated 1,073 signatures, while in Moravia and Silesia there were even fewer attempts to garner signatures.[10]

The study of these petitions promises unusual insights. As they contain extensive handwritten marginalia and glosses, they reveal, if only in fragments, the opinions of individuals and selected urban and rural milieus.[11] The petition campaign from Galicia, one of the poorest regions in Europe at the time, serves as an illustrative example in this chapter. The uniformly structured petition forms often contained information about the petitioners' occupations, religion, and place of

[4] The petition registered 123,560 signatures, almost half of the German-speaking Tyrolean population. Roman Bacher, *Der Tiroler Provinziallandtag von 1848 im Rahmen der allgemeinen österreichischen Verfassungsentwicklung*. Innsbruck, 1991, 84–5, 93–5.

[5] Hoerhan, *Petitionen*, 262.

[6] Anton Springer, *Protokolle des Verfassungsausschusses im Österreichischen Reichstage 1848–1849*. Leipzig, 1885, 35.

[7] Petition der Slowenen an den Kaiser (dem Petitionsaussschuss des Kremsierer Reichstags vorgelegt) of 21 June 1848, Az. 5013/RT 1848–49. ÖStA, HHStA LA ÖRT 1848/49, Karton 86, fol. 194. Joachim Hösler, *Von Krain zu Slowenien*. Munich, 2006, 288.

[8] Interpellation der dalmatinischen Abgeordneten an das Ministerium of 17 Dec. 1848, Az. 3080/RT 1848–49. ÖStA, HHStA, LA ÖRT 1848/49, Box 85, fols. 265–6.

[9] Vorgedruckte Petitionsbögen Salzburgischer Pfarrgemeinden an die 'Hohe österreichische Deputierten-Kammer' of 30 May 1848, e.g. Az. 4392/RT 1848–49. ÖStA, HHStA, LA ÖRT 1848/49, Box 86, fol. 169.

[10] František Roubík, 'Doslov'. In Roubík (ed.), *Petice venkovského lidu z Čech k Národnimu Výboru z roku 1848*. Prague, 1954, 514–15.

[11] For the evaluation of the glosses Jana Osterkamp, 'Imperial Diversity in the Village: Petitions for and against the Division of Galicia in 1848', *Nationalities Papers*, 44/5 (2016), 731–50.

residence, and allow conclusions to be drawn about their use of language, writing, and script. They open a window onto the edges of the empire.

The petitions for and against the partition of Galicia reflect the great expectations for political change that came not only from the political elite, but also from large sections of the population. In deciding to add their own signatures, many petitioners demonstrated their fundamental political interest. Through other innumerable, unconscious, and imperceptible everyday decisions about how to write, speak, and pray, urban and rural populations gradually became aware that their own environment was part of a larger community. In 1848, the buzzword 'nation' was used for such notions of belonging, a convenient cover for distinguishing oneself from the supposed Other.

In terms of language, religion, and social status, Galicia was populated by roughly equal populations of Polish-speaking Catholics (predominantly in the west) and Ukrainian-speaking Greek Catholics and Orthodox Christians in the east. There was also a numerically significant Jewish community. The population numbered almost 4.6 million. While the 1849 statistics for Galicia show a linguistic-national distribution of 45.9 per cent Poles, 46.8 per cent Ukrainians (then called Ruthenians), 6.7 per cent Jews, and 0.55 per cent Germans, the proportion in eastern Galicia was 71 per cent Ukrainians, 20.4 per cent Poles, and 7.9 per cent Jews. The *Holovna Rada Rus'ka* (Ruthenian Central Council), which assumed a higher Ukrainian proportion, disputed the latter figures.[12] The ruling elite was Polonized and therefore spoke Polish. The peasant community was both Polish and Ukrainian, both Catholic and 'Orthodox'. Jews, who mainly spoke Yiddish, a language not officially recognized by the authorities, often occupied intermediate social positions between the lives of the landlords and those of the peasants.

The Galician petition campaign reflected the European dimension of the Habsburg reorganization plans and cannot be understood without reference to the eighteenth-century partitions of Poland. Ever since a sovereign Poland had been wiped from the map, Polish elites had yearned for statehood. Two years on from their failed independence uprising in 1846, Polish nationalists felt the time was ripe for the re-establishment of a Polish state. The idea of a Polish nation state found many sympathizers among European intellectuals, all of whom invoked the idea of 'atonement'. The Frankfurt pre-parliament, later the *Paulskirche*, the Slav Congress, as well as pro-government Austrian writers such as Sommaruga, argued that the wrongs committed against Poland by the European Great Powers should now be redressed.[13] However, by the end of 1848, as the constitution was

[12] Cf. Jan Kozik, *Między reakcją a rewolucją: Studia z dziejów ukraińskiego ruchu narodowego w Galicji w latach 1848–1849*. Warsaw, 1975, 185; Rudolf A. Mark, *Galizien unter österreichischer Herrschaft*. Marburg, 1994, 53–65.

[13] Günter Wollstein, *Das 'Großdeutschland' der Paulskirche: Nationale Ziele in der bürgerlichen Revolution 1848/49*. Düsseldorf, 1977, 132; 'Proklamation der ersten Slavenversammlung in Prag an

finalized, many of the *Paulskirche* delegates had moved away from the idea of separate nation states for all. The territorial losses associated with such a drastic reorganization threatened the new Germany's status as a major European power. As a result, they increasingly vacillated and manoeuvred their way around the territorial demands of the Polish, Italian, and Hungarian nation-state movements.[14] The governments of the partitioning powers also refused concessions and continued to deny Poland's existence. After all, Austria, Prussia, and Russia derived much of their power in Europe from their rule over Polish territories.[15]

The petition campaign for and against the partition of Galicia epitomized Polish-Ukrainian antagonism.[16] After the Viennese government initially rejected a petition for Polish independence,[17] the Galician *Rada Narodowa Polska* (Polish National Council) dispatched another deputation to the imperial court in June 1848—again without success.[18] The Ukrainians, meanwhile, sought to counter the Polish machinations. On 2 June 1848, the Ruthenian National Council decided to promote a territorial 'division by nationality' in favour of the Ukrainians.[19] The association advocated for the creation of a politically autonomous Ukrainian Galicia within the Habsburg Monarchy and asked its rural branches to submit statements of solidarity.[20] Some Ukrainians opposed the annexation of Galicia to a future Poland with simple words (written in Polish, incidentally): 'Signing with the holy sign of the cross,...we ask to remain forever under the sceptre of the most illustrious Austrian Emperor'.[21] In a similar vein, the German colony of

die Völker Europas', 12 June 1848, printed in Jan Peter Jordan, *Aktenmäßiger Bericht über die Verhandlungen des ersten Slawenkongresses in Prag.* Prague, 1848, 38; Franz von Sommaruga, *Österreichs Zukunft und dessen Stellung in Deutschland.* Stuttgart, 1848, 8. Cf. Chapter 4.

[14] Wollstein, *Großdeutschland*, 223–42; Christof Dipper, *Revolution und Risorgimento: Italien 1848/49 aus deutscher Perspektive.* Munich, 2000, 73–89; Hans Günter Telle, *Das österreichische Problem im Frankfurter Parlament im Sommer und Herbst 1848.* Marburg, 1933, 20–1, 63–70.

[15] On the 'negative policy against Poland' of Prussia, Russia, and Austria cf. Martin Schulze Wessel, *Russlands Blick auf Preußen.* Stuttgart, 1995.

[16] Hans-Christian Maner, *Galizien: Eine Grenzregion im Kalkül der Donaumonarchie im 18. und 19. Jahrhundert.* Munich, 2007, 92–105.

[17] The Galician governor Stadion initially advocated for 'a national government under Austrian protection'. Council of Ministers of 17 Apr. 1848. In Thomas Kletečka (ed.), *Protokolle des Österreichischen Ministerrates* (hereafter *ÖMR*), 1/1: *Die Ministerien des Revolutionsjahres 1848 (20. März 1848–21. November 1848).* Vienna, 1996, No. 14, 78–81. On the deputation and petition cf. Council of Ministers of 5 Apr. 1848. In: *ÖMR*), 1/1, No. 4, 21–5.

[18] Stadion petitioned the Council of Ministers in vain to stop them. Cf. Council of Ministers of 5 June 1848. In Kletečka (ed.), *ÖMR* I/1, No. 62, 376–80. On the comparison of the Prussian and Austrian partition territories Hans Henning Hahn, 'Die polnische Nation in den Revolutionen von 1846–49'. In Dowe et al., *Europa 1848*, 242.

[19] The characterization of the Ruthenians as a nationality did not go unchallenged from within their own ranks. Adam Świątek, *Gente Rutheni, natione Poloni. Z dziejów Rusinów narodowości polskiej w Galicji.* Kraków, 2014, 211. The Ruthenians were initially encouraged by Vienna. Erledigung durch den Ministerrat, 10 May 1848. In Kletečka (ed.): *ÖMR* 1/1, No. 33, 191–8.

[20] The 'Ukrainian idea' is already embedded here, cf. Oleh Turij, *Holovna Rus'ka Rada 1848–1851.* Lviv, 2002, pp. xv, 30; Ivan L. Rudnytsky, 'The Ukrainians in Galicia under Austrian Rule'. In Andrei Markovits and Frank E. Sysyn (eds), *Nationbuilding and the Politics of Nationalism.* Cambridge, MA, 1982, 32.

[21] 'Podpisuje się znakiem krzyza swietego, do ruskoj rady, i prosiny takze abysmy pod Berlem Najasniejszego Cesarza Auwstryjakciego, nazawszy zostawali.' Petition von Grzymałowski, n.d. ÖStA, HHStA, LA ÖRT 1848/49, Box 132, fol. 949 (county Tarnopol).

Beckersdorf declared its dynastic loyalty, wishing 'never to separate from Austria, never to unite with the Poles, and to live and die with our beloved monarch Ferdinand'.[22] In response to the Ukrainian petition, the Polish elite organized a counter-petition, the so-called protestations.

Institutionally, three associations represented the Polish–Ukrainian opposition. At the one end of the spectrum, the aforementioned *Rada Narodowa Polska* (Polish National Council) sought Polish independence. At the other was the Austro-Slavic *Holovna Rada Rus'ka* (Rusyn Central Council), conservative, loyal to the emperor, and supported by the governor Franz von Stadion.[23] Between the two, the *Sobor Ruskyi* (Rusyn Assembly), an association of Polonophiles and Polonized Ukrainians subsidized by the Polish National Council, occupied an intermediate position.[24] Based on ecclesiastical institutions, each of these associations established an extensive network of branches in the towns and villages of Galicia. In rural areas, peasants participated in the respective campaigns alongside the dominant clergy.[25] The involvement of the churches led to the religious permeation of national and ethno-linguistic affiliations.

At first glance, the religious landscape of Galicia was clearly divided into large camps. A Catholic, predominantly Polish-speaking population occupied the western part; a Greek Catholic, mostly Ukrainian-speaking community inhabited the eastern part; while Bukovina in the far east (still part of Galicia in 1848/49) was settled by an Orthodox majority of Ukrainians and Romanians. The Ukrainians of Galicia thus belonged to two different churches: the Greek Catholic, formerly 'Uniate' Church, and the Greek Orthodox Church with an archbishopric in Czernowitz (Chernivtsi).[26] Just as the Ukrainian language was classified as either a dialect of Polish or Russian, there were attempts, lasting until the twentieth century, to bring the Greek Catholic Church into line with 'Polish' Roman Catholicism or Eastern ('Russian') Orthodoxy. The battle for the faithful was waged with the full knowledge and support of the governments of the two competing empires, and was used as a yardstick to measure (dis)loyalty to Vienna or St Petersburg.[27] Denominational ties thus became a dividing line, interpreted by both contemporaries and historians alike as differences between Poles,

[22] Beckersdorf bei Podhajce, county Tarnopol, Petition of 24 Aug. 1848. Box 132, fol. 660.

[23] Cf. Turij, *Holovna Rus'ka Rada*; Anna Veronika Wendland, Die Russophilen in Galizien. Vienna, 2001, 31. On the influence of Stadion cf. Council of Ministers of 7 May 1848. In Kletečka (ed.), *ÖMR* 1/1, No. 30, 170–8.

[24] Cf. Mar'ian Mudry'i, 'Rus'ky'j Sobor 1848 roku: Organizaciya ta chleny'. In Yaroslav Isayevych (ed.), *Yuvilejny'j zbirny'k na poshanu Ivana Patera*. Lviv, 2008, 107–26. Comprehensively Świątek, *Gente Rutheni, natione Poloni*.

[25] Turij, *Holovna Rus'ka Rada*, p. xxiv. Not a single peasant was represented in the Holovna Rada, but peasant participation was pushed for in the local branches. Kai Struve, *Bauern und Nation in Galizien*. Göttingen, 2005, 88–9.

[26] For further internal differentiation, which is still important today, cf. Michal Danilák, *Halyc'ki, bukovyns'ki, zakarpats'ki ukraïnci v revoljuciï 1848–1849 rokiv*. Bratislava, 1972.

[27] Wendland, *Die Russophilen in Galizien*; Alexei Miller, 'National Identities and the Forging of Political Loyalties'. In Jana Osterkamp and Martin Schulze Wessel (eds), *Exploring Loyalty*. Göttingen, 2017, 61–72.

Ukrainians, and Russians.[28] In everyday life, however, common religious experiences connected people, especially the Ukrainians of Galicia.[29] Greek Catholics and Orthodox believers shared a close bond forged by their common adherence to the Byzantine Orthodox rite in liturgy and spiritual life. The Ukrainian national movement built a national consciousness on these religious commonalities.[30] As a result, notwithstanding the existing ecclesiastical boundaries, there was little distinction between religious and national affiliations.

Initially, the Viennese government opposed the demands for a partition of Galicia. The new minister of the interior (and former Galician governor) Stadion, Vice-Governor Agenor Gołuchowski, and the Polish affairs officer in the Ministry of the Interior and new governor Wenzeslaus (Wacław) Zaleski, rejected plans to divide Galicia into a Ukrainian-speaking east and a Polish-speaking west.[31] Thus Gołuchowski added disparaging remarks to the Ukrainians petition to the emperor for the partition of the province before referring it to the government, recommending an administrative rather than territorial division.[32] Indeed, on 19 June the government decided to reorganize Galicia into two administrative units (rather than two separate crown lands, as a partition would imply), with effect from 1 August.[33] Dissatisfied with this compromise, the Ukrainian National Association reaffirmed its demand for greater independence and submitted additional memoranda to the government and the Imperial Diet to this effect on 17 July.[34] On 27 July, the Doblhoff government postponed the administrative partition, which was already under way, whereupon the Holovna Rada Rus'ka further intensified the petition movement.[35]

At the same time, polemics in the media intensified the dispute within the administrative apparatus. Zaleski, an intimate connoisseur and promoter of Ukrainian culture and language, now accused the Ruthenians of Russophilia.[36] To his mind, a Ukrainian crown land with the right to self-determination was a gateway for an expansion of Russian power. Although the Russophile movement was still weak in 1848 and only gained momentum after the disappointments of

[28] On the division by religion Keely Stauter-Halsted, *The Nation in the Village*. Ithaca, NY, 2004, 8; John-Paul Himka, 'Confessional Relations in Galicia'. In Christopher Hann and Paul Magocsi (eds), *Galicia: A Multicultured Land*. Toronto, 2005, 28; Wendland, *Die Russophilen in Galizien*.

[29] Heiko Haumann, 'Juden in der ländlichen Gesellschaft Galiziens am Ende des 19. und zu Beginn des 20. Jahrhunderts'. In Andrea Löw, Kerstin Robusch, and Stefanie Walter (eds), *Deutsche, Juden, Polen*. Frankfurt am Main, 2004, 40 and 47–50.

[30] Nationalization did not proceed in a straight line. Cf. Harald H. Jepsen, 'Orthodoxy and Autocephaly in Galicia'. In Hann and Magocsi, *Galicia*, 71–81.

[31] Iryna Vushko, *The Politics of Cultural Retreat*. New Haven, 2015, 237.

[32] Ivan Krevecz'ky'j, 'Sprava podyilu Halychyny w rr. 1846–1850', *Zapysky Naukovoho Tovarystva Imeni Sevchenka* (1910), 94: 68–9.

[33] Jan Kozik, *The Ukrainian National Movement in Galicia 1815–1849*. Edmonton, 1986, 266.

[34] Signed on 31 July 1848. Turij, *Holovna Rus'ka Rada*, 46 and 50.

[35] The reasons for this are unclear. Georg Christoph Berger Waldenegg, 'Die Bukowina war glücklicher'. In František Stellner (ed.), *Staletí objevů, diplomacie a válek*. Prague, 2005, 35.

[36] On Michael Zaleski Moser, 'Das Ukrainische ("Ruthenische") der galizischen Polen und Polonophilen zwischen 1830 und 1848/1849', *Zeitschrift für Slavische Philologie*, 62/2 (2003), 322–3.

the Revolution,[37] Zaleski dispatched memoranda expressing his concerns to the Council of Ministers.[38] Accusations of Russophilia not only fed diffuse fears of a 'Slavic danger' among the German-speaking population, but induced acute alarm amongst the Galician peasantry. Having only been released from serfdom in 1848, they feared that a rise in Russian power (and a subsequent union with Russia) would put them in chains once again.[39]

The petition movement touched on the fundamental concerns of the nobility, the middle classes, and the peasants of Galicia. The result was a political mobilization encompassing all tiers of society. The 1848/49 petitions for the partition of Galicia collected almost 200,000 signatures in the summer of 1848, to which '67,745 signatures' were added in the autumn.[40] Doubts were immediately raised about their credibility, with the remarkably high number of signatures prompting accusations of forgery from contemporaries and historians alike.[41] On the petition sheets, many signatures were represented by the crosses of the illiterate.[42] Sometimes, a Greek Catholic village priest would present a list of the names of his 'flock', arranged by family.[43] They justified their actions by pointing out that the peasants had been urged by their landlords to support the counter-petition and had therefore given their consent anonymously.[44]

Many sheets contain a considerable number of handwritten signatures, each indicating the petitioners' class, profession, and denomination (Figure 5.1). They can be considered genuine. The widespread politicization of the rural inhabitants in Galicia can be better understood against the backdrop of the national and social conflicts between landlords and peasants, on the one hand, and Poles and Ukrainians, on the other hand, during the pre-March period. The rural population experienced further political mobilization in the spring of 1848 with the elections to the Reichstag. A bitter power struggle raged between Poles, Ukrainians, and Austrian provincial officials over the Galician voters, 80 per cent of whom were peasants.[45]

[37] Wendland, *Russophile in Galizien*, 131–4.

[38] Cf. Council of Ministers of 28 Dec. 1848. In Kletečka (ed.), *ÖMR* 2/1: *Das Ministerium Schwarzenberg (5. Dezember 1848–Jänner 1850)*. Vienna, 2002, No. 10, 63–8.

[39] As a result, adherence to peasant liberation was explicitly noted on the petition forms, cf. Krevecz'ky'j, 'Sprava', 94: 72.

[40] Letter from the main initiator of the petition Michael Kuziemski to the Reichstag dated 13 Sept. 1848. ÖStA, HHStA, LA ÖRT 1848/49, Box 132, fol. 606.

[41] For a contemporary take, see the speech by Florian Ziemiałkowski. Springer, *Protokolle des Verfassungsausschusses*, 20; Anton Dabczański, *Die ruthenische Frage in Galizien*. Lviv, 1848, 34. From a historiographical perspective on the petitions cf. Hoerhan: *Petitionen*; Krevecz'ky'j, 'Sprava', 96: 105–54.

[42] Contrary to contemporary perception, this concerned both the Ruthenian and the Polish petition. The petition sheets of both sides in ÖStA, HHStA, LA ÖRT 1848–1849 'Petitionen gegen eine Teilung Galiziens'. Boxes 130–2. The wording is misleading, petitions from both sides are archived.

[43] Examples among many include Horozianka, county Komarno, petition of 21 August, and Czarnoszowice, county Lemberg, Petition n. d. ÖStA, HHStA, LA ÖRT 1848/49, Box 132, fols. 841 and 768.

[44] Kozik, *Ukrainian National Movement*, 267.

[45] Kozik, *Ukrainian National Movement*, 237–50; Struve, *Bauern und Nation in Galizien*, 98–9.

The professionally produced ballot sheets contained detailed information of the petitioners. They were the result of a lengthy process of successive Ukrainian and Polish petitions for and against the partition of Galicia launched by the two sides in Vienna. The first Ruthenian petitions contained simple demands: we want a partition of Galicia, and Ukrainian-speaking schools, authorities, and churches. The main concern of the Polish ruling elite, on the other hand, was to undermine the Holovna Rada as a mouthpiece for the Ukrainians in Galicia and its demands for a separate Ukrainian territory. The trick was to do so without appearing one-sidedly 'Polish' and thus falling prey to accusations of following an ethnic-nationalist agenda. In both its demand for Polish statehood and its rejection of a partition of Galicia along national lines, the Polish National Council referred to the pre-modern tradition of a political nation (*natio polona*) that integrated different ethnic tribes (*gentes*).

The Polish National Council first sent to Vienna the Sobor Ruskyi, which had collected some 577 signatures against the partition of Galicia.[46] The Sobor was considered the 'political organization of the 'gente rutheni, natione poloni' (Ruthenians by ethnicity, Polish by nationality).[47] The Sobor petitions were followed by more detailed petition ballots initiated by the Polish National Council, bearing the handwritten motto 'Wolność! Równość! Braterstwo!' (Liberty! Equality! Fraternity!). These were protests against any partition that was 'more than purely administrative'. Their glosses and clarifying notes emphasized that a territorial division according to linguistic and religious criteria was simply impossible, especially in Galicia's western reaches.[48] From Złoczów, the petitioners warned of violence and even civil war, invoking the 'terrible consequences that had followed the partition of Hungary and Croatia'.[49] To strengthen the argument of a political and historical Polish nation, the Polish National Council's protestations meticulously listed professions and religions of the petitioners to underscore the ethno-confessional diversity of the crown land.[50]

The Ruthenian Holovna Rada subsequently urged all its regional councils to take part in the petition campaign. Personal data were added to the petitioners' names and a delegation prepared for dispatch to the imperial court.[51] In response to Polish accusations that one-sided nationalism underlay its call for the partition of Galicia, the Rada modified and refined its approach. If there were a significant

[46] The Sobor included Polish or Polonized nobles and intellectuals of Ruthenian origin, e.g. Leon Sapieha and Kasper Cięglewicz, but also Ivan Vahylevych, member of the Ruthenian triad. Antony Polonsky, 'The Revolutionary Crisis of 1846–1849 and its Place in the Development of Nineteenth-Century Galicia', *Harvard Ukrainian Studies*, 22 (1998), 457.

[47] So Krevecz'ky'j, 'Sprava', 94: 78. Also Świątek, *Gente Rutheni, natione Poloni*, 219–20.

[48] ÖStA, HHStA, LA ÖRT 1848/49, Box 131 on Czortków.

[49] Petition n.d. Box 131, fol. 27.

[50] 'Protestationen gegen die Teilung Galiziens'. ÖStA, HHStA, LA ÖRT 1848/49 'Petitionen gegen eine Teilung Galiziens'. Boxes 131 and 132.

[51] Turij, *Holovna Rus'ka Rada*, 44, 76, 101–2, 104, 107.

number of ethnic Poles living in eastern Galicia, the Holovna Rada argued, they and the other 'nations, such as: Germans, Armenians, Jews, and Karaites' were to be granted 'equal nationality rights'. Despite this rhetoric of national equality, however, the image of the Other did not become any friendlier. In the same breath, Poles and Jews were dubbed 'plagues of the land'. The Poles 'probably travelled abroad out of boredom' or took part 'in the barricade battles in the capitals of Europe', while the 'Ruthenians, oppressed by the Poles, neglected by the government, without influence, without power' were unknown in Europe.[52] The authors thus adopted a platitude that had been circulating since Metternich, namely that Poles had manned every insurrectionist barricade in Europe and were notorious troublemakers.[53] The Holovna Rada, on the other hand, emphasized 'the integrity of the Austrian Monarchy' as a 'great power of the first rank in the family of European states'.[54]

When the Kremsier Constitutional Committee discussed the partition of Galicia, the opposing factions clashed in public. Florian Ziemiałkowski, a delegate from Lemberg (Lwów, Lviv), 'representative of the Polish intelligentsia in Eastern Galicia',[55] and after 1873 *Landsmannminister* (nationality minister) for Galicia, denied the existence of a Ukrainian nation: 'Until March, Ruthenians were those who were Greek, Poles those who were Catholic; therefore there were Ruthenians and Poles in one and the same family.'[56] For many Poles, Ukrainian was really just a Polish dialect, the difference between the groups purely religious, and a Ruthenian nation an invention of Stadion's.[57] Memoranda by Anton Dabczański and Kasper Cięglewicz, written especially for the members of the Austrian Reichstag and translated into German by the Polish National Council, offered further justifications for discounting the Ukrainians as an independent nation.[58] The Ukrainian side, in turn, responded with their own German-language disquisitions to convince the Reichstag of the contrary.[59]

[52] Memorandum of the Holovna Rada Rus'ka to the Ministry of Interior of 28 Oct. 1848. Krevecz'ky'j, 'Sprava', 96: 111–12.

[53] Hahn 'Die polnische Nation in den Revolutionen von 1846–49', 247.

[54] Memorandum of the Holovna Rada Rus'ka to the Ministry of Interior of 28 Oct. 1848, Krevecz'ky'j, 'Sprava', 96: 114.

[55] Zbigniew Fras, *Florian Ziemiałkowski (1817–1900): Biografia polityczna*. Wrocław, 1991, 54.

[56] Springer, *Protokolle des Verfassungsausschusses*, 20. Against this František Palacký. *Protokolle des Verfassungsausschusses*, 26–7.

[57] A critical view, but nonetheless representing the superiority of Polish culture Stanisław Smolka, *Die reussische Welt: Historisch-politische Studien*. Vienna, 1916, 51–3, 75.

[58] Dabczański, *Die ruthenische Frage 1848*; Dabczański, *Wyjaśnienie sprawy ruskiej*. Lviv, 1848; Kasper Cięglewicz, *Die roth-reussischen Angelegenheiten im Jahre 1848*. Vienna, 1848; Cięglewicz, *Rzecz czerwono-ruska 1848 roku*. Lviv, 1848. Stadion tried to intervene against Dabczański's presence in the Vienna Galician Committee. Cf. Council of Ministers of 29 Apr. 1848. In Kletečka (ed.), *ÖMR* 1/1, No. 22, 120–6.

[59] The pamphlet 'An die Russinen' (To the Ruthenians) was sent to Vienna in 600 copies. Turij, *Holovna Rus'ka Rada*, 52, 56.

The rise of a Ukrainian national consciousness did not come as a surprise in 1848. It was the result of a gradual process that had begun with the Josephinian educational reforms and ultimately led to attempts to codify a Ukrainian language in the pre-March period by the 'Ruthenian Triad', a circle of three intellectuals from the Lemberg Greek Catholic seminary: Markijan Šaškevyč, Ivan Vahylevyč, and Jakiv Holovac'kyj. The mutual Ukrainian–Polish estrangement deepened as a result of the 1846 uprising.[60] While Galician provincial officials, including more than a few Czechs from Bohemia, and Governor Stadion, supported the development of cultural independence for the Ukrainians, the Greek Catholic clergy resisted 'nationalization' as late as the 1840s. The Church feared a decline of the importance of religion.[61] In the March Revolution, however, the Greek Catholic clergy took the lead in supporting the Ukrainians. The Holovna Rada Rus'ka, to which only members of the Greek Catholic Church were admitted, turned the petition campaign into a test of loyalty: anyone who opposed the partition of Galicia was discredited as a 'pseudo-Ruthenian'.[62]

Among the Ukrainians, as among the Poles, religion and nation were closely linked. The Ukrainian elite was represented by the Greek Catholic bishop Hryhorij Jachymovyč, who advocated for a confessional-linguistic understanding of nation in the Kremsier constitutional parliament. Based on the observation that 'the two nations…lived in a deep-rooted enmity', Jachymovyč also referred to the medieval history of Halicz and thus to 'the time when Ruthenia had been a large state and Poland a small principality'.[63] There was no 'difference of tribe, because they are both Slavs', he argued, yet the Ukrainians' Greek-Catholic denomination, Little Russian language, and Cyrillic script not only differed from the Poles', but had been violently suppressed under Polish rule. Only a partition of Galicia would allow the Ukrainians to develop freely.[64]

The example of Galicia shows once again that, although national affiliation was politicized and strengthened in 1848 and employed as an argument for federal reorganization, in many cases 'nation' remained a nebulous concept. None of the criteria used to separate Poles and Ukrainians—language, script, or religion—proved to be clear-cut.[65] While the Ukrainian proponents of the

[60] John-Paul Himka, *Galician Villagers and the Ukrainian National Movement in the Nineteenth Century*. Edmonton, 1988; Paul Magocsi, *The Roots of Ukrainian Nationalism*. Toronto, 2002, 73–82, 94–5; Marta Bohačevs'ka-Chom'jak, *The Spring of a Nation: The Ukrainians in Eastern Galicia in 1848*. Philadelphia, 1967, 17. On the 1820s Stanisław Stępień, 'Borderland City: Przemyśl and the Ruthenian National Awakening in Galicia'. In Hann and Magocsi, *Galicia*, 55–60.

[61] Polonsky, 'Revolutionary Crisis of 1846–1849', 455. On promoting the Ruthenians Berger Waldenegg, 'Die Bukowina war glücklicher', 25.

[62] Turij, *Holovna Rus'ka Rada*, 43. Municipalities against a partition were precisely recorded. Cf. for the Stanislau area Turij, *Holovna Rus'ka Rada*, 67.

[63] The Holovna Rada Rus'ka commissioned Anton Petrushevych to write a 'Ruthenian history' of Galicia to boost its historical legitimacy. Turij, *Holovna Rus'ka Rada*, 44 and 46.

[64] Springer, *Protokolle des Verfassungsausschusses*, 24–5.

[65] On the criteria Hoerhan, *Petitionen*, 252–61.

petition wanted to prove the division of the population into two nations, and the Polish actors the unity of a single nation, a close reading of the glosses instead reveals significant overlaps between the two.

5.1. Separation by Language, Script, and Religion

The more the political thinkers of the March Revolution discussed 'nation' and 'nationalities' in terms of federal territories, the more imprecise and blurred their conceptual frameworks became. When 'nation' related to an existing territory, its spatial parameters were obvious, but it remained unclear whether the *einborne volk eines landes* (native people of a land)[66] collectively constituted the 'nation', or if that honour was reserved for a smaller linguistic and cultural community within it. Conversely, those who understood 'nation' and 'nationality' primarily as a linguistic and cultural collective were often unable to draw clear territorial borders around imagined national spaces. Before the codification of standard languages, linguistic boundaries were fluid and the way someone spoke did not provide a clear-cut shibboleth between Ukrainians and Poles, Slovaks and Moravians, or Croats and Serbs. The same was true of the multitude of dialects of German, which rivalled Slavonic in its great variety.[67] Language and linguistic nation were not a prior given, but rather a political project, not limited to the Slavic national movements.[68] This explains the linguistic nationalism of various unification movements, i.e. the promotion of standard languages as genuine national concerns.[69]

In 1848, the Poles and Ukrainians of Galicia did not yet constitute territorially distinct linguistic nations. The Ukrainian national movement was characterized by the struggle for a separate standard language on an equal footing with Polish. The use of Ukrainian in schools, administration, and the church was the principal demand of the petition campaign and the wider activities of the Ruthenian Central Council.[70] The matter gained urgency when Zaleski, the first governor of Galicia of Polish origin, abolished German as the pre-existing 'imposed language',[71] medium of instruction, and *lingua franca* in favour of Polish in all crown land

[66] This is the original meaning of nation in the German language. Cf. 'Nation' in Jacob and Wilhelm Grimm, *Deutsches Wörterbuch*, vol. 13. Leipzig, 1889, col. 425.

[67] Martin Durell, 'Political Unity and Linguistic Diversity in Nineteenth-Century Germany'. In Maiken Umbach (ed.), *German Federalism: Past, Present, Future*. Basingstoke, 2002, 94.

[68] Hösler, *Von Krain zu Slowenien*, 153.

[69] Vladimír Macura, *Znamení zrodu a české sny*. Prague, 2015, 47–79. Generally Durell, 'Linguistic Diversity', 101.

[70] A deputation to the governor in the autumn of 1848 opposed, among other things, Polish as the school language in Eastern Galicia. Turij, *Holovna Rus'ka Rada*, 81, 112. Instructive about the role of language Magocsi, *Roots of Ukrainian Nationalism*, 84–7.

[71] Comprehensive Anna Maria Harbig, *Die aufgezwungene Sprache. Deutsch in galizischen Schulen 1772–1848*. Białystok, 2006.

schools.[72] The glosses to the petitions reflect this. The communities from Złoczów and Stanisławów counties asked for an 'official Rusyn language'.[73] Another petitioner from Katusz demanded that 'the partition should be completed as soon as possible, and at the same time the Ruthenian should become the language of the Church' (replacing Old Slavonic or Polish respectively).[74]

On the Ruthenian side, the demand for an officially Ukrainian-speaking territory did not necessarily imply that the petitioners practised monolingualism. Just as the Czechs or Slovenes formulated their national-political demands in German,[75] some Ukrainians raised key demands, such as the recognition of their language, in Polish. This applied to the western part of the province, but also to Stanislau county (Stanisławów, Stanyslaviv, now Ivano-Frankyvsk) in eastern Galicia.[76] The use of different languages in the petitions was therefore not a sign of affiliation, but simply served the purpose of making sure that the relevant addressees would be able to understand the petitions.[77] Only in September 1848 did the Holovna Rada Rus'ka decide that, for official documents, 'everything should be written in Ruthenian whenever possible'.[78]

Although the Ruthenian National Council declared that as a distinguishing feature script was as important as language, Cyrillic was by no means dominant among the Ukrainian population. A quantitative analysis of signatures shows this.[79] The Polish National Council, on the other hand, claimed that most literate

[72] Vushko, *Politics of Cultural Retreat*, 237. This issue was then the focus of the Holovna Rada's negotiations, and it initially supported German-language schools. Wendland, *Russophile in Galizien*, 45. The Poles intervened with the Reichstag for the introduction of the Polish school language. Cf. Interpellation by Marian Dylewski. ÖStA, HHStA, LA ÖRT 1848/49, Box 85 (Anträge, Beschlüsse), fol. 209.

[73] E.g. Mosty wielkie, county Zołkiew, petition of 15 Apr. 1848. Box 132, fol. 1059.

[74] Petition n.d. Box 132, fol. 867.

[75] Hösler, *Von Krain zu Slowenien*, 152–3. On bilingualism in Bohemia, Robert Luft, 'Nationale Utraquisten in Böhmen: Zur Problematik "nationaler Zwischenstellungen" am Ende des 19. Jahrhunderts'. In Maurice Godé (ed.), *Allemands, Juifs et Tchèques à Prague 1890–1924/Deutsche, Juden und Tschechen in Prag*. Montpellier, 1996, 37–51; Alice Velková and Luboš Velek, 'Vnímání národnostní identity u venkovského obyvatelstva v Čechách na začátku 19. Století'. In Alice Velková and Jiří Pokorný (eds), *Nacionalismus, společnost a kultura ve střední Evropě 19. a 20. století*. Prague, 2007, 39–51.

[76] Cf. the petition of the municipality of Rizdwiony in the Stanislau county of 6 Aug. 1848, which read: 'My Obywateli…prosymo i zydajemo, aby nasza Zemla Hałecka na kotroy my of predwika zyiemo, mała swoju guberniu, swoy Riad, swoy Jazyk swoi Szkoły ryzszyi i myzszyi ruskii.' [We the inhabitants…ask and demand that in our land of Galicia, in which we have lived since time immemorial, its gubernium, administration, language and imperial and local schools be Ruthenian.] ÖStA, HHStA, LA ÖRT 1848/49, Box 132, fol. 1165.

[77] On various occasions, the petitioners gave their occupational description in German, e.g. 'gr. k. Pfarrer' from the 'Marktflecken Mosty wielkie, Zołkiewer Kreis', petition of 15 Aug. 1848 or another from the 'ruthenischen Lemberger Dekanate', Petition n. d. ÖStA, HHStA, LA ÖRT 1848/49, Box 132, fols. 1059 and 981. Cf. Struve, *Bauern und Nation in Galizien*, 378–81. The Ruthenian clergy, however, were considered Polonized. See Svjatoslav Pacholkiv, Emanzipation durch Bildung. Vienna, 2002, 65.

[78] Turij, *Holovna Rus'ka Rada*, 62.

[79] Random sampling of the petition forms with regard to the script in Osterkamp, 'Imperial Diversity in the Village', 741. Also Magocsi, *Roots of Ukrainian Nationalism*, 83–98.

Ruthenians did not read Cyrillic at all. This accusation does not prove to be true either.[80] Every letterhead of the Ukrainian petitioners was accompanied by a short Cyrillic text. Although the Latin script invariably appears more practised, the Cyrillic was not necessarily clumsy by comparison.[81] Indeed, some petitioners switched between the two; one woman from Old Bohowczan (Bohorodczany) in Stanislau county signed her forename in Latin and her surname in Cyrillic.[82]

Codification efforts were intended to bring an end to this ambiguity in the everyday use of language and script. The language dispute with the Poles and the *azbuczna wojna* (war over the alphabet)[83] prompted the Holovna Rada to commission lithographs of the Cyrillic script so that officials could 'start reading submissions in Ruthenian'.[84] For the patriotic Polish governor Gołuchowski, Cyrillic was a red rag. Like Zaleski, he associated it with a Ukrainian-speaking area that tended towards separatism, Russophilia, and Orthodoxy. Alphabets thus not only denoted affiliations but were also interpreted as proof of disloyalty in an era charged with nationalist politics. In the 1850s, the Czech ethnographer and ministerial official Josef Jireček drew up a Latin-based Ukrainian alphabet at Gołuchowski's request.[85] The Viennese government, however, did not accept Gołuchowski's plan and retained Cyrillic for the Ruthenians.[86]

There is no significant correlation between signatories' membership of the Greek Catholic Church—for many Ruthenians the most important feature of their nationality—and their ethnic origin. Many signatories to the last major signature campaign for the partition of Galicia in September 1848 included their denominations next to their names. Almost 100 per cent of them were Greek Catholics.[87] This close overlap was due to the Holovna Rada Rus'ka, which had organized the petitions and whose statutes admitted as members only 'honourable Ruthenians of the Greek rite'.[88] Counter-petitions from the same regions, on the other hand, revealed many Roman Catholics among the 'Ruthenians' and many Greek Catholics among the 'Poles'.[89]

Following the European tradition of religious affiliation influencing political affiliation, religion and denomination remained factors of national exclusion in

[80] Krevecz'ky'j, 'Sprava', 96: 119.

[81] E.g. Złotniki, Tarnopole county, Petitionen of 12 Aug. 1848, and several municipalities from Zołkiew county. ÖStA, HHStA, LA ÖRT 1848/49, Box 132, fols. 951, 1011, 1013, 1015, 1059.

[82] Alt-Bohowczan, Stanislau county, Petition n.d., Box 132, fol. 1167.

[83] Magocsi, *Roots of Ukrainian Nationalism*, 89–91; Świątek, *Gente Rutheni, natione Poloni*, 253–7.

[84] Examples of authorities not accepting Ruthenian submissions at Turij, *Holovna Rus'ka Rada*, 49, 106, 117.

[85] Magocsi, *Roots of Ukrainian Nationalism*, 91.

[86] Conference of Ministers of 11 June 1859. In Stefan Malfér (ed.), *ÖMR* 4/1: *Das Ministerium Rechberg (19. Mai 1859–3. März 1860)*. Vienna, 2003, No. 12, 43–45.

[87] Belonging to the Roman Catholic faith was explicitly noted, with 'ritus latini' or 'rit. lat.' as a deviation from the norm, cf. petitions from Iwanowka, Kopyczynce, Okno, Dubkowce, and Czernieszówka, county Tarnopol. ÖStA, HHStA, LA ÖRT 1848/49, Box 132, fols. 945–50.

[88] Turij, *Holovna Rus'ka Rada*, p. xix.

[89] Reactions from Holovna Rada Rus'ka were negative. Turij, *Holovna Rus'ka Rada*, 115.

1848. This is illustrated by the Galician Jews, some of whom formed a separate linguistic group. When Jews joined a particular national group, the 'other side' resorted to stigmatization and accusations of disloyalty.[90] This exclusion, which could be observed throughout the Habsburg Monarchy, found its way into the glosses of the petitions through descriptions of the relationship between Poles and Ukrainians.[91] An anti-Jewish resentment was often expressed with nonchalant matter-of-factness. A gloss from the town of Strye (Stryy, Stryi), later a railway junction and industrial centre, stated: 'Trade is insignificant...and exclusively in the hands of Jews. The crown land has no steamers on the Dniester and other navigable rivers, no railway.'[92] The Ukrainian elite rejected Jewish emancipation, and various petitions called for a ban on Jewish settlement, as was the case in Inner Austria.[93] The Polish National Council and Czartoryski's circle also excluded Jews from the Polish national idea, even if individual Poles supported their emancipation.[94]

The petitions deepened, or in some cases created, religious, national, and social rifts between Ukrainians, Poles, and Jews.[95] Galicia's Jewish population in particular feared losing out in the conflict between Ruthenians and Poles. In their petitions of 1848, Galician Jews therefore regularly asked for emancipation and the abolition of discriminatory practices such as the Jewish tax, rather than the partition of the province.[96] After the abolition of serfdom, the Galician Jews, like the Polish landlords, demanded compensation for the loss of their propination privileges.[97]

Whenever Jewish communities, or individual Jewish professional groups, took a stand on the partition of Galicia, they uniformly came out in opposition. Lists

[90] Martina Niedhammer, *Nur eine 'Geld-Emancipation'? Loyalitäten und Lebenswelten des Prager jüdischen Großbürgertums 1800–1867*. Göttingen, 2013, 87, 93; Sophia Kemlein, *Die Posener Juden 1815–1848*. Hamburg, 1997, 299–300; Julia Richers, *Jüdisches Budapest: Kulturelle Topographien einer Stadtgemeinde im 19. Jahrhundert*. Cologne, 2009, 201–8.

[91] On Jews in the rural areas, Struve, *Bauern und Nation in Galizien*, 384–433.

[92] Stryy, county Lemberg, petition n.d. ÖStA, HHStA, LA ÖRT 1848/49, Box 130, fol. 194.

[93] Box 130, fol. 194. Generally, Polonsky, 'Revolutionary Crisis of 1846–1849', 461–5.

[94] On the relationship between Poles and Jews on the emancipation question in neighbouring Prussia cf. Kemlein, *Die Posener Juden 1815–1848*, 285–90, 310–11; Dan Gawrecki, 'Některé problémy slezských měst v procesu modernizace 1740–1914'. In Pavel Kladiwa (ed.), *Město a městská společnost v procesu modernizace 1740–1918*. Ostrava, 2009, 143.

[95] Polonsky, 'Revolutionary Crisis of 1846–1849'; Rudnytsky, 'The Ukrainians in Galicia under Austrian Rule', 34.

[96] Hoerhan, *Petitionen*, 233–49. Stadion, the governor, also spoke out against the tax on Jews (including the kosher meat surcharge and the tax on lights). However, due to its significant income of 800,000 fl. per year, the Council of Ministers rejected this in May 1848. Cf. Council of Ministers of 5 May 1848. In Kletečka (ed.), *ÖMR* 1/1, No. 28, 157–61. The abolition still took place in the course of the year. Cf. Council of Ministers of 24 Aug. 1848. *ÖMR* 1/1, No. 111, 595–7.

[97] Propination privileges were feudal monopolies granting landowners the exclusive right to produce and sell alcoholic beverages within their estates. In Galicia, these rights were often leased to Jewish innkeepers and tavern operators; see ÖStA, HHStA, LA ÖRT 1848/49, Box 92 IX 'Petitionen' File 2, fol. 24. On the propination law, cf. Council of Ministers of 10 Sept. 1848. In Kletečka (ed.), *ÖMR* 1/1, No. 118, 619–22.

of signatures exist from urban professional groups in Brody such as the Jewish 'master butchers', 'master furriers', merchants, and tradesmen, and 'porters'.[98] Here, Jewish residents had already been represented on the municipal council for several decades.[99] The protests referred to the common economic space and, in particular, the 'existing relations in industry and trade' between all regions of the crown land.[100] However, they did not mention concerns about the anti-Jewish violence that had broken out during the Revolution in Prague, Budapest, and elsewhere.[101]

5.2. Everyday Life Together

The petitions offer an intimate insight into everyday life in Galicia. In many cases, they reveal not only what separated people, but also what united them across ethnic and religious boundaries. The signatory's occupation, social class, and religion were entered on a single page of the petition ballot. A comparison of ballots reveals an unsystematic blend of religious and linguistic backgrounds. In the county of Złoczów, from the municipalities of Túrsza and Toporów, Jewish 'Holzhändler' (wood merchants), tradesmen, and 'Hütelmacher' (hat makers) signed alongside Roman Catholic and Greek Catholic residents who listed their occupations as 'officyalista prywatny' (private clerk), 'kowal' (blacksmith), 'mechanik', 'ekonom' (farmer), or 'slusarcz' (locksmith).[102] From the town of Zbaraz in Tarnopol county, the list reveals a multi-denominational community including Roman Catholic land and property owners, a Protestant police inspector, a Jewish tradesman, a Greek Catholic landowner, a Jewish master carpenter, and a Roman Catholic mechanic.[103] One could carry on with this kaleidoscope of denominations and professions at length. Many women also appear amongst the petitioners.

The reality of everyday life in the villages, market towns, and cities had little in common with the rhetoric and declarations found in the petitions. While in 1849

[98] Petition n.d. ÖStA, HHStA, LA ÖRT 1848/49, Box 131, fols. 70–7 and 88–9.

[99] The participation of Jews in political life in this municipality, where they made up 80 per cent of the residents, led to a controversy between the municipality, the county office, and the government during the Vormärz. For this Börries Kuzmany, *Brody: Eine galizische Grenzstadt im langen 19. Jahrhundert*. Vienna, 2011, 132–7.

[100] Examples from Zloczów or Zatoscy in ÖStA, HHStA, LA ÖRT 1848/49, Box 131, fols. 27 and 86.

[101] On the 'Judenkrawalle' in Prague Franz Joseph Schopf, *Wahre und ausführliche Darstellung der am 11. März 1848 zur Erlangung einer constitutionellen Regierungs-Verfassung in der königlichen Hauptstadt Prag begonnenen Volks-Bewegung*. Leitmeritz, 1848, 37–40. On Budapest Richers, *Jüdisches Budapest*, 182–92.

[102] Petition county Złoczów, n.d. ÖStA, HHStA, LA ÖRT 1848/49, Box 131, fol. 68.

[103] Petition from Zbaraz, county Tarnopol, n.d. Box 131, fol. 139. Cf. the illustration at the start of this chapter.

the ruling elites were increasingly distancing themselves from each other, postulating an incontrovertible opposition between different nations that could not but result in conflict, everyday life, or at least parts of it, looked very different. Poles, Ukrainians, and Jews lived together in business and domestic communities and communicated through simplified colloquial terms despite being separated from each other by script (Latin, Cyrillic, Hebrew) and religion. This does not mean, however, that everyday communality could not turn violent in times of crisis.[104]

The rhetoric of a clearly defined nation was a fiction. On the basis of language, script, and religion, the Galician population could not be clearly divided into two distinct territories. For the future, however, mobilization through the petitions for and against partition inevitably entailed politicization and division. The petition campaign thus became a crossroads in the ethnicization of the Polish and Ukrainian identities, and in the question of whether the crown land's citizenship should be determined historically-politically or ethnically religiously.

5.3. Galicia's Partition From Without

The outbreak of the Polish–Ukrainian conflict bewildered the other nationalities in the Austrian Diet. After all, it was supposed to have been settled at the Slav Congress in Prague in June 1848.[105] A federal partition of Galicia had not been included in Palacký's idea of a federal nationality state, nor was it considered in the Kremsier draft constitution of March 1849. Indeed, partition plans could not find a majority in Kremsier.[106] There were other, more pressing, problems facing the reorganization of the empire.

This disregard caused resentment among the Ukrainians. Because of their loyalty to the emperor, they saw themselves as 'Tyroleans of the East'.[107] They now found that, while similar partition plans for a German and an Italian Tyrol had been approved by the committee members in Kremsier, theirs had not.[108] The majority of the Constitutional Committee felt closer to the Italian liberals than to conservative clerics like Jachymovyč.

[104] Haumann, 'Juden in der ländlichen Gesellschaft Galiziens', 40 and 47–50. On socio-economic issues Józef Buszko, *Zum Wandel der Gesellschaftsstruktur in Galizien und in der Bukowina*. Vienna, 1978.

[105] Wendland, *Russophile in Galizien*, 43; Vladimir Hostička, 'Slovanský sjezd a ukrajinci'. In Václav Veber (ed.), *150 let Slovanského sjezdu (1848): Historie a současnost*. Prague, 2000, 69.

[106] Springer, *Protokolle des Verfassungsausschusses*, 7 and 348–9. See also 'Protokolle des Verfassungsausschusses vom 6.1. bis 4.3.1848'. ÖStA, HHStA, LA ÖRT 1848/49, Box 80 File 1 and 2, Teilung und der Emanzipation der Juden in Galizien. For a summary of the discussions of the constitutional committee over partition plans in Jan. 1849, Maner, *Galizien*, 99–101.

[107] Magocsi, *Roots of Ukrainian Nationalism*, 65.

[108] Krevecz'ky'j, 'Sprava', 95: 69, 72. However, the partition of Tyrol had not been met with the emperor's approval.

The Kremsier Diet was not the only stage for the reorganization of Galicia. The Austrian government under Schwarzenberg also took concrete steps.[109] After the Lemberg Uprising in early November 1848, Governor Zaleski was replaced by Agenor Gołuchowski, another Pole, who was considered to be less nationalistic. He won the sympathy of the Ruthenians by speaking Ukrainian at his first meeting with representatives of the Holovna Rada, but this ultimately turned out to be an empty diplomatic gesture.[110] Shortly afterwards, a Ukrainian deputation again demanded partition of the crown land. The government responded by creating a new, separate administrative region with its seat in Krakow.[111] Unlike the Transylvanian Saxons or the Romanians of Bukovina, however, the Ukrainians were not promised a crown land of their own.[112] In a political culture of fine distinctions, the Ruthenian question did not play a prominent role in either the Reichstag or the government.

The partition of Galicia 'from above', however, was more than a mere administrative reorganization; it amounted in fact to federalization. In a memorandum dated 30 March 1849, the Ruthenians reiterated their desire for their own crown land.[113] The minister of the interior, Stadion, signalled to them that this request was premature and appealed to their loyalty to the imperial house.[114] Hidden behind the veil of historic state law unity, nevertheless an ethnicization of public life was made possible in the plan for two separate curiae at the provincial diet.[115] The new Galician governor Gołuchowski protested vehemently against Vienna's decision. He envisaged Eastern Galicia being driven into the hands of Russia and even predicted a Ruthenian war of independence.[116] The new minister of the interior, Alexander von Bach, finally took the wind out or his sails. He divided Galicia not into two, but into three administrative units, based in Lemberg, Krakow, and Stanislau.[117] The Viennese authorities resorted to Karl Czoernig's ethnographic maps[118] to define the borders

[109] Comprehensively Berger Waldenegg, 'Die Bukowina war glücklicher', 23–46.

[110] Turij, *Holovna Rus'ka Rada*, 106.

[111] For the composition of the Galician counties see Mark, *Galizien unter österreichischer Herrschaft*, 4–9. Also, Council of Ministers of 4 May 1850. In Kletečka Schmied-Kowarzik (eds), *ÖMR* 2/3: *Das Ministerium Schwarzenberg (1. Mai 1850–30. September 1850)*. Vienna, 2006, No. 337, 12.

[112] Berger Waldenegg, 'Die Bukowina war glücklicher', 35; Danilák, *Halyc'ki, bukovyns'ki, zakarpats'ki ukraïnci*.

[113] Turij, *Holovna Rus'ka Rada*, 119; Krevecz'ky'j, 'Sprava', 94: 75.

[114] Krevecz'ky'j, 'Sprava', 95: 78.

[115] On this perception Krevecz'ky'j, 'Sprava', 95: 77.

[116] Krevecz'ky'j, 'Sprava', 95: 79–81. On the debate between Bach and Gołuchowski see Council of Ministers of 4 May 1850. In Kletečka and Schmied-Kowarzik (eds), *ÖMR* 2/3, No. 337, 11–15.

[117] Verordnung des Innenministers, 8 Oct. 1850, No. 383/1850 RGBl. See Krevecz'ky'j, 'Sprava', 95: 82. In the meantime, four counties were also being discussed. Council of Ministers of 4 May 1850. In Kletečka and Schmied-Kowarzik (eds), *ÖMR* 2/3, No. 337, 11–15. On the decision cf. Council of Ministers of 25 May 1850. *ÖMR* 2/3, No. 342, 34–8.

[118] Krevecz'ky'j, 'Sprava', 95: 108. Pieter M. Judson, *The Habsburg Empire: A New History*. Cambridge, MA, and London, 2016, 242–3. See also Steffi Marung, Matthias Middell, and Uwe Müller, 'Territorialisierung in Ostmitteleuropa bis zum Ersten Weltkrieg'. In Frank Hadler and Matthias Middell (eds), *Handbuch einer transnationalen Geschichte Ostmitteleuropas*. Vol. 1: *Von der Mitte des 19. Jahrhunderts bis um Ersten Weltkrieg*. Göttingen, 2017, 73.

of these three counties, which were not to be 'strictly separated but grouped according to nationalities'.[119]

From a typological perspective this reorganization combined elements of executive federalism and a federation of nationalities. Although the three 'governorate counties' were subordinate to the central crown land administration in Lemberg (Lwów, Lviv), they resembled federal constituent units. They had the right of self-governance and were entitled to make their own laws, except in matters affecting the entire crown land.[120] Their policy fields included infrastructure, finance, welfare, education, and religious affairs.[121] The three representative bodies were formally called curiae of the provincial diets but actually resembled provincial diets themselves. Thun, who was hostile to this plan, raised this point in the Council of Ministers:

> Galicia is to be one crown land, but in reality it is to be divided into three crown lands, with separate representation, taxation, provincial legislation and territorial division. A governor and a central committee are proposed to represent unity, but the central committee...is a nullity.[122]

Bach's intention was that the burgher and peasant classes should predominate in the representative bodies. However, this reorganization was never carried out.[123]

The revolutionary agenda of the year 1848 and its leitmotif of the 'national' not only captured the imagination of the population but also changed the thinking within the regime. This can be seen in the Schwarzenberg government's plans for the partition of Galicia during the neo-absolutist phase. A remarkable plan, again formulated by Bach, envisaged the creation of a separate crown land, 'Ruthenia', which would unite the territories of Galicia, Bukovina, and Transcarpathian Hungary and take into account the 'governing principle of equality of nationalities'.[124] In the autumn of 1851, when the Council of Ministers contemplated revision of the 'imposed' March Constitution, Bach submitted his own memorandum.[125]

[119] Council of Ministers of 1 July 1850. In Kletečka and Schmied-Kowarzik (eds), *ÖMR* 2/3, No. 359, 112–18.

[120] Kaiserliches Patent vom 29.09.1850 über die Landesverfassung Galiziens, No. 386/1850 RGBl.

[121] Krevecz'ky'j, 'Sprava', 95: 111. The provincial administration was also to push for the 'colonization' of Galicia. See Council of Ministers of 27 July 1850. In Malfér and Schmied-Kowarzik (eds), *ÖMR* 2/2: *Das Ministerium Schwarzenberg (8. Jänner 1850–30. April 1850)*. Vienna, 2005, No. 373.

[122] Council of Ministers of 2 Sept. 1850, In Kletečka and Schmied-Kowarzik (eds), *ÖMR* 2/3, No. 388, 236.

[123] Critical on this Krauß, Council of Ministers of 2 Sept. 1850. *ÖMR* 2/3, No. 388, here 235.

[124] On similar plans of the Bukovina Ruthenians Peter Burian, *Die Nationalitäten in 'Cisleithanien' und das Wahlrecht der Märzrevolution 1848/49*. Graz and Cologne, 1962, 115.

[125] The memorandum quoted below is not dated, but due to its content it is probably connected with Bach's proposals for an independent Ruthenian part of Galicia, as he presented them on 11 Nov. 1851 to the Commission for the Revision of the Constitution. He did not find a majority, see Berger Waldenegg, 'Die Bukowina war glücklicher', 25.

He called for the Carpathian Slavs to be 'treated as isolated from the Magyars'.[126] His political motive was to weaken the power of both Habsburg Poland and Hungary. The Ukrainians, by contrast, found Bach's favour for their 'monarchism' and loyalty to the emperor.[127]

Bach had to justify granting a separate crown land to a hitherto underprivileged group that had only been recognized as a 'nation' in 1848. In the memorandum to his ministerial colleagues, Bach therefore relied on other political views, including the predominantly liberal stance that equal nationality rights presupposed 'equal capability' of the nationalities. The Ukrainians, a majority peasant community, were regarded as an uneducated, 'inert mass'. Bach argued against this; the Ruthenians were 'oppressed, not inert'. Equal ability could only be achieved through equal rights, not vice versa. In the end, however, both Bach's idea of a 'Ruthenia' comprising Galician, Bukovinian, and Hungarian territories and his proposed partition of Galicia into three 'quasi crown lands' with representative bodies fell victim to his own turn towards neo-absolutism. In 1854, Galicia was divided into two purely administrative counties, the Lemberg and Krakow counties, whose borders were aligned with the Polish and Ukrainian majorities.[128] In 1868, Galicia as a whole was granted informal autonomy, consolidating the supremacy of the Polish-speaking ruling elite in the provincial diet, administration, and society. As in the neighbouring Russian Empire, however, the question of the national character of the Ukrainians remained topical in the Habsburg Monarchy, as did the inadequate political participation of the peasantry.

A Federal History of the Habsburg Empire, 1815–1918. Jana Osterkamp, Oxford University Press.
 DOI: 10.1093/9780198943631.003.0006

[126] All the following quotations, unless otherwise noted, are taken from Bach's Memorandum 'Karpathische Slawen und Ruthenen. Frage der Wiederzuteilung derselben an Ungarn'. In: ÖStA, Allgemeines Verwaltungsarchiv, Nachlass Bach, Box 33.

[127] On this argument of the 'Ruthenians as a means to an end' to weaken the position of the Poles, cf. Berger Waldenegg, 'Die Bukowina war glücklicher', 32–45; Andreas Kappeler, *Kleine Geschichte der Ukraine*. Munich, 2009, 122.

[128] Verordnung der Minister des Innern, der Finanzen und der Justiz, 19 Jan. 1853, No. 10/1853 RBGl. See also Verordnung des Ministers des Innern, 30 Apr. 1854, No. 112/1854 RGBl. Whether it is correct to speak of 'two new lands', as Wilhelm Brauneder does, would depend on future research into administrative practice. Cf. Wilhelm Brauneder, 'Die Habsburgermonarchie als zusammengesetzter Staat'. In Hans-Jürgen Becker (ed.), *Zusammengesetzte Staatlichkeit in der Europäischen Verfassungsgeschichte*. Berlin, 2006, 219.

Figure 6.1 'Viribus Unitis—Treue und Eintracht der österreichischen Völker' [Fidelity and Unity Among the Austrian Peoples]. Lithograph. Vienna, 1849.

6
Historic Crown Land Federalism and the Unfinished Constitutions, 1849 and 1860/61

It can be said that 4 March 1849 was the federal constitutional moment of the nineteenth century. In a manner typical of the Habsburg Monarchy, an anti-revolutionary, restorative attitude on the part of the emperor and the government was combined with a cautious will to reform. The emperor's 'Imperial Constitution', promulgated on this day, gave birth to a new type of federalism: historic crown land federalism. Its novel element was the constitutional principle of federal equality, to be further realized in a federation of nationalities. To balance the scales between restoration and revolution, however, this federation was linked to 'historical' countries rather than ethnic-nationally defined territories. The revolutionary ideas of the nation state and the federation of nationalities had failed. Nevertheless, a mood of cautious optimism prevailed, for the path from empire to federalism seemed to be clearly marked.

The government commissioned artistic depictions to illustrate the constitutional promise of federal unity.[1] By the mid-nineteenth century, mass-produced graphics had replaced historical painting as the state's preferred artistic medium. In this way, the government was able to disseminate its federal constitutional promise through the popular press, even if it ultimately failed to keep it. At Christmas 1849, Austrian newspapers advertised a lithograph illustrating the federal unity of the nationalities envisaged by the constitution. Before a portrait of the youthful Emperor Franz Joseph I and an allegorical figure of 'Austria', which presented the constitution to the viewer, 'men of every nationality in the empire clasp hands to seal the union' (Figure 6.1). They stood side by side 'without distinction'.[2] The lithograph, titled 'Loyalty and Concord of the Austrian Peoples—Viribus Unitis', bore Franz Joseph's imperial motto and was likely the result of discussions with the Austrian minister of the interior, Alexander von Bach.[3]

[1] Selma Krasa-Florian, *Allegorie der Austria: Die Entstehung des Gesamtstaatsgedankens in der österreichisch-ungarischen Monarchie und die bildende Kunst*. Vienna, 2007, 81–2.

[2] 'Kunst', *Österreichisches Bürgerblatt für Verstand, Herz und gute Laune*, 1 Dec. 1849, 768. Cf. also advertisements in *Illustrierte Zeitung*, 1 Dec. 1849, 350; *Die Geissel: Tagblatt aller Tagblätter*, 6 Dec. 1849, 1140.

[3] Krasa-Florian, *Allegorie der Austria*, 80.

The Imperial Constitution of March 1849, whose core idea is illustrated in this picture, was built on the Kremsier draft. The constitutional committee of the revolutionary Austrian Reichstag had agreed on a model of historic crown land federalism. However, its passage through parliament, scheduled for 4 March 1849, failed, as the emperor and the government dissolved the Kremsier Reichstag by military force and imposed Franz Joseph's 'Imperial Constitution', the so-called March Constitution, on all his lands, including Hungary and Lombardy-Venetia.[4] Its normative principle was historic crown land federalism, which was to become decisive for the Austrian part of the empire after 1867. Historic crown land federalism offered the constitutional drafters, both in 1849 and later, the means to acknowledge two completely different interpretations of 'nation' in their federal order. Today, these would be labelled *Sprachnation* (linguistic nation) and *Landesnation* (provincial nation). It is in this ambiguity of the 'nation' that the history of Habsburg federalism clearly differs from other federations in Europe and the rest of the world.

The double meaning of 'nation' was further echoed in contemporary advertising. The leaflet accompanying the lithograph 'Loyalty and Concord' drew the attention of potential buyers to the linguistic communities that spoke German, Czech, Polish, Ukrainian, Slovenian, or Italian. On the other hand, the confederated 'men of all nationalities' were described in the brochure as 'Silesians, Carniolans, Carinthians, Salzburgers, Serbs, Lodomers, Slavonians, Croats, Hungarians, Bohemians, Lombards and Venetians, Dalmatians, Galicians, Austrians, Styrians, Tyroleans, Moravians and Transylvanians'. It was thus artfully left open whether the federal union was based on a linguistic-ethnic communities or on historic territories, i.e. whether Germans, Czechs, and Poles shook hands as Austrian 'peoples' or representatives of the historical crown lands such as Bohemia and Galicia.

Although many liberals welcomed the tenor of the constitution as the dawn of a constitutional era, they found its unilateral imposition intolerable.[5] The restorative turn in Europe soon led to another about-face in Vienna. Less than three years after its adoption, at the end of 1851, Franz Joseph repealed the constitution.[6] It was replaced by neo-absolutism with its top-down territorialization and a multi-tiered, 'organic' executive federalism.[7] Vienna then ruled without

[4] Imperial Manifesto of 4 Mar. 1849, whereby the Diet of Kremsier is dissolved and the peoples of Austria are granted an Imperial Constitution for the entire Empire of Austria by the Emperor's own authority, No. 149/1849 RGBl., as well as Imperial Patent of 4 Mar. 1849, containing the Imperial Constitution for the Empire of Austria, No. 150/1849 (so-called March Constitution). Fundamental rights were granted for all provinces except Hungary: Imperial Patent of 4 Mar. 1849 on the political rights guaranteed by the constitutional form of government, No. 151/1849 RGBl.

[5] Pieter M. Judson, *The Habsburg Empire: A New History*. Cambridge, MA, and London, 2016, 215–17.

[6] On the deconstitutionalization recently Georg Seiderer, *Österreichs Neugestaltung: Verfassungspolitik und Verwaltungsreform im österreichischen Neoabsolutismus unter Alexander Bach 1849–1859*. Vienna, 2015, 110–33.

[7] Cf. the Imperial Patents of 31 Dec. 1851, No. 2 and No. 11/1852 RGBl. For more details, see Chapter 4.

a parliament until 1860. Paradoxically, the rapid growth and success of governmental and administrative activity often favoured precisely those parties which had been defeated in Kremsier: the liberal bourgeoisie and certain nationalities.[8] Politically, the 1850s meant the building of a 'liberal empire'.[9] The constitutional turning point only came a decade later, following serious setbacks in foreign policy and military affairs.

In 1860 the provincial parliaments reopened and a parliament for the entire empire, the Reinforced Imperial Council. Once again, discussions ensued about the future constitutional basis of the empire. The emperor, however, abhorred constitutional semantics and was concerned lest revolutionary tendencies be awakened. He would not countenance any infringement on his monarchical omnipotence.[10] Constitutional innovations were thus regularly concealed behind old-fashioned and pre-modern—and thus more acceptable—descriptors such as 'patents', 'diplomas', 'compensations', or 'provincial ordinances'.

6.1. Federal Equality: Kremsier and Olomouc, March 1849

The constitution of 4 March 1849 had been co-drafted by the government, the imperial court, high-ranking state officials, and, informally, members of the Kremsier Reichstag. Its ratification created a unique political-legal moment: for the first time in its history, Austria now had a uniform constitution for *all* Habsburg territories. Even the Hungarian and Italian lands, which in a secessionist temper had steered clear of the Kremsier Diet, now found Franz Joseph's constitution imposed upon them.

The foundations for this innovation had been laid at Kremsier. In March 1849, the constitutional committee approved the proposals of the German-Moravian representative Kajetan Mayer, who, in critical disagreement with Palacký, dismissed a federation of nationalities in favour of converting the historic crown lands into federal constituent states.[11] Franz Joseph and the Schwarzenberg government took their cue from this preliminary work, but enacted the constitution as an imperial patent, i.e. as a law of the sovereign, without the participation of parliament.[12]

The historic crown lands were to form the basis of the new state structure. On closer inspection, however, justifying the new layout of the crown lands by

[8] John Deak, *Forging a Multinational State*. Stanford, CA, 2015, 101.

[9] Judson, *Habsburg Empire*, 282.

[10] Helmut Rumpler, *Eine Chance für Mitteleuropa*. Vienna, 1997, 374

[11] Draft of the Constitutional Charter for the Austrian States, Resolution of the Constitutional Committee of 4 Mar. 1849 (Kremsier Draft), reprinted in josef Redlich, *Das österreichische Staats- und Reichsproblem*. Vol. 1: *Der dynastische Reichsgedanke und die Entfaltung des Problems bis zur Verkündigung der Reichsverfassung von 1861*. Part 2: *Exkurse und Anmerkungen*. Leipzig, 1920, 215–26.

[12] Imperial Constitution, No. 150/1849 RGBl. For this purpose, the Council of Ministers had adopted and revised the Kremsier draft constitution. Redlich, *Staats- und Reichsproblem*, 1/2. 86–100.

appealing to 'history' proved no less artificial and nebulous than the revolution's idea of 'nation'.[13] The final territorial division largely corresponded with the boundaries of the former princely and estates territories. Bohemia, Moravia, Silesia, Lower and Upper Austria, and other inner-Austrian lands continued to bear their ancient dynastic names. In the case of the 'Grand Duchy of Cracow', a suitably historic moniker was revived.[14] A profusion of wholly new independent crown lands sprang up across the empire: Bukovina, Gorizia-Gradisca, Istria with Trieste, Croatia-Slavonia with the Littoral, the Voivodeship of Serbia, Carniola, and Salzburg. Despite this constitutional upheaval, the Ruthenian and Polish parts of Galicia remained firmly, if uneasily, bound together.[15]

For a systematic view of the federal reorganization of March 1849, it is worth comparing the Kremsier draft constitution and the emperor's constitutional octroi. Their differences are easily identified. First, the fundamental ambition of the revolution—greater political participation, liberty, and legal protection—once again receded into the background in favour of an adherence to monarchical prerogatives as well as the search for a balance between states, provinces, and peoples. Second, the government's legitimacy was derived from long-established foundations such as history, state law, and monarchic-dynastic cohesion, rather than from modern ideas of the freedom and equality of 'one people, one nation', and the concurrent rights to self-government and individual self-determination. The equal rights of individuals and nationalities (in the double sense of linguistic nation and provincial nation) were nonetheless extended.

Independence and Equality of the Crown Lands

On this last point, the similarity between the Kremsier constitutional draft and the Olomouc constitutional octroi is particularly striking. The Habsburg model of the historic crown land federalism was based on a unique, multi-tiered system of equal rights. Both constitutions subdivided the crown lands according to their historic appellations—and thus according to their dynastic rank—into kingdoms, duchies, margravates, and counties. Despite such hierarchical concerns, the constitutions nevertheless guaranteed each crown land the same degree of 'independence' (Olomouc) or 'autonomy' (Kremsier).[16] Lithographs such as

[13] See Karl Brockhausen, *Organisation und Instanzenzug der politischen Behörden in Österreich*. Vienna and Leipzig, 1908, 55, who points out that ten historical countries were defined before 1849, whereas fourteen were defined afterwards.

[14] On Krauß's proposal Redlich, *Staats- und Reichsproblem*, 1/2. 87.

[15] §§ 1 and 4 Imperial Constitution, No. 150/1849 RGBl.

[16] § 4 Imperial Constitution, No. 150/1849 RGBl.; § 5 Kremsier Draft Constitution. The Kremsier draft explicitly mentioned the full equality of the crown lands. Cf. also Gerald Stourzh, 'Länderautonomie und Gesamtstaat in Österreich 1848–1918'. In Stourzh, *Der Umfang der österreichischen Geschichte*. Vienna, 2011, 46.

'Barque with Austria' or 'Loyalty and Concord' made this claim to independence and crown land equality clear. The allegorical figures of each province are the same size and arranged on the same horizontal plane.

The two constitutions nevertheless differed regarding the equality of the *Länder*. According to paragraph 4 of the Kremsier draft, the 'imperial provinces' shared 'a relationship of full equality' with one other. The emperor's constitutional octroi significantly limited this federal idea by granting some crown lands more privileges than others (paragraphs 71–7). The constitution honoured promises made to the 'Voivodeship of Serbia' in 'older patents of liberty and recent imperial declarations', while Lombardy and the Veneto were granted their own special status. Croatia-Slavonia, with the Littoral and Fiume, was promised 'its idiomatic institutions'. Transylvania, meanwhile, was to regain its independence from Hungary. The remaining Hungarian nationalities were guaranteed equality 'in all spheres of public and civil life' as well as the 'equality of all nations inhabiting the land' of Transylvania (paragraphs 71, 74).

In a manner typical of federations, the Chamber of the Crown Lands in the Kremsier draft was composed based on parity, with each land receiving the same number of votes. In the case of the imperial octroi, the future Chamber of Crown Lands was merely supposed to 'take into account' the different parts of the empire.[17] Otherwise, so the argument ran, the legislature would be 'very costly, very numerous, and—still—not at all well composed', since few qualified deputies could be found in the smallest provinces like Bukovina or Salzburg.[18] The most important restriction imposed on the federal legislature by the constitutional octroi, however, was to reduce the *Reichsrat* (Imperial Council) to a merely 'advisory' body. Contrary to ideas developed in Kremsier, the Council would not become an imperial parliament with legislative powers. Against this background, the intention to establish an Imperial Court that would adjudicate disputes between the empire and the crown lands, as well as between the crown lands themselves, appeared to be little more than a consolation prize.[19]

The choice of historic crown land federalism (rather than a federation of linguistic nations) strengthened provincial patriotism. Linguistic-national spaces, as reflected in the model of a federation of nationalities, did not play a role in shaping the territories of the crown lands. Nonetheless, the introduction of linguistic-national counties was still envisaged: the Kremsier draft constitution by Kajetan Mayer, and the Olomouc constitution by Minister of the Interior Franz

[17] § 99 Para. 2 Kremsier Draft Constitution provided for six representatives per crown land; § 97 Imperial Constitution, No. 150/1849 RGBl.

[18] Redlich, *Staats- und Reichsproblem*, 1/2. 90.

[19] § 106 Para. 1 Imperial Constitution, No. 150/1849 RGBl.; § 140 Para. 3 Kremsier Draft Constitution. This provision stands in the tradition of the 'Austrägal-Ordnung' [Arbitration Order] of 16 June 1817 in the German Confederation.

von Stadion still envisaged the introduction of linguistic-national counties.[20] Galicia, Styria, and provinces such as Bohemia were to be divided into counties with either single- or dual-language administrations. While this proposal, like so many others, was ultimately never realized, the idea of national counties remained a central topic in debates on federalization until 1918.

Although historic crown land federalism did not align territorial and linguistic boundaries in March 1849, it did create other effective mechanisms to nurture, preserve, and bolster linguistic nationalities (*Sprachnationen*) besides territorial ones (*Landesnationen*). Central passages in both the Kremsier and Olomouc constitutions declared that 'tribes', 'nationalities', and 'peoples' had 'equal rights'[21] and that the 'nationalities' were to have the right to preserve their nationality and language.[22]

Equality of Provincial and Linguistic Nations

The federalism of March 1849 thus guaranteed a two-fold equality for the territorial and linguistic nations. Due to the multi-ethnic and multinational character of the Habsburg Monarchy, it was clear to all sides that the territorial civic nation and the linguistic nation could not be reconciled in everyday reality, either on a small scale (in the provinces) or at large (in the empire). The innovation of Habsburg historic crown land federalism was to integrate these two concepts.

In the debate at the Conference of Ministers on the constitutional octroi in February 1849, the minister of the interior, Alexander von Bach, captured this idea of a federal equality of the provinces, peoples, and nations: 'If the unity of the monarchy is a postulate, it will be attainable.... There can be no privileged nations, otherwise the other provinces, even the Germans, would want to secede.'[23]

By introducing equal rights for the 'nationalities', the authors of the constitution modified the revolutionary demands for 'one nation, one state'. They integrated the concept of 'nation' in all its complexity. The drafters referred to the populations of the crown lands as 'nations' (e.g. Bohemians, Moravians, Tyroleans, Galicians) but also fixed constitutional standards of equality for the linguistic nations within and across the crown lands (e.g. Germans, Czechs, Italians). In so doing, they gave a *multi-ethnic* dimension to *historic* crown land federalism. In the Kremsier draft, the state was obliged to guarantee 'all languages customary in the province equal

[20] § 34 Imperial Constitution, No. 150/1849 RGBl. Dazu, Redlich, *Staats- und Reichsproblem*, 1/2. 88.

[21] The classic treatment is Gerald Stourzh, *Die Gleichberechtigung der Nationalitäten in der Verfassung und Verwaltung Österreichs 1848–1918*. Vienna, 1985.

[22] § 5 Imperial Constitution, No. 150/1849 RGBl.

[23] Council of Ministers of 20 Feb. 1849. In Thomas Kletečka, 'Einleitung'. In Kletečka (ed.), *Protokolle des Österreichischen Ministerrates* (hereafterr ÖMR). 2/1: *Das Ministerium Schwarzenberg (5. Dezember 1848–7. Jänner 1850)*. Vienna, 2002, No. 20, 119–25.

rights in schools, offices, and public life'.[24] The government, afraid of creating financially unfeasible demands, dropped this commitment in its own Imperial Constitution.[25]

Even without this constitutional obligation, the Austrian government nonetheless adopted far-reaching measures after March 1849 to promote the ten recognized languages of the provinces. Provincial and imperial laws were published in all provincial languages; in Galicia, this included printing them in Ukrainian Cyrillic alongside Polish.[26] In the provinces of St Stephen's Crown, the primacy of Hungarian, which had been established in 1830, was abolished.[27] The imperial language policy provided the nationalities with important building blocks for their future cultural development. The institutionalization of the respective standard languages kept scientific commissions busy, developing, for example, specific legal glossaries for Czech, Ukrainian, and Croatian. Part of this government policy was a mother-tongue school system, albeit with considerable regional differences.[28] The minister of education, Leo von Thun-Hohenstein, also allowed for variation in higher education. Ethno-religious nations such as the Ruthenians, Romanians, or Serbs have now developed further as linguistic and cultural nations.[29] In view of this diversity and complexity, German was imposed as an official language throughout the empire to provide a common foundation.

Individual Equality?

The third key element of the constitutional and federal system of equality was a general imperial right to citizenship. The two constitutions diverged most on the issues of civil rights and political participation. The Kremsier draft differed from the Olomouc octroi in that the latter granted only individual civil rights of 'burghers', whereas the former viewed citizens as politically self-determined 'citoyens'. The Kremsier draft referred collectively to all imperial citizens as the

[24] § 19 Para. 2 Kremsier Draft Constitution, Anhang 'Grundrechte'.

[25] Redlich, *Staats- und Reichsproblem*, 1/2. 87.

[26] Svjatoslav Pacholkiv, *Emanzipation durch Bildung*. Vienna, 2002, 71.

[27] Henrik Marczali, *Ungarische Verfassungsgeschichte*. Tübingen, 1910, 130 and 154. On the importance of Hungarian as an official language in the Hungarian national movement cf. István Deák, *The Lawful Revolution: Louis Kossuth and the Hungarians 1848–1849*. New York, 1979, 43–7.

[28] Comparing different crown lands, Hannelore Burger, *Sprachenrecht und Sprachgerechtigkeit im österreichischen Unterrichtswesen 1867–1918*. Vienna, 1995. For different priorities at the provincial level in the field of education, see Chapter 9.

[29] Cf. Pacholkiv, *Emanzipation durch Bildung*, 76 and 230; Emanuel Turczynski, *Konfession und Nation: Zur Frühgeschichte der serbischen und rumänischen Nationsbildung*. Düsseldorf, 1976, 271; Emilia Hrabovec, 'Zwischen Nation und Religion, Thron und Altar'. In Hrabovec, Dušan Kováč, and Arnold Suppan (eds), *Die Habsburgermonarchie und die Slowaken 1849–1867*. Bratislava, 2001, 79–109; Keith Hitchins, *Orthodoxy and Nationality: Andreiu Saguna and the Rumanians of Transylvania 1846–1873*. Cambridge, MA, 1977, 199–223.

'people'.[30] This meant a community entitled to parliamentary participation in the affairs of the state. Indeed, the Constitutional Committee had explicitly referred to the 'people' as the source of sovereignty. When the Schwarzenberg government remonstrated against this democratic idea, the committee rephrased this statement: 'The entirety of the citizens of the state is the people.'[31]

In the imperial constitutional octroi, the word 'people' was no longer present. Sovereignty radiated from the emperor to his 'peoples', not the other way round. The participation of popular representatives in the Imperial Council was limited to an advisory capacity and without any legislative authority. Consequently, there was no common term for all citizens of the *Reich*; there were individual 'peoples', but not one collective 'people'. At the personal level, however, all citizens were united by the 'imperial citizenship law'.[32]

This 'mark of political affiliation' was not to be underestimated.[33] Common citizenship assured equal rights and duties to all imperial citizens in the empire and its crown lands. The civic rights (which were, however, more extensive in the Kremsier draft than in the emperor's) guaranteed equality and legal protection.[34] The constitutional octroi thus laid the foundation for the *bourgeois* society of the nineteenth century, but not for a *civil* society based on political participation.

Multi-Tiered Equality Rights

The two constitutions of March 1849 revolutionized the empire's previously asymmetrical framework of governance. The *Vormärz* system had bound individual territories and communities to the imperial centre in an asymmetrical fashion. The legal equality of 1849, which resulted from the March Revolution, established both a federal territorial system and the equality of provincial nations, linguistic nations, and individual citizens. Only the equality of religions, which had featured in the Kremsier draft constitution, was unachievable once the emperor and the conservatives in his government took control and imposed their octroi.

[30] § 1 Para. 3 Kremsier Draft Constitution, Appendix 'Fundamental Rights'.

[31] § 1 Para. 3 Kremsier Draft Constitution, Appendix 'Fundamental Rights'. Cf. Kletečka, 'Einleitung'. In Kletečka, (ed.), *ÖMR* 2/1, pp. xix–xx.

[32] § 23 Imperial Constitution, No. 150/1849 RGBl. Cf. on this also Hannelore Burger, *Heimatrecht und Staatsbürgerschaft österreichischer Juden*. Vienna, 2014, 63. However, the implementing law on imperial citizenship was not enacted.

[33] Dieter Gosewinkel, 'Staatsbürgerschaft als politische Zugehörigkeit'. In Katrin Boeckh, Krisztina Busa, Antje Himmelreich, Edvin Pezo, and Natali Stegmann (eds), *Staatsbürgerschaft und Teilhabe*. Munich, 2014, 17. Cf. Hannelore Burger, 'Passwesen und Staatsbürgerschaft'. In Waltraud Heindl-Langer and Edith Saurer (eds), *Grenze und Staat*. Vienna, 2000, 161–7.

[34] § 1 Para. 3 Kremsier Draft Constitution, Appendix 'Fundamental Rights'; Imperial Patent on Fundamental Rights, No. 151/1849 RGBl.

6.2. The Emperor's 'Constitutions' in the Crown Lands

With the 'Imperial Constitution' of 4 March 1849, the monarch and his Conference of Ministers sought to impose crown land federalism. However, the practice of this federalism in everyday life could no longer be ordered 'from above'. A practised federalism is based on cooperation and cohesion. A true federal union between the empire and the provinces could therefore only have been achieved through collaboration with the provinces. The system of constitutional equality of provincial nations, linguistic nations, and citizens also depended on the support of the crown lands and the provincial elites, as well as a close alignment with the provincial constitutions. However, the liberally oriented Schwarzenberg government lost the support of the old elites when it abolished the pre-1848-era estates constitution.

The new federal constitution contradicted the traditional and de facto privileges of individual territories, as well as of particular social, religious, and national communities that had arisen under the political logic of the old empire. Resentment among the regional elites was caused not only by the planned federal equality of all crown lands, but also by the newly introduced equality of the linguistic nations. In Transylvania, for example, the Magyars, Szeklers, and Germans refused to recognize the previously underprivileged Romanians as their equals. The same tensions erupted between Poles and Ruthenians in Galicia and Italians and Slovenes in the Littoral.

Kremsier's draft constitution had given the provinces extensive freedom of self-organization. Within three months, they were to submit new provincial constitutions and elect their representatives to the Reichstag. In 1849, however, the government massively curtailed their right to constitutional autonomy. A commission, chaired by the minister of the interior and justice, Bach, was now charged with drafting new provincial constitutions. While he invited provincial representatives to participate, they were treated merely as 'confidants' and not as equal partners.[35] Deputies from the Kremsier Reichstag, meanwhile, arrived in Vienna, ostensibly to discuss the provincial constitutions, only to be confronted by the Austrian government with almost finished drafts. The Bohemian representatives, František Palacký and Adolf Maria Pinkas, left in protest.[36] The provinces had been disenfranchised.

Behind the silencing of the crown lands lay a desire for greater consistency among the provincial constitutions and, not least, the fear of the liberal government that, without central impetus, the crown lands' ruling elites would not voluntarily accept the principle of constitutional equality throughout the empire. The character of the planned federal state depended on the provincial constitutions

[35] Council of Ministers of 30 Mar. 1849. In Kletečka (ed.), *ÖMR* 2/1, No. 40, 194–9.

[36] Jiří Kořalka, *František Palacký (1798–1876)*. Vienna, 2007, 324.

and, in particular, on the provincial electoral system. After all, the provincial parliaments were to send their representatives to the Imperial Council and thus had a decisive influence over its composition.

The concerns of the liberal members of the government were not unfounded. A brief look back to March 1848 is enough to explain both the government's doubts about the provincial elites and the provinces' doubts about the new imperial constitution. At that time, the regional elites had attempted to surreptitiously perpetuate the estates' privileges (and the socially, nationally, or confessionally discriminatory regulations that underpinned them) by including them, if in a modified form, in the provincial constitutions, even when these practices and customs were due to be abolished at the imperial level.[37] The Styrian provincial parliament, for example, had written the national equality of Slovenes and Germans into its constitution and, in textbook fashion, provided for the reorganization of its counties on the basis of nationality.[38] Nevertheless, it also sought to maintain its 'existing privilege of excluding Jews from Styria'.[39] Upper Austria similarly wanted to restrict provincial suffrage to Christians.[40] Lower Austria, on the other hand, did support Jewish emancipation.[41] Tyrol, meanwhile, was socially inclusive vis-à-vis the clergy, nobility, bourgeoisie, and peasantry,[42] but nationally exclusive at the expense of the Italian-speaking Trentino.[43] The Tyrolean estates also disapproved of new Protestant neighbours.[44] In the Hungarian lands, Croatia claimed a privileged position for Catholics and Croats over Protestants, Orthodox, and Serbs.[45]

Considering these experiences during the nascent revolution in and after March 1848, the Viennese government's contributions to the provincial constitutions a

[37] Peter Burian, *Die Nationalitäten in 'Cisleithanien' und das Wahlrecht der Märzrevolution 1848/49*. Graz and Cologne, 1962, 209. Cf. Chapter 3.2.

[38] Burian, *Nationalitäten in 'Cisleithanien'*, 127.

[39] Burian, *Nationalitäten in 'Cisleithanien'*, 127.

[40] § 6 Draft Constitution for Upper Austria of 7 Sept. 1848. Österreichisches Staatsarchiv Vienna, Department Haus-, Hof- und Staatsarchiv, Landesangelegenheiten Österreichischer Reichstag 1848/49, Box 84 'Anträge, Beschlüsse', fols. 53–79.

[41] Karl Hugelmann, 'Die Landtagsbewegung des Jahres 1848 in Österreich unter der Enns', *Jahrbuch für Landeskunde in Niederösterreich*, 14–15 (1914–15), 514.

[42] Cf. Council of Ministers of 26 Apr.1848. In Kletečka (ed.), *ÖMR* 1/1: *Die Ministerien des Revolutionsjahres 1848 (20. März 1848–21. November 1848)*. Vienna, 1996, No. 20, 107–13.

[43] These then petitioned the emperor, the government, the Kremsier Reichstag, and the Frankfurt National Assembly for a separate province based on nationality. The most important documents can be found in Sergio Benvenuti, *L'autonomia trentina al Landtag di Innsbruck e al Reichsrat di Vienna*. Trento, 1978.

[44] Among other things, it still concerned the ability of Protestants to hold property. Conference of Ministers of 2 Aug. 1859. In Stefan Malfér (ed.), *ÖMR* 4/1: *Das Ministerium Rechberg (19. Mai 1859–2./3. März 1860)*. Vienna, 2003, No. 2, 8. Although the Federal Act had promised Christians equal political and civic rights, with respect to Tyrol this had always been disregarded. Cf. Conference of Ministers of 6 Aug. 1859. *ÖMR* 4/1, No. 4, 14–16. For the decision-making process cf. the Conference of Ministers of 1 Sept. 1859. *ÖMR* 4/1, No. 28, 97–101.

[45] Conference of Ministers of 6 Aug. 1859. *ÖMR* 4/1, No. 4, 14–16. Cf. Mirjana Gross, *Die Anfänge des modernen Kroatien*. Vienna, 1993, 58.

year later can be interpreted as a liberal undertaking. It is true that, formally speaking, the 'Imperial Constitution' and the new provincial constitutions and electoral regulations enacted for some provinces in 1849/50 were imposed from above by the emperor and the government. In terms of their content, however, they followed a uniform pattern based on individual legal equality, were compatible with the imperial March Constitution, and consolidated the emperor's power in the provinces.

This federal combination of the imperial and the provincial constitutions ultimately rested on the person of the emperor. His influence over the provinces was secured by law, including his rights to convene and dissolve the provincial diets, to approve provincial laws, or to enact provisional laws when the diet was not in session. The powers of the diets themselves were enumerated and therefore limited. Their fields of competence included agriculture, public works, charity, and accounting, as well as the municipal, church, and school systems within the imperial legal framework and, in the military sphere, 'quartering' and *Vorspannleistungen* (the impressment or requisition of draft animals and carts).[46]

The composition of these provincial assemblies, which were no longer called *Ständetage* (diet of the states) but *Landtage* (diet of the crown land), was only formally linked to the curial structure of the pre-March period. Opportunities for political participation had expanded considerably. The traditional estates had been composed predominantly of the clergy and nobility. They were now replaced by a new kind of estates representing the interests of the educated and property-owning classes.[47] The composition of the new 'provincial estates' generally comprised 'four interest groups: 1. agriculture, 2. industry, 3. commerce, 4. science' and consisted of deputies from the large estates, towns, and rural communities, as well as science and industry.[48] In Bohemia and in Upper Austria, the 'industrial towns' were represented separately in the provincial diets.[49]

As the provincial constitutions were drafted centrally, they reproduced the equal rights outlined in the 'Imperial Constitution' for the provincial nations, the linguistic nations, and the individual citizens. In the lands of Bohemia, Moravia, Silesia, Gorizia-Gradisca and Istria, Carinthia, Carniola, Styria, Tyrol, and Bukovina, the provincial constitutions guaranteed the 'equal rights of the nationalities present in the province' and their 'inviolable right to cultivate their nationality

[46] E.g. § 8 of the Provincial Constitution for Lower Austria of 30 Dec. 1849, No. 1/1850 RGBl.

[47] This was preceded between 1787 and 1844 by a 'bourgeoisification' of noble land ownership, e.g. when indebted nobles sold their estates, thus breaking the closed estates society. Cf. Hannes Stekl, 'Österreichs Hocharistokratie vom 18. bis ins 20. Jahrhundert'. In Hans-Ulrich Wehler (ed.), *Europäischer Adel 1750–1950*. Göttingen, 1990, 155–67.

[48] Karl Hugelmann, 'Der ständische Zentralausschuss in Österreich im April 1848', *Jahrbuch für Landeskunde von Niederösterreich*, 12 (1913), 170–260, 247.

[49] § 10 Provincial Constitution for Upper Austria of 30 Dec. 1849, No. 2/1850 RGBl.

and language'.[50] In Galicia, the corresponding passage explicitly emphasized the 'Polish' and 'Ruthenian' nationalities. The government wanted to leave no doubt about the existence of a Ruthenian 'nation' while also guaranteeing equality for 'the other nationalities'.[51]

Despite these promises of equality, the provincial electoral regulations were anything but neutral in the way different nations were treated. In Bohemia, the provincial electoral system was intended to guarantee 'the German element a larger number of votes' by providing a stronger representation of the (predominantly German) northern towns. According to the minister of the interior, this was to ensure 'that the Czech democratic element, which predominates in most Bohemian provincial towns, is given a counterweight in the provincial diet'.[52] In line with contemporary social hierarchy,[53] Bach added that 'the Germans and Czechs should maintain a balance, and even though the Czechs are greater in number, the Germans are superior to them in terms of property and industry'.[54]

The government did not complete the preparations for new provincial constitutions and electoral regulations. The constitutionalism of 1849/50 thus remained unfinished for the crown lands as well. Neither Transylvania nor Croatia-Slavonia with Dalmatia was granted the crown land autonomy promised to them in the 'Imperial Constitution'. Bukovina and Salzburg, however, were elevated to crown land status,[55] and Trieste and the Military Frontier received separate provincial constitutions,[56] whereas existing plans for a new constitution for Lombardy-Venetia were abandoned, leaving the province under military administration.[57]

[50] Council of Ministers of 28 Dec. 1849. In Kletečka (ed.), *ÖMR* 2/1, No. 239, 943–48. E.g. § 3 Provincial Constitution for Carinthia, No. 8/1850 RGBl.; § 3 Provincial Constitution for Carniola, No. 9/1850 RGBl.; § 3 Provincial Constitution for Silesia, No. 11/1850 RGBl.; § 3 Provincial Constitution for Tyrol, No. 22/1850 RGBl.; § 3 Provincial Constitution for the Bukovina, No. 387/1850 RGBl.

[51] § 3 Provincial Constitution for Galicia-Lodomeria, No. 386/1850 RGBl.

[52] Council of Ministers of 31 Dec. 1849. In Kletečka (ed.), *ÖMR* 2/1, No. 241, 952–4; Council of Ministers of 2 Jan.1850. *ÖMR* 2/1, No. 243, 957–9. It says: 'The intention here is to better represent the industrial towns in the north against the rural population in the west and in the centre and not to give the latter a preponderance. If this substitution were not to take place, 33 of the towns would be German and 46 Czech.'

[53] Judson, *Habsburg Empire*, 308–13.

[54] Council of Ministers of 2 Jan. 1850. In Kletečka (ed.), *ÖMR* 2/1, No. 243, 957–9.

[55] Thomas Kletečka and Anatol Schmied-Kowarzik (eds), 'Einleitung'. In Kletečka and Schmied-Kowarzik (eds), *ÖMR* 2/2: *Das Ministerium Schwarzenberg (8. Jänner 1850–30. April 1850).* Vienna, 2005, p. x.

[56] Constitution for the Immediately Imperial City of Trieste, 12 April 1850, No. 139/1850 RGBl.; Fundamental Law for the Croatian-Slavonian and Banat-Serbian Military Frontier, 7 May 1850, No. 243/1850 RGBl., which underscored the special character of a separate administration incorporated into the *Reichsheer* (imperial army), with extensive privileges for the *Grenzer* (frontier soldiers).

[57] The provincial administration was originally to be centred in Verona in order to limit the influence of the rebellious cities of Milan and Venice. Council of Ministers of 5 Oct. 1849. In Kletečka (ed.), *ÖMR* 2/1, No. 180, 736–8; in particular also Bach's report on his submission, Council of Ministers of 14 Oct. 1849. In Kletečka (ed.), *ÖMR* 2/1: *Das Ministerium Schwarzenberg*, No. 186, 756–8; Thomas Kletečka and Anatol Schmied-Kowarzik (eds), 'Einleitung'. In Kletečka and Schmied-Kowarzik (eds), *ÖMR* 2/2: *Das Ministerium Schwarzenberg (8. Jänner 1850–30. April 1850).* Vienna, 2005, p. x.

The Viennese government removed the Serbian Voivodeship from the Hungarian territorial union and put it under direct control. Deprived of a constitution, however, it was subordinated to a civil and military administration with three administrative districts, one Serbian, one German, and one Romanian.[58]

The efforts to draft a new constitution for Hungary—one of the most politically important constitutional projects of 1849—also came to a standstill.[59] The Imperial Constitution of March 1849, with its provision for equality of the provinces alongside the equality of the provincial nations, linguistic nations, and citizens, was taking aim at Hungary in particular. Hungary was to benefit from the new constitutional principle of the 'full equality of all nationalities'. However, former prerogatives and privileges, which had followed the logic of the pre-1848 empire, were to become obsolete.[60] In the eyes of the Hungarians, the level of provincial rights enshrined in the octroyed March Constitution not only lagged behind their historic state law privileges, but failed to match the Hungarian Constitution of March 1848 sanctioned by the emperor.

Convinced of its own military superiority and of the support for Hungary among the great European powers, the Hungarian Parliament, on the initiative of Lajos Kossuth, declared Hungarian independence and the deposition of the Habsburgs from St Stephen's throne on 14 April 1849.[61] It was not until August 1849 that Hungary was defeated by Vienna, albeit with Russian support. Placed under restrictive military rule, it was divided into five administrative districts.[62] The Hungarian constitution was declared null and void on the basis of the so-called 'forfeiture of rights' theory, according to which Hungary's rejection of the House of Habsburg and its declaration of independence implied a forfeiture of its former constitutional rights. Thus, the right to its own legislation, administration, and jurisdiction, which had been guaranteed by the Hungarian Constitution of March 1848, had lost its validity.

The 'Imperial Constitution' was a reform only on paper. During the two years of its legal validity, it neither came into force nor led to the transformation of the empire into a federal state. The federal Imperial Constitution of 4 March 1849, the provincial constitutions adopted in 1849/50, and the institutions they provided for remained hollow promises.[63] Several crown lands did not receive new

[58] Council of Ministers of 4 Oct. 1849. In Kletečka (ed.), *ÖMR* 2/1, No. 179, 732–5.

[59] Council of Ministers of 12 Oct. 1849. In Kletečka (ed.), *ÖMR* 2/1, No. 184, 749–50. Cf. Kletečka and Schmied-Kowarzik, 'Einleitung'. In Kletečka and Schmied-Kowarzik (eds), *ÖMR* 2/2, p. x. On the forfeiture theory cf. Karin Olechowski-Hrdlicka, *Die gemeinsamen Angelegenheiten der Österreichisch-Ungarischen Monarchie*. Frankfurt am Main, 2001, 59–60.

[60] Seiderer, *Österreichs Neugestaltung*, 101–2 and 107.

[61] This declaration, 'a document written by Hungarian lawyer-politicians for Hungarian lawyer-politicians', went back to Kossuth, who unrealistically and against the army's votes counted on support from the European powers and a Hungarian alliance with Italy and the Ottoman Empire. Deák, *Lawful Revolution*, 259–64 (quote p. 262).

[62] Oszkár Sashegyi, *Ungarns politische Verwaltung in der Ära Bach*. Graz, 1979, 45–6.

[63] An overview of the provincial constitutions at Seiderer, *Österreichs Neugestaltung*, 111.

constitutions even on paper. Faced with the resistance of the Hungarians, the Croats, and the Italians, the administrative elites in 1850s Vienna no longer resorted to constitutional forms of action to reorganize the empire. Instead, they relied on state-building through the administrative state (in the imperial centre) and rigid military administration (in the peripheries).

The executive federalism of neo-absolutism after 1851 was based on the *Vormärz* tradition of governance and administration without parliaments.[64] The provincial constitutions of 1849/50 were not implemented, existing provincial constitutions were suspended, and the provincial diets were not convened during the decade. Bach nonetheless worked behind the scenes on an 'Organic Statute' for the provinces and planned provincial diets that took into account old elites (nobility and clergy) and new communities (bourgeoisie and peasantry).[65] It was not until 1861, however, that the constitutions initiated by Bach in 1848/50 served as a blueprint for the provincial constitutions enacted after the February Patent.

6.3. The Emperor's Constitutional Phobia and 1859 as a Year of Crisis

After 1859, constitutional life in the monarchy slowly resurfaced, though discussions of a new federal beginning remained piecemeal. Habsburg politics regarding constitutionalism and federalization kept shifting, sometimes in a conservative-estate, sometimes in a liberal-parliamentary direction, or otherwise pooled, making little to no progress either way. Important milestones were the October Diploma of 1860 under a conservative minister of the interior, the February Patent of his more liberal successor in 1861, a renewed conservative, anti-constitutional turn in 1865, and finally, the Austro-Hungarian Compromise Acts and the five liberal Austrian Fundamental Laws in 1867.

The reappearance of antiquated terms like 'patent' and 'diploma' was no accident. The reason behind them was what one might call Franz Joseph's constitutional phobia. Indeed, the emperor initially rejected any new constitution, even one favoured by members of his own Conference of Ministers, as an unwelcome breach in the dam that secured his monarchical power. As late as 25 August 1859, he urged his ministers to refrain from any move that might 'nourish the constitutional desires that have been on the increase for some time; on the contrary, such desires must be resisted'.[66] In this context, a new constitutional order could at best be achieved gradually. It is thus not surprising that the political foundations of the monarchy at the end of the 1860s were based not on a *single*

[64] Cf. Chapter 3. [65] Seiderer, *Österreichs Neugestaltung*, 448–57.
[66] Conference of Ministers of 25 Aug. 1859. In Malfér (ed.), *ÖMR* 4/1, 85.

uniform constitutional document, but on a wide variety of more or less incongruous documents and treaties.

The singular attempt by Franz Joseph and his advisers to govern the monarchy as a comprehensive state according to uniform administrative principles resulted in the period of neo-absolutism from 1849 to 1859. Looking back, the imperial official Carl von Czoernig described the era in positive terms. The 'reorganization of Austria' had encompassed all public affairs; a few years of 'successful activity were sufficient to erect an edifice which, although not yet completed in all its details, has grown to a degree which otherwise could not have been achieved in centuries'.[67] In the Austrian and Bohemian heartlands, the edifice of the absolutist state was particularly grandiose. The oppressive military administration in the Italian south and in the Hungarian east and south-east, however, revealed cracks and crumbling mortar in its walls.

Under neo-absolutism, the monarchy in its heartland had become an administrative and territorial state, increasingly concerned with social issues.[68] With major infrastructure, railway, and telegraph projects such as the legendary Semmering Railway, as well as welfare and educational initiatives—the ambitious Thun-Hohenstein educational reform is just one example—the central authorities in Vienna extended their reach throughout the territory. Their influence could be felt in everyday life.[69] After 1849, public works were increasingly taken into public hands. The emperor no longer sought to interfere with the most important social achievements of the March Revolution: peasant emancipation and land relief. Instead, he instrumentalized them to support the building of his bureaucratic state. Patrimonial and manorial (or 'private') sovereign rights were systematically curtailed. The state, provinces, and municipalities became political territories, while large latifundia regressed to the status of 'private property' and no longer granted their owners 'public' judicial and administrative rights. Instead, in the new administrative and territorial state, citizens were confronted with an army of fresh civil servants who replaced the patrimonial administration at the lower levels of government.[70] In Hungary, they were called the 'Bach Hussars' after the minister of the interior and the style of their uniforms. Thanks to these sweeping state reforms, which mainly accommodated bourgeois and liberal interests, the majority was willing to overlook the lack of political representation. Austrian liberals and bourgeoisie were not necessarily democrats.[71]

The dream of the Monarchy as a modern comprehensive state, however, came to a sudden and drastic end. The year 1859 proved to be a diplomatic, military,

[67] Carl Czoernig, *Österreichs Neugestaltung 1848–1858*. Vienna, 1858, p. v.

[68] Cf. Jörg Ganzenmüller and Tatjana Tönsmeyer, 'Einleitung'. In Ganzenmüller and Tönsmeyer (eds), *Vom Vorrücken des Staates in die Fläche*. Vienna, 2016, 12–14.

[69] Judson, *Habsburg Empire*, 286–301.

[70] Comprehensively Deak, *Forging a Multinational State*, 112–35.

[71] Pieter M. Judson, *Exclusive Revolutionaries*. Ann Arbor, 1996.

and financial disaster.[72] Wars and the threat of war, such as in Kurhessen in 1850 and in the Crimea between 1853 and 1856, had already absorbed enormous resources and upset the European balance of power. The Austrian government felt they could no longer trust old allies like Great Britain and not yet depend on new allies like Russia. In the German Confederation, Austria was increasingly isolated in the face of Prussia's growing political and economic influence. Military defeat in the Second Italian War of Independence led to the loss of Lombardy to France; neither the allied partners nor the German Confederation had rallied to the Austrian standard. The devastating Battle of Solferino not only weakened the Austrian government's international standing as well as its position inside the German Confederation. It also amounted to a domestic setback and became a byword for disaster.[73]

The empire's long-depleted finances provided the final impetus for a political turnabout. Austria's incessant military engagements and the accompanying massive expansion of the army had rapidly increased the defence budget. The achievements of bureaucratic state-building, which Czoernig praised so highly, were also extremely costly and could no longer be pursued with the necessary vigour. In the neo-absolutist battle over resources, the bureaucratic comprehensive state was defeated by the military state, as the historian of Austrian administration John Deak noted: 'Bach's administration and the enormous state-building efforts would be sacrificed on Mars's altar.'[74]

On 15 July 1859, Emperor Franz Joseph declared in the Laxenburg Manifesto that the primacy of military and foreign policy should now give way to the primacy of domestic policy.[75] In view of the disastrous financial situation, his advisers argued that the only way to finance his lofty agenda was to give the political elites a say in domestic politics and grant them an active role in controlling the budget. After the end of Bach's neo-absolutist era, Agenor Gołuchowski, Bach's short-lived successor as minister of the interior, promised in his 'Government Programme' of 22 August 1859 to bring the state budget under control. He wanted to 'transfer a substantial part of the functions that are now carried out by the provincial authorities, where possible, to autonomous institutions belonging to the interested parties themselves' and, to this end, to 'establish estates' representations in the various crown lands'.[76] This opened the constitutional debate of the 1860s in the empire and the crown lands that Franz Joseph had tried so hard to avoid.

[72] Rumpler, Chance für Mitteleuropa, 373.

[73] Wolf D. Gruner, *Der Deutsche Bund 1815–1866*. Munich, 2012, 81.

[74] Deak, *Forging a Multinational State*, 133.

[75] Josef Redlich, *Das österreichische Staats- und Reichsproblem*. Vol. 1: *Der dynastische Reichsgedanke und die Entfaltung des Problems bis zur Verkündigung der Reichsverfassung von 1861*. Subvol. 1: *Darstellung*. Leipzig, 1920, 462.

[76] *Wiener Zeitung*, 22 Aug. 1859, 1. Cf. Stefan Malfér, 'Einleitung'. In Malfér (ed.), *ÖMR* 4/1, pp. xxviii–xxix.

6.4. 'Federalists' and 'Centralists'

The constitutional struggle of the 1860s between feudal conservatives and liberals, and between the nobility and the middle classes, for political, legal, and economic participation has been described by contemporaries and historians alike as a struggle between so-called federalists and so-called centralists.[77] However, from the perspective of federal history, it is important to emphasize that *all* protagonists were concerned in some way with federal constitutional change. None of the decision-makers of the time was advocating for taking the Monarchy down the path towards a unitary state. The 'federalists' fought for a conservative estates federalism, the 'centralists' for a liberal federalism with graduated legislative participation.

The 'centralists' were not concerned with a unitary state, but with state unity. 'Centralism' in mid-nineteenth century linguistic usage should not be translated according to today's sense of 'centralist' meaning 'non-federal'. For the 'centralists' of the time, such as the liberal minister of the interior Anton von Schmerling, 'centralism' meant state unity based on the legislative and administrative cohesion within the empire.[78] The 'centralists' continued to grant the crown lands their own constitutional room for manoeuvre. It was Schmerling in particular who separated the provinces' constitutional competences from those of the empire and enacted the provincial statutes that survived until 1918. Against this background, the 'centralism' of Schmerling and other liberals should not be contrasted with the federalism of today. Rather, it should be distinguished from the composite monarchy of the *Vormärz*, which knew a common ruler, but no common central authorities or institutions.[79]

It is a misleading but nevertheless persistent assumption that the October Diploma of 1860 was the 'federalist' and the February Patent of 1861 the 'centralist' contribution to the decade-long political movement towards constitutionalization.[80] Both acts laid the foundations for the monarchy's later federal development. In fact, the constitutional struggle of the 1860s is a striking example of how one and the same governing principle—in this case the federalist idea—could be filled with very different political content. The conservative nobility was concerned with preserving the old provincial-level prerogatives that distinguished their status as an imperial elite. The liberal nobility and propertied bourgeoisie, on the other hand, wanted to abandon the estates-based order once and for all. They favoured a constitutional and parliamentary organization of the empire and the crown lands.

[77] Rumpler, *Chance für Mitteleuropa*, 375.
[78] Redlich, *Staats- und Reichsproblem*, 1/1. 700; Éva Somogyi, *Vom Zentralismus zum Dualismus*. Wiesbaden, 1983, 29, 33.
[79] Cf. on this diversity of rule Chapter 2.
[80] Stefan Malfér, 'Einleitung'. In Malfér (ed.), *ÖMR* 4/3: *Das Ministerium Rechberg (21. Oktober 1860–2. Februar 1861)*. Vienna, 2009, p. xxxiii.

In the constitutional struggle, the old estates' elites initially seemed to have the upper hand. The 'Reinforced Imperial Council' was to advise on the tasks and the composition of the provincial delegations and thus on the new imperial constitution. While the Imperial Council had been a merely advisory body under neo-absolutism after 1851, in 1860 it was given the right to approve the financial affairs of the empire. As a comparatively small body, its personnel was enlarged, i.e. 'reinforced', to adapt to these new competences, hence its name change from 'Permanent' to 'Reinforced' Imperial Council.[81] Alongside representatives of the high nobility, the upper bureaucracy, and the recognized religious denominations, the institution now included a number of prominent, though still outnumbered, bourgeois figures from trade and industry.

Another novelty was the introduction of thirty-eight crown land representatives.[82] From 1859, the 'Reinforced Imperial Council' thus also functioned as a chamber of the provinces. It was the conservative Bohemian-Austrian and Hungarian aristocratic communities that dominated the discussions on the future constitution and the relationship between the empire and the crown lands.[83] Their core demands concerned the future participation of the provincial diets in imperial legislation. They called for a final renunciation of neo-absolutism and its guiding principle that the power to decide rests alone with the emperor. These demands united the influential 'federalist aristocratic party', which 'appeared as such for the first time' in the Imperial Council.[84] Their efforts culminated in the October Diploma of 20 October 1860, by which the emperor, out of 'his own authority', bound himself and his government to a 'permanent and irrevocable fundamental law of the state'.[85]

Political Revival of the Crown Lands after 1860

The October Diploma of 1860 abolished neo-absolutism with federal administration through which the emperor had ruled without constitutional limitations. The subsequent reorganization of the empire aligned closely with historical trajectories and distinguished between 'Hungarian' and 'German-Slavic' crown lands.[86] The Hungarian lands were granted participation 'in the sense of their

[81] Imperial Patent of 13 Apr. 1851 on the Statute of the Imperial Council, No. 92/1851 RGBl.; instructive on the preceding developments Kletečka, 'Einleitung'. In *ÖMR* 2/4: *Das Ministerium Schwarzenberg (14. Oktober 1850–30. Mai 1851)*. Vienna, 2011, p. xxxiii. On the right of consent, cf. Imperial Handwritten Letter of 17 July 1860, No. 181/1860 RGBl.

[82] Ministerial Conference of 23, 24, and 26 Jan. 1849 (collective minutes). In Malfér (ed.), *ÖMR* 4/1, No. 99, 386–91. See also Malfér, 'Einleitung'. In *ÖMR* 4/1, pp. liii–lvi.

[83] On the contacts between Hungarian conservatives and the government cf. *ÖMR* 4/1, pp. xxxvi–xlviii.

[84] Redlich, *Staats- und Reichsproblem*, 1/1. 468.

[85] Imperial Patent of 13 Apr. 1851 on the Statute of the Imperial Council.

[86] Cf. the meeting of the Ministerial Conference of 16 Oct. 1860. Stefan Malfér (ed.), *ÖMR* 4/2: *Das Ministerium Rechberg (6. März 1860–16. Oktober 1860)*. Vienna, 2007, No. 219, 461–70.

former constitutions' and the rest of the crown lands 'in the sense of and in accordance with their provincial statutes'.[87] Thus, the participation of the provinces in the legislative process varied considerably. As the governmental negotiations on this passage make clear, the 'actual difference between Hungary and the other crown lands…was that in the case of the latter no agreement between the Crown and the provincial diets or the Reinforced Imperial Council was actually necessary for the laws to take effect'.[88] In Hungary, on the other hand, no imperial legislation could be passed without the consent of the Hungarian parliament.[89]

Controversy persisted within government circles over whether the Hungarians' 'legislative attributes' should be extended to the other crown lands, lest 'the old dualism' be perpetuated.[90] The reluctance to augment the legislative powers of the Austrian provincial parliaments stemmed from the liberals' reservations regarding the old ruling elites that dominated them. Ignaz von Plener argued in the Conference of Ministers:

> The distribution of legislative powers among 21 provincial parliaments is unacceptable and, apart from a few aristocratic factions, is not desired by anyone in Austria; rather, the general desire—at least the majority of the German-Slavic population of the middle and bourgeois classes and probably also of the more rational part of the peasantry—is for a collective representation in the centre [and] for the establishment of a constitutional imperial body, through which the non-Hungarian subjects would receive only that which was also granted to the Hungarians.[91]

In terms of their rights and their renewed composition, the provincial parliaments thus fell short even of what Bach had envisaged in the provincial diet statutes of 1848/50.[92]

The October Diploma and the four provincial statutes issued at the same time for Styria, Carinthia, Salzburg, and Tyrol were unanimously rejected by the public.[93] The strategic compromise between the government and the liberal propertied bourgeoisie was no longer tenable. The Austrian people had firmly believed in the elevation of the provincial diets in line with the Hungarian model, but the four provincial statutes conferred only rights of consultation and no

[87] Imperial Diploma regulating the internal state law relations of the Monarchy of 20 Oct. 1860, No. 226/1860 RGBl.

[88] Cf. the meeting of the Ministerial Conference of 16 Oct.1860. In Malfér (ed.), *ÖMR* 4/2, No. 219, 464.

[89] This was a follow-up to the former Hungarian constitutional law. Malfér, 'Einleitung'. In ÖMR 4/3: *Das Ministerium Rechberg*, p. xix.

[90] Cf. the Ministerial Conference of 16 Oct. 1860, at which Szécsen spoke in favour and Plener only with reservations for a legislative power for all crown lands. Malfér (ed.), *ÖMR* 4/2, No. 219, 461–70.

[91] Cf. the Ministerial Conference of 16 Oct. 1860. *ÖMR* 4/2, No. 219, 465.

[92] Rumpler, *Chance für Mitteleuropa*, 376.

[93] Fritz Fellner, 'Das "Februarpatent" von 1861: Entstehung und Bedeutung', *Mitteilungen des Instituts für Österreichische Geschichtsforschung*, 63/3 (1955), 550.

legislative powers. In Styria, for example, the provincial statute only allowed the diet to 'express the wishes or objections of the province—to the best of its knowledge and in good faith—in matters concerning the welfare and needs of Styria and to submit requests and petitions to the emperor either directly or at its own discretion through the governor'.[94] The gap between this extremely vague right of consultation and the much more far-reaching powers of the Hungarian parliament was no longer tolerable. In Graz and Salzburg, the municipal councils resigned in protest; in Vienna, the press demanded legislative rights for the provincial parliaments.[95] Equally untenable was the continued adherence to an electoral law based on the estates, which divided the Styrian parliament into four curiae of the clergy, the wealthy nobility, the cities, and other municipalities.[96] Even the Hungarians, who now had their own parliament, court chancellery, supreme court, and pre-1848 style constitution, were dissatisfied with the concessions. In response, riots ensued accompanied by election boycotts, and an almost total refusal to pay taxes, both of which were engineered by the comitat authorities.[97]

Constitutional Distribution of Competences in Schmerling's Federalism

This unanimous rejection of the October Diploma was a clear indication that a fundamental reform was long overdue. Gołuchowski was forced to resign, but his sacrifice could not halt the political revival of the provincial representative bodies. Within a few months, the new minister of the interior, Schmerling, placed the empire and the crown lands on new federal foundations. The so-called February Patent of 1861, which, like its predecessor, was also issued by the emperor, served as a legal basis.[98] First, Schmerling made the Imperial Council a bicameral legislative body. Whereas the October Diploma had only vaguely referred to the right to participate in imperial legislation, the February Patent expressly granted the Imperial Council the right to approve government bills and to draft legislation of its own. Second, it distributed legislative powers between the empire and the crown lands. Thirdly, Schmerling abandoned the estate-based character of the provincial diets and introduced the liberal principle of a representation based

[94] § 24 Statute on the Provincial Representation in the Duchy of Styria of 20 Oct. 1860, No. 227/1860 RGBl.

[95] Redlich, *Staats- und Reichsproblem*, 1/1. 673–7.

[96] § 2 Statute on the Provincial Representation in the Duchy of Styria of 20 Oct. 1860, No. 227/1860 RGBl.

[97] Rumpler, *Chance für Mitteleuropa*, 376.

[98] On the following Malfér, 'Einleitung'. *ÖMR* 4/3, pp. xxx–xxxv.

on property ownership and level of education. The provincial statutes enacted in October 1860 were adjusted accordingly.[99]

The February Patent maintained the federal trajectories of the October Diploma. Schmerling granted the crown lands equal federal rights through the constitution, but the legislative powers of the Imperial Council continued to differ with regard to the affairs of the Hungarian and non-Hungarian crown lands. Schmerling thus prolonged the 'dualism' of the October Diploma. At the same time, the clear division of power between the empire as a whole and the crown lands opened the door for the later development of a constitutional crown land federalism which could potentially include Hungary. Thanks to the reformed composition of the provincial diets, this federal model would no longer have had an estate-like character.

Schmerling divided legislative power across three levels. The Enlarged Imperial Council (also known as the General Imperial Council) was responsible for matters affecting the entire state, i.e., the Hungarian *and* non-Hungarian crown lands. The Smaller Imperial Council was to decide on matters concerning the rest of, i.e. non-Hungarian, crown lands. Finally, regarding certain matters the provincial parliaments had exclusive legislative powers; the matters of legislative powers were not laid down in the February Patent itself, but rather in the provincial statutes.[100] The separation of the legislative powers of the Imperial Council for the whole state and for the non-Hungarian provinces gave this institution the dualistic character mentioned above.[101] According to Schmerling's adviser, Hans Perthaler, this multi-level legislative structure was intended to 'give effect to the federal principle without endangering the unitary state, and to the unitary state principle without damaging the federal elements of the Austrian state'.[102]

The February Patent was the last give the entire empire a uniform and legally binding federal foundation. Schmerling was a 'centralist' only insofar as his federalism aimed at the constitutional unity of the empire and at central federal institutions. In the tense foreign and domestic political situation of the 1860s, neither the February Patent nor the 'Enlarged Imperial Council' contributed to

[99] *ÖMR* 4/3, p. xxxii. On Bohemia Bernd Rottenbacher, *Das Februarpatent in der Praxis*. Frankfurt am Main, 2001; Harry Slapnicka, *Oberösterreich: Die politische Führungsschicht 1861–1918*. Linz, 1983; Richard Schober, *Geschichte des Tiroler Landtages im 19. und 20. Jahrhundert*. Innsbruck, 1984; Benedikt Bilgeri, *Geschichte Vorarlbergs*. Vol. 4: *Zwischen Absolutismus und halber Autonomie*. Vienna, 1982; Georg Schmitz, *Die Anfänge des Parlamentarismus in Niederösterreich*. Vienna, 1985.

[100] The provincial competences included agriculture, infrastructure measures financed from provincial funds, welfare and social policy, as well as the provincial budget and accounting; within the framework of the imperial laws, municipal, church, and school affairs were added, as well as rations and accommodation of the army. Cf. § 18 Provincial Statute and Provincial Election Statute for the Margraviate of Moravia of 26 Feb. 1861, No. 20/1861 RGBl., Appendix II m.

[101] Olechowski-Hrdlicka: *Die gemeinsamen Angelegenheiten der Österreichisch-Ungarischen Monarchie*, 71.

[102] Quoted in Redlich, *Staats- und Reichsproblem*, 1/1. 726. On autonomous self-government with Schmerling cf. also Stourzh, 'Länderautonomie und Gesamtstaat', 50–1.

the consolidation of the empire. Domestically, this was due to the resistance of Hungary, Transylvania, and Croatia-Slavonia. There, citing older constitutions,[103] the ruling elites boycotted the Imperial Council, and refused to provide the taxes and recruits that were so desperately needed.[104] The Polish uprising of 1863[105] further shook the integrity of the Habsburg Monarchy. Revolutionary secessionist movements loomed elsewhere in Galicia, Hungary, Transylvania, the southern Slavic territories, and the Italian territories.[106] When the General Imperial Council finally met in 1865, the government and the Imperial Council clashed over the budget issue. Just like Gołuchowski in 1860, Schmerling was forced to resign—another minister of the interior who came to grief on the federal question.

Nationality Equality versus Dualism

The arrival of Schmerling's successor, Richard Count Belcredi, in July 1865 marked a conservative, anti-constitutional turn. Faced with an incapacitated Imperial Council, Belcredi resorted to drastic measures, persuading the emperor to suspend the February Patent of 1861.[107] After his extensive experiences with the 'Slavic question' as county governor in Moravia, provincial governor in Silesia, vice-president of the governorate in Trieste, and governor in Prague, he fought for the greater integration of the Slavic population into the empire. He opposed Schmerling's vision of an Imperial Council that favoured a German-speaking majority in clear contravention of demographic realities.

By temporarily suspending the constitution, Belcredi sought to clear the way for new constitutional negotiations grounded in historic crown land rights.[108] He planned to divide the empire into five historical administrative regions (German

[103] Stefan Malfér, 'Einleitung'. In Malfér (ed.), *ÖMR* 5/3: *Die Ministerien Erzherzog Rainer und Mensdorff (5. November 1861–6. Mai 1862)*. Vienna, 1985, pp. xix–xlv. Cf. Council of Ministers of 11 Mar. 1862. *ÖMR* 5/3, No. 211, 337–39; Highest Handwritten Letter to the Hungarian Court Chancellor on account of the non-convening of the Hungarian Parliament [11 Mar. 1862]. *ÖMR* 5/3, No. 211a, 339. See Fellner, 'Februarpatent', 554.

[104] Redlich, *Staats- und Reichsproblem*, 1/1. 702. The Council of Ministers met several times on this question, on military execution, and on tax collection, cf. Council of Ministers of 5 Feb. 1862. In Malfér (ed.), *ÖMR* 5/3, No. 194, 255–60. On Transylvania cf. Council of Ministers of 17 Nov. 1861. *ÖMR* 5/3, No. 152, 26–32. On Hungary Council of Ministers of 15 Feb. 1862. *ÖMR* 5/3, No. 197, 268–75 and Council of Ministers of 4 Mar. 1862. *ÖMR* 5/3, No. 202, 297–300. For the following troop reduction cf. Council of Ministers of 22 Apr. 1862. *ÖMR* 5/3, No. 223, 403–6.

[105] Thomas Kletečka and Klaus Koch, 'Einleitung'. In Kletečka and Koch (eds), *ÖMR* 5/6: *Die Ministerien Erzherzog Rainer und Mensdorff (4. Mai 1863–12. Oktober 1863)*. Vienna, 1989, pp. xix–xlv.

[106] On this cf. Council of Ministers of 10 June 1863. In Kletečka and Koch (eds), *ÖMR* 5/6, No. 361, 97–100. See also Thomas Kletečka and Klaus Koch, 'Einleitung'. In Kletečka and Koch (eds), *ÖMR* 5/7: *Die Ministerien Erzherzog Rainer und Mensdorff (15. Oktober 1863–23. Mai 1864)*. Vienna, 1992, pp. xxv–xxvi; Hans-Christian Maner, Galizien. Munich, 2007, 117–20.

[107] The February Patent was suspended by Imperial Patent of 20 Sept. 1865. No. 89/1865 RGBl.

[108] Robert A. Kann, *Das Nationalitätenproblem der Habsburgermonarchie*. Vol. 2: *Ideen und Pläne zur Reichsreform*. 2nd edn. Graz and Cologne, 1964, 132–4.

Austria, Hungary, Bohemia-Moravia-Silesia, Poland-Ruthenia, and the South Slavic territories). This pentarchy was reminiscent of Metternich's deliberations during the pre-March period. Within these five groups of several provinces, each province would have a diet. The Imperial Council in Vienna was to be drawn from the provincial diets, but would no longer have legislative, but only advisory powers. The Austrian and Hungarian crown lands, however, were to have equal status.[109] The conservative newspaper *Vaterland* (Fatherland), financed by Belcredi's brother Egbert, wrote: 'Austria's salvation does not depend on whether the negotiations with the provincial diets of Hungary and Croatia last one or two or five years, but on the fact that they will never be granted anything that would be detrimental to the empire, such as dualism.'[110]

The opportunity to ratify another universal constitution had passed, however. Reactions to Belcredi's measures in the provincial diets revealed clearly demarcated national camps. While many German-Austrian provincial parliamentarians protested against the suspension of the 'February Constitution', the provincial diets of Bohemia, Galicia, Istria, and Bukovina sent letters of gratitude. Neither the non-German population nor the conservative aristocratic elites held the Imperial Council, which was dominated by German liberals, in high esteem. The dissolution of the Imperial Council, and with it the end of a central legislative body common to all crown lands, was seen by these groups as an opportunity to extend their powers at the provincial level. Even though the Imperial Council was temporarily 'suspended', the provincial diets continued to meet, and the new provincial statutes remained in force.[111]

German-Austrian deputies and liberals took a different view of Belcredi's actions. Loud protest arose from the seventeen provincial diets of the non-Hungarian crown lands when they convened in mid-November 1865. Numerous complaints, coordinated by the provincial parliaments, were sent to Vienna[112] outlining, in forthright terms, the apparent illegality of the suspension.[113] The German-Austrian provincial diets demanded an imperial legislature (superior to the provincial legislatures) and the reinstatement of the February Patent.[114] Members of two leading German liberal provincial parliaments, led by Karl Wilhelm von Tinti in Lower Austria and Moritz von Kaiserfeld in Styria, set up a commission. The task of these constitutional loyalists was to compile evidence of the positive effects the February Patent had had on the welfare of the provinces and, no less importantly,

[109] Clam's memorandum to Belcredi of Jan. 1867. In Anton Ottakar Zeithammer, *Zur Geschichte der böhmischen Ausgleichsversuche 1865–1871*. Vol. 1: *Von Belcredi zu Hohenwart*. Prague, 1912, 28.

[110] 'Wie lange soll die Sistierung dauern?', *Das Vaterland*, 260, 12 Nov. 1865, 1.

[111] Somogyi, *Vom Zentralismus zum Dualismus*, 50–2.

[112] Somogyi, *Vom Zentralismus zum Dualismus*, 52.

[113] *Neue Freie Presse*, 445, 23 Nov. 1865, 12.

[114] In the Graz *Landstube*, both groups formed the 'Constitution Party', see 'Die Physiognomie des Landtags', *Die Presse*, 319, 18 Nov. 1865, 3.

to convince the emperor of its merits.[115] These German-speaking representatives of the provincial diets explicitly advocated for a dual-speed constitutionalism, foreshadowing the dualism that was yet to come.[116] In the non-Hungarian territories, the February Patent was to remain in effect, while the final comprehensive imperial constitution would be negotiated first with Hungary and Croatia and then with the Imperial Council.[117]

Hungarian politicians and deputies also concentrated on their relations with the emperor, avoiding political cooperation with the other crown lands, even where they had personal contacts.[118] When lambasted by the German-Austrian liberals for failing to support the parliament 'on this side of the Leitha' after Belcredi's dissolution of the Imperial Council, the Hungarians defensively replied that they negotiated only with the king and not the other half of the empire.[119] A similar attitude can be observed in their internal dealings with the other Hungarian nations. Neither representatives of Croatia-Slavonia nor Transylvania were included in the compromise negotiations, which were already well under way at the time.[120] The Slavic provincial elites on both sides of the Leitha rejected a dualistic division of the empire. They feared German hegemony in the Austrian and Magyar hegemony in the Hungarian half.

In August 1866, Slavic national politicians with federalist inclinations met in Vienna and Baden. František Palacký, František Ladislav Rieger, and Alois von Pražák, as well as Josip Juraj Strossmayer, Ivan Mažuranić, and Gołuchowski intensively debated Belcredi's pentarchy.[121] They called for a constitution with ethnic-national and linguistic equality, but were met with fierce resistance in certain quarters.[122] The Austrian-Germans discredited the meeting, smearing it

[115] *Neue Freie Presse*, 445, 23 Nov. 1865, 11–12.

[116] On the contemporary perception of the 'dualism' of the Austrian liberals cf. Péter Hanák, 'Antezedenzien des Osterartikels Deáks', *Acta Historica Academiae Scientiarum Hungaricae*, 21/3–4 (1975), 276.

[117] Subsequently, the emperor and the government tried to avoid negotiations on two fronts with Hungary and Croatia. Cf. Ivan Žolger, *Der staatsrechtliche Ausgleich zwischen Österreich und Ungarn*. Leipzig, 1911, 28. In the throne speech before the Hungarian Parliament in Dec. 1865, the emperor suggested to both Croatia-Slavonia and Transylvania that they should merge with Hungary. Žolger, *Ausgleich zwischen Österreich und Ungarn*, 2–3.

[118] At a meeting with the Czech deputy Klaudy, Deák promised to advocate for state-law federalism. However, he never followed through on his promise. Cf. Jan Havránek, 'Die tschechische Politik und der Ausgleich von 1867'. In Ľudovít Holotík (ed.), *Der österreichisch-ungarische Ausgleich 1867*. Bratislava, 1971, 528.

[119] Somogyi, *Vom Zentralismus zum Dualismus*, 53.

[120] On the 'Croatian' question of whether the crown land, which had been independent since 1848, should become part of the Hungarian lands or be united with them in a union, as well as on the Croatians' refusal to agree to the settlement, cf. Žolger, *Ausgleich zwischen Österreich und Ungarn*, 25–34; Keith Hitchins, 'The Rumanians of Transylvania and the Ausgleich 1865–1867'. In Holotík, *Der österreichisch-ungarische Ausgleich*, 876 and 880.

[121] Detailed Zeithammer, *Geschichte der böhmischen Ausgleichsversuche*, 16–22.

[122] Somogyi, *Vom Zentralismus zum Dualismus*, 73. The plan of Rieger and Palacký, however, only met with Gołuchowski's approval; other Poles distanced themselves. Cf. *Fremdenblatt*, 230, 22 Aug. 1866, 1–2.

as a new 'Slav Congress'.[123] Elsewhere, conservative nobles such as Heinrich Clam-Martinic, Adolph Schwarzenberg, or Georg Lobkowicz in Bohemia, who otherwise shared a belief in the defence of historic state law, would not support the recognition of a linguistic nation, a constitution, or equal participation in the imperial and provincial parliaments.[124]

The years 1865 to 1867 were ultimately characterized by compromise with the Hungarian elites and their demands for a dualistic partition of the empire. The most popular and influential advocate of dualism was the Hungarian member of parliament Ferenc Deák, who wrote pamphlets and legal treatises and held secret talks with Belcredi.[125] Deák defended the Hungarian constitution of 1848, rejected the October Diploma and the February Patent as legally invalid, and agitated against an Austrian empire.[126] He called for Hungarian sovereignty in military, financial, and foreign affairs. The Hungarian Diet, convened in December 1865, adopted his stance, but conceded that cooperation in 'common affairs' between the crown lands was necessary.[127]

The Hungarian demands were aided by the disintegration of the German Confederation. With the appointment of Friedrich Ferdinand von Beust as foreign minister in October 1866 (and then as prime minister in February 1867) following a dispute with Belcredi, the Hungarians gained a powerful advocate. Within a few months, Beust made Austro-Hungarian dualism, based on a compromise between German and Magyar claims to authority, a reality.[128] As a former champion of a dualistic or even trialistic reorganization of the German Confederation, he adhered to a belief in the civilizing mission of 'Germans' within the Austrian Empire. He opposed granting an equal share in imperial politics to the Slavic population and urged the emperor to unite 'the German and Hungarian elements against pan-Slavism'.[129]

[123] 'Der Slavenkongreß-beendigt', *Fremdenblatt*, 219, 11 Aug. 1866, 1. Against anti-Slavic resentment, 'Grazer Tagespost', quoted in *Fremdenblatt*, No. 277, 9 Oct. 1866, 3.

[124] Havránek, 'Die tschechische Politik und der Ausgleich', 530 and 533.

[125] Somogyi, *Vom Zentralismus zum Dualismus*, 35. On the background cf. Hanák, 'Antezedenzien des Osterartikels Deáks', 271–308. Franz von Deák, *Ein Beitrag zum ungarischen Staatsrecht*. Pest and Leipzig, 1865. See Hanák, 'Antezedenzien des Osterartikels Deáks', 278. On the state law aspect and a concise overview Peter Berger, 'Der österreichisch-ungarische Dualismus 1867–1918 und die österreichische Rechtswissenschaft' *Der Donauraum*, 13/3 (1968), 156–70.

[126] Legally formulated by Wenzel Lustkandl, *Das ungarisch-österreichische Staatsrecht*. Vienna, 1863. The above-mentioned polemic by Franz von Deák (*Beitrag zum ungarischen Staatsrecht*) was directed against the dogma of imperial unity. Hungarian publicists had already refrained from dealing with the empire in the pre-March period. Ágnes Deák, 'Miklós Wesselényi on the Future of the Habsburg Empire and Hungary'. In Ignác Romsics and Béla K. Király (eds), *Geopolitics in the Danube Region*. Budapest, 1999, 23–4.

[127] Deák had previously also recognized 'common affairs' of the empire in the so-called Easter Articles. Somogyi, *Vom Zentralismus zum Dualismus*, 54.

[128] Cf. Gerald Stourzh, 'Die dualistische Reichsstruktur, Österreichbegriff und Österreichbewusstsein 1867–1918'. In Stourzh, *Umfang der österreichischen Geschichte*, 105–24; László Katus, 'József Eötvös and Ferenc Deák: Laws on Nationalities'. In Romsics and Király, *Geopolitics in the Danube Region*, 140–2.

[129] Havránek, 'Die tschechische Politik und der Ausgleich', 535.

At the decisive meeting of the Conference of Ministers on 1 February 1866, which led to Belcredi's resignation, Beust commented on the scepticism of the Slavic population towards dualism: 'the government will never be able to please all nationalities in its internal policy'. Instead of 'satisfying everyone's needs', he continued, 'it is [the government's] task to rely on those who have the most vitality, who are spiritually close to each other and who have direct contact in their mutual interests, namely the Germans and the Hungarians'.[130]

6.5. Protecting Liberty in a Complex Constitutional Reality

It was not until 1867 that the model of historic crown land federalism emerged triumphant, almost twenty years after it had been 'invented' and written into the constitution in March 1849. It was still a limited victory, however, for the establishment of the dualist confederation of Austria-Hungary in 1867 gave crown land federalism a leading role only in the Austrian part of the empire. There was no single constitutional document for the entire monarchy. However, what the empire lacked in unity, Austria made up for in durability. In 1867, it established a new constitutional system based on the five Fundamental State Laws and a revised version of Schmerling's February Patent of 1861. Unlike the 'constitutions', 'patents', and 'diplomas' of 1849, 1860, and 1861, this constitutional framework was destined to last, enduring until the collapse of the empire and the monarchy in 1918.

Historic crown land federalism was now one principle of the federal order among others. The Austro-Hungarian dualism of 1867 meant that crown land federalism could never take up its role as an organizing principle for the whole state, as envisioned by both the Kremsier draft constitution and Franz Joseph's 'Imperial Constitution' of 1849. The crown land federalism of the post-1867 constitutional period thus differed markedly from the federalism of March 1849. Most obviously, its territorial scope had narrowed; it no longer encompassed the Austria of 1806 including Hungary (and Lombardy-Venetia), but the Austria of 1867 without Hungary. Pursuing a vision for a political community of all the nationalities of Hungary, the Hungarian part of the empire developed—within the Austro-Hungarian confederation—towards a Hungarian-speaking unitary nation state.

On the Austrian side, the crown lands were entrusted with all matters not reserved for the empire as a whole (Austria-Hungary) or for the Austrian half as a whole (Austria). Agriculture and provincial infrastructure, public education, health, and social welfare became their most important fields of activity. In the

[130] Speech of Beust in the Council of Ministers of 1 Feb. 1867. In Horst Brettner-Messler (ed.), *ÖMR 6/2: Das Ministerium Belcredi (8. April 1866–6. Februar 1867)*. Vienna, 1973, No. 125, 401.

following decades, the Austrian crown lands increasingly acted like states, working together within the multi-tiered framework of a 'cooperative empire'.[131] The popularity of crown land federalism in the Austrian part of the empire is demonstrated not least by the reprinting of those lithographs which had illustrated crown land federalism back in 1849. Strixner's 'Barque with Austria' was reproduced as late as 1898 in the volume *Unser Kaiser*.[132]

The history of a unified 'Imperial Constitution' for the entire Habsburg Monarchy thus remained unfinished. It was replaced by a multitude of different fundamental state laws, treaties, and statutes. In political reality, however, they had a validity and stability bordering on constitutional status. In addition to the Austro-Hungarian Compromise Laws and the Austrian Fundamental State Laws of 1867, these included the historical provincial constitutions, as in Hungary, and the new provincial statutes in Austria. In addition, there were internal bilateral treaties, such as the Hungarian-Croatian Compromise of 1868, or international treaties, such as the Treaty of Berlin of 1878 with its mandate to administer Bosnia-Herzegovina.

The unfinished history of constitutionalism was not simply a discouraging tale of the failed 'Imperial Constitution' or repeatedly thwarted attempts at the universal and unitary constitutional reorganization of the empire. For individual citizens and the various national, regional, and religious communities, the monarchy's resultant multi-structured system of governance actually opened up new spaces of protection and freedom. The interplay between the constitutionally guaranteed equality of linguistic nations, provincial nations, citizens (and, from 1867, of religions) in the Austrian part of the empire and the equality and freedom rights of the constitutional system in the Hungarian part created a wide scope for legal protection and political participation. In society, this laid the foundation for multiple identities and loyalties. The political (judicial) practice in the Austrian half contributed to the legal safeguarding and thus endurance of both concepts of the nation: the linguistic nation and the provincial-territorial nation. In Hungary, religious equality rather than national equality played a decisive role in social coexistence.

The constitutional and administrative multiplicity of multi-level federalism and the social variety forged by these disparate loyalties were interdependent.[133] Both gave the federal history of the Habsburg Monarchy its unique imprint. The configuration of the monarchy provided a framework for very different loyalties

[131] The two crown lands of Tyrol and Vorarlberg as well as the three crown lands of Istria, Gorizia-Gradisca, and Trieste, each of which constituted an Austrian administrative area with a common governorate and were thus a federation in miniature, held a special position. Cf. Chapters 9 and 10.

[132] Carl Klopfer, *Unser Kaiser: Ein Gedenkbuch der fünfzigjährigen Regierung, zugleich ein Lebens- und Characterbild Kaiser Franz Josef I.* Vienna, 1898, 49.

[133] On the interdependence of administrative structures and multilingual society cf. Judson, *Habsburg Empire*, 349 and 352–3.

and affiliations, which could be related to the dynasty and the emperor, to the nations (as linguistic and provincial collectives), to religion, or to the 'state' as the civic community of Austria or Hungary. All citizens of the Habsburg Monarchy lived in a common confederal home, yet they occupied very different spaces within it, which they could organize and fill with life in their own particular ways.[134]

A Federal History of the Habsburg Empire, 1815–1918. Jana Osterkamp, Oxford University Press.
 DOI: 10.1093/9780198943631.003.0007

[134] Cf. Chapters 8 and 9.

Figure 7.1 Historical map of the Habsburg Empire, 1815–1918.

22°
26°
0 50 100 150 200 250 km
RUSSIAN EMPIRE
50°
Brody
SILESIA
Cracow
Lviv
GALICIA
Przemyśl
Tarnopol
Sambor
Stryj
RUSSIAN EMPIRE
Dniester
Košice
Czernowitz
Ungvár
Pruth
Miskolc
BUKOVINA
Debrecen
Gödöllö
Tisza
Budapest
Iaşi
HUNGARY
Oradea
Cluj
TRANSYLVANIA
46°
Arad
Sibiu
Braşov
Timişoara
Drave
Voivodina
ROMANIA (Kingdom 1881)
Save
Bucharest
Belgrade
Danube
Danube
SERBIA (Kingdom 1882)
Sarajevo
Mostar
(Kingdom 1910)
MONTENEGRO
Cetinje
Kotor
OTTOMAN EMPIRE
Skutari
46°
100 200 500 1000 1500 2000 2500 3000 4000 m
Frankfurt/Main
Lemberg
Danube
Vienna
Tatra
Eastern Carpathians
Alps
Budapest
Southern Carpathians
Genoa
Apennines
Dinaric Alps
Danube
Balkan Mountains
Sofia

Figure 7.2 Propaganda postcard 'Hoch das Vaterland! Österreich-Ungarn wird nie untergehen.' [Long live the fatherland! Austria-Hungary will never fall], c.1916.

7

K. u. K.—The Confederative Double House, 1867–1918

The Compromise Laws of 1867 made Austria-Hungary a confederative double house. The insignia used by its diplomatic missions abroad were symbols of this dual structure of the empire. Atop the 'imperial and royal' embassies and legations, the black-and-yellow flag of Austria fluttered on the left and the red-white-green of Hungary on the right.[1] Those approaching the chancery buildings were to understand the flags as an expression of the empire's divided statehood. In addition to the two states' banners, the ambassadors also hoisted the imperial standard with its double-headed eagle, a symbol of their common dynastic heritage. It was not until after the outbreak of the war that a common imperial coat of arms was introduced in 1915.[2]

The coexistence of three flags represented the ambiguity of where and how 'sovereignty' was located in this complex federation. The formative period of federalism between 1848 and 1867 had produced different models of federalism: the federal nationality state, historic crown land federalism, and executive federalism or, in relation to the German Confederation, dualism and trialism. After 1867, however, political reality did not follow these neat blueprints. Nor was the resultant dualist system based on a single federal treaty.[3] Rather, Austria-Hungary remained bound by a legal and political union, which, in the apt phrase of Edmund Bernatzik, was intended to make the 'unilateral demolition of the dualist edifice' impossible.[4]

After 1867, in this (con)federative double house many constitutional questions were left unanswered. In Cisleithania, the constitution—based on the five Fundamental Laws—remained fragmentary. In Transleithania, the constitutional traditions that shaped the political system were not even written down or codified. Only the two 'Compromise Laws' provided any sort of common constitutional basis for the whole empire. The Hungarian Compromise Act had been

[1] Rudolf Agstner, *Handbuch des Österreichischen Auswärtigen Dienstes*. Vol. 1: *1918–1938. Zentrale, Gesandtschaften und Konsulate*. Vienna, 2015, 259.

[2] Edmund Bernatzik, 'Unsere neuen Wappen und Titel', *Österreichische Zeitschrift für öffentliches Recht*, 2/5–6 (1915/16), 616–52.

[3] Bernatzik, 'Unsere neuen Wappen und Titel', 624.

[4] Bernatzik, 'Unsere neuen Wappen und Titel', 624.

promulgated by Franz Joseph as 'Hungarian King' on 12 June 1867.[5] Two and a half years later, on 21 December 1867, he signed the corresponding Austrian Delegation Act in the first-person, using 'I'. The first-person signature left ample ambiguity about its dynastic and constitutional meaning.[6] The two Compromise Laws contradicted each other in important details. They did, however, agree on the tasks and number of common institutions assigned to the empire. These included the three common ministries of foreign affairs, war, and finance, and the so-called delegations.

In Austro-Hungarian state theory, an open-ended scholarly polemic now began. The Habsburg Monarchy was to be aligned with central legal concepts of statehood and sovereignty, not least to clarify for the political decision-makers where political power was rooted and how it was limited. These concepts continue to influence the scholarly debate of constitutional history to this day.[7] If one applies today's concepts of federation to Habsburg rule, it is not possible to clearly define the state character of the empire as a whole, or of its two main parts, or the crown lands. This is particularly true if one draws on the triad of characteristics developed by Georg Jellinek and Max Weber around the turn of the twentieth century: the people, territory, and state authority.

The empire's responsibilities for foreign policy, defence, and common finances were key areas of sovereign agency. Nevertheless, the empire was not a state because there was neither a common 'imperial people' nor a common legislator and judiciary. Contemporaries would likely have classified the Austrian and Hungarian parts of the empire as states. Each had a bicameral parliament, a government, and its own judiciary, laws, and administration. But they too remained incomplete states for they exercised no sovereignty in the above-mentioned fields. The historic crown lands, the third piece of the puzzle, were more obviously not states in contemporary thinking. While they did determine key policy areas such as social welfare, education, and agriculture, they lacked fundamental governmental and judicial institutions.

However clean and precise the legal concepts of empire, state, and federalism may have seemed at the time, it remained far from clear how they applied to the historical reality of the Habsburg double house (as depicted in the map, Figure 7.1). This chapter applies modern-day frameworks for the interpretation of

[5] Article XII of the Law of 1867 on the Common Affairs between the Crown lands of Hungary and the Other Lands under His Majesty's Government and on the modus operandi of their treatment, sanctioned by the King on 12 June 1867.

[6] Fundamental Law of 21 Dec. 1867 on Matters Common to all Crown lands of the Austrian Monarchy and the modus operandi of their treatment, No. 146/1867 RGBl.

[7] Karin Olechowski-Hrdlicka, *Die gemeinsamen Angelegenheiten der Österreichisch-Ungarischen Monarchie*. Frankfurt am Main, 2001, 192–201. Gerald Stourzh, 'Verfassung und Verfassungswirklichkeit Altösterreichs in den Schriften Georg Jellineks'. In Stanley L. Paulson and Martin Schulte (eds), *Georg Jellinek: Beiträge zu Leben und Werk*. Tübingen, 2000, 251–3. Cf. Martin P. Schennach (ed), *Rechtshistorische Aspekte des österreichischen Föderalismus*. Vienna, 2015.

multi-tiered systems of rule to the Habsburg constitutional landscape. Central to this analysis is a concept of federation (synonymous with *Bund*, *Föderation*, *fédération*), borrowed from recent federalism theories, which enables us to describe the relationship between Austria and Hungary as a (con)federation that, at least on the Austrian side, had its own internal federal structure at the level of the crown lands.[8]

7.1. Austro-Hungarian History of Federal Ideas

Throughout the dualist period between 1867 and 1918, state theorists failed to reach a consensus on the classification of the Habsburg Monarchy as a confederation or federation (*Staatenbund* or *Bundesstaat*), a personal or functional union (*Personalunion* or *Realunion*), or a monarchy, empire, or state. Constant engagement with the concept of federalism produced heterogeneous and hybrid positions that combined federal components in multiple variants.[9] The disagreement over federal concepts was essentially, if not primarily, related to diverging political intentions hidden behind the curtains of state law.

The focal point of this debate was one of the most important innovations in state theory: 'sovereignty'.[10] The concept of 'state sovereignty', as many still understand it today, increasingly replaced earlier notions of princely sovereignty.[11] The liberal doctrine of 'the state' in the nineteenth century presented the state and its sovereignty as an almost physical entity with tangible and spatial characteristics: wherever there was a sovereign state, no other state could be sovereign.[12] Sovereignty was seen as exclusive and indivisible.[13]

In state theory, federal constructs such as the Habsburg Monarchy were measured against the two basic models of 'confederation' (*Staatenbund*) or 'federal state' (*Bundesstaat*), which differed primarily in where they located sovereignty.[14]

[8] Cf. Introduction.

[9] Ludwig Gumplowicz, *Das österreichische Staatsrecht: Verfassungs- und Verwaltungsrecht*. Vienna, 1907, 44–5; Fritz Keller, *Österreichisches und ungarisches Staatsrecht: Eine Einführung*. Berlin, 1917, 45.

[10] Critically Friedrich Tezner, *Die Wandlungen der österreichisch-ungarischen Reichsidee*. Vienna, 1905, 45–53, who argues Bodin's theory of sovereignty does not apply to composite states.

[11] On the perspectives of international and state law Bardo Fassbender, *Der offene Bundesstaat: Studien zur auswärtigen Gewalt und zur Völkerrechtssubjektivität bundesstaatlicher Teilstaaten in Europa*. Tübingen, 2007.

[12] In extreme cases, it was argued that federal states were not possible at all, see the Bavarian constitutionalist Max von Seydel, 'Der Bundesstaatsbegriff. Eine staatsrechtliche Untersuchung'. In Seydel, *Staatsrechtliche und politische Abhandlungen*. Freiburg and Leipzig, 1893, here 6–7.

[13] Exceptionally, the German Georg Waitz outlined the possibility of a 'divided sovereignty' in 1853, Georg Waitz, *Grundzüge der Politik nebst einzelnen Ausführungen*. Kiel, 1862.

[14] Cf. concise summary of the debate Christoph Schönberger, 'Die Europäische Union als Bund: Zugleich ein Beitrag zur Verabschiedung des Staatenbund—Bundesstaat-Schemas', *Archiv des öffentlichen Rechts*, 129 (2004), 81–120; Olivier Beaud, *Théorie de la Fédération*. 2nd edn. Paris, 2009; Beaud, 'Federation and Empire: About a Conceptual Distinction of Political Forms', *International Journal of*

The confederation was seen as an international relationship; its member states remained sovereign. The federation, on the other hand, was an independent legal entity. Its constituent states had relinquished their sovereignty and transferred it to the federal government. Notions of sovereignty distributed across several levels of rule—typical of today's theory of multi-tiered governance—were roundly dismissed by the majority of constitutional experts at the time.[15]

Whether scholars categorized the Habsburg Monarchy as a confederation or a federation depended on their political outlook. Whoever located 'sovereignty' in the empire or the two parts of the empire, in the emperor and his ministries, or in the crown lands, attributed to them supreme authority. Many Austrian and Hungarian jurists drew their arguments from state doctrine in the German Empire.[16] There, too, legal scholars discussed the character of Germany as a confederation or federation and were just as 'fixated on locating sovereignty'.[17] Some saw the German Empire of 1871 as a federal state, although remnants of a confederation of states were still evident. Their intention was to strengthen the highest legislative and executive powers through a democratically legitimized Reichstag. Others regarded the German Reich as a confederation of states (or even of princes), emphasizing both their independence and the power of their royal rulers.[18] In these power struggles, constitutional jurisprudence used the 'state as argument', as Christoph Möllers succinctly put it. By developing state theory in seemingly neutral terms, legal scholars indirectly participated in a debate about the distribution of political power and participation.[19]

Other, more traditional categorizations were also discussed for Austria-Hungary. By a Supreme Handwritten Decree of 14 November 1868, the emperor formalized the official names 'Austro-Hungarian Monarchy' and 'Austro-Hungarian Empire'.[20] Despite these appellations, however, the constitutions did not contain a

Constitutional Law, 16/4 (2018), 1199–1206; Stefan Oeter, '"Föderation" oder "Bund" als Oberbegriff'. In Eva Marlene Hausteiner (ed.), *Föderalismen: Modelle jenseits des Staates*. Baden-Baden, 2016, 235–66. Cf. Introduction.

[15] Cf. as an exception the book by Theodor Dantscher von Kollesberg, *Der monarchische Bundesstaat Oesterreich-Ungarn und der Berliner Vertrag nebst der Bosnischen Vorlage*. Vienna, 1880.

[16] Overview by Ewald Wiederin, *Bundesrecht und Landesrecht*. Vienna, 1995, 8–11; Michael Stolleis, *Geschichte des öffentlichen Rechts in Deutschland*. Vol. 2: *Staatsrechtslehre und Verwaltungswissenschaft 1800–1914*. Munich, 1992, 365–7.

[17] Sebastian Huhnholz and Eva Marlene Hausteiner, 'Ein Bund unter Gleichen? Zum (anti)hegemonialen Charakter föderaler Arrangements', In Gerold Ambrosius, Christian Henrich-Franke, and Cornelius Neutsch (eds), *Föderalismus in historisch vergleichender Perspektive*. Vol. 2: *Föderale Systeme. Kaiserreich—Donaumonarchie—Europäische Union*. Baden-Baden, 2015, 281.

[18] On the political implications of the 'Princely League' convincingly Herfried Münkler, 'Fürstenbund und Bundesstaat: Der Erste Weltkrieg als (letzter) Reichseinigungskrieg'. In Hausteiner, *Föderalismen*, 181–206.

[19] Christoph Möllers, *Staat als Argument*. Tübingen, 2011. Also Reinhart Koselleck, 'Bund (Bündnis, Föderalismus, Bundesstaat)'. In Otto Brunner et al (eds), *Geschichtliche Grundbegriffe*. Subvol. 1: *Historisches Lexikon zur politisch-sozialen Sprache in Deutschland*. Stuttgart, 2004, 649.

[20] Tezner, *Wandlungen der österreichisch-ungarischen Reichsidee*; Ivan Žolger, *Der staatsrechtliche Ausgleich zwischen Österreich und Ungarn*. Leipzig, 1911.

clear concept of empire. References to the 'Reich' in the Compromise Laws signified the whole of Austria-Hungary.[21] In the Hungarian and Austrian constitutions, however, 'empire' referred only to their respective parts. The parliaments were called the Hungarian *Reichstag* and the Austrian *Reichsrat*, which was joined by an Austrian *Reichsgericht*. In Austrian state theory, it became customary to refer to the whole of Austria-Hungary as the 'empire', rather than to one of its two parts.[22] Many Hungarians found the term 'Hungarian half of the empire', which was common in German-language state theory, derogatory and belittling.[23] Constitutionalists such as Georg Jellinek, on the other hand, saw 'empire' in the European context only as a general term for monarchical rule.[24] The Slovenian-born constitutionalist Ivan Žolger argued similarly in his seminal work on the Austro-Hungarian Compromise. Žolger opposed the views of his professional colleagues who believed that legal conclusions about the state—i.e. whether it was unitary or a confederation or federation—could be inferred merely from the name 'empire'.[25]

The concepts of 'real union' and 'personal union' applied by contemporary scholars to the Habsburg Monarchy were also based on European state theory. 'Union' was usually applied to the union of monarchical states.[26] A personal union was the unification of otherwise legally independent states under one ruling dynasty 'as a result of the accidental coincidence of their succession to the throne'.[27] The typical example was Great Britain-Hanover, which had existed since the year 1714.[28] A real union was the 'constitutional union of several states under the same sovereign'.[29] Personal unions were inconceivable with, real unions without, a constitutional foundation.

Hungarian state theorists, above all, argued that the Habsburg Monarchy was a personal union. Because there was no common dualistic constitution, they regarded the succession rights enshrined in the Pragmatic Sanction as the unifying bond of the polity. They derived the common powers of foreign policy and defence from the 'majesty rights of the king', as the Hungarian king, rather than

[21] Josef von Löwenthal, 'Die rechtliche Natur von Österreich-Ungarn: Eine Analyse der gemeinsamen Angelegenheiten', *Österreichische Zeitschrift für öffentliches Recht*, 3/6 (1918), 613. Cf. Introduction.

[22] Cf. summary Tezner, *Wandlungen der österreichisch-ungarischen Reichsidee.*

[23] Heinrich Marczali, *Ungarisches Verfassungsrecht.* Tübingen, 1911, 191; Žolger, *Ausgleich zwischen Österreich und Ungarn*, 100.

[24] Georg Jellinek, *Die Lehre von den Staatenverbindungen.* Vienna, 1882, 250–1.

[25] Žolger, *Ausgleich zwischen Österreich und Ungarn*, 100–1. Similar Löwenthal, 'Österreich-Ungarn', 613.

[26] Today, the union model comprises supranational relations of states such as the European Union. For a short typology of federalism Dirk Jörke, *Die Größe der Demokratie.* Berlin, 2019, 252–3.

[27] Tezner, *Wandlungen der österreichisch-ungarischen Reichsidee*, 1.

[28] Jellinek, *Lehre von den Staatenverbindungen*, 87.

[29] Josef Ulbrich, *Die rechtliche Natur der österreichisch-ungarischen Monarchie.* Vienna, 1879, 6; Jellinek, *Lehre von den Staatenverbindungen*, 197.

from a common legal basis.[30] Having experienced a first peak around 1868, the discourse of a 'personal union' regained popularity after 1903, when the Hungarian Independence Party won a majority of seats in the Hungarian Chamber of Deputies and the Hungarian Liberals lost their majority for the first time since 1867.[31] The idea that Austria-Hungary consisted of two legally unconnected states with two independent regents who 'just happened' to be the same person provided Hungarian nationalists like Ferenc Kossuth with the means to justify their political quest for greater Hungarian independence.[32]

In the eyes of Austrian constitutionalists, this approach unnecessarily undermined the unifying bond between the empire's two parts.[33] In response, they adopted the concept of a real union. In his widely acclaimed study, the statistician and state law expert Franz von Juraschek argued that, for Austria-Hungary to qualify as a real union, the existence of common organs of government, whose commonality was constitutionally established, was sufficient. The question whether this created a new state 'alongside or above the united states' was not significant.[34] The influential doctrines of state law, written by Josef Ulbrich and Friedrich Tezner, reinterpreted the Pragmatic Sanction as a guarantee of 'the continuance and commonality of the sovereign personality' and thus as the historical state-law basis of a real union.[35] Even after 1867, Tezner assumed the continued existence of a 'common state' as a 'common monarchy'.[36]

The attempt to categorize reality through legal concepts did not concern the sphere of law alone, but also the sphere of politics. Lawyers, politicians, and historians fought, as Tezner wryly observed, 'with berserk rage' and 'like dragons' over who would have final say on statehood.[37] The Austrian federalism theorist Ewald Wiederin speaks of a 'jousting field' for power-related 'questions of prestige and rank'.[38] Behind the controversy over legal concepts of federalism, the primordial question of Austro-Hungarian state theory looms once more—about the original locus of statehood and sovereignty, and thus of power.

Choosing a particular concept thus had far-reaching legal and political consequences.[39] The authors' backgrounds and the scholarly context in which they

[30] Marczali, *Ungarisches Verfassungsrecht*, 76.

[31] Franz von Juraschek, *Personal- und Realunion mit einem Anhange*. Berlin, 1878, 99. On the Hungarian view Emerich Korbuly, *Ungarns öffentliches Recht*. Budapest, 1874; Marczali, *Ungarisches Verfassungsrecht*.

[32] Tezner, *Wandlungen der österreichisch-ungarischen Reichsidee*, 1.

[33] Bernatzik, 'Unsere neuen Wappen und Titel'.

[34] Juraschek, *Personal- und Realunion mit einem Anhange*, 92 and 95.

[35] Ulbrich, *Natur der österreichisch-ungarischen Monarchie*, 53 f.

[36] Tezner, *Wandlungen der österreichisch-ungarischen Reichsidee*, 12.

[37] Tezner, *Wandlungen der österreichisch-ungarischen Reichsidee*, 1 and 234.

[38] Wiederin, *Bundesrecht und Landesrecht*, 28, with reference to Ulrich Scheuner, 'Das Bundesverfassungsgericht und die Bindungskraft seiner Entscheidungen', *Die Öffentliche Verwaltung*, 15 (1962), 644.

[39] Wiederin, *Bundesrecht und Landesrecht*, 30.

wrote reveal the politics behind the concepts. The characterization of Austria-Hungary as a confederation of states implied that the 'sovereign' states of Austria and Hungary, which had joined together, were entitled to dissolve the confederation at any time.[40] This was the view of some Hungarian scholars. They argued for Hungary's statehood with reference to its history and the Pragmatic Sanction; from their point of view, sovereignty originated in each part of the empire.[41] By contrast, the terms federal state or real union postulated firmer foundations for the Monarchy as a whole. Traditionally, German-Austrian state law experts regarded the 'Austrian Empire', established in 1804, as the source of 'sovereignty'.[42] The term 'federal state' first appeared with the expansion of Austria-Hungary in 1878. Inspired by the Treaty of Berlin and the occupation of Bosnia and Herzegovina, the Innsbruck expert scholar, Theodor Dantscher von Kollesberg, presented an impressive theory on Austria-Hungary as a federal monarchy.[43] Using the concept of the federal state, he established Austria-Hungary's unity of action in foreign and defence policy as a multi-tiered unit.[44]

The state theory proved to have a blind spot in its attempts to conceptualize federalism: the crown lands. Comparisons with European federations and unions suggested a similarity that did not exist. The German Empire after 1871 and Austria-Hungary after 1867 were compared by using the concepts of the federal monarchy, the confederation of states, or the princely league. The Norwegian-Swedish union of 1814, the relationship between Russia and Finland, Russia and Poland, or Denmark and Iceland in turn were compared with the union model of Austria-Hungary. However, none of these countries had a domestic order that contained more than two tiers of federal governance. When contemporaries brought Germany and Austria-Hungary under the same federal concept, Germany appeared only with the levels of the empire and the constituent states, while Austria-Hungary appeared with the empire and the two parts of the empire, Austria and Hungary. The crown lands were simply ignored by the vast majority of state experts.[45] Only sporadically can one find approaches which incorporate

[40] Jörke, *Größe der Demokratie*, 253.

[41] Marczali, *Ungarisches Verfassungsrecht*, 268. On the state-law controversies in the run-up to the Compromise Laws Wenzel Lustkandl, *Das ungarische-österreichische Staatsrecht*. Vienna, 1863; Ferencz (Franz) Deák, *Ein Beitrag zum ungarischen Staatsrecht: Bemerkungen über Wenzel Lustkandl's 'Ungarisch-österreichisches Staatsrecht'*. Budapest, 1865.

[42] Friedrich Tezner, *Der österreichische Kaisertitel, das ungarische Staatsrecht und die ungarische Publicistik*. Vienna, 1899, 148–55.

[43] Dantscher von Kollesberg, *Der monarchische Bundesstaat Oesterreich-Ungarn*, 37.

[44] On the state character of Austria-Hungary Hermann Bidermann, *Die rechtliche Natur der österreichisch-ungarischen Monarchie*. Vienna, 1877. Cf. Ulbrich, *Natur der österreichisch-ungarischen Monarchie*, 53–4.; Tezner, *Der österreichische Kaisertitel*, 223.

[45] This aspect is passed over by Wiederin, who elaborates on the continuities between the federalism debate before and after 1918. Wiederin: *Bundesrecht und Landesrecht*.

them. One exception is Jellinek's essay 'On State Fragments', in which he treats crown lands mathematically as 'remainders' after subtracting the state.[46]

The rooms of the Austro-Hungarian double house allocated to each crown land differed significantly. It was predominantly Czech, Polish, Croatian, and South Slav authors who, in their writings, dealt with the question of the significance of historic crown land state law within the dualism of the empire.[47] Josef Pliveric, a professor of state law in Zagreb, interpreted the relationship between Hungary and Croatia as a federal union.[48] Moreover, according to Slavic (specifically Czech) scholars, the Austro-Hungarian Compromise of 1867 did not diminish the historical statehood and sovereignty of crown lands such as Bohemia.[49] In the Austro-Hungarian nomenclature, the term 'federalism' came to describe these positions. In a survey organized by a law journal in 1916, the word 'federalist' referred to those currents, dogmas, and parties that wanted to grant the crown lands—based on historical precedent—greater decision-making power and autonomy.[50]

If one examines the Austro-Hungarian federal edifice from within, a much more multifaceted picture emerges than the dualistic exterior appearance would suggest. Flags, coats of arms, military symbols, and extensive libraries of historical treatises on state law from the Middle Ages to the present day all established other crown lands within the empire as 'states' (such as Croatia-Slavonia), or at least as potential ones (such as Bohemia).[51] These different dimensions of statehood could not, and still cannot, be adequately described and studied with contemporary concepts of the state and state unions. New and innovative analytical categories are required.

7.2. Multi-Tiered Federalism as an Analytical Perspective

For the first time, we will examine here post-1867 Austria-Hungary as a multi-tiered federation. Because the monarchy was not rooted in a *single* constitution, but in two Compromise Laws—albeit with almost identical content—contemporaries and historians were reluctant to interpret the Compromise Laws in federal terms. Yet it is precisely this heuristic perspective which we shall take now.

[46] Georg Jellinek, *Über Staatsfragmente*. Heidelberg, 1896. Jellinek, however, remained sceptical about the feasibility of crown land sovereignty and warned against the danger of secessionism. Cf. Jens Kersten, *Georg Jellinek und die klassische Staatslehre*. Tübingen, 2000, 263.

[47] Thomas Simon, 'Zur Stellung der Länder in der österreichischen und deutschen Staatsrechtslehre von 1867/71 und 1918'. In Schennach, *Rechtshistorische Aspekte des österreichischen Föderalismus*, 63–86.

[48] Georg Jellinek and Josef Pliveric, *Das rechtliche Verhältnis Kroatiens zu Ungarn*. Agram, 1885.

[49] Cf. Chapter 8.

[50] 'Die Stellung der Kronländer im Gefüge der österreichischen Verfassung. Eine Rundfrage', *Österreichische Zeitschrift für öffentliches Recht*, 3 (1916).

[51] On the particular role of the individual crown lands, cf. Chapter 8.

The concept of federation applied here draws on the recent legal-political theory of federalism developed by Olivier Beaud, who himself was inspired by the historical examples of American, Swiss, and German federalism in the eighteenth and nineteenth centuries, and by Christoph Schönberger, who wrote a diachronic comparison of German federalism and the European Union.[52] It has also found its way into the studies of Stefan Oeter, Katharina Mangold, Eva Hausteiner, and Dirk Jörke.[53] Fundamentally, federations are defined by a distribution of power between several levels of government. No single tier has absolute priority as none possesses undivided or original sovereignty. It is precisely this balance of power that is constitutive of a federation.

The concept of federation or *Bund* is broader than that of the federal *state*. The theory of multi-level federations[54] discards two commonly held assumptions about federal polities. The first assumption, which still has many adherents, not least in the history of German federalism, concerns the question of the state, statehood, and sovereignty. According to this assumption, federalism is understood as multi-tiered governance of states (federal state and constituent states) in which sovereignty is clearly located either at the upper level of rule (federal state) or at the lower level of rule (confederation of states).[55] In the understanding of federalism applied here, however, statehood and sovereignty are no longer considered essential to the concept of federalism. For example, the German Confederation of 1815, like the political system of Europe today, had many attributes and institutions that are characteristic of statehood without necessarily being considered a state in its entirety.[56]

Second, this post-modern conceptualization of federalism avoids assigning sovereignty solely on the grounds of the technical wording of foundational legal documents. Sovereignty is instead interpreted with reference to a 'living constitution' that manifests itself in the practice of governance within a federal state. Accordingly, a multi-tiered federation (which is 'sovereign' in its entirety, not in its parts) can only be considered sovereign if it is sustained as a multi-tiered political system over an extended period of time.[57]

Federalism is therefore understood here as *the vertical distribution of state power among different levels of decision-making within a long-term polity.* All levels of governance in a federal polity share in the exercise of state sovereignty.

[52] Schönberger, 'Die Europäische Union als Bund'; Beaud, *Théorie de la Fédération.*

[53] Anna Katharina Mangold, *Gemeinschaftsrecht und deutsches Recht.* Tübingen, 2011, 449–50; Jörke, *Größe der Demokratie*; Oeter, '"Föderation" oder "Bund" als Oberbegriff'; Huhnholz and Hausteiner, 'Ein Bund unter Gleichen?' Cf. also the Introduction in this book.

[54] In particular, I rely on the work of Beaud, *Théorie de la Fédération*; Schönberger, 'Die Europäische Union als Bund'.

[55] Oeter, '"Föderation" oder "Bund" als Oberbegriff', 235–66.

[56] Beaud, 'Federation and Empire', 1199.

[57] On the legal-political character of federations, cf. with recourse to Carl Schmitt Beaud, *Théorie de la Fédération*, 16–19. On federal loyalty Hartmut Bauer, *Die Bundestreue.* Tübingen, 1992; Armin Hatje, *Loyalität als Rechtsprinzip in der Europäischen Union.* Baden-Baden, 2001.

In federal systems, the cooperation, opposition, and mere coexistence of state powers and levels of governance are kept in a legal and political balance.[58] As a result, questions about how the state is organized cannot neatly be separated from questions about the political practice of the time. Thus, federalism is based not only on an original act of state law, but essentially on political practice. This concept of a multi-level federation (*Bund*) can be used to focus both on a federal state structure and the procedural nature of federal development.[59]

In the dual history of the legal organization and political practice of Habsburg federalism presented here, the question discussed at the time whether statehood and sovereignty belonged to the empire as a whole or Austria and Hungary as its constitutive parts is not decisive. Instead, the political reality is examined in terms of specific institutions and policies.[60] Taking in consideration the federal objectives of the Compromise Laws, we will try to understand the empire as a foreign policy and security union as well as an economic community; the relationship between Austria and Hungary as a confederation. In the two parts of this confederation, interior federal structures developed differently. In the Austrian part of the empire, we observe a regionalization of politics (*Verländerung*). In the Hungarian part, the federation of Hungary and Croatia-Slavonia envisioned in the 1868 constitution turned out to be increasingly centrist in practice. Bosnia and Herzegovina was a special case. Occupied in 1878 and annexed in 1908, it never became a legal part of the confederation and was considered a sort of 'colony'.[61] Rule over Bosnia was thus structurally imperial rather than federal.

7.3. A Shared Monarch and a Monarchical Federation

In the nineteenth century, monarchical federalism, unlike republican federalism, was considered an exception.[62] Nonetheless, already the contemporary federalism expert, Theodor Dantscher, considered it untenable 'to think that the concept of the federal state can be realized only in the form of a republic'.[63] More recently, the historians of federalism have interpreted the German Confederation of 1815 and the German Empire of 1871 as monarchical federations.[64] This reflects a more general shift in emphasis within political history. The nineteenth century

[58] Similarly, Carl Schmitt, *Verfassungslehre*. Berlin, 1928, 373–91.

[59] Oeter, '"Föderation" oder "Bund" als Oberbegriff', 236–7.

[60] Stefan Nellen and Thomas Stockinger, 'Staat, Verwaltung und Raum im langen 19. Jahrhundert. Einleitung', *Administory*, 2/1 (2017), 7.

[61] Ferdinand Schmid, *Bosnien und die Herzegovina unter der Verwaltung Österreich-Ungarns*. Leipzig, 1914, 1.

[62] Originally, almost all early modern federations had a monarchical character as 'princely confederations'. Beaud, *Théorie de la Fédération*, 388. On the nexus of federalism and democracy Roland Sturm, *Föderalismus: Eine Einführung*. 2nd edn. Baden-Baden, 2010, 17–20.

[63] Dantscher von Kollesberg, *Der monarchische Bundesstaat Oesterreich-Ungarn*, 21–2.

[64] Beaud, *Théorie de la Fédération*, 387–91.

is no longer seen only as the century of revolutions and the nation state, but also as the 'century of the monarchy'.[65] Typologically, a monarchical federation is located somewhere between dynasty and empire, federation and nation state. German history, for instance, is an example of the transition from a princely confederation to a federal union or confederation of states.[66]

The case of Austria-Hungary was different. The transition to federalism did not start from a princely confederation but was a gradual change to monarchical constitutionalism. While Germany had several monarchs under its federal umbrella, Austria-Hungary was ruled by a single person. After 1867, the role of the monarch was *constitutionally* divided into two. In Hungary, he was the head of a so-called parliamentary monarchy. In Austria, by contrast, he retained significant control of the government.[67] After 1867, there was no longer one monarchy of the Habsburgs, but two 'Habsburg monarchies'.

In both constitutional systems, the legislative power was exercised jointly by the respective bicameral parliament and the monarch, whose veto power was absolute.[68] Bills had to pass through the Imperial Chancellery and across the emperor's desk before they could be presented to parliament (pre-sanction). Bills passed by the parliament, meanwhile, were valid only if the monarch approved them (sanction). While some saw this procedure as an expression of the 'sovereign will of the states' of Hungary and Austria, others regarded it as an emanation of the monarchical principle or as a sharing of sovereignty between the ruler and the empire as a whole.[69]

The power of the parliaments in Budapest and Vienna diverged noticeably. In the Austrian constitutional monarchy, the legislature formally had no influence on the government.[70] Although ministers were accountable to parliament under the principle of ministerial responsibility, they could not be dismissed.[71] The Austrian government, therefore, consisted of the emperor's confidants. Hungary had a parliamentary form of government in which the parliament could impeach ministers and, by a vote of no confidence, overthrow the government. The government's dependence on parliament resulted in closer cooperation between the two as well as concerted action vis-a-vis the king.

[65] Dieter Langewiesche, *Die Monarchie im Jahrhundert Europas*. Heidelberg, 2013. Cf. Johannes Paulmann, *Pomp und Politik*. Paderborn, 2000 and on the multiple modernities of monarchies Heidi Hein-Kircher and Frederik Frank Sterkenburgh (eds), *Modernizing Europe's Imperial Monarchies: Germany, Austria-Hungary, and Russia in the Nineteenth Century*, London 2025.

[66] For the German Empire Münkler, 'Fürstenbund und Bundesstaat'.

[67] On the typology of monarchies Ernst-Wolfgang Böckenförde, 'Der deutsche Typ der konstitutionellen Monarchie im 19. Jahrhundert'. In Böckenförde, *Recht, Staat, Freiheit*. Frankfurt, 1991, 273–305.

[68] Böckenförde, 'Konstitutionelle Monarchie', 283.

[69] Bernatzik, 'Unsere neuen Wappen und Titel', 638.

[70] Böckenförde, 'Konstitutionelle Monarchie', 285.

[71] Böckenförde, 'Konstitutionelle Monarchie', 287.

Hungarian governments thus enjoyed longer periods of stability. In Austria, by contrast, dismissals by the emperor and threats of resignation by the government were a tactical means of exercising power.[72] In a confidential conversation with the state law expert and politician Josef Redlich, Prime Minister Koerber, referring to the emperor's readiness to dismiss his ministers, spoke 'of the inherited evil of Austrian governments under Franz Joseph, that they could never count on the reliability of their existence and purposeful perseverance'. With an apparent lack of irony, he then labelled his own threats of resignation as a successful strategy, boasting that he had 'achieved a great deal with the emperor by constantly emphasizing his readiness to resign'.[73]

The legitimation of rule in Austria was rooted in the so-called monarchical principle.[74] The monarchical principle had been developed in conservative German state theory as a secular response to divine grace, with reference to French and English authors. It was regarded as 'a main article of European public law'.[75] At Metternich's instigation, it was included in the Vienna Concluding Act in 1820 and applied to all members of the German Confederation. 'Sovereign' state power was not vested in the nation or in the ruler and the nation together, but in the monarch alone.[76] Constitutional barriers were imposed of his own free will while constitutional reforms were 'granted' from above, not 'agreed upon' by treaty.[77] The monarch and the constitutional monarchy 'placed themselves in a statutory order that binds them'.[78] Once the constitution was in place, however, constitutional amendments could only be made with the constitutional participation of the parliamentary representation. Given this constitutional self-restraint, the differences between imposed and treaty-based constitutions in Europe diminished over time.[79]

Even though Austria and Hungary shared one monarch, the narratives they used to legitimize their respective monarchical states differed. In Hungary, constitutional experts still regularly linked the legitimacy of rule not to the monarch, but to the doctrine of the Holy Crown. The leading Hungarian legal historian,

[72] National-political disputes between the ministers for the Czechs and for the Germans, for example, led to several resignations. For this Josef Redlich, *Schicksalsjahre Österreichs: Die Erinnerungen und Tagebücher Josef Redlichs 1869–1936*. Vol. 1: *1869–1914*. Vienna, 2011, 260–1, 265, and 297.

[73] Redlich, *Schicksalsjahre Österreichs*, 1, 261.

[74] Hugo Hantsch, 'Franz Joseph'. In *Neue Deutsche Biographie*. Vol. 5. Berlin, 1961, 364. For the monarchical principle see Stolleis, *Geschichte des öffentlichen Rechts*, 2. 102–105.

[75] Quoted in Stolleis, *Geschichte des öffentlichen Rechts*, 2. 105. Cf. Otto Brunner, 'Vom Gottesgnadentum zum monarchischen Prinzip'. In Brunner, *Neue Wege der Verfassungs- und Sozialgeschichte*. 2nd edn. Göttingen, 1968, 160–86. For a contemporary account of the 'German' or 'French' character of this principle. Karl Gottfried Hugelmann, 'Zur Lehre vom "monarchischen Prinzip"', *Österreichische Zeitschrift für öffentliches Recht*, 2/4 (1915), 472–86.

[76] Cf. Hans Kelsen, *Hauptprobleme der Staatsrechtslehre*. Tübingen, 1911, 612–16.

[77] Stolleis, *Geschichte des öffentlichen Rechts*, 2. 103.

[78] Böckenförde, 'Konstitutionellen Monarchie', 280.

[79] Böckenförde, 'Konstitutionelle Monarchie', 281.

Ákos von Timon, summarized this state narrative in 1904. Medieval public law had developed 'the concept of public authority rooted in the nation and vested jointly in the king and the nation'. 'The idea of public authority—the idea of the state—is given concrete form, in contrast to individual royal authority, in the public-law concept of the Holy Crown.'[80] The 'state', and not the monarch, was the embodiment of the Crown of St Stephen. In this respect, the Hungarian conceptualization of the state was 'ahead of all other peoples of the West'—an allusion to the doctrine of divine right, which was still partly adhered to in Austria.[81] Even constitutionalists like Marczali, who no longer regarded the medieval doctrine of the Holy Crown as a valid source of law, postulated the historical 'primacy of the crown over the king'.[82] Marczali equated the state with the Hungarian crown (but not the state of Austria-Hungary with the imperial crown).[83]

Given the existence of other 'crowns' besides the Crown of St Stephen and given other historic state laws and provincial statutes referring to their own respective 'princely sovereign', the Habsburg monarch could potentially be 'divided' and shared even further. On a historical and symbolic level, even after 1867, Franz Joseph I was ascribed various 'sovereign personalities', referring to his roles and rights as Austrian emperor, Hungarian king, Bohemian king, and so on. The coronation requests from the Kingdom of Bohemia around 1871, for example, referred to the tradition of the Wenceslas Crown, shared by the monarch and the 'nation'.[84]

In the debates about state law as well as in the popular state narratives, the emperor was, therefore, not seen as a symbol of the state unity of Austria-Hungary.[85] Instead, Franz Joseph I slipped into the roles of quite different personae. There was an ambiguous interplay between the Pragmatic Sanction, the Compromise Laws, the constitutions, and provincial statutory orders and their many contradictory interpretations. This enabled him to capitalize on his dynastic titles as well as on his constitutionally and regionally diverse monarchical personae. At home and abroad, he used his manifold titles as circumstances demanded. To his peoples, he was a 'shared monarch'. He provided the reference point for the proverbial loyalty of his subjects, not as an abstract organ of the *state*, but as *dynastic* ruler with interchangeable personae.[86]

[80] Ákos von Timon, *Ungarische Verfassungs- und Rechtsgeschichte mit Bezug auf die Rechtsentwicklung der westlichen Staaten*. Berlin, 1904, 510–11.

[81] Timon, *Ungarische Verfassungs- und Rechtsgeschichte*, 511.

[82] Marczali, *Ungarisches Verfassungsrecht*, 27–8.

[83] Marczali, *Ungarisches Verfassungsrecht*, 268.

[84] Comprehensively Antonín Otakar Zeithammer, *Zur Geschichte der böhmischen Ausgleichsversuche 1865–1871*. 2 vols. Prague, 1912, 1913.

[85] Given the many different titles used for the signatures, the Compromise Laws did not provide a basis for state unity either.

[86] Daniel Unowsky, 'Dynastic Symbolism and Popular Patriotism: Monarchy and Dynasty in Late Imperial Austria'. In Jörn Leonhard and Ulrike von Hirschhausen (eds), *Comparing Empires*. Göttingen, 2011, 237–65; Laurence Cole and Daniel L. Unowsky, *The Limits of Loyalty: Imperial*

7.4. Delegations as Substitute for a Federal Parliament

A common imperial parliament did not exist within the Austro-Hungarian dualism of 1867. Indeed, it was only genuinely considered as part of a reform programme as late as 1913–14 by the heir to the throne, Franz Ferdinand, and his circle of advisers.[87] In 1867, the so-called delegations had been appointed as a possible equivalent for a common Reichstag. According to the ideas of the Austrian negotiators of the Compromise, these were to become a substitute for a common legislative body. The Hungarian negotiators, on the other hand, were anxious to avoid any semblance of parliamentary representation for the whole empire.[88] By holding the delegations to the standards of a parliament in a constitutional state, contemporary constitutional lawyers (as well as many constitutional historians today) discredited and disqualified them as institutionally incomplete and legislatively dysfunctional. Having abandoned the understanding of rule as shared by Metternich, Kübeck, Bach, and Gołuchowski, many liberals in 1867 considered the lack of a unified legislative body a major shortcoming.

However, the delegations should not be perceived as an inferior form of parliament, but as a genuinely federal institution. It is historically misguided to compare the representative function of a federal institution with the representative function of a parliament in a liberal constitutional state.[89] In the theory of federalism, a tiered parliamentary system—consisting of a bicameral federal parliament with an upper chamber representing the states alongside parliaments in the constituent states—is considered the norm.[90] Here the primacy of statutory law (as the condition of legitimate governance) justifies the combination of federalism with republican parliamentarism. Accordingly, the 'sovereign will of the state' had to be articulated in the form of general parliamentary laws.[91] However, according to the French theorist of federalism Beaud, the delegations should not be understood as parliamentary, but as federal institutions. Beaud argues that the federal representative body is neither governmental nor intergovernmental, neither a conference under the law of nations nor a classical parliamentary chamber: 'la Diète reste une institution proprement fédérative: elle n'est ni interétatique ni étatique... elle diffère non seulement de la conférence diplomatique, mais aussi d'une chambre normale d'un Parlement classique'.[92] The reason for this weaken-

Symbolism, Popular Allegiances, and State Patriotism in the Late Habsburg Monarchy. New York, 2007; Jiří Rak, *Zachovej nám, Hospodine: Češi v Rakouském císařství 1804–1918*. Prague, 2013.

[87] Cf. Chapter 11.4.

[88] Éva Somogyi, *Der gemeinsame Ministerrat der österreichisch-ungarischen Monarchie 1867–1906*. Vienna, 1996, 78.

[89] Beaud, *Théorie de la Fédération*, 356.

[90] Arthur Benz, 'Shared Rule vs Self-Rule? Bicameralism, Power-Sharing and the Joint Decision Trap"', *Perspectives on Federalism*, 10/2 (2018), 30–48.

[91] Böckenförde, 'Konstitutionelle Monarchie', 284–5.

[92] Beaud, *Théorie de la Fédération*, 353.

ing of liberal principles in multi-level federalism, according to Beaud, is that the 'Diète fédérale' does not represent the general population, but the member states of a federation according to the principle of parity.[93] The principle of parity is a reminder of the equality of the federal member states and implies an equality de jure that does not exist de facto.[94]

Viewed as a federal body, the delegations appear in a more positive light than is generally the case in Habsburg political history. There were two delegations, one Austrian and the other Hungarian. Each consisted of sixty deputies who were sent by the parliaments of Vienna and Budapest, thus acquiring indirect parliamentary legitimacy. The Hungarian Compromise Act justified the equal number of members with explicit reference to the 'principle of parity' of Austria and Hungary, i.e. with a federal rationale.[95] However, the delegations did not only reflect the parity of the two parts of the empire; in the Austrian delegation, a fixed quota for the crown lands had been applied since 1873, with Bohemia being allocated the most seats.[96]

In the actual decision-making process, however, the separateness of the two parts of the empire was emphasized, not overcome. Compared with other examples of federal representative bodies, the situation here was anomalous as the Austrian and Hungarian delegations met separately. They convened at the same time, but in different places, and had to communicate in writing through embassies (the so-called '*Nuntien*').[97] Unanimity was required for decisions on common affairs and the common budget. The unanimous decision had then to be approved by the emperor. Parliamentary negotiation or discussion of opposing positions was thus non-existent. In the dry, unrealistic, and lofty language of constitutional law textbooks, it was said that 'such concurrence is usually attempted by mutual notification of the resolutions; for if the resolutions are the same, concurrence is achieved'.[98] The Hungarian legal experts had prevented conjoint consultations and negotiations. They feared the abolition of parity and the danger of a gradual loss of power if the two delegations met together and decided issues according to the majoritarian principle, because 'where there is a danger of majority rule, the end of sovereignty is near'.[99]

[93] Koselleck, 'Bund (Bündnis, Föderalismus, Bundestaat)', 650.

[94] Beaud, *Théorie de la Fédération*, 355.

[95] § 29 of the Hungarian Compromise Act. Cf. Žolger, *Ausgleich zwischen Österreich und Ungarn*, 323.

[96] Law of 2 Apr. 1873 on the Amendment of the Fundamental Law on the Representation of the Empire, No. 40/1873 RGBl.

[97] Exceptionally, a joint meeting was held only on 30 Aug. 1869. Gustav Kolmer, *Parlament und Verfassung in Österreich*. Vol. 1: *1848–1869*. Vienna and Leipzig, 1902, 395. Austrian politicians hoped for a future opportunity to reform the system. Richard Charmatz, *Deutsch-österreichische Politik: Studien über den Liberalismus und über die auswärtige Politik Österreichs*. Leipzig, 1907, 122–3.

[98] Gumplowicz, *Das österreichische Staatsrecht*, 129.

[99] Marczali, *Ungarisches Verfassungsrecht*, 187.

The delegations represented the interest that united Austria and Hungary. Their powers were far from insignificant. In the policy areas of foreign affairs, defence, and common finances (the three so-called common affairs), the delegations had important participatory rights. The ministers of common affairs had to report to the delegations, and the delegations could make policy proposals.[100] Minutes and diary entries document that ministers did indeed face controversial debates and interpellations.[101] Motions of no confidence from the delegates were not uncommon, affecting not only the common ministers but also the government and the royal court. In 1912, for example, Carl Bardolff, an aide-de-camp in the military chancellery, telegraphed his superior, the heir to the throne Franz Ferdinand, that the Hungarian National Party under Desider (Desző) Perczel had withdrawn a motion of no confidence against the Austrian minister of war, Moritz von Auffenberg, at the last moment. The latter had been appointed to his post at the instigation of Franz Ferdinand—an arrangement that was also criticized by Tomáš G. Masaryk in the Austrian delegation, which was meeting at the same time.[102] By engaging in such practices, the delegations exercised at least some control. In addition, it became customary to present the delegations every year with the 'Red Books'—as the collection of diplomatic correspondence and documents was called—in order to justify both foreign policy and foreign trade policy, as well as the expenses of defence.[103]

In day-to-day policymaking, the delegations had the power to prevent rather than actively shape policies. The delegations' most effective power was to influence the common finances, particularly defence spending. The delegations showed that they knew how to use this power. In 1910, a dispute arose over naval expenditure for a fleet of modern battleships, known as dreadnoughts. This was a delicate matter as it was an issue close to Franz Ferdinand's heart. In 1910, after fierce controversy, the delegations granted the navy only medium-term investments, but no permanent increase in its budget.[104]

The Compromise Acts permitted the delegations to make proposals on common issues, but this opportunity for active policymaking remained underexploited due to the lack of cooperation between the delegations. Political negotiations were shifted to non-public, informal channels, bypassing the delegations of the two imperial parliaments. Indeed, the parliaments of the two parts of the empire often passed identical bills on common issues, thus depriving the delegations of their

[100] Anatol Schmied-Kowarzik, *Unteilbar und untrennbar?* Innsbruck, 2010, 33; Lothar Höbelt, 'The Delegations: Preliminary Sketch of a Semi-Parliamentary Institution', *Parliaments, Estates and Representation*, 6/2 (1986), 149–54; Günther Kronenbitter, *Krieg im Frieden*. Munich, 2003, 149.

[101] Ministerial responsibility was also disputed between the two parts of the empire. Löwenthal, 'Österreich-Ungarn', 645 n. 54.

[102] Cable from Bardolff to Franz Ferdinand, 3 May 1912. In HHStA, Nl. Franz Ferdinand, Box 8 Korrespondenz File Karl Bardolff, Fasz. 8–2, fol. 38.

[103] Gumplowicz, *Das österreichische Staatsrecht*, 128.

[104] Milan N. Vego, *Austro-Hungarian Naval Policy 1904–14*. London, 1996, 75–8.

original rights of participation and policymaking.[105] Austrian deputies referred to the delegations as the 'silent chamber parliament' (*Schweigkammerparlament*) or the 'deaf and dumb assembly' (*Taubstummenversammlung*).[106]

Separate political communication prevented a political culture of shared responsibility. Due to the counterintuitive division of political debate between a Hungarian and an Austrian delegation, political antagonism came to the fore in public perceptions as well. The delegates were relieved of the communicative burden of parliamentary negotiations. Within the delegations, the speakers could rhetorically insist on the differences between the two parts of the empire without having to consider the compromises others would need to find. In public, they talked about each other, in the back rooms with each other.

It was only on individual issues that the delegations became a forum for a general Austro-Hungarian public. They provided the sole arena for the expression of public opinions on Austro-Hungarian common policies. In order to reach a wider public, the delegates engaged in 'interpellation', i.e. they submitted parliamentary questions which ministers had to answer, albeit very briefly. The questions covered matters of common interest, as well as minor matters such as assistance to municipalities in the event of floods, the award of public contracts, the erection of monuments, and the rates of pensions and salaries. Conversely, the common ministers also used the delegations to test public opinion for their policies and plans. In these cases, the decision-making powers, the decisions taken, the control exercised by the delegates over the executive, the public nature of their negotiations, and the possibility of interpellation brought the delegations typologically close to becoming a federal body, a 'diète fédérale'.

Individual delegates also took up the concerns of those sections of the population that were not represented in the delegations. These were mainly the citizens of Bosnia and Herzegovina, who had neither seats nor votes in the Imperial Parliaments in Budapest or Vienna but were administered by the common Austro-Hungarian treasury.[107] Before the annexation in 1908, interpellations on Bosnian affairs originated from a group around the Dalmatian Reichsrat politician Juraj Biankini; after 1908, Bosnia-Herzegovina became a dominant topic in the delegations.[108]

[105] Löwenthal, 'Österreich-Ungarn', 635.

[106] Quoted in Charmatz, *Deutsch-österreichische Politik*, 133.

[107] Cf. Chapter 11.3.

[108] In 1906 alone, Biankini intervened in the following cases: the expulsion of Serbian and Croatian journalists from the newspapers *Srpska riječ* and *Hrvatski Dnevnik* from Sarajevo; the service of Bosnian elementary school teachers and civil servants; the establishment of a Bosnian Administrative Court; the lack of elementary schools; and the circumstances of the death of an Uhlan in Sarajevo. *Stenographische Protokolle der Delegation des Reichsrats für die 41. Session vom 25.12.1906 und 7.1.1907, Personen- und Sachregister*, 22–3, the answers are also listed there.

7.5. Common Foreign Affairs and Defence

Federations often emerge from defence, security, and foreign policy alliances.[109] If a federation is strengthened externally, it can develop better internally. Conversely, the pacification of domestic conflicts reduces the risk of power-political intervention by foreign powers.[110] Security motivations have been crucial for federations as diverse as the United States of America in 1797, Switzerland in 1815 and 1848, and the German Confederation in 1815.

In our case, Austro-Hungarian dualism was a reaction to the loss of the Austro-Prussian War and the dissolution of the German Confederation in 1866, the loss of Lombardy in 1859 and of Venetia in 1866, and the quasi-civil wars in Hungary and Galicia. Foreign and military security was an important motive for the creation and continued existence of Austria-Hungary. The Compromise Acts had thus anchored the common foreign and defence policy at the highest level of the empire. The Hungarian constitutional lawyer Marczali described these policies as the two 'main attributes of any independent state'.[111] Responsibility was legally divided between the monarch with his prerogatives, the common ministers, and the delegations. In practice, it also involved the governments of both parts of the empire.

Common Foreign Policy

Cooperation in foreign policy had federal characteristics. Even if contemporaries did not classify this foreign and defence community conceptually as a federation, lawyers and politicians—including Hungarian representatives—agreed in substance that the Compromise Acts enshrined a defence community and required joint foreign policy action.[112] The exception was the Hungarian Independence Party, led by Albert Apponyi since 1874, which rejected the Hungarian privileges in the Compromise of 1867 as insufficient. After 1906, it provided three ministers in the cabinet of the Hungarian prime minister, Sándor Wekerle. The Hungarian minister at the royal court, the liberal magnate Julius Andrássy, invoked the protective function of the alliance in a 1897 pamphlet targeted at the party: 'If two states can only declare war together, can only make peace together..., can only form alliances together, they can only be of one mind in all international

[109] On federalism as a security and defence union Thomas Fröschl, 'Confoederationes, uniones, ligae, Bünde'. In Fröschl (ed.), *Föderationsmodelle und Unionsstrukturen*. Vienna, 1994, 21–44; Koselleck, 'Bund (Bündnis, Föderalismus, Bundestaat)', 582–671; Beaud, *Théorie de la Fédération*, 286–7.

[110] Beaud, *Théorie de la Fédération*, 289.

[111] Marczali, *Ungarisches Verfassungsrecht*, 226.

[112] Löwenthal, 'Österreich-Ungarn', 643.

questions'.[113] According to Andrássy, the desire for separation endangered Hungary's power and security.[114]

From the late 1890s, however, the common foreign policy of Austria-Hungary was challenged not only by the Independence Party but by the entire Hungarian government. Hungary wanted to act as its own 'state' in foreign policy. Politicians and constitutional lawyers argued that the empire only had the power of representation in foreign 'common affairs', citing the different wording of the Hungarian and Austrian Compromise Acts.[115] In nineteenth-century Europe more generally, an independent foreign policy of the constituent states of a federation was nothing unusual.[116] Such a practice also developed in the multi-tiered Habsburg federation.

The Habsburg Monarchy appeared on the international stage in various guises. The actors were the empire, its constituent parts, and the monarch. In the vast majority of cases, Austria-Hungary acted as a subject of international law. In diplomatic circles, the term 'l'Autriche-Hongrie' became common after 1867. In the Treaty of Berlin of 13 July 1878, for example, 'Austria-Hungary' was entrusted with the administration of Bosnia-Herzegovina.[117] The two parliaments in Vienna and Budapest had to approve international agreements.[118] Even when international agreements were concluded with only one part of the empire, it was always Austria-Hungary as a solidary whole that shouldered the legal rights and obligations.[119]

Occasionally, the monarch made an appearance. It was 'Austria-Hungary' that signed the revised Geneva Convention of 1906 but 'Franz Joseph I' who signed the final treaty of The Hague Peace Conferences. Significantly, he chose neither the title Emperor of Austria nor King of Hungary, but his dynastic title 'divina favente clementia Austriae Imperator, Bohemiae Rex etc. et Hungariae Rex Apostolicus'.[120] For outsiders, this multiplicity was difficult to handle. It was not until 1908 that the Foreign Ministry under Alois Lexa von Aehrenthal issued official rules on which international treaties should be concluded by which negotiating parties.[121]

[113] Julius Andrássy, *Ungarns Ausgleich mit Österreich vom Jahr 1867*. Leipzig, 1897, 276.

[114] Andrássy, *Ungarns Ausgleich mit Österreich*, 273.

[115] The history of the Hungarian Compromise Act, which dates to 1866, shows that the Hungarian negotiators merely wanted to clarify that Hungary should not be affected by obligations arising from Austria's membership in the German Confederation, which still existed at the time. Žolger, *Ausgleich zwischen Österreich und Ungarn*, 90–4.

[116] On the German states Fassbender *Der offene Bundesstaat*.

[117] For the contemporary view Dantscher von Kollesberg, *Der monarchische Bundesstaat Oesterreich-Ungarn*. Cf. Chapter 111.3.

[118] Löwenthal, 'Österreich-Ungarn', 647.

[119] Löwenthal, 'Österreich-Ungarn', 648.

[120] Convention for the Improvement of the Condition of the Wounded and Sick in the Armies in the Field, No. 191/1911 RGBl.

[121] Stephan Verosta and Ignaz Seidl-Hohenveldern (eds), *Die völkerrechtliche Praxis der Donaumonarchie von 1859 bis 1918*. Vol. 1. Vienna, 1996, 83–8.

There was a decisive divergence between the Austrian and the Hungarian Compromise Acts with regard to the division of competences and areas of cooperative interdependence in foreign policy. While the Austrian version made the emperor and the common foreign minister responsible, the Hungarian version also added the Austrian and Hungarian governments into the mix. In practice, therefore, foreign affairs were regularly discussed, negotiated, and decided not only by the emperor and the common ministers, but also by a wider circle, including the departmental ministers of the two imperial governments.[122] In theory, Hungarian jurists insisted on the political separation of the empire and its parts.[123] In practice, decision-making required their interaction and collaboration.

The conflicting economic interests of Austria and Hungary became increasingly apparent in international negotiations after 1900. In 1903, Hungary briefly asserted itself as an independent subject of international law, turning *against* Austria and thus against the confederation.[124] This turning point was marked by the Brussels Sugar Convention.[125] In the global competition between 'colonial sugar' from overseas and beet sugar from Europe, the Habsburg Monarchy had built up a world-leading beet sugar industry with the help of a system of premiums. Large, small, and medium-sized refineries flourished in Lower Austria, Bohemia, Moravia, and some Galician regions; by 1903, there were more than 200.[126] As other European countries followed suit, the result was a prolonged collapse in the world market price. Great Britain's cane sugar colonies came under increasing pressure; only by managing to abolish these premiums under international law was the country able to liberalize the market.[127] Within the Habsburg Monarchy, Hungary in particular feared a decline in exports and wanted to restrict the 'influx of Austrian sugar'.[128] Hungary thus signed the Sugar Convention separately, and in return, the Austrian parliament approved the sugar exports quota between the two parts of the empire.

Hungary's success was short-lived. The Sugar Convention was the first worldwide commodity agreement and provided for a further novelty, a supranational supervisory body called the Brussels Sugar Commission.[129] Before long, a deci-

[122] Löwenthal, 'Österreich-Ungarn', 645–6; László Katus, *Hungary in the Dual Monarchy 1867–1914.* New York, 2008, 26. Comprehensively Olechowski-Hrdlicka, *Die gemeinsamen Angelegenheiten*, 469–73, 478–80.

[123] Marczali, *Ungarisches Verfassungsrecht*, 228.

[124] Kolmer, *Parlament und Verfassung in Österreich*, 8. 577.

[125] Hans Jacobs, *Die internationale Zuckerkonvention.* Berlin, 1928, 36–7 and 53.

[126] In Hungary, there was no refinery and a total of twenty sugar factories, Ludwig Bettelheim-Gabillon, 'Eugen von Böhm-Bawerk und die Brüsseler Zuckerkonvention (1903): Ein Beitrag zu seiner Wirksamkeit als Finanzminister', *Zeitschrift für Nationalökonomie*, 7/5 (1936), 611.

[127] The liberalization of the premiums was welcomed by the signatory states, which expected a greater revenue from the sugar tax. Cf. the statement of the Austrian finance minister Böhm-Bawerk, reprinted in Bettelheim-Gabillon, 'Zuckerkonvention', 613.

[128] Bettelheim-Gabillon, 'Zuckerkonvention', 610.

[129] In the European sugar policy of the 1970s, the constellation of 1903 was repeated again because Great Britain was obliged to purchase cane sugar from the Commonwealth countries. Christoph

sion made by the new Commission in June 1903 forced the withdrawal of Austrian and planned Hungarian sugar laws, which sought to seal off the two markets from each other.[130] When Hungary urged the Austrian government to withdraw from the Brussels Convention immediately, the Austrian minister of finance, Eugen von Böhm-Bawerk, replied succinctly: 'In case of doubt, one adheres to binding international treaties.'[131]

By and large, Austria-Hungary pursued a common foreign and security policy, despite all the quarrels. As the age of 'calculated wars'[132] dawned in Europe, it was reluctant to take up arms after the military losses of the 1860s. Instead, it successfully used diplomatic channels, such as the Dual Alliance with Germany, which was expanded into the Triple Alliance with Italy in 1882, to maintain its status as a great power.[133] The occupation of Bosnia and Herzegovina was a notable example of how the empire and its constituent parts held together.

Common Defence Policy

The common defence policy, like the foreign policy, demonstrated a high degree of cooperative interdependence; it had provided the foundation for the Compromise of 1867 but subsequently became an important arena for the growing competition between Austria and Hungary.[134] The Ministry of War was the most powerful of the common ministries and wielded the largest financial resources.[135] Every year, annual budget consultations and confirmation of recruitment quotas triggered arguments between Austria and Hungary over the reform, expansion, and financing of the armed forces.[136] After the defence debate of 1889, these disputes only intensified.[137]

Maria Merki, 'Zucker'. In Merki and Christoph Hengartner (eds), *Genussmittel: Ein kulturgeschichtliches Handbuch*. Frankfurt and New York, 1999, 231–56, 248–9.

130 Bettelheim-Gabillon, 'Zuckerkonvention', 629–30.

131 Bettelheim-Gabillon, 'Zuckerkonvention', 631.

132 Wolfram Siemann, *Vom Staatenbund zum Nationalstaat: Deutschland 1806–1871*. Frankfurt am Main and Vienna, 1995, 390 and 425. Using the example of the Crimean War Winfried Baumgart, *The Crimean War 1853–1856*. London, 1999.

133 Hew Strachan, 'Das europäische Mächtesystem und das Habsburgerreich in der Julikrise 1914'. In Helmut Rumpler (ed.), *Die Habsburgermonarchie 1848–1918*. Vol. 11: *Die Habsburgermonarchie und der Erste Weltkrieg*. Subvol. 1: *Der Kampf um die Neuordnung Mitteleuropas*. Part 1: *Vom Balkankonflikt zum Weltkrieg*. Vienna, 2016, 137–8.

134 Detailed Kronenbitter, *Krieg im Frieden*. Cf. Ivan Žolger, 'Die staatsrechtlichen Grundlagen der Wehrmacht Österreich-Ungarns', *Österreichische Zeitschrift für öffentliches Recht*, 2/5–6 (1915/16), 525–615.

135 Cf. Chapter 10.1.1.

136 Kronenbitter, *Krieg im Frieden*, 154. On the complex military constitution, see also Hans Kelsen, 'Zur Reform der verfassungsrechtlichen Grundlagen der Wehrmacht Österreich-Ungarns (1917/1918)'. In *Hans Kelsen Werke*. Vol. 3: *Veröffentlichte Schriften 1911–1917*. Ed. Matthias Jestaedt. Tübingen, 2010, 620–1. Also Olechowski-Hrdlicka, *Die gemeinsamen Angelegenheiten*, 269–70.

137 László Péter, *Hungary's Long Nineteenth Century*. Leiden, 2012, 369–74.

The introduction of conscription in 1868 had disappointed the Hungarians. They had interpreted the Compromise Acts as granting them the right to have their own armed forces and viewed the Hungarian Landwehr (Honvéd) as feeble, symbolic compensation.[138] From this moment on, Austria-Hungary maintained three armies: a common army for Austria-Hungary as well as the Landwehr in Austria, and the Honvéd in Hungary.[139] In 1903, the dispute escalated when the Hungarian Independence Party unilaterally decided to introduce artillery into the Honvéd.[140] Politicians and senior figures like Austrian Prime Minister Koerber, Archduke Franz Ferdinand, and Franz Conrad von Hötzendorf, the common army's chief of the general staff, saw the unity of the monarchy threatened by demands for a dualistic separation of the army.[141] They persuaded the emperor to withdraw the concessions he had already made.[142]

Tensions and competition between the two halves of the empire persisted until the acute military emergencies of the First World War demanded cooperation. Indeed, the common army proved to be the central institution of the Austro-Hungarian federation with a significance for the federal cohesion of the Habsburg Monarchy that expanded beyond its formal military power (as symbolized by patriotic postcards, Figure 7.2). Historians have long assumed that, of all common imperial institutions, the army was unique in making the monarchy tangible to the wider population.[143] Through universal conscription, the army presented a cross-section of the social, national, and religious diversity of the empire. It allowed a degree of social mobility virtually unheard of outside the army and permitted members of non-Magyar nationalities, especially Croatian military officers, to rise to prominence in the Hungarian units.[144] Catholic, Protestant, and Orthodox military chaplains, as well as field rabbis and imams, represented religious diversity in everyday military life.[145] In the Italian-speaking veterans'

[138] Kronenbitter, *Krieg im Frieden*, 156.

[139] Kronenbitter, *Krieg im Frieden*, 151–2. Cf. Peter Melichar and Alexander Mejstrik, 'Die bewaffnete Macht'. In Helmut Rumpler and Peter Urbanitsch (eds), *Die Habsburgermonarchie 1848–1918*. Vol. 9: *Soziale Strukturen*. Part 1: *Von der Feudal-Agrarischen zur Bürgerlich-industriellen Gesellschaft*. Subvol. 2: *Von der Stände- zur Klassengesellschaft*. Vienna, 2010, 1263–1326. For an overview Žolger, 'Grundlagen der Wehrmacht Österreich-Ungarns'.

[140] Kolmer, *Parlament und Verfassung in Österreich*, 8. 491–508 and 512.

[141] Fredrik Lindström, *Empire and Identity*. West Lafayette, IN, 2008, 58–9; Strachan, 'Das europäische Mächtesystem und das Habsburgerreich', 137.

[142] Lindström, *Empire and Identity*, 58–9.

[143] So far, little research has been done on the actual social acceptance of the army. Cf. Christa Hämmerle, 'Ein gescheitertes Experiment? Die Allgemeine Wehrpflicht in der multiethnischen Armee der Habsburgermonarchie', *Journal of Modern European History*, 5/2 (2008), 233.

[144] Catherine Horel, *Soldaten zwischen nationalen Fronten*. Vienna, 2009, 137–40. Magyars, in contrast to the other nations, were underrepresented in the ranks of professional officers, but had greater opportunities for rapid advancement. István Deák, *Der K. (u.) K. Offizier 1848–1918*. Vienna, 1991, 224–6.

[145] Kai Drewes, *Jüdischer Adel*. Frankfurt am Main and New York, 2013, 223; Robert Luft, 'Zivilgesellschaft im cisleithanischen Teil der Habsburgermonarchie bis 1914', In Jörg Hackmann and Klaus Roth (eds), *Zivilgesellschaft im östlichen und südöstlichen Europa in Geschichte und Gegenwart*. Munich, 2011, 199.

associations, as Laurence Cole has shown, loyalty and allegiance to the emperor were cultivated even among the peasantry, taking them beyond their small social circles.[146]

The common foreign and defence policy illustrates the peculiarities of the Austro-Hungarian federation. Time and again, federal, imperial, and national policies competed with one other, whether over foreign trade policy, a separate Hungarian artillery or fleet, the status of Hungarian as a command language,[147] the question of balance between the empire and its component parts, and the unifying purpose of the alliance. Both sides negotiated modi vivendi and adapted to changing circumstances, producing a federal equilibrium that never tilted permanently in favour of either Austria or Hungary.

7.6. Economic Community on Probation

The years after 1867 saw the emergence of an integrated monetary and economic area of Austria-Hungary which linked the two parts of the empire together and allowed for two-speed economic development.[148] If foreign policy, defence, and common finances were designed as non-negotiable components of the federation, the question of a common economic, customs, and trade policy was in principle up for discussion. The Compromise Acts provided that certain 'matters, though not administered commonly, shall be dealt with according to the same principles as may be agreed upon from time to time' (the so-called agreed matters or *paktierte Angelegenheiten*).[149] The parts of the empire used this opportunity to form an economic community on probation.[150]

Federations depend on economic prosperity.[151] Without a stable national economy, a federation can neither fulfil its core foreign and security policy functions, nor provide for the well-being of its peoples. In a federation, the fruits of common economic, financial, and welfare policies ideally benefit both the whole and the parts, for the very purpose of an (economic) alliance is to bring benefits to all

[146] Laurence Cole, *Military Culture and Popular Patriotism in Late Imperial Austria*. Oxford, 2014.

[147] The armies were a 'language Babylon' with eleven regimental languages; in operations, the command language should be uniform. Tamara Scheer, 'K. u. k. Regimentssprachen: Institutionalisierung der Sprachenvielfalt in der Habsburgermonarchie in den Jahren 1867/8–1914'. In Klaas-Hinrich Ehlers, Marek Nekula, Martina Niedhammer, and Hermann Scheuringer (eds), *Sprache, Gesellschaft und Nation in Ostmitteleuropa*. Göttingen, 2014, 75–92.

[148] Schmied-Kowarzik, *Unteilbar und untrennbar?* Björn Lemke, 'Zwischen zentrifugalen und zentripetalen Kräften: Ökonomische Integration in der Habsburgermonarchie'. In Ambrosius et al., *Föderalismus in historisch vergleichender Perspektive*, 2. 169–95.

[149] § 2 Fundamental State Law of 21 December 1867 Concerning the Matters Common to all the Lands of the Austrian Monarchy and the Manner of their Treatment, No. 146/1867 RGBl.

[150] On economic integration in the mirror of economic theory Lemke, 'Zwischen zentrifugalen und zentripetalen Kräften', 175–6.

[151] Beaud, *Théorie de la Fédération*, 301–20.

sides. Should significant inequalities exist within a federation, then divergent interests must be balanced in a federally acceptable way, while maintaining federal differences, so as to avoid a permanent shift in power towards one member state away from another.[152]

In the United States of America in 1777 and 1797, and in Switzerland in 1848, the common concern for economic welfare and economic unity was explicitly highlighted as a reason for federation in the treaties that brought it about. In the German Confederation, a different approach was taken after 1815. The liberal desire for economic integration as part of national unification, theoretically underpinned by the writings of Friedrich List, did not prevail against the resistance of Metternich, who predicted and feared Prussian supremacy through the Zollverein.[153] From the founding of the German Customs Union in 1833, the security alliance and economic union of this federation were thus separated.

In Austria-Hungary, federal economic unity was standard political practice. At ten-year intervals, Austria and Hungary negotiated the so-called economic compromises. Rhetorically and for strategic reasons, economic unity was repeatedly questioned during the negotiations, but in reality never touched. The economic compromises bundled together issues including the common customs and trade union (the common customs territory had only existed since 1850), a common central bank, and a common financial equalization system (the so-called quota). Economic historians have pointed to the mutually beneficial effect of this system which encouraged greater economic integration between the two halves of the empire in the lead-up to the outbreak of war.[154]

At the same time, however, dualism allowed Hungary and Austria to pursue economic policies at different speeds and with different economic ideas. Hungary benefited from the federal situation by being able to participate in the common market while pursuing an independent economic policy. Recent concepts of economic history speak of 'uneven and combined development' in the light of such practices.[155] The preferential treatment of Hungarian industrialists in Hungarian

[152] For discussions of today cf. Michael Hüther and Klaus Hafemann, 'Öffentliche Güter, Wettbewerb, Kompetenzverteilung—ökonomische Analysen zum Föderalismus'. In Ines Härtel (ed.), *Handbuch Föderalismus*. Vol. 1: *Grundlagen des Föderalismus und der deutsche Bundesstaat*. Heidelberg, 2012, 333–58. On federal competition Charles M. Tiebout, 'A Pure Theory of Local Expenditures', *Journal of Political Economy*, 64/5 (1956), 416–24; Wallace E. Oates, 'An Essay on Fiscal Federalism', *Journal of Economic Literature*, 37/3 (1999), 1120–49.

[153] Cf. Siemann, *Vom Staatenbund zum Nationalstaat*, 337–42.

[154] Different assessments occurred and continue to occur on the question of customs unions in the Balkans. John Komlos, *Die Habsburgermonarchie als Zollunion*. Vienna, 1986, 140. Similarly, already the professor at the consular academy Richard Schüller, Schutzzoll und Freihandel. Vienna and Leipzig, 1905, 250–6. Some areas were initially exempted, such as the free port of Trieste, which was opposed by Franz Xaver von Neumann-Spallart, *Österreichs maritime Entwicklung und die Hebung von Triest*. Stuttgart, 1882, 85–9. Cf. Chapter 10.

[155] On the concept 'uneven and combined development' Mladen Medved, 'Trotsky or Wallerstein? Approaching the Habsburg Monarchy in the Nineteenth Century', *East Central Europe*, 45 (2018), 39–62. Cf. Lemke, 'Zwischen zentrifugalen und zentripedalen Kräften', 180.

state contracts and the establishment of state-owned enterprises in Hungary were directed against Austrian producers, among others.[156] It is not surprising, therefore, that Hungarian economic nationalism inflamed passions in Austria and was branded as undermining solidarity and contradicting the dualistic spirit.[157] Notwithstanding the rhetoric, the financial volume of Hungarian industrial support was only moderate.[158]

Divergent paths of economic development are not unusual in a federation, but they must be reconciled with the federal economic community. The common economic space of Austria-Hungary always existed under the Damocles sword of possible dissolution. As mentioned above, the economic interests of both sides had to be renegotiated every ten years. In this cycle, the interests of the two sides were constantly rebalanced, and the conclusion of each subsequent economic, customs, and trade union was always shaped by the new context. These so-called junctims also had a political dimension.[159] In the public eye, the negotiations on economic compromises were dominated by mutual competition. In order to assert one's own interests, one had to showcase them effectively.

The fact that the economic community could be revoked allowed particularistic economic interests to come to the fore. Many economists, industrialists, and national activists argued against the assumption that a common economic area would necessarily produce the greatest possible prosperity for the population, the highest profits for entrepreneurs, and the most profitable tax revenues for the respective part of the empire. In times of crisis, such as the Great Depression after 1873, both Austrian industrialists and Hungarian agrarians argued for different protective tariffs to reflect the unequal economic characters of their respective regions.[160] In 1903, competition in the sugar industry even triggered the above-mentioned attempt to seal the two markets off from one other.[161] In times of economic prosperity, however, both sides relied on free-trade exports.

The Austro-Hungarian economic community therefore intertwined both competitive and cooperative strands. As economic policy could not permit a common ministry for economic matters, institutions and political actors were more

[156] Uwe Müller, 'Regionale Wirtschafts- und Nationalitätenpolitik in Ostmitteleuropa 1867–1939'. In Müller (ed.), *Ausgebeutet oder alimentiert?* Berlin, 2006, 40.

[157] On the Federation of Austrian Industrialists Lemke, 'Zwischen zentrifugalen und zentripedalen Kräften', 185–6.

[158] Lemke, 'Zwischen zentrifugalen und zentripedalen Kräften', 179–80.

[159] In the mid-1890s, for example, the Austrian prime minister used this channel to demand an increase in the Hungarian share of the quota. On mutual juntimization cf. Schmied-Kowarzik, *Unteilbar und untrennbar?*, 185–6.

[160] In domestic politics, they repeatedly demanded the abrogation of the Austro-Hungarian trade and customs treaties. Herbert Matis, *Österreichs Wirtschaft 1848–1913*. Berlin, 1972, 371–6. Cf. Adolf Beer, *Die österreichische Handelspolitik im neunzehnten Jahrhundert*. Vienna, 1891, 479, 509–14; Alexander (Sándor) von Matlekovits, *Das Königreich Ungarn: Volkswirtschaftlich u. statistisch dargestellt*. Vol. 2. Leipzig, 1900, 23–4.

[161] This compartmentalization was seen as contradictory to the Sugar Convention adopted by both. See Jacobs, *Zuckerkonvention*, 53–4.

interdependent here than in the other common affairs. The system lacked a single central institution;[162] responsibility for foreign trade lay with the common foreign ministry while the minister of common finances was responsible for customs revenue and fiscal equalization through quotas. Both common ministers were accountable to the delegations in these matters. The Austrian and Hungarian finance ministers, in turn, harmonized certain indirect taxes within the framework of the economic community, above all the highly profitable excise duties on sugar, spirits, and beer, and later also on petroleum.[163] Domestic economic policy was additionally determined by the respective Austrian and Hungarian governments and trade ministries.[164]

The advantages of an economic, customs, and trade union for all parties were obvious. In foreign trade, Austria-Hungary was a stronger negotiating and a more desirable economic partner than either Austria or Hungary alone. Both parts of the empire, and thus indirectly the empire itself, benefited economically from the tariff reductions and most-favoured-nation clauses negotiated by the common foreign ministry.[165] Despite public debates about protectionism and economic nationalism, the economic community lasted, even surviving crisis moments when new economic settlements could not be finalized at the end of the ten-year period. The best-known near-emergency occurred in 1897.[166] Even amidst this pressure, the economic compromise was not suspended but continued in the interests of all sides as a 'provisional arrangement' instigated by the emperor and negotiated by the governments. The particularistic economic egoism of the imperial halves was restricted by the interests of the empire as a whole.

The empire also instrumentalized its common economic policy for imperial purposes. Its global foreign trade policy was focused not only on Austrian and Hungarian markets, but also aimed to open up regions in the Levant, East and South Asia, Africa, and South America to the empire's economy.[167] Such foreign trade policy initiatives had been part of Vienna's diplomacy since the end of the eighteenth century and were resurrected around 1900 by Alexa von Aehrenthal who determined to establish the empire as a global player in the trade power struggle between the Great Powers.[168] Trieste, for example, one of the largest port cities in Europe, became a vital hub for the empire's overseas trade. In the context

162 Lemke, 'Zwischen zentrifugalen und zentripedalen Kräften', 174–5.

163 Hans Patzauer, *Österreichs und Ungarns Staatswirthschaften*. Vienna, 1916, 8.

164 Alois Brusatti, 'Die wirtschaftlichen Folgen des Ausgleichs von 1867'. In Peter Berger (ed.), *Der österreichisch-ungarische Ausgleich von 1867*. Vienna and Munich, 1967, 127–42; Schmied-Kowarzik, *Unteilbar und untrennbar?*, 35–6.

165 Overview at Matlekovits, *Das Königreich Ungarn*, 2. 506–7.

166 Comprehensively Schmied-Kowarzik, *Unteilbar und untrennbar?*

167 Alison Frank, 'Continental and Maritime Empires in an Age of Global Commerce', *East European Politics and Societies*, 25/4 (2011), 783.

168 On Aehrenthal's reform William D. Godsey, 'Der österreichisch(-ungarische) Diplomatische Dienst zwischen Stände- und Nationalgesellschaften'. In Rumpler and Urbanitsch, *Die Habsburgermonarchie 1848–1918*, 9/1/2. 1257.

of the British Empire, economic relations and power dynamics are often said to have forged an 'informal empire' just as important as the network of formal colonial relations.[169] For the architects of Austro-Hungarian foreign policy, the same idea applied: economic stature was synonymous with political power.

In 1907, however, the historian Richard Charmatz warned that the Monarchy's economic policy was far too 'impulsive' to compete on the world market.[170] After two decades of export surpluses, by 1907 the balance had reversed, leading to increasingly large foreign trade deficits.[171] The Habsburg Monarchy never fulfilled its potential roles as a hegemon in the world economy or an arbiter of an 'informal empire'. As economic historians have argued, the ruling elites simply failed to pursue a consistent policy.[172]

Against the background of the empire's global economic ambitions, it is understandable that neither the ruler nor his common ministers wished to disturb the domestic economic union. After all, it was there to provide a foundation for the empire's global economic position. It cannot be denied that the system was periodically dysfunctional, that it produced deficits, or that legal procedures had to be circumvented to ensure its survival.[173] Nevertheless, practical adherence to the economic community was fundamental, as is testified by plans for its future consolidation. The Belvedere Circle around Franz Ferdinand, for example, drew up a constitutional plan around 1914, which would finally make economic matters a permanent common concern of the Austro-Hungarian confederation.[174]

7.7. Centrifugal and Centripetal Forces of Multi-Level Federalism

The Habsburg Monarchy is broadly presented here as a multi-level federation, an interpretation which emphasizes not only the Hungarians' insistence on federal differences, for example, but also the integrative binding forces of dualism after 1867. Until now, state theory, politics, and history stressed the apparently divisive nature of the Austro-Hungarian Compromise Acts, which were considered neither functional nor sustainable. Only very isolated voices have highlighted the unifying aspect of dualism as a 'unio amicorum'.[175] A federal view allows both perspectives to be accommodated. On the one hand, the Compromise stands for

[169] Frank, 'Continental and Maritime Empires', 782.

[170] Charmatz, *Deutsch-österreichische Politik*, 203 and 207.

[171] There were German protective tariffs and tariff wars with Serbia and Romania. Matis, *Österreichs Wirtschaft*, 382–3.

[172] Frank, 'Continental and Maritime Empires', 781–2.

[173] For more detail Andrea B. Hölzl, *Die wirtschaftlichen Ausgleichsverhandlungen zwischen Österreich und Ungarn 1867–1918* (university diss.). Graz, 1989; Schmied-Kowarzik, *Unteilbar und untrennbar?*

[174] Cf. Chapter 12.

[175] Löwenthal, 'Österreich-Ungarn', 654.

a policy of demarcation under national auspices. On the other hand, it is a reminder that, until 1918, Austria-Hungary was a largely stable foreign, defence, financial, and economic community despite, or perhaps because of, the highly controversial and conflict-heavy power struggles it contained within.

When viewed collectively, the Compromise Acts, along with Austrian and Hungarian constitutional law, bilateral treaties, and informal agreements, allow scholars to construct a clear federal division of powers (even if only in outline) for the multi-tiered system of Habsburg Monarchy after 1867, despite the lack of a single, unifying founding document. Imperial powers existed for foreign affairs, defence, and finance; to these was added a common economic area, negotiated every ten years. Beyond the executive, the equal representation of the bicameral parliaments of Budapest and Vienna within the so-called delegations, which supervised the common ministers, budget, and army, indicates the federal character of this institution. In day-to-day decision-making, the empire and its component parts cooperated through the monarch, the common ministers, the two governments and parliaments—all signs of a federal practice that found both formal and informal ways of organizing commonality while preserving the differences allowed in the Austro-Hungarian confederation.

A Federal History of the Habsburg Empire, 1815–1918. Jana Osterkamp, Oxford University Press.
 DOI: 10.1093/9780198943631.003.0008

Figure 8.1 'Tyrolia'. Allegory. Woodcut, Munich, c.1890.

8
Longing for Home of One's Own, 1867–1871

The Austro-Hungarian confederative double house was fronted by a clearly structured façade, which, after 1867, looked particularly impressive on the Hungarian side. The Austro-Hungarian Compromise paved Hungary's path to modernity. However, its increasing prosperity, growing economic power, and greater political privilege nurtured desires among the other occupants of the federal house for their autonomy. Metaphorically speaking, there was a longing for a federal home under the shared roof of the monarchy, or even for states entirely their own, detached from the protection of the Habsburgs.

Immediately following the Compensation Laws, between 1867 and 1871, the ruling elites in the crown lands fought for imperial privileges and 'compensations'. The 'heavyweights' of the empire, Bohemia and Galicia, negotiated privileges on a par with Hungary.[1] Galicia, meanwhile, received only informal concessions, referred to as the 'Galician Compromise'.[2] In Prague, the nobility and the bourgeoisie dreamed of the trialist reorganization of the empire into 'Austria-Hungary-Bohemia', but came away empty-handed.[3] Elsewhere, Croatia achieved the so-called *nagodba* (compromise) in the Hungarian part of the empire,[4] while Tyrol was able to retain its existing historic state law privileges (see Figure 8.1).

8.1. Hungary's Economic Miracle

Hungary had experienced an enormous upswing after 1867. As a new component of the empire, it invested consistently in geopolitical, economic, and financial

[1] Cf. Peter Urbanitsch, 'Die nationalen Ausgleichsversuche in den Ländern Cisleithaniens in den Jahren vor dem Ersten Weltkrieg: Gemeinsamkeiten und Unterschiede'. In Lukáš Fasora, Jiří,Hanuš, and Jiří Malíř (eds), *Moravské vyrovnání z roku 1905: Možnosti a limity národnostního smíru ve střední Evropě*. Brno, 2006, 43–58.

[2] Harald Binder, '"Galizische Autonomie": Ein streitbarer Begriff und seine Karriere'. In Fasora et al., *Moravské vyrovnání*, 239–66.

[3] Valentin Urfus, 'Die Ausprägung der Idee des historischen böhmischen Staatsrechtes in den sechziger Jahren des 19. Jahrhunderts und der österreichisch-ungarische Dualismus'. In Ľudovít Holotík (ed.), *Der österreichisch-ungarische Ausgleich 1867*. Bratislava, 1971, 545; Joseph F. Zacek, 'Palacký and the Austro-Hungarian Compromise of 1867'. In Holotík, *Der österreichisch-ungarische Ausgleich*, 555–73.

[4] Croatian federalization plans did not find sufficient support among the quarrelling Austro-Slavs. Imre Ress (ed.), 'The Hungarian-Croat Compromise of 1868'. In Ignác Romsics and Béla K. Király (eds), *Geopolitics in the Danube Region*. Budapest, 1999, 187.

infrastructure. By 1873, the Budapest government's investments in railways, industries, and banks had increased sixfold.[5] Systematic transport planning augmented the pre-existing common imperial railway[6] as train and telegraph networks already begun by the Viennese authorities were enlarged and Budapest became a central transport and communication hub.[7] It quickly grew into the second capital of the empire, becoming the first east-central European city after Vienna to reach a population of one million. It was now the political, economic, social, and cultural centre of Hungary.[8]

With regard to its national economy, Hungary succeeded in emancipating itself from Austria through a moderate economic modernization starting in the 1880s. The previous division of labour between the two halves of the empire, which, up to the pre-1848 period, had cemented Hungary's position as a peripheral economy, continued to exist: manufacturing and processing industries were concentrated in Austria, while Hungary remained primarily a supplier of food and raw materials.[9] Nonetheless, the Compromise Laws appeared to have sparked a change. After 1867, Hungary's economic opportunities by far exceeded those of the imperial periphery. Its areas of economic concentration were deliberately chosen to complement those in the Austrian half of the empire.[10]

Hungary took advantage of the opportunities offered by dualism to develop independently and pursue a firmly national economic policy.[11] Industries that produced goods not yet manufactured in Hungary were given tax privileges or given land for their factories free of charge.[12] The expansion of the milling industry from the late 1870s, for example, paved the way for industrial food processing. Mechanical engineering companies, meanwhile, were encouraged to build up

[5] Ivan T. Berend, *History Derailed: Central and Eastern Europe in the Long Nineteenth Century*. Berkeley, CA, 2003, 134–58.

[6] On the multi-stage expansion of the railways Herbert Matis, *Österreichs Wirtschaft 1848–1913*. Berlin, 1972, 186–94.

[7] On the coexistence of imperial, Hungarian, and regional economic policies cf. Zoltán Kaposi, 'Der Staat, die wirtschaftliche Entwicklung und die Nationalitäten auf dem Gebiet des Königreichs Ungarn 1867–1918'. In Uwe Müller (ed.), *Ausgebeutet oder alimentiert?* Berlin, 2006, 101–18. On Budapest as a hub of global telegraphy Roland Wenzlhuemer, *Connecting the Nineteenth-Century World*. Cambridge, 2013, 143.

[8] Budapest ranked sixth in Europe. On urbanization Péter Hanák, *Ungarn in der Donaumonarchie*. Vienna, 1984, 327–32; Hanák, 'Verbürgerlichung und Urbanisierung: Ein Vergleich der Stadtentwicklung Wiens und Budapests'. In Ferenc Glatz and Ralph Melville (eds), *Gesellschaft, Politik und Verwaltung in der Habsburgermonarchie 1830–1918*. Budapest, 1987, 203–35.

[9] László Katus, 'The Common Market of the Austro-Hungarian Monarchy'. In András Gerö (ed.), *The Austro-Hungarian Monarchy Revisited*. New York, 2009, 21–50; György Kövér, 'The Economic Achievements of the Austro-Hungarian Monarchy'. In Gerö, *Austro-Hungarian Monarchy Revisited*, 51–83.

[10] Andrea Komlosy, *Grenze und ungleiche regionale Entwicklung*. Vienna, 2003, 108–11.

[11] Due to the ban on tariff barriers to trade, the focus was on non-tariff foreclosure policies. Björn Lemke, 'Zwischen zentrifugalen und zentripetalen Kräften'. In Gerold Ambrosius, Christian Henrich-Franke, and Cornelius Neutsch (eds), *Föderalismus in historisch vergleichender Perspektive*. Vol. 2: *Föderale Systeme*. Baden-Baden, 2015, 178–9.

[12] Alexander (Sándor) von Matlekovits, *Das Königreich Ungarn*. Vol. 2. Leipzig, 1900, 24–33.

manufacturing around Budapest.[13] Hungarian economic policy relied on public subsidies such as these, and therefore less on private initiative, in order to overcome internal economic differences and the west–east divide within the empire.[14] The largest local investor was the Hungarian government.[15]

8.2. Croatian-Hungarian Compromise (*Nagodba*)

In 1868, Croatia-Slavonia secured a privileged position among the Hungarian territories through its own Compromise Agreement with the Hungarian government (*Nagodba*).[16] Because the province and its military leadership had won plaudits in the war against the secessionist Hungarians in the March Revolution of 1848, the emperor conceded these privileges. However, he was careful not to infringe upon Austro-Hungarian dualism by doing so.

Thanks to this 'sub-dualism', Croatia-Slavonia was the only crown land apart from Hungary to possess a fully articulated separation of powers with a parliament (Sabor), administration, and judiciary.[17] The underlying power struggle was reflected in the scholarly debate regarding statehood and sovereignty. Croatian jurists interpreted the Nagodba as a 'federal treaty' and thus demanded political parity for Hungary and Croatia-Slavonia.[18] Referring to historic state law, they traced the statehood of the 'triune kingdoms of Dalmatia, Croatia, and Slavonia'

[13] On the individual sectors Kaposi, 'Der Staat, die wirtschaftliche Entwicklung und die Nationalitäten', 110–15. Statistical information on the milling industry Matlekovits, *Das Königreich Ungarn*, 2. 96–112.

[14] Cf. Uwe Müller, 'Regionale Wirtschafts- und Nationalitätenpolitik in Ostmitteleuropa 1867–1939'. In Müller, *Ausgebeutet oder alimentiert?*, 25–9 and 35–7; Ágnes Pogány, 'Wirtschaftsnationalismus in Ungarn im 19. und 20. Jahrhundert'. In Pogány, Eduard Kubů, and Jan Kofman, *Für eine nationale Wirtschaft*. Berlin, 2006, 11–71. Berend, *History Derailed*, 139–42. On industrial development László Katus, *Hungary in the Dual Monarchy 1867–1914*. New York, 2008, 243–77.

[15] Ákos Paulinyi, 'Die Industriepolitik in Ungarn und in Österreich und das Problem der ökonomischen Integration 1880–1914', *Zeitschrift für Wirtschafts- und Sozialwissenschaften*, 97/2 (1977), 131–66. Overall, however, these subsidies were too small to have a significant impact. John Komlos, *Die Habsburgermonarchie als Zollunion*. Vienna, 1986, 103–6.

[16] Overview at Georg Jellinek and Josef Pliverić, *Beiträge zum Ungarisch-kroatischen Bundesrechte*. Agram, 1886; Branko Pešelj, 'Der ungarisch-kroatische Ausgleich vom Jahre 1868: Verfassungsrechtlicher Überblick'. In Peter Berger (ed.), *Der österreichisch-ungarische Ausgleich von 1867*. Vienna and Munich, 1967, 169–85. Summarizing Ivo Perić, *Hrvatski državni sabor 1848–2000*. Vol. 2: *1868–1918*. Zagreb, 2000; Alexandra Kolaric, 'Probleme der staatsrechtlichen Verhältnisse'. In Heiner Timmermann (ed.), *Entwicklung der Nationalbewegungen in Europa: 1850–1914*. Berlin, 1998, 87–99. With a focus on Croatian-Serbian relations cf. Vasilije Jellinek, *Hrvatsko-Ugarska nagodba 1868. godine*. Belgrade, 1969.

[17] Charles Jelavich, 'The Croatian Problem in the Habsburg Empire in the Nineteenth Century', *Austrian History Yearbook*, 3/2 (1967), 100.

[18] Mirjana Gross, 'Der kroatische Sabor (Landtag)'. In Helmut Rumpler and Peter Urbanitsch (eds), *Die Habsburgermonarchie: 1848–1918*. Vol. 7: *Verfassung und Parlamentarismus*. Subvol. 2: *Die regionalen Repräsentativkörperschaften*. Vienna, 2000, 2283–2316; Pešelj, 'Der ungarisch-kroatische Ausgleich', 172–5; Dalibor Čepulo, 'Entwicklung der Regierungsinstitutionen des Königreiches Kroatien und Slawonien 1868–1918'. In Gábor Máthé and Barna Mezey (eds), *Kroatisch-ungarische öffentlich-rechtliche Verhältnisse zur Zeit der Doppelmonarchie*. Budapest, 2015, 43–8.

back to early modern treaties between the monarch and the estates. Magyar jurists, on the other hand, saw the Austro-Hungarian Compromise of 1867 as the ultimate source of authority in deciding question of sovereignty. In their eyes, only the Hungarian territory in its collective entirety had the quality of a state, not the *Nebenländer* (secondary territories) such as Croatia-Slavonia, which were subordinate to Budapest.[19]

While European international law experts took great interest in the question of Croatia-Slavonia's debatable sovereignty, Georg Jellinek, a Vienna-educated constitutional law expert from Heidelberg, criticized the reasoning behind the debate. Instead, he argued, Croatia clearly demonstrated,

> that the existence or non-existence of a state is first and foremost a historical fact…In their common affairs, the Hungarians have sovereignty to act and since the 'common', i.e. Hungarian, ministry is exclusively responsible to the Hungarian Diet, the Croats lack any legal guarantee that the Hungarian-Croatian Compromise will be respected by the ruling Magyar nation.[20]

The independence promised by Budapest, as the legal historian Dalibor Čepulo later put it, was 'controlled and conditioned' by Hungarian hegemony.[21]

Despite, or rather because of this Magyar hegemony, the idea, that its historic state law entitled Croatia to greater autonomy or even 'statehood', persisted until the end of the Habsburg Monarchy.[22] In provincial politics, the dream of a fully separated status of Croatia continued to gain political traction. In the 1880s, the so-called Rights Party (Party of Croatian State Law) became increasingly popular and even sought secession from the empire and the independence of an enlarged Croatia.[23] Ideas of a 'Greater Croatia' drew their legitimacy not only from historic state law, but also from a notion of South Slavic nationhood. This could be seen in party leader Mile Starčević's declaration that Serbs, Croats, Bosnians, Herzegovinians, and Dalmatians were all 'Croatian'.[24]

In practice, political competences were distributed among Hungary and Croatia across multiple tiers. The common affairs of Hungary and Croatia-Slavonia included

[19] This viewpoint was also held by the so-called Magarons, the high nobility native to Croatia and Hungary. Daniel Lalić, *Der Hochadel Kroatien-Slawoniens*. Munich, 2017, 55.

[20] Georg Jellinek, 'Rezension zu Jellinek, Georg, Josef Pliveric, *Beiträge zum ungarisch-kroatischen Bundesrechte. Rechtliche und politische Erörterungen*. Agram 1886', *Kritische Vierteljahresschrift für Gesetzgebung und Rechtswissenschaft*, NF 12 (1889), 326–7. Cf. Georg Jellinek, *Die Lehre von den Staatenverbindungen*. Vienna, 1882, 76 n. 13.

[21] Čepulo, 'Regierungsinstitutionen des Königreiches Kroatien und Slawonien', 52.

[22] Katus, *Hungary in the Dual Monarchy*, 465; Mirjana Gross, *Die Anfänge des modernen Kroatien*. Vienna, 1993, 200.

[23] Mirjana Gross, *Izvorno pravaštvo: Ideologija, agitacija, pokret*. Zagreb, 2000.

[24] Luciano Monzali, 'Pokus o chorvatsko-srbsko-italské vyrovnání v Dalmácii 1903–1907'. In Fasora et al., *Moravské vyrovnání*, 221–37. Between Serbs and Croats, the claim to regional hegemony was especially contested. Katus, *Hungary in the Dual Monarchy*, 468.

finances, the economy, trade, and defence, as well as common citizenship.[25] In Agram (Zagreb), the Sabor retained significant latitude for taking action in areas like the interior, the judiciary, education, and religion.[26] Regarding education and sciences, elementary schools were expanded according to the model of the Cisleithanian Imperial Elementary School Act of 1869. The university and the Academy of Sciences were also founded in Agram. The most contentious issue in the expansion of education in Croatia-Slavonia was the inadequate integration of the Serbs, who were forbidden to use the Cyrillic script.[27] The administration and the judiciary in Croatia-Slavonia were modernized and centralized according to European models. Self-government in the comitats, meanwhile, was more limited than in Hungary.[28] In rural areas, the feudal system was abolished and a credit system created to facilitate agrarian reforms.[29] In infrastructure policy, however, Agram regularly had to acquiesce to the interests of Vienna and Budapest in the planning of railways and their routes.[30] The railway connection between Hungary, the Mediterranean ports, and the Balkan lands disregarded Croatian-Slavonian needs for improved access of their cities and mining sector to the world market.[31]

The fiscal system tied Croatia to the benevolence of Budapest.[32] Unlike the crown lands of Cisleithania, Croatia did not enjoy fiscal autonomy. The Budapest Diet determined taxes and duties, which were then collected by the common

[25] Čepulo, 'Regierungsinstitutionen des Königreiches Kroatien und Slawonien', 50.

[26] On the reform laws of the 1870s James Paul Krokar, 'Liberal Reform in Croatia 1872–75: The Beginnings of Modern Croatia under Ban Ivan Mažuranić'. University dissertation, Indianapolis, 1980. These were prepared in the 1860s. Iskra Iveljić, 'Die Rolle der Großkaufleute in der Modernisierung und in der nationalen Bewegung Zivil-Kroatiens in den sechziger Jahren des 19. Jahrhunderts'. In Hannes Stekl, Peter Urbanitsch, Ernst Bruckmüller, and Hans Heiss (eds), *Durch Arbeit, Besitz, Wissen und Gerechtigkeit. Bürgertum in der Habsburgermonarchie*. Vienna, 1992, 231–43; Dalibor Čepulo, 'Building of the Modern Legal System in Croatia 1848–1918 in the Centre-Periphery-Perspective'. In Tomasz Giaro (ed.), *Modernisierung durch Transfer im 19. und frühen 20. Jahrhundert*. Frankfurt am Main, 2006, 47–91.

[27] Mirjana Gross, 'The Character of Croatian Autonomy in the First Decade after the Hungarian-Croatian Compromise of 1868'. In Solomon Wank, Heidrun Maschl, Brigitte Mazohl-Wallnig, and Reinhold Wagnleitner (eds), *The Mirror of History*. Santa Barbara, CA, 1988, 280; Jelavich, 'Croatian Problem', 105–6; Jan Rychlík, 'Uhersko-chorvatské vyrovnání roku 1868 a národnostní konflikty v Chorvatsku'. In Fasora et al. (eds), *Moravské vyrovnání*, 175–87.

[28] The Cisleithanian Fundamental Law on the Judiciary of 1867 served as an important model. On the reforms generally Čepulo, 'Building of the Modern Legal System in Croatia', 70–80; Gross, 'Croatian Autonomy in the First Decade', 281. On the role of the Hungarian comitats as a 'mixture of district governorate and provincial committee': Attila Pók, 'Neue Staatsstruktur des Habsburgerreiches: Neues Verwaltungssystem nach dem Ausgleich mit Ungarn'. In Glatz and Melville, *Gesellschaft, Politik und Verwaltung*, 199. On administrative reforms Katus, *Hungary in the Dual Monarchy*, 135–40.

[29] Gross, 'Der kroatische Sabor (Landtag)', 2304–7; Čepulo, 'Building of the Modern Legal System in Croatia', 76.

[30] Mirko Valentić, 'Das Eisenbahnnetz in der Militärgrenze: Pläne und Verwirklichung'. In Richard G. Plaschka, Anna M. Drabek,and Birgitta Zaar (eds), *Eisenbahnbau und Kapitalinteressen in den Beziehungen der österreichischen mit den südslawischen Ländern*. Vienna, 1993, 99–131.

[31] Valentić, 'Das Eisenbahnnetz', 124–31; Gross, 'Croatian Autonomy in the First Decade', 283.

[32] Gross places the Croatian fiscal system in the overall context of the Habsburg Monarchy. Mirjana Gross, 'Financijski temelji nagodbene autonomije civilne Hrvatske i Slavonije 1868–1880', *Historijski Zbornik*, 41/2 (1988), 89–122.

Hungarian-Croatian Ministry of Finance. Croatia could not impose taxes or duties by itself but received 45 per cent of the taxes collected in Croatia-Slavonia for provincial affairs. This sum was insufficient even to cover the cost of administration.[33] Hungary, therefore, accused Croatia of allowing itself to be supported financially. For their part, the Croatian decision-makers had little idea of the actual value of tax income in their territory. Mistrust towards Hungary naturally followed. In 1879, Croatian nationalist politicians, including the leader of the Rights Party, Josip Frank, accused the Hungarians of exploiting Croatia and of concealing and downplaying the true tax revenue it generated.[34]

Demands for greater fiscal autonomy for Croatia were thus accompanied by calls for Croatian independence.[35] Almost a century later, the Yugoslav writer Miroslav Krleža described the annual fiscal negotiations between Hungary and Croatia in his novel *The Flags* (1967), perhaps the first and only time a fictional work about the birth of a nation has opened with the details of a fiscal settlement. In a fictional newspaper article, a Croatian journalist uncovers 'a basketful of fraud, amounting to millions, at Croatia's expense'.[36] Krleža traces the journey of this biting newspaper article from a desk in the 'Cabinet of the Royal Croatian-Slavonian-Dalmatian Political Provincial Administration' via the tables in Budapest's coffeehouses up to the office of the Hungarian prime minister.

Informal rules further reduced Croatian-Slavonian influence. If the Sabor passed decisions and draft bills that Vienna did not approve of, it was simply dissolved or adjourned by the Banus, the governor in Croatia-Slavonia.[37] In the 1870s, Banus Ivan Mažuranić did attempt to increase Croatian autonomy but his reform plans were thwarted by Budapest.[38] This and other examples consistently demonstrated that the Croatian governor was equally dependent on both Budapest *and* Vienna; he was nominated by the Hungarian prime minister and appointed by the king.[39]

[33] Čepulo, 'Regierungsinstitutionen des Königreiches Kroatien und Slawonien', 53.

[34] Josip Frank, *Die Quote Kroatiens: Eine Studie über das finanzielle Verhältniss zwischen Kroatien und Ungarn anlässlich der bevorstehenden Verhandlungen der Regincolar-Deputationen*. Agram, 1879, 3 and 7.

[35] Cf. Bela Lukacs, 'Über das finanzielle Verhältnis zwischen Ungarn und Kroatien-Slawonien'. *Pester Lloyd*, 4/5 Apr. 1879, 93–5. On the connection between finances and autonomy with detailed figures cf. Karlo Boehm [pseudonym B. Karlović], *Financijalna nagodba*. Zagreb, 1904.

[36] Miroslav Krleža, *Die Fahnen*. 5 vols. Klagenfurt, 2016, 1. 7, 9, 15–23.

[37] Gross, 'Der kroatische Sabor (Landtag)', 2293–4, 2299–2300. The electoral regulations were also adapted to Viennese ideas of an 'obedient' majority in the provincial diet, and the census electoral law was the most restrictive in the empire. Lalić, *Hochadel Kroatien-Slawoniens*, 54 and 66–8; Vasilije Krestić, 'Über einige politisch-historische Bedingungen der Entstehung des kroatisch-ungarischen Ausgleichs 1868'. In Holotík, *Der österreichisch-ungarische Ausgleich*, 822; Čepulo, 'Building of the Modern Legal System in Croatia', 83.

[38] Gross, 'Croatian Autonomy in the First Decade', 278.

[39] The inauguration of Banus Levin Rauch in 1867 amounted to a 'small coronation'. For this Lalić, *Hochadel Kroatien-Slawoniens*, 53, 57–61. However, Rauch took a hard line against nationalist Croatian politicians, professors, and teachers. Krestić, 'Bedingungen der Entstehung', 814–16. On constitutional history cf. Čepulo, 'Regierungsinstitutionen des Königreiches Kroatien und Slawonien', 64; Mark Cornwall, 'Loyalty and Treason in Late Habsburg Croatia: A Violent Discourse before the

The 'Croatian-Slavonian-Dalmatian minister'[40] in the Transleithanian government was no better placed to fulfil Croatian expectations. It was hoped that this office would bring representation of and support for Croatian interests to the common Budapest government. Only Croats loyal to Hungary were appointed to this position, however. They routinely sided with Hungarian causes when conflicts arose. On several occasions, they even delayed Croatian draft bills before they could reach the monarch and the common government—a necessary stage in the approval process.[41] In the Austrian half of the empire, the so-called compatriot ministers for the Poles, Czechs, and Germans successfully lobbied for their respective national policies,[42] but the Croatian minister noticeably shirked this role.

Croatia's standing in the empire, and within the Hungarian sphere, changed over time. With the demilitarization of the Military Border and its territorial incorporation into Croatia-Slavonia, the province's political weight significantly increased.[43] The occupation of Bosnia-Herzegovina offered ambitious Croatian politicians a further opportunity to improve Croatia's position. After centuries under Ottoman rule, the populations of Bosnia and Herzegovina possessed little in the way of a distinct national-language consciousness. However, they did identify along religious lines. Croation nationalist politicians, therefore, were eager to win Bosnian Catholics over to the Croatian side.[44] In 1878, the Sabor of Agram petitioned the monarch in Vienna—ultimately in vain—to obtain Bosnia-Herzegovina for Croatia.[45]

Despite the Nagodba, Transleithania was acquiring the characteristics of a centralist state. Indeed, it was the elites in Budapest and Vienna who controlled the political fate of Croatia, which lacked the finances and resources to practise truly independent politics. Croatia may have been blessed with an extraordinary wealth of formal institutions—its own parliament, judiciary, and administration, as well as a minister in the Hungarian government—but unlike in Hungary, this did not translate into financial success. There was no 'economic miracle' to boast of.

First World War'. In Jana Osterkamp and Martin Schulze Wessel (eds), *Exploring Loyalty*. Göttingen, 2017, 97–120.

[40] The reference to Dalmatia lacked a factual basis, since it belonged to the Cisleithanian half of the empire, but it had great symbolic power.

[41] In the event of divergent views between the Croatian Banus and the Hungarian Council of Ministers, Franz Joseph always took the Hungarian point of view. The Banus Mažuranić adjusted his approach to first consult with the Minister. Gross, 'Croatian Autonomy in the First Decade', 281; Čepulo, 'Building of the Modern Legal System in Croatia', 67; Čepulo, 'Regierungsinstitutionen des Königreiches Kroatien und Slawonien', 55–7.

[42] Cf. below.

[43] The territorial dispute over the Military Border and Dalmatia was also a dispute over the dualistic balance of power. Gross, 'Croatian Autonomy in the First Decade', 282. On the tenacious negotiations Éva Somogyi, *Der gemeinsame Ministerrat der österreichisch-ungarischen Monarchie 1867–1906*. Vienna, 1996, 213–17.

[44] Hannes Grandits, *Herrschaft und Loyalität in der spätosmanischen Gesellschaft*. Vienna, 2008, 681; Gross, 'Der kroatische Sabor (Landtag)', 2307.

[45] Jelavich, 'Croatian Problem', 104.

8.3. 'Galician Compromise'

If we compare the Habsburg Empire to a building, then the floors in the Austrian wing followed a more uniform blueprint, formally based on the constitutional equality of the crown lands. Each was more or less as magnificently decorated and appointed as the next. Beyond these façades, however, as in Hungary, certain Austrian crown lands possessed greater power than others, despite their supposed equality being enshrined in constitutional law and parliamentary practice.[46] In 1868, Galicia succeeded in gaining informal concessions from Vienna which practically granted it a special status among the crown lands.

The exceptional position of the province resulted from an alliance between the emperor and the Polish nobility.[47] The term 'Galician autonomy', though frequently used, is misleading. Unlike Hungary or Croatia-Slavonia, Galicia did not receive legal privileges. Nor did the entire crown land benefit. It was the Polish nobility, above all, that Vienna chose to elevate as a nationally and socially distinguished population group, both within Galicia and within the empire.[48]

Disputes over a 'Compromise' for Galicia show that the foundations of the Austro-Hungarian edifice took time to settle in the years after 1867. As in Croatia, the Galicians based claims to greater independence on historic state law. In the decade before 1867, the Polish-Galician representatives of the Imperial Council had sought comprehensive reform of the entire state territory based on historical precedent.[49] After 1867, they were restricted to seeking the 'autonomy' of their homeland within the new dualist regime.[50]

The 'resolution campaign' of the Galician Diet (Sejm) between 1868 and 1871 aimed at a fundamental increase in power.[51] Politicians and leading officials had elevated Galicia to the level of statehood in their minds and thus needed the

[46] After 1873, the House of Representatives continued to be filled along regional lines, although the provincial diets no longer had the right of appointment. Franz Adlgasser, *Die Mitglieder der österreichischen Zentralparlamente 1848–1918: Ein biographisches Lexikon*. Vol. 1: *Konstituierender Reichstag 1848–1849, Reichsrat 1861–1918*. A–L. Vienna, 2014, p. xxxviii. Through the state governor's office and its authorities, the state authorities of Vienna were also present in the provinces in addition to the provincial authorities (the so-called double-track administration).

[47] Stanisław Pijaj, *Między polskim patriotyzmem a habsburskim lojalizmem*. Kraków, 2004; Roman Kochnowski, *Przy Tobie Najjaśniejszy Panie stoimy i stać chcemy*. Kraków, 2009.

[48] Binder, 'Galizische Autonomie', 243.

[49] Binder, 'Galizische Autonomie', 241–2. On the wavering attitude of the Koło, see also Pijaj, *Między polskim patriotyzmem a habsburskim lojalizmem*, 162–4.

[50] The Polish minister of culture and education Stanisław Madeyski, was an embodiment of this autonomist and concurrently anti-federalist attitude. See also Joanna Radzyner, *Stanisław Madeyski 1841–1910: Ein austro-polnischer Staatsmann im Spannungsfeld der Nationalitätenfrage in der Habsburgermonarchie*. Vienna, 1983, 240–5.

[51] For the wording of the resolution and the corresponding bills of the House of Representatives in Vienna cf. Edmund Bernatzik (ed.), *Die österreichischen Verfassungsgesetze, mit Erläuterungen*. 2nd edn. Vienna, 1911, 1132–42; Stanisław Grodziski, 'Der Landtag des Königreiches Galizien und Lodomerien'. In Rumpler and Urbanitsch, *Die Habsburgermonarchie 1848–1918*. 7/2. 2163–5; Stanisław Grodziski, *Sejm krajowy galicyjski 1861–1914*. Vol. 1. Warsaw, 1993, 149–61. More speeches from the Galician Diet appear in Grodziski: *Sejm krajowy galicyjski*. Vol. 2. Warsaw, 1993, 295–315.

formal institutions to match: a Galician Supreme Court and Court of Cassation, a provincial administration responsible to the diet, and greater fiscal autonomy. Local finances were precarious; important sources of domestic income such as the salt mines were in the hands of the Austrian Treasury and the province regularly clashed with Vienna over debts from land relief and peasant liberation.[52] In Vienna, however, the resolution campaign was seen very differently, as a battle cry in nationality politics. Flexing his symbolic muscle, the emperor cancelled a planned trip to Galicia to disparage the Polish ruling class.[53]

In 1871, a motion submitted by the government of Prime Minister Karl Sigmund von Hohenwart suggested at least some openness towards concessions to the Polish conservatives. The bill was nonetheless rejected by the Austrian Chamber of Deputies. Ever fearful of further federalization, the German Liberals saw the move as a possible opening for the scattering of imperial competences among other crown lands. Their stance was not unfounded; the government was also planning greater autonomy for the provinces of Bohemia and Tyrol.[54] From the Liberals' point of view,

> an agreement should be reached with the Resolutionist party... as for the party of Galician federalists, who want to win for Galicia today what they may want to help win tomorrow for Bohemia and the crown lands of our other rivals, we cannot possibly come to an agreement.[55]

As a result, the Viennese government established only informal privileges for the Poles. From April 1871, with only a brief initial interruption, a minister without portfolio sat in the Austrian Council of Ministers. He was responsible exclusively for Galician affairs and has recently been described by the historian Damian Szymczak as a one-man embassy or provincial delegate in the capital.[56] This role followed the model laid down by the 'Croatian-Slavonian-Dalmatian minister'.[57] While the office was not constitutionally grounded, as in Hungary, the Galician

[52] The Imperial Patent of 18 Apr. 1848 (for Galicia) had, in contrast to the Patent of 7 Sept. 1848 (for the empire), spoken of compensation for the abolition of the robot by the Imperial Treasury. In fact, in 1882 the Polish Club finally achieved a removal of the provincial debts resulting from land relief. Józef Buszko, *Polacy w parlamencie wiedeńskim 1848–1918*. Warsaw, 1996, 116. Nevertheless, resources remained low. Hans Peter Hye, *Das politische System in der Habsburgermonarchie*. Prague, 1998, 171.

[53] Michał Oberc, *Wizyty cesarza Franciszka Józefa I w Galicji*. Rzeszów, 2016, 40–4.

[54] Helmut Rumpler, *Eine Chance für Mitteleuropa*. Vienna, 1997, 430.

[55] Deputy Sturm in the budget debate on 7 June 1871, quoted in Gustav Kolmer, *Parlament und Verfassung in Österreich*. Vol. 2: *1869–1879*. Vienna and Leipzig, 1903, 139.

[56] Damian Szymczak, *Galicyjska 'ambasada' w Wiedniu*. Poznan, 2013. Among the 'Resolutionists' and in the government bill, however, the original passage had read: 'The Kingdom of Galicia is represented by a Minister in the Council of the Crown'. Kolmer, *Parlament und Verfassung in Österreich*, 2. 137.

[57] Szymczak, *Galicyjska 'ambasada' w Wiedniu*, 78.

minister proved to be much more empowered than his Croatian counterpart in Budapest.[58]

Historians, politicians, and legal scholars interpreted this office as either that of a provincial minister for the interests of Galicia[59] or of a compatriot minister for the interests of the Poles.[60] In practice, the prime minister and the emperor appointed only high-ranking Poles, usually the chairman of the Polish Club (*koło polskie*) in the Chamber of Deputies.[61] Even though the original bill spoke of a provincial minister for all of Galicia, Polish interests were decisive in the appointment and dominated the minister's activities. Czechs, Germans, Ruthenians, Jews, or Slovenes, who fought for similar representation in the Council of Ministers, also perceived the office as serving exclusively Polish national interests.

These views were shaped by the actions of the first incumbent, Florian Ziemiałkowski, who held office from 1873 to 1888 and emphasized provincial as well as Polish national interests.[62] The Ruthenians of Galicia refused to accept him because of his anti-Ruthenian stance: he had declared the Ukrainian-speaking population a mere branch of the Polish nation and took action against their Greek Catholic clergy.[63] In his first years in office, Ziemiałkowski was committed, among other things, to the founding of a technical university, the autonomy of the Polonized Provincial School Board,[64] and the establishment of cooperative banks. At the same time, he supervised and influenced Vienna's political communication with the Ruthenians.[65] His successors also looked after Polish interests in other crown lands as well as in the other partition territories, above all the Russian Empire.[66]

[58] The number of employees varied between three and six, and the workload involved, among other things, the processing of several hundred files on Galician affairs each month, answering enquiries from the self-government bodies as well as petitions, and organizing inter-ministerial conferences. Szymczak, *Galicyjska 'ambasada' w Wiedniu*, 71–4 and 78.

[59] This was the official description by the Galician Poles. Binder, 'Galizische Autonomie', 257.

[60] On the different names and designations Szymczak, *Galicyjska 'ambasada' w Wiedniu*, 59–60. The author tends to characterize it as a provincial minister. His numerous examples, however, instead show the office as a Polish institution.

[61] However, this did not mean that the minister and the Polish Club cooperated successfully thereafter. See Szymczak, *Galicyjska 'ambasada' w Wiedniu*, 113; Binder, 'Galizische Autonomie', 256–7.

[62] On the Polish-Ruthenian conflict see also Chapter 5. On the 'Provisions on the Sphere of Action of Minister Dr. Ziemialkowski' cf. the corresponding supplement in Johannes Kalwoda, *Zur Institution des deutschen 'Landsmannministeriums' in Altösterreich 1891–1910* (Dipl.-Arb.). Vienna, 1995, 129–30.

[63] They therefore demanded their own minister. Szymczak, *Galicyjska 'ambasada' w Wiedniu*, 81 and 84–5. After the failed 'Compromise' between Poles and Ruthenians, anti-Polish sentiment prevailed among the Ruthenian elite. Stanisław Pijaj, 'Pokusy o polsko-ukrajinskou dohodu v Haliči'. In Fasora et al. (eds), *Moravské vyrovnání*, 273. The Russophile trends had indeed strengthened. See Anna Veronika Wendland, *Die Russophilen in Galizien*. Vienna, 2001.

[64] On the discrimination against the Ruthenians Peter Urbanitsch, 'Das Schulwesen in Cisleithanien: Element eines kooperativen Imperiums?' In Jana Osterkamp (ed.), *Kooperatives Imperium: Politische Zusammenarbeit in der späten Habsburgermonarchie*. Göttingen, 2018, 98.

[65] Szymczak, *Galicyjska 'ambasada' w Wiedniu*, 113–27.

[66] Szymczak, *Galicyjska 'ambasada' w Wiedniu*, 83.

The influence of this ministerial post should not be overestimated, however. Just as the later compatriot ministers in the Viennese cabinet for the Czechs (1879–92 and 1900–9)[67] and the Germans (1891/1892 and 1906–10)[68] lobbied with few resources and competences, the minister for Galicia also had to make do without an administrative apparatus or budget of his own. His role was thus limited to informal interventions and initiatives[69] and his success largely depended on his ability to win the cooperation of the Polish Club in the Imperial Council.

Galician autonomy did nonetheless score some notable victories, including the Polonization of public life and an independent economic policy. In schooling and education, the Galician Diet became a pioneer of Polonization by exerting a nationalist influence on the Provincial School Board, teaching curricula, and personnel decisions. In this respect, it became a model for other mixed-language crown lands such as Bohemia.[70] The conservatives, who set the political tone, instrumentalized economic autonomy to pursue a policy that favoured agrarian over industrial interests.[71] While Hungary launched comprehensive industrial subsidy programmes, Galicia remained an agricultural province. The latifundia even increased in scale.[72] An economically conservative state administration and a provincial government that was financially too weak for large-scale economic initiatives prevented a broad promotion of industrialization in the province.[73]

Innovative economic incentives for development 'from above', which were repeatedly demanded by the bourgeoisie in view of the region's poverty, failed to materialize.[74] Although Galicia received an above-average share of the funds allocated to Cisleithania, it remained highly dependent on state aid for industrial and infrastructural development.[75] This proved fatal for the Galician oil industry.[76]

[67] Martin Klečacký, *Český ministr ve Vídni*. Prague, 2017.

[68] The willingness of the resort ministers to cooperate was generally low; from the parliamentary side, it was predominantly the German Liberals who voiced their concerns. Kalwoda, *Institution des deutschen 'Landsmannministeriums'*, 40 and 95.

[69] Within this framework, the minister also addressed common affairs such as emigration, education, soil improvement, or river regulation, but communication between the minister and the Ruthenians soon ceased. Szymczak, *Galicyjska 'ambasada' w Wiedniu*, 336 and 338.

[70] The 'Polonization' of the school system meant Polish dominance, but German- and Ruthenian-language schools continued to exist. Cf. Binder, 'Galizische Autonomie', 245–50; Joanna Falkowska, *Myśl wychowania narodowego w Galicji okresu autonomii: Twórcy i idee*. Toruń, 2013.

[71] Berend, *History Derailed*, 184–96.

[72] With respect to the level of industrialization, Galicia also lagged behind the other partition regions of Poland. Józef Buszko, *Zum Wandel der Gesellschaftsstruktur in Galizien und in der Bukowina*. Vienna, 1978, 15–31.

[73] Roger von Battaglia, 'Industrieförderung als künstliches Ausgleichsmittel', *Schriften des volkswirtschaftlichen Instituts des Obersten Polnischen Nationalkomitees*, Deutsche Folge, 1 (1917), 181.

[74] Cf. Klemens Kaps, *Ungleiche Entwicklung in Zentraleuropa*. Vienna, 2015, 373–6. On the unwillingness of local elites to invest Müller, 'Regionale Wirtschafts- und Nationalitätenpolitik in Ostmitteleuropa', 43–7.

[75] Franz Baltzarek, 'Zentralistische und föderalistische Aspekte der Wirtschaftspolitik am Beispiel Galiziens'. In Müller, *Ausgebeutet oder alimentiert?*, 59–90.

[76] Alison Frank, *Oil Empire: Visions of Prosperity in Austrian Galicia*. Cambridge, MA, 2005, 102–8; Uwe Müller, 'Transnationale Verflechtungen der Wirtschaft in Ostmitteleuropa während der

The achievements of 'Galician autonomy', the goals of Polish economic nationalism, and the actual economic development conflicted with each other and hindered a long-term economic upswing. Alison Frank rightly diagnoses with regard to the Galician politicians an 'incompatibility of their desire for Galician autonomy with the industry's need for economic integration with the rest of Austria. For the Galician oil industry, it was too much autonomy, not too little, that proved catastrophic.'[77]

The impact of the debates over a federal partition of Galicia that had left their mark on 1848 was hardly noticeable twenty years later. Attempts at Polish–Ruthenian reconciliation undertaken in 1869 and between 1890 and 1894 remained informal and short-lived.[78] Although Poles accounted for less than half of the Galician population, it was not until 1914—and only after pressure from the imperial government—that the Sejm allowed greater representation of the non-Polish population (as well as the peasantry).[79] Ruthenian deputies had been ousted from the Sejm in the decades before.[80] According to the reform proposals, national curiae were now to be established in the diet and electoral districts, as in Moravia in 1905[81] and Bukovina in 1914.[82] They were designed to ensure

ersten Globalisierung'. In Frank Hadler and Matthias Middell (eds), *Handbuch einer transnationalen Geschichte Ostmitteleuropas*. Vol. 1: *Von der Mitte des 19. Jahrhunderts bis zum Ersten Weltkrieg*. Göttingen, 2017, 314–19.

[77] Frank, *Oil Empire*, 255. Others emphasize the economic policy efforts favoured by autonomy, cf. Piotr Franaszek, 'Die wirtschaftspolitische Gesetzgebung der Wiener Regierung und die ökonomische Entwicklung Galiziens im langen 19. Jahrhundert'. In Müller, *Ausgebeutet oder alimentiert?*, 91–100.

[78] Nevertheless, the rapprochement led to the opening of a Ruthenian secondary school in Kolomea, a chair of Ukrainian history in Lemberg (Lwów, Lviv), a wider dissemination of Ruthenian in the school system, and the promotion of some cultural institutions. Pijaj, 'Pokusy o polsko-ukrajinskou dohodu', 274. Wendland, *Russophile in Galizien*, 158–168.

[79] Börries Kuzmany, 'Der Galizische Ausgleich'. In Elisabeth Haid, Stephanie Weismann, and Burkhard Wöller (eds), *Galizien: Peripherie der Moderne—Moderne der Peripherie*. Marburg, 2013, 124 and 141. However, the working class was not given greater consideration through universal suffrage. Józef Buszko, *Sejmowa reforma wyborcza w Galicji 1905–1914*. Warsaw, 1956. The Polish elite was among the strictest opponents of universal suffrage even at the imperial level. Instructively Hans Peter Hye, 'Ein politischer Preis des allgemeinen und länder- bzw. wahlbezirksweise gleichen Männerwahlrechts zum Abgeordnetenhaus: Die "lex Starzyński"'. In Kristina Kaiserová, (ed.), *Čechy a Sasko v proměnách dějin/Böhmen und Sachsen im Wandel der Geschichte*. Ústí nad Labem, 1993, 181–226.

[80] On the representation of the Ruthenians in the Sejm and the Imperial Council Franz Adlgasser, 'Neue Gesichter oder alte Bekannte? Das Abgeordnetenhaus im Spiegel der Wahlrechtsreformen'. In Thomas Simon (ed.), *Hundert Jahre allgemeines und gleiches Wahlrecht in Österreich*. Frankfurt am Main, 2010, 71.

[81] In Moravia, Czech and German curiae were established—in addition to the large estates. On this subject the anthology Fasora et al., *Moravské vyrovnání*.

[82] In Bukovina, other Romanian, Ruthenian, German, Jewish, and Polish curiae 'according to the Moravian model' were to be established in addition to the large landowner curia. The establishment of a Jewish curia failed due to the resistance of the Viennese bureaucracy and the locally acculturated Jewish bourgeoisie. Cf. John Leslie, 'Der Ausgleich in der Bukowina von 1910: Zur österreichischen Nationalitätenpolitik vor dem Ersten Weltkrieg'. In Emil Brix, Thomas Fröschl, and Josef Leidenfrost (eds), *Geschichte zwischen Freiheit und Ordnung*. Graz, 1991, 137–8.

parliamentary and political visibility for all sectors of the population, especially the underrepresented Ruthenians, a measure that, however, never took effect.[83]

In the final years of the Monarchy, 'Galician autonomy' was no longer considered a model worth imitating by other crown lands and nationalities. Within the 'normal' framework of the Austrian Fundamental Laws and the constitutions of their provinces, nationalities such as the Czechs or the Slovenes enjoyed significant opportunities for development without the need for a formal 'Compromise'. Moreover, Galicia's economic backwardness clearly set it apart from the Hungarian economic miracle. There was also the problem that large parts of the population were excluded from participation in Galician politics, both socially and nationally. The Polish historian Szymczak therefore stated that Galician autonomy had ultimately become 'a catchword without any real meaning'.[84]

8.4. Tyrolean Wilfulness

If one were to rifle through the history books to find a 'Tyrolean Compromise', you would come away empty-handed. Compared with the demands of other crown lands, however, Tyrol possessed considerable attributes of 'statehood'. It had a provincial militia and its own right to recruit, pursued a distinctive Catholic-conservative schooling policy, and rejected other imperial policies, claiming that imperial law could not override provincial or the 'historic state law'.[85] While other crown lands used state law arguments to negotiate more political agency for themselves, Tyrolean state law, with its elements of imperial 'loyalty in arms' and religious and regional unity, served as a justification for maintaining the status quo.

Metaphors such as the 'Tyrolean in arms' or 'Tyrol in arms' symbolized the territory's privileged relationship with its ruler.[86] For centuries, Tyrol had only enlisted citizens to defend their own land, i.e. in the service of the monarch as the local prince, rather than for the entire state.[87] Even after 1868, it was

[83] The new electoral rules now secured them at least 27.2 per cent of the mandates. Pijaj, 'Pokusy o polsko-ukrajinskou dohodu', 276. See Chapter 11.5.

[84] Damian Szymczak, 'Österreichisches rechtspolitisches System und die Bildung der Zivilgesellschaft in Galizien in der Autonomieära 1871–1914'. In Wilhelm Brauneder and Milan Hlavačka (eds), *Bürgerliche Gesellschaft auf dem Papier*. Berlin, 2014, 284–5.

[85] On historical state law federalism in Tyrol cf. Hans Lentze, 'Die Problematik der Föderalisierung in Österreich'. In Holotík, *Der österreichisch-ungarische Ausgleich*, 938–9.

[86] Martin Schennach, 'Der wehrhafte Tiroler: Zu Entstehung, Wandlung und Funktion eines Mythos', *Geschichte und Region/Storia e regione*, 14/2 (2005), 81–112; Laurence Cole, 'Province and Patriotism: German National Identity in Tirol 1850–1914', *Österreichische Zeitschrift für Geschichtswissenschaften*, 6/1 (1995), 66.

[87] Laurence Cole, *Military Culture and Popular Patriotism in Late Imperial Austria*. Oxford, 2014, 113.

incorporated separately into the imperial army organization; in 1861, the provincial ordinances of Tyrol and Vorarlberg had declared defence to be a purely provincial responsibility.[88] The Tyrolean and Vorarlberg militia could only be deployed to defend the provinces specifically, unless the entire monarchy was subject to attack by an overpowering enemy (as was the case in the First World War).[89] This myth was mined for political capital by German-speaking Tyroleans,[90] who were uniquely celebrated by the military through the ideal of the 'loyal German' rifleman at provincial parades.[91] The participation of the Tyrolean Italians, on the other hand, regularly caused problems.[92]

The state-law principle of 'unity in faith' led to further privileges. While state law in Hungary, Bohemia, and Croatia took a nationalist turn towards the end of the nineteenth century, in Tyrol it was the religious aspects of the law that were emphasized.[93] In view of the (re)secularization of education in the Austrian Empire after 1867, the majority of the Tyrolean Diet hoped to retain control over schooling together with the provincial bishops.[94] The Viennese government finally conceded the leadership of the local and provincial school boards to the Tyrolean clergy.[95] Twenty years later, the Innsbruck journal *The Catholic Primary School* still justified this exceptional educational policy with recourse to 'Tyrol's autonomy': the aim was 'to have Catholic primary schools, whatever the imperial school laws may be'.[96] Efforts to return primary schools to church control in the Austrian part of the empire with the help of Catholics of the Czech and Polish clubs in the Chamber of Deputies nevertheless failed.[97]

[88] On the quota system Günther Kronenbitter, *Krieg im Frieden*. Munich, 2003, 152. On the crown land's constitution Richard Schober, *Geschichte des Tiroler Landtages im 19. und 20. Jahrhundert*. Innsbruck, 1984, 148.

[89] On the incorporation of Tyrol into the three armies cf. Otto Stolz, *Geschichte der Verwaltung Tirols: Teilstück des 2. Bandes der Geschichte des Landes Tirol*. Innsbruck, 1998, 225–8. Another privilege was the election of officers by the enlisted men. Schober, *Geschichte des Tiroler Landtages*, 322.

[90] Laurence Cole, *'Für Gott, Kaiser und Vaterland': Nationale Identität der deutschsprachigen Bevölkerung Tirols 1860–1914*. Frankfurt am Main and New York, 2000, 395–412.

[91] 'Germanness' in Tyrol could have very different connotations and refer to the empire, Germany, or Tyrol. Laurence Cole and Hans Heiss, '"Unity vs. Difference": The Politics of Region-Building and National Identities in Tyrol 1830–1867'. In Laurence Cole (ed.), *Different Paths to the Nation: Regional and National Identities in Central Europe and Italy 1830–70*. Basingstoke, 2007, 53–6.

[92] Italian Tyroleans were initially to be excluded from the rifle companies. Schober, *Geschichte des Tiroler Landtages*, 321; Cole, *'Für Gott, Kaiser und Vaterland'*, 494–501.

[93] By joining the 'Iron Ring' of the Taaffe government in 1880, the Tyrolean conservatives nolens volens gave up their claim to 'historic state law', which they had propagated since 1861. Josef Fontana, *Der Kulturkampf in Tirol 1861–1892*. Bozen, 1978, 316 and 417; Schober, *Geschichte des Tiroler Landtages*, 190–9, 233–56.

[94] Pieter M. Judson, *Exclusive Revolutionaries*. Ann Arbor, 1996, 133.

[95] In matters of 'religion and morality', the three regional bishops had a right of veto. Schober, *Geschichte des Tiroler Landtages*, 241 and 252. In Bohemia, clergymen were represented in the school councils only as ordinary members. On the dispute over the liberalization of the school system there Stanislav Balík, Jiří Hanuš, Lukáš Fasora, and Marek Vlha, *Der tschechische Antiklerikalismus*. Vienna, 2016, 128–31.

[96] Fritz Maurer to the Provincial Governor Kathrein of 10 Oct. 1886, printed in Richard Schober (ed.), *Theodor Freiherr von Kathrein 1842–1916*. Innsbruck, 1992, 331.

[97] Promemoria of Governor Kathrein to the Catholic-Political People's Association for German Tyrol, end of Aug. 1887, reprinted in Schober, *Theodor Freiherr von Kathrein*, 333. However, an

This adherence to the 'unity in faith' principle and a Tyrolean Catholic religiosity was directed not least against the new religious freedoms of the Protestants.[98] The prince-bishops in the provincial diet suggested that the Tyrolean Protestants should in denominational terms not be counted as Tyroleans but belong to another Austrian province. The Viennese government did not give in to such exaggerated demands, but tolerated the intentional sluggishness of the provincial bureaucracy designed to inhibit the growth of Protestant congregations.[99] Even regional historians of the late twentieth century saw this as a success for the preservation of the 'unique character of the crown land' supported by the 'people'.[100] It was not until 1875 that Vienna enforced by decree the establishment of Protestant congregations in Merano and Innsbruck.[101] But when these new parishes sought leave to build churches, they were thwarted by the Tyrolean provincial committee as late as 1903, forcing the Administrative Court to intervene.[102] Even thereafter, the regional committee argued that the Tyrolean law on 'unity in faith' overrode any freedom of religion enshrined in imperial law.[103]

Dogmatic insistence on Tyrol's 'state law' and its precedence over Vienna gradually ebbed away once the Christian Socialists won a majority in the provincial diet after the turn of the century.[104] Conversative resistance to infrastructure projects as well as to agricultural and social reforms was also overcome and the crown land experienced an economic revival.[105] Road and railroad construction and, after several flood disasters, water engineering were now increasingly promoted by the province in cooperation with the empire, the municipalities, and the chambers of commerce and trade.[106] A regionally and financially

agreement with the Poles remained unsuccessful, note by Josef Neuner of 16 Jan. 1888, printed in Schober, *Theodor Freiherr von Kathrein*, 339.

[98] See below.

[99] Schober, *Geschichte des Tiroler Landtages*, 235 and 237; Hans Heiss, 'Die Evangelische Gemeinde A. B. Meran im Kontext der Südtiroler Geschichte'. In Hans H. Reimer (ed.), *Lutherisch in Südtirol*. Bozen, 2009, 622.

[100] Schober, *Geschichte des Tiroler Landtages*, 237. Notwithstanding his 'sympathy for the Catholic tradition', Schober diagnoses 'beginnings of anti-progressive intolerance towards people of other faiths'.

[101] This ministerial order by Stremayr led to bitter backlash as well as demonstrative Catholic piety, such as the revival of the Catholic Sacred Heart Men's League. Fontana, *Kulturkampf in Tirol*, 301–6, 417.

[102] Fontana, *Kulturkampf in Tirol*, 354.

[103] Schober, *Geschichte des Tiroler Landtages*, 240. On Merano Reimer, *Lutherisch in Südtirol*. From a legal perspective Hans Kelsen, *Reichsgesetz und Landesgesetz nach österreichischer Verfassung* (1914). In Matthias Jestaedt (ed.), *Hans Kelsen Werke*. Vol. 3: *Veröffentlichte Schriften 1911–1917*. Tübingen, 2010, 363.

[104] Lentze, 'Problematik der Föderalisierung in Österreich', 939.

[105] The agrarian reform was repeatedly delayed by different laws of inheritance in North and South Tyrol, by the lack of land registers, and the resulting lack of mortgage loans. Herbert Schlegel, *Die Tirolische Landes-Hypothekenanstalt*. Innsbruck, 1966, 12–35; Schober, *Geschichte des Tiroler Landtages*, 302.

[106] Schober, *Geschichte des Tiroler Landtages*, 306–19. On the role of the chambers since neo-absolutism Thomas Götz, *Bürgertum und Liberalismus in Tirol 1840–1873*. Cologne, 2001, 296–304.

differentiated banking sector provided the necessary capital.[107] The growth of regional debts during this period reflected less fiscal mismanagement than long overdue investment.

The theme of 'regional unity' in the Tyrolean state narrative had a dimension that was genuinely nationalist. Despite the rhetoric of unity, there was a clear lack of local patriotism that could have united German-speaking and Italian-speaking Tyroleans. While the German Tyroleans did feel a sense of belonging to the province of Tyrol, the Italian-speaking rural population cultivated loyalty to the emperor instead.[108] The Italian national-liberal bourgeoisie of Trentino insisted on the historical-cultural uniqueness of their region, developed great economic-political power within the framework of Trento's local self-administration, and—without always striving for separation—refrained from declarations of loyalty.[109] These urban elites acted pragmatically. They fostered contacts with Italy, cooperated with the institutions of the Austrian Empire, and resolutely tackled the modernization of their city. Later, their efforts were framed as an '"Alpine model" of coexistence and development'.[110]

As debates intensified over the potential reorganization of the Habsburg Monarchy, the call for 'autonomy' increasingly gained traction among Tyrol's Italians.[111] At the beginning of the 1860s, the Italian Tyroleans demanded a federal division of the province and their own provincial diet or, failing that, the national separation of the large landowner curia within the existing provincial parliament and more mandates for the Italian rural communities.[112] The German Tyroleans rejected any form of federalization, pointing to Tyrol's 'unity' as guaranteed by state law. In 1871, as negotiations were under way for the Bohemian Fundamental Articles and more far-reaching concessions for Galicia, the then Tyrolean governor Eduard von Taaffe drafted an administrative solution under instructions from the Hohenwart cabinet.[113]

[107] Manfred Martin, *Das Bankwesen in Tirol bis 1945*. Innsbruck, 1970, 84. Since the turn of the century, the province and the state governors, such as Markus von Spiegelfeld, distributed provincial investments equally between Italian and German Tyroleans. On the road construction programme for South Tyrol Schober, *Geschichte des Tiroler Landtages*, 312–13.

[108] Cole, *Military Culture and Popular Patriotism*, 169–216 and 310–11. The history of the Cisleithanian veterans' associations as a whole is still a desideratum. Robert Luft, 'Zivilgesellschaft im cisleithanischen Teil der Habsburgermonarchie bis 1914'. In Jörg Hackmann and Klaus Roth (eds), *Zivilgesellschaft im östlichen und südöstlichen Europa in Geschichte und Gegenwart*. Munich, 2011, 197.

[109] Götz, *Bürgertum und Liberalismus in Tirol*, 114–15, 156, 413–19, 525–9. On Trient Mariapia Bigaran, 'Notabeln und Stadtregierung: Ämter, Zensus und Berufe in Trient gegen Ende des 19. Jahrhunderts'. In Stekl et al., *Bürgertum in der Habsburgermonarchie*, 131–40.

[110] On Trient's municipal policy Mariapia Bigaran, 'Il governo municipale a Trento tra '800 e '900: Ordinamenti, gruppi sociali, politiche' (university diss.). Florence, 1996, 264.

[111] Schober, *Geschichte des Tiroler Landtages*, 256–78; Karl Bier, 'Der Autonomiekampf der Welschtiroler und die Stellung der deutschen Parteien und Regierungen', *Veröffentlichungen des Museum Ferdinandeum in Innsbruck*, 16 (1936/1938), 417–525; Sergio Benvenuti, *L'autonomia Trentina al Landtag di Innsbruck e al Reichsrat di Vienna*. Trento, 1978.

[112] Schober, *Geschichte des Tiroler Landtages*, 258.

[113] Schober, *Geschichte des Tiroler Landtages*, 260–1; Anton Bundsmann, *Die Landeschefs von Tirol und Vorarlberg in der Zeit von 1815–1913*. Innsbruck, 1954, 130–1; Bier, 'Autonomiekampf der Welschtiroler', 431.

The administrative reorganization of Tyrol planned by Taaffe and Hohenwart differed only in name from a federal division of the crown land.[114] A county council and a county committee were to take care of all Italian interests in the province. Competences that elsewhere were held by provincial committees and provincial parliaments were handed to these new institutions: road and water engineering, schooling, social welfare and poor relief, agriculture, and policing. These activities were to be funded by surcharges on direct taxes. The county council also had legislative powers, provided its decisions received approval from the emperor. Since the representatives of Italian Tyrol insisted on their own provincial diet, this compromise failed. Later reconciliation attempts revolved around the same points,[115] but unlike Hohenwart, the prime ministers Franz von Thun-Hohenstein and later Ernest von Koerber were no longer willing to make similar concessions.[116]

The nationalization of provincial politics progressed in small steps. Once the Italians abandoned their policy of obstruction in the provincial diet, the provincial governor Theodor von Kathrein initiated a compromise in 1901. He proposed national curiae for the provincial diet and provincial committee, and national self-government rights in municipal, school, health, and economic matters. Furthermore, he proposed proportional allocations from the provincial revenues, separate tax levying rights, as well as an Italian provincial school board.[117] The government and the state governor again refused to lend their support.[118] In turn, the provincial administration allowed at the local level for separate nationalist policies regarding school councils, the provincial agricultural councils, and even the fire brigades.

The administrative elites of the empire and the province regularly suspected Trentino of leaning towards Italian irredentism.[119] The question of an Italian-language university thus continued to be an explosive issue in Vienna and Innsbruck until the fall of the empire.[120] Markus von Spiegelfeld, then state governor, criticized the negative image of the disloyal Italian as late as 1912, saying that 'we have gone much too far in our obsession with suspecting irredentism everywhere... If we demand that they renounce the unitary state [of Italy]—their ideal—we must grant them all the more freedom and comfort.'[121]

[114] On the predecessor, the 'k. k. Court Councillor in Trento' cf. Stolz, *Geschichte der Verwaltung Tirols*, 49.

[115] On the various attempts at compromise Schober, *Geschichte des Tiroler Landtages*, 256–77.

[116] Schober, *Theodor Freiherr von Kathrein*, 52, 401–2, and 407–8.

[117] Minutes of the first meeting of the Autonomy Committee of 16 Jan. 1901, concept in Schober, *Theodor Freiherr von Kathrein*, 413–14. Reprinted in Benvenuti, *L'autonomia Trentina*, 190–201.

[118] Richard Schober, *La lotta sul progetto d'autonomie per il Trentino degli anni 1900–1902*. Trento, 1978.

[119] Cole and Heiss, 'Unity vs. Difference', 45 and 55.

[120] Gary B. Cohen, *Education and Middle-Class Society in Imperial Austria 1848–1918*. West Lafayette, IN, 1996, 112–13.

[121] Promemoria of the State Governor Markus von Spiegelfeld on the political situation in the Italian part of the Tyrol to Archduke Franz Ferdinand, 29 Sept. 1912, reprinted in Schober, *Theodor Freiherr von Kathrein*, 432 and 436–7. Spiegelfeld was replaced under Prime Minister Stürgkh as early

The example of Tyrol shows that a crown land's political privileges did not necessarily depend on the agreement of a 'compromise'. Tyrol's state narrative, with its core elements of loyalty in arms, unity in faith, and regional unity, corresponded to the political culture of the imperial court. Vienna did not sanction Tyrol's political privileges, but nonetheless tolerated them, especially with regard to religious policy and schooling. In political practice, however, the Tyrolean state narrative of 'regional unity' quickly became a hollow phrase. The provincial administration fragmented along ethnic lines and tended towards internal federalization or separation.

8.5. The Failed Compromise in Bohemia

The Kingdom of Bohemia and the three Bohemian lands (Bohemia, Moravia, and Silesia) enjoyed a prominent status in the Habsburg Monarchy and fulfilled all criteria for possible imperial privileges. State law and state narrative were both based on the history of a venerable kingdom. The influence of the provincial elite of high nobility and aspiring bourgeoisie extended economically and politically via Prague, Brno, and Troppau (Opava) to Vienna, Budapest, and beyond. Within the monarchy, the Bohemian lands ranked first in terms of economic and financial power. They were also at the forefront of building the modern state. Nevertheless, all attempts to formalize this exceptional position in a 'Bohemian Compromise' came to naught.

In the 1860s, Bohemian state law went through three phases of revision and reform. In the negotiations of the Imperial Council after 1861, it served as a template—alongside the 'state laws' of Hungary and Galicia—for establishing, on the basis of 'history', the necessary components of a greater autonomy for *all* crown lands. Demands for an independent administration, jurisdiction, and financial sovereignty, as well as regulatory competences in the areas of education, agriculture, and welfare, could be derived from 'historic state laws'. This led to a genuinely federalist vision of the empire as a whole. Later, from 1865 onwards, Bohemian state law helped to legitimate Bohemia's provincial privilege. After 1871, it was used to establish a statehood on Czech terms.[122]

After historic crown land federalism for the empire failed to gain acceptance in the Imperial Council, the Bohemian state law narrative was reprovincialized. It was now used to explain the relationship between the crown land and its sovereign and to justify political opposition. Since 1863, parts of the Bohemian (and later also the Moravian) Diet boycotted the Imperial Council and refused to send

as 1913. Cf. Bundsmann, *Die Landeschefs von Tirol und Vorarlberg*, 222–3. About the German school associations Judson, *Exclusive Revolutionaries*, 207–22.

[122] Jana Osterkamp, 'Geschichte als Argument: Das Böhmische Staatsrecht als politischer Leitbegriff im 19. Jahrhundert', *Střed/Centre*, 8/1 (2016), 17–23.

delegates.[123] Many wealthy landowners participated in the snub to express their rejection of Hungary's privileged position as a result in the February Patent and later in the Compromise.[124] Many Czechs saw the boycott as a means to oppose their discrimination by the Germans in the imperial and provincial electoral regulations, which in their view ran counter to their traditional rights.[125]

The Compromises with Hungary in 1867 and Croatia in 1868, and the 'Galician autonomy' in 1868, inspired a struggle for equal privileges. Bohemian representatives argued in numerous 'legal depositions'[126] with Vienna that the 'Lands of the Crown of Bohemia' had entered the association of states created by the Pragmatic Sanction with an independence and autonomy equal to that of Hungary. They had voluntarily accepted Hungary's privileged position in the dualist system only to 'bring the more than ten-year period of state legal turmoil to an end as soon as possible'.[127] This, however, did not mean that Bohemia had renounced its sovereignty. In the negotiations over the so-called Fundamental Articles of 1871, far-reaching privileges for Bohemia were discussed, planned, and promised by the monarch, who, however, withdrew them shortly afterwards.[128]

The Fundamental Articles promised independent legislative authority, administration, citizenship, fiscal sovereignty, and economic policy.[129] The 'legislation of the Bohemian Diet' and the 'administration of the Bohemian provincial government' were to be responsible for all matters that had not been declared common affairs of Austria and Hungary (Article 9). In matters of trade, customs, taxation and finance, infrastructure, and citizenship, Bohemia was merely 'willing' to make unifying agreements with the other crown lands (Articles 10, 11). The Viennese government was also to consist of 'appointed departmental ministers, then the court chancellors, and possibly the provincial ministers of equal rank, maintaining an appropriate voting ratio' (Article 13). Direct election of Bohemian deputies to the Austrian delegation would have ensured the crown land the greatest possible influence in the common affairs of Austria-Hungary (Article 4). Financial equalization occupied a major part of the agenda, with Bohemia having a say in the distribution of funds (Articles 6, 14).[130]

[123] Adlgasser, *Mitglieder der österreichischen Zentralparlamente*, 1, p. xlii.

[124] On the alleged 'dualism' of the February patent, cf. Chapter 4.

[125] Stanley Z. Pech, 'Passive Resistance of the Czechs 1863–1879', *Slavonic and East European Review* 36/87 (1958), 434–52. On the counter-position of the liberals cf. Jonathan Kwan, *Liberalism and the Habsburg Monarchy 1861–1895*. Basingstoke, 2013; Kwan, 'Austro-German Liberalism and Bohemian State Rights 1861–1879', *Střed/Centre*, 8/1 (2016), 109–50.

[126] Cf. Kolmer, *Parlament und Verfassung in Österreich*, 2. 287 and 525.

[127] Quotes in Antonín Otakar Zeithammer, *Zur Geschichte der böhmischen Ausgleichsversuche 1865–1871*. Vol. 2. Prague, 1913, 15–17.

[128] Zeithammer, *Geschichte der böhmischen Ausgleichsversuche*; Thomas Kletečka, *Der Ausgleichsversuch des Ministeriums Hohenwart-Schäffle mit Böhmen im Jahre 1871: Mit besonderer Berücksichtigung des reichsdeutschen Einflusses* (university diss.). Vienna, 1984.

[129] For the following, cf. the Fundamental Articles printed in Kolmer, *Parlament und Verfassung in Österreich*, 2. 191–7. Otto Urban, *Die tschechische Gesellschaft 1848–1918*. Vol. 1. Vienna, 1994, 367–75.

[130] Zeithammer, *Geschichte der böhmischen Ausgleichsversuche*, 2. 36–9.

The Fundamental Articles applied only to the Kingdom of Bohemia. Silesia and Moravia did not participate.[131] In Moravia, the parliamentarians invoked their own tradition of Moravian autonomy.[132] This was not least due to a 'power-saturated German majority in the diet'.[133] The Silesian Diet, which was dominated by the German propertied and educated elite, also rejected the extension of a Bohemian state law to its territory.[134]

However, the negotiations, which were on the verge of being finalized, ultimately failed. Historians emphasized different reasons for this failure. Thomas Kletečka stressed the changing foreign policy context after the founding of Germany. A quasi-sovereign Bohemia was no longer politically expedient to Berlin because the Kaiser's court, influenced by anti-Slavic resentment, feared destabilizing effects on its own eastern territories.[135] Domestic political opinion reflected this fear. For instance, Beust considered the possible rise of the Czechs a 'disruptive factor' for German-Magyar hegemony in Austria-Hungary; it should therefore be prevented.[136] Christian Scharf described how press coverage strongly polarized public opinion.[137] Lothar Höbelt, meanwhile, highlighted resentment in the other crown lands regarding the planned mode of financial redistribution (*Ausgleich*) in favour of Bohemia.[138]

If one considers Bohemia's standing in the monarchy, then it is clear that Vienna had neither an economic nor a political interest in Bohemia becoming autonomous. Unlike the relationship between Austria and Hungary, where both sides benefited from a disparity in political, legal, and economic development, Bohemia was an indispensable part of the imperial core.[139]

The history of the Fundamental Articles of 1871 also reveals a confusing variety of state law interpretations in Bohemia, which may well have prevented agreement.[140] There were three strong factions in the Prague Diet. The Bohemian nobility favoured sovereignty and state law, but only for the Kingdom of Bohemia, rather than the Bohemian lands as a whole. The Czech state politicians, above all František Palacký and František Ladislav Rieger, on the other hand, interpreted

[131] Urban, *Die tschechische Gesellschaft*, 1. 370–1.

[132] Urban, *Die tschechische Gesellschaft*, 1. 343–4 and 371.

[133] Jiří Malíř, 'Mähren und die Frage der Einführung des allgemeinen Wahlrechts 1848–1907'. In Simon, *Hundert Jahre allgemeines und gleiches Wahlrecht*, 259–60.

[134] Urban, *Die tschechische Gesellschaft*, 1. 370.

[135] Kletečka, *Ausgleichsversuch mit Böhmen*, 177–87. Modifying Lothar Höbelt, 'Devolution Aborted: Franz Joseph I and the Bohemian "Fundamental Articles" of 1871', *Parliaments, Estates and Representation*, 32/1 (2012), 47–50.

[136] Beust described the compromise as a 'serious threat to the empire and the dynasty'. Urban, *Die tschechische Gesellschaft*, 1. 372. See also Kwan, *Liberalism and the Habsburg Monarchy*, 81–2.

[137] Christian Scharf, *Ausgleichspolitik und Pressekampf in der Ära Hohenwart*. Munich, 1996.

[138] Höbelt, 'Devolution Aborted', 46–7.

[139] Cf. the Introduction in this book.

[140] Cf. Urban, *Die tschechische Gesellschaft*, 1. 283, 316–17, 354–61; Binder, 'Galizische Autonomie', 242; Hye, *Das politische System in der Habsburgermonarchie*, 167–70.

historic state law from a nationalist perspective and extended it to all Czech nationals within the Bohemian lands.[141] The third faction, the German-Bohemian liberals, were opposed to any kind of state autonomy for Bohemia; their ideal remained the Austrian Empire as a political unit.[142]

Later compromise attempts at reconciliation, such as the Emmersdorf Negotiations of 1878, the efforts to reach an understanding that began in 1887 and led to the so-called 'Punctuations' of 1890,[143] as well as the 'never-ending series of German-Czech attempts at reconciliation' after 1899 (which reached their height between 1909 and 1914) also remained unsuccessful.[144] The Emmersdorf negotiations still envisaged a federalization of the Habsburg Monarchy along liberal lines.[145] To support this, the Czech national politician Rieger proposed the foundation of a federalist party.[146] In contrast, the main agendas of the compromise attempts *after* the turn of the century revolved around language issues, a reform of the electoral regulations in the provincial committee, provincial institutions, and provincial parliamentary commissions, as well as the establishment of nationally separate electoral curiae.[147] A territorial division of Bohemia into national counties was demanded by German nationalists and considered by the Koerber cabinet.[148] Overall, the balancing of national political interests within Bohemia now took precedence over the relationship between the empire and the crown land.[149]

141 Urban, *Die tschechische Gesellschaft*, 1. 285.

142 Kwan, *Liberalism and the Habsburg Monarchy*, 73.

143 An implementation of the Punctuations failed not least because of a dispute within the Czechs. Luboš Velek, 'Národnostní vyrovnání jako cesta k soužití dvou národů v jedné země?' In Fasora et al., *Moravské vyrovnání*, 311. Cf. Karel Kazbunda, 'Krise české politiky a vídeňská jednání o t. zv. punktace roku 1890', *Český časopis historický*, 40 (1934), 80–108, 310–46, 491–528, and *Český časopis historický*, 41 (1935), 41–82, 294–320, 514–54.

144 Comprehensive in Czech and German language Luboš Velek, 'Úvod. Projekt česko-něměckého národnostního vyrovnání v Čechách v letech 1890–1915 a jeho geneze'. In Eva Drašarová, Roman Horský, Jiří Šouša, and Luboš Velek (eds), *Promarněná šance: Edice dokumentů k česko-německému vyrovnání před první světovou válkou. Korespondence a protokoly 1911–1912*. Vol. 1. Prague, 2008, 44; Jan Galandauer, 'Marný zápas Františka Thuna o česko-německé vyrovnání'. In Fasora et al., *Moravské vyrovnání*, 319–24.

145 Kwan, *Liberalism and the Habsburg Monarchy*, 106–21.

146 Rieger's effects contain the unfortunately undated dossier 'Preliminaries to a Programme of the Federal Party'. Archiv Národního muzea v Praze, Legacy F. L. Rieger, Carton 111. Content-wise, it is based on Constantin Frantz, 'Präliminarien zu einem Programm der föderativen Partei'. In Frantz, *Literarisch-politische Aufsätze*. Munich, 1876, 369–79. Cf. Kwan, *Liberalism and the Habsburg Monarchy*, 106; Urban, *Die tschechische Gesellschaft*, 1. 471–5.

147 A summary in Karl Urban's letter to the Minister President of 3 Jan. 1911. In Drašarová et al., *Promarněná šance*, 1., 109–11. On the changing nature of 'compromises' Velek, 'Úvod. Projekt česko-něměckého národnostního vyrovnání', 59–62 and 73–6. Detailed sources and studies on the negotiations at Karel Kazbunda, *Otázka česko-německá v předvečer velké války*. Prague, 1995.

148 Milan Hlavačka, *Zlatý věk české samosprávy. Samospráva a její vliv na hospodářský, sociální a intelektuální rozvoj Čech 1862–1913*. Prague, 2006, 139.

149 Velek, 'Národnostní vyrovnání jako cesta k soužití', 312; Urbanitsch, 'Die nationalen Ausgleichsversuche', 45–8.

The 'Czech minister' in Vienna helps to illustrate the divergent understandings of the Czech or Bohemian 'nation'. After the failure of the Fundamental Articles, the Czechs abstained from the provincial diet and the Imperial Council until 1879, when they entered a coalition with the conservative nobility. As a result of this cooperation, a Czech minister without portfolio was added to the Viennese cabinet as a compatriot minister.[150] As in Galicia, there was some debate whether this post was intended to be that of a provincial minister for the inhabitants of the Bohemian lands or that of a compatriot minister for the Czech-speaking population. From the evidence of ministerial appointments and activities, however, Czech interests clearly prevailed. Within these 'Czech' interests, crown land rivalries, i.e. between Bohemia, Moravia, and Silesia, became visible. When the Moravian-born compatriot minister Jan Žáček was accused of a lack of understanding of the situation in Bohemia, he had to resign.

When compared with the Galician minister, the Czech minister clearly possessed less authority and power. The highly differentiated Czech party landscape within the Bohemian lands meant that the minister did not receive the backing of a united parliamentary club as the minister for Galicia did through the Polish Club.[151] It was only under the Young Czech Antonín Rezek that ministers, deputies, parties, and the press took a harmonized approach towards Czech concerns.[152] Rezek's staff counted no more than three employees. Nevertheless, through his influence on personnel decisions, he succeeded at creating a 'Young Czech bureaucratic establishment' and placing the Bohemian administration in Czech hands.[153]

In public opinion and the press, the so-called nationalities struggle was increasingly perceived as insurmountable.[154] State Governor Franz Thun and Minister of the Interior Kasimir Badeni attempted to maintain neutrality in such matters.[155] Their intent was for the constitutionally guaranteed equality of nationalities to find its way into crown land and municipal politics and to break with the German tendency to set themselves apart politically from the other nationalities in the empire.[156] Stremayr's Language Ordinances of 1880 placed German and Czech on an equal footing in official dealings between the population and the provincial authorities. The Badeni Language Ordinances of 1897 extended this further, providing for linguistic equality in *internal* communications between the provincial government offices. After violent riots by the

[150] Klečacký, *Český ministr ve Vídni*, 264.

[151] Klečacký, *Český ministr ve Vídni*, 86.

[152] Klečacký, *Český ministr ve Vídni*, 61.

[153] Klečacký, *Český ministr ve Vídni*, 67 and 268.

[154] Velek, 'Úvod. Projekt česko-německého národnostního vyrovnání', 91. For the South Moravian region using the example of Znaim (Znojmo) Tereza Pavlíčková, *Die Entwicklung des Nationalitätenkonflikts in der Znaimer deutschen Presse 1850–1938*. Olomouc, 2013, 304.

[155] Jan Galandauer, *Franz Fürst Thun: Statthalter des Königreiches Böhmen*. Vienna, 2014.

[156] Velek, 'Úvod. Projekt česko-německého národnostního vyrovnání', 53–9.

Germans, these decrees were revoked.[157] Instead, the expansion of Czech in public life continued informally.[158] The Czech resort ministers and compatriot ministers in the Viennese government enforced bilingual practice by executive ordinances for the post office, telegraphy, and railways. In the law courts, public prosecutors' offices, tax authorities, and police stations, bilingualism was introduced, not officially but de facto.[159] Many politically active German Bohemians, however, were not prepared to give up the privileged status of their language. They settled their scores with the 'czechization of offices' in the press and in political pamphlets.[160] From 1908 onwards, they strove to paralyse the crown land's political life.

In Bohemia, the provincial budget was 'starved' due to the German Bohemians' prolonged obstruction in the provincial diet.[161] On the other hand the Czech majority in the provincial committee proved equally incapable of initiating a solution. In Istria, a similar nationally motivated boycott between Slovenes and Italians over municipal finances was settled in the provincial committee within a year.[162] In Bohemia, by contrast, the crown land's financial crisis permanently damaged the political culture of cross-national cooperation.[163] In 1913, with the so-called Anna Patent, the government replaced the paralysed provincial committee with a new state-run 'provincial administrative commission' designed to reorganize the provincial finances and to stop the cycle of debt.[164]

The curtain closed on the Bohemian Compromise. The dream of privileges like those enjoyed by Hungary, Galicia, or Tyrol went unfulfilled. Instead, Bohemia succumbed to a humiliating state curatorship in 1913. At first, people reacted with irony to this fall from grace. An ingenious entrepreneur printed Franz Joseph's broken promise to accept the Bohemian Crown on limited edition toilet paper.[165]

[157] Hlavačka, *Zlatý věk české samosprávy*, 136–9.

[158] Hlavačka, *Zlatý věk české samosprávy*, 139–40.

[159] Hlavačka, *Zlatý věk české samosprávy*, 139–40.

[160] Thus the nationalist writing of Anton Schubert, *Die Ämtervertschechung in Deutschböhmen*. Reichenberg, 1903.

[161] In 1913, the crown land was threatened with fiscal bankruptcy. On the background of the Anna patents cf. Galandauer, *Franz Fürst Thun*, 287–92; Hlavačka: *Zlatý věk české samosprávy*, 140; Jiří Klabouch, *Die Gemeindeselbstverwaltung in Österreich 1848–1918*. Vienna, 1968, 146–7.

[162] Frank Wiggermann, *K. u. k. Kriegsmarine und Politik: Ein Beitrag zur Geschichte der italienischen Nationalbewegung in Istrien*. Vienna, 2004, 109–11.

[163] Hlavačka, *Zlatý věk české samosprávy*, 140.

[164] On the unconstitutionality of the Anna Patent cf. Hans Kelsen, 'Die böhmische Verwaltungskommission vor dem Verwaltungsgerichtshof' (1913). In Jestaedt, *Hans Kelsen Werke*, 3. 106–11; Gerald Stourzh, 'Verfassungsbruch im Königreich Böhmen: Ein unbekanntes Kapitel zur Geschichte des richterlichen Prüfungsrechts im alten Österreich' (1992). In Stourzh, *Der Umfang der österreichischen Geschichte*. Vienna, 2011, 139–56. On the activities of the Provincial Administrative Commission, cf. Jaromír Patočka, 'Zemská správní komise pro Království české v letech 1913 a 1914' (diploma thesis). Univ. Karlova Prague, 2006.

[165] This was the old Czech press magnate Jan Stanislav Skrejšovský. For this Luboš Velek, 'Böhmisches Staatsrecht auf "weichem Papier": Tatsache, Mythos und ihre symbolische Bedeutung in der tschechischen politischen Kultur', *Bohemia*, 47/1 (2007), 112.

In the long run, however, repeated repudiations by the emperor and the government, the 'prison era' for national political activists, the dismissals of Czech nationals from the civil service in the 1870s, the fickle language policy of the 1890s, and the emergency policy of 1913 led contemporaries and historians to describe Bohemia (and the Czechs in particular) as having drawn the short end of the stick.[166]

This image of the disadvantaged Bohemian lands[167] and the crown land's disgraceful state curatorship should not, however, obscure the fact that, in many respects, the Bohemian lands and their inhabitants were able to shape the fate of their crown land. In the provincial diet and the provincial committee, in the numerous intermediary organizations such as chambers of commerce and trade,[168] bar associations,[169] and provincial councils of agriculture and education,[170] the elites of the Bohemian lands, sometimes in cooperation, sometimes in opposition, were able to urge the directions for new development in the region as well as across the empire. At the imperial level, politicians from the Bohemian lands had been sitting in Viennese cabinets since the 1860s. They came from the aristocratic or German bourgeois classes and were later joined by numerous Czech resort ministers such as Minister of Agriculture Albín Bráf or Minister of Finance Josef Kaizl.[171] It would be misleading, therefore, to describe Bohemia as peripheral by comparison to the centre of power in Vienna. Instead, it formed part of the imperial core.[172] Whereas Hungary (in the dualist empire), Croatia-Slavonia (in Hungary), and Galicia (in Cisleithania) were recipients of funds, the Bohemian lands, and the Kingdom of Bohemia in particular, were among the financially strongest and most resourceful donors.

Moreover, Bohemian state law provided not only a trove of arguments for greater crown land independence. Through foreign policy initiatives at the French

[166] Urban, *Die tschechische Gesellschaft*, 1. 344 and 377.

[167] The failure of a Bohemian Compromise is to this day linked in historiography to the failure of the Habsburg Monarchy as a whole. Recently Zoltán Szász, 'The Nation-State in a Multinational Empire'. In Gerö, *Austro-Hungarian Monarchy Revisited*, 181

[168] On Moravia Tomáš Jiránek, 'Česko-německé vztahy v obchodních a živnostenských komorách v Brně a v Olomouci v době moravského vyrovnání'. In Fasora et al., *Moravské vyrovnání*, 333–46.

[169] The parity composition improved the representation of class interests. Stanislav Balík, 'Česko-německé uspořádání v orgánech Advokátní komory v království Českém od počátku 20. století do r. 1918'. In Fasora et al., *Moravské vyrovnání*, 325–32.

[170] Following an intervention by the Young Czechs, elections to school councils were not part of the policy of obstruction. Urban, *Die tschechische Gesellschaft*, 1. 382.

[171] Urban, *Die tschechische Gesellschaft*, 1. 333–4.

[172] Komlosy, *Grenze und ungleiche regionale Entwicklung*, 194; Pieter Judson, 'L'Autriche-Hongrie était-elle un empire?', *Annales: Histoire, Sciences Sociales*, 63/3 (2008), 565; Robert Luft, 'Machtansprüche und kulturelle Muster nichtperipherer Regionen: Die Kernlande Böhmen, Mähren und Schlesien in der späten Habsburgermonarchie'. In Johannes Feichtinger, Moritz Csáky, and Ursula Prutsch (eds), *Habsburg Postcolonial: Machtstrukturen und kollektives Gedächtnis*. Innsbruck, 2003, 165–87; Solomon Wank, 'The Habsburg Empire'. In Karen Barkey and Mark von Hagen (eds), *After Empire. Multiethnic Societies and Nation-Building*. Boulder, CO, 1997, 51.

and Russian courts, Czechs such as František Palacký, František Ladislav Rieger, František Augustin Brauner, and Julius Grégr had made state law an object of European public interest as early as 1867.[173] After all, the historical state law of Bohemia—as a legitimizing narrative—outlasted the Habsburg Monarchy. During the peace negotiations in 1919, it underpinned the statehood of the new Czechoslovakia.[174]

A Federal History of the Habsburg Empire, 1815–1918. Jana Osterkamp, Oxford University Press.
 DOI: 10.1093/9780198943631.003.0009

[173] This Czech 'foreign policy' was tolerated by the Viennese government. Cf. Urban, *Die tschechische Gesellschaft*, 1. 329–33.

[174] Urban, *Die tschechische Gesellschaft*, 1. 345–8. On the role of international law cf. Natasha Wheatley, 'Law, Time, and Sovereignty in Central Europe: Imperial Constitutions, Historical Rights, and the Afterlives of Empire' (university diss.). Columbia, New York, 2016; now Wheatley, *The Life and Death of States: Central Europe and the Transformation of Modern Sovereignty*. Princeton: Princeton University Press, 2023.

Figure 9.1 Czech secondary school and technical secondary school in Moravian Ostrava. Photograph, 1907.

9

Acting Like States

The Crown Lands in a Cooperative Empire, 1867–1914

During the final third of the nineteenth century, *all* crown lands (including those not privileged through a bespoke 'Compromise', such as prosperous Bohemia) expanded their sovereignty by acting like independent states in an increasing number of policy fields. Collaboration among the crown lands and their cooperation with the imperial state took on an increasingly federal character. The contemporary buzzword for this process was *Verländerung* (provincialization). Thanks to the growing distribution of competences between the empire, its two parts, and the crown lands, and to the resulting collaboration between state and provincial institutions, the Habsburg Monarchy became a 'cooperative empire'.[1] It gradually abandoned the top-down rule typical of empires and the restrictions on communication and coordination among the crown lands. Instead, cooperation between the empire and its parts and collaboration among the provinces were increasingly favoured.

The importance of the crown lands for Habsburg federalism has remained all but unexplored. To date, the crown lands' history of federal statehood is yet to be written. Austrian and European state theory failed to consider Austria-Hungary as a federation. It is hardly surprising, then, that it would remain blind to the question whether the crown lands were members of a federation. Typically, the crown lands were regarded as mere 'administrative units' or 'municipal associations of the highest order' (*Kommunalverbände höchster Ordnung*) but certainly not as 'states'.[2] Legal scholars referred to the crown lands as states only within the

[1] See the contributions in Jana Osterkamp (ed.), *Kooperatives Imperium: Politische Zusammenarbeit in der späten Habsburgermonarchie*. Göttingen, 2018.

[2] For the classification as administrative units cf. the majority of contemporary scholars: Josef Ulbrich, *Das österreichische Staatsrecht*. 3rd edn. Tübingen, 1909; Friedrich Tezner, *Österreichisches Staatsrecht*. Vol. 2: *Die Volksvertretung*. Vienna, 1912; Franz Hauke, *Grundriß des Verfassungsrechts*. Leipzig, 1905; Ludwig Spiegel, 'Länder, Autonomie und Selbstverwaltung in der Gegenwart'. In Ernst Mischler and Josef Ulbrich (eds), *Österreichisches Staatswörterbuch: Handbuch des gesamten österreichischen öffentlichen Rechtes*. Vol. 3. 2nd edn. Vienna, 1907, 395–430. For a point of view of legal history cf. Wilhelm Brauneder, 'Die Habsburgermonarchie als zusammengesetzter Staat'. In Hans-Jürgen Becker (ed.), *Zusammengesetzte Staatlichkeit in der Europäischen Verfassungsgeschichte*. Berlin, 2006, 197–236; Martin P. Schennach (ed.), *Rechtshistorische Aspekte des österreichischen Föderalismus*. Vienna, 2015; Schennach, 'Gliedstaaten oder "Kommunalverbände höchster Ordnung"? Länder und Landesverfassungen in der österreichischen Staatsrechtslehre bis zum Ende der Monarchie'. In Gerold

context of 'historic state law' (and certainly not within that of contemporary constitutionalism).[3] The fact that the crown lands fulfilled modern state functions, especially on the Austrian side, thus went unnoticed.

The character of European statehood underwent fundamental changes in the nineteenth century. The military and interventionist state of the eighteenth century was augmented by the modern welfare state.[4] Statecraft no longer served purely to foster security and power, to collect taxes and military recruits, or to erect complex systems of 'surveillance and punishment'. Passive maintenance of the state was overtaken by active state building and welfare improvement. During the nineteenth century, the age of knowledge and science, the public sector provided primary and secondary schools, universities, and technical and agricultural colleges. It developed technical infrastructure programmes involving railways, telegraphy, canalization, and electrification in the cities and hydraulic engineering in rural areas. Social infrastructure was also expanded, inspired by conservative modernizers such as Lorenz von Stein, who provided the theoretical base for the state becoming active in the fields of welfare, poor relief, and public health. As a result, Austria—alongside Germany—became a pioneer of social security in Europe.

The Austrian crown lands played an indispensable role in the political history of the Habsburg welfare state. From 1867, the crown lands, on instruction of the imperial administration, designed, developed, and largely financed most of its activities. The same jurists who agreed that the crown lands were not, in legal terms, federal states, nonetheless conceded—unanimously—that they possessed many attributes of statehood. When, before the outbreak of the First World War, the leading *Zeitschrift für öffentliches Recht* (Journal of Public Law) surveyed constitutional and administrative lawyers for their opinions on the state-law status of the crown lands, it received fascinating answers. Karl Brockhausen, a Viennese administrative lawyer and expert on local self-government, believed there was no absolute answer as to 'whether the reins are held by the individual crown lands or by them collectively'.[5] Rudolf Herrnritt, an administrative and financial lawyer, also spoke of a 'steady increase in the powers of the crown land diets and their standing committees' and a deliberate expansion of their autonomy.[6] Their Prague-based colleague, Heinrich Rauchberg, emphasized that

Ambrosius, Christian Henrich-Franke, and Cornelius Neutsch (eds), *Föderalismus in historisch vergleichender Perspektive*. Vol. 6: *Integrieren durch Regieren*. Baden-Baden, 2018, 389–420.

[3] For Bohemia cf. Josef Kalousek, *Einige Grundlagen des böhmischen Staatsrechts*. Prague, 1871; Hugo Toman, *Das böhmische Staatsrecht und die Entwicklung der österreichischen Reichsidee von 1527 bis 1848*. Prague, 1871; Karel Kramář, *Das böhmische Staatsrecht*. Vienna, 1896.

[4] Hans-Peter Hye, 'Föderalistische Reformprojekte in der österreichischen Reichshälfte der Habsburgermonarchie: Eine gescheiterte Modernisierung'. In Wolfgang Kruse (ed.), *Andere Modernen: Beiträge zu einer Historisierung des Moderne-Begriffs*. Bielefeld, 2015, 220.

[5] Karl Brockhausen, 'Die Stellung der Kronländer im Gefüge der österreichischen Verfassung: Eine Rundfrage', *Österreichische Zeitschrift für öffentliches Recht*, 3 (1916), 6.

[6] Rudolf Herrnritt, 'Die Stellung der Kronländer im Gefüge der österreichischen Verfassung: Eine Rundfrage', *Österreichische Zeitschrift für öffentliches Recht*, 3 (1916), 40–1.

provincial patriotism, which was deeply rooted in the population, had arisen 'not only as a result of historical tradition, but also because of their present achievements'.[7] It was not only history and law that made the crown lands states, but their state-like activities.

What counts as a state activity and how policy fields develop are subject to constant historical change.[8] As Georg Jellinek argued in his 'Social Theory of the State', there is no 'conceptually necessary' purpose of a state; rather, what count as a state's goals fluctuate in accordance with the changing perceptions of different historical periods.[9] The nineteenth century in Europe, more than any other, saw an enormous transformation of state activity, state functions, and perceptions of the state.[10] Tasks that had previously been in the hands of individuals, society, and its institutions (especially with regard to education and social welfare), were transferred to the state. The boundaries between state and private responsibilities were redrawn.

Today's sociological theories of power and rule continue Jellinek's tradition.[11] Michael Mann is one prominent exponent. He describes the state not in terms of legal categories, but as a political power. The power of the 'state', referred to as *infrastructural power*, consists in its 'unique ability to provide a territorially-centralised form of organisation'.[12] According to Mann, the state's infrastructural capacity to penetrate civil society binds society to a territory.[13] Mann's sociology of rule, developed primarily for the centralized territorial state, will be applied below to a multi-level system of government.[14]

In this context, it is appropriate to speak of statehood tied to various policy fields and to examine the activities of the crown lands in light of these policies. The focus here will rest on the Cisleithanian half of the empire, where the Provincial Ordinances of 1861 gave the provincial diets and standing committees responsibility for education, regional infrastructure, public health, and social welfare.

[7] Heinrich Rauchberg, 'Die Stellung der Kronländer im Gefüge der österreichischen Verfassung: Eine Rundfrage', *Österreichische Zeitschrift für öffentliches Recht*, 3 (1916), 134.

[8] See Kathrin Loer, Renate Reiter, and Annette Elisabeth Töller, 'Was ist ein Politikfeld und warum entsteht es?', *Zeitschrift für Public Policy, Recht und Management*, 8/1 (2015) 7–28.

[9] Georg Jellinek, *Allgemeine Staatslehre*. 2nd edn. Berlin, 1905, 237 n. 1.

[10] Jellinek, *Allgemeine Staatslehre*, 250–6.

[11] Without reference to the older authors, Stefan Breuer, 'Von der sozialen Staatslehre zur Staatssoziologie: Georg Jellinek und Max Weber'. In Andreas Anter (ed.), *Die normative Kraft des Faktischen*. Baden-Baden, 2004, 89.

[12] Michael Mann, 'The Autonomous Power of the State: Its Origins, Mechanisms and Results', *European Journal of Sociology/Archives Européennes de Sociologie/Europäisches Archiv für Soziologie*, 25/2 (1984), 185. On the link between an economy based on regional division of labour, infrastructure development, and welfare activity, Josef Wysocki, *Infrastruktur und wachsende Staatsausgaben: Das Fallbeispiel Österreich 1868–1913*. Stuttgart, 1975, 8.

[13] Mann, *Autonomous Power of the State*, 211–12.

[14] Apparently, Mann perceives federalism as deficient because rule is not centrally bundled. Mann, *Autonomous Power of the State*, 205.

9.1. Education and Schooling

In nineteenth-century Europe, education and schooling were key policy areas appropriated and instrumentalized by the state for the extension of its power and influence within society.[15] In the eighteenth century, Empress Maria Theresa had already introduced compulsory mother-tongue primary schools to the Habsburg Monarchy, setting a long-term political trend.[16] The 1850s and 1860s saw rapid growth in the educational network.[17] After 1867, Cisleithania, under its liberal ministers, extended compulsory education and, unlike Hungary, systematically secularized the schools.[18] Under the conservative Taaffe government of the 1880s, the state again made concessions to the churches.[19] At the same time, it stepped up efforts to provide mother-tongue education in universities and secondary schools.[20] The division of the University of Prague into Czech- and German-speaking institutions is the most striking example of this policy.[21]

By the turn of the century, enrolment in secondary education in Austria was almost on par with Prussia, whose model many sought to emulate. Only Switzerland and Norway had better figures.[22] Enrolment in technical secondary and higher education was notably higher than in the rest of Europe.[23] Bohemia offered students a particularly differentiated technical education, enabling those from non-bourgeois backgrounds to enter technical professions and attracting scholars from across the Monarchy and abroad.[24] The performance of primary

[15] Jürgen Osterhammel, The Transformation of the World: A Global History of the Nineteenth Century. Princeton, 2014, 1111.

[16] Gustav Strakosch-Graßmann, *Geschichte des österreichischen Unterrichtswesens*. Vienna, 1905; Gary B. Cohen, *Education and Middle-Class Society in Imperial Austria 1848–1918*. West Lafayette, IN, 1996; Helmut Engelbrecht, *Geschichte des österreichischen Bildungswesens: Erziehung und Unterricht auf dem Boden Österreichs*. Vol. 3: *Von der frühen Aufklärung bis zum Vormärz*. Vienna, 1984; Margret Friedrich, Brigitte Mazohl, and Astrid von Schlachta, 'Die Bildungsrevolution'. In Helmut Rumpler and Peter Urbanitsch (eds), *Die Habsburgermonarchie 1848–1918*. Vol. 9: *Soziale Strukturen*. Part 1: *Von der Feudal-Agrarischen zur Bürgerlich-industriellen Gesellschaft*. Subvol. 1: *Lebens- und Arbeitswelten in der Industriellen Revolution*. Vienna, 2010, 67–107.

[17] Cohen: *Education and Middle-Class Society*, 55 and 66.

[18] Friedrich et al., 'Die Bildungsrevolution', 72–3.

[19] Church participation in the crown land's school board was at stake. The Reichsvolksschulgesetz was not amended, but special regulations prevailed in some crown lands as in Tyrol, Strakosch-Graßmann, *Geschichte des österreichischen Unterrichtswesens*, 298–308 and Chapter 8.4. Cf. on the reconfessionalization of schooling, Gustav Kolmer, *Parlament und Verfassung in Österreich*. Vol. 4: *1885–1891*. Vienna and Leipzig, 1907, 174–91.

[20] Harald Binder, Barbora Křivohlavá, and Luboš Velek (eds), *Místo národních jazyků ve výchově, školství a vědě v habsburské monarchii 1867–1918*. Prague, 2003.

[21] Hannelore Burger, *Sprachenrecht und Sprachgerechtigkeit im österreichischen Unterrichtswesen 1867–1918*. Vienna, 1995, 131.

[22] Cohen, *Education and Middle-Class Society*, 58.

[23] Cohen, *Education and Middle-Class Society*, 60, 75–84; Josef Schermaier, *Wirtschaftsförderung durch zentralstaatliche Bildungsmaßnahmen im Vielvölkerstaat Österreich*. Frankfurt am Main, 1999.

[24] Jiří Pokorný, 'Ingenieure in Böhmen und der Tschechoslowakei 1890–1939'. In Charles E. McClelland, Stephan Merl, and Hannes Siegrist (eds), *Professionen im modernen Osteuropa*. Berlin, 1995, 367–81; Cohen, *Education and Middle-Class Society*, 156. Milan Hlavačka refers to Czech technicians using their language in telegraphy and railways: *Zlatý věk české samosprávy: Samospráva a její vliv na hospodářský, sociální a intelektuální rozvoj Čech 1862–1913*. Prague, 2006, 143.

and elementary schools in Austria, by contrast, was moderate at best. Indeed, some crown lands languished at the bottom of the European tables for literacy and school attendance.[25] In the school year 1912/13, for example, more than half of the elementary schools in Tyrol and Dalmatia had a single class in which all age groups were taught together.[26] The economically successful crown lands were particularly committed to expanding education.[27] The elites demanded skilled workers to drive forward industrialization and agricultural modernization. At the same time, the continuously growing scope of state activity in public works and institutions required an equally growing number of experts.

One characteristic of Austrian education was that the power to shape educational policy rested with the funding institutions.[28] The universities were regulated, monitored, and maintained by Vienna.[29] The Cisleithanian state also had legislative control over the *Gymnasien* (academically rigorous secondary schools which prepared students for university), but financial maintenance was primarily the responsibility of the crown lands. By contrast, the commercial and technical secondary schools (*Realschulen*) were subject to provincial legislation, although Cisleithania made significant financial contributions to their maintenance. From the perspective of federal history, the crown lands' elementary schools (*Volksschulen*) and burgher schools (*Bürgerschulen*) are the most interesting. On the one hand, they gave rise to decades of conflict-ridden political negotiations between the imperial state and the individual crown lands. On the other, they led to multiple forms of cooperation between state and non-state actors: the empire, the crown lands, the provincial school boards, teachers' associations, parents and pupils, and the municipalities.

The development of education thus reveals a federal disparity. Galicia, Bukovina, Istria, and Dalmatia lagged behind in terms of school expansion and literacy. The Bohemian lands and Lower Austria by contrast enjoyed a relatively well-developed educational system.[30] The success or failure of educational initiatives rested not only on economic and financial circumstances, but on public perceptions. While

[25] Cohen, *Education and Middle-Class Society*, 63.

[26] Bureau der k. k. statistischen Zentralkommission (ed.), *Statistik der Unterrichtsanstalten in Österreich für das Jahr 1912/1913*. Vienna, 1917, 27*.

[27] On the link between economy and education Gabriel Tortella, 'Education and Economic Development since the Industrial Revolution: A Summary Report (The Less Developed Countries)'. In Tortella (ed.), *Education and Economic Development since the Industrial Revolution*. València, 1990, 3–45.

[28] Cf. Georg Schmitz, 'Organe und Arbeitsweise, Strukturen und Leistungen der Landesvertretungen'. In Rumpler and Urbanitsch, *Die Habsburgermonarchie 1848–1918*. Vol. 7: *Verfassung und Parlamentarismus*. Subvol. 2: *Die regionalen Repräsentativkörperschaften*. Vienna, 2000, 1458–93.

[29] Initially, only universities were administered by the imperial state. From 1872 onwards, with the exception of Galicia, it was also responsible for technical high schools. Schmitz, 'Organe und Arbeitsweise', 1491.

[30] Cohen, *Education and Middle-Class Society*, 64 and 69. In Bukovina, secondary education expanded. Constantin Ungureanu, 'Mittelschulen und höhere Lehranstalten in der Bukowina vor 1918: Nationen, Sprachen und Geschlechter. Ein statistischer Überblick'. In Markus Winkler (ed.), *Partizipation und Exklusion: Zur Habsburger Prägung von Sprache und Bildung in der Bukowina 1848–1918–1940*. Regensburg, 2015, 115–28.

representatives of the Catholic Church on the provincial school boards of Tyrol or Salzburg put the brakes on the expansion of compulsory education (*Verschulung*), national representatives in Bohemia, Moravia, or Galicia pursued an active, even aggressive education policy.[31]

In the clerically dominated crown lands such as Tyrol, Vorarlberg, Salzburg, and Upper (and initially) Lower Austria, reservations and suspicions persisted about liberal, and in particular, secular education.[32] The rural population was sceptical about state-driven compulsory education. Conversely, the liberal bourgeoisie and working class—predominantly in Bohemia and Moravia—joined forces to promote workers' educational associations under the slogan 'education policy is social policy'.[33]

Above all, however, education was a central site of the nationalization and ethnicization of politics. This affected Galicia, the Bohemian crown lands, crown lands with Slovene-speaking populations, the imperial capital Vienna, and South Tyrol.[34] The Czech national movement, in particular, possessed the resources to promote meaningful competition in education.[35] The excellent educational opportunities available to students in the Bohemian lands have repeatedly been linked to the territories' economic growth and the prosperity of their inhabitants, whether German-speaking or Czech.[36]

The national school controversy centred on minority schools. In the Bohemian lands, a battle was waged for Czech pupils with the aim of undermining the social prestige of German-language schools.[37] After the turn of the century, the Czech National Council in Moravia launched a remarkably successful campaign for 'Czech schools for Czech children!' Between 1890 and 1913, of fourteen new technical secondary schools in Moravia, ten were Czech-language, and of thirteen new secondary schools, only two were German-language (Figure 9.1).

[31] Cohen, *Education and Middle-Class Society*, 112; Tara Zahra, *Kidnapped Souls: National Indifference and the Battle for Children in the Bohemian Lands*. Ithaca, NY, and London, 2008.

[32] Strakosch-Graßmann, *Geschichte des österreichischen Unterrichtswesens*, 298. On the discussed reintroduction of religious education at secondary schools, Kolmer: *Parlament und Verfassung in Österreich*, 406–9.

[33] Wilhelm Wadl, *Liberalismus und soziale Frage in Österreich: Deutschliberale Reaktionen und Einflüsse auf die frühe österreichische Arbeiterbewegung 1867–1879*. Vienna, 1987, 159 and 178–9. Cf. Joseph Maria Baernreither, 'Socialreform in Österreich', *Zeitschrift für Volkswirtschaft, Sozialpolitik und Verwaltung*, 1 (1892), 34.

[34] Generally Cohen, *Education and Middle-Class Society*. On Slovenian-language schools, that were limited to the private sector, Monika Govekar-Okoliš, *Srednje šole na Slovenskem pri oblikovanju nacionalne identitete Slovencev v drugi polovici 19. stoletja*. Ljubljana ,2010; Burger, *Sprachenrecht und Sprachgerechtigkeit*, 71–3 and 116–25.

[35] Cohen, *Education and Middle-Class Society*, 91–2.

[36] On Czech workers cf. Ivan T. Berend, 'Economy and Education: The Hungarian Case in the 19th and 20th Centuries'. In Tortella, *Education and Economic Development*, 177–8.

[37] Jan Havránek, 'The Education of Czechs and Slovaks under Foreign Domination 1850–1918'. In Janusz J. Tomiak (ed.), *Schooling, Educational Policy, and Ethnic Identity*. Vol. 1: *Comparative Studies on Governments and Non-Dominant Ethnic Groups in Europe 1850–1940*. New York, 1991, 243 and 247–8; Burger, *Sprachenrecht und Sprachgerechtigkeit*, 100–14.

Before the First World War, there were more Czech-language than German-language schools in Moravia.[38] Those who suffered from the nationalization of education were bilingual and multilingual communities and families.[39] This included part of the Jewish population, which was traditionally multilingual.[40]

Among the winners of the nationalization of society, which made education a major issue, were schoolgirls and female students. Higher education for girls was only belatedly recognized as a public responsibility.[41] Slavic national movements focused particularly strongly on higher education for girls; here, women's and national movements were closely linked.[42] It was not a coincidence that the Monarchy's first secondary school for girls was founded as a Czech private institution in Prague in 1890. By 1910, nine out of thirteen all-girls secondary schools were located in Galicia.[43] Two years later, twenty-one of the thirty-two private girls secondary schools with public status were in Galicia.[44] The convergence of national and women's movements was also evident in the attendance rolls of female secondary school students: in the school year 1912/13, only fifty-one out of 956 schoolgirls in Bohemia and Moravia were German-speaking.[45] This 'Slavic' promotion of female education manifested itself further in the relatively high numbers of female students in Lviv, Kraków, and at the Czech University in Prague.[46]

The ethnicization of education was accompanied by structural changes in administration. The administration of the Bohemian school board, for example, was divided into national sections at an early stage. A common president and

[38] Before 1870, there were no Czech-language secondary and high schools. Petr Kadlec, *Střední školy a jejich studenti*. Ostrava, 2013, 104.

[39] Zahra, *Kidnapped Souls*, 13–48.

[40] Michael L. Miller, *Rabbis and Revolution: The Jews of Moravia in the Age of Emancipation*. Stanford, CA, 2011, 336. On Jewish pupils in German-language schools Pieter M. Judson, *Guardians of the Nation: Activists on the Language Frontiers of Imperial Austria*. Cambridge, MA, 2006, 48–52; Hillel J. Kieval, *The Making of Czech Jewry: National Conflict and Jewish Society in Bohemia 1870–1918*. New York, 1988.

[41] Friedrich et al., 'Die Bildungsrevolution', 69 and 86.

[42] Svjatoslav Pacholkiv, *Emanzipation durch Bildung: Entwicklung und gesellschaftliche Rolle der ukrainischen Intelligenz im habsburgischen Galizien 1890–1914*. Vienna, 2002, 277; Waltraud Heindl, 'Geschlechterbilder und Geschlechterrollen. Ideologie und Realitäten'. In Rumpler and Urbanitsch, *Die Habsburgermonarchie 1848–1918*, 9/1/1. 723–5.

[43] Cohen, *Education and Middle-Class Society*, 75.

[44] Most of them were run by Catholic orders such as the Ursulines and a few by Jewish educational associations. Burger, *Sprachenrecht und Sprachgerechtigkeit*, 233–4; Bureau, *Statistik der Unterrichtsanstalten in Österreich*, 76–83. On the associations in Galicia Maciej Janowski, 'Galizien auf dem Weg zur Zivilgesellschaft'. In Rumpler and Urbanitsch, *Die Habsburgermonarchie 1848–1918*. Vol. 8: *Politische Öffentlichkeit und Zivilgesellschaft*. Subvol. 1: *Vereine, Parteien und Interessenverbände als Träger der politischen Partizipation*. Vienna, 2006, 805–58. The Greek Catholic Church assumed patronage over some girls' secondary schools; Urszula Górska, *Drogi wolności: Ruch emancypacyjny kobiet w monarchii habsburskiej na podstawie publicystyki a twórczości literackiej w latach 1867–1918*. Warsaw ,2016, 98–100.

[45] Bureau, *Statistik der Unterrichtsanstalten in Österreich*, 78.

[46] Bureau, *Statistik der Unterrichtsanstalten in Österreich*, 4*.

vice-presidents provided a certain degree of uniformity.[47] The rapid growth of the Bohemian school system also led to an expansion of its administrative apparatus. In addition to the two national sections of the Bohemian school board, two separate ethnic-national administrative departments were established in 1907, with almost twenty *Konzeptsbeamten* (legally trained civil servants) and school inspectors. The competition between German- and Czech-speaking institutions, triggered by the nationalization of education, led to an overall increase in the range of educational services offered by the crown land's administration. The result was a gradual decline in the number of German-speaking students, who had traditionally been overrepresented in higher education.[48] Autonomous school boards with a Czech-speaking majority in cities like Prague, and medium-sized towns such as Plzeň, Pardubice, Chrudim, or Roudnice, prioritized school expansion and higher teacher salaries.[49] Nationally segregated institutions led to nationally segregated education even in cities like Plzeň, where German–Czech language contact was part of everyday life.[50]

In Galicia, the situation was different. As a result of the 'autonomy' of 1868, the Galician elite achieved a far-reaching Polonization of education which encompassed the crown land's most important steering institutions, such as the school board.[51] This process nonetheless left some room for Ukrainian-language education for the Ruthenian population. For many years, however, Ukrainian-language institutions suffered from a lack of prestige and could not open up the same career paths as Polish-language schools.[52] Mother-tongue Ukrainian education was offered in only thirteen of Galicia's eighty-one counties. The Galician Diet and its executive body, the Crown Land's Standing Committee, hindered the establishment of Ukrainian schools.[53] Many rural primary schools offered only two years of study. Attendance at secondary and technical schools, meanwhile, presupposed proficiency in German or, failing that, the certificate of completion

[47] National separation in the higher management of the regional school boards (office of the vice president) was revoked after a brief interlude in 1909, cf. Martin Klečacký, *Český ministr ve Vídni: Ve službách císaře, národa a politické strany*. Prague, 2017, 143–58.

[48] In education, the Czechs in Silesia were disadvantaged compared to Czechs in Bohemia and Moravia. Kadlec, *Střední školy a jejich studenti*. On the number of pupils Cohen, *Education and Middle-Class Society*, 150–1.

[49] Havránek, 'Education of Czechs and Slovaks', 235–6. This included girls' secondary schools in provincial towns such as Pardubitz and Valašské Meziříčí. Bureau, *Statistik der Unterrichtsanstalten in Österreich*, 78.

[50] Stefan Michael Newerkla, 'Wie toleranzintendierte Sprachengesetze zur nationalen Segregation führten—Die Aushöhlung des deutschen Schulwesens in Plzeň/Pilsen im langen 19. Jahrhundert'. In Hannes Philipp, Andrea Ströbl, Bernadette Weber, and Johann Wellner (eds), *Deutsch in Mittel-, Ost- und Südosteuropa*. Regensburg, 2018, 372–97.

[51] Renata Dutkowa, *Polityka szkolna w Galicji między autonomią a centralizmem 1861–1875*. Kraków, 1995.

[52] Ann Sirka, *The Nationality Question in Austrian Education*. Frankfurt am Main, 1980, 76–84.

[53] Peter Wozniak, 'Professionalisation and Nationalism in a Career Group: Secondary School Teachers in Galicia 1849–1914'. In McClelland et al., *Professionen im modernen Osteuropa*, 253.

from the seven-year 'committee school' (*Ausschussschule*) in one of the major towns. As a result, a majority of peasant children were denied educational advancement.[54] Of the fifty-seven public secondary schools, only five were 'Ukrainian'.[55] At the same time, publicly funded technical training was available only in Polish.[56] Demands by Ruthenian teachers' organizations for a nationally divided school board and regular and equal financing of Ukrainian schools, including the provision of textbooks, were repeatedly rejected.[57] A decision of the Imperial Supreme Court in favour of the Ruthenians, confirming the constitutionally granted rights to mother-tongue education, was largely ignored.[58] In the school year 1912/13, there were 3,200 Polish-speaking and 2,542 Ukrainian-speaking elementary schools in Galicia; but there was not a single Ukrainian-speaking secondary school.[59]

The educational revolution in Galicia led to a remarkable increase in the general education level in the Polish-dominated part of the crown land. Unlike in Bohemia, however, technical subjects remained largely underrepresented.[60] Polish-language primary and secondary schools, as well as universities, provided both a reservoir for the formation of a Polish national consciousness and a sounding chamber for the Polish intelligentsia.[61] The situation of the Poles in the Habsburg Monarchy was thus much better than that of their compatriots in the other partition territories, where education was subject either to Russification or Germanization.[62] On the other hand, many Ruthenian and Jewish schoolchildren were excluded from education in their mother tongue.[63]

Cisleithanian crown lands acted like states in the field of schooling and education, whether or not they actively promoted the expansion of education. The *Verländerung* of educational policy gave each crown land its own characteristic school system and led to a significant territorial disparity in educational opportunities.[64] Another indication of the divergent priorities of the crown

[54] Pacholkiv, *Emanzipation durch Bildung*, 96–7.

[55] Wozniak, 'Secondary School Teachers in Galicia', 243–4.

[56] Ukrainian technical schools rested on private initiatives. Pacholkiv, *Emanzipation durch Bildung*, 97.

[57] Pacholkiv, *Emanzipation durch Bildung*, 113–15.

[58] Burger, *Sprachenrecht und Sprachgerechtigkeit*, 126–9; Kolmer, *Parlament und Verfassung in Österreich*, 8. 410.

[59] Bureau, *Statistik der Unterrichtsanstalten in Österreich*, 328–9. After 'autonomy' was achieved, secondary schools were established disproportionately in Polish-dominated West Galicia, not in Ukrainian-dominated East Galicia. Pacholkiv, *Emanzipation durch Bildung*, 102.

[60] Cohen, *Education and Middle-Class Society*, 152.

[61] Wozniak, 'Secondary School Teachers in Galicia', 237–8.

[62] Jozef Miaso, 'Educational Policy and Educational Development in the Polish Territories under Austrian, Russian and German Rule 1850–1918'. In Tomiak, *Schooling, Educational Policy, and Ethnic Identity*, 1. 163–83. On Prussian Germanization and the fear of Polonization Sebastian Conrad, *Globalisierung und Nation im Deutschen Kaiserreich*. Munich, 2006, 124–44.

[63] Burger, *Sprachenrecht und Sprachgerechtigkeit*, 71 and 129–30. On the Orthodox and Reform Jewish schools, Bertha Pappenheim and Sara Rabinowitsch, *Zur Lage der jüdischen Bevölkerung in Galizien*. Frankfurt am Main, 1904.

[64] Cohen, *Education and Middle-Class Society*, 69.

lands was their fiscal commitment. The cost of education was immense, in some cases constituting the largest single component of the provincial budgets. In the debates over new fiscal transfers between Vienna and the crown lands after 1905, a major issue was whether the imperial state would assume these costs.[65]

Districts, cities, and municipalities took on important additional functions and shouldered further school expenditures.[66] The contemporary historian of education, Gustav Strakosch-Graßmann, while comparing the administrative capacity of crown lands and municipalities, stressed 'the superiority of the autonomous bodies in educational administration over the authorities of the imperial state'.[67] Gary Cohen also pointed out that the central authorities' ability to control education was diminishing.[68] However, these growing responsibilities were always accompanied by increased financial burdens. As a result, the introduction of liberal primary school laws was succeeded by never-ending complaints about the fiscal yoke borne by local authorities.[69]

The situation in Hungary was different. There, education was not primarily seen as a public service provided by the state. Educational traditions varied according to region, denomination, and nationality.[70] At the turn of the century, parochial schools accounted for 80 per cent of all primary schools, only dipping to 70 per cent by 1913.[71] The churches organized the school system autonomously, chose the language of instruction, and bore the main financial burden.[72] In Croatia-Slavonia, this led to the promotion of Croatian-Catholic over Serbian-Orthodox schools.[73] In Transylvania, however, the Protestant Saxons maintained their centuries-old school tradition, with a low illiteracy rate and their own teacher vocational training, even after unification with Hungary.[74] The Romanian schools of the Orthodox and Greek Catholic Church were more closely monitored by the state.[75] In Upper Hungary, today's Slovakia, Slovak-speaking primary schools were run by the Protestant Church, which functioned as the mouthpiece of the Slovak nationalist movement. This was the reason why several secondary

[65] Cf. Chapter 10.

[66] Hans Patzauer, *Österreichs und Ungarns Staatswirthschaften*. Vienna, 1916, 31.

[67] Strakosch-Graßmann, *Geschichte des österreichischen Unterrichtswesens*, 351.

[68] Cohen, *Education and Middle-Class Society*, 110.

[69] On municipal expenditures in Salzburg cf. Carl Chorinsky, *Die Salzburger Landesfinanzen um 1861–1878*. Vol. 1: *Die Landesfinanzen und die Schule*. Salzburg, 1880, 78–87. General data on the funding of education by municipalities are lacking.

[70] Alexander von (Sándor) Matlekovits, *Das Königreich Ungarn*. Vol. 2. Leipzig, 1900, 766–7.

[71] Péter Hanák, *Ungarn in der Donaumonarchie: Probleme der bürgerlichen Umgestaltung eines Vielvölkerstaats*. Vienna, 1984, 340; Matlekovits, *Das Königreich Ungarn*, 2. 787.

[72] Joachim von Puttkamer, *Schulalltag und nationale Integration in Ungarn*. Munich, 2003, 74; Matlekovits, *Das Königreich Ungarn*, 2. 788–99.

[73] Charles Jelavich, 'The Croatian Problem in the Habsburg Empire in the Nineteenth Century', *Austrian History Yearbook*, 3/2 (1967), 105.

[74] Puttkamer, *Schulalltag und nationale Integration in Ungarn*, 149–52.

[75] Puttkamer, *Schulalltag und nationale Integration in Ungarn*, 154.

schools were forced to close.[76] In terms of secondary, higher, and technical education, however, Hungary lagged behind Austria.[77]

9.2. Agriculture

Despite falling under state control in the Habsburg Monarchy and elsewhere across Europe, education typically continued to be shaped by social and religious institutions. Infrastructure, on the other hand, fell firmly within the remit of the state. References to infrastructure policy commonly conjure up visions of the great technical achievements of the nineteenth century, such as railways, newly navigable rivers, or telegraphy. The smaller, more inconspicuous infrastructures of everyday rural life, such as agricultural improvements and hydraulic engineering, are often forgotten.

Agricultural infrastructure attracted considerable attention at the time. It was *the* showcase of a state's technical capability. In recent research, however, it has long been overshadowed by the large-scale projects just mentioned.[78] Soil enrichment and ameliorations demonstrated a desire to create agrarian cultural landscapes out of marshes and wetlands. The invention of modern drainage, i.e. the underground installation of irrigation and drainage pipes that could be produced industrially at low cost, is considered one of the few 'real innovations' of modern agriculture in the mid-nineteenth century.[79] The idea was to turn boggy meadows and marshes into productive cattle pastures and cultivated peatlands. Parched summer meadows were to become well-watered fields. Nutritious alluvial soils would be sustainably restored, while the ever-present threat of flooding was to be limited.

Soil improvement, or melioration, was initially a field of experimentation for large landowners such as Anton von Doblhoff and Christian von Kinsky in Lower Austria or Johann Adolph zu Schwarzenberg in Bohemia.[80] Their knowledge was

[76] Puttkamer, *Schulalltag und nationale Integration in Ungarn*, 138–48 and 174; Havránek, 'Education of Czechs and Slovaks'. On the nationalization of the school system in other respects cf. Gerhard Seewann, *Geschichte der Deutschen in Ungarn*. Vol. 2: *1860–2006*. Marburg, 2012, 26–45.

[77] Matlekovits, *Das Königreich Ungarn*, 1, pp. xi–xii, and 2. 763–768, 808, and 828; Puttkamer, *Schulalltag und nationale Integration*. The admission of women to medical schools was related to the need for female physicians for Muslim women in Bosnia, Friedrich et al., 'Die Bildungsrevolution', 100–1.

[78] Cf. Rita Gudermann, *Morastwelt und Paradies*. Paderborn, 2000, 3. On Switzerland Daniel Speich, *Helvetische Meliorationen: Die Neuordnung der gesellschaftlichen Naturverhältnisse an der Linth. 1783–1823*. Zürich, 2003. On the Habsburg Monarchy Jana Osterkamp, 'Wasser, Erde, Imperium: Eine kleine Politikgeschichte der Meliorationen in der Habsburgermonarchie'. In Jörg Ganzenmüller and Tatjana Tönsmeyer (eds), *Vom Vorrücken des Staates in die Fläche*. Vienna, 2016, 179–98.

[79] Gudermann, *Morastwelt und Paradies*, 126 and 393.

[80] Anton von Doblhoff, *Über die Drainage: Ein Beitrag zur wissenschaftlichen Begründung und zur practischen Ausführung dieses Systems andauernder Bodenverbesserung und vermehrten Pflanzenbaues*. The Hague, 1850. Niederösterreichischen Landesausschuss (ed.), *Die Entwicklung und Förderung der technischen Bodenmelioration und der ländlichen Wasserversorgung im Erzherzogtume Österreich unter der Enns in den Jahren 1857–1917*. Vienna, 1918.

disseminated through agricultural societies, chambers of commerce and trade, and later by melioration associations.[81] Only after the emancipation of the peasants and the subsequent land relief process was there a state-sponsored promotion of agricultural modernization. The question of improving and intensifying yields could only be addressed once the matter of rural land ownership had been resolved.

Infrastructure depended on legal structure. The emergence of the modern state as a political actor and the displacement of landlords and landowners as the traditional holders of property rights led to modern agricultural policy.[82] In contrast to Great Britain and Ireland, Belgium, the Netherlands, France, and the individual states of the German Empire such as Saxony and Prussia, the Habsburg Monarchy was late in transforming soil amelioration from a 'bottom-up' initiative into a state-sponsored project. By law the power to effect change within the agricultural sector rested with the crown lands. After the devastating floods of 1882 and 1883, the Austrian parliament passed a package of bills that entrusted agricultural water management to the cooperation of the state, the crown lands, the districts, the municipalities, the water cooperatives, and waterside landowners.[83] This 'system of public aid' represented a significant turning point.[84] In previous years, unlike in other European countries, melioration had been promoted by means of loans rather than subsidies.[85] The remaining financial risk had often discouraged farmers and water co-operatives from taking action.[86] After 1884, the Cisleithanian Melioration Fund provided non-repayable grants for agricultural projects that met the requirements of provincial law as well as the technical standards of the provincial building authorities.[87] This process sometimes passed through eight stages and was extraordinarily cumbersome.[88] As critical comments

[81] Manuals were to facilitate implementation. Meliorační svaz v markrabstvé moravském v Brně (ed.), *Meliorační rádce: Pro podniky meliorační, regulační a hospodářské vodovody*. Brno, 1912. Wilhelm Wodiczka, *Die Bodenmeliorationen: Ihre Durchführungsorganisation und Finanzirung*. Vienna, 1898.

[82] Ulrich Pfister, 'Agrarreformen des 19. Jahrhunderts und die Entstehung der modernen Agrarpolitik'. Lecture, 16 Nov. 2018 in Vienna, Workshop 'Vom gesellschaftlichen Problem zum Politikfeld'.

[83] Institutional interfaces included the provincial commissions for water regulation, water construction co-operatives, and departments in the Ministry of Agriculture. On Tyrol cf. Herbert Killian, *Der Kampf gegen Wildbäche und Lawinen im Spannungsfeld von Zentralismus und Föderalismus*. Vol. 3/1: *Die Organisation*. Vienna, 1990, 50 and 127–31. Cf. David Blackbourn, *Die Eroberung der Natur: Eine Geschichte der deutschen Landschaft*. Munich, 2008, 256–8.

[84] Cf. the later minister of agriculture Albín Bráf, 'Über Meliorationscredit mit besonderer Berücksichtigung auf Österreich', *Zeitschrift für Volkswirtschaft, Socialpolitik und Verwaltung*, 1 (1892), 227.

[85] England was the role model. Bráf, 'Meliorationscredit', 235 and 243–4. The state did not fund French-style reforestation until after 1884. Killian, *Kampf gegen Wildbäche und Lawinen*.

[86] Niederösterreichischen Landesausschuss, *Förderung der technischen Bodenmelioration*, 20.

[87] Schmitz, 'Organe und Arbeitsweise', 1408.

[88] Ingenieur Neumann. In *Enquete der Kommission zur Förderung der Verwaltungsreform veranstaltet in der Zeit vom 21.10. bis 9.11.1912 zur Feststellung der Wünsche der beteiligten Kreise der Bevölkerung in Bezug auf die Reform der inneren und Finanzverwaltung*. Vienna, 1913, 277.

from individual crown lands suggest, the Ministry of Agriculture was granting melioration loans and subsidies without complying with legal requirements.[89] Grant practices also varied from one crown land to another. The Galician Land Improvement Fund granted interest-free loans that dwarfed the credit available elsewhere. Their cost was borne by Vienna—possibly a success of the Galician minister in the capital.[90]

Water engineering and soil melioration required technical expertise that was usually not available at the local level. Poorly executed infrastructure projects sometimes turned the dream of a rural paradise wrested from the swamp into a boggy or barren nightmare. Flooding and erosion turned meadows into marshland, while excessive evaporation led to the salinization of fields during summer.[91] The crown lands with the most resources at hand set up technical offices and hired specialists to plan melioration, river engineering, and other related measures.[92] Engineers for drainage, pasture, and cultivation had previously only been employed by a few agricultural corporations.[93]

Agricultural modernization proceeded at different speeds in different regions. In Salzburg, due to a general fiscal reluctance to invest, it was only after 1906 that the crown land considered public funding for land improvement and the establishment of a provincial technical service.[94] In crown lands such as Carinthia, Carniola, the Littoral, or Dalmatia, but also in Vorarlberg, there were neither separate technical institutions nor, more importantly, considerable provincial investments; the Cisleithanian state was obliged to send technicians and engineers itself.[95] In Bukovina, basic hydro-technical and geological data necessary for planning melioration projects were missing.[96] A quick look at Hungary shows that the state did not enforce soil improvement in the same way. The Hungarian Ministry of Agriculture established technical offices, the so-called Agricultural Engineer Offices (*Kultur-Ingenieurs-Ämter*), but did not provide credits and subsidies comparable to those in Austria.[97]

[89] Speech of the deputy Hrubý of 27 Dec. 1906. In Schlesischer Landtag in Troppau, Offizielle stenographische Berichte über die Verhandlungen der XLIII. Session des schlesischen Landtags in Troppau, 1. Sitzung am 27.12.1906. Troppau, 1907, 18–21.

[90] Schreiben der Landesbank des Königreichs Galizien und Lodomerien vom 7.1.1908 an k. k. Ackerbauminister Albín Bráf. Archiv Národního muzea v Praze (Archives of the National Museum in Prague, hereafter ANM), Nachlass Albín Bráf, Box 45, File 3604 'Meliorační práce na Moravě—půjčky zemědělské banky' 1907–1908. About Galicia Damian Szymczak, *Galicyjska 'ambasada' w Wiedniu: Dzieje ministerstwa dla Galicji 1871–1918*. Poznan, 2013, 336 and 338.

[91] V. Janský, *O úpravách řek i potoků a melioracích v království českém*. Prague, 1904, 36; Adolf Friedrich, *Die Bodenmeliorationen im Herzogthume Bukowina*. Vienna, 1903, 31–2.

[92] Tyrol was first to appoint an agricultural engineer in 1871/72, Vorarlberg following in 1878, Silesia in 1884, and Moravia in 1887; technical offices were established in Galicia in 1879, in Bohemia in 1884, in Lower Austria in 1886, and in Silesia also in 1886. Cf. Schmitz, 'Organe und Arbeitsweise', 1410–13.

[93] Schmitz, 'Organe und Arbeitsweise', 1399.

[94] Korrespondenz und Berichte zu 'Meliorationen'. Salzburger Landesarchiv, Landesausschuss II 10/06 (allgemein).

[95] Schmitz, 'Organe und Arbeitsweise', 1412.

[96] Friedrich, *Bodenmeliorationen*, 93–4.

[97] Matlekovits, *Das Königreich Ungarn*, 1. 399–404 and 520–2.

Moravia, on the other hand, institutionalized crown land melioration projects extensively and pursued a multi-year, long-term programme of 'wild water regulation' (*Wildbachverbauung*).[98] The Moravian Agricultural Technical Office grew within a few years from two hydraulic engineers in 1887 to forty-five expert technicians in 1912.[99] A special service was the cost-free design of projects, which motivated even small landowners to undertake larger construction projects and join water co-operatives. Its success eventually led to the appointment of the first Moravian provincial civil engineer to a professorship at the Vienna University of Natural Resources and Agriculture (*Hochschule für Bodenkultur*) in 1894. Originally initiated by an agricultural congress of large landowners, the monarchy's only university of agricultural sciences was charged with training the agricultural technicians of Cisleithania.[100]

The Austrian government contributed financially to melioration, river regulation, and hydraulic engineering. It set up large-scale, but time-consuming projects such as the Koerber Plan, which aimed at integrating the nationalities more effectively through economic policy.[101] The cooperative involvement of the crown lands, however, remained essential for the implementation of hydraulic works, as they provided institutions, technical expertise, and a substantial part of the financial resources. While Moravia, Silesia, Lower Austria, and other crown lands acted like states by planning melioration projects, raising funds from their fiscal resources, and seeking social acceptance for hydraulic engineering projects, others relied on the planning, financial, and technical assistance from central government institutions.

Political cooperation between the Austrian Ministry of Agriculture and the Imperial Parliament, as well as between the crown lands and municipalities, thus became fundamental for agricultural modernization. Georg Habermann, a contemporary jurist and central figure for modernization in the west Bohemian *Egerland*, wrote about hydraulic engineering projects:

> The interconnectedness of the state and the crown lands becomes increasingly obvious…imperial laws are drafted that make the state's fiscal contribution dependent on the cooperation of the crown land. Conversely, crown land bills are drafted in which the action of the crown land is made dependent on the contribution of the state.[102]

[98] Schmitz, 'Organe und Arbeitsweise', 1410. [99] Meliorační, *Meliorační rádce*, 1.

[100] Schmitz, 'Organe und Arbeitsweise', 1412; Manfried Welan and Paulus Ebner, 'Die k. k. Hochschule für Bodencultur 1872–1918. In Welan (ed.), *Die Universität für Bodenkultur Wien: Von der Gründung in die Zukunft 1872–1997*. Vienna, 1997, 21–64.

[101] Eibe Hinrichs, *Der Koerber-Plan. Wirtschaftspolitik als Integrationsfaktor für die Nationalitäten des Habsburgerreichs*. Frankfurt am Main, 2014, 247–53 and 307–8; Wysocki, *Infrastruktur und wachsende Staatsausgaben*, 36–40.

[102] Georg Habermann, 'Das Zusammenwirken lokaler Faktoren mit Staat und Land bei Lösung von Verwaltungsaufgaben', *Zeitschrift für Volkswirtschaft, Socialpolitik und Verwaltung*, 14 (1905), 150.

Infrastructure projects were created with regulating measures 'from above *and* from below'.[103] Modernization requires cooperation, Habermann said: 'It is undisputed that many tasks of public administration have been solved in this way in a satisfactory manner and that without this cooperation, in more than one policy field, what exists today would not have been achieved.'[104]

9.3. Public Health

In nineteenth-century Europe, public health similarly developed from a private and local concern into a public policy. The cholera epidemic of 1866 claimed more victims among soldiers in the war with Prussia than the conflict itself; it then spread to the urban population and killed more than 200,000 people.[105] This tragic experience, as well as other pandemics, raised awareness of health and hygiene as a public good at the global, imperial, and regional level.[106] In the early 1870s, Hungary still suffered more from cholera than most other European countries.[107] At the Austrian Welfare Exhibition in Vienna in 1898, these infectious diseases, with their horrendous mortality rates, came to symbolize the challenge to which the 'beneficial sea change in sanitary culture' had successfully responded.[108] The medical landscape of the Viennese Spitalgasse with its general hospital, maternity home, foundling home, and lunatic asylum—and its fundamental medical research—set the pattern for hospitals in other provincial capitals.[109]

About Georg Habermann Martin Krzoska, 'Das Egerland als Erinnerungsort'. In Miloš Řezník (ed.), *Regionale Erinnerungsorte: Böhmische Länder und Mitteldeutschland im europäischen Kontext.* Leipzig, 2013, 90.

[103] For the history of infrastructure in general Dirk van Laak, 'Infra-Strukturgeschichte', *Geschichte und Gesellschaft*, 3 (2001), 387.

[104] Habermann explicitly places the need for cooperation in a global context. Habermann, 'Zusammenwirken lokaler Faktoren', 149 and 158–9.

[105] Nachum T. Gross, 'Die Stellung der Habsburgermonarchie in der Weltwirtschaft'. In Adam Wandruszka and Peter Urbanitsch (eds), *Die Habsburgermonarchie 1848–1918*. Vol. 1: *Die wirtschaftliche Entwicklung*. Vienna, 1973, 16–17. According to local data in 1866, cholera killed 734 people in Trieste and the Küstenland, 254 in the Viennese General Hospital alone, and 160 in Kraków. Cf. Luigi Loy, *Relatione e documenti della commissione sanitaria centrale di Trieste sul cholera morbus nel 1866*. Trieste, 1867, 20; Leopold Oser, *Bericht über die Cholera-Abtheilung im k. k. allgemeinen Krankenhause während der Epidemie im Jahre 1866*. Vienna, 1867, 5; Józef Oettinger, *Cholera Nagminna w Krakowie r. 1866*. Kraków, 1867, 11.

[106] Osterhammel, Transformation of the World, 246; Tom Crook, *Governing Systems: Modernity and the Making of Public Health in England 1830–1910*. Oakland, CA, 2016, 201–9. State-funded sanitary measures such as vaccination date back to Maria Theresa and her physician van Swieten, who conducted vaccination experiments on orphans. Barbara Stollberg-Rilinger, *Maria Theresia*. Princeton, 2021, 495–506.

[107] Osterhammel, Transformation of the World, 260. In the 1890s, another epidemic occurred. For numbers cf. Matlekovits, *Das Königreich Ungarn*, 1. 159 and 162–3.

[108] E. [Emanuel] Kusý R. [Ritter] von Dúbrav, 'Entwicklung und Organisation des öffentlichen Sanitätswesens in Österreich'. In *Österreichs Wohlfahrts-Einrichtungen*. Vol. 3: *Gesundheitspflege*. Vienna, 1900, 3.

[109] Cf. the statistical analysis Bratassevic, 'Die Wiener k. k. Krankenanstalten während der Jahre 1892–1902', *Statistische Monatsschrift* (1906), 631–58. On conventional medicine in Vienna Hans Peter

Until the mid-nineteenth century, municipalities, denominational institutions, and private benefactors were responsible for health care. In the neo-absolutist Bach era, the authoritarian state decreed a state-run health system, but failed in its implementation.[110] The next attempt came via imperial legislation in Cisleithania after 1868, drafted jointly by the government, crown land representatives, and experts.[111] With the Imperial Sanitary Act No. 68/1870, the state ensured the supervision of public health through the Supreme Sanitary Authority and created control institutions in the provincial governorates and districts.[112] Hospitals, vaccination institutes, spas, pharmacies, and epidemic control, such as they were, came under state supervision, even though the crown lands had been shouldering their costs from the 1860s onward.[113]

The crown lands played an important role in the expansion of these state activities but were relatively late in making use of their scope for action.[114] In the 1860s, imperial statutory laws had given the crown lands and municipalities 'extremely wide-ranging agency regarding public health'.[115] They found themselves overburdened, however, and until the mid-1880s refused to pass the necessary provincial sanitary bills proposed by the empire.[116] The requirements, set by imperial law, included district physicians, municipal physicians, and midwives, as well as quarantine stations. The provincial diets deemed these provisions too costly. The 'action of the government', according to a ministry official, 'found the representatives of the crown lands still unprepared to grasp the necessity and desirability of securing a good medical service'.[117] Although public acceptance of government intervention in health and hygiene increased in the face of new 'cholera outbreaks',[118] important questions of funding remained unanswered. As late as 1908, the Congress of Cities criticized the fact that no Austrian city could 'fulfil its obligations to the population in the matter of sanitary policing'.[119]

Hye, 'Technologie und sozialer Wandel'. In Rumpler and Urbanitsch (eds), *Die Habsburgermonarchie 1848–1918*, 9/1/1. 57–8.

[110] Cf. Thomas N. Burg, *Sieches Volk macht siechen Staat*. Vienna, 1994, 68–77.

[111] Kusý von Dúbrav, 'Entwicklung', 6–7. [112] Kusý von Dúbrav, 'Entwicklung', 7–8.

[113] Schmitz, 'Organe und Arbeitsweise', 1442.

[114] The interplay between the state and regional and local institutions is typical of health care; on health governance in England, cf. Crook, *Governing Systems*; in Germany cf. Gabriele Metzler, *Der deutsche Sozialstaat: Vom bismarckschen Erfolgsmodell zum Pflegefall*. Stuttgart, 2003, 30–1.

[115] Kusý von Dúbrav, 'Entwicklung', 8. [116] Schmitz, 'Organe und Arbeitsweise', 1438–9.

[117] Kusý von Dúbrav, 'Entwicklung', 11; Jiří Pešek, 'Zur räumlichen Struktur großstädtischer Dienstleistungen im Gesundheitsbereich in Prag und Wien um 1900'. In Gerhard Melinz and Susan Zimmermann (eds), *Wien, Prag, Budapest: Blütezeit der Habsburgermetropolen*. Vienna, 1996, 177–84. The municipal physicians were financed by the municipalities and, in exceptional circumstances, by the crown land standing committee, cf. e.g. § 1 Law on the Implementation of the Sanitary Service in the Municipalities of 23 June 1892 no. 35/1892 LGVBl. Steiermark.

[118] Kusý von Dúbrav, 'Entwicklung', 14.

[119] Quoted in Gerhard Melinz and Susan Zimmermann, *Über die Grenzen der Armenhilfe*. Vienna and Zürich, 1991, 161.

As was typical for the emergence of new policy fields, public health was characterized by a high degree of regional disparity. There was no uniform regulation as to whether care facilities were paid for and administered by the imperial state, the crown lands, the districts, or the municipalities. Only in exceptional cases were hospitals in Cisleithania maintained by the empire or by provincial funds (and thus administered by the crown land standing committees).[120] Instead, they were usually run by district, municipal, or denominational trusts. Others were established specifically for 'industrial enterprises (mines, railways, factories) with their armies of workers'.[121] Nevertheless, crown lands and many communities felt overwhelmed by the cost of public health.[122] There was a notorious shortage of physicians in rural areas. To relieve the burden on the local authorities, the government of Silesia took over the funding of nursing care. It became the second largest expenditure in the crown land's budget after teachers' salaries.[123]

9.4. Social Welfare

In the 1880s, especially in Germany and Austria, social security emerged as a public state responsibility. It supplemented and sometimes replaced municipal welfare for the poor.[124] Social welfare policy in the Austrian part of the Habsburg Empire was characterized by vertical cooperation between the Austrian state, the crown lands, the districts, the municipalities, and private actors.[125] In the Hungarian territories, social policy relied on 'state-municipal cooperation'.[126] Across Europe, social welfare had initially been assigned even less importance than health care. While charitable care for the poor had been similar throughout

[120] Silesia was an exception, Karl Berthold, *Schlesiens Landesvertretung und Landeshaushalt.* Vol. 2: *Landeshaushalt.* Troppau, 1909, 506 and 537.

[121] Anton Ullmann, 'Die Krankenanstalten Österreichs diesseits der Leitha in den Jahren 1848–1898'. In *Österreichs Wohlfahrts-Einrichtungen.* Vol. 3: *Gesundheitspflege.* Vienna, 1900, 251 and 259; Kusý von Dúbrav, 'Entwicklung', 9.

[122] The 'public' hospitals were partly funded by the crown land funds. Ullmann, 'Krankenanstalten Österreichs', 253.

[123] Berthold, *Schlesiens Landesvertretung*, 2. 67. Anonymus, 'Erhebung über die finanziellen Verhältnisse in einzelnen Kronländern sowie über die Krankenverpflegskosten des Landes Schlesien', *Statistische Monatsschrift* (1910), 511.

[124] Cf. Monika Senghaas, *Die Territorialisierung sozialer Sicherung.* Wiesbaden, 2015, 80. On the concept of welfare under Koerber and Beck cf. Werner Drobesch, 'Ideologische Konzepte zur Lösung der "sozialen Frage"'. In Rumpler and Urbanitsch, *Die Habsburgermonarchie 1848–1918.* Vol. 9: *Soziale Strukturen.* Part 1: *Von der Feudal-Agrarischen zur Bürgerlich-industriellen Gesellschaft.* Subvol. 2: *Von der Stände- zur Klassengesellschaft.* Vienna, 2010, 1441; Ludwig Brügel, *Soziale Gesetzgebung in Österreich von 1848 bis 1918.* Vienna, 1919.

[125] Austria's social security systems with their ties to existing political territories reflected 'federal ideas of order', Monika Senghaas, 'Föderalismus und Sozialpolitik in der Habsburgermonarchie'. In Ambrosius et al., *Föderalismus in historisch vergleichender Perspektive.* Vol. 2: *Föderale Systeme.* Baden-Baden, 2015, 238.

[126] Susan Zimmermann, 'Armen- und Sozialpolitik in Ungarn im Vergleich zu Österreich'. In Rumpler and Urbanitsch, *Die Habsburgermonarchie 1848–1918*, 9/1/2. 1465.

the continent until the eighteenth century, the 'liberal break' of the nineteenth century led to considerable differences. The more the political values of a state were aligned with the liberal principles of individual responsibility and initiative, the harder it became to justify public social programmes.[127]

The 'social question' had already become a recognizable problem during the industrial revolution. The social consequences of the capitalization of labour resulted in the dissolution of the traditional relationship of patronage between the imperial state (the 'whole house') and the workforce. However, social security was not established as a state task until much later.[128] Scholars such as Lorenz von Stein, who was appointed to the University of Vienna and coined the term 'welfare state', provided the intellectual impetus for this political change. In contrast to the laissez-faire doctrine of the liberals, Stein emphasized the ethical aspects of economics and economic policy.[129] In order to balance the structural differences between individual freedom and collective freedom, a society that wants to live up to its aspirations to freedom and equality, he argued, needs the 'social state (as an administrative state)'.[130] Social welfare thus began, in the words of the economic historian Herbert Matis, 'to advance into regions hitherto sacrosanct to liberalism'.[131] In the Habsburg Monarchy, distributive social welfare indeed contributed to a more equal allocation of wealth.[132]

After the depression of 1873, large sections of the population were impoverished. Pauperization increased the pressure for political action.[133] After 1879, the conservative Taaffe government set the course for the expansion of the social welfare state.[134] The idea of a 'patriarchal social state' replaced the laissez-faire of the liberal era, which had practised social engineering rather than social welfare, for example through workhouses or the deportation of the destitute to their home communities.[135] In the 1880s, after the constitutionalization of 1867, it was the

[127] Jens Alber, *Vom Armenhaus zum Wohlfahrtsstaat*. Frankfurt am Main, 1982, 107; Sandrine Kott, *Sozialstaat und Gesellschaft; Das deutsche Kaiserreich in Europa*. Göttingen, 2014, 26–32; Peter A. Köhler, *Ein Jahrhundert Sozialversicherung in der Bundesrepublik Deutschland, Frankreich, Großbritannien, Österreich und der Schweiz*. Berlin, 1981; Gerhard A. Ritter, *Der Sozialstaat: Entstehung und Entwicklung im internationalen Vergleich*. Munich, 2010, 46–60.

[128] On a deficit in socio-political theory cf. Drobesch, 'Ideologische Konzepte', 1422.

[129] Herbert Matis, *Österreichs Wirtschaft 1848–1913*. Berlin, 1972, 346–7.; Drobesch, 'Ideologische Konzepte', 1433–5, 1437; Michael Mann, *The Sources of Social Power*. Vol. 2: *The Rise of Classes and Nation-States 1760–1914*. Cambridge, 2012, 280–1.

[130] Ernst-Wolfgang Böckenförde, 'Lorenz von Stein als Theoretiker der Bewegung von Staat und Gesellschaft zum Sozialstaat'. In Böckenförde, *Recht, Staat, Freiheit*. Frankfurt am Main, 1991, 191 and 193.

[131] Matis, *Österreichs Wirtschaft*, 352–3.

[132] Michael Pammer, *Entwicklung und Ungleichheit: Österreich im 19. Jahrhundert*. Wiesbaden, 2002, 279.

[133] Drobesch, 'Ideologische Konzepte', 1442–3.

[134] Cf. Kurt Ebert, *Die Anfänge der modernen Sozialpolitik in Österreich: Die Taaffesche Sozialgesetzgebung für die Arbeiter im Rahmen der Gewerbeordnungen 1879–1885* (Habil.). Graz, 1972.

[135] Matis, *Österreichs Wirtschaft*, 346; Andrea Komlosy, 'Der Staat schiebt ab. Zur nationalstaatlichen Konsolidierung von Heimat und Fremde im 18. und 19. Jahrhundert'. In Komlosy and Sylvia Hahn (eds), *Ausweisung, Abschiebung, Vertreibung in Europa 16.–20. Jahrhundert*. Innsbruck, 2006, 88. Generally Derek Fraser, 'Das Armengesetz und die Ursprünge des britischen Wohlfahrtsstaates'.

state administration that was expected to achieve socio-political pacification and social cohesion. The conflict between politically liberal and conservative ideas was also reflected in the dispute over costs.[136] Jürgen Osterhammel speaks of the 'conflict between cheap government and expensive public services', in other words between a liberal low-tax state and an interventionist welfare state.[137] In the Habsburg Monarchy, state subsidies for social security were primarily intended to integrate the working classes.[138] Compared with the German Empire, Cisleithania's contribution by itself remained fairly small.[139] However, it increased significantly through the addition of the contributions of the crown lands, districts, and municipalities.[140]

The involvement of society in welfare, as well as in the field of education, remained high. When leading social politicians such as Joseph Maria Baernreither, one of the initiators of the Austrian Ministry of Social Affairs in 1916,[141] called for state intervention in social policy, they meant the interaction of public institutions with society. Baernreither argued: 'no one should be fooled into thinking that the state can be the executor of social policy alone; on the contrary, the more effective lever lies not in the state but in society'.[142] Recent research on social welfare underpins this view. For example, Sandrine Kott examines the welfare state in the German Empire, the development of which ran often parallel to that of the welfare state of the Habsburg Monarchy. She speaks of a two-way process of the welfare state integrating the state into society, on the one hand, and society into the state, on the other.[143]

Social welfare in the imperial state of Cisleithania was enacted by the conservative Taaffe government, particularly in the 1880s, as 'social policy from above'.[144] With the introduction of workers' accident insurance in 1887 and workers' health insurance in 1888, the Habsburg Monarchy pioneered social policy in Europe,

In Wolfgang J. Mommsen (ed.), *Die Entstehung des Wohlfahrtsstaates in Großbritannien und Deutschland 1850–1950*. Stuttgart, 1982, 45. Comparing Bernhard Kittel, Herbert Obinger, and Uwe Wagschal, 'Die gezügelten Wohlfahrtsstaaten im internationalen Vergleich: Politisch-institutionelle Faktoren der Entstehung und Entwicklungsdynamik'. In Herbert Obinger (ed.), *Der gezügelte Wohlfahrtsstaat*. Frankfurt am Main, 2000, 329–64.

[136] Osterhammel, Transformation of the World, 790.

[137] Osterhammel, Transformation of the World, 790.

[138] Peter Becker, 'Stolpersteine auf dem Weg zum kooperativen Imperium: Bürokratische Praxis, gesellschaftliche Erwartungen und sozialpolitische Strategien'. In Osterkamp, *Kooperatives Imperium*, 26–7; Helmut Fiereder, *125 Jahre soziale Krankenversicherung in Oberösterreich 1869–1994*. Linz, 1994, 61.

[139] Mann, *Sources of Social Power*, 2. 502. Comparing both systems Baernreither, 'Socialreform in Österreich', 20–5.

[140] Milan Hlavačka, Pavel Cibulka, Jiří Pokorný, Olga Fejtová, and Pavel Bek, *Sociální myšlení a sociální praxe v českých zemích 1781–1939*. Prague, 2015, 584–5.

[141] Harald Bachmann, *Joseph Maria Baernreither 1845–1925: Der Werdegang eines altösterreichischen Ministers und Sozialpolitikers*. Neustadt an der Aisch, 1977.

[142] Baernreither, 'Socialreform in Österreich', 41; Baernreither, *Grundfragen der sozialen Versicherung in Österreich: Ergebnisse der Beratungen des Arbeitsbeirates*. Vienna, 1908.

[143] Kott, *Sozialstaat und Gesellschaft*, 16.

[144] Emmerich Talos, *Staatliche Sozialpolitik in Österreich*. Vienna, 1981, 80.

alongside Germany.[145] Socio-political intervention in the form of compulsory insurance gradually replaced the liberal institutions based on voluntary insurance between employees and employers and 'auxiliary funds' (*Hilfscassen*).[146] The Kingdom of Hungary followed this development belatedly, introducing health insurance in 1891 and accident insurance in 1907. In contrast to Austria, auxiliary funds continued to play an important role in Hungary.[147]

Later, pension and invalidity insurance was introduced in Cisleithania, with the crown lands of Bohemia and Lower and Upper Austria as forerunners.[148] Negotiations on unemployment insurance, however, were unsuccessful. The legislative focus on the industrial workforce moreover regularly excluded the rural workers from the social security systems.[149] Only Hungary provided for a minimal coverage of agricultural workers, although the number of insured persons was low.[150] In Cisleithania, the protection of dependent agricultural workers was left to the crown lands. As a result of the overrepresentation of agrarian landowners in the provincial diets, rural workers were not covered by health insurance.[151]

State measures were supplemented by provincial and municipal welfare offices. These included the so-called victualling stations (*Naturalverpflegsstationen*) for the merely 'accidentally destitute'—the contemporary expression for the unemployed as opposed to the criminalized 'skivers'.[152] Based on the Lower Austrian model, offices were established in seven provinces. This shows how closely the provincial diets followed socio-political innovations in the other crown lands.[153] Located

[145] Senghaas, *Territorialisierung sozialer Sicherung*, 84. For a typology Hicks, Alexander Hicks, Joya Misra, and Tang Nah Ng, 'The Programmatic Emergence of the Social Security State', *American Sociological Review*, 60/3 (1995), 330. On Germany Kott, *Sozialstaat und Gesellschaft*, 17.

[146] Cf. Hlavačka et al., *Sociální myšlení a sociální praxe*, 420–95. The 9th International Statistical Congress held in Budapest in the summer of 1876 dealt with social insurance systems in Europe, cf. Adolf Ficker, 'Die IX. Versammlung des internationalen statistischen Kongresses', *Statistische Monatsschrift* (1876), 440.

[147] Zimmermann, 'Armen- und Sozialpolitik in Ungarn', 1501; Matlekovits, *Das Königreich Ungarn*, 2. 365–70.

[148] Ferdinand Schmid, 'Der gegenwärtige Stand der Invaliditäts- und Altersversicherung in Österreich'. In *Österreichs Wohlfahrts-Einrichtungen 1848–1898*. Vol. 4: *Sociale Hilfspflege*. Vienna, 1900, 154–260. On the negotiations Brügel, *Soziale Gesetzgebung in Österreich*; Fiereder, *125 Jahre soziale Krankenversicherung*.

[149] Liberals thought this put agricultural employers, who were exempt from insurance benefits, at an advantage over industrial employers. Senghaas, *Territorialisierung sozialer Sicherung*, 103. However, liberals developed a peasantry-oriented programme only in Carinthia. Wadl, *Liberalismus und soziale Frage*, 209.

[150] Zimmermann, 'Armen- und Sozialpolitik in Ungarn', 1503–4 and 1514.

[151] Gerhard Siegl and Guenther Steiner, *Ja, jetzt geht es mir gut... Entwicklung der bäuerlichen Sozialversicherung in Österreich*. Vienna, 2010. On local exceptions Fiereder, *125 Jahre soziale Krankenversicherung*, 66.

[152] Friedrich Probst, 'Naturalverpflegsstationen in Österreich', *Statistische Monatsschrift*, 20 (1894), 65–6.

[153] In 1909, victualling stations in Bohemia received 228,610 crowns, in Styria 185,975 crowns, in Moravia 156,618 crowns, in Lower Austria 57,149 crowns, in Silesia 25,689 crowns, in Upper Austria 12,992 crowns, and in Vorarlberg 5,814 crowns, while in the other provinces they were not subsidized

along the main roads, the victualling stations offered food and shelter to itinerant labourers and craftsmen in return for work. The fact that convictions under the Vagrancy Act decreased is proof of the success of this measure.[154] The stations also assisted in filling vacancies free of charge, but at less than 1 per cent the success rate was negligible.[155] The costs were borne either by the crown lands, districts, or associations.[156] Municipal support for the unemployed, such as soup kitchens or employment offices, was established only in a few cities.[157] These included Vienna, Budapest, and Prague, as well as rural towns such as the Moravian Proßnitz (Prostějov) or Mährisch-Trübau (Moravská Třebová).[158] Later, an Imperial Act on Employment Services failed to pass, partly because of battles over the division of labour between the empire and the provinces.[159] A slowing down of social welfare measures in federal states, as claimed by today's sociologists, can therefore be confirmed from a historical perspective, at least in some cases.[160]

The organization of social security fell within the remit of the provinces.[161] There was no central accident insurance agency in Vienna; instead, the crown lands or groups of several crown lands formed the territorial framework for the insurance agencies.[162] A comparison of the territorial coverage of the insurances and their funding shows that the social state emerged at different speeds and intensities in the crown lands.[163] The Salzburg Accident Insurance Agency, which was responsible for Upper Austria, Salzburg, Tyrol, and Vorarlberg, insured only

at all, *Statistisches Jahrbuch der autonomen Landesverwaltung in den im Reichsrate vertretenen Königreichen und Ländern*, 11 (1913), 250–1. See Ernst Mischler, 'Übersicht über die öffentliche Armenpflege und die private Wohltätigkeit in Österreich'. In *Österreichs Wohlfahrts-Einrichtungen 1848–1898*. Vol. 1: *Armenpflege und Wohltätigkeit in Österreich*. Vienna, 1899, p. xxvii. On the discussions in the Diet, cf. Jan Janák, *Morava v národním ruchu 19. století*. Brno, 2007, 452–60.

[154] Probst, 'Naturalverpflegsstationen', 72–3; Hugo Herz, 'Die Vagabundage in Österreich in ihren Beziehungen zur Volkswirtschaft und zum Verbrechertume', *Zeitschrift für Volkswirtschaft, Socialpolitik und Verwaltung*, 14 (1905), 581.

[155] Cities and municipalities lacked comparable public institutions but relied on private or cooperative initiatives, Richard Boleslawski von der Trenck, 'Die Arbeitsvermittlung in Österreich'. In *Österreichs Wohlfahrts-Einrichtungen 1848–1898*, 4. 340. Cf. also the table 'Naturalverpflegsstationen'. In K. k. statistische Zentral-Kommission (ed.), *Statistisches Handbuch der autonomen Landesverwaltung in den im Reichsrate vertretenen Königreichen und Ländern*. Vol. 1. Vienna, 1900, 60–1.

[156] Probst, 'Naturalverpflegsstationen', 74.

[157] Unemployment relief primarily benefited male workers. Susan Zimmermann, 'Das Geschlecht der Fürsorge: Kommunale Armen- und Wohlfahrtspolitik in Budapest und Wien 1870–1914', *L'Homme*, 5/2 (1994), 37.

[158] Janák, *Morava v národním ruchu*, 453. [159] Janák, *Morava v národním ruchu*, 461.

[160] Cf. Kittel et al., 'Die gezügelten Wohlfahrtsstaaten', 340. Differenzierend Josef Schmid, 'Sozialpolitik und Wohlfahrtsstaat in Bundesstaaten'. In Gerhard Lehmbruch and Arthur Benz (eds), *Föderalismus: Analysen in entwicklungsgeschichtlicher und vergleichender Perspektive*. Wiesbaden, 2002, 279–305.

[161] The organization by territories was criticized and was to be replaced by professional associations. Senghaas, *Territorialisierung sozialer Sicherung*, 170, 180.

[162] Territorial administration was maintained for the pension insurance for salaried employees, introduced in 1906; Senghaas, 'Föderalismus und Sozialpolitik in der Habsburgermonarchie', 238–41.

[163] Kittel et al., 'Die gezügelten Wohlfahrtsstaaten', 334.

12.5 per cent of workers in these territories. The highest coverage was achieved by the Prague and Brno Accident Insurance Agencies for the Bohemian Lands, with over 40 per cent. The lowest percentage was recorded by the Lemberg insurance office, which was responsible for Bukovina and Galicia.[164] At a participation of only 9 per cent, Hungary also had limited insurance coverage; only the social security system in the metropolis of Budapest reflected the situation in the Cisleithanian provinces.[165] The picture differs only slightly with regard to health insurance.[166] Hungary lingered at the bottom of the scale, where the proportion of workers covered by health insurance was one-quarter of that in Austria.[167]

The reason for this was again of a fiscal nature. The uneven expansion of social welfare measures aligned with the uneven mobilization of fiscal resources in the crown lands. The costs of social welfare and indirect costs, such as the professional institutional organization of the insurance systems, were the burden of the crown lands. Representatives of the ministerial bureaucracy strongly opposed any kind of financial involvement by the imperial state.[168] Unlike in agricultural modernization, where the crown lands were obliged to employ trained technicians, there was often a lack of personnel trained in social law, especially at the middle and lower levels of the administration.[169] In Hungary, in particular, the welfare state was much less developed. Private protection of the needy was considered sufficient. Public authorities pointed out that caring factory owners were 'always concerned about the material wellbeing of their workers'—which, of course, was not necessarily the case.[170]

These varying degrees of commitment reflected the different political priorities of the provincial elites. In 1911, for example, Polish deputies from the conservative spectrum of the upper bourgeoisie and aristocracy prevented the introduction of the Imperial Self-Employment Insurance (*Reichsselbständigenversicherung*) in Galicia and Bukovina. Allegedly, the entrepreneurs could not afford the necessary premiums.[171] Other social security measures were also suspended. Galicia and Bukovina thus opposed the imperial state's authority regarding the enforcement of a uniform social policy. At the same time, they failed to develop a social policy of their own. In relation to the other provinces, they called into question the rudimentary principle of solidarity between the insurance institutions, which, in

[164] Senghaas, *Territorialisierung sozialer Sicherung*, 93.

[165] Zimmermann, 'Armen- und Sozialpolitik in Ungarn', 1515–16.

[166] Senghaas, *Territorialisierung sozialer Sicherung*, 94; Zimmermann, 'Armen- und Sozialpolitik in Ungarn', 1515.

[167] Matlekovits, *Das Königreich Ungarn*, 2. 70.

[168] Otto Stöger, 'Die Unfallversicherung der Arbeiter'. In *Österreichs Wohlfahrts-Einrichtungen 1848–1898*. Vol. 4: *Sociale Hilfspflege*. Vienna, 1900, 61.

[169] Becker, 'Stolpersteine', 42.

[170] Matlekovits, *Das Königreich Ungarn*, 2. 345. On worker protection in Hungary Zimmermann, 'Armen- und Sozialpolitik in Ungarn', 1488–92, 1500.

[171] Senghaas, *Territorialisierung sozialer Sicherung*, 168.

theory, should have provided coverage from common funds in the event of deficits in individual crown land institutions.[172]

The crown lands played a crucial role in distributing resources. Some of them took on a pioneering role in the establishment of social security schemes for a number of professions and social groups. Examples included the pension insurance schemes for municipal and district physicians, hydraulic engineers, and civil servants in provincial institutions, as well as the insurance of agricultural workers in Hungary.[173] If, on the other hand, individual crown lands did not prioritize social welfare, they particularly burdened the poorer sections of the population and migrant workers. The division of this policy area among the various levels of the multi-level governance system thus had its drawbacks and hampered the expeditious expansion of social security systems. Although the Cisleithanian governments had been considering proposals for the reform of workers' social security since 1904, the dispute over competencies, fuelled by the nationality conflict, prevented their parliamentary adoption.[174] It was only under the pressure of war that the Ministry of Social Welfare was established in Cisleithania in December 1917.[175]

9.5. Social Policy at Different Paces

The crown lands thus developed their 'state activity' in various modern policy areas at different paces. Austrian state ministries in Vienna were not alone in building up extensive staffs of civil servants and experts to find solutions to new challenges. The same held true for most provincial administrations.[176] Crown lands such as Bohemia, Lower Austria, or Silesia, with their high economic and financial capacity and the corresponding administrative resources, acted independently. Whether or not a crown land acted like a state toward its citizens in certain policy areas was not determined by the conclusion or non-conclusion of a 'Compromise'. It depended on the decisions taken by the political actors in the respective policy area, but also on the resources available and their mobilization in the crown land.

[172] In principle, territorial insurance institutions bore the financial risk; in addition, there was an insignificant reserve fund at the Ministry of the Interior. Senghaas, *Territorialisierung sozialer Sicherung*, 183–4. Only the Brno Accident Insurance Fund covered the obligations. Stöger, 'Unfallversicherung der Arbeiter', 57.

[173] The crown lands acted on their own initiative or, as with the Teachers' Pension Fund, were assigned the legislative powers to do so. E.g. Pension Statute for Civil Servants and Servants of the Crown Land and for the Crown Land Institutions, no. 53/1889 LGBl. Galizien.

[174] Fiereder, *125 Jahre soziale Krankenversicherung*, 68.

[175] Senghaas, *Territorialisierung sozialer Sicherung*, 125.

[176] Statistical evidence at Schmitz, 'Organe und Arbeitsweise'.

The activities of imperial and provincial institutions were linked by a dense network of interdependencies. In important policy areas, the asymmetrical nature of rule between the central authorities in Vienna and the institutions in the crown lands was modified by cooperation 'from above' and 'from below'. This coexistence of imperial 'top-down' politics and cooperative structures of rule characterized the 'cooperative empire' the Habsburg Monarchy had become since the last third of the nineteenth century.[177]

In addition to *vertical* interdependence in modern welfare administration, there was an increasing need for *horizontal* cooperation among the crown lands. One example is the negotiation of a new fiscal equalization system between 1890 and 1914. Attempts to reform public finances were driven by the so-called Crown Lands Conferences. Controversies arose over financial resources for the provincial policy areas and, under the increasing influence of social democracy, over their allocation to various social groups. The dispute over fiscal equity thus became a dispute over social participation, parliamentarization, and democratization. It was a dispute about federal solidarity and financial self-responsibility, and thus about the basic principles of federalism.

A Federal History of the Habsburg Empire, 1815–1918. Jana Osterkamp, Oxford University Press.
 DOI: 10.1093/9780198943631.003.0010

[177] Cf. Osterkamp, *Kooperatives Imperium*.

Figure 10.1 'Gemeinsames Erfordernis' [Joint Financial Requirement]. Austrian postcard, pen-and-ink drawing, c.1899.

10

The Price of Statehood

Negotiating Fiscal Federalism, 1896–1914

At the end of the nineteenth century, the public service state expanded into the political territories of Europe. The construction of railways, roads, and canals, and the building of schools, hospitals, and homes for the elderly, created an ever-denser network of infrastructure and social security. New channels of social communication through mass media, associations, parties, and parliaments created networks of political spaces. Under these political and social initiatives, territories began to 'crackle' and 'pulsate' with energy, as Charles S. Maier described it, as if under electrical tension.[1]

Territorialization and public service administration had their price. Throughout nineteenth-century Europe, debt and financial crises in the public sector accompanied the expansion of the fiscal state.[2] The disparity in territorialization between Austria and Hungary, and between the crown lands, as highlighted in this book so far,[3] was reflected in public finances. Who paid how much and for what? Did schools, roads, or local railways take priority? The answers were an expression of different regional preferences and multi-level investment strategies typical of federalism.[4]

The regional approach to fiscal history thus provides, first, insights into the uneven development of federal statehood.[5] As postulated by national economists such as Lorenz von Stein, a public service state's goal of generating and maintaining social wellbeing and, in turn, deriving macroeconomic prosperity from it could be implemented more sustainably in resource-rich lands such as Bohemia

[1] Charles S. Maier, 'Transformations of Territoriality 1600–2000'. In Gunilla Budde, Sebastian Conrad, and Oliver Janz (eds), *Transnationale Geschichte: Themen, Tendenzen und Theorien*. Göttingen, 2006, 45.

[2] Wolfgang Reinhard, *Staatsmacht und Staatskredit: Kulturelle Tradition und politische Moderne*. Heidelberg, 2017; Hans-Peter Ullmann, *Der deutsche Steuerstaat: Geschichte der öffentlichen Finanzen vom 18. Jahrhundert bis heute*. Munich, 2005; José Luís Cardoso and Pedro Lains, *Paying for the Liberal State*. Cambridge, 2010; Wolfgang Renzsch, 'Föderale Finanzverfassungen: Ein Vergleich Australiens, Deutschlands, Kanadas, der Schweiz und der USA aus institutioneller Perspektive', *Jahrbuch des Föderalismus* (2000), 42–54. Imperial financial history is still under-researched, cf. Ekaterina A. Pravilova, *Finansy imperii: Den'gi i vlast' v politike Rossii na nacional'nych okrainach 1801–1917*. Moscow, 2006.

[3] Cf. Chapters 7, 8, and 9.

[4] Cf. Charles M. Tiebout, 'A Pure Theory of Local Expenditures', *Journal of Political Economy*, 64/5 (1956), 416–24.

[5] Stefan Korioth, *Der Finanzausgleich zwischen Bund und Ländern*. Tübingen, 1997, 96.

or Lower Austria than in less developed regions.[6] The current of statehood did not pulsate evenly in all Habsburg territories. The monarchy's most industrialized land, Bohemia, pushed investment in infrastructure. Neither Vorarlberg, which also had a high level of industrialization, nor rural Salzburg followed the path of investment, thereby avoiding high public debt.[7] Dalmatia, on the other hand, lacked the money to expand its provincial roads.[8] Pandemic-weary Bukovina, meanwhile, complained of a lack of hospitals.[9] Per capita, Silesia demanded even more funds for public health.[10]

Fiscal history, secondly, illuminates an emerging sense of community between the crown lands. In the field of public finances, the Austrian crown lands, despite the many differences in provincial policies, succeeded in articulating common fiscal interests. In their financial policy towards Vienna, they acted jointly as a special-purpose association. The prohibition on interprovincial communication, laid down in the Austrian provincial constitutions and typical of empires, was still in force. Accordingly, no provincial institution was allowed to engage in political contact with a counterpart in another crown land.[11] More often than not, this rule was simply disregarded. There was no common political body of the provinces, such as a parliamentary 'House of the Provinces', so they created their own informal forums to fulfil the same purpose. These meetings took place in the Lower Austrian Diet in Vienna's Herrengasse as the so-called crown lands' conferences. As a result, a new financial equalization scheme was initiated and promoted—together with the Imperial-Royal Ministry of Finance—and passed as a parliamentary bill in 1914.

The community of the crown lands acted as a common interest group *against* the 'state', i.e. the Viennese ministerial bureaucracy. At their meetings in the Lower Austrian Diet's building, belligerent statements echoed off the walls. 'One should not care about the state at all in this hall, it does not care about how the provinces cover their fiscal needs.'[12] The increasing power of the crown lands' community as a political lobby is also illustrated by the remark of a fiscal statistician and

[6] On Stein's 'reproductive state' concept, Jan Pieter Schulz, *Finanzwissenschaft im deutschsprachigen Raum und in den Vereinigten Staaten 1865–1917*. Marburg, 2013, 119.

[7] Speech by Jodok Fink, *Stenographisches Protokoll der Enquete über die Landesfinanzen vom 7. bis 12. März 1908*. Vienna, 1908, 160–1.

[8] Speech by Vinzenz Ivčevič, *Enquete über die Landesfinanzen*, 155.

[9] Speech by Johann Wolczynski, *Enquete über die Landesfinanzen*, 32.

[10] Speech by Zdenko Sedlnitzky, *Enquete über die Landesfinanzen*, 140.

[11] In more detail Jana Osterkamp, 'Cooperative Empires: Provincial Initiatives in Imperial Austria', *Austrian History Yearbook*, 47 (2016), 128–46.

[12] Speech by Hermann Bielohlawek, *Stenographisches Protokoll über die am 16., 17. und 18. Februar 1905 im niederösterreichischen Landhause zu Wien abgehaltene Konferenz der Landesausschüsse der im Reichsrate vertretenen Königreiche und Länder betreffend die Regelung der Landesfinanzen*, Vienna, 1905, 57. This statement was later quoted critically, Speech by Karl Brockhausen, *Enquete über die Landesfinanzen*, 51.

ministerial public servant: 'Other states have other problems. Our specifically Austrian problem is: strong self-governing bodies, without a weakening of the state.'[13]

The state was not exclusively characterized as an adversary, however. In isolated cases, the crown lands evoked a solidary community of the provinces *with* the state.[14] At least some emphasized the need for such cooperation to fulfil public service tasks.[15] 'The state and the lands must not be regarded as opposites, but as cooperators in their common work of developing the state and the lands', stated the director of the Galician Provincial Bank and national economist Josef Milewski in 1908 during deliberations on a new fiscal equalization scheme.[16] The expert in the law of administration Karl Brockhausen went back to Shakespeare's *King Lear* to illustrate the dangers of separate action by the state and the provinces; a focus on strengthening the power of just one party would destroy both sides.[17]

Thirdly, the history of public finances is a history of social and political participation. It shows which social concerns were funded, who was to benefit from these public expenses, and who made the decisions. In modern democracies, all citizens are potential beneficiaries of public goods. In addition, they elect—and can be elected—decision-makers who distribute these goods, and they pay the taxes which fund them. Such congruence was absent in a monarchy like the Austro-Hungarian Empire.[18] This resulted in a vivid discussion among Habsburg financial scholars. They not only analysed technocratic aspects of public finances but also focused on socio-philosophical questions. The Czech national economist Josef Kaizl was one example. He emphasized that regional differences in the tax burden and the range of public services are not merely an expression of fiscal federalism but also pose risks to social development that need to be addressed.[19]

Fiscal justice in a federal context was not a topic other financial scholars considered worthy of discussion at the end of the nineteenth century.[20] Indeed, it

[13] Speech by Ferdinand Schmid, *Enquete über die Landesfinanzen*, 234.

[14] For detail on this 'loyalty polygon' Jana Osterkamp, 'Kooperatives Imperium: Loyalitätsgefüge und Reich-Länder-Finanzausgleich', *Geschichte und Gesellschaft*, 42/4 (2016), 617–20.

[15] Speech by Thaddäus Pilat, *Konferenz der Landesausschüsse betreffend die Regelung der Landesfinanzen* (1905), 42.

[16] Speech by Josef Milewski, *Enquete über die Landesfinanzen*, 68.

[17] Speech by Karl Brockhausen, *Enquete über die Landesfinanzen*, 50.

[18] On the principle of institutional congruence, cf. Charles B. Blankart and Erik R. Fasten, 'Die ökonomische Grammatik des Föderalismus: Von den Anfängen des Grundgesetzes bis zur Föderalismusreform II'. In Ines Härtel (ed.), *Handbuch Föderalismus*. Vol. 1: *Grundlagen des Föderalismus und der deutsche Bundesstaat*. Heidelberg, 2012, 323–4.

[19] Josef Kaizl, *Finanzwissenschaft*. Vol. 2. Vienna, 1901, 201.

[20] Korioth, *Finanzausgleich*, 310. On the state of the debate today, cf. Michael Hüther and Klaus Hafemann, 'Öffentliche Güter, Wettbewerb, Kompetenzverteilung. Ökonomische Analysen zum Föderalismus'. In Härtel, *Handbuch Föderalismus*, 1. 333–58. On federal competition Tiebout, 'Pure Theory'; Wallace E. Oates, 'An Essay on Fiscal Federalism', *Journal of Economic Literature*, 37/3 (1999), 1120–49.

only entered the theory of federalism in the latter half of the twentieth century.[21] Today, the question of how public tasks, expenditures, and revenues are to be distributed and coordinated within a multi-level political system is central for federal polities.[22]

10.1. Austria-Hungary

Fiscal practice in the Habsburg Monarchy was even more bewildering than the state structure itself.[23] Austria-Hungary (the entire state), Austria and Hungary (its two halves), the crown lands, the districts, municipalities, and statutory cities all enjoyed fiscal sovereignty, albeit in a declining order.[24] Many public tasks were financed simultaneously across several levels through a system of 'multi-tiered cost recovery'.[25]

This fiscal system of multi-level financing did not clearly separate state, provincial, and municipal finances, as would be typical in the United States of America, for example.[26] The most important centres of fiscal autonomy were Austria-Hungary, both parts of the empire, and the Austrian crown lands. Croatia-Slavonia and Bosnia-Herzegovina had no fiscal autonomy. Since the turn of the century, at least in the Austrian crown lands, we can observe the gradual development from a cooperative empire to cooperative federalism.[27] The latter is characterized by its goal of common legal standards and equal living conditions across the provinces.

Within Austria-Hungary's confederative framework, the two parts enjoyed equal rights as far as the common organs, such as the delegations, and the common affairs were concerned. Legally, the Austrian and Hungarian treasuries were on an equal footing and acted independently of one another. At the same time,

[21] Olivier Beaud, *Théorie de la Fédération*. 2nd edn. Paris, 2009, 319–20.

[22] Ullmann, *Der deutsche Steuerstaat*, 72; Hans Stumpp, *Die Entwicklung des Finanzausgleichs in Deutschland von 1871 bis zur Gegenwart* (diss. univ.). Würzburg, 1964, 2. Financial equalization does exist also in the unitary state, e.g. between municipalities. Korioth, *Finanzausgleich*, 34–43.

[23] Experts spoke of the 'almost insurmountable task for a non-specialist' of gaining an overview of the financial system. For a concise take on the national and imperial level Hans Patzauer, *Österreichs und Ungarns Staatswirthschaften*, Vienna, 1916, 3. The President of the Statistical Central Commission still lacked conclusive data on provincial and municipal finances in 1908, cf. speech by Franz Juraschek, *Enquete über die Landesfinanzen*, 254–6; on the policy field-specific analysis of finances in Moravia and Silesia see Pavel Kladiwa, Andrea Pokludová, and Renata Kafková, *Lesk a bída obec ních samospráv Moravy a Slezska 1850–1914*. Vol. 2/2: *Finance a infrastruktura*. Ostrava, 2009.

[24] Ernst Mischler, *Der öffentliche Haushalt in Böhmen*. Leipzig and Vienna, 1887.

[25] Speech by Ernst Mischler, *Enquete über die Landesfinanzen*, 221.

[26] On the systematics of interlinked and separated systems Korioth, *Finanzausgleich*, especially part 1 'Grundlagen', 19–56; Albert Hensel, *Der Finanzausgleich im Bundesstaat in seiner staatsrechtlichen Bedeutung*. Berlin, 1922, 33–144 and 149–50. Cf. Reichsschatzamt (ed.), *Denkschriftenband*. Part 3: *Die Finanzen von Frankreich, Großbritannien und Irland, Italien, Japan, Österreich-Ungarn, Rußland, der Schweiz, den Vereinigten Staaten von Amerika*. Berlin, 1908.

[27] On loyalty and fiscal equalization Osterkamp, 'Kooperatives Imperium'.

however, transfers of capital and, conversely, absorption of expenses disproportionately benefited the Hungarian lands. The caricature shown at the beginning of this chapter (Figure 10.1) illustrates how many residents in the Austrian half of the empire felt: fiscal transfers were depriving them of the fruits of their labour. In the image, an Austrian farmer tends to a dairy cow named 'common requirement', i.e. common budget, while inhabitants of Transleithania milk it and carry off the goods towards Budapest.[28]

The caricature reflects feelings of envy, if not resentment, which are not uncommon in fiscal federalism. It also highlights the distribution of public burdens. For the common affairs of defence, finance, and foreign affairs, the Austro-Hungarian Monarchy as a whole was entitled to all customs revenues.[29] If this was insufficient, the two parts of the empire had to make up the shortfall from other revenues. Every ten years, a ratio was agreed for the distribution of this burden, the so-called quota.[30] In the last year of peacetime, 1913, Austria-Hungary's net revenue amounted to 964 million crowns. Of this, only 227 million were customs duties (81.5 per cent from Austria, 18.5 per cent from Hungary). The vast majority of the remaining 737 million was supplied by the quota (63.6 per cent for Austria, 36.4 per cent for Hungary).[31] It was calculated according to a proportional formula based on the respective economic strengths of the two parts of the empire and therefore demanded more of the Austrians than the Hungarians. Austria's per capita contribution was initially 50 per cent (until 1889), and later 31 per cent (from 1907), higher than Hungary's per capita contribution. This resulted in the aforementioned transfer of wealth.[32]

Before 1867, Hungary's contribution to the costs of the state had been even lower. At the beginning of the 1860s, the Hungarian lands bore only a quarter of all common expenses. After 1867, this increased to one-third.[33] Here, one can see the fiscal flipside of the Compromise Laws: Hungary may have gained significant political independence, but it was now obliged to contribute far more to the state's financing.

The empire could not levy taxes on its own. Fiscal sovereignty, an important attribute of statehood, belonged to Austria and Hungary, but not to Austria-Hungary as a whole. According to the constitutional-liberal understanding of statehood, a 'Treasury of the Empire' would have necessitated parliamentary oversight and control of the budget. In reality, there were only the delegations, i.e. the

[28] Rudolf Jaworski, 'Einer gegen alle! Zur Visualisierung des deutschen Michels auf Bildpostkarten der späten Habsburgermonarchie', *Österreichische Zeitschrift für Volkskunde*, 122/1 (2019), 61–3.

[29] Patzauer, *Österreichs und Ungarns Staatswirthschaften*, 8 and 78.

[30] Between 1908 and 1917, the rate was 63.6 per cent for Austria and 36.4 per cent for Hungary.

[31] Cf. Patzauer, *Österreichs und Ungarns Staatswirthschaften*, 29 and 60.

[32] Michael Pammer, 'Public Finance in Austria-Hungary'. In Cardoso and Lains, *Paying for the Liberal State*, 140.

[33] Cf. the records of the years 1860–5 in Adolf Beer, *Die Finanzen Österreichs im 19. Jahrhundert nach archivalischen Quellen*. Prague, 1877, 351.

parliamentary committees of the Austrian Imperial Council and the Hungarian Imperial Diet, which approved the budget for common affairs. This federal substitute parliament[34] exercised its regulatory function only to a limited extent. Furthermore, the empire's financial revenue lagged behind that of the imperial halves. When combined, Austria and Hungary enjoyed revenues six times greater than the empire as a whole.

If one views the history of fiscal federalism as a double-sided story of federal statehood and multi-level participation, Austria-Hungary, in terms of its most financially dominant policy field, was a military state. Its military expenditure was, to some degree, controlled by the two delegations. A century earlier, the *fiscal-military state* had already been characterized by the dominance of military expenditures, but in the nineteenth century—as in the rest of Europe—Austria-Hungary's defence budget now dwarfed all other portfolios.[35] Even so, when one factors in the ongoing armaments race and measures military expenditure per capita, the Habsburg Empire still trailed Great Britain, France, Germany, Italy, and Russia.[36]

The share of the budget allocated for defence increased considerably when, at the instigation of Archduke Franz Ferdinand, a large naval investment programme was launched in 1910. Austria-Hungary now began to join in the European race for military dominance at sea.[37] Military newspapers published emphatic reports on the new battleships, the 'dreadnoughts'.[38] Investment in the navy reached comparable proportions to those in Germany. As in Germany, there was also widespread resistance by a public that had become increasingly wary of fiscal policy.[39] To secure his dream of a global naval force in the Adriatic, the heir

[34] Cf. Chapter 7.4.

[35] For a long-term overview of military expenditure in the German Empire, see Wilhelm Gerloff, 'Der Staatshaushalt und das Finanzsystem Deutschlands'. In Gerloff and Franz Meisel (eds), *Handbuch der Finanzwissenschaft*. Tübingen, 1929, 18. On the fiscal military state cf. Michael Hochedlinger, 'The Habsburg Monarchy: From "Military-Fiscal State" to "Militarization"'. In Christopher Storrs (ed.), *The Fiscal-Military State in Eighteenth-Century Europe*. Farnham, 2009, 55–94.

[36] Agnes Pogány, 'Finanzgebarung, Kriegskosten und Kriegsschulden'. In Helmut Rumpler (ed.), *Die Habsburgermonarchie 1848–1918*. Vol. 11: *Die Habsburgermonarchie und der Erste Weltkrieg*. Subvol. 1: *Vom Balkankonflikt zum Weltkrieg*. Vienna, 2016, 544. For an overview see Eric Brose, 'Arms Race prior to 1914, Armament Policy'. In *1914-1918-online. International Encyclopedia of the First World War*. Ed. Ute Daniel et al. Berlin, 2014.

[37] Milan N. Vego, *Austro-Hungarian Naval Policy 1904–14*. London, 1996, 69–78. Spending on naval issues ordered by Franz Ferdinand without prior consultation led to controversy in the delegations. See: Press collection. Österreichisches Staatsarchiv, Abteilung Haus-, Hof- und Staatsarchiv, Archduke Franz Ferdinand's Estate, Box 157 and 158 Delegations.

[38] Cf. 'Die "Dreadnoughts" der Welt', *Militär-Zeitung*, 65/19 (4 June 1910), 866–7; 'Der Stand des Dreadnoughtbaues in der Welt', *Danzers Armee-Zeitung*, 12/40 (3 Oct. 1907), 8–9; 'Unsere Erzherzog Franz Ferdinand-Klasse und die Dread noughts', *Danzers Armee-Zeitung*, 15/22 (2 June 1910), 4–5.

[39] Vego, *Austro-Hungarian Naval Policy*. On the Fleet Laws and the militarization of financial policy in the empire see Peter-Christian Witt, *Die Finanzpolitik des Deutschen Reiches von 1903 bis 1913*. Hamburg, 1970; Witt, 'Reichsfinanzen und Rüstungspolitik 1898–1914'. In Herbert Schottelius and Wilhelm Deist (eds), *Marine und Marinepolitik im kaiserlichen Deutschland 1871–1914*. Düsseldorf, 1981, 146–75.

to the throne had to assert himself towards both the Austrian and Hungarian delegations. The delegates, however, refused to allocate permanent funds for the navy in the common budget and supported only medium-term investment.[40]

When it came to servicing the general debt of the empire (*allgemeine Staatsschuld*) and paying the accumulated interest, the division of responsibility between Austria and Hungary diverged even more. In 1913, the interest on the general debt of the empire reached 208 million crowns, of which Hungary paid only 58 million and Austria the lion's share of 150 million crowns.[41] This 'general debt of the empire' quantified the financial obligations of the monarchy in 1867, before the Compromise Laws divided the empire into two fiscally independent parts. It had accumulated as a result of the monarchy's military endeavours, such as the defeat against Prussia, but also included the state's contributions to the cost of peasant liberation and land relief, as well as major investments in common railway and infrastructure development during the neo-absolutist era.[42]

10.2. Austria and Hungary

The costs of the administrative and public service state were borne primarily by Austria and Hungary. Their finances bore the brunt of the bulging costs of the service state. It was the expenditure on 'infrastructural power' that increased the most following the Compromise of 1867.[43] By contrast to other European countries, state activity expanded between 1868 and 1913 not only in absolute terms but also in relation to the national product. Financial expenditure grew not only because price increases and inflation required higher spending, but also because the public sector spent increasingly more money per capita. As the economic historian Josef Wysocki has shown in an influential study, per capita public expenditure on public service tasks in Austria-Hungary was significantly higher than in Germany or France.[44]

The Austro-Hungarian Compromise of 1867 allowed for a two-speed state-building process and separate investment policies. After the Austrian liberal government had initially pursued a somewhat restrained fiscal policy, Cisleithania became an investment state under the conservative Taaffe administration in the 1880s.

[40] Vego, *Austro-Hungarian Naval Policy*, 75–8; Frank Wiggermann, *K. u. k. Kriegsmarine und Politik*. Vienna, 2004, 168–9.

[41] Cf. Patzauer, *Österreichs und Ungarns Staatswirthschaften*, 27–8, 58–9, 77.

[42] On the state debt as of the reference year 1867 cf. Beer, *Die Finanzen Österreichs*, 341, 346–85 and 412; Hans-Peter Hye, 'Föderalistische Reformprojekte in der österreichischen Reichshälfte der Habsburgermonarchie'. In Wolfgang Kruse (ed.), *Andere Modernen: Beiträge zu einer Historisierung des Moderne-Begriffs*. Bielefeld, 2015, 221.

[43] The areas that Wysocki counted as 'infrastructure spending' largely coincide with the components of Michael Mann's infrastructural power. On their growth see Josef Wysocki, *Infrastruktur und wachsende Staatsausgaben: Das Fallbeispiel Österreich 1868–1913*, Stuttgart, 1975, 114–20.

[44] Wysocki, *Infrastruktur*, 108.

Hungary, by contrast, immediately took advantage of its new statehood, as is revealed by statistics and studies on the expansion of state activity. Indeed, the relative share allocated for railways and telegraphy, education, and the promotion of industry and agriculture was *higher* than in Austria.[45] While Austria apportioned only 19 per cent of its budget to such projects in 1913, Hungary spent 29 per cent.[46] Only in the fields of education and social welfare expenditure did Austrian expenditure noticeably increase after 1867, doubling in percentage terms to 13 per cent in 1900. Infrastructure subsidies, which initially concentrated primarily on railway construction, declined in percentage terms after 1880 despite the wave of railway nationalization.[47] In the long run, costs for administration and justice remained constant in both Cis- and Transleithania.

For a deeper understanding of public finances, we must take a closer look at the federal structure. The fiscal significance of the individual policy areas in the Habsburg Monarchy can only be weighed and analysed, either in comparison with other European countries or within the empire itself, if one considers the multi-level system of rule.[48] The *political* interdependence between the empire, its two parts, and the crown lands corresponded to a high degree of *fiscal* interdependence.

Policy interdependence between the empire, Austria, and Hungary was centred on the military and defence.[49] In addition to the military expenditures of Austria-Hungary as a whole, the two halves each spent 20 per cent of their budget on their militia (*Landwehr, Landsturm*). At the top of the list, however, with 38 per cent, was the bureaucratic apparatus needed to procure customs duties, levies, and taxes, to administer state enterprises and monopolies, and to finance the common institutions.[50]

In addition to the Austro-Hungarian confederation, there was vertical policy interdependence within the Austrian part of the empire among the Austrian central authorities, the crown lands, and the municipalities. This went hand in hand with a comparable fiscal interdependence.[51] If the Viennese central authorities

[45] On investments Alexander von (Sándor) Matlekovits, *Das Königreich Ungarn.* Vol. 2. Leipzig, 1900, 922–3.

[46] Patzauer, *Österreichs und Ungarns Staatswirthschaften*, 97; Pammer, 'Public Finance in Austria-Hungary', 143–4, 151–7. Szende estimates annual expenditure of 96 to 105 million crowns for the Hungarian Landwehr before 1914. Paul Szende, 'Der Staatshaushalt und das Finanzsystem Österreichs und Ungarns'. In Wilhelm Gerloff and Franz Meisel (eds), *Handbuch der Finanzwissenschaft.* Tübingen, 1929, 215.

[47] Pammer, 'Public Finance in Austria-Hungary', 143; Reichsschatzamt, 'Österreich und Ungarn'. In *Denkschriftenband,* part 3, 242–3.

[48] Similarly on Germany Eckart Schremmer, *Steuern und Staatsfinanzen während der Industrialisierung Europas.* Berlin and Heidelberg, 1994, 176–208.

[49] A similar picture emerges in Germany after 1871 cf. Julia Cholet, *Der Etat des Deutschen Reiches in der Bismarckzeit.* Berlin, 2012, 244.

[50] Since Austria-Hungary as a whole had no tax sovereignty, this concerned the revenues for the empire and the imperial halves.

[51] Cf. Chapter 9.

approved funding for a policy, these were supplemented (and often exceeded) by provincial and municipal contributions. From this perspective, many financial statistics of the time appear in a new light.

By way of an example, comparative statistics for both parts of the empire show that Hungarian per capita expenditure on education was higher than that in Austria.[52] Concluding that Austria spent less on education and was thus less committed to this public service would be misguided, however. Unlike in Hungary, education financing in Austria was largely in the hands of the crown lands and municipalities.[53] In Bohemia and Dalmatia, the share of costs for primary and secondary schools in the total provincial budget reached up to 50 per cent. The municipalities also contributed a large share.[54] Collectively, expenditure on education in Austria was therefore significantly higher than in Hungary.

Other policy areas such as hydraulic engineering and melioration were also funded by multiple parties. In the Austrian part of the empire, they were characterized by cooperative administration: the water construction funds, part of the provincial budgets, flowed from both provincial and central Austrian coffers.[55] Karl Urban, a Bohemian politician and later minister of trade during the First World War, was critical of the financial interdependence prevalent in the promotion of education, arts, public health, and business: 'However, the fact that the land and the state [meaning Austria as a whole, not Austria-Hungary] cooperate in the same area at the same time disturbs the uniformity of administrative policy'.[56] While Urban wanted to reduce these entanglements, others argued that they could not be unravelled. 'The modern state has long since ceased to be this simple, crude, brutal machine', administrative expert Josef Redlich observed, but is 'an infinitely complex construct of a multitude of heterogeneous organizations'.[57] The interdependence of the different levels of government proved effective in state-building both 'from above' and 'from below'.[58] But although it brought the public service state closer to the citizens, the complexity of this cooperation meant that in many cases the ultimate responsibilities for decision-making and financial expenditure became blurred.[59]

[52] Pammer, 'Public Finance in Austria-Hungary', 143–4.

[53] Patzauer, *Österreichs und Ungarns Staatswirthschaften*, 62, esp. nn. 23–4.

[54] In 1905, according to the statistics of the Ministry of Finance, the municipalities accounted for 1 per cent of the total provincial budget in Galicia, 2 per cent in Bukovina, 6 per cent each in Lower Austria, Tyrol, and Bohemia, 8 per cent in Moravia, 14 per cent in Gorizia and Gradisca, and 27 per cent in Vorarlberg; in the other provinces they accounted for less than 1 per cent. Cf. K. k. Finanzministerium (ed.), *Die Landeshaushalte der im Reichsrate vertretenen Königreiche und Länder. Nach den Vorschlägen für das Jahr 1905*. Vol. 1: *Bearbeitungsgrundsätze und Gesamtübersichten*. Vienna 1907, 122–3 and 130–1.

[55] Speech by Anton Pogatschnig, Istria's Provincial Audit Council, *Enquete über die Landesfinanzen*, 91.

[56] Speech by Karl Urban, *Enquete über die Landesfinanzen*, 181.

[57] Speech by Josef Redlich, *Enquete über die Landesfinanzen*, 128.

[58] Cf. Introduction.

[59] This was described by Fritz Scharpf as the 'policy entanglement trap' and has characterized cooperative federalism in Germany and Austria since the 1970s. Fritz W. Scharpf, Bernd Reissert, and Fritz Schnabel, *Politikverflechtung: Theorie und Empirie des kooperativen Föderalismus in der*

Despite their differences, Austria and Hungary were similar in character as fiscal states. In the Habsburg Monarchy, with its three federal levels, supreme fiscal sovereignty was vested in the imperial parts, and not in the crown lands or the empire as a whole. After 1867, this authority was exercised by both parliaments in Vienna and Budapest in cooperation with their respective ruler, the king-emperor. Accordingly, public finances and taxes developed in parallel in the two halves.[60] The fiscal expert Hans Patzauer stated in 1916 that 'there have hardly been two state economies anywhere and at any time...that show such great similarity as those of Austria and Hungary'.[61] This parallelism concerned, among other things, consumption taxes, such as on spirits, beer, sugar, or mineral oil, which could only be altered with the agreement of the other part of the empire.[62]

Taxation in the Habsburg Monarchy was thus far more uniform than in the German Empire, where some federal states preferred property and sales taxes and other personal income taxes.[63] Differences, nonetheless, emerged between Austria and Hungary in their ability to use taxation to facilitate their transformation from agricultural to industrial states and to tap new financial sources for state and society.

After several small and initially hesitant reforms in the mid-nineteenth century, Austria's tax system was, as in other European countries, increasingly oriented towards an 'ability-to-pay' model.[64] Older tax privileges were abolished. The centrepiece of the great tax and financial reform of 1896 was a progressive tax on all types of income. In particular, personal income taxes were strengthened at the expense of property taxes.[65] The new system was to be fairer while taking advantage of dynamic income growth. It had been developed jointly by financial policymakers and national economists with the input of economic elites[66] and was based on the theories of the Austrian School of National Economics.

In Hungary, land tax remained dominant over other taxes. It privileged large and medium estates over the small peasantry, which was disproportionately burdened.[67] Hungary did not have an income tax as a resource of state revenue.

Bundesrepublik. Kronberg im Taunus, 1976; Blankart and Fasten, 'Die ökonomische Grammatik des Föderalismus', 1. 326.

[60] On the history of taxation in Austria and Hungary Adolf Beer, *Der Staatshaushalt Österreich-Ungarns seit 1868*. Prague, 1881. Detailed and comparative Szende, 'Staatshaushalt und das Finanzsystem', 216–18; Matlekovits: *Das Königreich Ungarn*, 2. 844–5.

[61] Patzauer, *Österreichs und Ungarns Staatswirthschaften*, 95.

[62] The tax rates did not have to be the same after 1907. Patzauer, *Österreichs und Ungarns Staatswirthschaften*, 8.

[63] Ullmann, *Der deutsche Steuerstaat*, 44–7.

[64] Karsten von Blumenthal, *Die Steuertheorien der Austrian Economics: Von Menger zu Mises*. Marburg, 2007, 104. On the criterion of financial ability cf. Mark Spoerer, *Steuerlast, Steuerinzidenz und Steuerwettbewerb: Verteilungswirkungen der Besteuerung in Preußen und Württemberg 1815–1913*. Berlin, 2004, 33–4 and 95.

[65] Blumenthal, *Steuertheorien der Austrian Economics*, 107.

[66] Blumenthal, *Steuertheorien der Austrian Economics*, 106–7.

[67] Pammer, 'Public Finance in Austria-Hungary', 147. On taxes in Hungary: Reichsschatzamt, 'Österreich und Ungarn'. In *Denkschriftenband*, part 3, 294.

A systematic tax reform was also long overdue. At the same time, state activity intensified and state investment increased. Hungary's budget was thus regularly in the red.[68] In 1909, a tax reform based on the Austrian model to introduce a direct income tax failed due to resistance from the urban population.[69]

Disputes over tax and financial reforms in Austria and Hungary were always linked to the question of social and political participation in a dual monarchy with unequal suffrage. According to the liberal principle of 'no taxation without representation', the fiscal burden on the individual was only to be justified by his or her political participation in tax legislation. While direct taxation of land and property was accompanied by political participation rights, indirect taxation was not. Landowners enjoyed parliamentary participation rights, but the general 'consuming' population did not. At the same time, the numerous consumption taxes, especially on alcohol, meat, and sugar, accounted for the lion's share of tax revenues in both parts of the empire around 1900. (It will be recalled that these dues formed the fiscal background for the Austro-Hungarian conflict over the Brussels Sugar Convention.[70]) This reflected an international trend. During this period, consumption taxes showed dynamic growth in all countries. The upswing in alcohol excise taxes and the denial of political participation to consumers was criticized by Josef Redlich, the administrative and financial expert, in 1908: 'The invisible man in European financial policy is the brandy drinker, on whose back so much state expenditure is placed!'[71]

In retrospect, financial historians also assess indirect taxation as a strategy of the wealthy elites to pass on the costs of statehood to consumers who were not involved in parliamentary negotiations over expenditure.[72] With the introduction of universal suffrage for the Chamber of Deputies of the Austrian Imperial Council in 1907, this changed at least at the Cisleithanian level.

10.3. Crown Lands of Austria

In central policy areas, the crown lands in the Austrian part of the empire acted like states. They spent money like states but could finance themselves only to a limited extent. While the growing public service administration in Europe went hand in hand with the theoretical development[73] and practical expansion of the

[68] According to the final accounts for the years 1868 to 1897, the Hungarian budget registered a deficit twenty-two times and a surplus only eight times. Matlekovits: *Das Königreich Ungarn*, 2. 867.

[69] Szende, 'Staatshaushalt und das Finanzsystem', 218.

[70] After 1913, the sugar tax in Austria accounted for almost 40 per cent of consumption tax revenue. Cf. Pammer, 'Public Finance in Austria-Hungary', 147. Cf. Chapter 7.6.

[71] Speech by Josef Redlich, *Enquete über die Landesfinanzen*, 127.

[72] This instrumentalization was also evident in the empire, see Witt, 'Reichfinanzen und Rüstungspolitik', 146–7.

[73] On the Austrian perspective, cf. Lorenz von Stein, *Lehrbuch der Finanzwissenschaft*. Part 1: *Die Finanzverfassung Europas mit specieller Vergleichlands Englands, Frankreichs, Deutschlands,*

modern fiscal state,[74] the crown lands enjoyed only limited fiscal sovereignty. They were not fully formed fiscal states, as contemporary financial experts noted. The crown lands 'do not have a fully formed tax system, they have no transport taxes, no developed consumption tax system...And this gap in the tax system of the crown lands is not their fault, but results from the fact that the state has reserved all the most important types of revenue primarily for itself.'[75] Austria's financial system differed in this respect from the German Empire, where supreme fiscal sovereignty lay with the *Länder*.[76] Instead, it was more closely related to the Swiss system.[77]

Investments and Expenditures of the Crown Lands

In three of their major fields of activity—social welfare, schooling, and road infrastructure—many crown lands asserted themselves as investment states alongside Austria's overall activities. 'Investments are the characteristic sign of the last 50 years for the entire self-administration', the economist and social scientist Ernst Mischler emphatically noted. 'In no more than a single human lifetime, we have gone from nothingness in administration, from a blank sheet of paper, to a tremendous abundance of everything.'[78]

Mischler understood the growing political and fiscal power of the crown lands as a process of territorialization, 'which will perhaps never happen so quickly again in the history of state development'. It began with investments in land relief, road construction, public health, and education. In the future, the focus was to be on agricultural modernization.[79]

The dynamics of expenditure corresponded with policy development in public service administration.[80] With a share of 1.8 per cent of the total fiscal expenditure of the *Länder* in 1890, education and science policy claimed 38.9 per cent by

Österreichs, Italiens, Rußlands und anderer Länder. 5th edn. Leipzig 1885. Stein opposed both the classical economy of laissez-faire and Marx's class state. See Werner Drobesch, 'Ideologische Konzepte zur Lösung der "sozialen Frage"'. In Helmut Rumpler and Peter Urbanitsch (eds), *Die Habsburgermonarchie 1848–1918*. Vol. 9: *Soziale Strukturen*. Subvol. 1: *Von der Feudal-Agrarischen zur Bürgerlich-industriellen Gesellschaft*. Part 2: *Von der Stände- zur Klassengesellschaft*. Vienna, 2010, 1432–5; Schulz, *Finanzwissenschaft*, 112–123.

[74] Cf. Wolfgang Reinhard, *Staatsmacht und Staatskredit*. Heidelberg, 2017, 15.

[75] Speech by Josef Milewski, *Enquete über die Landesfinanzen*, 66.

[76] Stumpp, *Entwicklung des Finanzausgleichs*, 23.

[77] The Swiss cantons also had to provide free elementary schooling, care for non-cantonal residents, naturalization of foreign nationals, and other areas without compensation. See Korioth, *Finanzausgleich*, 311; Hensel, *Finanzausgleich im Bundesstaat*, 93.

[78] Speech by Ernst Mischler, *Enquete über die Landesfinanzen*, 224.

[79] Speech by Ernst Mischler, *Enquete über die Landesfinanzen*, 224, with reference to Mischler, *Der öffentliche Haushalt in Böhmen: Ein Beitrag zur Kenntnis und Beurteilung des Finanzwesens der Selbstverwaltung in Österreich*. Leipzig and Vienna, 1887.

[80] Cf. table 18 in Wysocki, *Infrastruktur*, 71.

1910. Transport and public buildings policy similarly rose from 7.4 per cent in 1890 to 14.8 per cent in 1919. Social welfare, meanwhile, remained at a continuously high level of 17.5 per cent. The field of agriculture and agrarian modernization, which Mischler had promised a great future, remained permanently low at under 5 per cent.

Crown Lands' Revenues

The crown lands in Austria differed considerably in expenditure and revenue, reflecting their diverging economic capacity and political will to act like states. In the economically booming core area of Cisleithania, crown land budgets were funded primarily through levies with a tax-like character. Provincial assets and publicly owned companies only accounted for between 2 and 5 per cent of revenue.[81] Crown lands such as Bohemia, Moravia, Silesia, or Lower Austria already engaged with their citizens and inhabitants like fiscal states, even if they did not formally enjoy tax sovereignty. Provincial demands for funding were justified with the new duties of the service state.[82] In other crown lands such as Galicia and Bukovina, revenues from provincial assets and companies comprised almost a third of the income. These regions financed themselves more like pre-modern polities and were late in employing modern forms of taxation.[83]

The reason for this disparity was the crown lands' confusing financial system. Provincial revenues were made up of an unsystematic mix of levies and surcharges on state taxes, provincial assets, provincial enterprises, and private-sector activities (e.g. local railways) as well as fees (such as stamp duties). Furthermore, the crown lands' financial sovereignty was formally limited. They could not levy taxes on their own authority but only surcharges up to 10 per cent on existing state taxes enacted by the Viennese Parliament.

However, the crown lands regularly levied far higher surcharges than they were legally entitled to; for while these additional quotas required the emperor's approval, this was rarely withheld. Despite their dependence on state taxes (accessoriality), the provincial surcharges reached considerable proportions and demonstrate the growing fiscal power of individual crown lands. As a rule, taxation through provincial surcharges easily exceeded the amount raised by underlying direct state taxes.[84] Regionally, the percentage ranged from 36 per cent in

[81] For the following cf. *Die Landeshaushalte*, 1. 83–101.

[82] On provincial taxes cf. Mischler, *Der öffentliche Haushalt in Böhmen*, 39, 42–4.

[83] On developments during the war, see the detailed study by the Polish conservative nationalist Stanisław Głąbiński, *Finanse samodzielnej Galicyi*. Lwów, 1916.

[84] In Lower and Upper Austria, Bohemia, Moravia, Silesia, and Vorarlberg, provincial surcharges were levied only on direct taxes; in the other crown lands they also applied to consumption taxes. Reichsschatzamt, 'Österreich und Ungarn'. In *Denkschriftenband*, part 3, 258.

Trieste to 203 per cent in Dalmatia.[85] As a result, the crown lands' budgetary policy was strongly dependent on the state's tax revenue. Vienna, in turn, could neither raise nor lower taxes without affecting the crown lands' finances.

Finally, the taxpayers' ability to bear the burden was limited. Increases and reductions in the tax burden at the various levels had to be coordinated. The fiscal expert Karl Urban found a fiscal-physical metaphor for this: the budgets of the state, provinces, and municipalities represented 'three superimposed zones, each with a special tax pressure coefficient'. If the tax pressure is reduced in one zone, it increases elsewhere, with the result that the overall 'tax pressure always remains the same'.[86]

An Outdated Funds System

Fundamental budget rules for sustainable, parliamentary-controlled public finances, long formulated and implemented in other European countries, were not observed in the crown lands.[87] These rules required budgets to be transparent, complete, uniform, specialized, and accurate.[88] Unlike the budgets of Austria and Hungary, the provincial budget was not a statutory law. As a remnant of premodern estates' rights, the budget estimate was neither subject to control by an independent Audit Court nor to the Supreme Sanction, i.e. the emperor's approval.[89] Due to this fiscal autonomy, there were no mechanisms to limit ordinary provincial expenditure to available provincial revenue.[90] Repayment plans for debts already accumulated, which had been part of a sustainable financial policy in Prussia since 1891, were missing.[91] 'Debt ceilings' for the constituent states are of relatively recent origin, even in modern-day federalism.[92]

[85] In 1905 the surcharges on direct taxes, measured against these, reached a percentage share of 36.7 in Trieste, 82.4 in Lower Austria, 110.3 in Carniola, 111.5 in Upper Austria, 126.0 in Carinthia, 131.5 in Styria, 155.7 in Bohemia, 157.0 in Bukovina, 154.6 in Tyrol, 154.7 in Galicia, 157.5 in Salzburg, 166.7 in Gorizia, 169.1 in Moravia, 177.3 in Istria, 194.6 in Vorarlberg, 202.1 in Silesia and 203.3 in Dalmatia. Cf. *Die Landeshaushalte*, 1. 174–5.

[86] Speech by Karl Urban, *Enquete über die Landesfinanzen*, 180.

[87] On budget rules in a European comparison cf. Stein, *Lehrbuch der Finanzwissenschaft*, 67–77, on self-government 131.

[88] These fundamental principles are laid down in the standard works on finance of the time, see Walther Lotz, *Finanzwissenschaft*. 2nd edn. Munich, 1931, 75–81 and 125–39; Josef Kaizl, *Finanzwissenschaft*. Vol. 1. Vienna, 1900, 78–98.

[89] Lower Austria and Tyrol were exceptions, *Enquete über die Landesfinanzen*, 69 and 115.

[90] For a long time, the significance of the provinces' financial laws had been underestimated; Adolph Wagner, *Finanzwissenschaft*. Vol. 1: *Einleitung, Ordnung der Finanzwirthschaft, Finanzbedarf, Privaterwerb*. 2nd edn. Leipzig and Heidelberg, 1877, 85; Kaizl, *Finanzwissenschaft*, 1. 87–91. Also Korioth, *Finanzausgleich*, 36, 99–103.

[91] Proposals for repaying the provincial debt were made by Karl Eppinger, Assessor to the Bohemian Provincial Committee, *Enquete über die Landesfinanzen*, 9.

[92] In the Federal Republic of Germany, a debt ban took effect from 2020 to cap the expenditure of the constituent federal states. For a concise overview, see Blankart and Fasten, 'Die ökonomische Grammatik des Föderalismus', 1. 330.

The provinces' fiscal system was fundamentally outdated. The crown lands did not operate with a uniform budget that recorded, determined, and disclosed revenues, expenditures, and debts. Instead, they still relied on the so-called funds system. Here, the budget was divided into many independent budget units, which ran in parallel. Individual administrative branches each had special purpose 'funds'.[93] The Lower Austrian provincial budget, for example, consisted of the principle provincial administration fund plus 104 additional designated funds. There were twenty-five individual special-purpose funds listed for 'insane asylums', thirteen for 'maternity homes and foundling homes', and varying numbers for 'widows' homes', 'infirmaries', and other institutions for the poor. In the area of river regulation, each river was assigned a budget of its own. Other special-purpose funds concerned education, agriculture, railways, and mortgage and insurance institutions. Despite formal purpose allocation, cross-financing between these funds regularly occurred.[94] In addition, some funds were jointly financed by Austria, the crown lands, and municipalities, while others were jointly administered.[95]

The opacity of the fund system was criticized by contemporary economists, but it persisted for political reasons. As late as 1907, the provincial accounting department of Lower Austria considered a unification of the individual funds into a single provincial fund to be feasible only 'to a very limited extent'. This reserved attitude must be seen as an expression of the provinces' scepticism about too much state control of 'their' finances.[96] In turn, this scepticism was motivated by different social dynamics.

'Social Levers' Behind the Crown Lands' Finances

The financial history of the crown lands, therefore, helps us to 'study the social levers' from the perspective of a 'fiscal sociology'. Motivated by their experience of the First World War, two Viennese economists, Rudolf Goldscheid and Joseph Schumpeter, pioneered this approach.[97] With the introduction of universal male

[93] Such special-purpose funds were designed to ensure that revenue was reserved for specific expenditures, cf. Ullmann, *Der deutsche Steuerstaat*, 17–18; for a critical view, see Mischler, *Der öffentliche Haushalt in Böhmen*, 19.

[94] Franz von Myrbach-Rheinfeld, *Grundriß des Finanzrechts*. Leipzig, 1906, 303–10.

[95] For an overview, *Die Landeshaushalte*, I. 7–15.

[96] Note by the Imperial-Royal Governorate of Lower Austria concerning the regulation of the provincial finances of 21 Aug. 1907 (Pattai). Niederösterreichisches Landesarchiv (further NÖLA), Regierungsarchiv, Präsidium des Landesauschusses (hereafter LA), Reg. I/10, Stammzahl 1138/1907 Vol. 'Sanierung der Landesfinanzen', without folio. The estates had previously held the same position. Cf. Ullmann, *Der deutsche Steuerstaat*, 18.

[97] Reprinted in Joseph Schumpeter, 'Die Krise des Steuerstaats'. In Schumpeter and Rudolf Goldscheid, *Die Finanzkrise des Steuerstaats: Beiträge zur politischen Ökonomie der Staatsfinanzen*. Frankfurt am Main, 1976, 332. For a summary, see: Wolfgang Fritz and Gertrude Mikl-Horke, *Rudolf Goldscheid: Finanzsoziologie und ethische Sozialwissenschaft*. Vienna, 2007, 163–5.

suffrage to the Austrian House of Deputies in 1907, the social effects of the fiscal system had become apparent to all. Many social groups had obtained a parliamentary mouthpiece at the state level.[98] Universal suffrage did not apply to the provincial parliaments, however.[99] This resulted in a deepening conflict between parliamentary majorities in the Vienna Imperial Council and those in the provinces.

The Social Democrats accused the provincial parliaments and provincial standing committees of restricting suffrage to the privileged and of focusing exclusively on the interests of the provincial elites, especially in agriculture and social welfare. The social concerns of the workers, it was argued, were insufficiently noted in the provinces, even though they paid the provincial levies and surcharges.[100] Karl Renner, the leading Social Democrat, criticized Habsburg fiscal federalism. 'In the state, crown land, and municipality, it is always a different class and different people that administer', he said, and that 'appropriate funds from the pockets of others'.[101] For the democrat Renner, the broader fiscal sovereignty of the provinces had necessarily to go hand in hand with the introduction of universal suffrage.

Josef Kaizl, the national economist, Young Czech nationalist, and short-term Austrian minister of finance, viewed the 'social levers' from a national perspective. He criticized the reality that some nationalities were privileged over others.[102] Kaizl pioneered the idea of a nationally just distribution of expenditures and taxation. Public services and goods should not be distributed in such a way 'that more is given to some circles or crown lands, or classes, or nationalities and less to others'.[103] If certain population groups were systematically discriminated against, even equally levied taxes would lose legitimacy. 'All too often', Kaizl argued, 'the advantages of institutions established and maintained by the state are limited to a few circles.'[104] In Istria or Dalmatia, for example, the Italian-dominated provincial committee delayed equal funding for Slovene-Croatian projects. In Galicia, the Ruthenians were similarly disadvantaged.[105] Kaizl emphasized the need for reciprocity in a community; since the citizens had to 'cooperate

[98] Cf. Chapter 11.

[99] Birgitta Bader-Zaar, 'The "Grande Affaire": Wahlrechtsreformen in Europa und Nordamerika im "langen" 19. Jahrhundert'. In Thomas Simon (ed.), *Hundert Jahre allgemeines und gleiches Wahlrecht in Österreich*. Frankfurt am Main, 2010, 13–35.

[100] Speech by Karl Renner, *Enquete über die Landesfinanzen*, 186 and 188.

[101] Speech by Karl Renner, *Enquete über die Landesfinanzen*, 69.

[102] Kaizl, *Finanzwissenschaft*, 2. 201.

[103] The Czech edition appeared in 1892, nine years before the German version.

[104] Kaizl, *Finanzwissenschaft*, 2. 201.

[105] Wiggermann, *Kriegsmarine und Politik*, 125. On the relationship between Italians and Croats in Dalmatia cf. Luciano Monzali, *The Italians of Dalmatia: From Italian Unification to World War I*. Toronto, 2009.

in the state's activities', they were entitled to regard themselves as 'the object of its care and efforts'.[106]

In the ethnically mixed crown lands where different nationalities already sat in the diets as equal partners, the nationalization of public services often led to an explosion in expenditure. 'In Austria, everything is duplicated, triplicated, and quadruplicated; everyone wants their own', one expert said.[107] In the 'dualism of national expenditure' in Bohemia and Moravia, 'every crown granted for German purposes is matched by at least one crown for Czech purposes'.[108] This exponentially growing provincial expenditure was concentrated on education, arts, and culture, as well as agriculture.

Verdicts on the distribution of financial means by nationality in the crown lands varied widely. Some financial experts considered it irresponsible due to the resulting debts, while others regarded it as necessary for national fiscal equality and tax fairness.[109] Some Germans, hitherto privileged, denounced the 'equality and equal rights machinations of the Slavic peoples of Austria' as a 'Potemkin village'. Without any historical justification, they decried 'the notorious "cultural demands" of the Czechs, Poles, Ruthenians, Slovenes and Croats [that] mean just as much looting and pillaging of the Germans' tax coffers'.[110] The caricature shown at the beginning of this chapter could also have been applied, with a different caption, to the relationship between 'Germans' and 'Slavs'. Conversely, Czech national economists accused their German compatriots of pursuing economic hegemony.[111] The nationality conflict, which was played out in the private sector in the form of growing economic nationalism, increasingly affected financial policy of the imperial state and the crown lands.

In addition to ethnicization, the crown lands' finances were also politicized. The party-political competition for votes and costly election promises drove up provincial expenditures. Members of the provincial diets habitually showed 'too little resistance to the many wishes that, although not unreasonable in themselves, were incompatible with the financial situation of the crown lands'.[112] Due to an

[106] Kaizl, *Finanzwissenschaft*, 2. 201. For a moral-philosophical justification, cf. Kaizl's Prague colleague Emil Sax, *Grundlegung der theoretischen Staatswirthschaft*. Vienna, 1887, 465–6.

[107] Speech by Ernst Mischler, *Enquete über die Landesfinanzen*, 228.

[108] Friedrich Kleinwächter, 'Die österreichische Enquete über die Landesfinanzen (March 1908)', *Jahrbücher für Nationalökonomie und Statistik*, 93 (1909), 52.

[109] See the instructive debates in the Bohemian Parliament on financial restructuring on 29 Dec. 1906. Cf. also Kaizl, *Finanzwissenschaft*, 2. 201. On ethnicizing the state administration, cf. also Karl Renner's speech, *Enquete über die Landesfinanzen*, 191.

[110] Anton Schubert, *Das Deutschtum im Wirtschaftshaushalte Österreichs: Ein Ausbauversuch der Schrift 'Deutschböhmen als Wirtschaftsgrossmacht' für ganz Österreich*. Vol. 1: *Der Besitzstand der Deutschen in Österreich*. Reichenberg, 1905, 5 and 8.

[111] Albín Bráf, *Národohospodářské potřeby české*. Prague, 1908, 9–10.

[112] Richard Pfaundler, *Der Finanzausgleich in Österreich: Ein Beitrag zur Entwicklungsgeschichte der finanziellen Beziehungen zwischen Staat, Ländern und Gemeinden in den Jahren 1896 bis 1927*. Vienna, 1927, 16. Cf. Paul Kompert, 'Die Reform der Budgetierung in den österreichischen Landesfinanzwirtschaften', *Jahrbuch für Gesetzgebung, Verwaltung und Volkswirtschaft im Deutschen*

'addiction to popularity', they would 'increasingly move away from being representatives of the whole land and see their main task in gaining as many advantages as possible for their constituency'.[113] One financial expert particularly criticized the 'unsuccessful local railway campaign' in Austria: a large number of the local railways built turned out 'on closer inspection to be nothing more than campaign expenses'. Conditions prevailed 'like in Hungary', which was notorious for the collusion between parliamentarians and railway consortia.[114] Indeed, the influence of party politicians, who promised their voters, like children at Christmas, a railway and received public loans in return, as for example in Bohemia, was hardly insignificant.

10.4. Cooperation on Fiscal Equalization

The Cisleithanian crown lands expanded their state activities, leading many to enter a debt spiral by the end of the nineteenth century. They now required support from the Austrian government in Vienna. In the negotiations on a new fiscal equalization system in 1896, Vienna treated the crown lands for the first time as a single political entity. Previously, the Austrian Ministry of Finance negotiated provincial surcharges on state taxes bilaterally, province by province. Now that state and crown lands sat together at the same table, it was possible to impose more uniform taxation across the board. The previous bilateral negotiations, which had led to inequality among the crown lands, gave way to a cooperative compromise.

The appreciation of the crown lands' ruling elites that they were collectively stronger than the sum of their parts gave them greater confidence and resilience. In 1905, an informal forum, the provincial conferences, was created through which the elites circumvented the imperial ban on political cooperation between the provinces. They stood shoulder to shoulder to protect their interests against Vienna. In Cisleithania, the crown lands coordinated their fiscal policy demands vis-à-vis the imperial authorities. In hyperbolical fashion, they characterized their alliance as bound by *solidarity*.

An innovative instrument—the federal fiscal equalization scheme—was produced to balance fiscal interests between the Austrian part of the empire and the crown lands. The term 'fiscal equalization' was only coined in the 1920s, but in

Reich, 34 (1910), 139–50; Paul Grünwald, 'Zur Finanzstatistik der autonomen Selbstverwaltung in Österreich', *Zeitschrift für Volkswirtschaft, Sozialpolitik und Verwaltung*, 19 (1910), 68–119.

[113] Speech by Otto Steinwender, *Enquete über die Landesfinanzen*, 119.

[114] Speech by Ferdinand Schmid, *Enquete über die Landesfinanzen*, 167. On local lobbyism in Bohemian railway construction in Bohemia cf. Milan Hlavačka, *Zlatý věk české samosprávy*. Prague, 2006, 125; Stanislav Pavlíček, *Naše lokálky*. Prague, 2002. On Hungary cf. András Cieger, 'The Ways of Enrichment and its Interpretations in Hungarian Politics after the Austro-Hungarian Compromise of 1867', *Střed/Centre*, 7/1 (2015), 38.

reality, it was first seen in late nineteenth-century Switzerland, where it regulated financial relations between the Swiss Confederation and the cantons.[115] Fiscal equalizations primarily distribute fiscal and tax sovereignty rights among the territorial units of a state.[116]

A necessary component of any fiscal equalization scheme is the vertical distribution between the entire state, its member units, and the municipalities. Horizontal distribution, which spreads finances among equal territorial units, such as provinces, is possible only in certain cases. These horizontal transfers allow reallocations that make the result of vertical tax distribution fairer. Such horizontal mechanisms became established in only a few countries worldwide, such as Germany, Austria, and Switzerland, as well as Canada and Australia, and even then only after the First World War.[117]

The Austrian State–Crown Lands Fiscal Equalization of 1896

Originally, fiscal equalization was only practised in the context of Austro-Hungarian dualism. It was not until 1896 that the Personal Income Tax Reform Bill introduced such an arrangement for Austria and its crown lands. This equalization of interests was initiated by the Austrian Ministry of Finance, but from 1898 the process included consultation with the provincial standing committees, an uncharted territory in the political landscape of the empire.[118]

Building on the experience of other European countries, the reform of 1896 tapped into a new source of revenue.[119] In contrast to stagnating property taxes, the personal income tax promised continuously growing revenues. In order to prevent additional provincial surcharges that would undermine taxpayer honesty and compliance and thus the effectiveness of the new state tax, the Austrian Ministry of Finance made sure to win the crown lands' approval.[120] The provinces waived their right to add surcharges on the tax and, in return, received transfers from the Austrian state funded by the new revenue. This windfall amounted to 6 million crowns in 1896, 8 million crowns in 1906, and 21 million crowns in 1909.[121]

115 Hensel, *Finanzausgleich im Bundesstaat*, 15; Pfaundler, *Finanzausgleich in Österreich*.

116 Korioth, *Finanzausgleich*, 22.

117 Korioth, *Finanzausgleich*, 22–3. and 28–33. For a global comparison cf. Roland Sturm, *Föderalismus: Eine Einführung*. 2nd edn. Baden-Baden, 2010, 113–22; Oates, 'Fiscal Federalism', 1127–8.

118 Hans Peter Hye, 'Die "Länderkonferenz". 1905–1907. Ein Versuch gemeinsamer politischer Willensfindung der politischen Eliten der Länder'. In Jan Janák (ed.), *Ústřední moc a regionální samospráva*. Brno, 1995, 282.

119 Pfaundler, *Finanzausgleich in Österreich*, 2.

120 On this and the following Pfaundler, *Finanzausgleich in Österreich*, 1–6.

121 Pfaundler, *Finanzausgleich in Österreich*, 329.

The Austrian state and the crown lands maintained their cooperation in subsequent years. In 1898, the Ministry of Finance proposed a new regulation for the taxation of spirits and beer. It once again wanted to replace the disparate state surcharges with direct state transfers.[122] In November 1899, every provincial standing committee communicated its agreement to the ministry. Their decision was fuelled by expectations of profits three times higher than the revenue from the personal income tax.[123] Ultimately, however, the Dalmatian Diet refused to approve this informal agreement between the Austrian government and the provincial standing committees, not for substantive but for domestic reasons.[124] A few months later, the Vienna Imperial Council therefore amended only the taxation of spirits. The provinces waived their provincial surcharges and, in return, received a share of the revenue.[125] Each year after 1906, the additional revenue for the crown lands from direct state transfers of the spirits levy was within a range of 20 to 22 million crowns.[126] An exclusive state beer tax, however, did not materialize; instead, the Austrian government agreed to separate beer levies in each province.[127]

The provincial beer levies became the most important revenue for the crown lands. To consumers, the provinces now appeared as new and independent tax and regulatory authorities, a status that had been impossible to attain under the previous regime of taxes, levies, and surcharges.[128] Indeed, the beer tax alone effectively turned the Austrian crown lands into fiscal states.[129] However, revenue from this source could not be increased as any attempts to do so were regularly met with strong opposition. As one brewery journal wrote, 'the liquid bread of the poor is burdened enough by taxes and levies as is'.[130]

[122] On the following Pfaundler, *Finanzausgleich in Österreich*, 6–13.

[123] Pfaundler, *Finanzausgleich in Österreich*, 8.

[124] The Dalmatian provincial budget would have benefited from the transfers, Haira Lacmanović-Heydenreuter, *Dalmatien in Wien: Die dalmatinischen Abgeordneten im Wiener Reichsrat 1867–1918*. Hamburg, 2011, 345–8. The prevailing view in the Dalmatian parliament was that the state was unduly siphoning off the fiscal power of the population. This view underlies recent studies on the Dalmatian Diet, such as Ivo Perić, *Dalmatinski sabor*. Zadar, 1978, 202–6; Alexander Buczynski, 'Der dalmatinische Landtag'. In Helmut Rumpler and Peter Urbanitsch (eds), *Die Habsburgermonarchie 1848–1918*. Vol. 7: *Verfassung und Parlamentarismus*. Subvol. 2: *Die regionalen Repräsentativkörperschaften*. Vienna, 2000, 1972–3.

[125] Gesetz über die Erhöhung der Branntweinabgabe und die Zuweisung eines Teils ihres Ertrages an die Landesfonde, No. 86/1901 RGBl. Provinces that expected a loss from a waiver of the surcharge were thereby placed in a better position.

[126] Pfaundler, *Finanzausgleich in Österreich*, 239.

[127] Pfaundler, *Finanzausgleich in Österreich*, 7 and 41–2.

[128] Review by Friedrich Wieser, *Enquete über die Landesfinanzen*, 277.

[129] On the renegotiations cf. *Stenographisches Protokoll über die am 27. Februar 1909 im Herrensaal des niederösterreichischen Landhauses stattgefundene Konferenz der Landesausschüsse in Angelegenheit der Landes-Bierauflage*. Vienna, 1909.

[130] 'Die Sanierung der Landesfinanzen', *Gambrinus. Brauerei- und Hopfenzeitung*, 32/3–4 (1905), 102 and 143.

The Crown Lands' Conferences on the Restructuring of Finances

The search for new fiscal sources led the Austrian crown lands to a new form of collaboration. In 1905, for the first time since the meeting of the Central Committee of the Estates in 1848, crown land representatives sought agreement and common ground among themselves before approaching the government.[131] Negotiations between the crown lands over financial reform reveal how political and financial interdependence was no longer limited to bilateral cooperation between the Austrian state and a single crown land. These conferences on the remediation of provincial finances are an expression of *horizontal* cooperation. The self-awareness of a community of equal provinces cooperating with each other is characteristic of federalism and distinguishes it from the asymmetrical distribution of power found in empires.

The development of fiscal equalization marks the transition from a cooperative empire to cooperative federalism, albeit only in Austria. The initiative was taken by the Moravian Provincial Committee, which in autumn 1904 invited all other Cisleithanian provincial committees, as well as some representatives of the Viennese government, to 'a congress dedicated to reforming the provincial finances'.[132] Moravia emphasized the urgent need for reforms. Growing provincial expenditure, together with consistently low revenues, produced ever higher debts, provincial taxes, and surcharges. Therefore, it was time to grant the crown lands a tax of their own. Through its proposal, the Moravian Provincial Committee was preaching to the choir. Even the Austrian Prime Minister Paul Gautsch admitted, in a speech during the budget debate in the Austrian Chamber of Deputies, that the provinces' financial situation was precarious and promised support.[133]

Following the Moravian initiative, other crown lands presented their reform ideas. The ideas of networking, solidarity, and institutionalizing political cooperation were central and help us to analyse the provincial elites' self-understanding within the federal system. These discussions not only illustrate fiscal policy details and innovations but reveal the possibilities and limits of fiscal solidarity and cooperation between the crown lands.

The most radical proposal came from the Istrian Provincial Committee. It sought to consolidate the idea of cooperation in financial matters initiated by

[131] The crown lands' conferences were initiated by Moravia and organized by Lower Austria in Vienna. Therefore, the authoritative records are held in the Moravský zemský archiv (Moravian Provincial Archives, hereafter MZA) and the Niederösterreichischen Landesarchiv.

[132] The initiative was based on a motion by the Young Czech member of the Moravian Diet Václav Šílený of Nov. 1903, supported by the Diet, cf. Moravian Provincial Committee of 17 Sept. 1904, ref. 64081/1904. MZA, Zemský výbor (hereafter ZV), Box 2772 Konference sanace 1905, fol. 596.

[133] Speech by Prime Minister Gautsch on 14 Feb. 1905. Stenographic Minutes of the House of Deputies, 17th Session, p. 27117.

Moravia and extend it to other political issues.[134] This proposal diametrically opposed the imperial logic of the provincial constitutions, in particular the ban on cooperation between the provinces. To the Istrian politicians, this prohibition seemed outdated. Mutual agreement on important political issues was 'not only advisable for the provinces, but also certainly successful in most cases'. Finances could be restructured 'more easily or at least more securely' if the conference of the crown lands planned for February 1905 was 'given a permanent character'.

Istria emphasized the common interests of the crown lands in relation to the empire. Imperial legislation, draft bills, and international treaties should be examined at an early stage to uncover their financial impact on the crown lands. As long as the Imperial Council could pass framework laws without having to take financial responsibility for their implementation (which devolved to the crown lands), the latter could not adequately draft their budgets. In fact, many policy areas were regulated by the Austrian state, but implemented and financed by provinces, which had no influence over them.

The first conference of the provincial committees on a new financial equalization system took place at Moravia's invitation from 16 to 18 February 1905 in the House of the Lower Austrian Diet in Vienna's Herrengasse.[135] Delegates of the provincial committees from all crown lands except Trieste attended. Among them were provincial governors (*Landeshauptmänner*), provincial audit counsellors (*Landesrechnungsräte*), a representative of the city of Vienna, as well as high-ranking officials from the Austrian Ministries of Finance and the Interior.[136] The event was well received by the press, with extensive and detailed coverage in the major newspapers.[137] The idea of institutionalized cooperation between the crown lands was the first item on the agenda. In the press, this idea was labelled the 'Austrian Council of Provinces'.[138] Since the Austrian crown lands were not represented by a parliamentary chamber, a 'Council of Provinces' would have served as their institutional mouthpiece.

The provincial representatives spoke in favour of such an approach for reasons of cooperation and solidarity. Within a few days, however, the Istrian initiative

[134] On this and the following, cf. letter from the provincial governor Ludovico Rizzi in Parenzo to the Moravian provincial committee in Brno, 18 Jan. 1905. MZA, ZV, Box 2772 Konference sanace 1905, fols. 397–9.

[135] Konferenz der Landesausschüsse betreffend die Regelung der Landesfinanzen 1905.

[136] Konferenz der Landesausschüsse betreffend die Regelung der Landesfinanzen 1905, 5–6. Cf. Österreichisches Staatsarchiv Wien, Abteilung Finanz- und Hofkammerarchiv, Finanzministerium (hereafter ÖStA, FHKA, FinMin), Reg. Dept. III, Zl. 5334/.1905, Länderkonferenz 1905, Teilnahme des Innen- und des Finanzministeriums.

[137] 'Die Konferenzen der österreichischen Landesausschüsse', *Vaterland* (Abendblatt), 18 Feb. 1905, 1–2; 'Ein österreichischer Länderrat', *Neues Wiener Tagblatt* (Tagesausgabe), 18 Feb. 1905, 8. The following articles are more concise: 'Ein österreichischer Länderrat', *Reichspost*, 19 Feb. 1905, 9; 'Ein österreichischer Länderrat', *(Linzer) Tages-Post*, 19 Feb. 1905, 3; 'Ein österreichischer Länderrat', *(Neuigkeits) Welt Blatt*, 19 Feb. 1905, 5.

[138] Other important topics had already been discussed, namely a comparative statistical study of provincial finances, studies on the fiscal connection of provincial revenue with 'modern social tendencies', administrative reforms, and reforms of the workers' insurance. For the press echo see above.

failed.[139] The Galician provincial committee had announced in advance that Galicia would not participate in a permanent 'conference of provinces'. It would only take part in occasional meetings on financial restructuring. Its delegates argued dryly and legalistically that a federation of the provincial committees 'would not be compatible with the provisions of the provincial statute and, moreover, would run counter to the political and constitutional position of the provincial diets and committees'.[140] Behind this coded reference to the prohibition of cooperation lay Galicia's easily decipherable strategy of maintaining the privileged position it had won in 1868. This victory was not to be jeopardized by new forms of negotiation that would recognize other provinces as Galicia's peers with equal rights. Self-interest prevailed over the common interest.

Bohemia was also less than enthusiastic. At the same time, however, the province's financial crisis had taken on breathtaking proportions.[141] In order to cover its ordinary provincial expenditure, the crown land was taking out loans at an unsustainable rate. By 1907, they already constituted a quarter of the budget.[142] In the Bohemian Diet, the German-speaking opposition repeatedly declared that this spending policy would lead to a 'slippery slope'.[143] Czech nationalists, on the other hand, welcomed the deficits because they served to ethnicize the education system. The expenses were also linked to a hypothetical Czech 'Compromise'. Karel Baxa, the Czech nationalist and future mayor of Prague, suggested that the loans would be repaid by a future independent 'Bohemian province'. His provocative argument implied that, if a settlement based on historic state law was not forthcoming, the Austrian imperial state would have to shoulder the enormous debts itself.[144] The gamble failed, however. In 1913, Bohemia, fiscally paralysed by the nationalities conflict, was placed under curatorship. The (unconstitutional) Anna Patents replaced the provincial diet and committee with a state-appointed '*Landesverwaltungskommission*' (provincial administrative commission).[145]

In earlier years, the Austrian Ministry of Finance had repeatedly made concessions to Bohemia to cover its deficits, as in 1905, when similar commitments were

[139] Tagesordnung für die erste Conferenz der Landesausschüsse der im Reichsrate vertretenen Königreiche und Länder. MZA, ZV, Box 2772 Konference sanace 1905, fol. 400.

[140] Galician Provincial Committee in Lemberg (Lwów, Lviv) to Moravian Provincial Committee in Brno, 6 Feb. 1905. MZA, ZV, Box 2772 Konference sanace 1905, fols. 420 and 438.

[141] Until the end of the 1880s, the Bohemian provincial budget was on a stable track. Mischler, *Der öffentliche Haushalt in Böhmen*, 3–4.

[142] The provincial budget for 1907 was 82 million crowns, which included a deficit of almost 19 million crowns.

[143] Karl Buquoy and Karl Max Zedtwitz, *Gutachten vom 15.4.1906, Bericht des Landesausschusses mit Vorlage der von den einzelnen Landtagsabgeordneten erstatteten Gutachten in Angelegenheit der Sanierung der Landesfinanzen*. Print No. 962/1906 of the Bohemian Diet, 43–64.

[144] Expert opinion by Karel Baxa of 5 Apr. 1906, quoted in the speech by Ferdinand Schmid, *Enquete über die Landesfinanzen*, 169.

[145] Lothar Höbelt, 'Bohemia 1913: A Consensual Coup d'état?', *Parliaments, Estates and Representation*, 20/1 (2000), 207–14. With a focus on the provincial finances cf. Jaromír Patočka, 'Zemská správní komise pro Království české v letech 1913 a 1914' [The State Administrative Commission for the Kingdom of Bohemia in 1913 and 1914] (university diss.). Charles University Prague 2006. Cf. Chapter 8.5.

made to Galicia.[146] Today, Vienna would be accused of a decades-long 'bail-out' of Bohemia's overspending.[147] At the same time, Bohemian representatives made sporadic attempts to create an authority within the ministerial bureaucracy to represent the fiscal interests of all the provinces. During an intensive discussion, the financial officer of the Bohemian provincial committee, Karl Urban, asked the Ministry of Finance to establish a legally backed advisory board to the government on the autonomous finances of the provinces.[148] The ministry flirted with the idea, especially with the possibility of having 'external manpower available to produce thorough reports on the individual provincial budgets', but ultimately rejected it.[149]

Lower Austria, like Bohemia a fiscal donor to the empire, wavered equally between solidarity among the provinces and its own fiscal interests. Robert Pattai, a member of the Lower Austrian Diet and disciple of the German nationalist, anti-clerical, and anti-Semitic Schönerer movement,[150] had initially adopted Istria's proposal for regular political cooperation at the conference of the crown lands. He justified this by saying 'that certain common points of interest in Austria must be maintained [and] that the crown lands must come closer together in certain respects'. He went on to declare 'that there are men and crown lands who are rigidly federalist and there are those who tend towards centralism. But…we are all autonomists (applause), even those of us from the German crown lands'.[151] In a nutshell, the crown lands should cooperate when it was in their common interest but be spared the influence of others when pursuing their individual provincial interests.

After three days of negotiations at the first conference of the crown lands in February 1905, the nearly fifty provincial representatives were unable to agree on a model for debt relief, financial distribution, or political cooperation. They did, however, set up a seventeen-member commission to work out more concrete 'principles of restructuring' by the summer and autumn of 1905. In their final resolution, the crown lands proposed a provincial share of the Austrian state's *total* tax revenues, as well as provincial taxes of their own. In addition, the state

[146] After the abolition of propination, Galicia had been promised an increase in the provincial beer surcharge. Bohemia, meanwhile, was promised an increase in the surcharges on direct taxes as well as an increase in the tax on spirits. The latter could not be implemented immediately due to a lack of agreement from Hungary, cf. Referentenerinnerung des k. k. Finanzministeriums. ÖStA, FHKA, FinMin, Reg. dept. III, Zl. 66229/1905.

[147] That the assumption of provincial debts by the state does not prevent further debt is shown by recent examples, see Blankart and Fasten, 'Die ökonomische Grammatik des Föderalismus', 1. 328–30. In theoretical terms, Oates, 'Fiscal Federalism', 1139.

[148] Rejecting note of the Imperial-Royal Ministry of Finance of 9 Nov. 1905. ÖStA, FHKA, FinMin, Reg. dept. III, Länderfinanzen, Zl. 72180/1905.

[149] Note by the Imperial-Royal Ministry of Finance. ÖStA, FHKA, FinMin, Reg. dept. III, Länderfinanzen, Zl. 72180/1905.

[150] On Pattai John W. Boyer, *Karl Lueger (1844–1910). Christian Social Politics as a Profession.* Vienna, 2010, 42.

[151] Konferenz der Landesausschüsse betreffend die Regelung der Landesfinanzen 1905, 72.

was to absorb the costs for security and 'military quartering', which had previously been covered by the provinces.[152]

Although a majority of the crown lands was in favour of permanent cooperation, the 'Commission of Seventeen', in its internal deliberations, soon abandoned the idea of a standing 'Council of Provinces'. As the rapporteur Hugo Fux, vice-governor of Moravia, noted, without Galicia and Bohemia, a permanent body of the remaining provinces made no sense. In an attempt to find a silver lining, Fux surmised that 'cooperation on a case-by-case basis will have the same weight as a permanent body, and I would argue that it will be even more effective because it will be driven solely by genuine interest'.[153]

Ministerial Reservations

Without the institutionalization of cooperation between the crown lands, the plans for a new fiscal equalization system initiated 'from below' soon faltered. The autumn deadline for the Commission of Seventeen's restructuring principles was not met, for what were later described as 'political reasons'.[154] In addition, the dates for further crown lands' conferences and ministerial meetings were repeatedly postponed.[155] Internal notes from the Ministry of Finance reveal the attitudes of central officials. They rejected the provinces' proposals 'because of the political nature of these negotiations' and considered them 'totally unacceptable from a government point of view'.[156] Behind the 'political reasons' lay concerns about further federalization: In a 1906 memorandum, Richard Reisch, an economist and ministerial councillor in the Ministry of Finance, noted, 'I make no secret of the fact that I am no friend of, if I may say so, the federalization of taxation and duties because...it is only too likely to promote federalization in the political sense and to shake the very essence of the modern unitary state: economic unity.'[157] In 1906, therefore, the crown lands did nothing to restructure provincial

[152] Report of the Moravian Provincial Committee on the Regulation of Provincial Finances, LA-Print No. 97/1905. MZA, ZV, Box 2772 Konference sanace 1905, fols. 4–7, here 5. However, provincial expenditure on the military rarely exceeded 1 per cent. See also *Die Landeshaushalte*, 1. 130–1.

[153] Paper by Dr Hugo Fux, Deputy Governor of Moravia, on the motion of the Istrian Provincial Committee concerning the regulation of joint action by the crown lands to safeguard common interests, and the motion by Dr Pattai on the same question, submitted at the meeting of 18 Feb. 1905 of the Conference of Provincial Committees, Brno in September 1905. MZA, ZV, Box 2772 Konference sanace 1905, fols. 314–17.

[154] Report of the Salzburg Provincial Committee of 6 Mar. 1907. In *Verhandlungen des Salzburger Landtages. IV. session of the 9th period 1906/1907*. Salzburg, 1907, 1177.

[155] Pfaundler, *Finanzausgleich in Österreich*, 15. On the convening and subsequent rescheduling, see the letters of various provincial committees and the Imperial-Royal Ministry of Finance. NÖLA, LA, Stammzahl 1138/1907.

[156] Note by the Imperial-Royal Ministry of Finance. ÖStA, FHKA, FinMin, Reg. dept. III, Länderfinanzen, Zl. 72180/1905, and Länderkonferenzen, Zl. 8685/1905.

[157] Analysis by Ministerialrat Reisch on the question of the restructuring of the provincial finances of 20 Feb. 1906. ÖStA, FHKA, FinMin, allgemeine Reihe, Zl. 12854/1906 without folio.

finances.[158] In the meantime, a new Department for Autonomous Provincial Finances was set up in the Imperial-Royal Ministry of Finance. As this department collected statistical data about the provincial finances, agency over fiscal policy was imperceptibly returned to the Viennese financial bureaucracy. The Ministry of Finance and the Central Statistical Commission took over the task of collecting the provincial data needed to plan reform. The complexity of the outdated fund system and the reluctance of many provinces to disclose financial information made this a difficult undertaking.[159] The first systematic statistical appraisal of provincial finances took several years to compile. Nevertheless, it laid a solid foundation for further financial research.[160] Moreover, the Ministry of Finance used the audit to impose its own timetable.[161] It had been well aware of the provinces' short time horizon and the public's expectations for overcoming the debt crisis as soon as possible. Within the ministry, however, 'the year 1909 was regarded as the year of the comet as far as provincial finances were concerned'.[162]

Despite having initiated discussions on a new system of fiscal equalization, the crown lands did not intervene in the planning process until 1907. In the meantime, provincial debts reached new heights. Following the example of Bohemia, Silesia, Moravia, and Styria now also resorted to loans to cover their ordinary expenses.[163] During discussions in the diets on the 1907 budget, the restructuring programme came up again. In order to achieve at least a temporary arrangement while the financial reform promised for 1909 was pending, Moravia again initiated a conference of the crown lands. The goal was 'not only extensive permanent state aid…but also rapid aid'.[164] The provincial representatives of Salzburg and

[158] The Lower Austrian members of the Commission of Seventeen for Provincial Finances were simultaneously tasked with preparing electoral reform. Therefore, the Commission did not convene in 1906. Cf. letter of Lower Austrian Provincial Governor Schmolk to the Moravian Provincial Committee, Vienna, 12 Nov. 1906. MZA, ZV, Box 2639 Sanování zemských financí, fol. 220.

[159] For missing information, cf. the letter of the Imperial-Royal Ministry of Finance to the Lower Austrian Provincial Committee of 19 Aug. 1907. NÖLA, LA, Stammzahl 1138/1907, fol. 2639.

[160] The results were published in eighteen volumes, see *Die Landeshaushalte*. As early as 1886, the lack of financial statistics was criticized. Mischler, *Der öffentliche Haushalt in Böhmen*, 2.

[161] Due to the 'highly political nature' of the provincial finances, the Imperial-Royal Ministry of Finance preferred consultations with the Ministries of the Interior, Education, and Agriculture; note by Section Councillor Reisch of 26 July 1905. ÖStA, FHKA, FinMin, Reg.

[162] Exposé by Ministerialrat Reisch on the question of restructuring the provincial finances of 20 Feb. 1906. In ÖStA, FHKA, FinMin, allgemeine Reihe, Zl. 12854/1906 without folio.

[163] *Stenographisches Protokoll über die am 9. Juni 1907 im niederösterreichischen Landhause zu Wien abgehaltene Konferenz der Landesausschüsse der im Reichsrate vertretenen Königreiche und Länder betreffend die Regelung der Landesfinanzen*. Vienna, 1907, 4 (quote), 8, 12, and 17.

[164] On 26 Oct. 1906, the Moravian Provincial Committee requested the Lower Austrian Provincial Committee to convene the next meeting on provincial finances as soon as possible, see note from the Moravian Provincial Committee to the Salzburg Provincial Committee of May 1906. MZA, ZV, Box 2639, fol. 217. Quote in note from the Moravian Provincial Committee to the Imperial-Royal Moravian Governorate, Brno of 3 May 1907. MZA, ZV, Box 2639, fols. 209–10.

Silesia joined forces with Moravia. They accused the government of being 'unwilling to listen to the cry of distress from the provinces'.[165]

The crown lands' conference of 9 June 1907 on the reorganization of provincial finances reached an even wider audience than the one in 1905. All members of the Imperial Council had received identical memoranda from the provincial committees in advance, asking them to bring forth an emergency motion. Most members of parliament signed, crossing national and ideological divides. They called on the government to 'fully and permanently restore the finances of the provinces'. A draft of the bill was to be presented to the 'Crown Lands' Conference of Provincial Committees' for consideration.[166] In his speech from the throne on 19 June 1907, the emperor promised that his government would 'submit certain proposals after extensive preparatory work has been completed'. It may have come from the emperor's mouth, but the promise was exceedingly vague.[167] After the introduction of universal suffrage on the state level, the Social Democrats had taken their seats in the Chamber of Deputies of the Imperial Council for the first time. They recognized the urgent need to restructure provincial finances but made support for a solution contingent on the introduction of universal suffrage in the provinces. This stalemate unveiled the social implications of the distribution conflict between the imperial state and the alliance of the provinces.

The provinces' accusation that the Imperial-Royal Ministry of Finance was deaf to their 'cry of distress' was unjustified. It is true, however, that the ministerial windmills turned more slowly than the crown lands' frantic merry-go-round of debt. The ministerial bureaucracy had long since realized, without saying so publicly, that it would 'have to initiate a major action in which a rather impressive number of millions would have to be set in motion'.[168] In setting course for the new system of financial equalization, it even drew on the resolutions of the crown lands' conferences of 1905 and 1907. There, the provinces had demanded, first, the transfer of an exclusively provincial tax; secondly, general fiscal transfers detached from specific purposes; and, thirdly, state responsibility for the costs of

[165] Quote in the circular letter from Salzburg Provincial Committee to Moravian Provincial Committee, Salzburg of 15 Apr. 1907. MZA, ZV, Box 2639, fols. 218–19. See also copy Silesian Provincial Committee to Imperial-Royal Ministry of Finance, Troppau of 25 Apr. 1907. MZA, ZV, Box 2639, fol. 215.

[166] Resolutions of the Conference. Konferenz der Landesausschüsse betreffend die Regelung der Landesfinanzen 1907, 27. On the Moravian instruction: Niederösterreichischer Landesausschuss in Angelegenheit der von der Länderkonferenz am 9. Juni in Wien in der Frage der Sanierung der Landesfinanzen gefassten Beschlüsse. Meeting document of the Moravian Provincial Committee, Brno, 13 June 1907. MZA, ZV, Box 2639, fol. 194.

[167] Specifically, he mentioned a new regulation of the building, inheritance, and gift tax, Throne Speech of 19 June 1907. *Stenographische Protokolle des Abgeordnetenhauses, 18th Session*, Supplement 1, 1–4, here 3.

[168] Analysis by Ministerial Councillor Reisch on the restructuring of the provincial finances of 20 Feb. 1906. ÖStA, FHKA, FinMin, allgemeine Reihe, Zl. 12854/1906, without folio.

primary education, the military, and the gendarmerie, as well as of the repatriation of the poor, public health, and river regulation.[169]

Within the ministry, the official in charge of the project won plaudits for his decision to transfer part of the cost of primary education to the treasury of the imperial state.[170] Attention now focused on this field; experts and statisticians sought to gain an 'exhaustive overview of the school system and expenditure on primary education in the individual provinces' by 'critically examining the individual provincial estimates'.[171] The Imperial-Royal Ministry of Finance refused to release any information before the task was complete.[172] This lack of communication and transparency was perceived by the provinces as indifference to their plight.

The Enquête on the Provincial Finances

The Imperial-Royal Ministry of Finance convened an investigation—known by the French term 'enquête'—in March 1908. Enquêtes were popular at the time as specialist forums for the exchange of knowledge and expert opinion. They dealt with issues as diverse as administrative reform, social welfare, trade and trade exports, property taxes, and marriage law.[173] In practice, the enquêtes provided an interface between the imperial state and society, representing a broad spectrum of opinions and involving experts from politics, society, and academia in the state's decision-making processes.[174]

The extensive material which informed the Enquête on the finances of the provinces was published in advance.[175] Through a questionnaire, the Imperial-Royal Ministry of Finance collected expert opinions on the causes of the provinces' various financial crises and on the three proposed solutions (the transfer of

[169] Konferenz der Landesausschüsse betreffend die Regelung der Landesfinanzen 1905, on the gendarmerie 9, 12, 15, 17, 19, 41, 55, 57; on repatration of the poor 12; on public health 12.

[170] Analysis by Ministerial Councillor Reisch on the restructuring of the provincial finances and outline of minutes of the respective meetings held at the Ministry of Finance on 21 Dec. 1905 and 4 Jan. 1906, both enclosures dated 20 Feb. 1906. ÖStA, FHKA, FinMin, general series, Zl. 12854/1906.

[171] ÖStA, FHKA, FinMin, general series, Zl. 12854/1906.

[172] Even later on, provincial representatives were not able to access essential data of the fiscal equalization, such as the crown lands' share in the state revenue. Cf. speech by Karl Eppinger, *Enquete über die Landesfinanzen*, 17.

[173] Selected grey literature of the time: *Stenographisches Protokoll der Enquete über die Reform der Gebäudesteuer*. Vienna, 1904; *Verhandlungen der Enquete betreffend die Förderung des Blindenfürsorgewesens*. Vienna, 1909; *Protokoll über die Enquete, betreffend die Sozialversicherung der Seeleute*. Vienna, 1910; *Enquete der Kommission zur Förderung der Verwaltungsreform veranstaltet in der Zeit vom 21.10. bis 9.11.1912 zur Feststellung der Wünsche der beteiligten Kreise der Bevölkerung in Bezug auf die Reform der inneren und Finanzverwaltung*. Vienna, 1913.

[174] Peter Becker, 'Stolpersteine auf dem Weg zum kooperativen Imperium'. In Jana Osterkamp (ed.), *Kooperatives Imperium: Politische Zusammenarbeit in der späten Habsburgermonarchie*. Göttingen, 2018, 32–3.

[175] *Landeshaushalte*, 18 vols.

a tax to the provinces, fiscal transfers reserved for specific policy areas such as education, or general all-purpose capital transfers).[176] In today's conceptual categories of fiscal equalization, the debate centred around variations of either a fiscal separation system (allocating taxes to different federal levels) or an interlinked system (collecting taxes at a single federal level and then transferring them to others).[177] This detailed and methodical approach made some provincial politicians impatient. At the beginning of the Enquête, Hermann Bielohlawek, a representative from Lower Austria, laconically summarized the situation. 'The fact is: the crown lands need money. The state administration should now reveal: does it have any?'[178]

Whereas the 1905 and 1907 crown lands' conferences had relied on bilateral negotiations with the Ministry of Finance, the ministry now brought in additional advisers. Having enjoyed the supportive company and camaraderie of their peers in the echo chamber of the conferences, the provinces now found that their lamentations over insufficient financial resources were met with scornful scepticism from the invited experts. Was there really a lack of funds?, probed Ferdinand Schmid, a statistician and professor at the University of Innsbruck.[179] Surely the crown lands can help themselves?, remarked Karl Renner, a leading Social Democrat.[180]

The Enquête on the reform of provincial finances thus sheds light on the social concerns, needs, and problems which lurked behind the details of the fiscal debate. In addition to Renner and Schmid, other administrative experts such as Karl Brockhausen and Josef Redlich made arguments that went far beyond previous exchanges between the provincial committees and the Ministry of Finance.

For Schmid, it was clear that the financial system had to follow the path of a modern territorial and constitutional state. He saw Austria and the crown lands 'stuck in the state-building process'. Alluding to Prussia, he noted pointedly that 'elsewhere former duchies, counties, etc. have been reduced to the level of modern provinces'.[181] Because of the strength of the provincial administrations, acting alongside the imperial state administration, Austria lacked both 'a unified territory' and 'a unified state power'. A consolidation of power was needed, such that 'autonomous bodies have to carry out the tasks assigned to them on the basis of their own resources' and 'in subordination to the state'.

The call for a more unitary state went hand in hand with the allegation that the provinces' restrictive electoral laws undermined their political legitimacy. The provincial fiscal and political systems could no longer be justified due to the

176 *Enquete über die Landesfinanzen*, pp. vii–x.
177 Renzsch, 'Föderale Finanzverfassungen', 44–6; cf. also Oates, 'Fiscal Federalism'.
178 Speech by Hermann Bielohlawek, *Enquete über die Landesfinanzen*, 8.
179 Speech by Ferdinand Schmid, *Enquete über die Landesfinanzen*, 164.
180 Speech by Karl Renner, *Enquete über die Landesfinanzen*, 69.
181 On the following: speech by Ferdinand Schmid, *Enquete über die Landesfinanzen*, 165.

democratic deficits in the crown lands. They hardly had 'any genuine self-government, in which society administers itself'. Instead, 'control [was exercised] by some over others and preferably at the expense of these others'.[182] For this reason, Renner, Schmid, and Friedrich Wieser, founder of the Austrian School of Economics, sociologist, and later trade minister, tied tax increases for the provinces to the introduction of universal suffrage.[183]

Provincial elites, on the other hand, argued that universal suffrage at the provincial level would make no difference to their policies. Most provincial spending on education, welfare, and infrastructure benefited the masses anyway.[184] Parliamentary representation that included the working class would only blow bigger holes in the budgets.[185] The provincial elites at the Enquête presented themselves as paternalistic statesmen who could be trusted to honour the common good without the pressure of broader popular participation. This was a far cry from how the underrepresented classes and nationalities really felt. In their eyes, the provincial committees only represented their own interests and not those of their territories.

The Enquête was thus a rematch between 'centralists' and 'federalists'.[186] The Lower Austrian politician Pattai spoke out against Schmid: 'Spare us the centralist ideal and anything that would lead to it'.[187] Other representatives argued similarly. The provinces were 'historic entities with their own national, social, economic, and philosophical characteristics, needs, and tendencies. They can only form a living, active and supportive part of the whole state by preserving and cultivating their autonomy'.[188] In short, Austria could not become a 'national unitary state' like Prussia.[189] On the other hand, economists and administrative experts such as Ernst Mischler argued that there was nothing 'absolutely encrusted' in the course of historical development. 'Lady Autonomy, too,' could 'undergo change and grow old'.[190]

When Josef Redlich asked: 'Do we all agree on what kind of state we are turning into? Is it a unitary state…or is it not something much closer to a federal state?',[191] a decidedly 'autonomist' mood emerged. This 'autonomist' attitude surprised many participants.[192] The Moravian politician and Czech nationalist Josef

[182] See a similar speech by Karl Renner, *Enquete über die Landesfinanzen*, 69.

[183] Expert opinion by Friedrich Wieser, *Protokoll der Enquete über die Landesfinanzen*, 281.

[184] Speech by Otto Steinwender, *Enquete über die Landesfinanzen*, 113f.

[185] Speech by Leopold Steiner, *Enquete über die Landesfinanzen*, 80–1; Josef Redlich, *Enquete über die Landesfinanzen*, 126. Similarly Stanisław Głabinski, *Enquete über die Landesfinanzen*, 192.

[186] On neo-absolutism and Schmerling, see Chapters 3 and 6.

[187] Speech by Robert Pattai, *Enquete über die Landesfinanzen*, 56.

[188] Speech by Stanisław Głabinski, *Enquete über die Landesfinanzen*, 193. See the similar speech by Josef Redlich, *Enquete über die Landesfinanzen*, 122.

[189] On this Robert Pattai, Otto Steinwender, and Stanisław Głabinski, *Enquete über die Landesfinanzen*, 112, 114, 193, and 238.

[190] Speech by Ernst Mischler, *Enquete über die Landesfinanzen*, 226.

[191] Speech by Josef Redlich, *Enquete über die Landesfinanzen*, 236.

[192] Speech by Robert Pattai, *Enquete über die Landesfinanzen*, 37; speech by Josef Redlich, *Enquete über die Landesfinanzen*, 124; speech by Stanisław Głabinski, *Enquete über die Landesfinanzen*, 191.

Koudela, a 'federalist' according to conventional perception, remarked to his 'centralist' colleague from Lower Austria that he was 'delighted to see that gentlemen who were rigid centralists only a short time ago have come to the conclusion that this principle must be overcome'.[193]

Indeed, with the introduction of universal male suffrage in 1907, the opposition between 'centralists' and 'federalists' was inverted. This came to the fore at the Enquête of 1908. In the preceding decades, the terms federalism and centralism had been charged with nationality and power politics. The German Austrians had sought their strength in a centralist unitary state, while the Slavic peoples had pursued it at the provincial level. After 1907, however, this constellation changed: Habsburg federalism now offered the propertied and educated elites guaranteed power at the provincial level, which they had long since lost in the Vienna Chamber of Deputies.

Ideological Disputes over Educational Spending

The experts' debate at the Enquête on how to improve provincial finances revolved around the proposal to support the crown lands in their educational expenditure. In the run-up to the Enquête, Bohemia and Moravia had already argued that the imperial state should assume this financial burden. Indeed, Bohemian jurists saw it as the state's duty and obligation to contribute to the costs of elementary education.[194] Salzburg also argued in favour of fiscal state transfers for education, describing all other measures as inadequate 'palliatives'.[195] The majority of provincial representatives took a similar view, calling for the state to pay half of teachers' salaries and pensions.[196]

Fiscal transfers for primary education would have offered enormous relief for the provincial budgets. In Bohemia, primary and secondary schooling accounted for half of all expenditure in 1905. In Moravia, it was a third, and in 1908 two-thirds.[197] Increases in salaries only worsened fiscal predictions for the coming years.[198] The justification for fiscal equalization in education policy was obvious: elementary education was a task for the whole state, not just a provincial one. The state would benefit from an educated population, which would increase the

[193] Speech by Josef Koudela, *Enquete über die Landesfinanzen*, 219.

[194] Copy of a letter from the Bohemian Provincial Committee to the Imperial-Royal Ministry of Finance of 24 Mar. 1908. MZA, ZV, Box 2639, fol. 68.

[195] Salzburg Provincial Committee to Moravian Provincial Committee of 24 Dec. 1908. MZA, ZV, Box 2639, fol. 901.

[196] Reading of the resolution by Karl Eppinger, *Enquete über die Landesfinanzen*, 244.

[197] Report of the Moravian Provincial Committee on the Regulation of Provincial Finances of 4 July 1908, Print No. 503/1908. MZA, ZV, Box 2639, fol. 644.

[198] Walter Loewenfeld, 'Die Finanzen der Österreichischen Kronländer', *Finanzarchiv*, 25/2 (1908), 177.

'earning power, tax capacity, and military strength of its inhabitants' and thus bring great benefits to the state.[199]

However, serious differences of opinion about fiscal transfers in education had already come to light at the 1907 crown lands' conference.[200] By its nature, educational policy was highly charged, both emotionally and ideologically.[201] Each crown land cultivated regional characteristics and used its financial resources differently.[202] Lower Austria refused to transfer the costs of primary schools to the state because it feared Vienna's influence over the appointment of teachers.[203] Lower Austria's representative Pattai, a member of the dominant Christian Social Party, painted this prospect in lurid colours. After the introduction of universal suffrage, the resulting paralysis of the Imperial Council would lead to the appointment of Social Democrats as school inspectors which the provincial government would be forced to accept.[204]

Galicia and Tyrol followed suit. They pursued more conservative education policies than the other provinces and shouldered a lower fiscal burden for schooling. Therefore, they had less to expect from the imperial state in terms of purpose-specific transfers.[205] The low level of spending on education in Galicia had long been considered a problem by the Ministry of Finance. On the one hand, Galicia particularly needed to develop its school system.[206] On the other, the province was already in receipt of large sums of state money as part of the Galician 'autonomy'. These handouts could not be increased at the expense of other regions.[207]

The representatives of powerful provinces like Lower Austria, Galicia, and Tyrol depicted transfers of capital for education as an undesirable gateway for Vienna's influence. Remarks from other crown lands to the effect that the existing

[199] Speech by Ernst Mischler, *Enquete über die Landesfinanzen*, 228; Report of the Moravian Provincial Committee on the Regulation of Provincial Finances of 4.71908, Print No. 503/1908. MZA, ZV, Box 2639, fol. 644–5.

[200] Konferenz der Landesausschüsse betreffend die Regelung der Landesfinanzen 1907, 21.

[201] Jana Osterkamp, 'Gefühlshaushalt in Mähren: Leistungsverwaltung, Landesschulden und Loyalitäten nach 1905', *Administory. Journal of Administrative History*, 3 (2018), 183–98.

[202] Cf. Tiebout, 'Pure Theory'.

[203] The practice of fiscal federalism suggests that purpose-specific financial allocations regularly go hand in hand with increased control and influence. Gunter Kisker, *Kooperation im Bundesstaat: Eine Untersuchung zum kooperativen Föderalismus in der Bundesrepublik Deutschland*. Tübingen, 1971, 34–45; Ulrich Scheuner, 'Kooperation und Konflikt: Das Verhältnis von Bund und Ländern im Wandel'. In Scheuner, *Staatstheorie und Staatsrecht: Gesammelte Schriften*. Berlin, 1978, 405.

[204] Speech by Robert Pattai, *Enquete über die Landesfinanzen*, 242.

[205] Outline of minutes of meetings held at the Ministry of Finance on 21 Dec. 1905 and 4 Jan. 1906 on the restructuring of provincial finances, supplement of 20 Feb. 1906. ÖStA, FHKA, FinMin, allgemeine Reihe, Zl. 12854/1906.

[206] Despite its size, Galicia spent less on education and science in absolute terms than the small-scale Moravia (in 1905, 14,487,456 crowns in Galicia and 15,299,979 crowns in Moravia). *Die Landeshaushalte*, 1. 68–9.

[207] Some ministry officials did not want to deprive the province of the already granted funds, while others wanted to consider all crown lands equally, cf. the contributions by Bernatzky, Engel, and Reisch, Outline of minutes of meetings held at the Ministry of Finance on 21 Dec. 1905 and 4 Jan. 1906 on the restructuring of provincial finances, supplement of 20 Feb. 1906. ÖStA, FHKA, FinMin, allgemeine Reihe, Zl. 12854/1906.

legislative framework already granted the imperial state influence over education were of no avail.[208] The Imperial-Royal minister of finance caved in to the resistance of the three large provinces. The costly path of purpose-specific transfers was not pursued any further. The meticulously prepared bill, which laid the foundations for the state's participation in the costs of primary education, was not even submitted to the Imperial Council.[209] The celebrated solidarity among the crown lands thus reached its limits when it came to the ideologically charged issue of schooling.

The principal alternative to fiscal transfers reserved for education was general capital transfers, which could be used for any purpose and would be funded by increased consumption taxes. Lower and Upper Austria, Galicia, and Tyrol favoured such a solution.[210] Vienna did not agree unconditionally, however. In order to create comparable provincial budgets, it demanded the abolition of the fund system. Moreover, financial control mechanisms were to ensure that provincial expenditures could not exceed provincial revenues. Only extraordinary expenditure should be covered by extraordinary sources of revenue such as loans.[211] These conditions were inspired by the findings of the so-called 'Austrian School of Economics' and the opinions of the financial experts gathered at the Enquête.[212]

The crown lands protested, not least against the obligation to balance their budgets. Moravia argued that transfers or surcharges were needed to enable the crown land 'to cover ordinary expenditure with ordinary income'.[213] Other provincial parliaments flatly rejected 'external control of their fiscal management...which in all likelihood would call into question the continued existence of the autonomy of the provinces'.[214] The lack of control over provincial finances suddenly became a symbol of provincial autonomy: 'The moment you give the provincial budgets the character of a law, you would bury provincial autonomy forever.'[215] While the crown lands had hitherto been able to pass their budgets

[208] Speech by Peter Grasselli, *Enquete über die Landesfinanzen*, 96.

[209] Pfaundler, *Finanzausgleich in Österreich*, 19.

[210] Lower Austrian Provincial Committee to Moravian Provincial Committee concerning the restructuring of provincial finances, Vienna, 10 Apr. 1908. MZA, ZV, Box 2639, fol. K 49; copy of the note of the Upper Austrian Provincial Committee to the Imperial and Royal Ministry of Finance of 2 Apr. 1908. MZA, ZV, Box 2639, fol. K 19.

[211] The neighbouring German Empire had already implemented this rule for municipal finances. Ullmann, *Der deutsche Steuerstaat*, 70–1.

[212] At the turn of the century, this was the most important difference between the German-speaking and Anglo-American financial theories. Schulz, *Finanzwissenschaft*, 292–6, 554–7.

[213] Memorandum of the Moravian Provincial Committee to the Imperial-Royal Ministry of Finance concerning the restructuring of the provincial finances, 29 Apr. 1909. MZA, ZV, Box 2639, fol. 862.

[214] Report of the Salzburg Provincial Committee. In *Verhandlungen des Salzburger Landtages. 1st Session, 10th Electoral Period 1909/1910*. Salzburg, 1910, 702. Similarly for Lower Austria, cf. note of the Imperial-Royal Provincial Governorate of Lower Austria concerning the regulation of provincial finances of 21 Aug. 1907 (Pattai). NÖLA, LA Stammzahl 1138/1907, without folio.

[215] Speech by Anton Pogatschnig, *Enquete über die Landesfinanzen*, 91.

without the emperor's approval, under this arrangement they would have been obliged to present their budgets to the emperor and the government. This was opposed not only by provincial lobbyists, but also by high-ranking academics such as Ernst Mischler.[216]

At the end of the Enquête, the Imperial-Royal minister of finance, Witold von Korytowski, ironically concluded that 'that ugly expression: the bankruptcy of the provinces...has been recognised as an exaggeration'. He pointed out that their 'enduring power to tax and to grant loans,...is still little used in many provinces'.[217] Korytowski made it clear to the crown lands, with a wink at their alleged 'desperate situation', that he would not bail them out. To the ministry, it was clear that the provinces could not be allowed to view the state 'as a reservoir from which they could try to quench their presumably insatiable thirst for revenue'.[218] In 1910, the deputies of the Imperial Council refused to approve draft bills presented by the Imperial-Royal Ministry of Finance that would reform the distribution of finances between the state and the provinces. Instead, the provisional measures already in place—transfers from spirits and personal income taxes as well as the provincial beer surcharges—were extended.[219]

Minor Financial Reform in 1914

After much wrangling, the Fiscal Transfer Act of January 1914 laid provisional foundations for fiscal equalization and a future 'minor financial reform'. The Imperial-Royal Ministry of Finance set an 'impressive number of millions in motion'.[220] It increased the provincial share of tax revenue from beer, spirits, and personal income.[221] There was a vertical element to this fiscal equalization: the financial flows were directed from the government to the provinces. In addition, a negotiated transfer ratio guaranteed the horizontal distribution of funds. The size of each province's quota depended on consumption and tax revenue, but also on the income provinces received from Vienna on the basis of previous bilateral arrangements, as for example in Galicia. As a result, the Austrian crown lands gained greater financial resources without extending political participation to the general population.

[216] Instructive on this debate are speeches by Ferdinand Schmid and Ernst Mischler, *Enquete über die Landesfinanzen*, 165 and 227, cf. also 8–9, 43, 91–2, 115, 120, 124, 139, 145–6, 168–9, 179, 183.

[217] Speech by Witold Korytowski, *Enquete über die Landesfinanzen*, 261.

[218] ÖStA, FHKA, FinMin, allgemeine Reihe, Zl. 11644/1907, fol. 25.

[219] Pfaundler, *Finanzausgleich in Österreich*, 39–44, with the detailed regulations.

[220] Analysis by Ministerial Councillor Reisch on the restructuring of the provincial finances of 20 Feb. 1906. ÖStA, FHKA, FinMin, allgemeine Reihe, Zl. 12854/1906, without folio.

[221] Gesetz über die Neuregelung der Überweisungen aus Staatsmitteln an die Landesfonds und die Herabsetzung des Ausmaßes der Realsteuern, No. 14/1914 RGBl.; detailed in Pfaundler, *Finanzausgleich in Österreich*, 45–57.

The financial equalization of 1914, however, did not eliminate the provinces' debts. In March 1914, Bukovina proposed a mutualization of debt 'with solidary liability of all provinces'.[222] This proposal was based on an idea from Salzburg, which in 1905 had suggested a Provincial Advance Fund (*Länder-Vorschuss-Fonds*). This fund would be jointly financed by the state and the crown lands and disburse emergency loans.[223] At the Enquête of 1908, Ernst Mischler had also advocated for the transfer of provincial obligations to the state.[224] The need to borrow for investment posed an unequal challenge to the crown lands, especially the poorer ones, as banks viewed their creditworthiness as poor.[225] It was not until the end of the nineteenth century that a system of provincial banks or state investment banks was established.[226] The proposed 'Habsburg bonds' would therefore have been a strong signal of solidarity among the provinces.

The First World War brought these initiatives to a halt. Tax revenues collapsed completely. While the empire was empowered by the War Economy Ordinance of August 1914 to raise funds for the military effort,[227] the crown lands did not have this option. Once again, it was the Ministry of Finance that meticulously identified the provinces' wartime needs and sought solutions.[228] After 1917, the government and the provinces not only negotiated additional transfers but also agreed to share the burden of new cost-of-living allowances for teachers.[229] Thus, the originally planned education transfers finally became reality.[230] After the war, a permanent fiscal equalization system was quickly worked out for the new Republic of Austria on the basis of preparatory work undertaken by the Imperial-Royal Ministry of Finance. The instruments of regional fiscal control were also applied in other successor states.[231] In the war years between 1914 and 1918, the

[222] This was to improve the creditworthiness of the less well-off crown lands, see note from the Bukovina Provincial Committee to the Moravia Provincial Committee of 3 Mar. 1914. MZA, ZV, Box 2639, fol. 225.

[223] Proposal of the Salzburg Provincial Committee concerning the creation of a Provincial Advance Fund. MZA, ZV, Box 2772 Konference sanace 1905, fols. 303–11.

[224] Speech by Ernst Mischler, *Enquete über die Landesfinanzen*, 232.

[225] On the problem of creditworthiness Osterkamp, *Gefühlshaushalt in Mähren*. For a general discussion Oates, 'Fiscal Federalism', 1139.

[226] František Vencovský (ed.), *Dějiny bankovnictví v českých zemích*. Prague, 1999. On industrial involvement cf. Richard L. Rudolph, *Banking and Industrialization in Austria-Hungary*. Cambridge, 1976. On the publicly funded investment bank of Galicia see Marc Ben-Joseph, *Adversities of Autonomy: Bank krajowy królestwa Galicyi i Lodomeryi and the Politics of Credit in Galicia*. Kraków, 1999. On the importance of public credit, see also Reinhard, *Staatsmacht und Staatskredit*, 22, 34–40.

[227] Kaiserliche Verordnung, betreffend die Vornahme von Kreditoperationen zur Bestreitung der Auslagen für außerordentliche militärische Vorkehrungen aus Anlaß der kriegerischen Verwicklungen, No. 220/1914 RGBl. In more detail, Pogány, 'Finanzgebarung, Kriegskosten und Kriegsschulden'.

[228] Cf. records of the Moravian Provincial Committee on the influence of the war on the autonomous financial economy, table for the Imperial-Royal Ministry of Finance, n.d. MZA, ZV, Box 2639, fol. 922.

[229] On these later conferences see Chapter 1.

[230] Richard Pfaundler, *Der Finanzausgleich in Österreich: Das System, seine Begründung und Durchführung*. Vienna, 1931, 66–78 and 243–5.

[231] Pfaundler, *Finanzausgleich in Österreich: System*, 66–78 and 243–5.

crown lands' conferences became an important institution for formulating and enforcing the common interests of the crown lands in the Austrian part of the empire; in the long run, they paved the way for the 'cooperative federal state' of the post-war period.[232]

10.5. Cooperation and Solidarity in Habsburg Europe

The history of Habsburg fiscal federalism allows us to draw conclusions about the fundamental structure of federal politics. In the complex negotiations over fiscal equalization, a *scale* of political interaction emerges that ranges from competition and rivalry to coordination and cooperation to mutual support and solidarity. Such scales are still relevant for comparative research on federalism today. Federalism can be seen as an order of shared politics that differs fundamentally from the hierarchical organization of the unitary state.[233]

The historical development of financial streams in Austria-Hungary thus reveals more than a dry fiscal topography. It not only shows how policy fields were distributed in the Habsburg Monarchy and who paid for them. The debates on fiscal policy also illustrate how fiscal equalization channelled competition and fostered coordination, collaboration, and solidarity among the Austrian crown lands.

By contrast, the Austro-Hungarian federation aimed at a healthy balance in the competition between the two parts of the empire, within a shared economic framework, but outside the core areas of defence, security, and foreign affairs. Deeper cooperation between the two parts of the empire in other policy areas was not considered desirable. Solidary cooperation—as the next level of federal coordination—was invoked only sparingly in political debates, even though Hungary was the recipient party in Austria-Hungary's fiscal equalization and, of course, fought alongside the Austrians in times of war.

In the relationship between the Austrian crown lands, unlike in the relationship between the two parts of the empire, solidarity counted as symbolic capital. It was rhetorically invoked at the crown lands' conferences.[234] However, this solidary community did not encompass all sections of the population. From 1907 at the latest, the opportunities for political participation began to differ

[232] Jana Osterkamp, 'Vom kooperativen Imperium zum kooperativen Bundesstaat? Föderale Motive in der österreichischen Revolution 1918–1920'. In Peter Bußjäger and Martin Schennach (eds), *1919: Länderkonferenzen und Landesverfassungen*. Innsbruck, 2020, 69–89; Ulrich Nachbaur, '1918. Selbständiges Land Vorarlberg'. In Peter Bußjäger, 3. *November 1918: Die Länder und der neue Staat*. Vienna, 2019, 75–9.

[233] For an overview, see Arthur Benz, 'Demokratisches Regieren im Föderalismus: Neue Literatur zu einem alten Thema', *Neue Politische Literatur*, 64 (2019), 517–18; Christoph Schönberger, 'Die Europäische Union als Bund—Zugleich ein Beitrag zur Verabschiedung des Staatenbund-Bundesstaat-Schemas', *Archiv des öffentlichen Rechts*, 129 (2004), 98.

[234] In more detail Osterkamp, 'Kooperatives Imperium:. Loyalitätsgefüge und Reich-Länder-Finanzausgleich'.

fundamentally at the various federal levels of government. The Social Democrats and underrepresented nationalities criticized the informal collaboration at the crown lands' conferences. They saw in those little else than the privileged elites closing ranks. As we shall see, the financial development of the Habsburg Empire, including the debates on fiscal equalization, are thus a direct reflection of fundamental political changes in the empire, society, and at the imperial court. After 1900, these changes led to renewed calls for a reform of federalism.[235]

A Federal History of the Habsburg Empire, 1815–1918. Jana Osterkamp, Oxford University Press.
 DOI: 10.1093/9780198943631.003.0011

[235] Cf. the following Chapters 11 and 12.

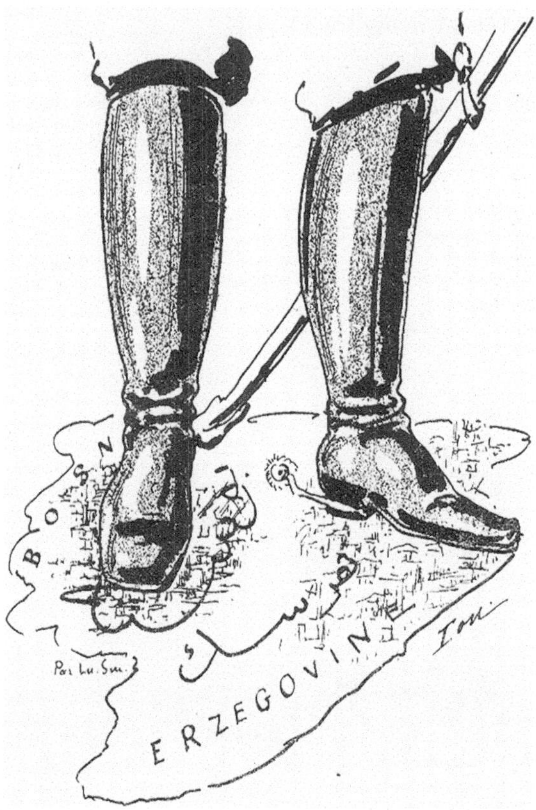

Figure 11.1 'Civilisation est en marche' [Civilization is on the march]. Turkish Caricature, pen-and-ink drawing, 1909.

11
Crisis Years
Dead Ends of Territorial Federalism and the New Model of Personal Autonomy, 1907–1918

Around 1900, the Habsburg Monarchy experienced a federal renaissance. Changes in the empire, in society, and at court during the second half of the nineteenth century triggered the need for extensive reform. In the fifty years since the outbreak of the March Revolution, Austria-Hungary had become a state with an expanded bureaucracy. The degree of *Durchstaatlichung*, that is, territorialization, bureaucratization, and juridification of public life, was high in comparison with the rest of Europe. It made Austria-Hungary a modern, multi-level administrative state.[1]

Even as an administrative state, Austria-Hungary remained a multi-ethnic empire. The coexistence of the individual nations and linguistic, religious, and social communities was characterized by an acceptance of diversity and, at the same time, a culture of distinction and the resulting hierarchies typical of empires. This was true not just across the empire, but within individual regions. While the imperial culture of fine distinctions felt natural to the elites, its acceptance among the wider population gradually eroded. Instead, a new sense of equality emerged in society, especially among the hitherto marginalized nationalities (such as the Ruthenians, Romanians, Slovenes, and Slovaks) and religious communities (such as Jews and Muslims), but also among the middle and lower classes. This awareness was underpinned by legal guarantees of equality for all citizens, nations, and languages, and of their corresponding institutions. This social and institutional twin-track development resulted in the comprehensive ethnicization of public and private life.

Unlike in many other European states, the Habsburg narratives of territorialization and nationalization failed to converge after 1900. The Habsburg Monarchy did not become a nation state.[2] The idea of national homogeneity could not be enforced without violent ruptures in a polity characterized by multinational and multi-religious diversity, not only at the imperial level but also within individual crown lands and regions. At the same time, the growing awareness of the equality of the various national, religious, and social groups made the imperial logic of rule by distinction unsustainable.

[1] See Peter Becker, 'Der Staat—Eine österreichische Geschichte?', *Mitteilungen des Instituts für Österreichische Geschichtsforschung* (hereafter *MIÖG*), 126 (2018), 317–40.

[2] Becker, 'Der Staat', 320.

The hour of federalism—a system based on the equality of differences—had arrived once more. At first glance, the federal options under consideration closely resembled those of earlier eras. As a large-scale application of federalism, trialism became the preferred option in place of dualism; Bohemia, Galicia, Croatia, and Bosnia were each scrutinized as potential third autonomous parts of the empire. Models of crown land federalism and executive federalism were also under discussion. And as before, proponents of a federation of nationalities continued to argue for linguistically and nationally defined provincial borders rather than historically informed ones.

This federal renaissance was informed by earlier experiences. By 1900, the limits and contradictions of a purely territorial federalist model had become clear. Now it was time to overcome them. Political theorists had been well aware that territorialization and nation-building were separate processes. In light of this, they concluded that neither the Austro-Hungarian federation (dualism) nor the elevation of provinces to state-like entities (crown land federalism) nor the administrative federalism experienced in neo-absolutism, nor the planned federation of nationalities, met contemporary expectations of a fair organization of the Habsburg Empire in all its diversity.

The innovative idea of personal autonomy led to a fundamental revision of previous federal concepts, which had always been territorial in nature. Inspired by this new idea of a federal association of legal persons, various models were discussed with the aim of representing the empire's religious, linguistic, and ethnic diversity without recourse to territorial autonomy. The idea of personal autonomy without a unified territory was reminiscent of pre-modern government structures that had preceded the concept of the modern territorial state. Given the social diversity of the monarchy, the more recent, 'modern' model of territorially unified rule was no longer considered viable on its own. With a return to elements of personal autonomy, pre-modernity thus once again proved surprisingly 'post-modern' in Habsburg history.[3]

By adding this new structural principle to the federal construction kit, federalism established itself as a politically flexible form of state organization. The new ideas were quickly implemented in individual crown lands: Moravia introduced non-territorial personal autonomy with national curiae in 1905. Bukovina followed suit in 1910 and Galicia in 1914. For Bosnia-Herzegovina, non-territorial personal autonomy with religious provincial curiae was implemented in 1910. In this way, federal innovations were tested on an individual basis. If successful, they were adopted by others. If not, potentially undesirable developments could be safely contained. This laboratory function is still considered an advantage of federalism today.[4]

[3] Cf. the Introduction.

[4] Charles Blankart, *Öffentliche Finanzen in der Demokratie*. 8th edn. Munich, 2011, 617; Wallace E. Oates, 'An Essay on Fiscal Federalism', *Journal of Economic Literature*, 37/3 (1999), 1132.

The ten years leading up to the outbreak of war in 1914 constituted a decade of crisis. The Austrian Emperor Franz Joseph had been in power for more than fifty years. Although he remained a fatherly figure, still inextricably linked in many of his subjects' minds with the empire, he was no longer expected to carry out sweeping reforms. After the suicide of his son, Crown Prince Rudolf, in 1889, the emperor's relationship with the new heir to the throne, Franz Ferdinand, was strained. Many questions about the division and distribution of political power between the two men and the impending transfer of the crown remained unanswered.

The elites that set the tone in politics, science, culture, education, and the arts had made the transition from an aristocratic to a bourgeois society.[5] Mass politicization through associations, parties, and the press empowered not only the working class but also the petty bourgeoisie and peasants; they now demanded greater rights of participation and protection. The ruling elites met the calls for democratizing the electoral law with isolated national (and increasingly socio-political) concessions, as well as the introduction of universal male suffrage for the Austrian Chamber of Deputies in 1907. Nonetheless, these moves did not end the national and social struggles.

Ultimately, the Habsburg Empire had to assert itself in a European and global environment that was increasingly fluctuating between nationalist and imperialist politics. On the one hand, the monarchy's new nation-state neighbours posed a challenge to the empire. With the emergence of Italy in 1866, Germany in 1871, Serbia in 1878, Bulgaria in 1878, and Romania in 1881, the Habsburg Empire found itself surrounded by new constitutional nation states. In past eras, imperial territorial expansion had guaranteed political, military, and economic power. Now, these new states illustrated the successes of the nation-state model—and did so on the Habsburgs' doorstep.

On the other hand, the development of nation states in the Balkans had long since become an integral part of the Great Powers' fight for global hegemony.[6] Austria joined the Great Game with the annexation of Bosnia-Herzegovina in 1908 (Figure 11.1). The emperor and his ministers hoped to counter the influence of the other Great Powers by expanding Austria's imperialist reach at the expense of the ailing and ossified Ottoman Empire. However, this expectation went unfulfilled. Instead, the annexation led to an international crisis, irreparable damage to diplomatic relations with Russia, and even threats of war from this erstwhile ally. The Balkan Wars after 1912 once again brought the empire to the brink of war.

In the face of these crises, the Habsburg balance between federation, state, and empire had to be recalibrated. The circle of federalist thinkers had widened

[5] On the middle classes see Ernst Bruckmüller, 'Was there a "Habsburg Society" in Austria-Hungary?', *Austrian History Yearbook*, 37 (2006), 1–16.

[6] Marie-Janine Calic, *The Great Cauldron: A History of Southeastern Europe*. Cambridge, MA, 2019, 318–23.

considerably since the rise of federalist ideas around 1848. In that time, social democracy had become a prominent voice of federalism. In addition, federalist ideas emanated for the first time from a high-ranking member of the court, the heir to the throne Franz Ferdinand, who had asked his advisers to develop plans for the federalist reconstruction of Austro-Hungarian dualism.[7] In short, federalism was widely perceived to be the response to the national, social, foreign, and domestic crises of the time. The Austro-Marxist programme of a federation of nationalities, for example, emerged in the 1890s in the context of the suffrage movement and was intended to defuse national and social conflicts. Trialist ideas and Franz Ferdinand's accession programme, meanwhile, were a response to political escalations in Hungary, Bosnia, and Bohemia.

The question whether the implementation of any of these federal ideas would ultimately have prevented the political disintegration of Austria-Hungary is impossible to answer from a historical perspective. The common view is that Austria-Hungary was doomed long before the outbreak of war because of the nationality conflict, the Balkan crisis, the weakness of its institutions, or simply because of its inability to implement change.[8] However, the hopes for a new federalist future at the time should not simply be disregarded. The period after 1900, with all its reforms—both planned and implemented—was more than a prelude to the allegedly *inevitable* disintegration of the Habsburg Monarchy. While acknowledging the apparent atmosphere of crisis and the decade's immense challenges, the federal history attempted here aims to shed light on what was thought possible—and what was achieved—in the struggle to maintain, and create, cohesion in the empire.

11.1. European Nation States and Habsburg Nationalism

Political thinkers in the Habsburg Monarchy developed their federal models after 1900 in the context of the modern European nation state, on the one hand, and the question of the sustainability and renewability of empires, on the other. Born in the French Revolution of 1789, the nation-state idea reached the peak of its popularity during the nineteenth century. Similar phenomena could be observed throughout Europe between 1848 and 1900: the middle classes increasingly dominated social and economic life, an industrial workforce emerged, and opportunities for educational advancement improved. Supported by a growing

[7] Cf. Chapter 7 (on the Austro-Hungarian Federation) and Chapter 12 (accession to the throne programme).

[8] For concise and critical examinations of such readings cf. Pieter M. Judson, *The Habsburg Empire: A New History*. Cambridge, MA, and London 2016, 382–4; Gary Cohen, 'Neither Absolutism nor Anarchy: New Narratives on Society and Government in Late Imperial Austria', *Austrian History Yearbook*, 29/1 (1998), 37–61.

bourgeois nationalism, the *idea* of the nation state took hold among the wider population.[9]

For Habsburg actors, the idea of the nation state became attractive not least because of what was happening in neighbouring states. State-building in Germany and Italy had fostered their political, economic, and cultural ascent. At the gates of the Habsburg Monarchy to the south and east, even smaller nation states such as Serbia, Bulgaria, or Romania were flexing their muscles. In the economic war between the Habsburg Monarchy and Serbia in 1906, known as the Pig War, Serbia emerged as the economic David against the Habsburg Goliath.

The reality of the complex, multi-ethnic Habsburg Monarchy was incompatible with the nation-state idea. By contrast with national developments in Great Britain, France, Germany, or Italy, the monarchy therefore developed its own unique varieties of nationalism.[10] Indeed, for many years, national activists in Austria-Hungary did not pursue the path to the nation state.[11] Instead, Austria-Hungary's various national movements sought to strengthen their respective national *societies* and to achieve autonomy as cultural, linguistic, and educational nations within the framework of the empire.[12] Their nationalism was, politically speaking, no less effective than that in other European states. However, due to its unique character, it falls outside the scope of modern definitions of nationalism.[13]

From the mid-nineteenth century onwards, the Habsburg Empire, like no other empire, offered its formerly marginalized nationalities, at least in the Austrian half, opportunities for independent cultural development.[14] With the centrally supported expansion of mother-tongue education from the 1850s onwards, the empire's linguistic groups increasingly cultivated their heritage. On the one hand, they shared a common goal in pursuing their respective cultural and political autonomy. On the other hand, they separated themselves from one another along

[9] Cf. John Breuilly, *Nationalism and the State*. New York, 1982, 102.

[10] On the comparison of these four nationalisms cf. Stefan Berger, 'Britischer und deutscher Nationalismus im Vergleich: Probleme und Perspektiven'. In Ulrike von Hirschhausen and Jörn Leonhard (eds), *Nationalismen in Europa*. Göttingen, 2001, 96–116; Miles Taylor, 'The British Empire in the Age of Nationalism 1815–1871'. In Hirschhausen and Leonhard, *Nationalismen in Europa*, 117–32; Robert Tombs, 'The Political Trajectory of Nationalism in France'. In Hirschhausen and Leonhard, *Nationalismen in Europa*, 133–53; Adrian Lyttelton, 'Between Piccola Patria and Grande Patria: National Identity and Nation-Building in Nineteenth-Century Italy'. In Hirschhausen and Leonhard, *Nationalismen in Europa*, 154–77.

[11] For a rejection of limiting the history of nationalism to a history of the nation state cf. Philip Ther, 'Schlesisch, deutsch oder polnisch? Identitätenwandel in Oberschlesien 1921–1956'. In Ther and Kai Struve (eds), *Die Grenzen des Nationalismus*. Marburg, 2002, 323–46.

[12] In detail Miroslav Hroch, *Národy nejsou dílem náhody. Příčiny a předpoklady utvá ření moderních evropských národů*. Prague, 2008; Miroslav Hroch, *Das Europa der Nationen*. Göttingen, 2005.

[13] John Breuilly, 'Nationalism and the History of Ideas', *Proceedings of the British Academy*, 105 (2000), 188; Ernest Gellner, *Nations and Nationalism*. Oxford, 1983, 1; Elie Kedourie, *Nationalism*. London, 1961, 1; Anthony Smith, *Nationalism and Modernism*. London and New York, 1998, 70–5. An overview in Hirschhausen and Leonhard, *Nationalismen in Europa*, 11–45.

[14] Judson, *Habsburg Empire*, 272.

regional language borders.[15] Non-discrimination on the basis of ethnicity, as well as multi-lingualism in schools, offices, and the courts, which were legally guaranteed in Cisleithania since 1867, were originally intended to promote the cultural development of each nationality. However, the legal and political disputes over the conditions under which the different mother tongues could be used in these arenas led in the long run to an ethnicization of politics and law that went beyond cultural concerns.[16] Better educational and professional opportunities for all population groups, if not for all regions (the east and south-east were disadvantaged), allowed for a social permeability that should not be underestimated. This distinguished the Habsburg region from, for example, the multinational state of Belgium in Western Europe.[17]

Despite the ethnicization of politics, people in most multi-ethnic regions continued with their multi-lingual everyday lives and maintained multiple national affiliations.[18] However, as soon as Germans were required to learn a Slavic language such as Czech for their civil service careers, multilingualism became a scandal.[19] When Prime Minister Kazimir Count Badeni pushed through this requirement in a 1897 decree, with the aid of the new 'clerical-Slavic' majority in the Imperial Council, riots and violence followed.[20] Badeni's resignation, the withdrawal of his Language Ordinance, and the further polarization of the dispute

[15] Pieter M. Judson, *Guardians of the Nation: Activists on the Language Frontiers of Imperial Austria*. Cambridge, MA, 2006, 19–65. An overview is provided by Marget Friedrich, Brigitte Mazohl, and Astrid von Schlachta, 'Die Bildungsrevolution'. In Helmut Rumpler and Peter Urbanitsch (eds), *Die Habsburgermonarchie 1848–1918*. Vol. 9: *Soziale Strukturen*. Subvol. 1: *Von der Feudal-Agrarischen zur Bürgerlich-industriellen Gesellschaft*. Part 1: *Lebens- und Arbeitswelten in der Industriellen Revolution*. Vienna, 2010, 67–107. On nationalized competition Beata Hock, 'Kulturelle Dimensionen der transnationalen Verflechtungen Ostmitteleuropas 1871–1914'. In Frank Hadler and Matthias Middell (eds), *Handbuch einer transnationalen Geschichte Ostmitteleuropas*. Vol. 1: *Von der Mitte des 19. Jahrhunderts bis um Ersten Weltkrieg*. Göttingen, 2017, 189–255.

[16] For further references cf. Gerald Stourzh, 'The Ethnicizing of Politics and "National Indifference" in Late Imperial Austria'. In Stourzh, *Der Umfang der österreichischen Geschichte*. Vienna, 2011, 283–323.

[17] Friedrich et al., 'Die Bildungsrevolution', 77. For a comparison, see Tim Mathias Schmidt, *Sprachnationale Konflikte, Staatsreformdiskurs und Sozialdemokratie. Ein Vergleich zwischen den böhmischen Ländern und Belgien 1894–1938* (university diss.). Munich, 2014.

[18] Especially Tara Zahra, 'Imagined Noncommunities: National Indifference as a Category of Analysis', *Slavic Review*, 69/1 (2010), 93–119; Jeremy King, *Budweisers into Czechs and Germans*. Princeton, 2002; Jeremy King, 'The Nationalization of East Central Europe: Ethnicism, Ethnicity, and Beyond'. In Maria Bucur and Nancy M. Wingfield (eds), *Staging the Past: The Politics of Commemoration in Habsburg Central Europe*. West Lafayette, IN, 2001, 112–52; Judson, *Guardians of the Nation*. For the neighbouring region of Upper Silesia, see also James E. Bjork, *Neither German nor Pole: Catholicism and National Indifference in a Central European Borderland*. Ann Arbor, 2008; Ther and Struve, *Grenzen des Nationalismus*, 323–46. For Transleithian examples cf. Roger Brubakers, Margit Feinschmidt, Jon Fox, and Liana Grancea, *Nationalist Politics and Everyday Ethnicity in a Transylvanian Town*. Princeton 2006.

[19] The Czechs perceived this as an expression of linguistic equality, cf. the brochure by Bedřich Pacák, *Skizzen zur Regelung der Sprachenverhältnisse im Königreiche Böhmen*. Kuttenberg, 1896.

[20] Hannelore Burger, 'Die "jüdische Frage" zwischen den Ausgleichsbewegungen in Mähren, der Bukowina und Galizien'. In Lukáš Fasora, Jiří Hanuš, and Jiří Malíř (eds), *Moravské vyrovnání z roku 1905: Možnosti a limity národnostního smíru ve střední Ev ro pě*. Brno, 2006, 77.

subsequently poisoned the domestic political climate.[21] Rising anti-Semitism was the flip side of German, Czech, Polish, or Ukrainian nationalism, which excluded Jews from their respective conceptions of nationhood.[22] Only a few national politicians fought publicly against this, among them Tomáš G. Masaryk during the so-called Hilsneriade, an affair reminiscent of the Dreyfus trial.[23]

The relationship between the nationalities changed fundamentally. Pre-existing hierarchies that placed the 'historical' or 'dominant nations' of Germans, Hungarians, Poles, and Italians above non-privileged 'peoples without history' and 'dominated nations' such as Czechs, Slovaks, Ruthenians, Slovenes, and others, had been called into question in 1848. By 1900, they appeared even less defensible.[24] The various nationalities' strength was not based solely on the machinations and commitment of their respective national movements. Equally important were factors such as the promotion of the economy, investment in infrastructure, and the development of culture and education by the state and the provincial institutions.[25]

In fin-de-siècle Austria-Hungary, the nation as a political principle was no longer limited to the sphere of culture. Nor was it necessarily related to issues of the nation state. In the face of the great European empires of their time, many national activists considered a Czech or Greater German nation state to be unrealistic. Given the historic and economic interdependence with other Central European regions, such a state was not even desirable.[26] Instead, their priority

[21] Hans Mommsen, '1897: Die Badeni-Krise als Wendepunkt in den deutsch-tschechischen Beziehungen'. In Detlef Brandes (ed.), *Wendepunkte in den Beziehungen zwischen Deutschen, Tschechen und Slowaken 1848–1989*. Essen, 2007, 111–18.

[22] Marsha L. Rozenblit, 'Die sozialen Grundlagen des Antisemitismus in der Habsburgermonarchie 1848–1918'. In Rumpler and Urbanitsch, *Die Habsburgermonarchie 1848–1918*, 9/1/2: *Von der Stände- zur Klassengesellschaft*. Vienna, 2010, 1370–1.

[23] The trial of Leopold Hilsner from Bohemia was based on anti-Semitic accusations of ritual murder, which were opposed with verve by the later Czechoslovak President T. G. Masaryk. On anti-Semitism in Bohemia cf. Vít Strobach, *Židé—národ, rasa, třída. Sociální hnutí a 'židovská otázka' v českých zemích 1861–1921*. Prague, 2015; Michal Frankl, *'Prag ist nunmehr antisemitisch': Tschechischer Antisemitismus am Ende des 19. Jahrhunderts*. Berlin, 2011. On Masaryk's role also Alain Soubigou, *Thomas Masaryk*. Paris, 2002.

[24] In political language, however, this distinction, which goes back to Marx and Engels, has continued to have an effect, see Ernst Hanisch, *Der kranke Mann an der Donau: Marx und Engels über Österreich*. Vienna, 1978, 179. Even Otto Bauer argued in a German-nationally superior way: *Die Nationalitätenfrage und die Sozialdemokratie*. Vienna, 1907, 188–238.

[25] Fredrik Lindström, 'Ernest von Koerber and the Austrian State Idea: A Reinterpretation of the Koerber Plan. 1900–1904', *Austrian History Yearbook*, 35 (2004), 143–84; Alfred Ableitinger, *Ernest von Koerber und das Verfassungsproblem im Jahre 1900*. Vienna, 1973, 221. Cf. Chapters 9 and 10.

[26] Edvard Beneš, *Le problème autrichien et la question tchèque*. Paris, 1908, 307; Jiří Kořalka, 'Von der ständisch-territorialen Verfassung zur Nation'. In: Hirschhausen and Leonhard, *Nationalismen in Europa*, 318–19 and 321; Holger Afflerbach, 'Die Deutschösterreicher zwischen Staatsraison und "Nibelungentreue"'. In Helmut Rumpler (ed.), *Die Habsburgermonarchie 1848–1918*. Vol. 11: *Die Habsburgermonarchie und der Erste Weltkrieg*. Subvol. 1: *Der Kampf um die Neuordnung Mitteleuropas*. Part 2: *Vom Vielvölkerstaat Österreich-Ungarn zum neuen Europa der Nationalstaaten*. Vienna, 2016, 653.

was not to separate their communities from the House of Habsburg, but to improve their standing within the existing imperial system.[27]

In some of the empire's peripheries, however, nationalism took a different trajectory. Communities in the north and south sought above all to establish an independent nation state. They dreamed of and promoted a territory linked to their fellow nationalists beyond the borders. In the north of the empire, the active pursuit of this goal was limited to small circles. The Russophiles in eastern Galicia, with Russian support, set their sights on a territory that would unite the Ruthenians of the Habsburg Empire and the Ukrainians of the Russian Empire.[28] Galician Poles maintained links with the Polish national movements in Prussia and Russia to achieve 'independence alongside the Habsburg Monarchy'.[29]

In the south, Croats, Serbs, and Romanians came to consider the nation state more and more as an option for the future. Each group fantasized about possible territories for their imagined state.[30] The formation of nation states in the south-eastern vicinity fuelled this desire to break away from the empire. As the equilibrium among the Great Powers began to crumble in the region, the more momentum nation-state thinking gained. On occasions, South Slav nationalists could even count on the goodwill of leading politicians in Vienna. The geopolitically trained publicist Leopold Chlumecký, who envisioned a new and powerful Austria-Hungary in the global competition for sea power, markets, and spheres of interest, wrote to the heir to the throne that a Greater Serbia would secure Austria-Hungary's economic hegemony in the region.[31] While the idea of a federation of nationalities was used by Franz Ferdinand to maintain imperial power, the Austro-Marxists took a different route.

11.2. Austro-Marxist Federation of Nationalities and Socialist Balkan Federation

The first proposal for a *democratic* federation came from the Austro-Marxists. Its foundations were laid by the Austrian Social Democrats, who adopted federal principles at their Party Congress in Brno on 29 September 1899.[32] Karl Renner's

[27] Judson, *Habsburg Empire*, 274–5.

[28] Harald Binder, 'Die Ukrainer: Von enttäuschter Staatstreue zum Kampf um Selbständigkeit'. In Rumpler, *Die Habsburgermonarchie 1848–1918*, 11/1/2. 854.

[29] Piotr Szlanta, 'Der lange Abschied der Polen von Österreich'. In Rumpler, *Die Habsburgermonarchie 1848–1918*, 111/1/2. 814–16.

[30] Calic, *Great Cauldron*, 323–7; Răzvan Părăianu, 'Von der kulturellen zur politischen Einheit der Rumänen'. In Rumpler, *Die Habsburgermonarchie 1848–1918*, 11/1/2. 768–71.

[31] Memorandum from Leopold Chlumecky to Franz Ferdinand, 'Austria-Hungary and the Balkans'. Österreichisches Staatsarchiv Wien, Abteilung Haus-, Hof- und Staatsarchiv (hereafter ÖStA, HHStA), Estates of Archduke Franz Ferdinand, Box 113 Memoranda.

[32] Cf. the text in Karl Renner [pseudonym Rudolf Springer], *Der Kampf der Österreichischen Nationen um den Staat*. Part 1: *Das nationale Problem als Verfassungs- und Verwaltungsfrage*. Leipzig

study *The Struggle of the Austrian Nations for the State* (1902) and Otto Bauer's work *The Nationality Question and Social Democracy* (1907), based on Renner's book, gave theoretical support to this idea. The Slovenian socialist Etbin Kristan provided further groundwork.[33]

The Austro-Marxist federation of nationalities took the nation seriously as an important political principle.[34] The party's primary goal, however, remained social justice and democratic participation. Draft plans produced by the Austro-Marxists were among the most innovative of any Austrian federalist thinkers. With their commitment to a federation of nationalities and to the nation as a politically relevant category, the Austro-Marxists also broke new ground within the Socialist International.[35] They opposed not only the exclusion of social democrats from the nation, but also the usual exclusion of the nation from socialist thought (though their theories were later rejected by Lenin and Stalin).[36] The Austro-Marxists were also responding to currents within the Austrian social democratic parties: for the Polish, Ukrainian, or Czech socialist movements, the affirmation of national thought was a matter of course.[37] However, Austrian social democracy limited the idea of a federation of nationalities to Cisleithania; Hungary was included only as an afterthought.[38]

The Austro-Marxists defined the concepts of nation, nationality, and federation of nationalities for themselves from the position of a marginalized minority. Political mechanisms excluded the social democratic electorate from many types of nation: the political nation of voters, the cultural nation of the educated, and even the ethnic nation, whose members were supposed to identify with their

and Vienna, 1902, 247. On the controversies and earlier drafts cf. *Arbeiterzeitung*, 28 Sept. 1899, 2–4, and 29 Sept. 1899, 4–5. See also Hans Mommsen, *Die Sozialdemokratie und die Nationalitätenfrage im habsburgischen Vielvölkerstaat*. Vol. 1: *Das Ringen um die supranationale Integration der zisleithanischen Arbeiterbewegung 1867–1907*. Vienna, 1963, 314–38.

[33] Franc Rozman, 'Etbin Kristan und seine Idee der Personalautonomie'. In Helmut Konrad (ed.), *Arbeiterbewegung und nationale Frage in den Nachfolgestaaten der Habsburgermonarchie*. Vienna and Zurich, 1993, 97–109.

[34] Bauer, *Nationalitätenfrage und Sozialdemokratie*, 538–9.

[35] Hans Mommsen, 'Otto Bauer, Karl Renner und die sozialdemokratische Nationalitätenpolitik in Österreich von 1905 bis 1914'. In Keith Hitchins (ed.), *Studies in East European Social History*. Leiden, 1977, 10. Austro-Marxism is understood as the theoretical-scientific examination of socialism, and social democracy as the practical, party-political side. Cf. Ernst Hanisch, *Der große Illusionist—Otto Bauer (1881–1938)*. Vienna, 2011, 112–16; Norbert Leser, *Zwischen Reformismus und Bolschewismus: Der Austromarxismus als Theorie und Praxis*. 2nd edn. Vienna, 1985.

[36] On the initial negation of the national by the Social Democrats cf. Raimund Löw, *Der Zerfall der Kleinen Internationale: Nationalitätenkonflikte in der Arbeiterbewegung des alten Österreich 1889–1914*. Vienna, 1984, 14; Bill Bowring, 'Burial and Resurrection: Karl Renner's Controversial Influence on the "National Question" in Russia'. In Ephraim Nimni (ed.), *National-Cultural Autonomy and its Contemporary Critics*. New York, 2005, 193–4.

[37] Kerstin S. Jobst, *Zwischen Nationalismus und Internationalismus: Die polnische und ukrainische Sozialdemokratie in Galizien von 1890 bis 1914*. Hamburg, 1996, 30.

[38] Hanisch, *Der große Illusionist*, 102. Therefore, even nation-building projects that, as in the Czechoslovak case, crossed the Austro-Hungarian internal border, were not systematically pursued by social democracy. Jan Galandauer, *Bohumír Šmeral 1880–1914*. Prague, 1981, 109–10.

'fatherland' rather than their class.[39] Until 1907, census suffrage, i.e. suffrage tied to property qualifications, prevented their participation in parliaments. At best, the working class was included in the cultural nation as the subjects of a mandate to civilize and educate.[40] The Slav social democrats, especially the Czechs, were also denied their share in the building of the ethnic and linguistic nation by the bourgeois national parties, on the grounds that they prioritized the struggle for social improvement over the fight for the nation.[41] Despite their vilification as 'fatherless', 'nationally neuter', or 'national traitors', many social democrats took 'nation' as a positive reference point.[42] Victor Adler, speaking in the Chamber of Deputies on 3 December 1908, said: 'We Social Democrats, who are called traitors to the state and the people in all the languages of the monarchy (laughter)...We stand united despite everything and we know: Austria lives in us alone.'[43]

The social democratic concept of the nation was democratic and equated the nation with the people.[44] The Brno party programme of 1899 called for a 'truly democratic polity based on universal, equal, and direct suffrage, in which all feudal privileges are abolished in the state and provinces'.[45] This concern for democratization affected all political levels: empire, crown lands, counties, and municipalities.[46] Unlike in many other parties, it also extended to women's rights.[47] The idea of the nation as an impetus for democratization was directed against bourgeois nationalism. Renner ridiculed national politicians who opposed universal suffrage as 'uninvited advocates...who represent only a small part of each nation'.[48] At the same time, Austro-Marxists were all too aware that democratic decision-making procedures alone would not create a nation. Otto Bauer thus stressed the need to educate the 'broad masses of the people' towards a

[39] For details see Jakub S. Beneš, *Workers and Nationalism: Czech and German Social Democracy in Habsburg Austria 1890–1918*. Oxford, 2017.

[40] See Bauer, *Nationalitätenfrage und Sozialdemokratie*, 164.

[41] In addition to Beneš, see also Strobach, *Židé*, 42.

[42] Cf. Seliger's speech at the Brno Party Congress, *Arbeiterzeitung*, 28 Sept. 1899, 2, and the preceding disputes. On the Czech see 'Die nationale Frage und die Sozialdemokratie', *Die Arbeiterzeitung*, 26 Sept. 1899, 4–5; Mommsen, *Sozialdemokratie und Nationalitätenfrage*, 1. 266–94.

[43] Victor Adler, 'Für die Nationen! Wider die nationalistischen Hetzer'. In *Victor Adlers Aufsätze, Reden und Briefe*. Vol. 8: *Österreichische Politik*. Ed. by the Parteivorstand der Sozialdemokratischen Arbeiterpartei Deutschösterreichs. Vienna, 1929, 164.

[44] Renner, *Kampf der Österreichischen Nationen*, 1. 171.

[45] Renner, *Kampf der Österreichischen Nationen*, 1. 247.

[46] The theoretical concerns were popularized through easily understandable pamphlets. Cf. for example, *Principles for the Activity of Social Democratic Municipal Representatives in the Municipalities of the 5th Agitation Circle* (adopted at the district conference on 7 July 1912). Bodenbach, 1912.

[47] Ilse Reiter, '"Das Wahlrecht gebt uns frei!": Kampf der Sozialdemokratie für das allgemeine und gleiche Reichsratswahlrecht'. In Thomas Simon (ed.), *Hundert Jahre allgemeines und gleiches Wahlrecht in Österreich*. Frankfurt am Main, 2010, 199–212.

[48] Renner, *Kampf der Österreichischen Nationen*, 1.163.

consciousness of national cohesion.[49] This insight into the man-made aspect of nationalism set him apart from most of his countrymen.[50]

Austro-Marxist Federalism

The democratic federation of nationalities developed by Renner and Bauer was based on two intertwined structural elements and principles: territoriality and personality. The territorial division of the federation was to be based on the linguistic and cultural borders between the nationalities. Crown land federalism would thus be abandoned with the crown lands becoming national counties.[51] The Czech Austro-Marxist Bohumír Šmeral also leaned towards this view, although he refrained from employing the term 'counties', which was unpopular with Czechs.[52] This idea of nationally delimited counties can be traced back to the Kremsier Reichstag of 1848, with periodic appearances in the intervening sixty years in proposals by various Austrian governments and state-law experts such as Bohuslav Rieger, Friedrich Tezner, Karl Brockhausen, and Joseph Maria Baernreither.[53] Even the Realist Party of Masaryk and Beneš advocated for national counties.[54] For his part, Karl Renner wanted to model the size of national counties on the smaller crown lands such as Carniola or Carinthia.[55] Factors like provincial territory and the 'provincial nation' in its historic state-law configuration, i.e. the sense of belonging to a historic area such as Bohemia, Moravia, Galicia, or Lower Austria, which had played a role in 1848, no longer seemed relevant.[56]

The second central element of the Austro-Marxist federation of nationalities was the principle of personal association. In order to organize the national diversity of the empire on a federal basis, i.e. to create federal cohesion amongst the various nationalities, they would have to organize themselves not only territorially in national counties, but also as public bodies or associations of

[49] Bauer, *Nationalitätenfrage und Sozialdemokratie*, 136. On Bauer's rejection of an essentialist understanding of nation, Olaf Leiße, *Der Untergang des österreichischen Imperiums: Otto Bauer und die Nationalitätenfrage in der Habsburg Monarchie*. Marburg, 2012, 364.

[50] Cf. Smith, *Nationalism and Modernism*, 145–59; Hroch, *Národy nejsou dílem náhody*, 42; Umut Özkirimli, *Theories of Nationalism*. 3rd edn. London, 2017, 51–80.

[51] The Koerber government set up plans for new counties as well. Renner, *Kampf der Österreichischen Nationen*, 1. 136–44.

[52] Many Czech nationalists regarded the division into counties as a betrayal of historic state law unity. Galandauer, *Šmeral*, 106–7.

[53] Ableitinger, *Koerber und das Verfassungsproblem*, 151–5; Solomon Wank, 'Zwei Dokumente Aehrenthals aus den Jahren 1898/99 zur Lösung der inneren Krise in Österreich-Ungarn', *Mitteilungen des Österreichischen Staatsarchivs*, 19 (1966), 349. See also contributions in the issue 'Länderautonomie' in *Österreichische Zeitschrift für öffentliches Recht*, 3/1 (1916).

[54] Beneš, *Le problème autrichien*, 286–7 and 300.

[55] Bohemia would have been divided into ten territories. Renner, *Kampf der Österreichischen Nationen*, 1. 136–44.

[56] Also Galandauer, *Šmeral*, 72–3.

persons.[57] Wherever possible, each nationality was granted its own county with the right to democratic self-government (the territorial principle). In addition, nationalities were regarded as non-territorial political associations with self-government rights, based on personal affiliation (the personality principle). The personality principle was intended to allow 'nations' democratic self-determination, especially in the fields of education, the arts, and culture, even if they did not occupy a contiguous, largely ethnically homogeneous territory but were scattered over several counties. At the highest echelons, the association's political representation was to be exercised in government by the national ministers. This was reminiscent of the pre-existing *Landsmannminister* (compatriot ministers).[58] Every citizen was to register with a national record office, thereby declaring his allegiance and paying taxes to one national collective.[59] With these arrangements for a federal state, Bauer and Renner sought to 'juridify national competition' and to 'juridify the nation'.[60] In order to clarify what the personality principle hoped to achieve, it is helpful to compare it with the self-organization of churches. Like the planned counties, churches also offer an organized community for members of a denomination without uniting them in a territory.[61] Renner himself compared the religious peace of the pre-modern period to the nationality peace sought by the Austro-Marxists.[62]

Federalism of Slavic Socialists

The Slavic Socialists rejected the Austro-Marxists' model of a federation of nationalities, precisely because of the personality principle and the separation of nation and territory.[63] They were convinced that the principle of personality would further favour the Austrian Germans. Among them was Edvard Beneš, who had written his dissertation in France on the Austrian nationality problem. He sympathized with the Czech socialists.[64] At home, many Slavic social democrats were confronted with the tradition of 'historic state law'. Separating the nation from the 'national territory' seemed unthinkable, as did conceiving of it as

[57] Renner, *Kampf der Österreichischen Nationen*, 1. 165–8 and 208.

[58] Unlike the compatriot ministers, who had few competences, the national ministers were to be heads of the national autonomous administrations, ministers at the emperor's court, and state secretaries in national affairs. Renner, *Kampf der Österreichischen Nationen*, 1. 201–9. Cf. Chapter 8.

[59] Renner, *Kampf der Österreichischen Nationen*, 1. 165–8 and 208.

[60] Cf. Karl Renner, *Die Nation als Rechtsidee und die Internationale*. Vienna, 1914, 16–17.

[61] Mommsen, *Sozialdemokratie und Nationalitätenfrage*, 1. 327.

[62] Renner, *Kampf der Österreichischen Nationen*, 1. 62. Similarly Bauer, *Nationalitätenfrage und Sozialdemokratie*, 133, 324–66.

[63] Mommsen, *Sozialdemokratie und Nationalitätenfrage*, 1. 322; Elza Tomac, 'Die sozialdemokratische Partei in Kroatien und die Krise des Dualismus Österreich-Ungarns vom Jahre 1903 bis zum 1. Weltkrieg'. In Hitchins, *Studies in East European Social History*, 52.

[64] Beneš, *Le problème autrichien*, 298.

a personal association of a cultural and linguistic community.[65] The form taken by a future federation of nationalities, whether according to a purely territorial principle or a mixed territorial-personal principle, thus depended on whether the nation was understood as a cultural-linguistic community (Renner, Bauer) or as a historical-territorial and socio-economic community (František Modráček).

Many Slavic social democrats continued to advocate a territorially organized federation of nationalities, in line with the model of historic crown land federalism. Initially, Czech social democrats denounced historic state law as a 'fantastic aberration of constitutional law' designed to divert attention from the economic plight of the lower and middle classes.[66] Nonetheless, representatives of the party's national wing aimed to preserve the entirety of Bohemia in a future federation of nationalities.[67] Renner noted the irony of this position, which was advocated by Josef Hudec, Alfréd Meissner, and Modráček.[68] 'It is self-evident that national rights can only be rights of nations. But the self-evident is never self-evident for us. With amazing persistence, our protagonists of the national idea have fought, for over fifty years, for the rights of... the crown lands.'[69]

The federation of nationalities raised a further controversy that preoccupied social democracy: financial justice. If the nationalities in the future federal state were to finance and regulate their affairs each from their own resources, the czech social democrats argued, they had to start off from an equal position of wealth.[70] A federal reorganization should not perpetuate existing differences in the economic power of the nationalities, as the Czech Socialist František Modráček noted: 'A compromise between the nationalities is only possible, therefore, where there is complete cultural and economic equality'.[71] Bauer then developed a form of fiscal federalism that took account of national differences.[72] In his view, the tax revenue of each nation should not be based on the nationality of those who owned the companies and businesses (mainly Germans, Poles, or Hungarians, depending on the region), but on those who paid the most income tax (the Czech, Ruthenian, and Slovak workers).[73] Bohumír Šmeral, one of the few Czech

[65] Mommsen, 'Bauer, Renner und die sozialdemokratische Nationalitätenpolitik', 4. Of the contemporary voices, cf. František Modráček, 'Zur nationalen Frage/K národnostní otázce'. In Löw, *Der Zerfall der Kleinen Internationale*. Appendix I, 217.

[66] Galandauer, *Šmeral*, 78–9, 102; Mommsen, *Sozialdemokratie und Nationalitätenfrage*, 1. 324.

[67] Mommsen, *Sozialdemokratie und Nationalitätenfrage*, 1. 324; Galandauer, *Šmeral*, 80 and 86.

[68] Galandauer, *Šmeral*, 80.

[69] Renner, *Kampf der Österreichischen Nationen*, 1. 69.

[70] On Bohemia Galandauer, *Šmeral*, 106.

[71] 'Die nationale Frage und die Sozialdemokratie', *Die Arbeiterzeitung*, 26 Sept. 1899, 5.

[72] A national quota for tax revenue was promoted in Bohemia by both nationalities. For the Czechs, Karel Kramář, *Anmerkungen zur böhmischen Politik*. Vienna, 1906, 121. Joseph Maria Baernreither and Ottokar Czernin, German Bohemians, argued for a national separation of the provincial finances, Memorandum by Joseph Maria Baernreither on the Bohemian Question [with notes by Ottokar Czernin] n.d. ÖStA, HHStA, NL Archduke Franz Ferdinand, Box 113 memoranda.

[73] Otto Bauer, 'Die Steuerkraft der Nationen', *Der Kampf*, 1/10 (1908), 446–52; Mommsen, 'Bauer, Renner und die sozialdemokratische Nationalitätenpolitik', 16–18.

Austro-Marxists, also wanted to pool all tax revenues and then distribute them among the nationalities.[74]

The Split of Social Democracy

The political struggle between the nationalities within social democracy led to a split in 1911. Ironically, this schism came at the time of the social democratic parties' greatest success, when they formed the strongest faction in the Chamber of Deputies (with 85 per cent of support coming from Czechs and Germans).[75] Czech trade unionists made the first move, forming their own organization, followed shortly afterwards by secession of a Czech Labour Party. In Galicia and Bukovina, the Ruthenian-speaking social democrats split into a pro-Polish and a pro-Ukrainian wing.[76] As a result, there was no longer a supranational, social democratic parliamentary grouping in the Austrian Chamber of Deputies.[77] Similarly, the Slovaks tried to leave the Hungarian Labour Party for national reasons.[78] The once straightforward socialist programme for a democratic federation of nationalities was thus lost and diluted amidst a tangle of new labour parties.

Despite this setback, the Austro-Marxist leaders in Vienna stuck to their version of a democratic federation of nationalities informed by the personality principle. Indeed, they would continue to do so until the end of the war. In 1918, Karl Renner republicized his ideas under the title 'The Right of Self-Determination of Nations in Special Application to Austria'.[79] In the preface, he noted the fact that the personality principle had since been implemented in Moravia, Bukovina, Galicia, and Bosnia-Herzegovina, albeit without the democratization he had intended and thus in a 'less than logical manner'. However, he paid tribute to the implementation itself: Austria had made 'the first and most interesting attempts at domestic international law; it may be regarded as an experimental field of domestic internationalism'.[80] In 1918, not only socialists, but politicians of all stripes and all over the world hoped that with 'internationalism' domestically applied the era of aggressive nationalism was finally on its demise.[81]

[74] Löw, *Der Zerfall der Kleinen Internationale*, 275–94; Galandauer, *Šmeral*, 82–122.

[75] Beneš, *Workers and Nationalism*, 2. On the composition of the Chamber of Deputies cf. Günther Schefbeck, 'Die Gewählten: Auf dem Weg zu einer Kollektivbiographie der österreichischen Parlamentsmitglieder'. In Simon, *Hundert Jahre allgemeines und gleiches Wahlrecht*, 121.

[76] Jobst, *Zwischen Nationalismus und Internationalismus*, 217–18.

[77] *Der Streit zwischen den tschechischen und deutschen Gewerkschaften in Österreich: Bericht an den Internationalen sozialistischen Kongress in Kopenhagen 1910*. Prague, 1910. See Löw, *Der Zerfall der Kleinen Internationale*, 86–96 and 132–65.

[78] In 1905, the Slovak Labour Party withdrew from the All-Hungarian Federation. It rejoined only under pressure from the Second International. Dušan Kováč, 'Die Flucht der Slowaken aus dem ungarischen Staatsverband'. In Rumpler, *Die Habsburgermonarchie 1848–1918*, 11/1/2. 739.

[79] Karl Renner, *Das Selbstbestimmungsrecht der Nationen in besonderer Anwendung auf Österreich*. Vol. 1: *Nation und Staat*. Leipzig and Vienna, 1918.

[80] Preface in Renner, *Das Selbstbestimmungsrecht der Nationen*, vol. 1, pp. i–ii.

[81] Glenda Sluga, *Internationalism in the Age of Nationalism*. Philadelphia, 2013, 11–18.

Balkan Socialist Federalism

One of the main competitors of the Austro-Marxist federation of nationalities, as a socialist design for the future, was the idea of a 'federation of free Balkan republics'. In the Balkans, the *socialist* movement and its multinational federalism was a response to the local *nationalist* movement. Karl Kautsky was the first to argue for a socialist Balkan federation of 'Bulgarians, Serbs, Greeks, Turks' in 1908. He found many supporters among Bulgarians, Serbians, but also Croatians.[82] In January 1910, the 'First Social Democratic Balkan Conference', attended by delegates from the labour parties of Bulgaria, Serbia, Romania, Montenegro, and Macedonia, as well as from the south of the Habsburg Monarchy (Croatia-Slavonia and Bosnia-Herzegovina), adopted his programme.

Unlike the detailed and well-crafted theory put forward by the Austro-Marxists, the Balkan federation was more of a slogan. Nevertheless, it had a major impact on the region. In the face of rampant and violent nationalism, as well as economic conflict and volatile struggles for local hegemony, federalism was once again perceived in its original role as a guarantor of peace and security.[83] It is little wonder, therefore, that the 1910 Congress of the Socialist International in Copenhagen spoke out strongly in its favour: 'Only the union of all the Balkan peoples in a federal republic can eliminate the danger of war and ensure the normal political development of the Orient.'[84] Social democrats from south-eastern Europe warned as early as 1912 that 'a Balkan war could lead to a world war'.[85]

But the socialists of south-eastern Europe did not speak with a unified voice. The movement for a Balkan federation was principally led by the Labour Party of the Kingdom of Serbia. At the Balkan Conference in 1910, the Serbs formulated a claim to leadership over all 'secretaries of the social democratic parties in the Balkans and south-eastern Europe'.[86] The response to this socialist version of 'Greater Serbia' was mixed. The reformist section of Bulgarian social democracy,

[82] Karl Kautsky, 'Die nationalen Aufgaben der Sozialisten unter den Balkanslawen', *Der Kampf*, 1 Dec. 1908, 106. Cf. Stefan Troebst, '"Hochverehrter Meister und Genosse!": Karl Kautsky und die sozialistische Bewegung in Bulgarien 1887–1934'. In Troebst, *Zwischen Arktis, Adria und Armenien: Das östliche Europa und seine Ränder*. Cologne, 2017, 96–7; Tomac, 'Die sozialdemokratische Partei in Kroatien', 49.

[83] On the peace function see Thomas Fröschl, 'Confoederationes, uniones, ligae, Bünde'. In Fröschl (ed.), *Föderationsmodelle und Unionsstrukturen: Über Staatenverbindungen in der frühen Neuzeit vom 15. zum 18. Jahrhundert*. Vienna, 1994, 39. On the socialist Balkan League as an alternative model to nationalism and imperialism cf. Calic, *Great Cauldron*, 337–8.

[84] 'Rapport au Bureau Socialiste International pour le Comité Central du Parti Socialdémocrate bulgare' ('Étroit') (D. Blagoeff, Chr. Kabaktchieff, G. Dimitroff) of March 1913. Verein für Geschichte der ArbeiterInnenbewegung (hereafter VGA), Internationales Büro, Box 127, File 790 Balkanländer 1908–1919, without folio.

[85] Memorandum 'Um die Frage der Abhaltung der zweiten sozialdemokratischen Balkankonferenz' from the Central Committee of the Bulgarian Social-Democratic Labour Party (D. Blagoev, G. Kyrkov, V. Kolarov, K. Kabachev, G. Dimitrov), 15/28 Sept. 1912. VGA, Internationales Büro, Box 127, File 790 Balkanländer 1908–1919, without folio. The position of Austrian social democracy towards the war was anything but clear. Jobst, *Zwischen Nationalismus und Internationalismus*, 224–32.

[86] 'Eine sozialdemokratische Balkankonferenz', *Arbeiterwille*, 22 Jan. 1910, 2.

the so-called *broad* section, as opposed to the revolutionary *narrow* section, was positive and hopeful of a Balkan federation.[87] The party congress in Croatia and Slavonia, however, feared Serbian dominance. Indeed, Croatians and Slavonians came to support the idea of a Balkan federation only in 1912, in the wake of the Balkan wars, when a solution to the South Slav question seemed possible outside the empire.[88] Incidentally, the Serbian socialist vanguard expressed its view to the International Bureau in Vienna that 'Bosnia and Herzegovina belong to them'.[89] In their reply, the Austrian Social Democrats defended Bosnia's membership of the Austro-Hungarian Empire. Later, however, they relaxed their stance, adopting a position of strict non-interference in south-eastern Europe under the slogan 'The Balkans for the Balkan peoples'.[90] Conversely, the Austro-Marxist ideas of democratic federalism, across all levels of government, came to fruition only after 1918.

11.3. National Personal Autonomy and the Participation of the Jewish Population, 1905–1918

Austria-Hungary remained a monarchical federation until 1918.[91] After the 1890s, the idea of political self-determination within a nation of citizens led to mass politicization not seen since 1848.[92] Hundreds of thousands took to the streets in the major cities to demand universal suffrage. In October 1905 alone, the police registered 100,000 demonstrators at a rally in Prague.[93] The suffrage movement owed its existence to the commitment of the social democrats. It gained the support of a middle-class electorate after electoral reforms were introduced in the Russian Empire in 1905 and in Belgium in 1906, following France, Great Britain,

[87] Memorandum 'Um die Frage der Abhaltung'. See Janko Sakasoff, 'Neoslawismus, Balkanföderalismus und Sozialdemokratie', *Der Kampf*, 1 Feb. 1911, 209–14. Generally, Augusta Dimou, *Entangled Paths towards Modernity*. Budapest, 2009.

[88] 'Ein Nationalprogramm der kroatischen Sozialdemokratie', *Arbeiterwille*, 19 Aug. 1910, 3. 'Ein Manifest der kroatischen Sozialdemokratie', *Volksstimme* (Budapest), 22 Oct. 1912. VGA, Internationales Büro, Box 127, File 791 Ungarn, Kroatien 1911–1921, fol. 275. Cf. Tomac, 'Die sozialdemokratische Partei in Kroatien', 60–1; Cvetka Knapic-Krhen, 'Karl Renner und die nationale Frage in den Nachfolgestaaten der Monarchie. Was blieb vom Personalitätsprinzip?' In Konrad (ed.), *Arbeiterbewegung und nationale Frage*, 115.

[89] Letter from N. Koschanin to the International Bureau in Vienna, Belgrade of 5 Feb. 1909. VGA, Internationales Büro, Box 127, File 790 Balkanländer 1908–1919, Folder 1908–1910, without folio. The letter referred to statements by Antonín Němec, who wanted Austria to keep these countries. On competing Serbian and Austrian social democracy cf. Enver Redžić, 'Die österreichische Sozialdemokratie und die Frage Bosniens und der Herzegowina'. In Hitchins, *Studies in East European Social History*, 102–5. The dispute is also documented in the *Arbeiterzeitung*, 9, 13, and 29 Oct. 1908, 30 Mar. 1909.

[90] Galandauer, *Šmeral*, 222–3.

[91] Cf. Chapter 7.

[92] William Alexander Jenks, *The Austrian Electoral Reform of 1907*. New York, 1950, 40; Reiter: 'Das Wahlrecht gebt uns frei!', 187. On the support of national liberals cf. Luboš Velek, 'Die Idee des allgemeinen Wahlrechts im politischen Lager der tschechischen Liberalen 1861–1914'. In Simon (ed.), *Hundert Jahre allgemeines und gleiches Wahlrecht*, 241–2.

[93] Beneš, *Workers and Nationalism*, 123, 129, and 143.

and the German Empire.[94] However, the democratization of electoral law and parliaments was limited. In 1907, universal, equal, and secret male suffrage was introduced for the Austrian Chamber of Deputies of the Imperial Council in Vienna (for Hungary, electoral reforms were extensively discussed but not implemented).[95] The curia system of the Austrian provincial diets, however, was retained and merely supplemented by a 'general electoral curia', based on universal suffrage.

Other electoral reforms in the crown lands were aimed not at democratic but at national or religious federalism.[96] In 1905, Moravia was the first country to introduce national curiae in the Provincial Diet and to implement the system of national personal autonomy. Galicia and Bukovina soon followed suit. In 1910, Bosnia-Herzegovina introduced religious curiae for Catholics, Orthodox, and Muslims in the provincial elections. The disparity between forms of representation in the two halves of the empire, in the crown lands, and in Bosnia-Herzegovina fundamentally changed the federal reality and once again made the monarchy a laboratory of federalism.

National Personal Autonomy in Moravia, Bukovina, and Galicia

The so-called Moravian Compromise of 1905 marks a watershed in the history of non-territorial federalism whose significance extends far beyond the era of the Habsburg Monarchy.[97] The electoral reform of the Moravian Diet introduced some elements of national personal autonomy, popularized by the social democrats.[98] In terms of content, however, the implementation took a socially conservative turn; the Austro-Marxists' goal of democratization was abandoned.

The innovation of the Moravian Compromise[99] was not only the addition of a 'general curia' to the diet, but the nationalization of the existing curiae.[100] Prior to

[94] Beneš, *Workers and Nationalism*, 102.

[95] From the circles of the heir to the throne, cf. memorandum by Dezső Bánffy, Ungarn und Wahlrecht 1910. ÖStA, HHStA, NL Erzherzog Franz Ferdinand, Box 113 Denkschriften, without folio; presentation by Andrássy to the emperor of 30 Oct. 1908. In: ÖStA, HHStA, Kabinettskanzlei Az. 3248/1908.

[96] On the connection between federalism and nationalism, Holly Case, 'The Strange Politics of Federative Ideas in East-Central Europe', *Journal of Modern History*, 85 (2013), 833–66.

[97] Börries Kuzmany, 'Habsburg Austria: Experiments in Non-Territorial Autonomy', *Ethnopolitics*, 15/1 (2016), 43–65; Börries Kuzmany, A History of Non-Territorial Autonomy: Accommodating National Diversity in Modern Europe, 1848-1939. Oxford 2027.

[98] Cf. above Chapter 11.2.

[99] The introduction of national curiae and national electoral classes was laid down in one of four provincial laws concerning the Moravian Compromise. The others regulated the working language of autonomous authorities, the national-political segregation of schooling, and the national organization of the medical and bar associations. Cf. Alfred Skene, *Der nationale Ausgleich in Mähren 1905*. Vienna, 1910; Horst Glassl, *Der mährische Ausgleich*. Munich, 1967; Fasora et al., *Moravské vyrovnání*.

[100] On the following cf. Gerald Stourzh, *Die Gleichberechtigung der Nationalitäten in der Verfassung und Verwaltung Österreichs 1848–1918*. Vienna, 1985, 222–6.

the reform, the diet had consisted of four curiae for (1) the clergy, (2) large, landed estates, (3) cities, industrial towns, and chambers of commerce and trade, and (4) rural municipalities.[101] As a modest concession to universal suffrage, a general electoral class was added, as in other Austrian crown lands.[102]

Now, mandates in the curiae were distributed according to a national quota. The mandates for cities, industrial towns, and trade, meanwhile, were divided equally between Czechs and Germans. Of the rural municipalities, thirty-nine were allocated to the Czechs and thirteen to the Germans, and of the general electoral curia, the Czechs received fourteen and the Germans six. Only the curiae for landed property and the clergy were exempt from this national division.[103] The personal autonomy principle was intended to ensure a more equitable distribution of seats in the diet between the two major national groups, the Germans and the Czechs. The Jews, as a third population group, were not considered.[104]

Constituencies and voters were also divided nationally. Municipalities registered voters in national cadastres, but individual citizens could object to this.[105] This legalization of national affiliation was based both on the subjective criterion of national self-identification and on 'objective', external criteria. In the complaints received in 1907, the Moravian state governorate tended towards the subjective principle of self-identification, while the Imperial Court subsequently reinforced supposedly more objective elements such as colloquial language.[106] The compulsion to have an 'unambiguous' national identity curtailed the possibility of having multiple national affiliations and, as a result, individual citizens' scope for action.[107]

The nationalization and ethnicization of politics had its limits. The nationalization of Moravian provincial politics was characterized less by legislation than by administration. In its legislative decisions, the Moravian Diet did not vote by curia and thus continued to embody a supranational, provincial entity. In the executive and administrative work of the diet, the national curiae gained fresh, practical importance. As soon as a newly elected diet convened, the national curiae appointed members to the Provincial Committee (which conducted the

[101] Malíř, 'Mähren und die Frage der Einführung des allgemeinen Wahlrechts 1848–1907'. In Simon, *Hundert Jahre allgemeines und gleiches Wahlrecht*, 257.

[102] The distribution of mandates was as follows: clergy (2 deputies), large property (30 deputies), cities, industrial towns, chambers of commerce and trade (46 deputies), and rural municipalities (53 deputies). The general curia comprised 20 deputies.

[103] Lothar Höbelt, 'Der Großgrundbesitz und der Ausgleich, oder Vom Nutzen aristokratischer Exklusivität'. In Fasora et al., *Moravské vyrovnání*, 64.

[104] One reason for this was that a separate Jewish curia would have weakened the German position. Unlike in Galicia or Bukovina, where the majority of Jews spoke Yiddish, in Moravia, language did not provide a clear criterion of demarcation. Jews were counted as either German or Czech.

[105] Overview of the cadastres in several articles under the title 'Národní katastr moravský', *Moravská orlice*, 13, 14, and 21 Dec. 1905, 1.

[106] Stourzh, *Gleichberechtigung der Nationalitäten*, 227.

[107] Zahra, 'Imagined Noncommunities'; Tamara Scheer and Rok Stergar, 'Ethnic Boxes: The Unintended Consequences of Habsburg Bureaucratic Classification', *Nationalities Paper*, 46/4 (2018), 575–91.

business of the diet, i.e. the *governance* of the province), as well as to various provincial parliamentary committees, expert commissions, provincial institutions, and public bodies such as the Provincial School Board or the Provincial Education Board (i.e. the provincial *administration*). Moreover, national proportional representation was from now on used to fill 'teaching, civil service, and administrative posts'. In the newspaper *Moravská orlice* (Moravian Eagle), Czech nationalists praised this arrangement: 'The provincial administration will thus pass from German to Czech hands.'[108]

The Moravian Compromise failed to resolve permanently either national or social conflicts and the fight continued in the newspapers.[109] Czech politicians doubted not only the supposedly neutral position of the landed property curia, but also the national justice of the whole Moravian Compromise. The negotiators of the Compromise, Alfred Skene, a member of the 'Middle Party'[110] with its supranational self-image of the landed nobility, and Jan Žáček, the party leader of the Moravian Old Czechs and later a hapless compatriot minister in the Viennese Cabinet under Richard von Bienerth, were defamed in the press as 'traitors'.[111] Newspaper reports, however, reveal that the Moravian Czechs and their umbrella organization, the Moravian National Council (*národní rada*), were in a better position than other crown lands and had greater political influence.[112] Moravia embarked on major investment programmes to modernize agriculture, education, and welfare, incurring huge debts in the process.[113] In the Habsburg laboratory of federalism, the Moravian Compromise developed considerable appeal and became a model for others.

Various drafts for similar compromises circulated informally among members of other provincial assemblies. By 1910, national personal autonomy was enshrined in Bukovina's provincial law; Galicia introduced it in 1914, but the imminent war prevented its implementation. Elsewhere, the matter was considered in Bohemia, Silesia, Styria, Carinthia, Tyrol, the Littoral, Dalmatia, and Transylvania.[114] The

[108] 'Správa země přejde tím z rukou německých do rukou českých', quoted from 'Českému lidu v markrabství Moravském', *Moravská orlice*, 21 Jan. 1906, 1.

[109] 'Po moravském "paktu"', *Moravská orlice*, 6 Jan. 1907, 1.

[110] Malíř, 'Mähren und die Frage', 261–5.

[111] 'Brněnský pakt', *Moravská orlice*, 24 Dec. 1905, 1.

[112] 'K zemským volbám', *Moravská orlice*, 19 Aug. 1906, 1; 'Nový moravský sněm', *Moravská orlice*, 28 Dec. 1906, 1; 'Náš sněm', *Moravská orlice*, 30 Dec. 1906, 1. However, a concentration of all Czech political forces in one parliamentary faction did not succeed. Cf. 'Soustředení českých stran', *Moravská orlice*, 2 Sept. 1906, 1; 'Z Prahy', *Moravská orlice*, 14 Dec. 1906, 1.

[113] Cf. Chapter 10; Jana Osterkamp, 'Gefühlshaushalt in Mähren: Leistungsverwaltung, Landesschulden und Loyalitäten nach 1905', *Administory. Journal of Administrative History*, 3 (2018), 183–98.

[114] In a collection of materials for a Bohemian settlement by Joseph Maria Baernreither, there are files on Tyrol, Moravia, Carniola, Silesia, Carinthia, and Styria. ÖStA, HHStA, NL Baernreither, Box 32 Bohemia, relations between Germans and Czechs, fol. 621. He received the material on Moravia from Josef Redlich, Redlich to Baernreither, n.d. Box 47 Korrespondenz, without folio. See also Burger, 'Jüdische Frage', 73; Aurel Constantin Onciul, *Aurel Ritter von Onciul und der nationale Ausgleich in der Bukowina*. Nuremberg, 1999, 107–8.

political motives varied from one crown land to the next. In Bukovina, with its five nationalities there was little danger of one nationality dominating the others, unlike in Moravia, Bohemia, Silesia, or Tyrol.[115] Stalemates between Ruthenians, Romanians, Jews, Germans, and Poles were nonetheless regular occurrences in the diet and the target of a national curia system proposed by the leader of the Romanian Democratic Party, Aurel Onciul.[116] A memorandum on the nationality question by Onciul, who had worked in the Brno district administration until 1906, can be found in the files of the Moravian Provincial Committee.[117] Later, he worked intensively on the Moravian Compromise, which he admired as a fair solution.[118] In Galicia, by contrast, the initiative for a national compromise came from the central government. Vienna's aim was to improve the representation of the Ruthenians, both to integrate the 'Ruthenian Irredenta' with its alarming Russian aspirations and to create a counterweight to the Polish elite.[119] Unsurprisingly, the negotiations met with prolonged resistance.

Each of these three electoral reforms adopted the original Austro-Marxist idea but added a social conservative twist. Their avowed aim was to prevent the social democrats from entering the provincial parliaments. Conservatives argued that the various social classes' 'different utility values' for the common good should be reflected in the organization of the provincial parliaments.[120] The juxtaposition of Austro-Marxist theory and provincial practice illustrates how the same organizing principle could be combined with very different national and socio-political intentions.

The Austro-Marxists had pinned their hopes on universal suffrage as a means of achieving democracy and social justice and, thus, of pacifying national conflicts. Conservatives such as Skene, on the other hand, believed that 'the establishment of national peace would surely lead to further developments in the social field'.[121] The nationalization of the provincial diets was deliberately carried out without thorough democratization.[122]

[115] See John Leslie, 'Der Ausgleich in der Bukowina von 1910: Zur österreichischen Nationalitätenpolitik vor dem Ersten Weltkrieg'. In Emil Brix, Thomas Fröschl, and Josef Leidenfrost (eds), *Geschichte zwischen Freiheit und Ordnung*. Graz, 1991, 113–44. According to the 1900 census, 730,195 inhabitants lived in Bukovina, of whom 297,798 were Ruthenians, 229,018 Romanians, 159,486 German-speaking Jews, 96,150 Jews of other national affiliations, 63,336 Germans, and 26,857 Poles. The number of Ruthenians increased steadily in relation to the Romanians, who formed the crown land's elite. Viorica Angela Crăciun, 'The Democratic Party of Bukovina and its National and Imperial Loyalties 1902–1918'. In Jana Osterkamp and Martin Schulze Wessel, *Exploring Loyalty*. Göttingen, 2017, 122.

[116] Crăciun, 'Democratic Party', 131.

[117] Moravský zemský archiv (Moravian Provincial Archives) Brno, Zemský sněm (Provincial Parliament), Box 453a Folder 'SA Brno Zemský sněm, Ritter Onciul: Sprachenkampf in Österreich', fols. 2–30.

[118] Crăciun, 'Democratic Party', 125 and 131; Onciul, *Aurel Ritter von Onciul*, 11.

[119] Börries Kuzmany, 'Der Galizische Ausgleich'. In Elisabeth Haid, Stephanie Weismann, and Burkhard Wöller (eds), *Galizien: Peripherie der Moderne—Moderne der Peripherie*. Marburg, 2013, 124–5.

[120] Skene, *Der nationale Ausgleich*, 50 and 52.

[121] Skene, *Der nationale Ausgleich*, 88.

[122] In Moravia, both German and Czech deputies voted against universal suffrage. Malíř, 'Mähren und die Frage', 270. On the political spectrum of German Moravians Pavel Cibulka, *Německé politické strany na Moravě 1890–1918: Ideje, programy, osobnosti*. Prague, 2012.

Crown Lands Avoiding Democracy

A new logic of citizenship emerged in the territories.[123] This was the result of the democratization of elections to the Lower House of the Vienna Imperial Council in 1907; the nationalization of elections to the three provincial diets of Moravia in 1905, Bukovina in 1910, and Galicia in 1914; and the organization of elections along religious lines to the Bosnian-Herzegovinian Provincial Diet in 1910 (and the maintenance of an estates-based feudal voting system in Hungary).

The electorate was determined in accordance with different principles in each case. The Viennese House of Representatives symbolized an idea of democracy that identified the political nation with the *demos*, which consisted of all adult male citizens. Non-territorial personal autonomy in the crown lands, in contrast to the Austro-Marxist theory, did not have a democratic character. National personal autonomy in Moravia, Galicia, and Bukovina promoted the nationalization and ethnicization of politics; in Bosnia-Herzegovina, religious personal autonomy increased the political influence of religious affiliations.

New political innovations were thus combined with the old curial system. Due to both the traditional system of census suffrage and the curia, the former ruling elites continued to be overrepresented in the representative bodies of the Austrian crown lands, as well as in Hungary and Bosnia-Herzegovina. From 1907 onwards, the emerging social and national groups from the middle and lower bourgeoisie, the peasantry, and the working class (and their parties) were only represented in the Lower House of the Imperial Council in Vienna.

Due to regionally differentiated electoral laws, political majorities at the various decision-making levels (Imperial Council, provincial parliaments, and municipal councils) rarely formed along party, national, or social lines. The policy areas of education, welfare, agricultural modernization, and regional infrastructure were of particular importance to those sections of the population that for the first time were enfranchised in 1907. However, they were for the most part not under the control of the representatives elected to the Chamber of Deputies. Rather, they fell within the purview of the provincial institutions. Reforms in these areas, then, could not be carried out by the Imperial Council alone, but only in conjunction with the provincial parliaments. At this subordinate level, however, the lower classes did not enjoy universal suffrage. The ingrained federal division of labour thus counteracted the democratic extension of the franchise at

[123] A classic on the sociology of 'citizenship': Thomas H. Marshall, *Citizenship and Social Class*. Cambridge, 1950. On the historical debate, cf. the contributions in Rudolf von Thadden, Steffen Kaudelka, and Thomas Serrier (eds), *Europa der Zugehörigkeiten: Integrationswege zwischen Ein- und Auswanderung*. Göttingen, 2007; Christoph Conrad and Jürgen Kocka (eds), *Staatsbürgerschaft in Europa*. Hamburg, 2001.

the state level. As a result, politicians who had fought for the universal right to vote[124] found themselves without the power to execute their political agenda.

The interdependence of federal policies was also central to Austro-Hungarian relations. For example, a reformed tax and financial system for Austria, which the Social Democrats and Christian Socialists had repeatedly demanded as a prerequisite for social and national justice, touched on the common affairs between Austria and Hungary.[125] Cooperation between Austrian deputies and Hungary, or the crown lands, against the interests of the Hungarian elites was not entirely hopeless, as the Financial Equalization Act of 1914 showed, but it was protracted and difficult.[126] Dogmatic adherence to the curia system in the Imperial Diet in Budapest and in the crown lands of Austria was felt most painfully in the very areas where the new electorate had hoped for change and participation.

The hard-won right to vote did not deliver the power its supporters had hoped for. This made it more difficult to form coalitions in the Chamber of Deputies and increased frustration within parliamentary groups (and thus their willingness to obstruct). Excessively long speeches, irrelevant questions, or interpellations that paralysed the parliamentary process soon became commonplace. Historians have often sought to explain obstruction in the Viennese Chamber of Deputies by the conditions that prevailed inside the parliament: the party landscape after 1907 was too fragmented for transnational coalitions, the rules of procedure were too weak to sufficiently prevent obstruction, and the electoral reform failed to make the government accountable to the parliament.[127] The federal history developed here, by contrast, sheds new light on the *political* motives: it was the increasing importance of the crown lands for central policy areas or, in other words, their *policy-dependent statehood and sovereignty*[128] in the areas of social welfare, education, agriculture, and infrastructure, which reduced the political weight of the Chamber of Deputies.

One modest achievement of the Chamber of Deputies in Vienna was that it provided a public forum for groups that hitherto had been socially or nationally marginalized. For example, the concerns of the Ukrainian-speaking population, which was underrepresented in the Polish-dominated Galician Diet, were first brought to wider public attention when Ruthenians sat in larger numbers in the Viennese parliament. They, too, wielded the weapon of obstruction. Political reports in the press, as well as reports and situation telegrams from the Military Chancellery to Franz Ferdinand, noted that Ruthenian obstruction occurred but

[124] On middle-class and socialist women's rights movements cf. Reiter: 'Das Wahlrecht gebt uns frei!', 199–212. A permanent residence was a precondition for the right to vote. This effectively disenfranchised peddlers and seasonal workers. Birgitta Bader-Zaar, 'Die Demokratisierung des Wahlrechts'. In Robert Kriechbaumer, Michaela Maier, Maria Mesner, and Helmut Wohnout (eds), *Die junge Republik: Österreich 1918/19*. Vienna, 2018, 108–9.

[125] Cf. Chapter 7. [126] Cf. Chapter 10.

[127] Ableitinger, *Koerber und das Verfassungsproblem*, 11–12. [128] Cf. Chapter 9.

failed to address the underlying issues. This is an important indicator of the extent to which 'obstruction' became part of everyday parliamentary folklore.[129] As explained above, however, visibility alone did not grant these social groups the power and influence to incorporate their concerns into general laws.

Personal Autonomy for Jews?

The limitations of a territorially based federalism were felt most acutely by those groups that could neither historically nor legally claim the right to a territory of their own, or that were spread over several crown lands. The right to federal self-government, based on the principle of personality, was therefore very attractive, especially for parts of Austrian Jewry, as a means of achieving greater political participation. In the uneven processes of electoral reform, with democratization, on the one hand, and representation based on national and religious affiliations, on the other, the Jews fell through the cracks.

After 1900, disputes within the Jewish community over its national, religious, or cultural identity intensified. This went hand in hand with competing demands for a territory in Palestine (Zionism), national autonomy in the homeland (diaspora nationalism), or assimilation. It was not always possible to match these demands with specific political blocks.[130] Within the same party, some might seek national autonomy, while others were advocating for a national territory in Eastern Europe that would also be confederated with Austria-Hungary.[131]

At an all-Austrian conference of their spokesmen in December 1905, the Zionists decided to fight for a Jewish curia in the Chamber of Deputies.[132] Large and increasingly politically mobilized Jewish populations existed in Moravia, Bukovina, and Galicia. As a result, Jewish representatives had also been fighting for greater rights of participation in the negotiations over the so-called

[129] The situation telegrams from the Military Chancellery to Franz Ferdinand never mentioned the motives for the obstruction. Thus, Bardolff wrote on 12 June 1912 'Announced obstruction of the Ruthenians not yet eliminated' (Fasz. 8–2, fol. 50), on 5 Nov. 1913 'In the Austrian Chamber of Deputies Ruthenians are to intensify obstruction today. In the Hungarian Chamber of Deputies, opposition will continue today with obstruction talk' (Fasz. 8–2, fol. 283), on 10 Dec. 1913 'Ruthenians deployed this morning with technical obstruction' (Fasz. 8–2, fol. 298) and finally 'Ruthenians stopped obstruction at seven o'clock in the evening due to the influence of Sylvester' (Fasc. 8–2, fol. 309) and on 29 Jan. 1914 'In the Austrian Chamber of Deputies Czech obstruction' (Fasc. 8-2, fol. 5). ÖStA, HHStA, NL Erzherzog Franz Ferdinand, Box 8 Korrespondenz, File Karl Bardolff.

[130] Adolf Gaisbauer, *Davidstern und Doppeladler. Zionismus und jüdischer Nationalismus in Österreich 1882–1918*. Vienna, 1988, 244–9. Henry Abramson, *A Prayer for the Government: Ukrainians and Jews in Revolutionary Times 1917–1920*. Cambridge, MA, 1999, 26–30. On parallels in Russia see Anke Hilbrenner, *Diaspora-Nationalismus: Zur Geschichtskonstruktion Simon Dubnows*. Göttingen, 2007, 119–31.

[131] David Rechter, 'Nationalism at the Edge: The Jüdische Volksrat of Habsburg Bukovina', *Ashkenaz*, 18–19/1 (2009), 65.

[132] Gaisbauer, *Davidstern und Doppeladler*, 178.

compromises. Zionists and diaspora nationalists worked together. In Galicia and Bukovina in particular, Jewish diaspora nationalism developed around political activists such as Nathan Birnbaum, Benno Straucher, and Max Diamant.[133] They wanted Yiddish to be recognized as the official dialect of Jews in Austria and thus as the necessary basis for the political, social, and cultural equality of the Jewish nationality. In Moravia, Galicia, and Bukovina, this would provide the foundation for Jewish national personal autonomy.[134] The issue was subsequently brought before the Austrian courts and administrative authorities.[135] Ultimately, the Imperial Court classified Yiddish as a dialect and not as a national language. As a result, the Jews officially retained the status of a religious community rather than that of a nation.[136]

While Jewish attempts to gain greater political representation through a separate registry were unsuccessful in Moravia (not least because such a development would reduce the number of German mandates in the diet),[137] the new electoral law negotiated for Bukovina in 1908 and 1909 envisioned a national electoral curia for the local Jewry[138] Once again, the Viennese government used the argument that the Jews were not a nationality to reject this proposal.[139] In response, Bukovina's provincial politicians cleverly redrew their electoral boundaries in such a way as to ensure a Jewish electoral majority in some constituencies.[140] Jews made up a larger proportion of the population in Bukovina than in Moravia, 13 per cent in total, and held leading positions in commerce, agriculture, politics, and civil society. The demands of the Jewish population for greater participation were therefore more openly discussed in Bukovina than in Vienna.[141]

A similar debate raged in Galicia. Here, too, the struggle for a Jewish national curia was ultimately unsuccessful. For the new urban curia, representing Galician towns and cities, however, the electoral boundaries were drawn in such a way as to guarantee a certain number of seats in the diet for Jewish deputies.[142] Assimilated Jews welcomed this compromise, which did not call into question their national identification as Poles or Germans.[143] Jewish nationalists in Galicia, however, vehemently opposed the denial of their nationality and spoke of a 'theft of electoral rights'.[144]

[133] Rechter, 'Nationalism at the Edge'.

[134] Gerald Stourzh, 'Max Diamant and Jewish Diaspora Nationalism in the Bukovina'. In Stourzh, *From Vienna to Chicago and Back*. Chicago, 2007, 192.

[135] Gerald Stourzh, 'Galten die Juden als Nationalität Altösterreichs? Ein Beitrag zur Geschichte des cisleithanischen Nationalitätenrechts', *Studia Judaica Austriaca*, 10 (1984), 73–117.

[136] Stourzh, 'Max Diamant', 203.

[137] Gerald Stourzh, 'The National Compromise in the Bukovina'. In Stourzh, *From Vienna to Chicago and Back*, 185.

[138] Kuzmany, 'Der Galizische Ausgleich', 138.

[139] Burger, 'Jüdische Frage', 81.

[140] From then on, some nationally minded Jews organized themselves in the Jewish 'People's Council'. On this *Volksrat* as a precursor of the Jewish national councils in the interwar period, see Rechter, 'Nationalism at the Edge', 76–89.

[141] Burger, 'Jüdische Frage', 80–1.

[142] Kuzmany, 'Der Galizische Ausgleich', 128–9.

[143] Burger, 'Jüdische Frage'.

[144] Kuzmany, 'Der Galizische Ausgleich', 129 n. 25.

Demands for Jewish personal autonomy found not only little resonance with the conservative provincial diets but also led to conflicts within the Social Democratic Party. The Austrian Social Democrats were forced to take a stand because of the large number of Jewish members in their ranks.[145] When, in 1905, a separate organization of Jewish workers in Galicia, the 'Poale Zion', split off from the Polish-speaking labour party, the central office in Vienna had to decide whether or not to integrate it as an independent party into the wider federation.[146] The Jewish workers of Galicia, referring to the Brno Programme, demanded national autonomy within the Social Democratic Party and thus within a future federation of nationalities.[147] In Galicia itself, the Polish Social Democrats opposed the recognition of Jewish Social Democrats as equal members of the party's federation, while the Ruthenian faction supported it.[148]

Otto Bauer, who openly professed both his Jewish origins and German nationality, followed the mainstream of the assimilated Jews or, as he called them, 'Jews of the West'.[149] In line with inner Jewish debates between 'Eastern Jews' and 'Western Jews', Bauer described Jewish assimilation as an irreversible and historically and culturally necessary process that should not be artificially delayed by national autonomy.[150] Both the German and the Polish Social Democrats of Austria dismissed the 'Poale Zion' as a backward-looking 'national Jewish' party that had no place in social democracy.[151] In 1915, when the socialist Jewish party 'Poale Zion of Austria' celebrated the 'awakening of the Jewish masses of Eastern Europe to national consciousness' as the dawn of modernity, they accused their German and Polish comrades of lacking 'the least bit of understanding'.[152]

The question of a Jewish nation not only preoccupied Austrian social democracy but eventually reached the International Bureau in Vienna and the European International Bureau in Brussels. Ever more supporters around the world rallied behind the idea of national personal autonomy for Jews. The General Jewish Workers' Federation reported to the International Social Democracy Bureau in

[145] On this cf, Gaisbauer, *Davidstern und Doppeladler*, 368–414; Robert S. Wistrich, *Socialism and the Jews*. London and Toronto, 1982.

[146] Bauer, *Nationalitätenfrage und Sozialdemokratie*, 366–81.

[147] The first split took place in 1905. In 1911 a 'Unification Congress' brought together the Jews still organized in the Polish Labour Party in the Jewish Party of Galicia which merged with the Jewish Labour Party of Bukovina in 1913. In 1914, the party counted about 6,000 members. Cf. Bericht der Jüdisch-Sozialdemokratischen Partei Galiziens und der Bukowina zum internationalen Sozialisten- und Gewerkschaftskongress in Wien 1914. Krakow, 2 May 1914. VGA, International Bureau, Box 128, File 798 Gesamtexekutive, without folio.

[148] Jobst, *Zwischen Nationalismus und Internationalismus*, 223.

[149] Bauer, *Nationalitätenfrage und Sozialdemokratie*, 375.

[150] Bauer, *Nationalitätenfrage und Sozialdemokratie*, 379.

[151] Letter K. Krysztón to Imperial Party Secretariat, 23 Aug. 1913. VGA, Internationales Büro, Box 128, File 798 Gesamtexekutive, without folio.

[152] Erklärung der Jüdischen Sozialistischen Arbeiterpartei Poale-Zion Österreichs, Vienna, Aug. 1915. VGA, Internationales Büro, Box 128, File 806 Jüdische Organisationen in Österreich 1915–1918, 1919, fol. 19.

Copenhagen in 1910 that more than 11,000 signatures from twenty-four cities had been collected in support of Russian Jewry's demands for national-cultural autonomy.[153] A tug-of-war broke out between the various party offices over where the Jewish Social Democrats of Galicia belonged. The office in Vienna obstructed the admission of the Jewish National Social Democrats of Galicia to the Socialist International.[154] Within the International, opinions only changed after the onset of war. In November 1917, leading European social democrats spoke out in favour of recognizing the Jews as a nation.[155]

11.4. The Annexation of Bosnia-Herzegovina: Trialism and Religious Personal Autonomy, 1908/10

The political transformation of the fin-de-siècle Habsburg Monarchy was inspired by social renewal. Attempts to include hitherto neglected social, national, and religious groups led to wider participation in political and public life. At the same time, this transformation was accompanied by the empire's territorial expansion to the south-east. Bosnia-Herzegovina, occupied by Austria in 1878 and annexed in 1908, was a product of Europe's crumbling old imperial order, which had begun to disintegrate at the furthest reaches of the Ottoman Empire, leading to the creation of new nation states in Bosnia's immediate vicinity.

Bosnia-Herzegovina represents an imperialist turn taken by the Habsburg Monarchy in the late nineteenth century. Its occupation and annexation shook the foundations of the Austro-Hungarian federation and highlighted the pressing need for a renewal of the Monarchy through federal reforms. Once again, the hegemonic elites in Vienna attempted to overcome the limitations of a purely territorial political organization by adding elements of federalism based on the personal principle in the new province. Unlike in Moravia, Galicia, or Bukovina, the federal integration of Bosnia-Herzegovina was based on existing legal traditions, namely the millet system from the Ottoman period of rule. It was therefore different in character.

[153] *Bericht über die Tätigkeit des Allgemeinen Jüdischen Arbeiterbundes in Litauen, Polen und Russland ('Bund') an den Internationalen Sozialistischen Kongress in Kopenhagen.* Geneva, 1910, 4 (one copy available in VGA, International Bureau, Box 125, File 778 Berichte 1910 Galizien, Böhmen, Juden, fol. 429).

[154] This question returned in 1914. Adolf Feldmann of the 'Executive Committee of the Jewish Social Democratic Party of Galicia and Bukovina' asked the Secretariat of the Imperial Social Democratic Party for admission to the International. Correspondence between Adolf Feldmann and F. Skaret of 11, 15 and 24 July 1914. VGA, International Bureau, Box 128, File 798, Gesamtexekutive, fols. 4–6.

[155] Memorandum No. 8 of the Jewish Press Office in Stockholm, 25 Nov. 1918, 'Der kommende Friede und die Judenfrage. Ansichten führender Sozialisten' (opinions by Camille Huysmann, Pieter Jelles Troelstra, J. Goldenberg, Gustav Moller, P.A. Hansson, Paul Axelrod, and S. Zorian). VGA, Internationales Büro, Box 128, File 806 Jüdische Organisationen in Österreich 1915–1918, 1919, fols. 7–12.

Austria-Hungary's imperial disposition towards Bosnia-Herzegovina is controversial. The historiographical debate over Bosnia's status—as a colony, a 'proxy colony', a 'situation coloniale',[156] an 'ersatz colony',[157] an 'imperial supplementary space' or an 'informal empire'[158]—continues to this day.[159] What is clear, however, is that contemporaries perceived the region as a colony. The statistician Ferdinand Schmid, for example, wrote in his well-researched regional geography of 1914 'that Bosnia and Herzegovina were acquired by Austria-Hungary as a colonial territory and have largely remained so to the present day'.[160]

Imperialism of International Law

The *situation coloniale* in Bosnia-Herzegovina was rooted in international law—Austria's policy had been sanctioned by the 1878 Treaty of Berlin—which made it difficult to integrate the region into Austria-Hungary's confederative framework. Despite the geostrategic importance of the Balkans, Vienna had only an informal influence in the region since the pre-March period. After the dissolution of the German Confederation, however, it discovered an 'Austrian vocation for Oriental policy'.[161] This reorientation of Vienna's foreign policy and its push southwards was facilitated by uprisings and unrest in the region, particularly after 1873, as well as the Russo-Turkish War of 1877 and its consequences for local power politics.

The logic of imperialist action, as exercised by the European Great Powers, was given a fresh theoretical grounding. British, German, and Austrian experts in international law developed new legal concepts such as 'occupation' or 'annexation' to justify expansive political interventions on foreign soil; the claim to be conducting a 'civilizing mission' was one notable example.[162] The Great Powers tailored international law to suit their needs. Through myriad treaties, agreements,

[156] Georges Balandier, 'La situation coloniale: Approche théorique', *Cahiers Internationaux de Sociologie*, 11 (1951), 44–79.

[157] Robert J. Donia, 'The Proximate Colony: Bosnia-Hercegovina under Austro-Hungarian Rule'. In Clemens Ruthner (ed.), *Wechselwirkungen: Austria-Hungary, Bosnia-Herzegovina, and the Western Balkans, 1878–1918*. New York, 2015, 67–82.

[158] Calic, *Great Cauldron*, 320.

[159] For a new account on political belonging, paths to citizenship and confessional sovereignty, Emily Greble, Muslims and the Making of Modern Europe. New York, 2021; Benno Gammerl, *Staatsbürger, Untertanen und Andere*: Göttingen, 2010, 151–79.

[160] Ferdinand Schmid, *Bosnien und die Herzegovina unter der Verwaltung Österreich-Ungarns*. Leipzig, 1914, 1. The Bosnian civil service newspaper also spoke of colonies in the broader sense, 'Erreichtes und Erstrebtes', *Beamtenzeitung für Bosnien-Herzegovina*, 15 Sept. 1908, 1.

[161] Speech by the delegate Dr [Josef] Redlich on Bosnian affairs of 27 Oct. 1908 before the Austrian delegation. ÖStA, HHStA, NL Baernreither, Box 42, fol. 710–15, here 711.

[162] Sebastian Conrad, *Globalisierung und Nation im Deutschen Kaiserreich*. Munich, 2006, 329. Antony Anghie, *Imperialism, Sovereignty and the Making of International Law*. Cambridge, 2004; Martti Koskenniemi, *The Gentle Civilizer of Nations*.Cambridge, 2001, 127.

and conventions, they legally overwhelmed and subjugated the Ottoman Empire under their hegemony.[163] Only twenty years after Turkey had been admitted to the 'European concert' in 1856, the Great Powers cancelled its membership in the community of European states and culture. Allegedly, Turkey's renewal and reform process was not keeping pace with the rest of the continent. According to the renowned international law expert Franz Liszt, Turkey could no longer count on the solidarity of the 'civilized' states.[164] Within the local population, this process led to a readjustment of affiliations and loyalties that were no longer based solely on religion but also on nationality.[165]

In 1878, the Congress of Berlin awarded Austria-Hungary the administration of Bosnia-Herzegovina. It invoked the 'peace-making' and 'civilizing' functions of international law to justify this transfer of power. Vienna mobilized a quarter of a million soldiers to occupy a country of only two million inhabitants in a violent three-month campaign. For Bosnia-Herzegovina and its people, the Berlin Treaty brought nothing but war, legal uncertainty, and political instability. Under Article 25, the country was to be 'occupied and administered by Austria-Hungary' while remaining part of the Ottoman Empire.[166] Territorial sovereignty still resided with Turkey, but the practical exercise of sovereign power was entrusted to Austria-Hungary.[167] On 21 April 1879, Austria-Hungary signed a treaty with Turkey that regulated important everyday matters by mutual agreement. In administrative practice, however, Austria's occupational regime soon disregarded this.[168]

The power of 'administration' granted to Vienna by the Treaty of Berlin was broadly interpreted as a general power to 'govern'. Austria-Hungary imposed its own as the exclusive currency, sovereignty over the passport system, and a monopoly over mineral resources.[169] Bosnians and Herzegovinians were also required to serve in the common army through compulsory military service.[170]

The authorities acted arbitrarily against their new subjects. Unwelcome foreigners were quickly labelled *personae non gratae* and forced to leave the country;

[163] Under international law, only occupations of 'stateless territories' were justified. Franz Liszt, *Das Völkerrecht systematisch dargestellt*. 5th edn. Berlin, 1907. Miloš Vec, 'From the Congress of Vienna to the Paris Peace Treaties of 1919', in Bardo Fassbender and Anne Peters (eds), *The Oxford Handbook of the History of International Law*. Oxford, 2012, 672.

[164] On the Ottoman reaction through law Aimée Genell, Empire by Law: The Ottoman Origins of the Mandate System in the Middle East. Columbia, 2026; see also Christoph K. Neumann, 'Bad Times and Better Self: Definitions of Identity and Strategies for Development in Late Ottoman Historiography'. In Fikret Adanir and Suraiya Faroqhi (eds), *The Ottomans and the Balkans: A Discussion of Historiography*. Leiden, 2002, 57–78.

[165] Hannes Grandits, Nathalie Clayer, and Robert Pichler (eds), *Conflicting Loyalties in the Balkans*. London, 2011.

[166] Georg Jellinek, *Die Lehre von den Staatenverbindungen*. Vienna, 1882, 116.

[167] According to international law textbooks, Austria-Hungary legally exercised territorial and personal sovereignty. Liszt, *Völkerrecht*, 103. The 'sovereignty' promised to Turkey was only an empty shell.

[168] Schmid, *Bosnien und die Herzegovina*, 16.

[169] Mining Act for Bosnia and Hercegovina of 14 May 1881, No. 230 LGBl.

[170] Provisional Military Act for Bosnia and Hercegovina of 24 Oct. 1881, No. 236 LGBl.

others were compelled to serve in the army as 'imperial subjects'.[171] The Bosnian administration was headed by the Bosnian Office, part of the Common Imperial and Royal Ministry of Finance, the army inspector of the province, and a subordinate civil administrator. It soon took on the character of a military administration.[172] Austria-Hungary's exercise of genuine sovereign rights was in open contradiction to international law. Nevertheless, it prevailed in everyday colonial reality and was tolerated by the other signatories of the Berlin Treaty.[173] Within a few years, Ottoman control of Bosnia and Herzegovina had become a mere shadow of its former self.[174]

Between Sultan and Emperor

The local population was caught between the sultan and the emperor. According to one census, it comprised 23 per cent Croatian Catholics, 32 per cent Bosnian Muslims, and 44 per cent Serbian Orthodox, with more or less identical ethnic and religious boundaries.[175] The Ottoman tradition of the millet system continued to divide the Bosnian-Herzegovinian population into political groups.[176] While Muslims had led the state in the Ottoman Empire, other religious communities had enjoyed extensive rights of self-government in matters related to religion, as well as in matters such as family, education, culture, social affairs, and taxation.

Vienna's occupational regime under Governor Bénjamin Kállay disadvantaged both the former Ottoman elites and the peasantry. The Muslim magnates continued to enjoy the protection of their feudal estates. However, it was now Croatian Catholics who were disproportionately appointed to new public offices.[177] The Orthodox Serbs suffered a curtailment of their existing rights of religious and political self-administration, which were very extensive by Ottoman standards, and were regularly harassed by the Austrian administration.[178] Representatives of the Serbian Orthodoxy complained to the emperor about their lack of legal

[171] Gammerl, *Staatsbürger, Untertanen und Andere*, 161.

[172] In the 1880s, the emperor signed no more than a dozen laws, while the number of ordinances was in the four-digits. On the civil authorities, Schmid, *Bosnien und die Herzegovina*, 54–60.

[173] For the illegality under international law cf. Hans Schneller, *Die staatsrechtliche Stellung von Bosnien und Herzogowina*. Leipzig, 1892, 155. On state legal incorporation cf. Emil Lingg, 'Die staatsrechtliche Stellung Bosniens und der Herzegowina', *Archiv für öffentliches Recht*, 5 (1890), 484. Cf. Joseph Maria Baernreither, *Bosnische Eindrücke*. Vienna, 1908, 46–7.

[174] Schmid, *Bosnien und die Herzegovina*, 18.

[175] Statistisches Departement der Landesregierung für Bosnien und die Hercegovina. 1912. Die Ergebnisse der Volkszählung in Bosnien und der Hercegovina vom 10. Oktober 1910. Sarajevo, p. xxxix.

[176] On the Millet system, Karen Barkey, *Empire of Difference*. Cambridge, 2008, 130–42.

[177] Bojan Aleksov, 'Habsburg Confessionalism and Confessional Policies in Bosnia and Herzegovina'. In Ruthner, *Wechselwirkungen*, 100.

[178] On Serbian self-government, Mustafa Imamović, *Bosnia and Herzegovina: Evolution of its Political and Legal Institutions*. Sarajevo, 2006, 148–51.

protection.[179] Meanwhile, the regime was reluctant to improve the peasantry's situation through land reform. Agrarian unrest thus continued into 1910.[180] The development and promotion of education and culture were also neglected.[181] Contemporaries even suggested that this was a calculated move to avoid the undesirable 'self-empowerment of the population'.[182]

The Bosnian governor Kállay, who administered the region for more than two decades,[183] tried to pursue simultaneous policies of 'territorialization' and *étatisation*. This was intended to unify the province but ultimately failed. With the neologism *bošnjatsvo* (Bosniaks), Kállay offered the inhabitants a new common provincial identity. At first glance, the idea of a provincial identity that transcended religions and nations was quite promising, especially since the languages spoken by the inhabitants were very similar.

In the end, however, national, ethno-religious, as well as religious loyalties that transcended Bosnia's borders proved more attractive than Kállay's all-encompassing idea of a unified provincial nation. Serbian Orthodox and Bosnian Muslims, for example, sought (re)integration into the Kingdom of Serbia or the Ottoman Empire.[184] Many Croatian Catholics in Bosnia flirted with incorporation into the crown land of Croatia-Slavonia.[185] This must be seen in the context of national-political and constitutional changes in south-eastern Europe at the time. Following mass protests against Károly Khuen-Héderváry, the authoritarian Banus of Croatia-Slavonia in 1903, a coup against the Austrophile Obrenović dynasty in Serbia in the same year, and an uprising against the Turkish Sultan in 1908, the region was in turmoil and upheaval. In the wake of this volatility, Serbs and Turks gained both constitutional freedoms and their own parliaments. After Khuen's fall, Croatia-Slavonia also regained greater freedoms.

The harsh regime in Bosnia-Herzegovina also relented somewhat following Kállay's death and his succession by Stephan Burián. Separate political parties and press organs were developed for the three population groups. A glance at the newspapers of 1908 reveals popular expectations for the future of the country. Serbs and Muslims opposed the possibility of annexation, which was already on the cards in early 1908. In a series of editorials, the Serbian Sarajevo press organ *Srpska riječ* (Serbian Word) demanded a constitution for Bosnia and autonomy under international law. It opposed an Austrian annexation as well as the

[179] Memorandum der serbisch-orthodoxen Kirchen- und Schulgemeinden aus Bosnien und Herzegowina bezüglich Kirche, Schule und Nationalität vom 7.12.1896 an die ah. kaiserliche Hofkanzlei. ÖStA, HHStA, NL Baernreither, Box 42, fols. 749–60, here 756.

[180] Moritz Auffenberg von Komarów, *Aus Österreichs Höhe und Niedergang: Eine Lebensschilderung*. Munich, 1921, 138.

[181] Gammerl, *Staatsbürger, Untertanen und Andere*, 152.

[182] Schmid, *Bosnien und die Herzegovina*, 51–3.

[183] On Kállay, Robin Okey, *Taming Balkan Nationalism*. New York, 2007.

[184] Calic, *Great Cauldron*, 323–7; Baernreither, *Bosnische Eindrücke*, 38–9.

[185] Okey, *Taming Balkan Nationalism*, 167.

introduction of a trialism.[186] Muslim newspapers such as *Bošnjak* (The Bosniak), *Muslimanska svijest'*(Muslim Consciousness), and *Musavat* (Equality) also rejected a possible annexation. They insisted on the status quo under international law, the sovereignty of the sultan.[187] Only the Bosnian Croats, in their newspapers *Hrvatski Dnevnik* (Croatian Daily Gazette) and *Osvit* (Dawn), welcomed the annexation and sketched out trialist visions of the future for a 'Southern Slavia' as a third element of the Austro-Hungarian Empire. After thirty years of occupation, the majority of Bosnian-Herzegovinians still opposed Habsburg rule.

The Annexation Crisis after 1908

With the annexation of Bosnia-Herzegovina on 5 October 1908, the emperor formally extended his sovereignty and the Habsburg law of succession to the territory he had occupied thirty years earlier. Constitutional rights were promised to the population of some two million.[188] To justify annexation, he argued in the official communication that his exercise of power in Bosnia-Herzegovina since 1878 had invalidated Turkish sovereignty. He wrote: 'Administration is rule, for rule in the modern state cannot be expressed in any other way than through administration, which is conceptually the application of all state power in the broadest sense of the word.' According to the emperor, Austria-Hungary had acquired not only territorial sovereignty, but also sovereignty over new subjects through the Berlin Treaty. This was 'absolutely incompatible with the future continuation of Turkish sovereignty over both countries.'[189]

The annexation caused one of Austria's greatest foreign policy crises since the 1860s. Although the local Bosnian press had reported the possibility of annexation as early as January 1908, the great European powers were taken by surprise and felt betrayed.[190] War with Serbia and Russia—secret negotiations with the latter having failed—was only narrowly averted. The annexation and the subsequent crisis made Bosnia-Herzegovina a topic of public debate. Many Austrian and Hungarian politicians, civil servants, and lawyers argued that the annexation was merely a legal consummation of the power exercised and internationally

[186] Bosna i aneksija [Bosnia and the Annexation]. In: Srpska Riječ of 9.2.1908, 2; Aneksija ili ne [Annexation, yes or no]. In: Srpska Riječ of 26.4.1908, 1; Memorandum. In: Srpska Riječ of 28.8.1908, 1.

[187] Ne propustimo priliku! [Let's not miss the opportunity!]. In: Bošnjak, 1.5.1908, 1; Našim čitaocima [To our readers]. In: Muslimanska Svijest of 2.9.1908, 1; S kim ćemo? [With whom are we walking?]. In: Musavat, 29.5.1908, 1; O aneksiji Bosne i Hercegovine [On the annexation of Bosnia-Herzegovina]. In: Musavat, 4.9.1908, 1.

[188] Documents printed in Wiener Zeitung No. 231 of 7 Oct. 1908.

[189] Vortrag über die Einbringung des Annexionsgesetzes vom 9.11.1908. ÖStA, HHStA, Kabinettskanzlei Az. 3406/1908.

[190] Holger Afflerbach, Der Dreibund. Europäische Großmacht- und Allianzpolitik vor dem Ersten Weltkrieg. Vienna et al., 2002, 626–636.

tolerated since 1878.[191] They declared that Austria-Hungary had 'nothing to annex'.[192] It could not be denied, however, that the Bosnian question further fanned the flames of the empire's nationalities conflict.

In the eyes of many, the integration of Bosnia-Herzegovina into one half of the Austro-Hungarian confederation would have created new imbalances between the nationalities. As in the days of the Badeni crisis, German nationalists invoked threatening visions of a 'Slav danger' if Bosnia-Herzegovina were to become part of the Austrian half.[193] For the Magyar elites, integration into Hungarian territory would have similarly tipped the 'Slavic' scales in favour of the Croats.

Trialism thus became the most popular buzzword for the integration of Bosnia and Herzegovina after 1908.[194] It offered a template that suited the widest range of geostrategic and national-political interests. Bosnia would become a state on an equal footing with Austria and Hungary, either on its own or in association with other South Slavic regions. Upgrading Bosnia as the 'third half of the empire' was perceived by other aspirants to this honour as a slap in the face. The Slavs of the north opposed federal reorganization in the south. There was no shortage of expressions of pan-Slavic solidarity; the leading Young Czech Karel Kramář, for example, declared that the now '150 million Slavs have a common feeling and thinking'.[195] But Václav Klofáč, a Czech nationalist socialist, argued that the 'Czechs could not be indifferent to trialism. As soon as federalization takes place in the south, we must also federalize the north.'[196]

Trialist ideas were combined with arguments of historic state law. Croatian nationalists like Josip Frank, for instance, hoped to elevate Croatia-Slavonia (augmented by Dalmatia and Bosnia-Herzegovina) to the status of an imperial territory alongside Austria and Hungary.[197] Other, more moderate Croatian-Slavonic plans left the crown land's status within Austria-Hungary's dualist framework untouched. Instead, they proposed territorial expansion into Dalmatia and Bosnia-Herzegovina within that system.[198] In Carniola, Slovenian national politicians such as Ivan Šusteršić used the annexation debate and the catchword

[191] As an example, see Theodor von Sosnosky: Die Balkanpolitik Österreich-Ungarns seit 1866. Mit 2 Karten und einem Anhang. Vol. 2. Stuttgart, 1914, 154 f.; Schmid, *Bosnien und die Herzegovina*, 25–7; Stephan Verosta, Theorie und Realität von Bündnissen. Heinrich Lammasch, Karl Renner und der Zweibund 1897–1914. Vienna, 1971, 77 f.

[192] Baernreither, *Bosnische Eindrücke*, 51; Baernreither, *Fragmente eines politischen Tagebuches. Die südslawische Frage und Österreich-Ungarn vor dem Weltkrieg*. Ed. Josef Redlich. Berlin, 1928, 86 and 90.

[193] Ableitinger, *Koerber und das Verfassungsproblem*, 28–9.

[194] Baernreither, *Bosnische Eindrücke*, 38 and 52. This was already the case in 1878. Imamović, *Bosnia and Herzegovina*, 197–8.

[195] Stenographic Minutes, Delegation of the Imperial Council, 43rd Session, 3rd Meeting, Budapest 28 Oct. 1908, 139.

[196] Stenographic Minutes, Delegation of the Imperial Council, 43rd Session, 2nd Meeting, Budapest 27 Oct. 1908, 31.

[197] Mirjana Gross, *Izvorno pravaštvo: Ideologija, agitacija, pokret*. Zagreb, 2000.

[198] Andrej Rahten, *Ivan Šusteršič, der ungekrönte Herzog von Krain*. Vienna, 2012, 149.

'trialism' to advocate even greater reorganization in favour of all 'Southern Slavs'. This included the crown lands of Croatia-Slavonia, Dalmatia, the Serbian Voivodeship, and the Slovene-populated sub-regions of Carniola, Carinthia, the Littoral, and Gorizia-Gradisca.[199] Šusteršić wanted trialism to counterbalance 'Magyar Chauvinism and Italian and Serbian irredentism' and to bring nation states such as the Kingdom of Serbia under the monarchy's sway, an argument that reached the sympathetic ears of the heir to the throne Franz Ferdinand.[200]

While these trialist ideas were almost always accompanied by power struggles between Serbs and Croats, intellectuals such as the Slavist Vatroslav Jagić and military officers like the Austro-Hungarian general Emil Woinovich shared a different vision. They used informal channels and wrote memoranda to high-ranking political contacts to promote trialism as an opportunity for rapprochement between Croats and Serbs.[201] While Jagić wrote to Baernreither, who had previously toured the region and was touted in the Sarajevo press as a future 'Minister for Bosnia', Woinovich addressed his concerns to Archduke Franz Ferdinand.[202] Whether in correspondence, speeches, or pamphlets, one phrase appeared over and over again: the time was 'not yet ripe' for trialism.[203] In August 1908, at the instigation of the Hungarians, the Common Council of Ministers had explicitly ruled out a trialist restructuring.[204] Discussions on trialism remained vague and unresolved.

To maintain the existing balance of power and end the tug-of-war between Austria, Hungary, and Croatia over the question 'to whom does Bosnia belong?', Bosnia-Herzegovina ultimately became an 'imperial land'—a 'tributary land', special territory, or *corpus separatum* directly under the sovereign.[205] The Monarchy

[199] Initially, there was only talk of an 'administrative territory'. Cf. Rahten, *Šusteršič, der ungekrönte Herzog von Krain*, 142.

[200] On the heir to the throne and Hungary, see Alma Hannig, *Franz Ferdinand: Die Biografie*. Vienna, 2013, 104–7.

[201] Letter from Vratoslav Jagić to Joseph Maria Baernreither, 29 June 1909. In ÖStA, HHStA, NL Baernreither, Box 42, fol. 3. Cf. also Baernreither, *Fragmente eines politischen Tagebuches*, 155.

[202] Letter from Vratoslav Jagić to Joseph Maria Baernreither, 29 June 1909. ÖStA, HHStA, NL Baernreither, Box 42, fol. 3. Cf. also Baernreither, *Fragmente eines politischen Tagebuches*, 155; 'Dr. Baernreither in Sarajevo', *Sarajevoer Tagblatt*, 2 June 1909, 1. On Woinovich cf. Gedanken von Emil von Woinovich über die Lösung der südslavischen Frage. ÖStA, HHStA, NL Franz Ferdinand, Box 115 Denkschriften.

[203] Letter from Vratoslav Jagić to Joseph Maria Baernreither, 29 June 1909. ÖStA, HHStA, NL Baernreither, Box 42, fol. 3; Baernreither: *Fragmente eines politischen Tagebuches*, 116; manuscript by Freiherr von Schwegel 'Aus den Verhandlungen des Krainischen Landtags', Laibach 16. ÖStA, HHStA, NL Baernreither, Box 43, fol. 248. Cf. also the assessment by Moritz von Auffenberg to Franz Ferdinand 'Politische Situation im Annexionsgebiet Ende 1909'. ÖStA, HHStA, NL Franz Ferdinand, Box 113 memoranda. Auffenberg later informed the heir to the throne about the situation in Bosnia-Herzegovina. Auffenberg von Komarów, *Österreichs Höhe und Niedergang*, 131–2 and 137.

[204] Hungarian Prime Minister Wekerle in the Common Council of Ministers of 19 Aug. 1908, In Anatol Schmied-Kowarzik (ed.), *Die Protokolle des gemeinsamen Ministerrates der österreichisch-ungarischen Monarchie 1908–1914*. Vol. 4: *1908–1914*. Budapest, 2011, No. 3, 185.

[205] On the disputed concepts cf. Gustav Steinbach, 'Die bosnische Verfassung', *Jahrbuch des öffentlichen Rechts der Gegenwart*, 4 (1910), 481.

now consisted of three parts, but did not form a confederate trialism. The foundations of the confederative semi-home remained untouched; it was, so to speak, merely augmented by a colonial annex. Despite the ruler's constitutional promises, the *situation coloniale* of the occupation period continued, albeit in a slightly modified form.

The province was not formally included in the common affairs and common institutions of the Habsburg Monarchy. Bosnian deputies were denied admittance to both the Imperial Council in Vienna and the Imperial Diet in Budapest. As a consequence, the province's inhabitants did not enjoy the same rights as the other citizens of Austria-Hungary.[206] Even a modest proposal by Alois Lexa von Aehrenthal to send Bosnian representatives to the delegations failed; having been established by the Austro-Hungarian Compromise, they had been entrusted with Bosnian affairs since 1878.[207] Although a Bosnian Diet was inaugurated in 1910, its decision-making powers were minimal. Any provincial law had to be approved by the governments of both Austria and Hungary and by the Common Imperial and Royal Ministry of Finance. The province was also denied its own financial resources.[208] In terms of competences and revenues, Bosnia-Herzegovina was thus barely comparable to the other crown lands.[209]

The reorganization of Bosnia-Herzegovina through the Provincial Constitution of 1910 was nevertheless an experiment of supra-regional significance. It was based on the personality principle already established in Moravia in 1905, with a modification in the design of the curia system: now, religious criteria determined the division of constituencies and mandates. The composition of the Sarajevo Diet marked a return to religion as a political principle. In the pre-modern period, religious affiliation, together with social affiliation, had largely determined the political rights of individuals and communities. In the nineteenth century, these categories were gradually replaced by political and national affiliations. As the ethnicization and nationalization of the various Bosnian communities were still in their infancy, a political classification according to religion offered a means of reflecting social diversity.[210]

After 1900, religious affiliation continued to be a more significant criterion for identification than national allegiance in Bosnia-Herzegovina.[211] Nationalization had only affected the Serbian Orthodox and Croatian Catholics, who aspired to a political community with their compatriots and coreligionists beyond the borders. For the other third of the population, the national framework remained

[206] Gammerl, *Staatsbürger, Untertanen und Andere*, 158–161.

[207] Anatol Schmied-Kowarzik, 'Einleitung'. In Schmied-Kowarzik (ed.) , *Die Protokolle*, 4. 50.

[208] Joseph Maria Baernreither noted critically that even Bosnia's share in the common customs revenues had not been clarified. Speech by the delegate Dr Baernreither on Bosnian affairs of 29 Oct. 1908, here 9–10. ÖStA, HHStA, NL Baernreither, Box 43, fols. 318–23.

[209] Kowarzik-Schmied, 'Einleitung', 83–107.

[210] Okey, *Taming Balkan Nationalism*.

[211] Hannes Grandits, *Herrschaft und Loyalität in der spätosmanischen Gesellschaft*. Vienna, 2008, 680–1.

imprecise.[212] In official documents, Bosnian Muslims referred to themselves exclusively by their religious affiliation as 'Musulmen'. Bosnian Serbs and Croats petitioned for the protection of their religious self-determination *and* their 'nationality'. The Habsburg authorities encouraged Muslim self-identification by recognizing Islam as a religious community in 1909 and granting Bosnia-Herzegovina full religious and educational autonomy.[213] It remains a matter of debate whether Bosnia's Muslims possessed a national or provincial affiliation distinct from their religion under the Ottoman Empire.[214] In the Austrian Empire, and later in Yugoslavia, Serbs and Croats competed to claim the Bosnian Muslims as members of their respective nations.[215]

The new minister in charge, Burián, availed himself of these religious divides in Bosnian society to reorganize the province. As the annexation unfolded, the question had arisen as to how the three communities could be equally integrated into a 'Bosnian constitution'.[216] In the Sarajevo parliament, Burián successfully advocated for religious equality. The composition of the Bosnian Diet thus reflected not only the typical neo-estate system common elsewhere in the Austrian and Hungarian crown lands, with representation for large landowners, cities, and a general curia, but also the interests of the Bosnian nobility. Rather, these curiae overlapped with an additional curia system based on religious identification. The mandates of the traditional curiae were distributed among the three groups according to a fixed quota, using constituencies defined by religious affiliation.[217] The three main religious groups were each represented in the presidium of the Bosnian Diet by the president, whose office rotated between them, and his two deputies.[218] The Bosnian curia system added a religious component to the model of non-territorial personal autonomy already tested in other crown lands. The colonial situation in Bosnia-Herzegovina thus allowed religion to return as a political and, at the same time, federal category for the region.[219]

[212] Okey, *Taming Balkan Nationalism*, 167–9.

[213] Petar Vrankić, *Religion und Politik in Bosnien und der Herzegowina 1878–1918*. Paderborn, 1998, 708; Gammerl, *Staatsbürger, Untertanen und Andere*, 175.

[214] Fikret Adanir, 'The Formation of a "Muslim" Nation in Bosnia-Hercegovina'. In Adanir and Faroqhi, *The Ottomans and the Balkans*, 267–304.

[215] The recognition of the Bosnian Muslims as a nation dates only to the 1960s. Iva Lučić, *Im Namen der Nation: Der politische Aufwertungsprozess der Muslime im sozialistischen Jugoslawien 1956–1971*. Wiesbaden, 2018; Sevan Pearson, *Wem gehört Bosnien?* Stuttgart, 2019.

[216] According to Okey, the author is Burián, not Foreign Minister Alexa von Aehrenthal. Okey, *Taming Balkan Nationalism*, 177.

[217] The Catholics elected sixteen, the Muslims twenty-four, and the Serbian Orthodox thirty-one of the seventy-two elected deputies. There was also one Jewish mandate. Schmid, *Bosnien und die Herzegovina*, 34–5; Gammerl, *Staatsbürger, Untertanen und Andere*, 178.

[218] Schmid, *Bosnien und die Herzegovina*, 36.

[219] On colonies as an experimental field for reforms, cf. Sebastian Conrad, 'Doppelte Marginalisierung. Plädoyer für eine transnationale Perspektive auf die deutsche Geschichte', *Geschichte und Gesellschaft*, 28/1 (2002), 155; Dirk van Laak, 'Kolonien als "Laboratorien der Moderne"?' In Sebastian Conrad and Jürgen Osterhammel (eds), *Das Kaiserreich transnational: Deutschland in der Welt 1871–1914*. Göttingen, 2004, 257–79.

This alignment of electoral law and provincial politics with religious affiliations remained unique in the monarchy. Other ethnic-religious groups, notably the Bukovinian and Galician Jews, who had also fought for representation in their provincial diets, were denied the same on the grounds that they did not comprise a nation.[220]

11.5. Federal Personal Autonomy as a Prospective Principle

Despite isolated reforms, the Habsburg Monarchy remained a monarchical federation until 1918. The oft-proclaimed correlation between federalism and democracy cannot be found in Habsburg federal history. The uneven extension of the franchise at the various levels of political decision-making led to a plurality of political cultures in the regions. For the Austro-Hungarian federation as a whole, however, there was no comparable drive to modernize.

Federal ideas and structures around 1900 reflected the experience of previous decades. The 'old' types of federalism—dualism and trialism, crown land federalism, federation of nationalities, and executive federalism—were enriched and modified. Historical, legal, economic, social, national, and religious factors were all considered in the fair organization of the monarchy's diversity. The limitations of territorial federalism were to be alleviated by the idea of a federalism based on personal association, which was later translated into a mixed constitution. In so doing, the federalist thinkers demonstrated an unprecedented degree of innovation in the history of federalism.

While the democratic federation of nationalities, trialism for the monarchy, or a transnational Balkan federation in the south-east remained abstract ideas akin to political slogans, the concept of non-territorial personal autonomy had a very concrete impact on practical politics after 1900. The innovative idea of a non-territorial association of persons points far beyond the Habsburg Monarchy in the history and theory of federalism.

When national or religious diversity is the driving force behind federalism, it should not be reduced to a territorial order. Where nationalities and religions are scattered across the various constituent states, the idea of a federal union without strict territorial boundaries guarantees federal justice. It allows the self-determination of different communities and prevents the hegemony of parliamentary majorities over minorities. As late as 1917, the international law expert and short-lived prime minister Heinrich Lammasch, in a keynote speech on foreign policy, proposed national personal autonomy as an element of future

220 Stourzh, 'Juden als Nationalität Altösterreichs?'

peace treaties.[221] During the interwar period, Estonia incorporated the idea of personal autonomy into its nationality policy and constitution. To this day, elements of non-territorial personal autonomy rights can be found in the constitutions of European states such as Russia, Romania, and Hungary, whose origins can be traced to the multifaceted Habsburg school of federal thought.[222]

A Federal History of the Habsburg Empire, 1815–1918. Jana Osterkamp, Oxford University Press.
 DOI: 10.1093/9780198943631.003.0012

[221] Speech by Heinrich Lammasch on 28 June 1917 in the Herrenhaus, quoted in Verosta, *Theorie und Realität von Bündnissen*, 240.

[222] Kuzmany, *History of Non-Territorial Autonomy*; David J. Smith and Joe Hiden (eds), *Ethnic Diversity and the Nation State*. Abingdon, 2012.

Figure 12.1 Dreadnought *Viribus Unitis*. Launch ceremony attended by the Crown Prince and Princess. Photograph, 1911.

12
The Eternal Heir to the Throne, his 'Thinktank', and the Accession Programmes, 1911/1914

In his twilight years, Emperor Franz Joseph was opposed to any reorganization of Austria-Hungary's confederative framework. However, the heir to the throne was expected to undertake far-reaching reforms. Franz Ferdinand and the 'Belvedere Circle', his coterie of advisers in the Military Chancellery named after their base in the Lower Belvedere, represented a new balance between federalism, empire, and the state. The plans for federalism they discussed have since fuelled the imaginations of many counterfactual historians. One question dominates all others: would further federalization have saved the Habsburg Empire from disintegration?

Franz Ferdinand's meticulous plans for constitutional reform that were to follow his accession to the throne have often been outlined, not least by those in his inner circle:

> We were on the terrace of the magnificent imperial Miramar Palace.... We had just completed a detailed examination of the drafts prepared, with painstaking care and much honest skill, to form—at the given moment—the foundations and starting point for the reorganization of Austria-Hungary, the creation of the 'United States of Greater Austria'.

These recollections from the spring of 1914—with their wistful references to the 'beautiful south', the 'shining blue of the Adriatic', the 'black-green cypresses', and other mournful motifs of pre-war Europe—were those of Johann Andreas von Eichhoff, a departmental councillor in the Austrian Ministry of the Interior and responsible within in the Military Chancellery for constitutional restructuring.[1]

The Miramar Palace overlooks Trieste and the shipyard of the Stabilimento Tecnico Triestino in Muggia. On 24 July 1911, it witnessed the launch of the first Mediterranean 'dreadnought', in the presence of Franz Ferdinand, who had initiated its construction with his 'Naval Action'. The battleship was christened *Viribus*

[1] Johann Andreas Eichhoff, 'Die geplante Gründung der "Vereinigten Staaten von Großösterreich": Das vorbereitete Thronmanifest des Erzherzogs Franz Ferdinand—ein tragisches, geschichtliches Dokument', *Reichspost*, 28 Mar. 1926, 1.

Unitis in allusion to the coronation motto of the 'old' emperor. This was a third-choice moniker: the Belvedere had preferred *Tegetthoff*, while the government promoted *Emperor Franz Joseph* in the press.[2] In light of the protracted and public tension between the Hofburg of the emperor and the Belvedere of his heir, the compromise *Viribus Unitis* almost bordered on sarcasm. The empire's two most senior royals hardly cooperated 'with united forces', as the name implied.

The photograph in Figure 12.1 was taken on the day of the ship's launch, providing a symbolic maritime parallel with the past. Franz Joseph's coronation motto and his ultimately short-lived constitution of 4 March 1849 were illustrated in the lithograph *Barke mit der Austria* (Barque with Austria),[3] which evokes a decidedly peaceful, companionable, almost idyllic atmosphere. Seventy years later, it was the ultra-modern, lethal battleship so beloved of Franz Ferdinand that was making the federalist waves. For him, reform was first and foremost a means to greater power. Even the restructuring of the confederation was primarily aimed at strengthening the empire militarily, diplomatically, and economically, and only secondly at containing social and national conflicts.[4]

The power-political thrust of Franz Ferdinand's federalist plans was confirmed by his confidants, such as the Hungarian minister of the interior, Josef Kristóffy. He credited the heir to the throne with an imperialist 'drive towards the east'. In terms of foreign policy, the empire should expand 'to the south-east with Thessaloniki as its goal', while 'Serbia, Albania, Romania, Bulgaria should be federally linked to the "Hungarian empire"'.[5] The need for territorial expansion to the south-east was postulated by many politicians at the time. The liberal Josef Redlich noted in his diary that labelling 'Austria-Hungary as a great power' made no sense 'if it does not strive for the unification of all Yugoslavs under its sceptre and the conquest of Thessaloniki'.[6] Two leading nationalists in the Hungarian parliament, Milan Hodža (for the Slovaks) and Iuliu Maniu (for the Romanians), expressed very similar views in a 'promemoria' to Franz Ferdinand: 'Small empires have no future... It is a vital precondition for the survival of the Habsburg Empire to secure for itself exclusive political and economic influence in the Balkans. This is, of course, only conceivable if the empire continues to exist as a world power.'[7]

[2] Letter from Alexander Brosch to Franz Ferdinand dated 27 Feb. 1911. Österreichisches Staatsarchiv Wien, Abteilung Haus-, Hof- und Staatsarchiv (hereafter ÖStA, HHStA), Nachlass Erzherzog Franz Ferdinand, Abt. 5: Korrespondenz, Box 10, Folder C, fols. 107–9.

[3] Cf. Chapter 0 (Introduction).

[4] Robert A. Kann, *Erzherzog Franz Ferdinand: Studien*. Munich, 1976, 45; see also Alma Hannig, *Franz Ferdinand: Die Biografie*. Vienna, 2013, 192–4.

[5] Quoted from Josef Kristóffy, *Magyarország kálváriája*. Vol. 1. Pest, 1928, 439-40. Printed in Georg Franz, *Erzherzog Franz Ferdinand und die Pläne zur Reform der Habsburgermonarchie* (university diss.). Munich, 1943, 96 and 162.

[6] Cf. Josef Redlich, *Schicksalsjahre Österreichs: Die Erinnerungen und Tagebücher Josef Redlichs 1869–1936*. Vol. 1: *Erinnerungen und Tagebücher 1869–1914*. Vienna, 2011, 471.

[7] 'Promemoria', written by Milan Hodža and Iuliu Maniu, handed in 25 Nov. 1911. ÖStA, HHStA, NL Franz Ferdinand, Abt. 5: Denkschriften und Broschüren, Folder: H–Sch.

Franz Ferdinand's constitutional plans were often glorified, despite their imperialist core. In their interwar hagiographies, his closest advisers, such as Eichhoff, celebrated them as a future model for a peaceful federation of the 'United States of Europe'.[8] Eichhoff even asserted in 1926 that a federalization of the empire would have made 'the declaration of war by these "United States of Greater Austria" impossible' and that 'contrary to all tendentious rumours... "Greater Austria" was intended as a haven of peace and welfare for its peoples'.[9]

12.1. The Belvedere Circle as a Federal Thinktank

Over the years, Franz Ferdinand and his Military Chancellery became a 'kind of imperial chancellery', a 'subsidiary government', and a 'supervisory authority for the court and the government'.[10] As the Military Chancellery had its own budget, Franz Ferdinand employed permanent advisers and staff to keep him informed of current affairs using the most modern media (such as the telegraph), to prepare for his accession to the throne, and to draw up reform plans. The Belvedere Circle was assembled by Alexander Brosch von Aarenau, aide-de-camp and inaugural head of the Military Chancellery, between 1906 and 1911. His newly won and arguably excessive power ultimately led to his dismissal by the emperor and his replacement by Carl von Bardolff.[11]

Franz Ferdinand's advisers included Conrad von Hötzendorf, chief of the general staff, for military affairs; Alexander von Spitzmüller, governor general of the Credit Institute, for economic and financial matters; and Richard Riedl, head of department in the Ministry of Trade, for questions of trade. They were joined by a cadre of lawyers, including the constitutional law expert Johann Andreas Eichhoff, the international law scholar Heinrich Lammasch, the administrative lawyer Edmund Bernatzik, and Gustav Turba, a specialist in Austro-Hungarian constitutional and legal relations.[12] The archduke's circle of acquaintances among the Bohemian high nobility included Heinrich Clam-Martinitz, later prime minister under Emperor Karl, Ottokar Czernin, a future foreign minister, and Karl Schwarzenberg. Mooted as a potential head of government under Emperor Franz Ferdinand, the Istrian governor Konrad Hohenlohe was a descendant of a south

[8] Eichhoff, 'Gründung der "Vereinigten Staaten von Großösterreich"', 2.

[9] Eichhoff, 'Gründung der "Vereinigten Staaten von Großösterreich"', 2. Cf. also Johann Andreas Eichhoff, 'Franz Ferdinand: Gedenkworte zum 20. Jahrestage seines Todes', *Neue Freie Presse*, 29 June 1934, 1–2.

[10] Hannig, *Franz Ferdinand*, 94–7.

[11] Ludwig Jedlicka, 'Alexander Brosch von Aarenau und Moritz von Auffenberg-Komarów: Dokumente einer Freundschaft'. In Emil Franzel (ed.), *Virtute fideque: Festschrift für Otto von Habsburg*. Vienna, 1965, 91.

[12] Franz, *Erzherzog Franz Ferdinand*, 69–70.

German princely house, the son of Emperor Franz Joseph's long-serving lord great chamberlain, and a member of the high society.[13]

The inner circle included representatives of various nationalities such as Josef Kristóffy, who had prepared the ground for the aborted introduction of universal suffrage in 1905–6, and the Croatians Josip Frank and Pavao Rauch.[14] Later prime ministers of the Habsburg successor states, Romania and Czechoslovakia, were also involved, including Alexandru Vaida-Voevod and the above-mentioned Iuliu Maniu and Milan Hodža. Another important figure in federalist constitutional reforms was Aurel Popovici, a Romanian Transylvanian who wrote the 1906 book *The United States of Greater Austria*. Also present was Edmund Steinacker, the leader of the Hungarian German People's Party. The non-Hungarian nationalities from the Hungarian territories were in the ascendancy at the Belvedere, where their concerns were welcomed as arguments for the political weakening of the Magyars.

Friedrich Funder of the *Reichspost* (The Imperial Post), Leopold Chlumecký of the *Österreichische Rundschau* (Austrian Review), Carl M. Danzer of the *Armeezeitung* (Army Gazette), and the political writer Theodor von Sosnovsky were engaged in working the press on Franz Ferdinand's behalf.[15] In a memorandum, Carl Danzer proposed the establishment of an Austrian-Hungarian newspaper.[16] The weekly newspaper *Groß-Österreich: Organ zur Vertretung der Reichsinteressen* (Greater Austria: Organ of Imperial Interests), which had a Christian-conservative tone and advocated a transformation of the monarchy along national federalist lines, was such a publication. It stood in the Belvedere camp but struggled financially. *Groß-Österreich* was nurtured by Aurel Popovici, who in June 1907 informally asked Brosch, the director of the Military Chancellery, for donations because the Austrian government was 'threatening to suppress the paper completely'.[17] When the newspaper later published an article which, as Brosch wrote, could have been found 'in an all-German or social democratic newspaper', the Belvedere reacted with indignation.[18]

[13] For the personnel table, cf. 'Personalverzeichnis für den Thronwechsel, gez. Brosch im November 1911' und 'Programm für den Thronwechsel'. In: ÖStA, HHStA, NL Franz Ferdinand, Abt. 1: Persönliche Dokumente und Schriften, Box 167, fols. 92–100, here 96. On Hohenlohe's imperial biography cf. Marion Wullschleger, '"Gut österreichische Gesinnung": Imperiale Identitäten und Reichsbilder der letzten österreichischen Statthalter in Triest (1904–1918)'. In Tim Buchen and Malte Rolf (eds), *Eliten im Vielvölkerreich: Imperiale Biographien in Russland und Österreich-Ungarn. 1850–1918*. Oldenbourg, 2015, 92.

[14] On Rauch see Mark Cornwall, 'Loyalty and Treason in Late Habsburg Croatia: A Violent Discourse before the First World War'. In Jana Osterkamp and Martin Schulze Wessel (eds), *Exploring Loyalty*. Göttingen, 2017, 97–120.

[15] Jean-Paul Bled, *Franz Ferdinand: Der eigensinnige Thronfolger*. Vienna, 2013, 133–4.

[16] Memorandum by Carl Danzer on the founding of an empire-wide newspaper. ÖStA, HHStA, NL Franz Ferdinand, Abt. 5: Denkschriften und Broschüren, Box 113.

[17] The conversation between Aurel Popovici and Alexander Brosch also dealt with Belvedere's concern that the newspaper might swing to the government camp or be bought by 'backers of the government', letter from Alexander Brosch to Franz Ferdinand dated 17 June 1907. ÖStA, HHStA, NL Franz Ferdinand, Abt. 2: Korrespondenz, Box 9, Folder C, fols. 445–7.

[18] Letter from Alexander Brosch to Franz Ferdinand, 16 Dec. 1907. Korrespondenz, Box 9, Folder C, fols. 535–7.

The press policy of the Belvedere Circle contemplated anything but a free press, as a passage in the 1911 accession programme makes clear. It spoke of 'the creation of a reputable press, which is neither Christian-social nor clerical' for 'the effort would be fruitless without the intentional formation of public opinion'. The influence of 'Jewish newspapers such as the *Neue Freie Presse*, the *Neues Wiener Tagblatt* and the *Zeit*' had to be broken.[19] Unpopular measures were to be blamed in the press on the Austrian government rather than on the crown.[20] After his accession to the throne, Franz Ferdinand's public relations network would be run by 'a staff of legal scholars, historians, and civil servants,...led by the head of the cabinet'.[21]

Franz Ferdinand's world of federal ideas and practices was not, however, fed solely by the views of this inner circle. The heads of the Military Chancellery, first Brosch and later Bardolff, also solicited outside expert opinions, memoranda, and background papers on pressing issues of the day. The provenance of these memoranda reveals the involvement of high-ranking personalities such as the general and short-lived minister of war Moritz von Auffenberg, the Hungarian-Transylvanian nationalist Dezső Bánffy, the Croatian general Emil Woinovich, and economic and financial experts such as Karl Leth.

Most of the memoranda related to tasks of the Military Chancellery. Even a 1911 memorandum on the reorganization of the state finances, written by Karl Leth, vice-governor of the Postal Savings Bank and later Austrian finance minister in 1915/1916, was put in the context of an anticipated war and outlined ways of achieving 'financial war readiness' through war bonds and new taxation.[22] The memoranda also included military situation reports from the crisis regions of the empire, such as Bosnia-Herzegovina, Croatia, and Hungary, which discussed reform projects and their chances of successful implementation.[23]

Whatever else they offer, this plethora of memoranda provides little insight into Franz Ferdinand's own position on federalism. Contemporaries and historians have repeatedly emphasized that the heir to the throne neither committed himself to a specific federal reorganization of the empire nor left behind a blueprint for a draft constitution, despite the programme of 1911 drawn up under Brosch.[24] In his memoirs published in 1938, the last head of the Military

[19] Programm für den Thronwechsel [Version 1911]. ÖStA, HHStA, NL Franz Ferdinand, Abt. 1: Persönliche Dokumente und Schriften, fols. 713–69, here fol. 768–9. Publicly accessible in 'Franz Ferdinands Regierungsprogramm: Ein welthistorisches Dokument', *Neues Wiener Journal*, 1 Jan. 1924, 8.

[20] Programm für den Thronwechsel [Version 1911].

[21] Programm für den Thronwechsel [Version 1911].

[22] Memorandum 'Finanzwesen Österreichs von Dr. Leth, Vicegouverneur des k. k. Postsparkassenamtes'. ÖStA, HHStA, NL Franz Ferdinand, Abt. 5: Denkschriften, Box 114, fols. 1–102, here fols. 15–20.

[23] The corresponding memoranda by Auffenberg, Bánffy, Chlumecký, Czernin, Shek, Vetter, and Woinovich can be found in ÖStA, HHStA, NL Franz Ferdinand, Abt. 5: Denkschriften, Box 113 and 115.

[24] Richard Lein, 'Das Thronwechselprogramm der Militärkanzlei Erzherzog Franz Ferdinands aus dem Jahr 1911', *Prague Papers on the History of International Relations*, 2 (2011), 86–109;

Chancellery, Carl von Bardolff, wrote that he encountered a series of such reform proposals when he took office in 1911.[25]

When one examines federal reform ideas attributed to the heir to the throne, it is striking how he adapted familiar models of federalism from earlier epochs to his worldview. Franz Ferdinand was politically conservative with anti-Semitic and anti-socialist leanings; he was not a liberal and certainly not a democrat.[26] In his words and deeds, political Catholicism and militarism were ambiguously combined. The latter aimed at a 'renewed' Habsburg state as a global and naval power and served as an important foundation for his political friendship with the Prussian ruler Wilhelm II.[27] Franz Ferdinand was well aware of the monarchy's military weaknesses and advocated military restraint in foreign policy crises, in opposition not least to the chief of the general staff, Franz Xaver Josef Conrad von Hötzendorf.[28]

The heir to the throne explored political Catholicism as a potential unifying force for the empire. In 1912, he patronized the International Eucharistic World Congress in Vienna and received widespread media coverage.[29] Franz Ferdinand's policy of piety provided the blueprint for later ideas of a federal 'Christian Empire' under Emperor Karl and the latter's political alliance with the Austrian bishops.[30] In a pastoral letter addressed to the Habsburg population on 4 August 1918, the bishops continued to emphasize the 'Christian origin of the reign' and presented the war as a test of the Christian Empire.[31]

Franz Ferdinand detested the existing Austro-Hungarian dualist system and the domineering Magyar aristocracy. In his eyes, the recurring disputes with Hungary over the military budget undermined the Monarchy's military standing.[32] Various reform options appear in the memoranda that involved breaking the back of the Magyar elite's power base. These included such radical manoeuvres as

Günther Kronenbitter, 'Verhinderter Retter? Erzherzog Franz Ferdinand und die Erhaltung der Habsburgermonarchie'. In Ulrich E. Zellenberg (ed.), *Konservative Profile: Ideen und Praxis in der Politik zwischen FM Radetzky, Karl Kraus und Alois Mock*. Graz and Stuttgart, 2003, 268–9 and 279; Rudolf Kiszling, 'Erzherzog Franz Ferdinand und seine Pläne für den Umbau der Donaumonarchie'. *Der Donauraum*, 8 (1963), 262–3.

[25] On this and the following Carl von Bardolff, *Soldat im alten Österreich*. Jena, 1938, 151–4; Franz, *Erzherzog Franz Ferdinand*, 75–6.

[26] Bled, *Franz Ferdinand*, 120–4.

[27] Hannig, *Franz Ferdinand*, 106, 149, and 189–90. On rising military expenditures in the Habsburg Monarchy, which were, however, moderate by European standards, cf. Chapter 10.1.

[28] Cf. Bled, *Franz Ferdinand*, 254; Hannig, *Franz Ferdinand*, 184; Günther Kronenbitter, *Krieg im Frieden: Die Führung der k. u. k. Armee und die Grossmachtpolitik Österreich-Ungarns 1906–1914*. Munich, 2003, 413.

[29] Diary entry from 12 Sept. 1912. In Redlich, *Schicksalsjahre Österreichs*, 1. 470.

[30] The theoretical basis was the writing of the later precursor of the *Ständestaat* (corporist state) after 1934 Ignaz Seipel, *Nation und Staat*. Vienna, 1916. It was through this brochure that contact was made with Heinrich Lammasch. Cf. Klemens von Klemperer, *Ignaz Seipel: Staatsmann einer Krisenzeit*. Graz, 1976.

[31] 'Die Erzbischöfe und Bischöfe Österreichs: Hirtenbrief gegeben am 4.8.1918', *Wiener Diözesanblatt*, 24 Aug. 1918, 97–105. Cf. Chapter I.

[32] Bled, *Franz Ferdinand*, 127.

the complete abolition of dualism or the transformation of the Monarchy into a federal nationality state. Aurel Popovici's work *United States of Greater Austria*, which envisioned sixteen autonomous nation states, was used as a guideline, but without the democratization of the franchise advocated by Karl Renner and Otto Bauer.[33]

Franz Ferdinand is often cast in an almost mythical role in the story of trialism.[34] Memoranda from the Belvedere entourage, some of which were leaked to the press (deliberately or not), alternately envisaged the creation of a Bohemian or later, against the background of the Bosnian crisis, South Slavic group of crown lands (comprising Croatia-Slavonia, Dalmatia, Bosnia-Herzegovina, and the coastal region with Trieste). With the help of his allegedly trialist plans, Franz Ferdinand was able to win over potential supporters and to exert political pressure on his opponents. After 1908, for example, his alleged preference for trialism gained Franz Ferdinand backers in Croatia, while simultaneously fanning fears in Hungary and Serbia.[35] Some in the Belvedere hoped that a third constituent part of the empire would exert hegemonic influence over the whole of south-eastern Europe.[36] Franz Ferdinand envisaged the Catholic Croats taking a leadership role in unifying the imperial south in the spirit of Roman Catholicism.[37] These trialist plans were, however, perennially vague and did not produce a fully fledged draft constitution.

12.2. Accession Programme of 1911

As the federalist plans of Franz Ferdinand's circle became more definite, they distanced themselves from the dazzling idea of 'trialism'. The creation of a third imperial component, comprising 'Croatia, Bosnia and Herzegovina, Dalmatia, and the coastal region' was seen by many Austrian politicians as a 'secret elixir [*Arcanum*] for forcing Hungary to its knees', in the words of Brosch. However, trialism was merely a 'pretty good scare tactic against the Hungarian chauvinists, but without bringing any real advantages for the dynasty or for Austria'. The only

[33] Aurel C. Popovici, *Die Vereinigten Staaten von Groß*-Österreich: Politische Studien zur Lösung der nationalen Fragen und staatsrechtlichen Krisen in Österreich-Ungarn. Leipzig, 1906, 320 und 324–5. On Popovici's anti-democratic and anti-republican attitude Alina Teslaru-Born, *Ideen und Projekte zur Föderalisierung des Habsburgischen Reiches mit besonderer Berücksichtigung Siebenbürgens 1848–1918* (university diss.). Frankfurt am Main, 2006, 316.

[34] On individual reform plans of trialism cf. Hannig, *Franz Ferdinand*, 99–103; Bled, *Franz Ferdinand*, 208–13.

[35] Hannig, *Franz Ferdinand*, 101.

[36] In addition to Eichhoff's articles, the reports of the French economic historian Gonnard, who travelled through the region in 1912 and analysed the plans for the Belvedere, are instructive. René Gonnard, 'Le trialisme', *Revue politique et parlementaire*, 19 (1912), 223–44 and 20 (1913), 55–71.

[37] Cf. Hannig, *Franz Ferdinand*, 108–9; Wilhelm Schüssler, *Österreich und das deutsche Schicksal*. Leipzig, 1925, 70.

'advantage of a trias' was that it made possible 'the later annexation of Serbia and Montenegro'. But this 'ideal, which is probably still a long way off' did not justify the imponderable risk of constitutional reorganizsation, especially since, according to Brosch, 'the southern Slav politicians are all more or less unreliable'.[38] Heinrich Lammasch, an expert in constitutional and international law, who had to assess the accession programme legally, was convinced by Brosch's 'illuminating explanations of the difficulties of trialism'.[39] The memoranda of the Belvedere, which had dealt with various options for a trialist reorganization of the empire, thus became obsolete.

Instead, the 1911 accession programme retained dualism in a modified form. As early as 1907, Franz Ferdinand had told Kristóffy that 'it is not necessary to demolish the edifice of dualism'. 'Dualism is essentially a federative arrangement', he continued, 'it is the first step towards federalism' and thus a way to move forward.[40] To facilitate this 'moving forward' in the federal evolution of dualism, the accession programme envisaged expanding and empowering the common institutions (the common ministers and delegations). The Monarchy's three-tiered federal structure of Austria-Hungary, Austria and Hungary, and the crown lands was to be retained. If Franz Ferdinand has sometimes been described as a 'centralist', this is true only insofar as he planned to expand the highest 'central' level of the empire.[41]

At the symbolic-political level of state semantics, however, the Monarchy was to be wholly re-evaluated. One of the accession programme's very first points stipulated the 'elimination of the terminology "the two states of the monarchy" as approved by Dr Beck's government' and the 'restoration of the imperial term in the title of the monarchy as Austria-Hungary: *Reich* (Empire)'. Beck, for whom Franz Ferdinand harboured 'an unquenchable hatred', was of course, not to be blamed for the semantics of statehood criticized here. Instead, they reflected a controversy over fundamental principles of constitutional law.[42] The dispute that had been smouldering for decades in Habsburg state theory about whether 'sovereignty' was vested in the monarch, the monarchy as a whole, or both parts of the empire would have been settled by a uniform concept of 'empire'.[43]

[38] 'Programm für den Thronwechsel'. ÖStA, HHStA, NL Franz Ferdinand, Abt. 1: Persönliche Dokumente und Schriften, Box 167, fols. 713–69, here fols. 734–5.

[39] 'Bemerkungen des Hofrates Lammasch zum Exposé des Oberstleutnants von Brosch über den Thronwechsel'. ÖStA, HHStA, NL Franz Ferdinand, Abt. 1: Persönliche Dokumente und Schriften, Box 167, fols. 776–803, here fol. 796.

[40] According to Kristóffy, quoted in Franz, *Erzherzog Franz Ferdinand*, 68.

[41] For this assessment as a centralist Robin Okey, *The Habsburg Monarchy: From Enlightenment to Eclipse*. New York, 2001, 366.

[42] On the relationship between Beck and Franz Ferdinand, cf. Lammasch's report on the change of throne plans, printed as an annex to Stephan Verosta, *Theorie und Realität von Bündnissen: Heinrich Lammasch, Karl Renner und der Zweibund 1897–1914*. Vienna, 1971, 583.

[43] Cf. Chapter 8.

As part of this symbolic package, the conceptually renewed 'Reich' would be governed by common ministers called *Reichsminister* (or the Hungarian equivalent) who would serve under a *Reichskanzler*. A copy of a letter in which Franz Ferdinand objected to the 'Imperial Minister of War' becoming merely 'Minister of War', as stipulated by Franz Joseph on 20 September 1911, shows how important this symbolism was to him. Franz Ferdinand sharply criticized this semantic simplification as 'deference to Hungarian national demands and a concession to the separatist course'.[44]

The focus on the state's symbolic unity generated extensive explanations of new coats of arms and flags. Pre-existing vexillological practice with the coexistence of different state flags in front of the Austro-Hungarian embassies and consulates abroad—one for Hungary, one for Austria, and one for the monarch—was considered 'unsustainable'. It should be replaced by a uniform heraldic regime.[45] The necessary designs received considerable attention during preparations for the transfer of the crown.[46] Indeed, Brosch's accession programme stated that demands 'concerning the independent state law position of Hungary' could only be met 'in agreement with the unresolved question of the flag and coat of arms'. It was:

> not surprising at all if citizens of the two parts of the monarchy…should have no sense of kinship; after all, they see that the state itself [meaning here the entire monarchy] does everything in its power to highlight the separation between Austria and Hungary abroad through its flags and emblems.[47]

The most important and substantive reorganization of Austro-Hungarian federalism was the planned strengthening of the delegations.[48] The Compromise Acts of 1867 had established the Austrian and Hungarian delegations as para-parliamentary institutions to enable representatives of both parts of the empire to participate in the common matters of defence, foreign policy, and finances. As the delegations did not constitute an imperial parliament, they could only monitor and supervise but not legislate. While they approved the common budget and could hold the common ministers accountable, laws on common affairs were passed elsewhere, by the parliaments in Vienna and Budapest.

[44] The copy of his letter from Schloss Blühnbach of Oct. 1911 'Erklärung zur Änderung des Titels "Reichskriegsminister"' is filed with the drafts of the constitution. ÖStA, HHStA, NL Franz Ferdinand, Abt. 1: Persönliche Dokumente und Schriften, Box 167, fol. 775.

[45] On the symbolism of flags cf. Chapter 8.

[46] 'Franz Ferdinands Regierungsprogramm: Ein welthistorisches Dokument', *Neues Wiener Journal*, 30 Dec. 1923, 8.

[47] 'Programm für den Thronwechsel'. ÖStA, HHStA, NL Franz Ferdinand, Abt. 1: Persönliche Dokumente und Schriften. Box 167, fol. 740.

[48] Cf. Chapter 8.

Brosch's accession programme proposed a significant expansion of the delegations' competences and power. From a passive supervisory organ, they would have become the central legislative body for imperial affairs. With this reform, therefore, the highest level of the empire (Austria-Hungary) would have gained its own parliamentary body. Hitherto, parliaments had existed solely in the two halves of the empire and in the crown lands. The 'common affairs' of Austria-Hungary, meanwhile, were to be extended to include infrastructure policy 'for the railways, merchant navy, Danube navigation, and air navigation'.[49] As Lammasch noted, this would have further expanded the circle of common imperial ministers.[50] In addition to the military and finances, infrastructure (both for civilian and military purposes) was seen as a new and important power issue.

One obvious dysfunctionality of the delegations, in place since 1867, was that the Austrian and Hungarian groups did not meet in person. This was about to change, as the key parameters of the accession programme laid out in bullet points: 'Joint meetings of both delegations (e.g. ministerial speeches only given once); prevent the Hungarian delegation from thwarting a joint vote'.[51] These joint negotiations were to give the delegations the character of 'an independent legislative body'.[52] Representatives to the delegations would continue to be appointed by the parliaments in Vienna and Budapest, in addition to a new delegation from the Bosnian-Herzegovinian Diet.[53] Until then, the Bosnian population had had neither seats nor votes in the delegations.

Although Franz Ferdinand was known to the public as an enemy of dualism, the 1911 accession programme was *not* fundamentally opposed to Austria-Hungary's existing federal, multi-tiered system. In drafting a new constitution, Franz Ferdinand was pursuing neither a 'centralist' abolition of the imperial halves nor of the crown lands, but merely the containment of the Magyar elite.[54] The planned introduction of universal suffrage in the Hungarian parliament also served this purpose. According to Belvedere's calculations, the electoral reform would have given 55 per cent of the 453 seats in the Chamber of Deputies to non-Magyar representatives, such as Croats, Romanians, Slovaks, and Germans residing in Hungary, whom Franz Ferdinand considered particularly loyal to the state.[55]

[49] 'Programm für den Thronwechsel'. ÖStA, HHStA, NL Franz Ferdinand, Abt. 1: Persönliche Dokumente und Schriften, Box 167, fol. 737. The addition of shipping and airships was done on Lammasch's advice, cf. 'Bemerkungen des Hofrates Lammasch zum Exposé des Oberstleutnants von Brosch über den Thronwechsel'. ÖStA, HHStA, NL Franz Ferdinand, Abt. 1: Persönliche Dokumente und Schriften, Box 167, fol. 797.

[50] Lammasch, 'Bemerkungen', fol. 797

[51] 'Programm für den Thronwechsel'. ÖStA, HHStA, NL Franz Ferdinand, Abt. 1: Persönliche Dokumente und Schriften, Box 167, fol. 737.

[52] ÖStA, HHStA, NL Franz Ferdinand, Abt. 1: Persönliche Dokumente und Schriften, Box 167, fol. 737.

[53] Cf. Lammasch, 'Bemerkungen', fols. 796–7. On Bosnia see Chapter 11.4.

[54] Franz, Erzherzog Franz Ferdinand, 84–5.

[55] Robert A. Kann, *Das Nationalitätenproblem der Habsburgermonarchie*. Vol. 2: *Ideen und Pläne zur Reichsreform*. 2nd edn. Graz and Cologne, 1964, 196.

The planned introduction of universal suffrage in Hungary was thus based on power politics rather than democratic convictions. According to Brosch:

> the worst thing that can possibly happen is that the parliament becomes ineffective because of endless quarrelling between the nationalities, as has been the case in Austria for years now. This would have the advantage, however, of denying the Hungarian government the ability to invoke the will of the 'nation'—as it has always done in the past—if it wanted to stage a raid against one of the few common institutions in Vienna.[56]

The accession programme was conservative, anti-liberal, and implicitly anti-parliamentary. Although it ostensibly followed the Habsburg constitutional order and merely sought to resolve inconsistencies between the Austrian and Hungarian versions of the Compromise, it nevertheless pointed to the 'slippery slope of constitutional violations'.[57] Brosch explicitly suggested 'the hard way' if the Belvedere's ideas did not succeed through negotiation. If necessary, he wanted to impose a constitution 'from above' and defend it with military force.[58] Unfortunately, the 1911 drafts for such a constitution are missing in the archives.[59] Instead, Franz Ferdinand's papers contain a surprising and until now undetected source.

12.3. Accession Programme of 1914

Until recently, the second programme for the accession to the throne from 1914 was considered lost. Recent research and biographies do not reference it.[60] Franz Ferdinand's papers, however, contain the very constitutional plans that Eichhoff discussed with him at the Miramar Palace just weeks before the heir's assassination. In addition to a meticulous timetable for the transfer of the crown—which in fact resembles the 1911 plans—the bundle of documents includes *two* constitutional drafts for a new 'Fundamental Law'. These two alternatives were to accommodate different scenarios for the succession to the throne envisaged by the Military Chancellery.

[56] 'Programm für den Thronwechsel'. ÖStA, HHStA, NL Franz Ferdinand, Abt. 1: Persönliche Dokumente und Schriften, Box 167, fol. 723.

[57] Kann, *Nationalitätenproblem der Habsburgermonarchie*, 2. 193 and 195.

[58] 'Franz Ferdinands Regierungsprogramm: Ein welthistorisches Dokument', *Neues Wiener Journal*, 1 Jan. 1924, 8–9.

[59] Detailed Lein, 'Thronwechselprogramm der Militärkanzlei', 89 and 108.

[60] Kann, *Franz Ferdinand*, 36. Broucek mentions the constitutional works, but only used the Eichhoff files, from which, in contrast to Franz Ferdinand's files, no preferences for the different models can be traced. Peter Broucek, 'Reformpläne aus dem Beraterkreis Erzherzog Franz Ferdinands und Kaiser Karls'. In Richard G. Plaschka, Horst Haselsteiner, Arnold Suppan, Anna M. Drbek, and Birgitta Zaar (eds), *Mitteleuropa-Konzeptionen*. Vienna, 1995, 113. Cf. Franz, *Erzherzog Franz Ferdinand*, 91–5. Similar Hannig, *Franz Ferdinand*, 103. No mention at Bled, *Franz Ferdinand*.

This second accession programme can be dated to 1914 from biographical accounts such as Eichhoff's memoirs and other circumstantial evidence. A reference to Henry W. Steed's book, *The Hapsburg Monarchy*, first published in October 1913, appears in an accompanying internal note from the Military Chancellery. The Austrian censors had banned Steed's work for allegedly insulting Franz Joseph's majesty.[61] In the Belvedere's note, Steed's book became a placeholder for public opinion in Austria. Accordingly, the expected 'mission' of the heir to the throne lay in 'a meaningful act' to 'push the Magyars back into a position corresponding to their numerical strength and to replace the dualistic system by centralist unity'.[62] A marginal note referring to the Hungarian prime minister, István Tisza, who only took office in June 1913, is equally relevant.[63]

An even more precise dating to the spring of 1914 can be deduced from Eichhoff's above-quoted testimony and the fact that the 'old' emperor was then suffering from 'catarrh and fever' which did not subside for several weeks. Telegrams exchanged between Bardolff and Franz Ferdinand over a number of weeks suggest that, in April and May 1914, the heir to the throne and his closest advisers were anticipating the emperor's death and an imminent change in office.[64] As early as 1911, Lammasch had made biting remarks over Franz Ferdinand's tendency to preface comments on the emperor's passing (which the court physician had long predicted) with 'clearly not seriously meant platitudes' such as 'God forbid'.[65]

The roadmap for the 'succession that never was' included an 'Aide mémoire für Seine Majestät den Kaiser'.[66] Somewhat prematurely, 'His Majesty the Emperor' already referred to Franz Ferdinand. The 1914 accession programme adopted the 1911 plan in many details including symbolic policy and protocol (such as the new imperial title and the draft design of coats of arms), Franz Joseph's obituary, and a 'manifesto' to the Habsburg peoples. The draft 'People's Manifesto' announced the accession to the throne and the postponement of the constitutional oath until contradictions between the Austrian and Hungarian Compromise Acts had been resolved. This strategy for justifying the postponement can be traced to Heinrich

[61] Henry Wickham Steed, *The Hapsburg Monarchy*. 3rd edn. London, 1914, p. viii.

[62] ÖStA, HHStA, NL Franz Ferdinand, Abt. 1: Persönliche Dokumente und Schriften. Box 167, fol. 148. Such a passage is not found in Steed's remarks on the succession to the throne. Steed, *Hapsburg Monarchy*, pp. vii and 282–7. For Steed's view of the crown cf. Peter Schuster, *Henry Wickham Steed und die Habsburgermonarchie*. Vienna, 1970, 124–32.

[63] ÖStA, HHStA, NL Franz Ferdinand, Abt. 1: Persönliche Dokumente und Schriften, Box 167, fols. 204–5.

[64] Karl Bardolff's telegrams on the emperor's health were sent to Franz Ferdinand almost daily from 20 April 1914 until the end of May. ÖStA, HHStA, NL Franz Ferdinand, Abt. 2: Korrespondenzen, Box 8, Folder Karl Bardolff, Fasz. 8, fols. 101, 192, 104–13, 116.

[65] Lammasch quoted in Verosta, *Theorie und Realität von Bündnissen*, 583.

[66] 'Aide mémoire für S. Majestät den Kaiser'. ÖStA, HHStA, NL Franz Ferdinand, Abt. 1: Persönliche Dokumente und Schriften, Box 167, fol. 143.

Lammasch.[67] Nonetheless, the Belvedere firmly believed that either the Austrian or Hungarian government would refuse to publish the Manifesto in order to prevent a constitutional reorganization.[68]

In this case, the 'Aide mémoire' made provisions for an immediate dismissal of the government and the appointment of a loyal successor (the names of whose members were already listed). A 'reliable general' was to take charge of the government on an interim basis. He would propose appointments to the various ministries if a new government could not be formed quickly.[69] In a worst-case scenario, the accession to the throne would be announced by the minister of war and the commanders-in-chief of the *Landwehr* forces.[70] The possibility of entrusting a general with the power to govern the empire was a novelty. In preceding decades, Habsburg policy had resorted to military administration on several occasions in crisis regions such as Hungary or Lombardy-Venetia, but never in the empire as a whole.

The obvious objective of this pithy plan was to either create governments in Vienna and Budapest that were loyal to the 'new' emperor or to establish a military government. In any case, the planned constitutional change was to take place *before* the new ruler was sworn in.[71] Formally, the minister of foreign affairs would have been responsible for negotiating constitutional reforms. Under normal circumstances, he was obliged to consult 'the Austrian, the Hungarian, and the common minister for the affairs of BH [Bosnia-Herzegovina]'.[72] The plan gave him little such leeway, however. The Military Chancellery was determined to present him with an already complete 'draft of an imperial constitution'.[73] To prevent the dissemination of this draft 'from above' too early, the foreign minister was to be permitted to inform the other parties only 'by telephone'.[74]

The parliamentary option originally envisaged by the Belvedere—namely, submitting the draft constitution 'to the parliaments' if the foreign minister and the governments failed to reach an agreement—was later deleted from the memorandum.[75] The reason given was that parliamentary involvement would 'in all likelihood reduce the prepared Fundamental Law to a torso, lacking all the elements

67 Heinrich Lammasch, 'Erzherzog Franz Ferdinand'. In Marga Lammasch and Hans Sperl (ed.), *Heinrich Lammasch: Seine Aufzeichnungen, sein Wirken und seine Politik*. Vienna and Leipzig, 1922, 81–2.

68 On the constitutional oath Lammasch, 'Erzherzog Franz Ferdinand', 82–8.

69 Lists of persons for this purpose were prepared by both Brosch and Bardolff. ÖStA, HHStA, NL Franz Ferdinand, Abt. 1: Persönliche Dokumente und Schriften, Box 167, Folder 'Thronwechsel, Ablauf', fols. 1–2, 92–100, and 224–5.

70 'Aide mémoire für S. Majestät den Kaiser'. Box 167, fol. 143.

71 On Czernin's role Lammasch, 'Erzherzog Franz Ferdinand', 82–3.

72 'Aide mémoire für S. Majestät den Kaiser'. Box 167, fol. 177.

73 'Aide mémoire für S. Majestät den Kaiser'. Box 167, fol. 177.

74 Cf. 'Aide mémoire für S. Majestät den Kaiser'. Box 167, fol. 204.

75 'Aide mémoire für S. Majestät den Kaiser'. Box 167, fol. 177 [reverse side].

important for the preservation of the unity of the state'.[76] A 'failure to reorganize the constitution would, however, forever dash hopes of freeing the empire from the shackles that have paralysed its political and economic power for decades and of placing the throne on a firm footing'.[77] One should not get involved in the ministerial, parliamentary, or 'academic discussion of the constitutional issues'.[78] All these reasons justified the 'octroi of the Fundamental Law'.[79]

In advance of the apparently imminent transfer of the crown, the Military Chancellery had already prepared envelopes addressed to incumbent officeholders for the dispatch of the People's Manifesto and the draft constitutions, including to the common minister for foreign affairs, Leopold Berchtold.[80] Such extensive preparations were almost certainly approved by the heir to the throne, whose agreement in principle to these draft constitutions can therefore be assumed. Because of their different scopes for reform, they will be referred to below as the 'minor' and the 'major' federalism reforms.

The Minor Federalism Reform of 1914

The file in Franz Ferdinand's papers on the 1914 accession programme contains constitutional drafts for *two* federalist reforms. The 'minor' reform constitution bore clear similarities to Brosch's 1911 plan.[81] Many of its provisions presupposed the continued existence of the Austrian and Hungarian constitutions, as well as those of the crown lands. Major changes only affected the highest level—that of the empire as a whole—whose power was expanded. This was based on the codification of the Austro-Hungarian economic community, which until then had to be renegotiated every ten years (the so-called agreed matters).[82] In addition to defence, foreign policy, and finance, the policy areas of customs, trade, state monopolies, monetary affairs, maritime law, and railways were to be added to the imperial portfolio. To cover the costs, the empire was empowered to take 'common loans'. Thus, strengthening the empire did not necessarily imply weakening the other federal levels. The common economic space could no longer be terminated unilaterally or, more importantly for everyday politics, threatened with termination.

[76] 'Aide mémoire für S. Majestät den Kaiser'. Box 167, fol. 147.
[77] 'Aide mémoire für S. Majestät den Kaiser'. Box 167, fol. 147.
[78] 'Aide mémoire für S. Majestät den Kaiser'. Box 167, fol. 147.
[79] 'Aide mémoire für S. Majestät den Kaiser'. Box 167, fols. 148 and 234.
[80] 'Aide mémoire für S. Majestät den Kaiser'. Box 167, fol. 244. Berchtold had held this office since Feb. 1912.
[81] It concerns the 'Gesetzesentwurf über die gemeinsamen Angelegenheiten des österreichisch-ungarischen Reiches'. ÖStA, HHStA, NL Franz Ferdinand, Abt. 1: Persönliche Dokumente und Schriften, Box 167, fols. 249–56. Cf. for the discussion of the earlier draft of 1911 Lein, 'Thronwechselprogramm der Militärkanzlei'.
[82] On the confederation of Austria-Hungary cf. Chapter 5.

The expansion of the empire's powers was to be accompanied by a bolstering of its institutions, including the creation of an 'imperial chancellor' to assist the common ministers.[83] A 'Customs and Tariff Parliament', meanwhile, would be established for the 'new' common policy area of economic affairs.[84] A crucial innovation, as in 1911, concerned the delegations. The Austrian and Hungarian delegations were to be supplemented by a Bosnian and Herzegovinian delegation. This quasi-parliamentary 'triumvirate' would henceforth decide on legislation affecting the common affairs, thus effectively repealing earlier provisions of the 1867 Compromise Acts.

From 1912 to 1914, the question of a Bosnian-Herzegovinan delegation became the subject of sharp criticism within the Military Chancellery. With the outbreak of the Balkan Wars, the Military Chancellery revised this constitutional scenario. 'Since the successes of the Balkan War, the mood of the Croatian population in Bosnia, Croatia-Slavonia, and Dalmatia has deteriorated considerably, loyalty and dynastic fidelity are declining, treasonous currents seem to be heading towards the establishment of an independent South Slavic Empire.'[85] Against this background, the 'intention of the drafted Fundamental Law to vote down the presumptuous Magyarism with the help of the Bosnian-Herzegovinian delegation' could produce the opposite effect. An alliance of 'Magyars hostile to the empire with the southern Slavs' was to be feared. The loyalty of the Croats, therefore, had to be assessed before they could be granted increased influence in the empire. Such remarks echoed concerns about the population's waning loyalty to the emperor. Here, the motive for trialism in the south-east becomes clear once again: strengthening the Croats to contain Magyar power.

A commentary in Franz Ferdinand's papers, probably written by Bardolff, therefore suggested a different direction for reform. This 'reorganization would comprise the complete abandonment of dualism and the representation of individual crown lands and territories—according to the Great Austrian recipe—in a central parliament in Vienna.'[86] As early as 1911, Lammasch had also advocated proportional representation of the parts of the empire in a 'central parliament' instead of 'three juxtaposed delegations'.[87] The idea of an ethno-federal 'Greater Austria' along the lines of Aurel Popovici's proposal was thus back on the table.

[83] On the dispute about this function Lammasch, 'Erzherzog Franz Ferdinand', 83–4.

[84] Another draft law can be found in the papers outlining this institution's composition and responsibilities. Cf. ÖStA, HHStA, NL Franz Ferdinand, Abt. 1: Persönliche Dokumente und Schriften, Box 167, fols. 654–81.

[85] ÖStA, HHStA, NL Franz Ferdinand, Abt. 1: Persönliche Dokumente und Schriften, Box 167, fol. 242.

[86] ÖStA, HHStA, NL Franz Ferdinand, Abt. 1: Persönliche Dokumente und Schriften, Box 167, fol. 242.

[87] Lammasch, 'Erzherzog Franz Ferdinand', 88. On Lammasch's self-image cf. Verosta, *Theorie und Realität von Bündnissen*.

By intervening against the dissolution of the historic crown lands, Franz Ferdinand made sure that its stint was brief.[88] The result was another compromise.

The Major Federalism Reform of 1914

The second 1914 draft constitution for the accession to the throne provided for a major reform of federalism.[89] The strength of this proposal lay in its reliance on relatively few resources to engineer a fundamental reconstruction of the Habsburg Monarchy. Its federal structure, which with its three levels of governance remained unusual in European comparison, was once again retained. As in the 'minor' reform, the focus rested on empowering the highest level of the empire. The vision was not, therefore, to transform the Habsburg Monarchy into a 'classical' two-tiered, federal state.

The core of the reform was rather the abolition of the delegations. In their place, a new institution, a federal parliament for common affairs, the *Reichsvertretung*, would be established. Comprising a representative chamber for the states (Upper House) and one for the nationalities (Lower House), this bicameral parliament would have become the empire's third supreme legislative body alongside the parliaments in Vienna and Budapest. The crown land diets would remain untouched.

The powers of the whole empire were extended as foreseen in the 'minor federalism reform' and the 1911 accession programme; they also included a common economic policy. In all other respects, the constitutions of Austria and Hungary were to remain in place as the middle tier of the federal system. Therefore, the policy fields falling in the remits of the Austrian and Hungarian parts of the empire would have been distributed among the existing federal tiers. Development at different speeds would have remained possible and probable. Pre-existing electoral laws were to remain in force in the crown lands, thus preserving the regional diversity of the ruling elites.

Compared with all previous plans, the most radical innovation of the new imperial parliament was the composition of the nationality chamber (Lower House) according to the principle of national personal autonomy. The Slovak national politician Milan Hodža, for example, had previously advocated such a step in internal memoranda.[90] With typical efficiency, the Military Chancellery had prepared the corresponding national register of the entire empire soon

[88] Kiszling, 'Erzherzog Franz Ferdinand und seine Pläne', 265.

[89] 'Gesetzentwurf über die gemeinsamen Angelegenheiten des österreichisch-ungarischen Reichs'. ÖStA, HHStA, NL Franz Ferdinand, Abt. 1: Persönliche Dokumente und Schriften, Box 167, fols. 259–65.

[90] Memorandum from Milan Hodža to Franz Ferdinand in 1911. ÖStA, HHStA, NL Franz Ferdinand, Abt. 5: Denkschriften, Box 114.

thereafter. The Lower House was to consist of 100 representatives, divided among national electoral groups (curiae), from the Austrian House of Representatives (the Lower House of the Vienna Reichsrat), the Hungarian House of Representatives (the Lower House of the Budapest *Reichstag*), and the Bosnian-Herzegovinan Diet. Eight nations were considered worthy of inclusion: (1) Germans (with the highest share of votes), (2) Hungarians, (3) 'Bohemians, Moravians, Slovaks', (4) 'Serbo-Croats, Slovenes', (5) Poles, (6) Ruthenians, (7) Romanians, and (8) Italians. After convening the Imperial Parliament, the deputies would declare their affiliation to one of the designated national curiae, which were further subdivided into Austrian, Hungarian, and Bosnian electoral bodies.[91]

Despite formal plans for parliamentarization, nationalization (in the sense of ethnicization), and the introduction of non-territorial personal autonomy, this construction had a primarily anti-democratic bent, as was betrayed by an internal memorandum. The national curiae, for instance, were primarily intended to curb the influence of the mass parties at the imperial level. As the memorandum explains, 'the Social Democrats [and] the Radicals among the Germans and Czechs' would be only weakly represented in the *Reichsvertretung* (Imperial Assembly).[92] By prescribing the number of votes for each national electoral group as an 'appendix to the Fundamental Law', the planned 'Electoral Regulations' put an end to the free formation of parliamentary groups on a party-political and democratic basis.[93]

With the planned introduction of national personal autonomy at the imperial level, the Belvedere Circle broke new ground. Karl Renner and Otto Bauer's original idea of a federal, non-territorially organized nationality state was, ironically, turned in a conservative direction against the social democrats. A handwritten note by Bardolff on the planned electoral regulations—both for the formation of national electoral groups and for the preservation of delegations—meticulously lists the nationalities which would sit in the Lower House, ominously labelling each as 'loyal to the state' or 'unreliable'.[94] While the majority of Germans were classified as loyal, not a single 'loyalist' could be found among the Croats, Bosnians, or magnates in the Hungarian Upper House. A second projection compared the party-political distributions of seats if the delegates to the 'new' imperial parliament were sent by the municipalities or, alternatively, by the parliaments in Vienna and

[91] ÖStA, HHStA, NL Franz Ferdinand, Abt. 1: Persönliche Dokumente und Schriften, Box 167, fol. 226.

[92] ÖStA, HHStA, NL Franz Ferdinand, Abt. 1: Persönliche Dokumente und Schriften, Box 167, fol. 147.

[93] On the electoral regulations cf. ÖStA, HHStA, NL Franz Ferdinand, Abt. 1: Persönliche Dokumente und Schriften, Box 167, fols. 226–9.

[94] 'Kräfteverhältnis in der Reichsvertretung bei Beibehaltung der Delegationen' and 'Kräfteverhältnis in der Reichsvertretung bei Bildung von nationalen Wahlgruppen'. ÖStA, HHStA, NL Franz Ferdinand, Abt. 1: Persönliche Dokumente und Schriften, Box 167, fols. 135–6.

Budapest.[95] In the first case, the German and Czech Social Democrats would be clearly outnumbered by the national and conservative parties; in the second, they would have no voice at all.[96] It is no exaggeration to suggest that the final draft of the electoral law, which was based on this second variant, was the result of the anti-socialist reservations of the heir to the throne and his Belvedere circle.

Incidentally, the composition of the national electoral groups for the new imperial parliament did not impede either Austro-Hungarian dualism or historic crown land federalism. Indeed, the Belvedere's 1914 constitutional plans preserved the historic crown lands as the lower federal level and the dualistic imperial division as the middle federal level, with Bosnia as an 'imperial land' directly subordinated to Vienna.[97] Franz Ferdinand's assassination in the Bosnian capital Sarajevo put a premature end to these reforms.

12.4. Before the 'Peoples' Manifesto': A Diary of Demise, 1917/18

Without the constitutional preparations of Franz Ferdinand's Military Chancellery, Emperor Karl's famous *Völkermanifest* (Peoples' Manifesto) of 15 October 1918 would not have existed. The young emperor's ideas, as described in detail in the first chapter of this book, aligned closely with those of the Belvedere. These similarities were augmented by a continuity in personnel; following the death of Franz Joseph in 1916, many of the late Franz Ferdinand's advisers rose to high positions under the new emperor. Clear parallels exist between the Peoples' Manifesto of 1918 and the Belvedere tradition of thought.[98]

Karl may have consulted and adopted Franz Ferdinand's constitutional plans, but the onset of war meant that his empire was a very different place from the world of 1911 or early 1914. By 1917/18, cohesion in the Habsburg interior, not just between the nationalities, but also between military and civil authorities, and imperial, state, and provincial institutions, had become increasingly precarious. The war economy, the food crisis, rampant disease, unemployment, poverty, and growing war-weariness—in short, a veritable quagmire of political, economic, social, and psychological factors all collided. What had once stood for the unity

[95] 'Verteilung der Mandate des Unterhauses auf die Länder im Falle der Wahlen durch die Gemeinden' and 'Verteilung der Mandate des Unterhauses auf die Reichsratsparteien im Falle der Entsendung aus dem Reichrate'. ÖStA, HHStA, NL Franz Ferdinand, Abt. 1: Persönliche Dokumente und Schriften, Box 167, fols. 139–40.

[96] 'Verteilung der Mandate des Unterhauses auf die Reichsratsparteien im Falle der Entsendung aus dem Reichrate'. ÖStA, HHStA, NL Franz Ferdinand, Abt. 1: Persönliche Dokumente und Schriften, Box 167, fol. 140.

[97] Cf. the state-law debates in Chapter 11.

[98] Ludwig Jedlicka, 'Erzherzog Franz Ferdinand (1863–1914)'. In Hugo Hantsch (ed.), *Gestalter der Geschicke Österreichs*. Innsbruck, 1962, 534. Cf. Chapter 1.

of the Monarchy—the dynasty; a paternalistic, symbolically potent emperor like Franz Joseph; widely taught visions of the state as a peaceful House of Peoples and civilizing bulwark against the east; and the advantages of a common market as well as a common security and defence policy—had all been thrown into doubt.

The legitimacy of Habsburg rule was now challenged by modern ideas like democracy, the nation state, and socialism. In the wake of the Russian Revolution, the latter gained support in Austria-Hungary. Debates about the future among the ruling elites around 1917–18 reveal an undeniable unease regarding these world-historical developments. Many parliamentary politicians, high-ranking diplomats, government officials, and Karl's own advisers wanted to renew the conservative forces that had bound the monarchy together. Once again, the principle of federalism offered a possible solution.

Federalist Reform Programmes in 1917/1918

The political diaries of Josef Redlich offer a panopticon of contemporary Vienna, giving a fine picture of the tendencies and trends amidst the capital's 'highest circles'. Redlich led an animated political and social life and harboured ambitions of becoming the Austrian prime minister or minister of finance in 1918. He sought potential supporters for his 'federalist reform programme', which his diaries develop in systematic detail.[99] His roles as a high-ranking Austrian politician, an internationally renowned and connected scientist, a friend of leading contemporary artists such as Hugo von Hofmannsthal, and a popular socialite opened many doors for Redlich. He enjoyed access to the political *séparées* in the coffeehouses of Vienna's first district, to the illustrious Jockey Club frequented by the Austrian nobility, to bourgeois and aristocratic salons, to the club and committee rooms in Vienna's Imperial Council on the Ringstrasse, and finally to the emperor's audience apartments in the Hofburg.

By 1917/18, the basic models for imperial reform had changed little since the days of the Belvedere Circle. Some adaptations were made to accommodate the alliance with Germany, however. One imperialist reformer in Redlich's circle was the Austro-Hungarian diplomat Alexander Graf von Hoyos, who had ties to Otto von Bismarck's family. In the spring of 1918, Hoyos advocated to Redlich the new 'great Berlin idea', namely, 'a gigantic empire' and a 'deepened' alliance with Germany.[100] This empire should include 'the German Baltic regions, Finland, and Ukraine' as 'independent affiliated states' so that, if necessary, it could be in a

[99] Diary entry from 18 Feb. 1918. In Redlich, *Schicksalsjahre Österreichs*. Vol. 2: *Tagebücher 1915–1936*. Ed. Fritz Fellner and Doris A. Corradini. Vienna, 2011, 379.

[100] The following quotations come from the diary entry from 26 May 1918. In Redlich, *Schicksalsjahre Österreichs*, 2. 405–6.

state of economic autarky and therefore negotiate with the Anglo-Saxon group and the Chinese-Japanese group on the basis of parity'. Hoyos's statements and actions make him a paradigm of Austria-Hungary's disposition towards imperialism after 1900. This inclination has been comparatively little explored and is often disputed in the historiography.[101] From the time he entered the diplomatic service, he was a renowned 'hawk' in the Foreign Ministry.[102] In 1908, he won German support for the annexation of Bosnia-Herzegovina. In 1912, at the Ballhausplatz, he drew up plans for the expansion of the Habsburg Monarchy to the north or, alternatively, to Salonika.[103] In 1914, he secured German backing for the war against Serbia with the 'Hoyos Mission'. Now, in 1918, he joined the ranks of the 'Ludendorffites' with his remarks on a 'gigantic empire', as Redlich disparagingly remarked. The cohesion of this *Reich* was to be achieved not by reconciling nationalities in domestic politics, but by Great Power politics in international affairs.[104] The future belonged to empires because, as Hoyos reminded Redlich, 'after the war, 'small enterprises' like Austria-Hungary would no longer make any sense'.

These grandiloquent views from the ranks of the Foreign Ministry were not shared by many domestic politicians, most of whom believed that any federalist reform had to be part of a sustainable nationality policy. Redlich, for his part, believed that, after the war, Austria would 'exist only as a federal state, and this must be accepted by Berlin'.[105] In November 1917, within Karl's inner circle, Foreign Minister Czernin and Cabinet Chancellery Director Arthur Polzer-Hodlitz clashed over the future course. Polzer was forced to leave his post. A short time later, Polzer called on Redlich to discuss a memorandum on the future of the Habsburg Empire.[106] Polzer wanted to preserve the Central Powers, but pursued a 'vigorous peace policy contrary to Czernin and Wekerle' and was opposed to the positions of privilege of Germans and Magyars in the empire.[107] As late as the summer of 1917, Joseph Maria Baernreither, a member of the House of Lords and the first Austrian minister of social affairs, confided to Redlich that the emperor was under Polzer's influence and wanted to take a stand on the principle of the 1848 Kremsier Constitution: 'No nation may rule over another'.[108] The Meinl circle, which included political and legal experts such as Redlich, Ignaz Seipel, and Heinrich Lammasch, also reached the conclusion[109] that the empire could not be

[101] Jürgen Osterhammel, *The Transformation of the World: A Global History of the Nineteenth Century*. Princeton, 2014, 562.

[102] Kronenbitter, *Krieg im Frieden*, 392.

[103] Redlich, *Schicksalsjahre Österreichs*, 1. 151 and 471.

[104] Cf. Fritz Fellner, 'Die "Mission Hoyos"'. In Fellner and Heidrun Maschl (eds), *Vom Dreibund zum Völkerbund: Studien zur Geschichte der internationalen Beziehungen 1882–1919*. Vienna, 1994, 115.

[105] Diary entry from 26 Apr. 1918. In Redlich, *Schicksalsjahre Österreichs*, 2. 397–8.

[106] Redlich, *Schicksalsjahre Österreichs*, 2. 365.

[107] Redlich, *Schicksalsjahre Österreichs*, 2. 366.

[108] Diary entry from 3 June 1917. In Redlich, *Schicksalsjahre Österreichs*, 2. 303.

[109] Cf. Klemperer, *Ignaz Seipel*; Lammasch and Sperl (eds), *Heinrich Lammasch*.

governed according to the German nationalist 'recipes of Count Czernin' or the nationalist-imperialist ideas of the Central Powers.[110]

When it came to reforms within the Habsburg Monarchy, the transitions between imperialist and federalist arguments were fluid. Redlich himself advocated a 'strengthening of the federalist elements in the Austrian constitution' and a revision of the Austro-Hungarian Compromise. At times, he was also a supporter of Austro-Polish trialism, which had imperial implications. In this hypothetical situation, the crown land of Galicia was to be annexed to an 'independent' Poland, which in turn would be 'annexed to Austria'.[111] While Franz Ferdinand had considered a new 'southern Slavia' as a possible third confederative part of the empire, the war shifted the balance to the north.

Redlich's political diary bears witness to the slow death of the Monarchy. In the eyes of Slavic political nationalists, 'Austria', as a system that favoured Magyars and Germans, had outlived its purpose by the summer of 1917.[112] Their expectations were fixed on a sovereign nation state. Those who would have supported its federalization in May 1917 now distanced themselves from the empire altogether.[113] When the Seidler government lost its parliamentary majority in September, the Czech deputies, feeling that international recognition was imminent, informed Redlich that they would be satisfied only with a sovereign state.[114] The nation-building process among the 'South Slavs' was even more radical than among the Czechs.[115] Slovenes like Ivan Šusteršić and Janez Krek advocated a 'Greater Croatia' that would include Slovenia.[116] On the other hand, leading politicians from the Bosnian government, such as the Croat Adalbert Shek, did not see the 'South Slavs' as morally or economically capable of forming an independent 'South Slavic crown land'.[117]

The 'Czech', 'South Slavic', 'Polish', and 'Ukrainian' questions intersected closely with the foreign policy and peace plans of the Allies. The dissolution of the Habsburg Monarchy and the establishment of small democratic constitutional states, as finalized by the Paris Agreements of 1919/20, did not follow any preconceived plan. The Allies had long considered a reformed Habsburg Monarchy desirable for maintaining the balance of power in Europe and as a bulwark

[110] Cf. Josef Redlich, *Österreichische Regierung und Verwaltung im Weltkriege*. Vienna, 1929, 256.

[111] Diary entry from 29 July 1917. In Redlich, *Schicksalsjahre Österreichs*, 2. 325. Later, Redlich considered this solution 'impossible'. Diary entry from 5 Sept. 1918. In Redlich, *Schicksalsjahre Österreichs*, 2. 431.

[112] For an overview cf. Mark Cornwall (ed.), *The Last Years of Austria-Hungary*. Exeter, 2002; Étienne Boisserie, *Les Tchèques dans la Première Guerre mondiale*. Paris, 2017, 279–322.

[113] Cf. Chapter 1.

[114] Diary entry from 30 Sept. 1917. In Redlich, *Schicksalsjahre Österreichs*, 2. 344.

[115] Janko Pleterski, 'The Southern Slav Question'. In Cornwall, *The Last Years of Austria-Hungary*, 119–48.

[116] Diary entry from 9 Jan. 1917. In Redlich, *Schicksalsjahre Österreichs*, 2. 256.

[117] Diary entry from 25 June 1916. In Redlich, *Schicksalsjahre Österreichs*, 2. 180.

against the perceived threat of 'Bolshevism'.[118] In August 1917, the Hungarian social democratic journalist Josef Diner-Dénes told Redlich about his mission to Switzerland and his conversations with the 'political agent of the French Republic in Bern', to whom he had proposed a confederation of Austria-Hungary, Serbia, Romania, and Montenegro. He assured Redlich that France had abandoned the idea of partitioning the Habsburg Monarchy and considered the 'idea of a federation worthy of discussion'.[119] On the other hand, by early 1918 the Habsburg experts Henry Wickham Steed and William Seton-Watson, employed in the British propaganda department, were already publicly advocating the dissolution of the Danube monarchy in the journal *New Europe*.[120] Redlich, who had been on friendly terms with Steed during his time in Vienna, was unpleasantly surprised when he learned of this shortly before the end of the war.[121] In the spring of 1918, his political confidant, Heinrich Lammasch, had travelled to Switzerland on a secret mission to discuss ideas for a federal reorganisation of the Habsburg Monarchy with the American and British correspondent George Herron, on behalf of the imperial government.[122]

As defeat in the war and the break-up of the empire became increasingly likely, plans for a post-war federation proliferated. Schemes for a 'Danube federation' or a federal 'Central Europe' are among the better-known examples.[123] The envisioned external and internal territorial borders appeared as changeable as the respective democratic, republican, or monarchical regimes.[124] The longer the war went on, the less Austria-Hungary figured in the plans for a federation as an indivisible entity. After a speech by Hungarian Prime Minister Stephan Tisza on 5 June 1918, Redlich noted with relief that at least 'Hungary has no intention of

[118] Ulrike Harmat, 'Untergang, Auflösung, Zerstörung der Habsburgermonarchie? Zeitgenössische Bedingungen der Erinnerung und Historiographie'. In Ulrike Harmat and Helmut Rumpler (eds), *Die Habsburgermonarchie 1848–1918*. Vol. 12: *Bewältigte Vergangenheit? Die nationale und internationale Historiographie zum Untergang der Habsburgermonarchie als ideelle Grundlage für die Neuordnung Europas*. Vienna, 2018, 68–9.

[119] Diary entry from 20 Aug. 1917. In Redlich, *Schicksalsjahre Österreichs*, 2. 334.

[120] On war propaganda from Austria and the Allied cf. Mark Cornwall, *The Undermining of Austria-Hungary*, 257–308.

[121] Diary entry from 6 Oct. 1918. In Redlich, *Schicksalsjahre Österreichs*, 2. 439.

[122] George D. Herron, 'Heinrich Lammasch's Suggestion for Peace in Bern 1918'. In Lammasch and Sperl, *Heinrich Lammasch*, 186–97. Cf. also Heinrich Benedikt, *Die Friedensaktion der Meinlgruppe 1917/18: Die Bemühungen um einen Verständigungsfrieden nach Dokumenten, Aktenstücken und Briefen*. Graz and Cologne, 1962, 230–45.

[123] Cf. besides the works mentioned so far, the compilations Ahmet Esroy, Maciej Górny, and Vangelis Kechriotis (eds), *Discourses of Collective Identity in Central and Southeast Europe*. Vol. 3: *Modernism I. The Creation of Nation States*. Budapest, 2010, 301–90; Włodzimierz Borodziej (ed.), *Option Europa: Deutsche, polnische und ungarische Europapläne des 19. und 20. Jahrhunderts*. 3 vols. Göttingen, 2005.

[124] Cf. Helmut Rumpler, 'Die Todeskrise Cisleithaniens 1911–1918: Vom Primat der Innenpolitik zum Primat der Kriegsentscheidung'. In Rumpler (ed.), *Die Habsburgermonarchie 1848–1918*. Vol. 11: *Die Habsburgermonarchie und der Erste Weltkrieg*. Subvol. 1: *Der Kampf um die Neuordnung Mitteleuropas*. Part 2: *Vom Vielvölkerstaat Österreich-Ungarn zum neuen Europa der Nationalstaaten*. Vienna, 2016, 1188–1195 and 1211–22.

forming a "Central Europe" with Romania, Serbia, and Bulgaria'.[125] In early October 1918, Redlich spoke privately with Czech deputies, including the agrarian František Staněk. They had already turned their backs on Austria and the dynasty and sought a federal 'union of the Polish, Bohemian, Slovak, and Yugoslav states'.[126] Later, Romania was also included in Czech plans for an alliance as a necessary geographical link between north and south.[127]

When we spatially overlay these various ideas of federalism, the result is a confusing and conflicting mosaic that gives the impression that almost everything was possible. The last promise of federalization made by an Austro-Hungarian ruler in October 1918 finally heralded the end of the empire. At that moment, the possibility of a nation state and a democratic future began to eclipse the imperial past.

Karl's Manifesto to his Peoples, with which this book began, no longer struck the right chord for reconciling the nationalities and their nationalism within a federally reorganized Habsburg Empire. The idea of a federal state standing proud under the banner of 'Viribus Unitis' had outlived its time. The eponymous battleship, christened in 1911 in the presence of Franz Ferdinand, had carried the body of the assassinated heir in 1914. On 31 October 1918, it was ceded by Admiral Miklós Horthy to the fleet of newly established Yugslavian state and symbolically renamed *Jugoslavija*. That very evening, this proud symbol of both the old empire and the new Yugoslav nation state was sunk by a pair of Italian military divers.

A Federal History of the Habsburg Empire, 1815–1918. Jana Osterkamp, Oxford University Press.
 DOI: 10.1093/9780198943631.003.0013

[125] Diary entry from 6 June 1918. In Redlich, *Schicksalsjahre Österreichs*, 2. 408.

[126] Diary entry from 2 and 10 Oct. 1918. In Redlich, *Schicksalsjahre Österreichs*, 2. 437 and 441.

[127] Frank Hadler, 'Weltkrieg und Friedenskongress: Laboratorien für Konzipierung und Realisierung der tschechoslowakischen Selbstbestimmung'. In Steffen Höhne (ed.), *Zusammenbruch, Trauma, Triumph*. Wiesbaden, 2020, 151–4.

Outlook

The Federal House of Europe

The European nineteenth century was a century of federalism. Just like great empires and emerging nation states, federations were woven into the continent's constitutional fabric. Territories like Germany or Switzerland, with federal internal structures, or dualistic and trialistic unions like Sweden-Norway, Denmark-Iceland, Russia-Finland, and England-Scotland-Ireland, all shaped a unique chapter in the history of European statehood. Interest in this history is fed by two sources: the inherent appeal of an abstract, even utopian, ideal of a federal community, and the integrating force of everyday, concrete federal practice.

The Habsburg Monarchy offers a rich narrative of federalism, both in ideas and in practice. Its unique feature lay in the combination of an internal federal division into crown lands—from Bohemia in the west to Bukovina in the east, and Galicia in the north to Lombardy-Venetia in the south—with external membership of the German Confederation or, after 1867, of the dualistic union of Austria-Hungary. Because of this complex territorial interweaving at the heart of Europe, the Habsburg Monarchy offers a unique perspective on the political reorganization of the continent between the Congress of Vienna and the First World War.

The Habsburg Monarchy was one of the most innovative laboratories of federal thought, even though—or perhaps because—it did not possess a unified federal constitution until shortly before its demise. The driving force behind its unique federalist course was the innate diversity of a multi-tiered and territorially convoluted, multi-religious, and polyethnic empire. Over the course of a century, between 1818 and 1918, a distinct federal typology emerged, comprising administrative federalism, the federal nationality state, historic crown land federalism, dualism and trialism, and non-territorial personal autonomy. It served as a construction kit for various reform designs and organizational theories. Concepts which originated from political sources as varied as State Chancellor Klemens von Metternich, the Belvedere Circle around Archduke Franz Ferdinand, the advisers to the young Emperor Karl, nascent social democracy, and the South Slavic, Romanian, or Jewish autonomy movements were amalgamated in assorted ways to form countless visions of a federal future. It is therefore no coincidence that federal reforms of the monarchy were discussed until the very last days of its existence in October 1918.

The intellectual debates surrounding the federal future of the Habsburg *Europe in miniature* and the possible integrative as well as centrifugal forces that can consolidate and support federations, or inhibit and overthrow them, are reminiscent of discussions about the *Europe in large* after the two world wars and up to the present day. Abstract debates about the sense and nonsense of a 'United States of Europe' and a federal constitution stand side by side with an already lived federal reality. The Habsburg Monarchy did not have a federal constitution until 1918, but it had a federal structure, just like the united Europe of today. As in the European Union, the integrating power of federalism in the Habsburg Monarchy can best be described in terms of specific policy areas. What is more, the Austro-Hungarian Compromise of 1867 contoured a confederative union whose achievements in foreign, defence, financial, and economic policy are often overlooked.

A living federal order, today as in the past, is based on cohesion through cooperation. In the late Habsburg Monarchy, key areas of modern policy, such as the construction of railways, flood protection facilities, primary schools, and hospitals, were planned, decided, and financed in cooperation between the institutions of the empire, the two imperial halves, and the crown lands and comitats. The elites increasingly recognized cooperative interaction as an asset that benefited all sides when trying to solve urgent political problems. The categories of sovereignty, statehood, and ultimate decision-making in the federal state, which were then (and still are) hotly debated in academic circles, receded into the background in these practical disputes. Although Vienna claimed sole control over all important decisions, it tolerated cooperation between the crown lands in the Austrian part of the empire after the turn of the century. The Austrian community of crown lands constituted itself as a *new* political tier, acting *with* Vienna rather than *against* it. Cooperation between them, nonetheless, always retained an informal character.

Because the community of crown lands was not institutionalized and the empire's political culture of divide and rule was officially maintained, Habsburg federalism remained unstable. The sword of Damocles, namely the threat of prohibition, always hung over the cooperative political structures of the crown lands, no matter how successful they might be. At any time, Vienna could stop collaboration across provinces and nationalities. Even if the Viennese central institutions worked with the crown lands and recognized their importance, the imbalance of power in favour of the imperial centre and the de facto privileges enjoyed by certain nationalities and religions ultimately had a negative effect on the overall loyalty to the Monarchy.

Moreover, the federal structures of the Monarchy were insufficiently supported by political and social enfranchisement. In the eyes of its critics, the promises of solidarity and collaboration among the Austrian crown lands were a project of the imperial elites. After the turn of the century, up-and-coming political groups regarded federal cooperation as little more than favouritism. In 1907, universal suffrage was introduced, but only for the Austrian Imperial Council and not for Hungary or the crown lands. Important social groups remained disenfranchised. This lack of legitimacy proved particularly precarious in the case of the new addition to the empire, Bosnia-Herzegovina. The federal dream of equality between regions and cultures, communities and individuals remained unfulfilled. Instead, political visions of the future increasingly identified a just order of equality and freedom with the guiding idea of the nation state.

The federal history of the Habsburg Monarchy thus also reveals its increasingly limited ability to generate a sense of legitimacy and loyalty among its citizens. Since the last third of the nineteen century, both the crown lands and the institutions and organizations of the nationalities had established themselves as reference points of social cohesion, while the Monarchy was steadily losing acceptance. This was due not least to the successes of the cooperative welfare and benefits administration in the provinces. A 'Habsburg' loyalty in a supranational, civic, and cultural sense, on the other hand, weakened precisely because it failed to adapt to the growing need for wider political participation. The peoples of the Monarchy were denied the democratic and federal experience of a Habsburg community of equals, legitimized by broad political and social engagement. The unifying effect of dynastic affiliation completely eroded after Franz Joseph's death, leaving nothing in its wake. An alternative, all-encompassing binding force was simply missing.

The fragile foundation of legitimacy and loyalty on which the Habsburg Monarchy was built is captured in a central passage of Ingeborg Bachmann's *Malina*, published in 1971. The novel is set in the small nation state of Austria, which at the time lay on the spatial dividing lines of the Cold War and outside the Western European economic and political union. Bachmann deals with the attraction and repulsion of the Habsburg past in literary terms. The protagonist, who lives in the Ungargasse (Hungarian Street) in Vienna, comes to terms with the horrors of her own wartime experience because her hometown, that 'Galician village... always fell right in the path of the pen on Allied staff maps'. In a dream, the protagonist experiences an emotional attraction to different languages, cultures, and architectural styles within the same Habsburg house. At the same time, she is repelled by the imperial violence and the illegitimacy of an outdated, involuntarily inherited monarchy, which makes the place she dreamt of uninhabitable:

> 'The House of Austria' has always been my favourite expression because it best explains my ties to Austria, better than all the others at my disposal. I must have lived in this house at different times, as I can immediately call to mind the streets of Prague and the port of Trieste, I dream in Czech, in Windish, in Bosnian, I have always been at home in this house—without the slightest desire to reinhabit it... to raise any claim, for the crown lands fell to me, and I abdicated: at the Imperial Church *Am Hof* I renounced the oldest crown.[1]

[1] Quotations from Ingeborg Bachmann, *Malina*. Tr. Philip Boehm. New York, 2019 (first German edn 1971).

Emperor Karl, the final monarch of the 'House of Austria', did not take this obvious step. In November 1918, he renounced his participation in government but refused to abdicate, clinging to his 'divine rights'. Democracy nevertheless stripped the dynasty of its power. Since then, the Habsburg Monarchy no longer existed as a political entity, but only as a cultural and literary space.

With its federal history, it has left an important legacy. In today's united Europe, too, there is talk of the 'common house' that should offer a permanent home for all peoples and inhabitants. However, the national framework has not lost its importance for social coexistence. Just as the nation state mobilized many communities in the nineteenth century as a place of political longing, a similar development can be observed at the beginning of the twenty-first century in the face of a global crisis. The exit of Britain from the European Union is significant. This development, which is perceived as a crisis, is accompanied by the growing imperial and hegemonic influence of Russia and China in eastern and south-eastern Europe. Security, peace, and cohesion in the European house remain fragile achievements.

A federal history of nineteenth-century Europe, with its interwoven perspectives of empire and nation state, thus leads far beyond the history of the Habsburg Empire into the European present. It tells of what unites and what divides. It is the story of a balance between unity and diversity, of abstract blueprints for the complex management of both coordination and individuality, of practical cooperation that must prove itself in concrete tasks, and not least the will to live together in the European house—a will, which must be regenerated again and again.

A Federal History of the Habsburg Empire, 1815–1918. Jana Osterkamp, Oxford University Press.
 DOI: 10.1093/9780198943631.003.0014

Glossary

Models of Federalism and Governance

Administrative/Executive Federalism A mode of governance characteristic of neo-absolutist and the pre-March bureaucratic periods, whereby the imperial centre retained legislative supremacy and devolved administrative implementation to subordinate tiers such as the crown lands without meaningful parliamentary involvement.

Balkan Socialist Federalism A proposed union of Balkan southeastern European peoples advocated by social-democratic and labour movements in the late 19th and early 20th centuries as an alternative to imperial domination and national fragmentation.

Cooperative Empire A analytical concept describing the late Habsburg Monarchy's late 19th-century shift from 'radial rule'—in which the imperial centre controlled political communication and agency—toward informal but tolerated cooperation among imperial elites, crown land institutions, and societal actors in response to modern governance challenges.

Dualism The legal arrangement of 1867 dividing the Habsburg empire into two partly autonomousblocks: Austria (Cisleithania) and Hungary (Transleithania), connected by the common policies finances, defence, war, and economy.

Federal Nationality State (Ethno-federalism) Administrative and political units are drawn along ethno-linguistic lines, making nationality rather than historical crown land the basis of federal governance.

Fiscal Federalism The distribution of public tasks, expenditures, and revenues among the levels of a federal or multi-tiered polity, central to debates over the financial viability of crown land and municipal autonomy in the late Habsburg Monarchy.

Historical Crown Land Federalism A model based on the historic hereditary lands (crown lands) rather than ethnic lines, thereby preserving the legal continuity and territorial integrity of the crown lands as the legitimate framework of state organization.

Historic State Law A doctrine asserting the uninterrupted sovereignty of a crown land on the basis of ancient charters, treaties, and legal traditions, invoked against centralising imperial legislation and serving as the primary legal-political argument of Bohemian Czech, Hungarian, and Croatian political movements, but also Tyroleans, claiming autonomy within the Monarchy.

Monarchical Federalism A federal model characterised by the gradual transition of a confederation of princes into a constitutional monarchy, in which dynastic legitimacy and emerging constitutionalism negotiated the distribution of sovereign power.

Multi-Tiered Federalism An analytical perspective viewing federalism as the vertical distribution of legislative, executive, and fiscal competences across multiple levels of governance, from the Empire down through intermediate (e.g. Cisleithenia, crown lands) and local tiers (e.g. counties, comitats, municipalities).

Non-Territorial Personal Autonomy A model granting self-government rights to national or religious communities defined as 'associations of persons' rather than to territorially bounded units, thereby decoupling collective rights' protection from geographic concentration.

Trialism A proposed federal restructuring of the Monarchy after 1867 that would have added a third component—most commonly a Galician, Bosnian, or Bohemian crown land bloc—to the existing dualist framework.

Historical Institutions and Administrative Bodies

Belvedere Circle A 'thinktank' of military, political, and legal advisers assembled by Archduke Franz Ferdinand to prepare for his accession to the throne and for imperial reorganization.

Common Ministries The indispensable institutional framework of dualism, comprising the three ministries of common affairs—Foreign Affairs, Defence, Finance—ensuring the Monarchy's coherence as a great power and a customs union while preserving the autonomy of Austria and Hungary in all other domains.

Compatriot Minister (Landsmannminister) A minister without portfolio in the Cisleithanian central government representing the interests of a specific nationality, a pragmatic device for managing national tensions within the imperial cabinet without conceding formal institutional autonomy to individual peoples.

County Offices (Kreisämter) Intermediate state authorities in several crown lands, already in the pre-1848 period, to monitor local and seigneurial administration and to act as a liaison to the centre.

Crown Lands (Kronländer) Historic administrative, political, and dynastic territories (e.g. Bohemia, Galicia) acting as the primary sub-units within the Monarchy.

Curia System An stratified electoral system dividing enfranchised population into separate curiaes, first, defined by property, taxation, or social standing, structurally over-representing landed and bourgeois interests; subsequently repurposed—most notably in Moravia (1905) and Bukovina (1910)—as a mechanism for allocating mandates along national lines, transforming the curia from an instrument of class representation into one of negotiated national coexistence.

Delegations A federal institution after 1867 consisting of sixty members from both the Austrian and the Hungarian Imperial Parliaments overseeing the common affairs and the common budget.

Enforced Imperial Council (*Verstärkter Reichsrat*) A advisory council of the 1860s expanded by the inclusion of regional representatives from Austria and Hungary to lend broader legitimacy to imperial legislation, preceding the dualism and constitutional settlements of 1867 without constituting a fully elected representative assembly.

Imperial Council (*Reichsrat*) The bicameral parliament for the Austrian part of the empire, after 1867, consisting of a House of Lords and a House of Representatives.

Kremsier Parliament (1848–9) The most significant constitutional deliberative body of the 1848 revolution in the Habsburg lands, producing a sophisticated draft constitution that proposed a federalist reorganization of the Habsburg Monarchy on the basis of national and historic crown land principles—dissolved by military force in March 1849 before its work could be enacted.

Millet System (Ottoman Empire) A Ottoman legal tradition of organising political and legal rights along confessional rather than territorial or national lines, partially adapted by Habsburg authorities in Bosnia-Herzegovina, where religious community membership continued to structure civil status, personal law, and educational organisation under Austro-Hungarian rule.

Patrimonial Jurisdiction (*Patrimonialgerichtsbarkeit*) Seigneurial justice in which juridical competence over peasants and rural dependants was vested in the manorial lord rather than the state, abolished in the Habsburg Monarchy in the course of the 1848 reforms as part of the emancipation of the peasantry and the construction of a modern bureaucratic judiciary.

Paulskirche Parliament (1848–9) The Frankfurt revolutionary assembly of 1848–49 debated the boundaries and form of a unified German state, confronting the Habsburg Monarchy with the unresolved *Großdeutsch/Kleindeutsch* question—whether Austria's German lands would join a greater Germany—, standing in direct tension with the Kremsier Parliament's vision of a reformed multinational Habsburg federation.

Provincial Diets (Landtage) Representative assemblies in each crown land, successor institutions to the pre-1848 estates assemblies (*Ständetage*), exercising autonomous legislative competence in defined domains like education, welfare, and regional infrastructure.

Quota The financial cornerstone of 1867 dualism, fixing by decennial negotiation the share of common imperial expenditures borne by Cisleithania and Transleithania respectively, its periodic revision functioning as a barometer of the shifting balance of power between Vienna and Budapest within the framework of the *Ausgleich*.

Sabor The historic Diet of Croatia-Slavonia, which maintained autonomous powers within the Hungarian half of the empire.

Standing Committee (*Landesausschuss*) The executive body of a Provincial Diet in Cisleithania, responsible for the day-to-day administration and governance of a crown land.

United Court Chancellery (*Vereinigte Hofkanzlei*) The central administrative authority in Vienna for the non-Hungarian lands during the *Vormärz* period, combining legislative, executive, and judicial competences in a single chancellery until its abolition in the wake of the 1848 reforms.

Constitutional Acts, Laws, and Legal Theories

Anna Patents (1913) Series of imperial decrees issued in 1913 that dissolved the Bohemian Diet and its Standing Committee, replacing elected provincial self-governance with a state-appointed administrative commission, widely condemned as unconstitutional and emblematic of the irreconcilable conflict between Czech and German political forces in the crown land.

Comprehensive State Idea (Gesamtstaatsidee) The constitutional doctrine conceiving the Habsburg Monarchy as a single, indivisible state unified under the dynasty, developed as a counterweight to federalist, nationalist, and traditional historic-crown-land claims to autonomy.

Compromise Laws (Ausgleich) of 1867 The legal settlement transforming the Austrian Empire into the Dual Monarchy of Austria-Hungary, establishing two autonomous halves bound together solely by the common ministries and by the person of the emperor-king.

February Patent (1861) A constitutional act that created a bicameral Imperial Council (Reichsrat) for the non-Hungarian lands and distributed powers between the empire and crown land diets, thereby institutionalising a form of historic crown land federalism.

Fundamental Articles (1871) A failed draft for a 'Bohemian Compromise' negotiated between the imperial government and Bohemian Czech political leaders that would have granted Bohemia a status analogous to Hungary under the 1867 Compromise, recognising historic state right laws and establishing a separate Bohemian chancellery.

Fundamental State Laws (1867) Five constitutional laws of the Austrian half of the Dual Monarchy that codified fundamental civic and political rights—including equality of nationalities and freedom of association—and defined the competences of the *Reichsrat*, the courts, and the executive, remaining formally in force until 1918.

Nagodba (1868) The 1868 Croatian-Hungarian Compromise agreement subordinating Croatia-Slavonia to the Hungarian half of the Dual Monarchy while granting it limited internal autonomy in administration, judiciary, and education—creating an asymmetric 'sub-dualism' that mirrored the logic of the 1867 *Ausgleich.*

October Diploma (1860) A rescript that dismantled neo-absolutism by restoring legislative participation to the crown land diets, grounding imperial reform in the traditions of the estates rather than liberal constitutionalism—superseded within months by the February Patent of 1861.

Peoples' Manifesto (1918) Emperor Karl's belated attempt to reform the Monarchy representing the final—and futile—invocation of federalism as an instrument of imperial survival in the closing days of the Great War.

Pragmatic Sanction (1713) A fundamental dynastic law by Emperor Charles VI establishing uniform succession rules across all Habsburg hereditary lands and declaring them 'indivisible and inseparable', providing the foundation for the unity of the Monarchy and the basis for the centralist *Gesamtstaatsidee.*

Sylvester Patent (1851) The imperial decree of 31 Dec. 1851 that repealed the 1849 constitution formally initiated the era of neo-absolutism by restoring centralised bureaucratic governance and suspending representative institutions until the forced constitutional reopening of 1860.

Bibliography

Archival Sources

Archiv národního muzea (ANM), Prague
Albín Bráf Estates
František L. Rieger Estates
Moravský zemský archiv (MZA), Brno
Zemský výbor
Zemský sněm
Národní archiv (NA), Prague
Zemský výbor
Niederösterreichisches Landesarchiv (NÖLA), St. Pölten
Regierungsarchiv
Österreichisches Staatsarchiv (ÖStA), Vienna
Abteilung Haus-, Hof- und Staatsarchiv (HHStA)
Ministerium des Äußern (MdÄ) Erzherzog Franz Ferdinand Estates Joseph Maria Baernreither Estates Landesangelegenheiten Österreichischer Reichstag 1848/49 (LA ÖRT 1848/49)
Abteilung Allgemeines Verwaltungsarchiv (AVA)
Alexander von Bach Estates Karl Hugelmann Estates
Abteilung Finanz- und Hofkammerarchiv (FHKA)
Salzburger Landesarchiv (SLA), Salzburg
Landesausschuss (LA)
Regierungsarchiv
Slezský zemský archiv (SZA), Opava
Zemský výbor
Verein für Geschichte der ArbeiterInnenbewegung (VGA), Archiv, Vienna
Parteistellenarchiv
Internationales Büro

Journals

Arbeiterzeitung
Az Est
Beamtenzeitung für Bosnien-Herzegowina
Blochs Österreichische Wochenschrift
Bohemia
Brünner Zeitung
Carinthia
Čech
Český socialista
Danzers Armee-Zeitung
Das Vaterland
Dělnické listy
Der Morgen
Der Tiroler
Deutsches Volksblatt
Die Presse
Fremdenblatt
Gambrinus. Brauerei- und Hopfenzeitung

Grenzboten
Hlas
Jüdische Zeitung
Kikeriki
Lidové noviny
(Linzer) Tages-Post
Linzer Volksblatt
L'Istria
Militär-Zeitung
Mír
Národní politika
Népszava
Neue Freie Presse
Neues Pester Journal
Neues Wiener Journal
Neues Wiener Tagblatt
(Neuigkeits) Welt Blatt
Obzor národohospodářský
Österreichische Landzeitung
Pester Lloyd
Pilsener Tagblatt
Prager Tagblatt
Právo lidu
Reichspost
Salzburger Chronik
Salzburger Zeitung
Sarajevoer Tagblatt
Vaterland
Vídenský denník
Vorarlberger Volksblatt
Vorarlberger Wacht
Wiener Diözesanblatt
Wiener Zeitung
Zeit

Published Works

Ableitinger, Alfred, *Ernest von Koerber und das Verfassungsproblem im Jahre 1900*. Vienna, 1973.

Ableitinger, Alfred (ed.), *Demokratiserung und Verfassung in den Ländern 1918–1920*. Vienna, 1983.

Abramson, Henry, *A Prayer for the Government. Ukrainians and Jews in Revolutionary Times 1917–1920*. Cambridge, MA, 1999.

Adanir, Fikret, The Formation of a 'Muslim' Nation in Bosnia-Hercegovina: A Historiographic Discussion. In Adanir, Fikret, and Faroqhi, Suraiya (eds), *The Ottomans and the Balkans: A Discussion of Histogriography*. Leiden, 2002, 267–304.

Adler, Victor, Für die Nationen! Wider die nationalistischen Hetzer. In *Victor Adlers Aufsätze, Reden und Briefe. Ed. v. Parteivorstand der Sozialdemokratischen Arbeiterpartei Deutschösterreichs.* Vol. 8: *Österreichische Politik*. Vienna, 1929, 144–64.

Adlgasser, Franz, Neue Gesichter oder alte Bekannte? Das Abgeordnetenhaus im Spiegel der Wahlrechtsreformen. In Simon, Thomas (ed.), *Hundert Jahre allgemeines und gleiches Wahlrecht in Österreich: Modernes Wahlrecht unter den Bedingungen eines Vielvölkerstaates*. Frankfurt am Main, 2010, 53–87.

Adlgasser, Franz, *Die Mitglieder der österreichischen Zentralparlamente 1848–1918: Ein biographisches Lexikon*. 2 vols. Vienna, 2014.

Adlgasser, Franz, Die Zivilgesellschaft im Parlament. Verbands- und Vereinswesen im Wiener Reichsrat. In Osterkamp, Jana (ed.), *Kooperatives Imperium. Politische Zusammenarbeit in der Habsburgermonarchie.* Munich, 2018, 75–93.

Afflerbach, Holger, Die Deutschösterreicher zwischen Staatsraison und 'Nibelungentreue'. In Rumpler, Helmut (ed.), *Die Habsburgermonarchie 1848–1918.* Vol. 11: *Die Habsburgermonarchie und der Erste Weltkrieg.* Subvol. 1: *Der Kampf um die Neuordnung Mitteleuropas.* Part 2: *Vom Vielvölkerstaat Österreich-Ungarn zum neuen Europa der Nationalstaaten.* Vienna, 2016, 651–78.

Agstner, Rudolf, *Handbuch des Österreichischen Auswärtigen Dienstes.* Vol. 1: *1918–1938: Zentrale, Gesandtschaften und Konsulate.* Vienna, 2015.

Alber, Jens, *Vom Armenhaus zum Wohlfahrtsstaat: Analysen zur Entwicklung der Sozialversicherung in Westeuropa.* Frankfurt am Main, 1982.

Albrich, Thomas, Einleitung. In Albrich, Thomas (ed.), *Von Salomon Sulzer bis 'Bauer & Schwarz': Jüdische Vorreiter der Moderne in Tirol und Vorarlberg.* Innsbruck, 2009, 7–10.

Aleksov, Bojan, Habsburg Confessionalism and Confessional Policies in Bosnia and Herzegovina. In Ruthner, Clemens (ed.), *Wechselwirkungen: Austria-Hungary, Bosnia-Herzegovina, and the Western Balkans. 1878–1918.* New York, 2015, 82–121.

Allmayer-Beck, Johann-Christoph, Der Ausgleich von 1867 und die k. u. k. bewaffnete Macht. In Berger, Peter (ed.), *Der österreichisch-ungarische Ausgleich von 1867: Vorgeschichte und Wirkungen.* Vienna and Munich, 1967, 113–26.

Ambrosius, Gerold, Henrich-Franke, Christian, and Neutsch, Cornelius (eds), *Föderalismus in historisch vergleichender Perspektive.* Vol. 2: *Föderale Systeme. Kaiserreich—Donaumonarchie—Europäische Union.* Baden-Baden, 2015.

Ammerer, Gerhard, Godsey, William D. Junior, Scheutz, Martin, Urbanitsch, Peter, and Weiss, Alfred Stefan, Die Stände in der Habsburgermonarchie: Eine Einleitung. In Ammerer, Gerhard, Godsey, William D. Junior, Scheutz, Martin, Urbanitsch, Peter, and Weiss, Alfred Stefan (eds), *Bündnispartner und Konkurrenten des Landesfürsten? Die Stände in der Habsburgermonarchie.* Vienna and Munich, 2007, 13–41.

Andics, Erzsébet, *Metternich und die Frage Ungarns.* Budapest, 1973.

Andrássy, Julius, *Ungarns Ausgleich mit Österreich vom Jahr 1867.* Leipzig, 1897.

Anghie, Antony, *Imperialism, Sovereignty, and the Making of International Law.* Cambridge, 2004.

Anter, Andreas, Modernität und Ambivalenz in Georg Jellineks Staatsdenken. In Anter, Andreas (ed.), *Die normative Kraft des Faktischen: Das Staatsverständnis Georg Jellineks.* Baden-Baden, 2004, 37–59.

Apollonio, Almerigo, Gli esperimenti d'autogoverno comunale del governatore Francesco Stadion in Istria e nel Gorizano 1844–47. *Quaderni Giuliani di Storia,* 7/2 (1996), 31–98.

Aretin, Karl Otmar von, *Vom Deutschen Reich zum Deutschen Bund.* Göttingen, 1980.

Aretin, Karl Otmar von, *Das Alte Reich 1648–1806.* Vol. 3: *Das Reich und der österreichisch-preußische Dualismus 1745–1806.* Stuttgart, 1997.

Armour, Ian D., 'Like the Lord Lieutenant of a County': The Habsburg Monarchy and Milan Obrenović of Serbia 1868–1881. *Canadian Slavonic Papers,* 55/3–4 (2013), 305–42.

Auffenberg von Komarów, Moritz, *Aus Österreichs Höhe und Niedergang: Eine Lebensschilderung.* Munich, 1921.

Augustynowicz, Christoph, *Grenze(n) und Herrschaft(en) in der kleinpolnischen Stadt Sandomierz 1772–1844.* Vienna and Münster, 2015.

Aust, Martin, and Schenk, Benjamin Frithjof (eds), *Imperial Subjects: Autobiographische Praxis in den Vielvölkerreichen der Romanovs, Habsburger und Osmanen im 19. und frühen 20. Jahrhundert.* Cologne, 2015.

Avrutin, Eugene M., Dekel-Chen, Jonathan L., and Weinberg, Robert (eds), *Ritual Murder in Russia, Eastern Europe, and Beyond: New Histories of an Old Accusation.* Bloomington, IN, 2017.

Baár, Monika, *Historians and Nationalism: East-Central Europe in the Nineteenth Century.* New York, 2010.

Bacher, Roman, *Der Tiroler Provinziallandtag von 1848 im Rahmen der allgemeinen österreichischen Verfassungsentwicklung*. Innsbruck, 1991.

Bachleitner, Norbert, *Die literarische Zensur in Österreich von 1751 bis 1848*. Vienna, 2017.

Bachmann, Harald, *Joseph Maria Baernreither 1845–1925: Der Werdegang eines altösterreichischen Ministers und Sozialpolitikers*. Neustadt an der Aisch, 1977.

Bachmann, Ingeborg, *Malina*. Tr. Philip Boehm. New York, 2019 (first German edn 1971).

Bader-Zaar, Birgitta, Die 'grande affaire': Wahlrechtsreformen in Europa und Nordamerika im 'langen' 19. Jahrhundert. In Simon, Thomas (ed.), *Hundert Jahre allgemeines und gleiches Wahlrecht in Österreich: Modernes Wahlrecht unter den Bedingungen eines Vielvölkerstaates*. Frankfurt am Main, 2010, 13–35.

Bader-Zaar, Birgitta, Die Demokratisierung des Wahlrechts. In Kriechbaumer, Robert, Maier, Michaela, Mesner, Maria, and Wohnout, Helmut (eds), *Die junge Republik: Österreich 1918/19*. Vienna, 2018, 101–12.

Baernreither, Joseph Maria, Socialreform in Österreich. *Zeitschrift für Volkswirtschaft, Sozialpolitik und Verwaltung*, 1 (1892), 11–42.

Baernreither, Joseph Maria, *Bosnische Eindrücke: Eine politische Studie*. Vienna, 1908.

Baernreither, Joseph Maria, *Grundfragen der sozialen Versicherung in Österreich: Ergebnisse der Beratungen des Arbeitsbeirates*. Vienna, 1908.

Baernreither, Joseph Maria, *Fragmente eines politischen Tagebuches: Die südslawische Frage und Österreich-Ungarn vor dem Weltkrieg*. Ed. Josef Redlich. Berlin, 1928.

Bahm, Karl F., Demokratie, Nationalismus und das Schicksals eines 'nationalen Zwitters': Uffo Horn und die 1848er Revolution in Böhmen. In Velková, Alice, Velek, Luboš, and Pokorný, Jiří (eds), *Nacionalismus, společnost a kultura ve střední Evropě 19. a 20. století. Pocta Jiřímu Kořalkovi k 75. narozeninám/Nationalismus, Gesellschaft und Kultur in Mitteleuropa im 19. und 20. Jahrhundert. Festschrift für Jiří Kořalka zum 75. Geburtstag*. Prague, 2007, 53–69.

Bakunin, Michael, *Aufruf an die Slaven*. Koethen, 1848.

Balandier, Georges, La situation colonial: Approche théorique. *Cahiers Internationaux de Sociologie*, 11 (1951), 44–79.

Balík, Stanislav, Česko-německé uspořádání v orgánech Advokátní komory v království Českém od počátku 20. století do r. 1918. In Fasora, Lukáš, Hanuš, Jiří, and Malíř, Jiří (ed.), *Moravské vyrovnání z roku 1905: Možnosti a limity národnostního smíru ve střední Evropě*. Brno, 2006, 325–32.

Balík, Stanislav, Hanuš, Jiří, Fasora, Lukáš, and Vlha, Marek, *Der tschechische Antiklerikalismus: Quellen, Themen und Gestalt des tschechischen Antiklerikalismus in den Jahren 1848–1938*. Vienna, 2016.

Baltzarek, Franz, *Die Geschichte der Wiener Börse: Öffentliche Finanzen und privates Kapital im Spiegel einer österreichischen Wirtschaftsinstitution*. Vienna, 1973.

Baltzarek, Franz, Zentralistische und föderalistische Aspekte der Wirtschaftspolitik. In Müller, Uwe (ed.), *Ausgebeutet oder alimentiert? Regionale Wirtschaftspolitik und nationale Minderheiten in Ostmitteleuropa 1867–1939*. Berlin, 2006, 59–90.

Barany, George, Ungarns Verwaltung 1848–1918. In Wandruszka, Adam, and Urbanitsch, Peter (eds), *Die Habsburgermonarchie 1848–1918*. Vol. 2: *Verwaltung und Rechtswesen*. Vienna, 1975, 306–468.

Bardolff, Carl von, *Soldat im alten Österreich: Erinnerungen aus meinem Leben*. Jena, 1938.

Barkey, Karen, *Empire of Difference: The Ottomans in Comparative Perspective*. Cambridge, 2008.

Bartal, Israel, *Geschichte der Juden im östlichen Europa 1772–1881*. Göttingen, 2010.

Barth, Anna, *Agrarpolitik im Vormärz: Die Steirische Landwirtschaftsgesellschaft unter Erzherzog Johann*. Graz, 1980.

Barton, Arnold H., *Sweden and Visions of Norway: Politics and Culture 1814–1905*. Carbondale, IL, 2003.

Barton, Peter, Die evangelische Kirche im Lande und Erzstift Salzburg. In Dopsch, Heinz, and Spatzenegger, Hans (eds), *Geschichte Salzburgs: Stadt und Land*. Vol. 2/3. Salzburg, 1991, 1521–50.

Bataković, Dušan T., *The Foreign Policy of Serbia 1844–1867: Ilija Garašanin's Načertanije.* Belgrade, 2014.

Battaglia, Roger von, Industrieförderung als künstliches Ausgleichsmittel. In *Schriften des volkswirtschaftlichen Instituts des Obersten Polnischen Nationalkomitees.* Deutsche Folge, 1. Krakow, 1917.

Bauer, Hartmut, *Die Bundestreue: Zugleich ein Beitrag zur Dogmatik des Bundesstaatsrechts und zur Rechtsverhältnislehre.* Tübingen, 1992.

Bauer, Otto, *Die Nationalitätenfrage und die Sozialdemokratie.* Vienna, 1907.

Baumann, Zygmunt, *Moderne und Ambivalenz: Das Ende der Eindeutigkeit.* Hamburg, 2005.

Baumgart, Winfried, *The Crimean War 1853–1856.* London, 1999.

Bayly, Christopher A., *Empire and Information: Intelligence Gathering and Social Communication in India. 1780–1870.* Cambridge, 1996.

Beaud, Olivier, *Théorie de la Fédération.* 2nd edn. Paris, 2009.

Beaud, Olivier, Federation and Empire: About a Conceptual Distinction of Political Forms. *International Journal of Constitutional Law,* 16/4 (2018), 1199–1206.

Beck, Ulrich, and Grande, Edgar, Die reflexive Modernisierung Europas. In Beck, Ulrich, and Grande, Edgar, *Das kosmopolitische Europa.* Frankfurt am Main, 2004, 49–80.

Becker, Peter, Der Staat: Eine österreichische Geschichte? *Mitteilungen des Instituts für österreichische Geschichtsforschung,* 126 (2018), 317–40.

Becker, Peter, Stolpersteine auf dem Weg zum kooperativen Imperium: Bürokratische Praxis, gesellschaftliche Erwartungen und sozialpolitische Strategien. In Osterkamp, Jana (ed.), *Kooperatives Imperium: Politische Zusammenarbeit in der späten Habsburgermonarchie.* Göttingen, 2018, 23–53.

Bedeus von Scharberg, Joseph, *Die Verfassung des Großfürstenthums Siebenbürgens aus dem Gesichtspunkte der Geschichte, der Landesgesetze und des bestehenden öffentlichen Rechtes.* Vienna, 1844.

Beer, Adolf, *Die Finanzen Österreichs im 19. Jahrhundert nach archivalischen Quellen.* Prague, 1877.

Beer, Adolf, *Der Staatshaushalt Österreich-Ungarns seit 1868.* Prague, 1881.

Beer, Adolf, *Die österreichische Handelspolitik im neunzehnten Jahrhundert.* Vienna, 1891.

Beer, Adolf, Die Finanzverwaltung Oesterreichs 1749–1816. *Mitteilungen des Instituts für Österreichische Geschichtsforschung,* 15 (1894), 237–366.

Beer, Adolf (ed.), *Kübeck und Metternich. Denkschriften und Briefe.* Vienna, 1897.

Begert, Alexander, *Böhmen, die böhmische Kur und das Reich vom Hochmittelalter bis zum Ende des Alten Reiches: Studien zur Kurwürde und zur staatsrechtlichen Stellung Böhmens.* Husum, 2003.

Behschnitt, Wolf D., *Nationalismus bei Serben und Kroaten 1830–1914. Analyse und Typologie der nationalen Ideologie.* Munich, 1980.

Beidtel, Ignaz, *Die politischen Zustände der österreichischen Staaten nach dem Zustande vom 16. April 1848.* Vienna, 1848.

Beidtel, Ignaz, *Geschichte der österreichischen Staatsverwaltung 1740–1848.* Vol. 2: *1792–1848.* Innsbruck, 1898.

Bellabarba, Marco, *Das Habsburgerreich 1765–1918.* Berlin and Boston, 2020.

Beller, Steven, *The Habsburg Monarchy 1815–1918.* Cambridge, 2018.

Benedek, Gábor, Ministerialbeamte zur Zeit des Ausgleichs. In Bácskai, Vera (ed.), *Bürgertum und bürgerliche Entwicklung in Mittel- und Osteuropa.* Vol. 2. Budapest, 1986, 555–89.

Benedek, Gábor, Die Beamten in Ungarn. In Rumpler, Helmut, and Urbanitsch, Peter (eds), *Die Habsburgermonarchie 1848–1918.* Vol. 9: *Soziale Strukturen.* Part 1: *Von der Feudal-Agrarischen zur Bürgerlich-industriellen Gesellschaft.* Subvol. 2: *Von der Stände- zur Klassengesellschaft.* Vienna, 2010, 1211–43.

Benedikt, Heinrich, *Die Friedensaktion der Meinlgruppe 1917/18: Die Bemühungen um einen Verständigungsfrieden nach Dokumenten, Aktenstücken und Briefen.* Graz and Cologne, 1962.

Beneš, Edvard, *Le problème autrichien et la question tchèque: Étude sur les luttes politiques des nationalités slaves en Autriche.* Paris, 1908.

Beneš, Jakub S., *Workers and Nationalism: Czech and German Social Democracy in Habsburg Austria 1890–1918*. Oxford, 2017.

Ben-Joseph, Marc, *Adversities of Autonomy: Bank krajowy królestwa Galicyi i Lodomeryi and the Politics of Credit in Galicia 1870–1913*. Crakow, 1999.

Benvenuti, Sergio, *L'autonomia Trentina al Landtag di Innsbruck e al Reichsrat di Vienna: Proposte e progetti 1848–1914*. Trento, 1978.

Benz, Arthur, Demokratisches Regieren im Föderalismus: Neue Literatur zu einem alten Thema. *Neue Politische Literatur*, 64 (2019), 513–35.

Berding, Helmut, and Ullmann, Hans-Peter, Veränderungen in Deutschland an der Wende vom 18. zum 19. Jahrhundert. In Berding, Helmut, and Ullmann, Hans-Peter (eds), *Deutschland zwischen Revolution und Restauration*. Königstein im Taunus, 1981, 11–40.

Berend, Ivan T., Economy and Education: The Hungarian Case in the 19th and 20th Centuries. In Tortella, Gabriel (ed.), *Education and Economic Development since the Industrial Revolution*. Valencia, 1990, 173–84.

Berend, Ivan T., *History Derailed: Central and Eastern Europe in the Long Ninetheenth Century*. Berkeley, CA, 2003.

Berger, Peter (ed.), *Der österreichisch-ungarische Ausgleich von 1867: Vorgeschichte und Wirkungen*. Vienna and Munich, 1967.

Berger, Peter, Der österreichisch-ungarische Dualismus 1867–1918 und die österreichische Rechtswissenschaft. Der Donauraum, 13/3 (1968), 156–70.

Berger, Stefan, Britischer und deutscher Nationalismus im Vergleich. Probleme und Perspektiven. In Hirschhausen, Ulrike von, and Leonhard, Jörn (eds), *Nationalismen in Europa: West- und Osteuropa im Vergleich*. Göttingen, 2001, 96–116.

Berger, Stefan, and Miller, Alexey, *Nationalizing Empires*. Budapest, 2015.

Berger Waldenegg, Georg Christoph, Die Bukowina war glücklicher: Die administrative und staatsrechtliche Stellung der Ruthenen in Galizien von Anfang 1848 bis Herbst 1850. In Stellner, František (ed.), *Staletí objevů, diplomacie a válek: Sborník k 60. narozeninám profesora Aleše Skřivana*. Prague, 2005, 23–46.

Bernadello, Adolfo, *Veneti sotto l'Austria. Ceti popolari e tensioni sociali 1840–1866*. Verona, 1997.

Bernatzik, Edmund (ed.), *Die österreichischen Verfassungsgesetze: Mit Erläuterungen*. 2nd edn. Vienna, 1911.

Bernatzik, Edmund, Unsere neuen Wappen und Titel. *Österreichische Zeitschrift für öffentliches Recht*, 2/5–6 (1915/16), 616–52.

Bernstorff, Jochen von, Georg Jellinek: Völkerrecht als modernes öffentliches Recht im fin de siècle. In Paulson, Stanley L., and Schulte, Martin (eds), *Georg Jellinek. Beiträge zu Leben und Werk*. Tübingen, 2000, 183–206.

Berthold, Karl, *Schlesiens Landesvertretung und Landeshaushalt: Von ihren Anfängen bis zur neuesten Zeit*. Vol. 2: *Landeshaushalt*. Opava, 1909.

Bettelheim-Gabillon, Ludwig, Eugen von Böhm-Bawerk und die Brüsseler Zuckerkonvention (1903): Ein Beitrag zu seiner Wirksamkeit als Finanzminister. *Zeitschrift für Nationalökonomie*, 7/5 (1936), 596–636.

Bibl, Viktor, *Die niederösterreichischen Stände im Vormärz. Ein Beitrag zur Vorgeschichte der Revolution des Jahres 1848*. Vienna, 1911.

Bibl, Viktor, *Der Zerfall Österreichs*. Vol. 2: *Von Revolution zu Revolution 1848–1918*. Vienna, 1924.

Bidermann, Hermann Ignaz, *Legislation autonome de la Croatie et apercu de l'histoire du droit Croate*. Gant, 1876.

Bidermann, Hermann Ignaz, *Die rechtliche Natur der österreichisch-ungarischen Monarchie*. Vienna, 1877.

Bidermann, Hermann Ignaz, *Geschichte der österreichischen Gesamt-Staats-Idee 1526–1804*. Vol. 1: *1526–1705*. Innsbruck, 1867. Vol. 2: *1705–1740*. Innsbruck, 1889.

Bier, Karl, Der Autonomiekampf der Welschtiroler und die Stellung der deutschen Parteien und Regierungen. *Veröffentlichungen des Museum Ferdinandeum in Innsbruck*, 16 (1936/1938), 417–525.

Bigaran, Mariapia, Notabeln und Stadtregierung: Ämter, Zensus und Berufe in Trient gegen Ende des 19. Jahrhunderts. In Stekl, Hannes, Urbanitsch, Peter, Bruckmüller, Ernst, and Heiss, Hans (eds), *Durch Arbeit, Besitz Wissen und Gerechtigkeit: Bürgertum in der Habsburgermonarchie*. Vienna, 1992, 131–40.

Bigaran, Mariapia, Il governo municipale a Trento tra '800 e '900. Ordinamenti, gruppi sociali, politiche. University dissertation. Florence, 1996.

Bilgeri, Benedikt, *Geschichte Vorarlbergs*. Vol. 4: *Zwischen Absolutismus und halber Autonomie*. Vienna, 1982.

Binder, Harald, 'Galizische Autonomie': Ein streitbarer Begriff und seine Karriere. In Fasora, Lukáš, Malíř, Jiří, and Hanuš, Jiří (eds), *Moravské vyrovnání z roku 1905: Možnosti a limity národnostního smíru ve střední Evropě/Der Mährische Ausgleich von 1905: Möglichkeiten und Grenzen für einen nationalen Ausgleich in Mitteleuropa*. Brno, 2006, 239–66.

Binder, Harald, Die Ukrainer von enttäuschter Staatstreue zum Kampf um Selbständigkeit. In Rumpler, Helmut (ed.), *Die Habsburgermonarchie 1848–1918*. Vol. 11: *Die Habsburgermonarchie und der Erste Weltkrieg*. Subvol. 1: *Der Kampf um die Neuordnung Mitteleuropas*. Part 2: *Vom Vielvölkerstaat Österreich-Ungarn zum neuen Europa der Nationalstaaten*. Vienna, 2016, 853–85.

Binder, Harald, Křivohlavá, Barbora, and Velek, Luboš (eds), *Místo národních jazyků ve výchově, školství a vědě v habsburské monarchii 1867–1918/Position of National Languages in Education, Educational System and Science of the Habsburg Monarchy 1867–1918*. Prague, 2003.

Binder, Iris, Der Kärntner Landtag. In Rumpler, Helmut, and Urbanitsch, Peter (eds), *Die Habsburgermonarchie 1848–1918*. Vol. 7: *Verfassung und Parlamentarismus*. Subvol. 2: *Die regionalen Repräsentativkörperschaften*. Vienna, 2000, 1719–37.

Bjork, James E., *Neither German nor Pole: Catholicism and National Indifference in a Central European Borderland*. Ann Arbor, 2008.

Blackbourn, David, *Die Eroberung der Natur: Eine Geschichte der deutschen Landschaft*. Munich, 2008.

Blankart, Charles, *Öffentliche Finanzen in der Demokratie*. 8th edn. Munich, 2011.

Blankart, Charles B., and Fasten, Erik R., Die ökonomische Grammatik des Föderalismus: Von den Anfängen des Grundgesetzes bis zur Föderalismusreform II. In Härtel, Ines (ed.), *Handbuch Föderalismus: Föderalismus als demokratische Rechtsordnung und Rechtskultur in Deutschland, Europa und der Welt*. Vol. 1: *Grundlagen des Föderalismus und der deutsche Bundesstaat*. Heidelberg, 2012, 319–32.

Bled, Jean-Paul, *Franz Ferdinand: Der eigensinnige Thronfolger*. Vienna, 2013.

Blumenthal, Karsten von, *Die Steuertheorien der Austrian Economics: Von Menger zu Mises*. Marburg, 2007.

Böckenförde, Ernst-Wolfgang, Der deutsche Typ der konstitutionellen Monarchie im 19. Jahrhundert. In Böckenförde, Ernst-Wolfgang, *Recht, Staat, Freiheit: Studien zur Rechtsphilosophie, Staatstheorie und Verfassungsgeschichte*. Frankfurt am Main, 1991, 273–305.

Böckenförde, Ernst-Wolfgang, Der Staat als Organismus: Zur staatstheoretisch-verfassung spolitischen Diskussion im frühen Konstitutionalismus. In Böckenförde, Ernst-Wolfgang, *Recht, Staat, Freiheit. Studien zur Rechtsphilosophie, Staatstheorie und Verfassungsgeschichte*. Frankfurt am Main, 1991, 263–72.

Böckenförde, Ernst-Wolfgang, Lorenz von Stein als Theoretiker der Bewegung von Staat und Gesellschaft zum Sozialstaat. In Böckenförde, Ernst-Wolfgang, *Recht, Staat, Freiheit. Studien zur Rechtsphilosophie, Staatstheorie und Verfassungsgeschichte*. Frankfurt am Main, 1991, 170–208.

Boehm, Karlo [Pseudonym Karlović, B.], *Financijalna nagodba*. Zagreb, 1904.

Bohačevs'ka-Chom'jak, Marta, *The Spring of a Nation: The Ukrainians in Eastern Galicia in 1848*. Philadelphia, 1967.

Boisserie, Ètienne, *Les Tchèques dans la Première Guerre mondiale: 'Nous ne croyons plus aucune promesse'*. Paris, 2017.

Boleslawski von der Trenck, Richard, Die Arbeitsvermittlung in Österreich. In *Österreichs Wohlfahrts-Einrichtungen 1848–1898*. Vol. 4: *Sociale Hilfspflege*. Vienna, 1900, 311–54.

Bolzano, Bernard, *Über das Verhältnis der beiden Volksstämme in Böhmen: Drei Vorträge im Jahre 1816 an der Hochschule zu Prag gehalten*. Vienna, 1849.

Bormann, Patrick, Furcht und Angst als Faktoren deutscher Weltpolitik 1897–1914. In Bormann, Patrick, Freiberger, Thomas, and Michel, Judith (eds), *Angst in den Internationalen Beziehungen*. Göttingen, 2010, 71–90.

Borodziej, Włodzimierz (ed.), *Option Europa. Deutsche, polnische und ungarische Europapläne des 19. und 20. Jahrhunderts*. 3 vols. Göttingen, 2005.

Borodziej, Włodzimierz, Brzostek, Błażej, and Górny, Maciej, Polnische Europa-Pläne des 19. und 20. Jahrhunderts. In Borodziej, Włodzimierz (ed.), *Option Europa. Deutsche, polnische und ungarische Europapläne des 19. und 20. Jahrhunderts*. Vol. 1: *Essays*. Göttingen, 2005, 43–134.

Borsi-Kálmán, Béla, *Hungarian Exiles and the Romanian National Movement: 1849–1867*. New York, 1991.

Bosbach, Franz, and Hiery, Hermann, Einleitung. In Bosbach, Franz, and Hiery, Hermann (eds), *Imperium—Empire—Reich: Ein Konzept politischer Herrschaft im deutsch-britischen Vergleich*. Munich, 1999, 11–16.

Botušans'kyj, Vasyl', Die Ukrainer und der Prager Slavenkongress. In Moritsch, Andreas (ed.), *Der Prager Slavenkongress 1848*. Vienna, 2000, 115–22.

Bourdieu, Pierre, *Die feinen Unterschiede. Kritik der gesellschaftlichen Urteilskraft*. Frankfurt am Main, 1987.

Bowring, Bill, Burial and Resurrection: Karl Renner's Controversial Influence on the 'Question' in Russia. In Nimni, E. (ed.), *National-Cultural Autonomy and its Contemporary Critics*. New York, 2005, 191–206.

Boyer, John W., *Karl Lueger (1844–1910): Christlichsoziale Politik als Beruf*. Vienna, 2010.

Bráf, Albín, Über Meliorationscredit mit besonderer Berücksichtigung auf Österreich. *Zeitschrift für Volkswirtschaft, Socialpolitik und Verwaltung*, 1 (1892), 227–48.

Bráf, Albín, *Národohospodářské potřeby české*. Prague, 1908.

Brandt, Harm-Hinrich, Von Bruck zu Naumann: 'Mitteleuropa' in der Zeit der Paulskirche und des Ersten Weltkrieges. In Brandt, Harm-Hinrich, Gehler, Michael, Schmidt, Rainer F., and Steininger, Rolf (eds), *Ungleiche Partner? Österreich und Deutschland in ihrer gegenseitigen Wahrnehmung: Historische Analysen und Vergleiche aus dem 19. und 20. Jahrhundert*. Innsbruck, 2009, 315–52.

Brandt, Harm-Hinrich (ed.), *Der österreichische Neoabsolutismus als Verfassungs- und Verwaltungsproblem: Diskussionen über einen strittigen Epochenbegriff*. Vienna, 2014.

Bratassević, Eduard, Die Wiener k.k. Krankenanstalten während der Jahre 1892–1902. *Statistische Monatsschrift* (1906), 631–58.

Brauneder, Wilhelm, Das Gutsgebiet: Vom monarchisch-ständischen Staatselement zum lokalen Verwaltungssprengel. In Kovács, Kálmán (ed.), *Entwicklung der städtischen und regionalen Verwaltung in den letzten 100 Jahren in Mittel- und Osteuropa*. Vol. 3. Budapest, 1979, 51–65.

Brauneder, Wilhelm, *Leseverein und Rechtskultur: Der Juridisch-politische Leseverein zu Wien 1840–1990*. Vienna, 1992.

Brauneder, Wilhelm, Die Pragmatische Sanktion. In Brauneder, Wilhelm (ed.), *Studien I: Entwicklung des Öffentlichen Rechts I*. Frankfurt am Main, 1994.

Brauneder, Wilhelm, Die Habsburgermonarchie als zusammengesetzter Staat. In Becker, Hans-Jürgen (ed.), *Zusammengesetzte Staatlichkeit in der Europäischen Verfassungsgeschichte: Tagung der Vereinigung für Verfassungsgeschichte in Hofgeismar vom 19.3.–21.3.2001*. Berlin, 2006, 197–236.

Brawer, A. J., *Galizien wie es an Österreich kam: Eine historisch-statistische Studie über die inneren Verhältnisse des Landes im Jahre 1772*. Leipzig, 1910.

Brennan, Christopher, Reforming Austria-Hungary: Beyond his Control or Beyond his Capacity? The Domestic Policies of Emperor Karl I November 1916–May 1917. University dissertation. London School of Economics and Political Science, 2012.

Brettner-Messler, Horst (ed.), *Protokolle des Österreichischen Ministerrates VI/1: Das Ministerium Belcredi (29. Juli 1865–26. März 1866)*. Vienna, 1971.

Brettner-Messler, Horst (ed.), *Protokolle des Österreichischen Ministerrates VI/2: Das Ministerium Belcredi (8. April 1866–6. Februar 1867)*. Vienna, 1973.

Breuer, Stefan, Von der sozialen Staatslehre zur Staatssoziologie: Georg Jellinek und Max Weber. In Anter, Andreas (ed.), *Die normative Kraft des Faktischen. Das Staatsverständnis Georg Jellineks*. Baden-Baden, 2004, 89–112.

Breuilly, John, *Nationalism and the State*. New York, 1982.

Breuilly, John, Nationalism and the History of Ideas. *Proceedings of the British Academy*, 105 (2000), 187–223.

Brie, Siegfried, *Theorie der Staatenverbindungen*. Stuttgart, 1896.

Brockhausen, Carl, *Organisation und Instanzenzug der politischen Behörden in Österreich*. Vienna and Leipzig, 1908.

Brose, Eric, Arms Race prior to 1914: Armament Policy. In Daniel, Ute, et al. (eds), *1914–1918-Online: International Encyclopedia of the First World War*. Berlin, 2014.

Broucek, Peter, Reformpläne aus dem Beraterkreis Erzherzog Franz Ferdinands und Kaiser Karls. In Plaschka, Richard G., Haselsteiner, Horst, Suppan, Arnold, Drabek, Anna M., and Zaar, Birgitta (eds), *Mitteleuropa-Konzeptionen*. Vienna, 1995, 111–21.

Brubakers, Roger, Feischmidt, Margit, Fox, Jon, and Grancea, Liana, *Nationalist Politics and Everyday Ethnicity in a Transylvanian Town*. Princeton, 2006.

Bruckmüller, Ernst, *Nation Österreich: Kulturelles Bewußtsein und gesellschaftlich-politische Prozesse*. 2nd edn. Vienna, 1996.

Bruckmüller, Ernst, 'Kein Robot! Kein Zehent mehr!': Die Bauern, der Reichstag und die Grundentlastung. In Bruckmüller, Ernst, and Häusler, Wolfgang (eds), *1848: Revolution in Österreich*. Vienna, 1999, 89–127.

Bruckmüller, Ernst, Was There a 'Habsburg Society' in Austria-Hungary? *Austrian History Yearbook*, 37 (2006), 1–16.

Brügel, Ludwig, *Soziale Gesetzgebung in Österreich von 1848–1918: Eine geschichtliche Darstellung*. Vienna and Leipzig, 1919.

Brunner, Otto, Vom Gottesgnadentum zum monarchischen Prinzip. In Brunner, Otto, *Neue Wege der Verfassungs- und Sozialgeschichte*. 2nd edn. Göttingen, 1968, 160–86.

Brusatti, Alois, Die wirtschaftlichen Folgen des Ausgleichs von 1867. In Berger, Peter (ed.), *Der österreichisch-ungarische Ausgleich von 1867: Vorgeschichte und Wirkungen*. Vienna and Munich, 1967, 127–42.

Bryce, James, *Studies in History and Jurisprudence*. Vol. 2. Oxford, 1901.

Buchen, Tim, and Rolf, Malte (eds), *Eliten im Vielvölkerreich: Imperiale Biographien in Russland und Österreich-Ungarn, 1850–1918*. Berlin and Boston, 2015.

Buchholz, Stephan, Zur Rechtsvereinheitlichung in Deutschland in der zweiten Hälfte des 19. Jahrhunderts. *Rabels Zeitschrift für ausländisches und internationales Privatrecht*, 50 (1986), 77–110.

Buczynski, Alexander, Der dalmatinische Landtag. In Rumpler, Helmut, and Urbanitsch, Peter (eds), *Die Habsburgermonarchie 1848–1918*. Vol. 7: *Verfassung und Parlamentarismus*. Subvol. 2: *Die regionalen Repräsentativkörperschaften*. Vienna, 2000, 1951–89.

Bundsmann, Anton, *Die Landeschefs von Tirol und Vorarlberg in der Zeit von 1815–1913*. Innsbruck, 1954.

Buquoy, Georg von, *Einige der wesentlichen Punkte, die jeder Theorie des Debattirens in den Kammern einer echten Volks-Repräsentativ Verfassung entsprechen müssen, gleichsam als eine Vorschule zu den Kammer-Debatten im Oesterreichischen Staate*. Prague, 1848.

Bureau des Industrierates im k.k. Handelsministerium (ed.), *Verhandlungen und Beschlüsse des Industrierates*. Heft 20: *Verbesserung der österreichischen Straßenverhältnisse*. Vienna, 1909.

Bureau der k.k. statistischen Zentralkommission (ed.), *Statistik der Unterrichtsanstalten in Österreich für das Jahr 1912/1913*. Vienna, 1917.

Burg, Peter, Die Triaspolitik im Deutschen Bund. In Rumpler, Helmut, and Lutz, Heinrich (eds), *Österreich und die deutsche Frage*. Munich, 1982, 136–61.

Burg, Thomas N., *Sieches Volk macht siechen Staat: Arzt, Stand und Staat im 19. Jahrhundert.* Vienna, 1994.

Burger, Hannelore, *Sprachenrecht und Sprachgerechtigkeit im österreichischen Unterrichtswesen 1867–1918.* Vienna, 1995.

Burger, Hannelore, Passwesen und Staatsbürgerschaft. In Heindl-Langer, Waltraud, and Saurer, Edith (eds), *Grenze und Staat: Paßwesen, Staatsbürgerschaft, Heimatrecht und Fremdengesetzgebung in der österreichischen Monarchie 1750–1867.* Vienna, 2000, 3–172.

Burger, Hannelore, Die jüdische Frage zwischen den Ausgleichsbewegungen in Mähren, der Bukowina und Galizien. In Fasora, Lukáš, Hanuš, Jiří, and Malíř, Jiří (eds), *Moravské vyrovnání z roku 1905. Možnosti a limity národnostního smíru ve střední Evropě.* Brno, 2006, 71–85.

Burger, Hannelore, *Heimatrecht und Staatsbürgerschaft österreichischer Juden: Vom Ende des 18. Jahrhunderts bis in die Gegenwart.* Vienna, 2014.

Burgess, Michael, *Comparative Federalism: Theory and Practice.* New York, 2006.

Burgess, Michael, Das Paradox der Diversität. Asymmetrischer Föderalismus aus vergleichender Perspektive. *Jahrbuch des Föderalismus: Föderalismus, Subsidiarität und Regionen in Europa.* Vol. 9, Baden-Baden, 2008, 103–16.

Burian, Peter, *Die Nationalitäten in 'Cisleithanien' und das Wahlrecht der Märzrevolution 1848/49.* Graz and Cologne, 1962.

Burián von Rajecz, Stephan, *Drei Jahre aus der Zeit meiner Amtsführung im Kriege.* Berlin, 1923.

Bußjäger, Peter, Föderalismus durch Macht im Schatten? Österreich und die Landeshauptmännerkonferenz. *Jahrbuch des Föderalismus: Föderalismus, Subsidiarität und Regionen in Europa.* Vol. 4, Baden-Baden, 2003, 79–99.

Buszko, Józef, *Sejmowa reforma wyborcza w Galicji 1905–1914.* Warsaw, 1956.

Buszko, Józef, *Zum Wandel der Gesellschaftsstruktur in Galizien und in der Bukowina.* Vienna, 1978.

Buszko, Józef (ed.), *Österreich Polen: 1000 Jahre Beziehungen.* Crakow, 1996.

Buszko, Józef, *Polacy w parlamencie wiedeńskim 1848–1918.* Warsaw, 1996.

Calhoun, Craig, Cooper, Frederick, and Moore, Kevin W. (eds), *Lessons of Empire: Imperial Histories and American Power.* New York, 2006.

Calic, Marie-Janine, *The Great Cauldron: A History of Southeastern Europe.* Cambridge, MA, 2019.

Čapková, Kateřina, *Czechs, Germans, Jews? National Identity and the Jews of Bohemia.* New York and Oxford, 2015.

Čapková, Kateřina, and Kieval, Hillel J. (eds), *Prague and Beyond: Jews in the Bohemian Lands.* Philadelphia, 2021.

Capra, Carlo, Die Zentralbehörden für die italienischen Provinzen 1713–1796. In Maťa, Petr, Hochedlinger, Michael, and Winkelbauer, Thomas (eds), *Verwaltungsgeschichte der Habsburgermonarchie in der Frühen Neuzeit.* Vol. 1/1: *Hof und Dynastie, Kaiser und Reich, Zentralverwaltungen, Kriegswesen und landesfürstliches Finanzwesen.* Vienna, 2019, 522–33.

Case, Holly, The Strange Politics of Federative Ideas in East-Central Europe. *Journal of Modern History,* 85 (2013), 833–66.

Ceauşu, Mihai-Ştefan, Zur sozioökonomischen Gesamtsituation der Bukowina im Vormärz vom Josephinischen Kataster 1786 bis 1848. In Rumpler, Helmut, Scharr, Kurt, and Ungureanu, Constantin (eds), *Der Franziszeische Kataster im Kronland Bukowina/Czernowitzer Kreis (1817–1865): Statistik und Katastralmappen.* Vienna, 2015, 17–24.

Čepulo, Dalibor, Building of the Modern Legal System in Croatia 1848–1918 in the Centre-Periphery-Perspective. In Giaro, Tomasz (ed.), *Modernisierung durch Transfer im 19. und frühen 20. Jahrhundert.* Frankfurt am Main, 2006, 47–91.

Čepulo, Dalibor, Entwicklung der Regierungsinstitutionen des Königreiches Kroatien und Slawonien 1868–1918. In Máthé, Gábor, and Mezey, Barna (eds), *Kroatisch-ungarische öffentlich-rechtliche Verhältnisse zur Zeit der Doppelmonarchie.* Budapest, 2015, 31–103.

Cerman, Ivo, Opposition oder Kooperation? Der Staat und die Stände in Böhmen 1749–1789. In Ammerer, Gerhard, Godsey, William D., Scheutz, Martin, Urbanitsch, Peter, and Weiß,

Alfred Stefan (eds), *Bündnispartner und Konkurrenten der Landesfürsten? Die Stände in der Habsburgermonarchie.* Vienna, 2007, 374–93.

Cerman, Ivo, and Velek, Luboš (eds), *Adel und Wirtschaft: Lebensunterhalt der Adeligen in der Moderne.* Munich, 2009.

Černý, Jan M., *Boj za právo: Sborník aktů politických u věcech státu a národa českého od roku 1848.* Vol. 1. Prague, 1893.

Cetnarowicz, Antoni, Die Polen und der Prager Slavenkongress. In Moritsch, Andreas (ed.), *Der Prager Slavenkongress 1848.* Vienna, 2000, 103–14.

Charmatz, Richard, *Deutsch-österreichische Politik: Studien über den Liberalismus und über die auswärtige Politik Österreichs.* Leipzig, 1907.

Cholet, Julia, *Der Etat des Deutschen Reiches in der Bismarckzeit.* Berlin, 2012.

Chorinsky, Carl, *Die Salzburger Landesfinanzen um 1861–1878.* Vol. 1: *Die Landesfinanzen und die Schule.* Salzburg, 1880.

Cibulka, Pavel, *Německé politické strany na Moravě 1890–1918: Ideje, programy, osobnosti.* Prague, 2012.

Cieger, András, Interests and Strategies; An Investigation of the Political Elite of the Sub-Carpathian Region in the Age of Dualism 1867–1918. In Pál, Judit, and Popovici, Vlad (eds), *Elites and Politics in Central and Eastern Europe 1848–1918.* Frankfurt am Main, 2014, 191–210.

Cieger, András, The Ways of Enrichment and its Interpretations in Hungarian Politics after the Austro-Hungarian Compromise of 1867. *Střed/Centre,* 7/1 (2015), 34–65.

Cięglewicz, Kasper, *Die roth-reussischen Angelegenheiten im Jahre 1848: Eine Berichtigung der Denkschrift der Ruthenen in Galizien zur Aufklärung ihrer Verhältnisse.* Vienna, 1848.

Cięglewicz, Kasper, *Rzecz czerwono-ruska 1848 roku.* Lviv, 1848.

Clewing, Konrad, *Staatlichkeit und nationale Identitätsbildung: Dalmatien in Vormärz und Revolution.* Munich, 2001.

Clewing, Konrad, Der begrenzte Wert strategischen Wertes: Dalmatien als habsburgische Randprovinz. In Maner, Hans-Christian (ed.), *Grenzregionen der Habsburgermonarchie im 18. und 19. Jahrhundert: Ihre Bedeutung und Funktion aus der Perspektive Wiens.* Münster, 2005, 217–34.

Cohen, Gary B., *Education and Middle-Class Society in Imperial Austria 1848–1918.* West Lafayette, IN, 1996.

Cohen, Gary B., Neither Absolutism nor Anarchy: New Narratives on Society and Government in Late Imperial Austria. *Austrian History Yearbook,* 29/1 (1998), 37–61.

Cohen, Gary B., Nationalist Politics and the Dynamics of State and Civil Society in the Habsburg Monarchy 1867–1914. *Central European History,* 40/2 (2007), 241–78.

Cole, Laurence, Province and Patriotism: German National Identity in Tirol 1850–1914. *Österreichische Zeitschrift für Geschichtswissenschaften,* 6/1 (1995), 61–83.

Cole, Laurence, *'Für Gott, Kaiser und Vaterland': Nationale Identität der deutschsprachigen Bevölkerung Tirols 1860–1914.* Frankfurt am Main and New York, 2000.

Cole, Laurence, *The Limits of Loyalty: Imperial Symbolism, Popular Allegiances, and State Patriotism in the Late Habsburg Monarchy.* New York, 2007.

Cole, Laurence, *Military Culture and Popular Patriotism in Late Imperial Austria.* Oxford, 2014.

Cole, Laurence, and Heiss, Hans, 'Unity vs. Difference': The Politics of Region-Building and National Identities in Tyrol 1830–1867. In Cole, Laurence (ed.), *Different Paths to the Nation: Regional and National Identities in Central Europe and Italy 1830–70.* Basingstoke, 2007, 37–59.

Confino, Alon, Federalism and the Heimat Idea in Imperial Germany. In Umbach, Maiken (ed.), *German Federalism: Past, Present, Future.* Basingstoke, 2002, 70–90.

Conrad, Christoph, and Kocka, Jürgen (eds), *Staatsbürgerschaft in Europa: Historische Erfahrungen und aktuelle Debatten.* Hamburg, 2001.

Conrad, Sebastian, Doppelte Marginalisierung: Plädoyer für eine transnationale Perspektive auf die deutsche Geschichte. *Geschichte und Gesellschaft,* 28/1 (2002), 145–69.

Conrad, Sebastian, *Globalisierung und Nation im Deutschen Kaiserreich.* Munich, 2006.

Cooper, Frederick, *Colonialism in Question: Theory, Knowledge, History*. Berkeley, CA, 2005.

Coreth, Anna, *Pietas Austriaca: Österreichische Frömmigkeit im Barock*. Munich, 1982.

Coreth, Anna, *Pietas Austriaca*. West Lafayette, IN, 2004.

Cornwall, Mark, *The Last Years of Austria-Hungary: A Multi-National Experiment in Early Twentieth-Century Europe*. Exeter, 2002.

Cornwall, Mark, *The Undermining of Austria-Hungary: The Battle for Hearts and Minds*. Basingstoke, 2010.

Cornwall, Mark, Loyalty and Treason in Late Habsburg Croatia: A Violent Discourse before the First World War. In Schulze Wessel, Martin, and Osterkamp, Jana (eds), *Exploring Loyalty*. Göttingen, 2017, 97–120.

Cornwall, Mark, Treason in an Era of Regime Change: The Case of the Habsburg Monarchy. *Austrian History Yearbook*, 50 (2019), 124–49.

Correnti, Cesare, *L'Austria e la Lombardia*. Italia, 1847.

Cova, Ugo, Der Landtag der reichsunmittelbaren Stadt Triest und ihres Gebietes. In Rumpler, Helmut, and Urbanitsch, Peter (eds), *Die Habsburgermonarchie 1848–1918*. Vol. 7: *Verfassung und Parlamentarismus*. Subvol. 2: *Die regionalen Repräsentativkörperschaften*. Vienna, 2000, 1919–49.

Crăciun, Viorica Angela, The Democratic Party of Bukovina and its National and Imperial Loyalties. 1902–1918. In Osterkamp, Jana, and Schulze Wessel, Martin (eds), *Exploring Loyalty*. Göttingen, 2017, 121–35.

Crook, Tom, *Governing Systems: Modernity and the Making of Public Health in England 1830–1910*. Oakland, CA, 2016.

Csáky, Moritz, *Von der Aufklärung zum Liberalismus. Studien zum Frühliberalismus in Ungarn*. Vienna, 1981.

Csáky, Moritz, *Das Gedächtnis Zentraleuropas: Kulturelle und literarische Projektionen auf eine Region*. Vienna, 2019.

Čubrilovič, Vasa, *Istorija političke misli u Srbiji XIX veka*. Belgrade, 1958.

Cvirn, Janez, Die Slovenen und der Prager Slavenkongress. In Moritsch, Andreas (ed.), *Der Prager Slavenkongress 1848*. Vienna, 2000, 127–35.

Czoernig, Carl, *Die lombardische Gemeinde-Verfassung nach ihrer Entstehung und Ausbildung, ihrem Verfalle und ihrer Wiederherstellung*. Heidelberg, 1843.

Czoernig, Carl, *Österreichs Neugestaltung 1848–1858*. Stuttgart and Augsburg, 1858.

Dabczański, Anton, *Die ruthenische Frage in Galizien*. Lviv, 1848.

Dabczański, Anton, *Wyjaśnienie sprawy ruskiej*. Lviv, 1848.

Daimer, Josef, Die Erkrankungs- und Sterblichkeitsverhältnisse in Österreich im Allgemeinen und mit Rücksicht auf übertragbare Krankheiten und deren Bekämpfung insbesondere. In *Österreichs Wohlfahrts-Einrichtungen*. Vol. 3: *Gesundheitspflege*. Vienna, 1900, 27–96.

Danilák, Michal, *Halyc'ki, bukovyns'ki, zakarpats'ki ukraïnci v revoljucii 1848–49 rokiv*. Bratislava, 1972.

Dann, Philipp, *Parlamente im Exekutivföderalismus: Eine Studie zum Verhältnis von föderaler Ordnung und parlamentarischer Demokratie in der Europäischen Union*. Berlin, 2004.

Dann, Philipp, The Gubernative in Presidential and Parliamentary Systems: Comparing Organizational Structures of Federal Governments in the USA and Germany. *Zeitschrift für ausländisches öffentliches Recht und Völkerrecht*, 66 (2006), 1–40.

Dantscher von Kollesberg, Theodor, *Der monarchische Bundesstaat Österreich-Ungarn und der Berliner Vertrag nebst der bosnischen Vorlage*. Vienna, 1880.

Deák, Ágnes, Miklós Wesselényi on the Future of the Habsburg Empire and Hungary. In Romsics, Ignác, and Király, Béla K. (eds), *Geopolitics in the Danube Region: Hungarian Reconciliation Efforts 1848–1998*. Budapest, 1999, 21–40.

Deák, Franz, *Ein Beitrag zum ungarischen Staatsrecht: Bemerkungen über Wenzel Lustkandl's 'Ungarisch-Österreichisches Staatsrecht': Vom Standpunkte der Geschichte des ungarischen Staatsrechts*. Pest and Leipzig, 1865.

Deák, István, *The Lawful Revolution: Louis Kossuth and the Hungarians, 1848–1849*. London, 1979.

Deák, István, *Der K. (u.) K. Offizier 1848–1918*. Vienna, 1991.

Deak, John, *Forging a Multinational State: State Making in Imperial Austria from the Enlightenment to the First World War*. Stanford, CA, 2015.

D'Elvert, Christian, *Die Verfassung und Verwaltung von Österreichisch-Schlesien in ihrer historischen Ausbildung*. Brno, 1854.

Demmerle, Eva, *Kaiser Karl I. 'Selig, die Frieden stiften…': Die Biographie*. Vienna, 2005.

Denis, Ernest, *La Bohème depuis la Montagne Blanche*. Vol. 1. Paris, 1903.

Deringil, Selim, *Conversion and Apostasy in the Late Ottoman Empire*. Cambridge, 2012.

Derndarsky, Michael, Österreich und der Deutsche Bund 1815–1866: Anmerkungen zur deutschen Frage zwischen dem Wiener Kongreß und Königgrätz. In Lutz, Heinrich, and Rumpler, Helmut (eds), *Österreich und die deutsche Frage im 19. und 20. Jahrhundert: Probleme der politisch-staatlichen und soziokulturellen Differenzierung im deutschen Mitteleuropa*. Munich, 1982, 92–116.

Derndarsky, Michael, Österreich und die Deutsche Frage zwischen 1848 und 1866/71: Konzeptionelles Dilemma und situative Probleme der Donaumonarchie gegenüber Deutschland. In Rumpler, Helmut, and Lutz, Heinrich (eds), *Österreich und die deutsche Frage*. Munich, 1982, 63–90.

Derndarsky, Michael, Vormacht im Bund mit Preußen? Österreichs Deutschlandpolitik 1860–1867 und ihr Scheitern. In Gehler, Michael, Schmidt, Rainer F., Brandt, Harm-Hinrich, and Steininger, Rolf (eds), *Ungleiche Partner? Österreich und Deutschland in ihrer gegenseitigen Wahrnehmung: Historische Analysen und Vergleiche aus dem 19. und 20. Jahrhundert*. 2nd edn. Stuttgart, 2009, 223–46.

Dimou, Augusta, *Entangled Paths towards Modernity: Contextualizing Socialism and Nationalism in the Balkans*. Budapest, 2009.

Dinhobl, Günter, '…die Cultur wird gehoben und verbreitet'. In Hárs, Endre (ed.), *Zentren, Peripherien und kollektive Identitäten*. Tübingen, 2006, 79–96.

Diószegi, István, *Hungarians in the Ballhausplatz: Studies on the Austro-Hungarian Common Foreign Policy*. Budapest, 1983.

Diószegi, István, Die Liberalen am Steuer: Der Ausbau des bürgerlichen Staatssystems in Ungarn im letzten Drittel des 19. Jahrhunderts. In Langewiesche, Dieter (ed.), *Liberalismus im 19. Jahrhundert*. Göttingen, 1988, 484–98.

Dipper, Christof, *Revolution und Risorgimento: Italien 1848/49 aus deutscher Perspektive. Die Revolutionen von 1848 in der europäischen Geschichte. Ergebnisse und Nachwirkungen*. Munich, 2000.

Doblhoff, Anton von, *Über die Drainage: Ein Beitrag zur wissenschaftlichen Begründung und zur practischen Ausführung dieses Systems andauernder Bodenverbesserung und vermehrten Pflanzenbaues*. Leipzig, 1850.

Doering-Manteuffel, Anselm, *Vom Wiener Kongress zur Pariser Konferenz: England, die deutsche Frage und das Mächtesystem 1815–1856*. Göttingen and Zürich, 1991.

Donia, Robert J., The Proximate Colony. Bosnia-Hercegovina under Austro-Hungarian Rule. In Ruthner, Clemens (ed.), *Wechselwirkungen: Austria-Hungary, Bosnia-Herzegovina, and the Western Balkans 1878–1918*. New York, 2015, 67–82.

Donia, Robert J., and Fine, John V. A., *Bosnia and Hercegovina: A Tradition Betrayed*. New York, 1994.

Dowe, Dieter, Haupt, Heinz-Gerhard, and Langewiesche, Dieter (eds), *Europa 1848: Revolution und Reform*. Bonn, 1998.

Drašarová, Eva, Horský, Roman, Šouša, Jiří, and Velek, Luboš (eds), *Promarněná šance: Edice dokumentů k česko-německému vyrovnání před první světovou válkou. Korespondence a protokoly 1911–1912*. Vol. 1. Prague, 2008.

Drewes, Kai, *Jüdischer Adel: Nobilitierungen von Juden im Europa des 19. Jahrhunderts*. Frankfurt am Main and New York, 2013.

Dreyer, Michael, *Föderalismus als ordnungspolitisches Prinizip: Das föderative Denken der Deutschen im 19. Jahrhundert*. Frankfurt am Main, 1987.

Drobesch, Werner, *Grundherrschaft und Bauer auf dem Weg zur Grundentlastung: Die 'Agrarrevolution' in den innerösterreichischen Ländern*. Klagenfurt, 2003.

Drobesch, Werner, Kärnten-Böhmen: Annotationen zum Strukturwandel von Gesellschaft und Wirtschaft während des Vormärz. In Fräss-Ehrfeld, Claudia (ed.), *Kärnten und Böhmen, Mähren, Schlesien*. Klagenfurt, 2004, 257–76.

Drobesch, Werner, Ideologische Konzepte zur Lösung der 'sozialen Frage'. In Rumpler, Helmut, and Urbanitsch, Peter (eds), *Die Habsburgermonarchie 1848–1918*. Vol. 9: *Soziale Strukturen*. Part 1: *Von der Feudal-Agrarischen zur Bürgerlich-industriellen Gesellschaft*. Subvol. 2: *Von der Stände- zur Klassengesellschaft*. Vienna, 2010, 1419–63.

Drobesch, Werner, and Fräss-Ehrfeld, Claudia (eds), *Die Bauern werden frei. Innerösterreichs Landwirtschaft zwischen Beharren und Modernisierung im frühen 19. Jahrhundert*. Klagenfurt, 2007.

Dubow, Saul (ed.), *The Rise and Fall of Modern Empires*. Vol. 2: *Colonial Knowledges*. Farnham, 2013.

Durell, Martin, Political Unity and Linguistic Diversity in Nineteenth-Century Germany. In Umbach, Maiken (ed.), *German Federalism: Past, Present, Future*. Basingstoke, 2002, 91–112.

Dutkowa, Renata, *Polityka szkolna w Galicji między autonomią a centralizmem 1861–1875*. Kraków, 1995.

Dvořák, Jindřich, *Moravské sněmování roku 1848–49: Na padesátiletou památku novodobého sněmu a zrušení roboty na Moravě, jakož i nastoupení císaře a krále Františka Josefa I. na trůn*. Telč, 1898.

Dvořák, Rudolf, *Jednání sněmů moravských v letech 1792–1835*. 2 vols. Brno, 1904, 1906.

Džaja, Srećko M., Der bosnische Konfessionalismus: Ein Phänomen der weltgeschichtlichen Peripherie. *Saeculum: Jahrbuch für Universalgeschichte*, 35/3–4 (1984), 267–92.

Ebert, Kurt, *Die Anfänge der modernen Sozialpolitik in Österreich: Die Taaffesche Sozialgesetzgebung für die Arbeiter im Rahmen der Gewerbeordnungen 1879–1885*. Habil. Graz, 1972.

Edlbacher, Ludwig, *Landeskunde von Oberösterreich: Geschichtlich-geographisches Handbuch für Leser aller Stände*. 2nd edn. Vienna, 1883.

Eisenmann, Louis, *Le compromis austro-hongrois de 1867: Étude sur le dualisme*. Paris, 1904.

Eisenstadt, Shmuel N., Multiple Modernities: Analyserahmen und Problemstellung. In Bonacker, Thorsten, and Reckwitz, Andreas (eds), *Kulturen der Moderne: Soziologische Perspektiven der Gegenwart*. Frankfurt am Main, 2007, 19–45.

Elliott, John H., A Europe of Composite Monarchies. *Past and Present*, 137 (1992), 48–71.

Engelbrecht, Helmut, *Geschichte des österreichischen Bildungswesens: Erziehung und Unterricht auf dem Boden Österreichs*. Vol. 3: *Von der frühen Aufklärung bis zum Vormärz*. Vienna, 1984.

Engel-Janosi, Friedrich, Die Theorie vom Staat im deutschen Österreich 1815–1848. *Zeitschrift für öffentliches Recht*, 2 (1921), 360–94.

Engel-Janosi, Friedrich, Einleitung. In Brettner-Messler, Horst, *Protokolle des Österreichischen Ministerrates VI/1: Das Ministerium Belcredi (29. Juli 1865–26. März 1866)*. Vienna, 1971, pp. vii–lxiii.

Erhebung über die finanziellen Verhältnisse in einzelnen Kronländern sowie über die Krankenverpflegskosten des Landes Schlesien. *Statistische Monatsschrift* (1910), 511.

Enquete der Kommission zur Förderung der Verwaltungsreform veranstaltet in der Zeit vom 21.10. bis 9.11.1912 zur Feststellung der Wünsche der beteiligten Kreise der Bevölkerung in Bezug auf die Reform der inneren und Finanzverwaltung. Vienna, 1913.

Enquete über die Landesfinanzen vom 7. bis 12. März 1908. Vienna, 1908.

Eötvös, Joseph, *Die Reform in Ungarn*. Leipzig, 1846.

Eötvös, Joseph, *Garantien der Macht und Einheit Österreichs*. Leipzig, 1859.

Esch, Michael G., Migration: Transnationale Praktiken, Wirkungen und Paradigmen. In Hadler, Frank, and Middell, Matthias (eds), *Handbuch einer transnationalen Geschichte Ostmitteleuropas*. Vol. 1: *Von der Mitte des 19. Jahrhunderts bis zum Ersten Weltkrieg*. Göttingen, 2017, 131–87.

Esroy, Ahmet, Gorny, Maciej, and Kechriotis, Vangelis (eds), *Discourses of Collective Identity in Central and Southeast Europe*. Vol. 3: *Modernism I: The Creation of Nation States*. Budapest, 2010.

Evans, Robert J. W., The Habsburgs and the Hungarian Problem 1790–1848. *Transactions of the Royal Historical Society—Essays in Modern History*, 39 (1989), 41–62.
Falkowska, Joanna, *Myśl wychowania narodowego w Galicji okresu autonomii. Twórcy i idee*. Toruń, 2013.
Fasora, Lukáš, Hanuš, Jiří, and Malíř, Jiří (eds), *Moravské vyrovnání z roku 1905. Možnosti a limity národnostního smíru ve střední Evropě*. Brno, 2006.
Faßbender, Bardo, *Der offene Bundesstaat: Studien zur auswärtigen Gewalt und zur Völkerrechtssubjektivität bundesstaatlicher Teilstaaten in Europa*. Tübingen, 2007.
Feichtinger, Johannes, and Heiss, Johann (eds), *Kritische Studien zur 'Türkenbelagerung'*. Vol. 2: *Der erinnerte Feind*. Vienna, 2013.
Feichtinger, Johannes, Csáky, Moritz, and Prutsch, Ursula (eds), *Habsburg Postcolonial: Machtstrukturen und kollektives Gedächtnis*. Innsbruck, 2003.
Feigl, Helmut, Der Adel in Niederösterreich 1780–1861. In Reden-Dohna, Armgard von (ed.), *Der Adel an der Schwelle des bürgerlichen Zeitalters 1780–1860*. Stuttgart, 1988, 191–223.
Fellner, Fritz, Das 'Februarpatent' von 1861: Entstehung und Bedeutung. *Mitteilungen des Instituts für Österreichische Geschichtsforschung*, 63/3–4 (1955), 549–64.
Fellner, Fritz, Die Historiographie zur österreichisch-deutschen Problematik als Spiegel der nationalpolitischen Diskussion. In Lutz, Heinrich, and Rumpler, Helmut (eds), *Österreich und die deutsche Frage im 19. und 20. Jahrhundert: Probleme der politisch-staatlichen und soziokulturellen Differenzierung im deutschen Mitteleuropa*. Munich, 1982, 34–59.
Fellner, Fritz, Die 'Mission Hoyos'. In Fellner, Fritz, and Maschl, Heidrun (eds), *Vom Dreibund zum Völkerbund: Studien zur Geschichte der internationalen Beziehungen 1882–1919*. Vienna, 1994, 112–41.
Ficker, Adolf, Die IX. Versammlung des internationalen statistischen Congresses. *Statistische Monatsschrift* (1876), 397–450.
Fiereder, Helmut, *125 Jahre soziale Krankenversicherung in Oberösterreich 1869–1994*. Linz, 1994.
Fischel, Alfred, *Der Panslawismus bis zum Weltkrieg*. Stuttgart and Berlin, 1919.
Fischer, Jens Malte, *Karl Kraus: Der Widersprecher. Biografie*. Vienna, 2020.
Florea, Cristina, *Bukovina: The Life and Death of an East European Borderland*. Princeton, 2025.
Földes, Béla, *Finanzwissenschaft*. Jena, 1920.
Fontana, Josef, *Der Kulturkampf in Tirol 1861–1892*. Bozen, 1978.
Franaszek, Piotr, Die wirtschaftspolitische Gesetzgebung der Wiener Regierung und die ökonomische Entwicklung Galiziens im langen 19. Jahrhundert. In Müller, Uwe (ed.), *Ausgebeutet oder alimentiert? Regionale Wirtschaftspolitik und nationale Minderheiten in Ostmitteleuropa 1867–1939*. Berlin, 2006, 91–100.
Frančíková, Dáša, *Women as Essential Citizens in the Czech National Movement: The Making of the Modern Czech Community*. Lanham, MD, 2017.
Frank, Alison F., *Oil Empire: Visions of Prosperity in Austrian Galicia*. Cambridge, MA, 2005.
Frank, Alison, Continental and Maritime Empires in an Age of Global Commerce. *East European Politics and Societies*, 25/4 (2011), 779–84.
Frank, Josip, *Die Quote Kroatiens. Eine Studie über das finanzielle Verhältniss zwischen Kroatien und Ungarn anlässlich der bevorstehenden Verhandlungen der Regnicolar-Deputationen*. Agram, 1879.
Frank, Tibor, *Picturing Austria-Hungary: The British Perception of the Habsburg Monarchy 1865–1870*. Boulder, CO, 2005.
Frankl, Michal, *'Prag ist nunmehr antisemitisch': Tschechischer Antisemitismus am Ende des 19. Jahrhunderts*. Berlin, 2011.
Frantz, Constantin, Präliminarien zu einem Programm der föderativen Partei. In Frantz, Constantin, *Literarisch-politische Aufsätze*. Munich, 1876, 369–79.
Franz, Georg, *Erzherzog Franz Ferdinand und die Pläne zur Reform der Habsburgermonarchie*. University dissertation. Munich, 1943.
Franz, Georg, *Die deutschliberale Bewegung in der habsburgischen Monarchie*. Munich, 1955, 134–52.

Fras, Zbigniew, *Florian Ziemiałkowski 1817–1900: Biografia polityczna*. Wrocław, 1991.

Fraser, Derek, Das Armengesetz und die Ursprünge des britischen Wohlfahrtsstaates. In Mommsen, Wolfgang J. (ed.), *Die Entstehung des Wohlfahrtsstaates in Großbritannien und Deutschland 1850–1950*. Stuttgart, 1982, 17–39.

Fräss-Ehrfeld, Claudia (ed.), *Napoleon und seine Zeit. Kärnten-Innerösterreich-Illyrien*. Klagenfurt, 2009, 111–48.

Friedensfels, Eugen von, *Joseph Bedeus von Scharberg: Beiträge zur Zeitgeschichte Siebenbürgens im 19. Jahrhundert*. Vol. 2. Vienna, 1877.

Friedrich, Adolf, *Die Bodenmeliorationen im Herzogthume Bukowina*. Vienna, 1903.

Friedrich, Margret, Mazohl, Brigitte, and von Schlachta, Astrid, Die Bildungsrevolution. In Rumpler, Helmut, and Urbanitsch, Peter (eds), *Die Habsburgermonarchie 1848–1918*. Vol. 9: *Soziale Strukturen*. Part 1: *Von der Feudal-Agrarischen zur Bürgerlich-industriellen Gesellschaft*. Subvol. 1: *Lebens- und Arbeitswelten in der Industriellen Revolution*. Vienna, 2010, 67–107.

Fritz, Wolfgang, and Mikl-Horke, Gertraude, *Rudolf Goldscheid: Finanzsoziologie und ethische Sozialwissenschaft*. Vienna, 2007.

Fröschl, Thomas, Confoederationes, uniones, ligae, Bünde. In Fröschl, Thomas (ed.), *Föderationsmodelle und Unionsstrukturen: Über Staatenverbindungen in der frühen Neuzeit vom 15. zum 18. Jahrhundert*. Vienna, 1994, 21–44.

Gaisbauer, Adolf, *Davidstern und Doppeladler: Zionismus und jüdischer Nationalismus in Österreich 1882–1918*. Vienna, 1988.

Gaj, Ljudevit, *Gedanken zum Ausgleich Croatiens und Slavoniens*. Agram, 1864.

Galandauer, Jan, *Bohumír Šmeral 1880–1914*. Prague, 1981.

Galandauer, Jan, Marný zápas Františka Thuna o česko-německé vyrovnání. In Fasora, Lukáš, Hanuš, Jiří, and Malíř, Jiří (ed.), *Moravské vyrovnání z roku 1905: Možnosti a limity národnostního smíru ve střední Evropě*. Brno, 2006, 319–324.

Galandauer, Jan, *Franz Fürst Thun: Statthalter des Königreiches Böhmen*. Vienna, 2014.

Gall, Lothar, Gemeinde und Staat in der politischen Theorie des frühen 19. Jahrhunderts. In Blickle, Peter (ed.), *Theorien kommunaler Ordnung in Europa*. Munich, 1996, 63–74.

Gammerl, Benno, *Staatsbürger, Untertanen und Andere: Der Umgang mit ethnischer Heterogenität im britischen Weltreich und im Habsburgerreich 1867–1918*. Göttingen, 2010.

Gatti, F. A., *Die Ereignisse des Jahres 1848 in der Steiermark: Auf Grundlage authentischer Quellen zusammengestellt*. Graz, 1850.

Gawrecki, Dan, Schlesien als Randgebiet der Habsburgermonarchie nach 1742. In Maner, Hans-Christian (ed.), *Grenzregionen der Habsburgermonarchie im 18. und 19. Jahrhundert: Ihre Bedeutung und Funktion aus der Perspektive Wiens*. Münster, 2005.

Gawrecki, Dan, Některé problémy slezských měst v procesu modernizace 1740–1914. In Kladiwa, Pavel (ed.), *Město a městská společnost v procesu modernizace 1740–1918*. Ostrava, 2009, 133–46.

Gawrecki, Dan (ed.), *Dějiny Českého Slezska 1740–2000*. Vol. 1. Opava, 2003.

Gebhardi, Ludwig Albrecht, *Geschichte der Königreiche Dalmatien, Kroatien, Szlavonien, Servien, Raszien, Bosnien, Rama und des Freystaats Ragusa*. Pest, 1808.

Gednánj pánů stawů Morawských: Übersetzt von Alois W. Šembera. Brno, 1849.

Geist-Lányi, Paula, *Das Nationalitätenproblem auf dem Reichstag zu Kremsier 1848/1849: Ein Beitrag zur Geschichte der Nationalitäten in Österreich*. Munich, 1920.

Gellner, Ernest, *Nations and Nationalism*. Oxford, 1983.

Genell, Aimée, *Empire by Law: The Ottoman Origins of the Mandate System in the Middle East*. Columbia, 2026.

Georgiev, Jiří, *Až do těch hrdel a statků? Konzervativní myšlení a otázka samosprávy v politických strategiích české státoprávní šlechty po roce 1848*. Prague, 2011.

Gergely, András, Der ungarische Adel und der Liberalismus im Vormärz. In Langewiesche, Dieter (ed.), *Liberalismus im 19. Jahrhundert: Deutschland im europäischen Vergleich*. Göttingen, 1988, 458–83.

Gergely, András, Das Bündnis zwischen Frankfurt und Pest-Buda und die österreichische Frage. In Jaworski, Rudolf, andLuft, Robert (ed.), *1848/49 Revolutionen in Ostmitteleuropa*. Munich, 1996, 257–78.

Gerloff, Wilhelm, Der Staatshaushalt und das Finanzsystem Deutschlands. In Gerloff, Wilhelm, and Meisel, Franz (eds), *Handbuch der Finanzwissenschaft*. Tübingen, 1929, 1–69.

Gernert, Angelica, *Liberalismus als Handlungskonzept: Studien zur Rolle der politischen Presse im italienischen Risorgimento vor 1848*. Stuttgart, 1990.

Gernert, Angelica, Italien 1848: Revolution auf italienisch. In Timmermann, Heiner (ed.), *1848: Revolution in Europa. Verlauf, politische Programme, Folgen und Wirkungen*. Berlin, 1999, 265–80.

Gerö, András, *The Hungarian Parliament 1867–1918: A Mirage of Power*. New York, 1997.

Gerö, András, *Emperor Francis Joseph: King of the Hungarians*. New York, 2001.

Glassheim, Eagle, *Noble Nationalists: The Transformation of the Bohemian Aristocracy*. Cambridge, MA, 2005.

Glassl, Horst, *Der mährische Ausgeich*. Munich, 1967.

Glassl, Horst, *Das österreichische Einrichtungswerk in Galizien 1772–1790*. Wiesbaden, 1975.

Godsey, William D., *Aristocratic Redoubt: The Austro-Hungarian Foreign Office on the Eve of the First World War*. West Lafayette, IN, 1999.

Godsey, William D., Der österreichisch(-ungarische) Diplomatische Dienst zwischen Stände- und Nationalgesellschaften. In Rumpler, Helmut, and Urbanitsch, Peter (eds), *Die Habsburgermonarchie 1848–1918*. Vol. 9, *Soziale Strukturen*. Part 1: *Von der Feudal-Agrarischen zur Bürgerlich-industriellen Gesellschaft*. Subvol. 2: *Von der Stände- zur Klassengesellschaft*. Vienna, 2010, 1245–61.

Godsey, William D., *The Sinews of Habsburg Power: Lower Austria in a Fiscal-Military State 1650–1820*. Oxford, 2018.

Gönczi, Katalin, *Die europäischen Fundamente der ungarischen Rechtskultur: Juristischer Wissenstransfer und nationale Rechtswissenschaft in Ungarn zur Zeit der Aufklärung und im Vormärz*. Frankfurt am Main, 2008.

Gonnard, René, Le trialisme. *Revue politique et parlementaire*, 19 (1912), 223–244; 20 (1913), 55–71.

Górny, Maciej, Das ethnographische Motiv in den polnischen Föderationsplänen des 19. Jahrhunderts. In Borodziej, Włodzimierz (ed.), *Option Europa: Deutsche, polnische und ungarische Europapläne des 19. und 20. Jahrhunderts*. Vol. 1: *Essays*. Göttingen, 2005, 187–203.

Górska, Urszula, *Drogi wolności: Ruch emancypacyjny kobiet w monarchii habsburskiej na podstawie publicystyki a twórczości literackiej w latach 1867–1918*. Warsaw, 2016.

Gosewinkel, Dieter, Staatsbürgerschaft als politische Zugehörigkeit: Eine Grundlinie europäischer Geschichte im 20. Jahrhundert. In Boeckh, Katrin, Busa, Krisztina, Himmelreich, Antje, Pezo, Edvin, and Stegmann, Natali (eds), *Staatsbürgerschaft und Teilhabe: Bürgerliche, politische und soziale Rechte im östlichen Europa*. Munich, 2014, 15–34.

Gosewinkel, Dieter, *Schutz und Freiheit? Staatsbürgerschaft in Europa im 20. und 21. Jahrhundert*. Berlin, 2016.

Gottas, Friedrich, *Die Frage der Protestanten in Ungarn in der Ära des Neoabsolutismus: Das ungarische Protestantenpatent vom 1.9.1859*. Munich, 1965.

Gottas, Friedrich, *Ungarn im Zeitalter des Hochliberalismus: Studien zur Tisza-Ära 1875–1890*. Vienna, 1976.

Gotthard, Axel, Die habsburgischen Länder und das Alte Reich. In Mat'a, Petr, Hochedlinger, Michael, and Winkelbauer, Thomas (eds), *Verwaltungsgeschichte der Habsburgermonarchie in der Frühen Neuzeit*. Vol. 1/1: *Hof und Dynastie, Kaiser und Reich, Zentralverwaltungen, Kriegswesen und landesfürstliches Finanzwesen*. Vienna, 2019, 360–74.

Gottsmann, Andreas, *Der Reichstag von Kremsier und die Regierung Schwarzenberg: Die Verfassungsdiskussion des Jahres 1848 im Spannungsfeld zwischen Reaktion und nationaler Frage*. Munich, 1995.

Gottsmann, Andreas, *Venetien 1859–1866: Österreichische Verwaltung und nationale Opposition*. Vienna, 2005.

Gottsmann, Andreas, *Rom und die nationalen Katholizismen in der Donaumonarchie: Römischer Universalismus, habsburgische Reichspolitik und nationale Identitäten 1878–1914*. Vienna, 2010.

Gottsmann, Andreas, and Malfèr, Stefan, Die Vertretungskörperschaften und die Verwaltung in Lombardo-Venetien. In Rumpler, Helmut, and Urbanitsch, Peter (eds), *Die Habsburgermonarchie 1848–1918*. Vol. 7: *Verfassung und Parlamentarismus*. Subvol. 2: *Die regionalen Repräsentativkörperschaften*. Vienna, 2000, 1592–1632.

Götz, Thomas, *Bürgertum und Liberalismus in Tirol 1840–1873: Zwischen Stadt und 'Region', Staat und Nation*. Cologne, 2001.

Govekar-Okoliš, Monika, *Srednje šole na Slovenskem pri oblikovanju nacionalne identitete Slovencev v drugi polovici 19. stoletja*. Ljubljana, 2010.

Grandits, Hannes, *Herrschaft und Loyalität in der spätosmanischen Gesellschaft: Das Beispiel der multikonfessionellen Herzegowina*. Vienna, 2008.

Grandits, Hannes, Clayer, Nathalie, and Pichler, Robert (eds), *Conflicting Loyalties in the Balkans: The Great Powers, the Ottoman Empire and Nation-Building*. London, 2011.

Grasse, Alexander, *Italiens langer Weg in den Regionalstaat. Die Entstehung einer Staatsform im Spannungsfeld von Zentralismus und Föderalismus*. Opladen, 2000.

Grawert, Rolf, *Staat und Staatsangehörigkeit: Verfassungsgeschichtliche Untersuchung zur Entstehung der Staatsangehörigkeit*. Berlin, 1973.

Greble, Emily, *Muslims and the Making of Modern Europe*. New York, 2021.

Green, Abigail, *Fatherlands: State-Building and Nationhood in Nineteenth-Century Germany*. Cambridge, 2001.

Grimm, Jacob, and Grimm, Wilhelm, *Deutsches Wörterbuch*. Vol. 13. Leipzig, 1889.

Grodziski, Stanisław, *Sejm krajowy galicyjski 1861–1914*. 2 vols. Warsaw, 1993.

Grodziski, Stanisław, Justizreformen in Galizien in der Regierungszeit Maria Theresias und Josephs II. In Buszko, Józef (ed.), *Österreich Polen: 1000 Jahre Beziehungen*. Kraków, 1996, 123–33.

Grodziski, Stanisław, Der Landtag des Königreiches Galizien und Lodomerien. In Rumpler, Helmut, and Urbanitsch, Peter (eds), *Die Habsburgermonarchie 1848–1918*. Vol. 7: *Verfassung und Parlamentarismus*. Subvol. 2: *Die regionalen Repräsentativkörperschaften*. Vienna, 2000, 2131–69.

Gross, Mirjana, Financijski temelji nagodbene autonomije civilne Hrvatske i Slavonije 1868–1880. *Historijski zbornik*, 41/2 (1988), 89–122.

Gross, Mirjana, The Character of Croatian Autonomy in the First Decade after the Hungarian-Croatian Compromise of 1868. In Wank, Solomon, Maschl, Heidrun, Mazohl-Wallnig, Brigitte, and Wagnleitner, Reinhold (eds), *The Mirror of History: Essays in Honor of Fritz Fellner*. Santa Barbara, CA, 1988, 275–94.

Gross, Mirjana, *Die Anfänge des modernen Kroatien: Gesellschaft, Politik und Kultur in Zivil-Kroatien und -Slawonien in den ersten dreißig Jahren nach 1848*. Vienna, 1993.

Gross, Mirjana, Der kroatische Sabor (Landtag). In Rumpler, Helmut, and Urbanitsch, Peter (eds), *Die Habsburgermonarchie 1848–1918*. Vol. 7: *Verfassung und Parlamentarismus*. Subvol. 2: *Die regionalen Repräsentativkörperschaften*. Vienna, 2000, 2283–2316.

Gross, Mirjana, *Izvorno pravaštvo: Ideologija, agitacija, pokret*. Zagreb, 2000.

Gross, Nachum Th., Die Stellung der Habsburgermonarchie in der Weltwirtschaft. In Brusatti, Alois (ed.), *Die Habsburgermonarchie 1848–1918*. Vol. 1: *Die wirtschaftliche Entwicklung*. Vienna, 1973, 1–28.

Grüne, Niels, *Dorfgesellschaft—Konflikterfahrung—Partizipationskultur: Sozialer Wandel und politische Kommunikation in Landgemeinden der badischen Rheinpfalz 1720–1850*. Stuttgart, 2011.

Gruner, Wolf D., *Der Deutsche Bund 1815–1866*. Munich, 2012.

Grünwald, Paul, Zur Finanzstatistik der autonomen Selbstverwaltung in Österreich. *Zeitschrift für Volkswirtschaft, Sozialpolitik und Verwaltung*, 19 (1910), 68–119.

Grünwald, Paul, Das Finanzproblem im Bundesstaat. *Zeitschrift für Verwaltung*, 54, NF 1/1 (1921), 16–27, 35–49.

Grzeszick, Bernd, *Vom Reich zur Bundesstaatsidee: Zur Herausbildung der Föderalismusidee als Element des modernen deutschen Staatsrechts*. Berlin, 1996.

Gudermann, Rita, *Morastwelt und Paraid: Ökonomie und Ökologie in der Landwirtschaft am Beispiel der Meliorationen in Westfalen und Brandenburg 1830–1880*. Paderborn, 2000.

Gumplowicz, Ludwig, *Das österreichische Staatsrecht: Verfassungs- und Verwaltungsrecht*. 3rd edn. Vienna, 1907.

Gutheil-Knopp-Kirchwald, Carl, *Vom K. K. Ministerium für Soziale Fürsorge zum Bundesministerium für Soziale Verwaltung: Die Errichtung des Österreichischen Sozialministeriums*. Vienna, 1998.

Haas, Arthur G., Kaiser Franz, Metternich und die Stellung Illyriens. *Mitteilungen des Österreichischen Staatsarchivs*, 11 (1958), 373–98.

Haas, Arthur G., *Metternich, Reorganization and Nationality 1813–1818: A Story of Foresight and Frustration in the Rebuilding of the Austrian Empire*. Wiesbaden, 1963.

Haas, Hanns, Salzburg in der Habsburgermonarchie: Vormärz, Revolution und Neoabsolutismus. In Dopsch, Heinz, and Spatzenegger, Hans (eds), *Geschichte Salzburgs: Stadt und Land*. Vol. 2/2. Salzburg, 1988, 661–717.

Haas, Hanns, Postmeister, Wirt, Kramer, Brauer, Müller und Wundarzt: Trägerschichten und Organisationsformen des Liberalismus. Das Salzburger Beispiel—vom frühen Konstitutionalismus zum Kulturkampf. In Bruckmüller, Ernst, Döcker, Ulrike, Stekl, Hannes, and Urbanitsch, Peter (eds), *Bürgertum in der Habsburgermonarchie*. Vienna and Cologne, 1990, 257–73.

Haas, Hanns, and Hellmuth, Thomas, Der Salzburger Landtag. In Rumpler, Helmut, and Urbanitsch, Peter (eds), *Die Habsburgermonarchie 1848–1918*. Vol. 7: *Verfassung und Parlamentarismus*. Subvol. 2: *Die regionalen Repräsentativkörperschaften*. Vienna, 2000, 1769–1820.

Habermann, Georg, Das Zusammenwirken lokaler Faktoren mit Staat und Land bei Lösung von Verwaltungsaufgaben. *Zeitschrift für Volkswirtschaft, Socialpolitik und Verwaltung*, 14 (1905), 148–59.

Habermas, Jürgen, Das Zeitbewusstsein der Moderne und ihr Bedürfnis nach Selbstvergewisserung. In Habermas, Jürgen, *Der philosophische Diskurs der Moderne*. Frankfurt am Main, 1985, 9–33.

Habermas, Jürgen, *Der philosophische Diskurs der Moderne*. Frankfurt am Main, 1985.

Habermas, Jürgen, Im Sog der Technokratie: Ein Plädoyer für europäische Solidarität. In Habermas, Jürgen, *Im Sog der Technokratie: Kleine politische Schriften*, 12. Berlin, 2013, 82–111.

Hachtmann, Rüdiger, *Epochenschwelle zur Moderne: Einführung in die Revolution von 1848/49*. Tübingen, 2002.

Hadler, Frank, 'Nevertheless, a Great Theatrical Exhibition of Slav Solidarity': Der Prager Slawen-Kongress von 1908 als Hauptaktion des Neoslawismus. In Hadler, Frank, and Makowski, Krzysztof A. (eds), *Approaches to Slavic Unity. Austro-Slavism, Pan-Slavism, Neo-Slavism, and Solidarity among the Slavs Today*. Poznan, 2013, 131–52.

Hadler, Frank, Weltkrieg und Friedenskongress: Laboratorien für Konzipierung und Realisierung der tschechoslowakischen Selbstbestimmung. In Höhne, Steffen (ed.), *Zusammenbruch, Trauma, Triumph: Das Epochenjahr 1918 und sein Nachleben in Zentral-, Ostmittel- und Südosteuropa*. Wiesbaden, 2020, 141–65.

Hadler, Frank, and Middell, Matthias (eds), *Handbuch einer transnationalen Geschichte Ostmitteleuropas*. Vol. 1: *Von der Mitte des 19. Jahrhunderts bis um Ersten Weltkrieg*. Göttingen, 2017.

Hahn, Hans Henning, *Außenpolitik in der Emigration: Die Exildiplomatie Adam Jerzy Czartoryskis 1830–1840*. Munich and Vienna, 1978.

Hahn, Hans Henning, Die polnische Nation in den Revolutionen von 1846–49. In Dowe, Dieter, Haupt, Heinz-Gerhard, and Langewiesche, Dieter (eds), *Europa 1848: Revolution und Reform*. Bonn, 1998, 231–52.

Hall, Catherine, *Cultures of Empire: Colonizers in Britain and the Empire in the 19th and 20th Centuries. A Reader*. Manchester, 2000.

Hall, Catherine (ed.), *Civilising Subjects: Metropole and Colony in the English Imagination 1830–1867*. Cambridge, 2002.

Haller, Carl Ludwig von, *Restauration der Staatswissenschaft oder Theorie des natürlich-geselligen Zustands, der Chimäre des künstlich-bürgerlichen entgegengesetzt*. 6 vols. Aalen, 1964 (1st edn. 1820).

Halmos, Károly, Verbürgerlichung als Veradeligung: Zivilisation in Ungarn. Grenzland und Peripherie. In Stekl, Hannes, Urbanitsch, Peter, Bruckmüller, Ernst, and Heiss, Hans (eds), *Durch Arbeit, Besitz, Wissen und Gerechtigkeit: Bürgertum in der Habsburgermonarchie*. Vienna, 1992, 180–92.

Halmos, Károly, Das Besitz- und Bildungsbürgertum in Ungarn. In Rumpler, Helmut, and Urbanitsch, Peter (eds), *Die Habsburgermonarchie 1848–1918*. Vol. 9: *Soziale Strukturen*. Part 1: *Von der Feudal-Agrarischen zur Bürgerlich-industriellen Gesellschaft*. Subvol. 2: *Von der Stände- zur Klassengesellschaft*. Vienna, 2010, 909–50.

Hämmerle, Christa, Ein gescheitertes Experiment? Die Allgemeine Wehrpflicht in der multiethnischen Armee der Habsburgermonarchie. *Journal of Modern European History*, 5/2 (2008), 222–43.

Hammermayer, Ludwig, Die letzte Epoche des Erzstifts Salzburg: Politik und Kirchenpolitik unter Erzbischof Graf Hieronymus Colloredo 1772–1803. In Dopsch, Heinz, and Spatzenegger, Hans (eds), *Geschichte Salzburgs. Stadt und Land*. Vol. 2, part 1. Salzburg, 1988, 453–535.

Hanák, Péter, Antezedenzien des Osterartikels Deáks. *Acta Historica Academiae Scientiarum Hungaricae*, 21/3–4 (1975), 271–308.

Hanák, Péter, *The First Attempt at the Austro-Hungarian Compromise 1860*. Budapest, 1975.

Hanák, Péter, *Ungarn in der Donaumonarchie: Probleme der bürgerlichen Umgestaltung eines Vielvölkerstaats*. Vienna, 1984.

Hanák, Péter, Verbürgerlichung und Urbanisierung: Ein Vergleich der Stadtentwicklung Wiens und Budapests. In Glatz, Ferenc, and Melville, Ralph (eds), *Gesellschaft, Politik und Verwaltung in der Habsburgermonarchie 1830–1918*. Budapest, 1987, 203–35.

Hanebrink, Paul A., *In Defense of Christian Hungary: Religion, Nationalism, and Antisemitism 1890–1944*. Ithaca, NY, 2006.

Hanisch, Ernst, *Der kranke Mann an der Donau: Marx und Engels über Österreich*. Vienna, 1978.

Hanisch, Ernst, *Der große Illusionist: Otto Bauer (1881–1938)*. Vienna, 2011.

Hannick, Christian, Das Problem der Konfession am Prager Slavenkongress. In Moritsch, Andreas (ed.), *Der Prager Slavenkongress 1848*. Vienna, 2000, 39–46.

Hannig, Alma, *Franz Ferdinand: Die Biografie*. Vienna, 2013.

Hantsch, Hugo, Lemma Franz Joseph. In *Neue Deutsche Biographie*. Vol. 5. Berlin, 1961, 361–4.

Harbig, Anna Maria, *Die aufgezwungene Sprache: Deutsch in galizischen Schulen 1772–1848*. Białystok, 2006.

Harmat, Ulrike, Magnaten und Gentry in Ungarn. In Rumpler, Helmut, and Urbanitsch, Peter (eds), *Die Habsburgermonarchie 1848–1918*. Vol. 9: *Soziale Strukturen*. Part 1: *Von der Feudal-Agrarischen zur Bürgerlich-industriellen Gesellschaft*. Subvol. 2: *Von der Stände- zur Klassengesellschaft*. Vienna, 2010, 1043–89.

Harmat, Ulrike, Untergang, Auflösung, Zerstörung der Habsburgermonarchie? Zeitgenössische Bedingungen der Erinnerung und Historiographie. In Harmat, Ulrike, and Rumpler, Helmut (eds), *Die Habsburgermonarchie 1848–1918*. Vol. 12: *Bewältigte Vergangenheit? Die nationale und internationale Historiographie zum Untergang der Habsburgermonarchie als ideelle Grundlage für die Neuordnung Europas*. Vienna, 2018, 49–95.

Hárs, Endre, Müller-Funk, Wolfgang, Reber, Ursula, and Ruthner, Clemens (eds), *Zentren, Peripherien und kollektive Identitäten in Österreich-Ungarn*. Tübingen, 2006.

Härtel, Ines (ed.), *Handbuch Föderalismus: Föderalismus als demokratische Rechtsordnung und Rechtskultur in Deutschland, Europa und der Welt*. Vol. 1: *Grundlagen des Föderalismus und der deutsche Bundesstaat*. Heidelberg, 2012.

Hartig, Franz de Paula von, *Das kaiserliche Manifest vom 20.9.1848. Oder: Freimüthige Bemerkungen über die österreichische Herrschaft im lombardisch-venetianischen Königreiche*. Prague, 1848.

Hartig, Franz de Paula von, *Genesis der Revolution in Oesterreich im Jahre 1848.* Leipzig, 1850.

Haselsteiner, Horst, *Die Serben und der Ausgleich: Zur politischen und staatsrechtlichen Stellung der Serben Südungarns in den Jahren 1860–1867.* Cologne, 1976.

Haslinger, Peter, *Nation und Territorium im tschechischen politischen Diskurs 1880–1938.* Munich, 2010.

Hassenpflug, Eila, Die böhmische Adelsnation als Repräsentantin des Königreichs Böhmen: Von der Inkraftsetzung der Verneuerten Landesordnung bis zum Regierungsantritt Maria Theresias. *Bohemia*, 15/1 (1974), 71–91.

Hatje, Armin, *Loyalität als Rechtsprinzip in der Europäischen Union.* Baden-Baden, 2001.

Hauch, Gabriella, Frauen-Räume in der Männer-Revolution 1848. In Dowe, Dieter, Haupt, Heinz-Gerhard, and Langewiesche, Dieter (eds), *Europa 1848: Revolution und Reform.* Bonn, 1998, 841–900.

Hauke, Franz, *Die geschichtlichen Grundlagen des Monarchenrechts: Ein Beitrag zur Bearbeitung des österreichischen Staatsrechts.* Vienna and Leipzig, 1894.

Hauke, Franz, *Grundriß des Verfassungsrechts.* Leipzig, 1905.

Haumann, Heiko, Juden in der ländlichen Gesellschaft Galiziens am Ende des 19. und zu Beginn des 20. Jahrhunderts. In Löw, Andrea, Robusch, Kerstin, and Walter, Stefanie (eds), *Deutsche, Juden, Polen: Geschichte einer wechselvollen Beziehung im 20. Jahrhundert.* Frankfurt am Main, 2004, 35–58.

Haupt, Heinz-Gerhard, and Langewiesche, Dieter, Die Revolution in Europa 1848: Reform der Herrschafts- und Gesellschaftsordnung—Nationalrevolution—Wirkungen. In Dowe, Dieter, Haupt, Heinz-Gerhard, and Langewiesche, Dieter (eds), *Europa 1848: Revolution und Reform.* Bonn, 1998, 11–41.

Hauptmann, Ferdinand, *Die österreichisch-ungarische Herrschaft in Bosnien und der Hercegovina 1878–1918:. Wirtschaftspolitik und Wirtschaftsentwicklung.* Graz, 1983.

Hausteiner, Eva Marlene (ed.), *Föderalismen: Modelle jenseits des Staates.* Baden-Baden, 2016.

Havránek, Jan, Die tschechische Politik und der Ausgleich von 1867. In Holotík, L'udovít (ed.), *Der österreichisch-ungarische Ausgleich 1867.* Bratislava, 1971, 520–44.

Havránek, Jan, The Education of Czechs and Slovaks under Foreign Domination 1850–1918. In Tomiak, Janusz J. (ed.), *Schooling, Educational Policy and Ethnic Identity.* Vol. 1: *Comparative Studies on Governments and Non-Dominant Ethnic Groups in Europe 1850–1940.* New York, 1991, 235–61.

Heffter, Heinrich, *Die deutsche Selbstverwaltung im 19. Jahrhundert: Geschichte der Ideen und Institutionen.* 2nd edn. Stuttgart, 1969.

Heindl, Waltraud, Geschlechterbilder und Geschlechterrollen: Ideologie und Realitäten. In Rumpler, Helmut, and Urbanitsch, Peter (eds), *Die Habsburgermonarchie 1848–1918.* Vol. 9: *Soziale Strukturen.* Part 1: *Von der Feudal-Agrarischen zur Bürgerlich-industriellen Gesellschaft.* Subvol. 1: *Lebens- und Arbeitswelten in der Industriellen Revolution.* Vienna, 2010, 701–41.

Heindl, Waltraud, *Josephinische Mandarine: Bürokratie und Beamte in Österreich.* Vol. 2: *1848–1914.* Vienna, 2013.

Heindl, Waltraud, Verwaltungseliten im Neoabsolutismus: Professionelles und politisches Profil vor dem Horizont der Modernisierung. In Brandt, Harm-Hinrich (ed.), *Der österreichische Neoabsolutismus als Verfassungs- und Verwaltungsproblem: Diskussionen über einen strittigen Epochenbegriff.* Vienna, 2014, 145–57.

Heinemann-Grüder, Andreas, *Föderalismus als Konfliktregelung: Indien, Russland, Spanien und Nigeria im Vergleich.* Opladen, 2011.

Hein-Kircher, Heidi, and Sterkenburgh, Frederik Frank (eds), *Modernizing Europe's Imperial Monarchies: Germany, Austria-Hungary, and Russia in the Nineteenth Century*, London, 2025.

Hein-Kircher, Heidi, *Lembergs 'polnischen Charakter' sichern: Kommunalpolitik in einer multiethnischen Stadt der Habsburgermonarchie zwischen 1861/62 und 1914.* Stuttgart, 2020.

Heiss, Hans, Die Evangelische Gemeinde A. B. Meran im Kontext der Südtiroler Geschichte. In Reimer, Hans H. (ed.), *Lutherisch in Südtirol: Die Geschichte der Evangelischen Gemeinde Meran. Eine Spurensuche zum Protestantismus in Südtirol und im Trentino.* Bozen, 2009, 620–7.

Heiss, Hans, Ein neues Land: Tirol in Restauration und Vormärz. In Hastaba, Ellen, and Rachewiltz, Siegfried de (eds), *'Für Freiheit, Wahrheit und Recht!': Joseph Ennemoser und Jakob Philipp Fallmerayer. Tirol von 1809 bis 1848/49*. Innsbruck, 2009, 33–48.

Heiss, Hans, and Götz, Thomas, *Am Rand der Revolution. Tirol 1848/49*. Vienna, 1998.

Helcel, Antoni Zygmunt, and Lubomirski, Jerzy, Akt der slawisch-österreichischen Union (1848). In Borodziej, Włodzimierz (ed.), *Option Europa: Deutsche, polnische und ungarische Europapläne des 19. und 20. Jahrhunderts*. Vol. 3: *Texte*. Göttingen, 2005, 73–80.

Helfert, Joseph Alexander, *Oesterreich und die Nationalitäten. Ein offenes Wort an Herrn Frz. Palacky*. Vienna, 1850.

Helfert, Joseph Alexander, *Zur Geschichte des lombardo-venezianischen Königreichs*. Vienna, 1908.

Helmedach, Andreas, Integration durch Verkehr: Das Habsburger Reich. *Osteuropa*, 3 (2005), 18–32.

Hensel, Albert, *Der Finanzausgleich im Bundesstaat in seiner staatsrechtlichen Bedeutung*. Berlin, 1922.

Herbert, Ulrich, Europe in High Modernity; Reflections on a Theory of the 20th Century. *Journal of Modern European History*, 5 (2007), 5–20.

Herdepe, Klaus, *Die Preußische Verfassungsfrage 1848*. Neuried, 2003.

Herron, George D., Heinrich Lammasch's Suggestion for Peace in Bern 1918. In Lammasch, Marga (ed.), *Heinrich Lammasch: Seine Aufzeichnungen, sein Wirken und seine Politik*. Vienna, 1922, 186–97.

Herz, Hugo, Die Vagabundage in Österreich in ihren Beziehungen zur Volkswirtschaft und zum Verbrechertume. *Zeitschrift für Volkswirtschaft, Socialpolitik und Verwaltung*, 14 (1905), 571–626.

Heumos, Peter, 'Kartoffeln her oder es gibt eine Revolution': Hungerkrawalle, Streiks und Massenproteste in den böhmischen Ländern 1914–1918. *Mitteilungsblatt des Instituts für soziale Bewegungen*, 3 (2000), 158–76.

Hicks, Alexander, Misra, Joya, and Ng, Tang Nah, The Programmatic Emergence of the Social Security State. *American Sociological Review*, 60/3 (1995), 329–49.

Hilbrenner, Anke, *Diaspora-Nationalismus: Zur Geschichtskonstruktion Simon Dubnows*. Göttingen, 2007.

Hillemann, Ulrike, *Asian Empire and British Knowledge: China and the Networks of British Imperial Expansion*. Basingstoke, 2009.

Himka, John-Paul, The Greek Catholic Church and Nation-Building in Galicia, 1772–1918. *Harvard Ukrainian Studies*, 8 (1984), 426–52.

Himka, John-Paul, *Galician Villagers and the Ukrainian National Movement in the Nineteenth Century*. Edmonton, 1988.

Himka, John-Paul, Confessional Relations in Galicia. In Hann, Christopher, and Magocsi, Paul (ed.), *Galicia: A Multicultured Land*. Toronto, 2005, 22–35.

Hinrichs, Eibe, *Der Koerber-Plan: Wirtschaftspolitik als Integrationsfaktor für die Nationalitäten des Habsburgerreichs. Die Regierungszeit Ernest von Koerbers 1900–1904 aus wirtschaftlicher Perspektive*. Frankfurt am Main, 2014.

Hirschhausen, Ulrike von, Leonhard, Jörn, Europäische Nationalismen im West-Ost-Vergleich. Von der Typologie zur Differenzbestimmung. In Hirschhausen, Ulrike von, and Leonhard, Jörn (eds), *Nationalismen in Europa. West- und Osteuropa im Vergleich*. Göttingen, 2001, 11–45.

Hitchins, Keith, The Rumanians of Transylvania and the Ausgleich 1865–1867. In Holotík, Ľudovít (ed.), *Der österreichisch-ungarische Ausgleich 1867*. Bratislava, 1971, 860–96.

Hitchins, Keith, *Orthodoxy and Nationality: Andreiu Saguna and the Rumanians of Transylvania 1846–1873*. Cambridge, MA, 1977.

Hlavačka, Milan, *Zlatý věk české samosprávy: Samospráva a její vliv na hospodářský, sociální a intelektuální rozvoj Čech 1862–1913*. Prague, 2006.

Hlavačka, Milan, *České země v 19. Století: Proměny společnosti v moderní době*. 2 vols. Prague, 2014.

Hlavačka, Milan, Cibulka, Pavel, Pokorný, Jiří, Fejtová, Olga, and Bek, Pavel, *Sociální myšlení a sociální praxe v českých zemích 1781–1939: Ideje, legislativa, instituce*. Prague, 2015.

Höbelt, Lothar, The Delegations: Preliminary Sketch of a Semi-Parliamentary Institution. *Parliaments, Estates and Representation*, 6/2 (1986), 149–54.

Höbelt, Lothar, Die Deutschfreiheitlichen Österreichs: Bürgerliche Politik unter den Bedingungen eines katholischen Vielvölkerstaates. In Langewiesche, Dieter (ed.), *Liberalismus im 19. Jahrhundert: Deutschland im europäischen Vergleich*. Göttingen, 1988, 161–71.

Höbelt, Lothar, Bohemia 1913: A Consensual Coup d'État? *Parliaments, Estates and Representation*, 20/1 (2000), 207–14.

Höbelt, Lothar, Der Großgrundbesitz und der Ausgleich, oder: Vom Nutzen aristokratischer Exklusivität. In Fasora, Lukáš, Hanuš, Jiří, and Malíř, Jiří (eds), *Moravské vyrovnání z roku 1905: Možnosti a limity národnostního smíru ve střední Evropě*. Brno, 2006, 59–69.

Höbelt, Lothar, Devolution Aborted: Franz Joseph I and the Bohemian 'Fundamental Articles' of 1871. *Parliaments, Estates and Representation*, 32/1 (2012), 37–52.

Höbelt, Lothar, Die austro-polnische Lösung. Eine unendliche Geschichte. In Heeresgeschichtlichen Museum Wien (ed.), *Der Erste Weltkrieg und der Vielvölkerstaat*. Vienna, 2012, 35–54.

Höbelt, Lothar, *'Stehen oder Fallen?' Österreichische Politik im Ersten Weltkrieg*. Vienna, 2015.

Hochedlinger, Michael, The Habsburg Monarchy: From 'Military-Fiscal State' to 'Militarization'. In Storrs, Christopher (ed.), *The Fiscal-Military State in Eighteenth-Century Europe*. Farnham, 2009, 55–94.

Hock, Beata, Kulturelle Dimensionen der Transnationalen Verflechtungen Ostmitteleuropas 1870er Jahre bis 1914. In Hadler, Frank, and Middell, Matthias (eds), *Handbuch einer transnationalen Geschichte Ostmitteleuropas*. Vol. 1: *Von der Mitte des 19. Jahrhunderts bis um Ersten Weltkrieg*. Göttingen, 2017, 189–255.

Hoerhan, Otto, *Die Petitionen an den Kremsierer Reichstag 1848/49*. University dissertation. Vienna, 1965.

[Hörmann von Hörbach, Joseph], *Tirol unter der baierischen Regierung: Mit Aktenstücken*. Vol. 1. Aarau, 1816.

Hoffmann, Robert, Die Stadt Salzburg in Vormärz und Neoabsolutismus 1803–1860. In Dopsch, Heinz, and Spatzenegger, Hans (eds), *Geschichte Salzburgs: Stadt und Land*. Vol. 2/4. Salzburg, 1991, 2241–80.

Hofmeister, Herbert, Pläne und Ansätze zu einer Kreis(Selbst)Verwaltung in der neueren österreichischen Verfassungsgeschichte. In Kovács, Kálmán (ed.), *Entwicklung der städtischen und regionalen Verwaltung in den letzten 100 Jahren in Mittel- und Osteuropa*. Vol. 3. Budapest, 1979.

Hoke, Rudolf, Österreich. In Jeserich, Kurt, Pohl, Hans, and Unruh, Georg Christoph von (eds), *Deutsche Verwaltungsgeschichte*. Vol. 2: *Vom Reichsdeputationshauptschluß bis zur Auflösung des Deutschen Bundes*. Stuttgart, 1983, 354–68.

Holec, Roman, Die ungarische Wirtschafts- und Industriepolitik bis 1914 aus slowakischer Sicht. In Müller, Uwe (ed.), *Ausgebeutet oder alimentiert? Regionale Wirtschaftspolitik und nationale Minderheiten in Ostmitteleuropa 1867–1939*. Berlin, 2006, 119–39.

Holenstein, André, Introduction: Empowering Interactions. Looking at Statebuilding from Below. In Holenstein, André, Blockmans, Wim, and Mathieu, Jon (eds), *Empowering Interactions: Political Cultures and the Emergence of the State in Europe 1300–1900*. Abingdon and New York, 2009, 1–31.

Holotík, L'udovít (ed.), *Der österreichisch-ungarische Ausgleich 1867*. Bratislava, 1971.

Hölzl, Andrea B., *Die wirtschaftlichen Ausgleichsverhandlungen zwischen Österreich und Ungarn 1867–1918*. University dissertation, Graz, 1989.

Hořejš, Miloš, Die nationalen Schutzvereine in Böhmen, Mähren und Schlesien 1900–1938: Mitgliedschaft, finanzielle Einnahmen und Wirkung. In Kubů, Eduard, and Schultz, Helga (eds), *Wirtschaftsnationalismus als Entwicklungsstrategie ostmitteleuropäischer Eliten*. Prag and Berlin, 2004, 197–220.

Horel, Catherine, *Soldaten zwischen nationalen Fronten: Die Auflösung der Militärgrenze und die Entwicklung der königlichungarischen Landwehr (Honvéd) in Kroatien-Slawonien 1868–1914*. Vienna, 2009.

Horel, Catherine, La France et l'Empire d'Autriche 1815–1918. *Bulletin de l'Institut Pierre Renouvin*, 32/2 (2010), 57–79.

Hösler, Joachim, *Von Krain zu Slowenien: Die Anfänge der nationalen Differenzierungsprozesse in Krain und der Untersteiermark von der Aufklärung bis zur Revolution 1768 bis 1848*. Munich, 2006.

Hostička, Vladimir, Slovanský sjezd a ukrajinci. In Veber, Václav (ed.), *150 let Slovanského sjezdu (1848): Historie a současnost*. Prague, 2000, 63–71.

Hrabovec, Emilia, Zwischen Nation und Religion, Thron und Altar: Der slowakische Katholizismus in der 'Ära Bach'. In Hrabovec, Emilia, Kováč, Dušan, and Suppan, Arnold (eds), *Die Habsburgermonarchie und die Slowaken 1849–1867*. Bratislava, 2001, 79–109.

Hroch, Miroslav, Das Bürgertum in den nationalen Bewegungen des 19. Jahrhunderts: Ein europäischer Vergleich. In Kocka, Jürgen (ed.), *Bürgertum im 19. Jahrhundert: Deutschland im europäischen Vergleich*. Vol. 3. Munich, 1988, 337–59.

Hroch, Miroslav, *Das Europa der Nationen: Die moderne Nationsbildung im europäischen Vergleich*. Göttingen, 2005.

Hroch, Miroslav, *Národy nejsou dílem náhody: Příčiny a předpoklady utváření moderních evropských národů*. Prague, 2008.

Huber, Florian, *Grenzkatholizismen: Religion, Raum und Nation in Tirol, 1830–1848*. Göttingen, 2016.

Hugelmann, Karl Gottfried, Der ständische Zentralausschuss in Österreich in April 1848. *Jahrbuch für Landeskunde von Niederösterreich*, 12 (1913), 170–260.

Hugelmann, Karl Gottfried, Die Landtagsbewegung des Jahres 1848 in Österreich unter der Enns. *Jahrbuch für Landeskunde in Niederösterreich*, 14–15 (1914–15), 495–530.

Hugelmann, Karl Gottfried, Zur Lehre vom 'monarchischen Prinzip'. *Österreichische Zeitschrift für öffentliches Recht*, 2/4 (1915), 472–86.

Hugelmann, Karl Gottfried, Das kaiserliche Kabinettschreiben vom 8. April 1848 und das Ministerium Pillersdorf. *Jahrbuch für Landeskunde von Niederösterreich*, 15–16 (1916–17), 492–512.

Huhnholz, Sebastian, and Hausteiner, Eva Marlene, Ein Bund unter Gleichen? Zum (anti) hegemonialen Charakter föderaler Arrangements. In Ambrosius, Gerold, Henrich-Franke, Christian, and Neutsch, Cornelius (eds), *Föderalismus in historisch vergleichender Perspektive*. Vol. 2: *Föderale Systeme: Kaiserreich—Donaumonarchie—Europäische Union*. Baden-Baden, 2015, 279–98.

Hüther, Michael, Hafemann, Klaus, Öffentliche Güter, Wettbewerb, Kompetenzverteilung—ökonomische Analysen zum Föderalismus. In Härtel, Ines (ed.), *Handbuch Föderalismus: Föderalismus als demokratische Rechtsordnung und Rechtskultur in Deutschland, Europa und der Welt*. Vol. 1: *Grundlagen des Föderalismus und der deutsche Bundesstaat*. Heidelberg, 2012, 333–58.

Hye, Hans Peter, Ein politischer Preis des allgemeinen und länder- bzw. wahlbezirksweise gleichen Männerwahlrechts zum Abgeordnetenhaus: Die lex Starzyński. In Kaiserová, Kristina (ed.), *Čechy a Sasko v proměnách dějin/Böhmen und Sachsen im Wandel der Geschichte*. Ústí nad Labem, 1993, 181–226.

Hye, Hans Peter, Die 'Länderkonferenz' (1905–1907): Ein Versuch gemeinsamer politischer Willensfindung der politischen Eliten der Länder. In Janák, Jan (ed.), *Ústřední moc a regionální samospráva*. Brno, 1995, 281–9.

Hye, Hans Peter, *Das politische System in der Habsburgermonarchie: Konstitutionalismus, Parlamentarismus und politische Partizipation*. Prague, 1998.

Hye, Hans Peter, Kommunale Selbstverwaltung und Öffentlichkeit im Hochliberalismus: Carl Georg Wolfrum und die Entwicklung der Stadt Aussig (Ústí nad Labem) 1848–1885. In Fasora, Lukáš, Hanuš, Jiří, and Malíř, Jiří (eds), *Občanské elity a obecní samospráva 1848–1948*. Brno, 2005, 254–70.

Hye, Hans Peter, Technologie und sozialer Wandel: In Rumpler, Helmut, andUrbanitsch, Peter (eds), *Die Habsburgermonarchie 1848–1918*. Vol. 9: *Soziale Strukturen*. Part 1: *Von der*

Feudal-Agrarischen zur Bürgerlich-industriellen Gesellschaft. Subvol. 1: *Lebens- und Arbeitswelten in der Industriellen Revolution*. Vienna, 2010, 15–65.

Hye, Hans Peter, Föderalistische Reformprojekte in der österreichischen Reichshälfte der Habsburgermonarchie: Eine gescheiterte Modernisierung. In Kruse, Wolfgang (ed.), *Andere Modernen. Beiträge zu einer Historisierung des Moderne-Begriffs*. Bielefeld, 2015, 219–40.

Ilwof, Franz, *Der Protestantismus in Steiermark, Kärnten und Krain vom 16. Jahrhundert bis in die Gegenwart*. Graz, 1900.

Imamović, Mustafa, *Bosnia and Herzegovina: Evolution of its Political and Legal Institutions*. Sarajevo, 2006.

Inama-Sternegg, Karl Theodor von, *Die Tendenz der Gross-Staatenbildung in der Gegenwart: Eine politische Studie*. Innsbruck, 1869.

Ivanišević, Alojz, Integration und Desintegration zwischen Serben, Kroaten und Muslimen. *Der Donauraum*, 37/1–2 (1997), 67–90.

Ivantyšynová, Tatiana, Die slovakische Politik und der Austroföderalismus. In Moritsch, Andreas (ed.), *Der Austroslavismus: Ein verfrühtes Konzept zur politischen Neugestaltung Mitteleuropas*. Vienna, 1996, 44–54.

Ivasyuk, Lesya, *Die polnische Revolution von 1846 in Galizien: Österreichische, ukrainische und polnische Wahrnehmungen*. Wiesbaden, 2017.

Iveljić, Iskra, Die Rolle der Grosskaufleute in der Modernisierung und in der nationalen Bewegung Zivil-Kroatiens in den sechziger Jahren des 19. Jahrhunderts. In Stekl, Hannes, Urbanitsch, Peter, Bruckmüller, Ernst, and Heiss, Hans (eds), *Durch Arbeit, Besitz, Wissen und Gerechtigkeit: Bürgertum in der Habsburgermonarchie*. Vienna, 1992, 231–43.

Iveljić, Iskra, 'Stiefkinder Österreichs': Die Kroaten und der Austroslavismus. In Moritsch, Andreas (ed.), *Der Austroslavismus: Ein verfrühtes Konzept zur politischen Neugestaltung Mitteleuropas*. Vienna, 1996, 124–37.

Iveljić, Iskra, Die Kroaten und der Prager Slavenkongress. In Moritsch, Andreas (ed.), *Der Prager Slavenkongress 1848*. Vienna, 2000, 171–81.

Jackson, Alvin, *The Two Unions: Ireland, Scotland, and the Survival of the United Kingdom 1707–2007*. Oxford, 2012.

Jacobs, Hans, *Die internationale Zuckerkonvention*. Berlin, 1928.

Janák, Jan, *Morava v národním ruchu 19. století*. Brno, 2007.

Janowski, Maciej, Galizien auf dem Weg zur Zivilgesellschaft. In Rumpler, Helmut, and Urbanitsch, Peter (ed.), *Die Habsburgermonarchie 1848–1918*. Vol. 8: *Politische Öffentlichkeit und Zivilgesellschaft*. Subvol. 1: *Vereine, Parteien und Interessenverbände als Träger der politischen Partizipation*. Vienna, 2006, 805–58.

Janský, V., *O úpravách řek i potoků a melioracích v království českém*. Prague, 1904.

Jaworski, Rudolf, Einer gegen alle! Zur Visualisierung des deutschen Michels auf Bildpostkarten der späten Habsburgermonarchie. *Österreichische Zeitschrift für Volkskunde*, 122/1 (2019), 55–75.

Jedlicka, Ludwig, Erzherzog Franz Ferdinand (1863–1914). In Hantsch, Hugo (ed.), *Gestalter der Geschicke Österreichs*. Innsbruck, 1962, 527–38.

Jedlicka, Ludwig, Alexander Brosch von Aarenau und Moritz von Auffenberg-Komarów: Dokumente einer Freundschaft. In Franzel, Emil (ed.), *Virtute fideque. Festschrift Otto von Habsburg*. Vienna, 1965, 90–102.

Jelavich, Charles, The Croatian Problem in the Habsburg Empire in the Nineteenth Century. *Austrian History Yearbook*, 3/2 (1967), 83–115.

Jellinek, Georg, *Die Lehre von den Staatenverbindungen*. Vienna, 1882.

Jellinek, Georg, Rezension zu Jellinek, Georg, Josef Pliveric, *Beiträge zum ungarisch-kroatischen Bundesrechte: Rechtliche und politische Erörterungen. Agram 1886. Kritische Vierteljahresschrift für Gesetzgebung und Rechtswissenschaft*, NF 12 (1889).

Jellinek, Georg, and Pliveric, Josef, *Das rechtliche Verhältnis Kroatiens zu Ungarn*. Agram, 1885.

Jellinek, Georg, and Pliveric, Josef, *Beiträge zum ungarisch-kroatischen Bundesrechte. Rechtliche und politische Erörterungen*. Agram, 1886.

Jepsen, Harald H., Orthodoxy and Autocephaly in Galicia. In Hann, Christopher, and Magocsi, Paul (eds), *Galicia a Multicultured Land*. Toronto, 2005, 71–81.

Jindra, Zdeněk, *Hospodářský vzestup českých zemí od poloviny 18. století do konce monarchie*. Prague, 2015.

Jiránek, Tomáš, Česko-německé vztahy v Obchodních a živnostenských komorách v Brně a v Olomouci v době moravského vyrovnání. In Fasora, Lukáš, Hanuš, Jiří, and Malíř, Jiří (eds), *Moravské vyrovnání z roku 1905: Možnosti a limity národnostního smíru ve střední Evropě*. Brno, 2006, 333–46.

Jobst, Kerstin S., *Zwischen Nationalismus und Internationalismus: Die polnische und ukrainische Sozialdemokratie in Galizien von 1890 bis 1914. Ein Beitrag zur Nationalitätenfrage im Habsburgerreich*. Hamburg, 1996.

Jordan, Jan Peter, *Aktenmäßiger Bericht über die Verhandlungen des ersten Slawenkongresses in Prag*. Prague, 1848.

Jordan, Jan Peter, Die Entwicklung des Eisenbahnnetzes auf dem Gebiet des heutigen Jugoslawien (bis 1918). In Plaschka, Richard G., Drabek, Anna M., and Zaar, Birgitta (eds), *Eisenbahnbau und Kapitalinteressen in den Beziehungen der österreichischen mit den südslawischen Ländern*. Vienna, 1993, 13–30.

Jörke, Dirk, *Die Größe der Demokratie: Über die räumliche Herrschaft und Partizipation*. Berlin, 2019.

Joyce, Patrick, *The State of Freedom: A Social History of the British State since 1800*. Cambridge, 2013.

Judson, Pieter M., *Exclusive Revolutionaries: Liberal Politics, Social Experience, and National Identity in the Austrian Empire 1848–1914*. Ann Arbor, 1996.

Judson, Pieter M., *Guardians of the Nation: Activists on the Language Frontiers of Imperial Austria*. Cambridge, MA, 2006.

Judson, Pieter M., L'Autriche-Hongrie était-elle un empire? *Annales. Histoire, Sciences Sociales*, 63/3 (2008), 563–96.

Judson, Pieter M., Do Multiple Languages Mean a Multicultural Society? Nationalist Frontiers in Rural Austria 1880–1918. In Feichtinger, Johannes, and Cohen, Gary (ed.), *Understanding Multiculturalism: The Habsburg Central European Experience*. New York and Oxford, 2014, 61–82.

Judson, Pieter M., *The Habsburg Empire: A New History*. Cambridge, MA, and London, 2016.

Judson, Pieter M., *Habsburg: Geschichte eines Imperiums 1740–1918*. Munich, 2017.

Judson, Pieter M., Zahra, Tara, *The Great War and the Transformation of Habsburg Central Europe*. New York, 2025.

Juraschek, Franz von, *Personal- und Realunion mit einem Anhange: Das rechtliche Verhältniss zwischen Oesterreich und Ungarn*. Berlin, 1878.

Kadlec, Petr, *Střední školy a jejich studenti: K formování inteligence na severní Moravě a ve Slezsku ve druhé polovině 19. a na počátku 20. století*. Ostrava, 2013.

Kaernbach, Andreas, *Bismarcks Konzepte zur Reform des Deutschen Bundes: Zur Kontinuität der Politik Bismarcks und Preußens in der deutschen Frage*. Göttingen, 1991.

Kaernbach, Andreas, Hegemonie oder Interessensphärenteilung? Bismarcks Handlungsalternativen mit Blick auf Österreich im Reichgründungsjahrzehnt. In Kaernbach, Andreas, Gehler, Michael, Schmidt, Rainer F., and Steininger, Rolf (eds), *Ungleiche Partner? Österreich und Deutschland in ihrer gegenseitigen Wahrnehmung: Historische Analysen und Vergleiche aus dem 19. und 20. Jahrhundert*. Innsbruck, 2009, 247–67.

Kaizl, Josef, *Finanzwissenschaft*. 2 vols. Vienna, 1900, 1901.

Kajčev, Naum, *Ilirija. Ot Varna do Vilach. Chărvatskoto nacionalno văzraždane, sărbite i bălgarite. Do 1848 g*. Sofija, 2015.

Kalmár, János, and Hochedlinger, Michael, Die Hofkommission (Hofdeputation) in Transylvanicis, Banaticis et Illyricis und die Illyrische Hofkanzlei. In Maťa, Petr, Hochedlinger, Michael, and Winkelbauer, Thomas (eds), *Verwaltungsgeschichte der Habsburgermonarchie in der Frühen Neuzeit*. Vol. 1/1: *Hof und Dynastie, Kaiser und Reich, Zentralverwaltungen, Kriegswesen und landesfürstliches Finanzwesen*. Vienna, 2019, 516–20.

Kalousek, Josef, *Einige Grundlagen des böhmischen Staatsrechts*. Prague, 1871.

Kalousek, Josef, *České státní právo*. 2nd edn. Prague, 1892.

Kalwoda, Johannes, *Zur Institution des deutschen Landsmannministeriums in Altösterreich 1891–1910*. Dipl.-Arb. Univ. Vienna, 1995.

Kann, Robert A., *The Multinational Empire: Nationalism and National Reform in the Habsburg Monarchy 1848–1918*. 2 vols. New York, 1950.

Kann, Robert A., *Erzherzog Franz Ferdinand: Studien*. Munich, 1976.

Kaposi, Zoltán, Der Staat, die wirtschaftliche Entwicklung und die Nationalitäten auf dem Gebiet des Königreichs Ungarn 1867–1918. In Müller, Uwe (ed.), *Ausgebeutet oder alimentiert? Regionale Wirtschaftspolitik und nationale Minderheiten in Ostmitteleuropa 1867–1939*. Berlin, 2006, 101–18.

Kaps, Klemens, *Ungleiche Entwicklung in Zentraleuropa: Galizien zwischen überregionaler Verflechtung und imperialer Politik 1772–1914*. Böhlau and Vienna, 2015.

Kaser, Karl, *Freier Bauer und Soldat: Die Militarisierung der agrarischen Gesellschaft an der kroatisch-slawonischen Militärgrenze 1535–1881*. Vienna, 1997.

Katus, László, József Eötvös and Ferenc Deák: Laws on Nationalities. In Romsics, Ignác, and Király, Béla K. (eds), *Geopolitics in the Danube Region: Hungarian Reconciliation Efforts 1848–1998*. Budapest, 1999, 133–60.

Katus, László, *Hungary in the Dual Monarchy 1867–1914*. New York, 2008.

Katus, László, The Common Market of the Austro-Hungarian Monarchy. In Gerö, András (ed.), *The Austro-Hungarian Monarchy Revisited*. New York, 2009, 21–50.

Kazbunda, Karel, *Otázka česko-německá v předvečer velké války. Zrušení ústavnosti země České tzv. annenskými patenty z 26. července 1913*. Prague, 1995.

Kedourie, Elie, *Nationalism*. London, 1961.

Keller, Fritz, *Österreichisches und ungarisches Staatsrecht. Eine Einführung*. Berlin, 1917.

Kelsen, Hans, *Hauptprobleme der Staatsrechtslehre: Entwickelt aus der Lehre vom Rechtssatze*. Tübingen, 1911.

Kelsen, Hans, Industrieförderung in Rumänien (1912). In Jestaedt, Matthias (ed.), *Hans Kelsen Werke*. Vol. 3: *Veröffentlichte Schriften 1911–1917*. Tübingen, 2010, 65–72.

Kelsen, Hans, Die böhmische Verwaltungskommission vor dem Verwaltungsgerichtshof (1913). In Jestaedt, Matthias (ed.), *Hans Kelsen Werke*. Vol. 3: *Veröffentlichte Schriften 1911–1917*. Tübingen, 2010, 106–11.

Kelsen, Hans, Reichsgesetz und Landesgesetz nach österreichischer Verfassung (1914). In Jestaedt, Matthias (ed.), *Hans Kelsen Werke*. Vol. 3: *Veröffentlichte Schriften 1911–1917*. Tübingen, 2010, 259–425.

Kelsen, Hans, Zur Reform der verfassungsrechtlichen Grundlagen der Wehrmacht Österreich-Ungarns (1917/1918). In Jestaedt, Matthias (ed.), *Hans Kelsen Werke*. Vol. 3: *Veröffentlichte Schriften 1911–1917*. Tübingen, 2010, 615–29.

Kemlein, Sophia, *Die Posener Juden 1815–1848: Entwicklungsprozesse einer polnischen Judenheit unter preußischer Herrschaft*. Hamburg, 1997.

Kempter, Klaus, *Die Jellineks 1820–1955: Eine familienbiographische Studie zum deutschjüdischen Bildungsbürgertum*. Düsseldorf, 1998.

Kersten, Jens, *Georg Jellinek und die klassische Staatslehre*. Tübingen, 2000.

Kersten, Jens, Warum Georg Jellinek? Georg Jellinek und die Staats- und Europarechtslehre der Gegenwart. In Anter, Andreas (ed.), *Die normative Kraft des Faktischen: Das Staatsverständnis Georg Jellineks*. Baden-Baden, 2004, 175–99.

Kieval, Hillel J., *The Making of Czech Jewry: National Conflict and Jewish Society in Bohemia 1870–1918*. New York, 1988.

Killian, Herbert, *Der Kampf gegen Wildbäche und Lawinen im Spannungsfeld von Zentralismus und Föderalismus: Eine historische Studie*. Vol. 3/1: *Die Organisation*. Vienna, 1990.

King, Jeremy, The Nationalization of East Central Europe: Ethnicism, Ethnicity, and Beyond. In Bucur, Maria, and Wingfield, Nancy M. (eds), *Staging the Past: The Politics of Commemoration in Habsburg Central Europe. 1848 to the Present*. West Lafayette, IN, 2001, 112–52.

King, Jeremy, *Budweisers into Czechs and Germans: A Local History of Bohemian Politics 1848–1948*. Princeton, 2002.

Kirilina, Ljubov' A., *Slovency i revoljucija 1848–1849 gg*. Moscow, 2000.

Kisker, Gunter, *Kooperation im Bundesstaat: Eine Untersuchung zum kooperativen Föderalismus in der Bundesrepublik Deutschland.* Tübingen, 1971.

Kiszling, Rudolf, Erzherzog Franz Ferdinand und seine Pläne für den Umbau der Donaumonarchie. *Der Donauraum*, 8 (1963), 261–6.

Kittel, Bernhard, Obinger, Herbert, and Wagschal, Uwe, Die gezügelten Wohlfahrtsstaaten im internationalen Vergleich: Politisch-institutionelle Faktoren der Entstehung und Entwicklungsdynamik. In Obinger, Herbert (ed.), *Der gezügelte Wohlfahrtsstaat: Sozialpolitik in reichen Industrienationen.* Frankfurt am Main, 2000, 329–64.

K. k. Finanzministerium (ed.), *Die Landeshaushalte der im Reichsrate vertretenen Königreiche und Länder: Nach den Vorschlägen für das Jahr 1905.* 18 vols. Vienna, 1907.

K.k. statistische Zentral-Kommission, *Statistisches Handbuch der autonomen Landesverwaltung in den im Reichsrate vertretenen Königreichen und Ländern.* Vols. 1–14. Vienna, 1900–18.

Klabouch, Jiří, *Die Gemeindeselbstverwaltung in Österreich 1848–1918.* Vienna, 1968.

Klabouch, Jiří, Die Lokalverwaltung in Cisleithanien. In Wandruszka, Adam, and Urbanitsch, Peter (eds), *Die Habsburgermonarchie 1848–1918.* Vol. 2: *Verwaltung und Rechtswesen.* Vienna, 1975, 270–305.

Kladiwa, Pavel, Pokludová, Andrea, and Kafková, Renata, *Lesk a bída obecních samospráv Moravy a Slezska 1850–1914.* Vol. 2/2: *Finance a infrastruktura.* Ostrava, 2009.

Klečacký, Martin, *Český ministr ve Vídni. Ve službách císaře, národa a politické strany.* Prague, 2017.

Kleinwächter, Friedrich, Die österreichische Enquete über die Landesfinanzen (März 1908). *Jahrbücher für Nationalökonomie und Statistik*, 93 (1909), 43–63.

Klemperer, Klemens von, *Ignaz Seipel: Staatsmann einer Krisenzeit.* Graz, 1976.

Kletečka, Thomas, *Der Ausgleichsversuch des Ministeriums Hohenwart-Schäffle mit Böhmen im Jahre 1871. Mit besonderer Berücksichtigung des reichsdeutschen Einflusses.* University dissertation, Vienna, 1984.

Kletečka, Thomas, Einleitung. In Kletečka, Thomas (ed.), *Protokolle des Österreichischen Ministerrates.* Vol. 1/1: *Die Ministerien des Revolutionsjahres 1848 (20. März 1848–21. November 1848).* Vienna, 1996, pp. ix–xlviii.

Kletečka, Thomas (ed.), *Protokolle des Österreichischen Ministerrates.* Vol. 1/1: *Die Ministerien des Revolutionsjahres 1848 (20. März 1848–21. November 1848).* Vienna, 1996.

Kletečka, Thomas, Einleitung. In Kletečka, Thomas (ed.), *Protokolle des Österreichischen Ministerrates.* Vol. 2/1: *Das Ministerium Schwarzenberg (5. Dezember 1848–7. Jänner 1850).* Vienna, 2002, pp. ix–lii.

Kletečka, Thomas (ed.), *Protokolle des Österreichischen Ministerrates.* Vol. 2/1: *Das Ministerium Schwarzenberg (5. Dezember 1848–7. Jänner 1850).* Vienna, 2002.

Kletečka, Thomas, Staat und Kirche(n) im Zeichen der Revolution. In Velková, Alice, Velek, Luboš, and Pokorný, Jiří (eds), *Nacionalismus, společnost a kultura ve střední Evropě 19. a 20. století. Pocta Jiřímu Kořalkovi k 75. narozeninám/Nationalismus, Gesellschaft und Kultur in Mitteleuropa im 19. und 20. Jahrhundert. Festschrift für Jiří Kořalka zum 75. Geburtstag.* Prague, 2007.

Kletečka, Thomas, Einleitung. In Kletečka, Thomas (ed.), *Protokolle des Österreichischen Ministerrates.* Vol. 2/4: *Das Ministerium Schwarzenberg (14. Oktober 1850–30. Mai 1851).* Vienna, 2011, pp. ix–xliv.

Kletečka, Thomas (ed.), *Protokolle des Österreichischen Ministerrates.* Vol. 2/4: *Das Ministerium Schwarzenberg (14. Oktober 1850–30. Mai 1851).* Vienna, 2011.

Kletečka, Thomas, and Koch, Klaus (ed.), *Protokolle des Österreichischen Ministerrates.* Vol. 5/6: *Die Ministerien Erzherzog Rainer und Mensdorff (4. Mai 1863–12. Oktober 1863).* Vienna, 1989.

Kletečka, Thomas, and Koch, Klaus, Einleitung. In Kletečka, Thomas, and Koch, Klaus (eds), *Protokolle des Österreichischen Ministerrates.* Vol. 5/6: *Die Ministerien Erzherzog Rainer und Mensdorff (4. Mai 1863–12. Oktober 1863).* Vienna, 1989, pp. xix–xlv.

Kletečka, Thomas, and Koch, Klaus, Einleitung. In Kletečka, Thomas, and Koch, Klaus (eds), *Protokolle des Österreichischen Ministerrates.* Vol. 5/7: *Die Ministerien Erzherzog Rainer und Mensdorff (15. Oktober 1863–23. Mai 1864).* Vienna, 1992, pp. ix–xxxiv.

Klečka, Thomas, and Koch, Klaus (ed.), *Protokolle des Österreichischen Ministerrates.* Vol. 5/7: *Die Ministerien Erzherzog Rainer und Mensdorff (15. Oktober 1863–23. Mai 1864).* Vienna, 1992.

Klečka, Thomas, and Schmied-Kowarzik, Anatol, Einleitung. In Klečka, Thomas, and Schmied-Kowarzik, Anatol (eds), *Protokolle des Österreichischen Ministerrates.* Vol. 2/2: *Das Ministerium Schwarzenberg (8. Jänner 1850–30. April 1850).* Vienna, 2005, pp. ix–xxix.

Klečka, Thomas, and Schmied-Kowarzik, Anatol (eds), *Protokolle des Österreichischen Ministerrates.* Vol. 2/2: *Das Ministerium Schwarzenberg (8. Jänner 1850–30. April 1850).* Vienna, 2005.

Klečka, Thomas, and Schmied-Kowarzik, Anatol (ed.), *Protokolle des Österreichischen Ministerrates.* Vol. 2/3: *Das Ministerium Schwarzenberg (1. Mai 1850–30. September 1850).* Vienna, 2006.

Klečka, Thomas, and Schmied-Kowarzik, Anatol, Einleitung. In Klečka, Thomas, and Schmied-Kowarzik, Anatol (eds), *Protokolle des Österreichischen Ministerrates.* Vol. 2/5: *Das Ministerium Schwarzenberg (4. Juni 1851–5. April 1852).* Vienna, 2013, pp. ix–lviii.

Klimó, Árpád von, *Nation, Konfession, Geschichte: Zur nationalen Geschichtskultur Ungarns im europäischen Kontext 1860–1948.* Munich, 2003.

Klopfer, Carl (ed.), *Unser Kaiser: Ein Gedenkbuch der fünfzigjährigen Regierung, zugleich ein Lebens- u. Characterbild Kaiser Franz Josef I.* Vienna, 1898.

Klüber, Johann Ludwig, *Öffentliches Recht des Teutschen Bundes und der Bundesstaaten.* 3rd edn. 2 vols. Franfurt am Main, 1831.

Knapic-Krhen, Cvetka, Karl Renner und die nationale Frage in den Nachfolgestaaten der Monarchie: Was blieb vom Personalitätsprinzip? In Konrad, Helmut (ed.), *Arbeiterbewegung und nationale Frage in den Nachfolgestaaten der Habsburgermonarchie.* Vienna and Zürich, 1993, 111–43.

Knecht, Ingo, *Der Reichsdeputationshauptschluß vom 25. Februar 1803.* Berlin, 2007.

Koch, Matthias, *Pillersdorf und die Wahrheit: Oder Beleuchtung seiner 'Rückblicke' auf die politische Bewegung in Österreich in den Jahren 1848 und 1849.* Vienna, 1849.

Koch, Ursula E., Macht und Ohnmacht der Presse um 1848: Frankreich und Deutschland im Vergleich. In Dowe, Dieter, Haupt, Heinz-Gerhard, and Langewiesche, Dieter (eds), *Europa 1848: Revolution und Reform.* Bonn, 1998, 771–812.

Kochnowski, Roman, *Przy Tobie Najjaśniejszy Panie stoimy i stać chcemy: Monarchia habsburska w polskiej myśli politycznej lat 1860–1914.* Kraków, 2009.

Köhler, Peter A., *Ein Jahrhundert Sozialversicherung in der Bundesrepublik Deutschland, Frankreich, Großbritannien, Österreich und der Schweiz.* Berlin, 1981.

Koskenniemi, Martti, *The Gentle Civilizer of Nations: The Rise and Fall of International Law 1870–1960.* Cambridge, 2001.

Kolaric, Alexandra, Probleme der staatsrechtlichen Verhältnisse. In Timmermann, Heiner (ed.), *Entwicklung der Nationalbewegungen in Europa 1850–1914.* Berlin, 1998, 87–99.

Kolejka, Josef, Der Slawenkongress in Prag im Juni 1848: Die slawische Variante einer österreichischen Föderation. In Jaworski, Rudolf, and Luft, Robert (eds), *1848/49 Revolutionen in Ostmitteleuropa.* Munich, 1996, 129–47.

Kolmer, Gustav, *Parlament und Verfassung in Österreich.* Vol. 1: *1848–1869.* Vienna and Leipzig, 1902.

Kolmer, Gustav, *Parlament und Verfassung in Österreich.* Vol. 2: *1869–1879.* Vienna and Leipzig, 1903.

Kolmer, Gustav, *Parlament und Verfassung in Österreich.* Vol. 6: *1895–1898.* Vienna and Leipzig, 1910.

Kolmer, Gustav, *Parlament und Verfassung in Österreich.* Vol. 8: *1900–1904.* Vienna and Leipzig, 1914.

Komlos, John, *Die Habsburgermonarchie als Zollunion: Die Wirtschaftsentwicklung Österreich-Ungarns im 19. Jahrhundert.* Vienna, 1986.

Komlosy, Andrea, *Grenze und ungleiche regionale Entwicklung: Binnenmarkt und Migration in der Habsburgermonarchie.* Vienna, 2003.

Komlosy, Andrea, Der Staat schiebt ab. Zur nationalstaatlichen Konsolidierung von Heimat und Fremde im 18. und 19. Jahrhundert. In Komlosy, Andrea, and Hahn, Sylvia (eds), *Ausweisung, Abschiebung, Vertreibung in Europa 16.–20. Jahrhundert*. Innsbruck, 2006, 87–114.

Kompert, Paul, Die Reform der Budgetierung in den österreichischen Landesfinanzwirtschaften. *Jahrbuch für Gesetzgebung, Verwaltung und Volkswirtschaft im Deutschen Reich*, 34 (1910), 139–50.

Kořalka, Jiří, Bedingtheiten und Entscheidungen angesichts der Krise der multinationalen Monarchie: Prag-Frankfurt im Frühjahr 1848: Österreich zwischen Großdeutschtum und Austroslawismus. In Lutz, Heinrich, and Rumpler, Helmut (eds), *Österreich und die deutsche Frage im 19. und 20. Jahrhundert: Probleme der politisch-staatlichen und soziokulturellen Differenzierung im deutschen Mitteleuropa*. Munich, 1982, 117–39.

Kořalka, Jiří, Welche Nationsvorstellungen gab es 1848 in Mitteleuropa? In Jaworski, Rudolf, and Luft, Robert (eds), *1848/49 Revolutionen in Ostmitteleuropa*. Munich, 1996, 29–45.

Kořalka, Jiří, Revolutionen in der Habsburgermonarchie. In Dowe, Dieter, Haupt, Heinz-Gerhard, and Langewiesche, Dieter (eds), *Europa 1848: Revolution und Reform*. Bonn, 1998, 197–230.

Kořalka, Jiří, František Palacký und die böhmischen Bolzanisten. In Rumpler, Helmut (ed.), *Bernard Bolzano und die Politik: Staat, Nation und Religion als Herausforderung für die Philosophie im Kontext von Spätaufklärung, Frühnationalismus und Restauration*. Vienna, 2000, 201–20.

Kořalka, Jiří, Von der ständisch-terrorialen Verfassung zur Nation. Tschechische Nationalbildung und nationale Identität im 19. Jahrhundert. In Hirschhausen, Ulrike von, and Leonhard, Jörn (eds), *Nationalismen in Europa: West- und Osteuropa im Vergleich*. Göttingen, 2001, 306–21.

Kořalka, Jiří, *František Palacký (1798–1876): Der Historiker der Tschechen im österreichischen Vielvölkerstaat*. Vienna, 2007.

Korbuly, Emerich, *Ungarns öffentliches Recht*. Budapest, 1874.

Korioth, Stefan, *Integration und Bundesstaat: Ein Beitrag zur Staats- und Verfassungslehre Rudolf Smends*. Berlin, 1990.

Korioth, Stefan, *Der Finanzausgleich zwischen Bund und Ländern*. Tübingen, 1997.

Korunić, Petar, *Jugoslavizam i federalizam u hrvatskom nacionalnom preporodu 1835–1875: Studija o političkoj teoriji i ideologiji*. Zagreb, 1989.

Koselleck, Reinhart, *Preußen zwischen Reform und Revolution: Allgemeines Landrecht, Verwaltung und soziale Bewegung von 1791 bis 1848*. Munich, 1989.

Koselleck, Reinhart, Art. Bund (Bündnis, Föderalismus, Bundestaat). In Koselleck, Brunner, Otto, Conze , Werner (eds), *Geschichtliche Grundbegriffe*. Subvol. 1: *Historisches Lexikon zur politisch-sozialen Sprache in Deutschland*. Stuttgart, 2004, 582–671.

Kossuth, Lajos, Der Donaubund (1862). In Borodziej, Włodzimierz (ed.), *Option Europa: Deutsche, polnische und ungarische Europapläne des 19. und 20. Jahrhunderts*. Vol. 3: *Texte*. Göttingen, 2005, 111–16.

Kotík, Antonín (ed.), *Pláč koruny české: Některé dokumenty jako příspěvek k dějinám prusko-rakouské války roku 1866*. Prague, 1919.

Kott, Sandrine, *Sozialstaat und Gesellschaft. Das deutsche Kaiserreich in Europa*. Göttingen, 2014.

Kováč, Dušan, Die Flucht der Slowaken aus dem ungarischen Staatsverband. In Rumpler, Helmut (ed.), *Die Habsburgermonarchie 1848–1918*. Vol. 11: *Die Habsburgermonarchie und der Erste Weltkrieg*. Subvol. 1: *Der Kampf um die Neuordnung Mitteleuropas*. Part 2: *Vom Vielvölkerstaat Österreich-Ungarn zum neuen Europa der Nationalstaaten*. Vienna, 2016, 735–65.

Kovács, Elisabeth, *Untergang oder Rettung der Donaumonarchie?* Vol. 1: *Die österreichische Frage. Kaiser und König Karl I./IV. und die Neuordnung Mitteleuropas 1916–1922*. Vienna, 2004.

Kövér, György, The Economic Achievements of the Austro-Hungarian Monarchy. In Gerö, András (ed.), *The Austro-Hungarian Monarchy Revisited*. New York, 2009, 51–83.

Kozik, Jan, *Między reakcją a rewolucją: Studia z dziejów ukraińskiego ruchu narodowego w Galicji w latach 1848–1849*. Warsaw, 1975.

Kozik, Jan, *The Ukrainian National Movement in Galicia 1815–1849*. Edmonton, 1986.

Krahwinkler, Harald, Die Landtage von Görz-Gradisca und Istrien. In Rumpler, Helmut, and Urbanitsch, Peter (eds), *Die Habsburgermonarchie 1848–1918*. Vol. 7: *Verfassung und Parlamentarismus*. Subvol. 2: *Die regionalen Repräsentativkörperschaften*. Vienna, 2000, 1873–1918.

Kramář, Karel, *Das böhmische Staatsrecht*. Vienna, 1896.

Kramář, Karel, *Anmerkungen zur böhmischen Politik*. Vienna, 1906.

Krasa-Florian, Selma, *Allegorie der Austria: Die Entstehung des Gesamtstaatsgedankens in der österreichisch-ungarischen Monarchie und die bildende Kunst*. Vienna, 2007.

Krasinski, Valerian, *Panslavism and Germanism*. London, 1848.

Kraus, Karl, *Die letzten Tage der Menschheit: Bühnenfassung des Autors*. Frankfurt am Main, 1992.

Krestić, Vasilije, *Hrvatsko-Ugarska nagodba 1868. godine*. Belgrade, 1969.

Krestić, Vasilije, Über einige politisch-historische Bedingungen der Entstehung des kroatisch-ungarischen Ausgleichs 1868. In Holotík, L'udovít (ed.), *Der österreichisch-ungarische Ausgleich 1867*. Bratislava, 1971, 783–829.

Kretschmann, Carsten, Bismarck und das deutsch-österreichische Problem. *Mitteilungen des Instituts für österreichische Geschichtsforschung*, 111 (2003), 429–44.

Krevecz'ky'j, Ivan, Sprava podyilu Halychyny w rr. 1846–1850. *Zapysky Naukovoho Tovarystva Imeni Sevchenka*, 93 (1910), 54–69; 94, 58–83; 95, 54–115; 96, 105–54.

Kristóffy, Josef, *Magyarozszág kálváriája*. Vol. 1. Pest, 1928.

Krleža, Miroslav, *Die Fahnen*. 5 vols. Klagenfurt, 2016.

Krokar, James Paul, Liberal Reform in Croatia 1872–75: The Beginnings of Modern Croatia under Ban Ivan Mažuranić. University dissertation, Indianapolis, 1980.

Kronenbitter, Günther, *Krieg im Frieden: Die Führung der k. u. k. Armee und die Grossmachtpolitik Österreich-Ungarns 1906–1914*. Munich, 2003.

Kronenbitter, Günther, Verhinderter Retter? Erzherzog Franz Ferdinand und die Erhaltung der Habsburgermonarchie. In Zellenberg, Ulrich E. (ed.), *Konservative Profile: Ideen und Praxis in der Politik zwischen FM Radetzky, Karl Kraus und Alois Mock*. Graz and Stuttgart, 2003, 267–83.

Krzoska, Martin, Das Egerland als Erinnerungsort. In Řezník, Miloš (ed.), *Regionale Erinnerungsorte: Böhmische Länder und Mitteldeutschland im europäischen Kontext*. Leipzig, 2013, 85–98.

Kübeck, Max von (ed.), *Metternich und Kübeck: Ein Briefwechsel*. Vienna, 1910.

Kubů, Eduard, Wirtschaftsnationalismus in Parteiprogrammen der böhmischen Länder und der Ersten Tschechoslowakischen Republik. In Kubů, Eduard, Pogány, Ágnes, and Kofman, Jan (eds), *Für eine nationale Wirtschaft: Ungarn, die Tschechoslowakei und Polen vom Ausgang des 19. Jahrhunderts bis zum Zweiten Weltkrieg*. Berlin, 2006, 73–133.

Kühl, Joachim, *Föderationspläne im Donauraum und in Ostmitteleuropa*. Munich, 1958.

Kuk, Leszek, *Wielka emigracja a powstanie słowianofilstwa francuskiego: W kręgu działalności Cypriana Roberta*. Toruń, 1991.

Kukuljević Sakcinski, Ivan, *Die legitimen und historischen Rechte Croatiens und der Ausgleich mit Ungarn*. 2nd edn. Agram, 1883.

Kürnberger, Ferdinand, *Siegelringe: Eine ausgewählte Sammlung politischer und kirchlicher Feuilletons*. Hamburg, 1874.

Kusý Ritter von Dúbrav, Emanuel, Entwicklung und Organisation des öffentlichen Sanitätswesens in Österreich. In *Österreichs Wohlfahrts-Einrichtungen*. Vol. 3: *Gesundheitspflege*. Vienna, 1900, 3–24.

Kutnar, František, Sociální neklid zemědělského obyvatelstva v Čechách za Bachova absolutismu. *Historický sborník*, 17 (1970), 31–65.

Kuzmany, Börries, *Brody: Eine galizische Grenzstadt im langen 19. Jahrhundert*. Vienna, 2011.

Kuzmany, Börries, Der Galizische Ausgleich. In Haid, Elisabeth, Weismann, Stephanie, and Wöller, Burkhard (eds), *Galizien: Peripherie der Moderne—Moderne der Peripherie*. Marburg, 2013, 122–41.

Kuzmany, Börries, Habsburg Austria: Experiments in Non-territorial Autonomy. *Ethnopolitics*, 15/1 (2016), 43–65.

Kuzmany, Börries, *A History of Non-Territorial Autonomy: Accommodating National Diversity in Modern Europe, 1848–1939*. Oxford, 2027.

Kwan, Jonathan, *Liberalism and the Habsburg Monarchy 1861–1895*. Basingstoke, 2013.

Kwan, Jonathan, Austro-German Liberalism and Bohemian State Rights 1861–1879. *Střed/Centre*, 8/1 (2016), 109–50.

Kymlicka, Will, Is Federalism a Viable Alternative to Secession? In Lehning, Percy B. (ed.), *Theories of Secession*. London, 1998, 111–50.

Laak, Dirk van, Infra-Strukturgeschichte. *Geschichte und Gesellschaft*, 3 (2001), 367–93.

Laak, Dirk van, Kolonien als 'Laboratorien der Moderne'? In Conrad, Sebastian, and Osterhammel, Jürgen (eds), *Das Kaiserreich transnational: Deutschland in der Welt 1871–1914*. Göttingen, 2004, 257–79.

Lacmanović-Heydenreuter, Haira, *Dalmatien in Wien: Die dalmatinischen Abgeordneten im Wiener Reichsrat 1867–1918*. Hamburg, 2011.

Lalić, Daniel, *Der Hochadel Kroatien-Slawoniens: Zwischen Verlust, Verteidigung und Neuerwerb gesellschaftlicher Elitenpositionen 1868–1918*. Munich, 2017.

Lambert, David, and Lester, Alan (ed.), *Colonial Lives Across the British Empire. Imperial Careering in the Long Nineteenth Century*. Cambridge, 2006.

Lammasch, Heinrich, Erzherzog Franz Ferdinand. In Lammasch, Marga, and Sperl, Hans (eds), *Heinrich Lammasch: Seine Aufzeichnungen, sein Wirken und seine Politik*. Vienna and Leipzig, 1922, 77–95.

Landauer, Karl, *Literatur zur Frage der deutsch-österreichischen-ungarischen Wirtschaftsannäherung*. Jena, 1916.

Láng, Lajos, *Hundert Jahre Zollpolitik*. Vienna and Leipzig, 1906.

Langewiesche, Dieter, Liberalismus und Bürgertum in Europa. In Kocka, Jürgen (ed.), *Bürgertum im 19. Jahrhundert: Deutschland im europäischen Vergleich*. Vol. 3. Munich, 1988, 360–94.

Langewiesche, Dieter, Revolution in Deutschland: Verfassungsstaat-Nationalstaat-Gesellschaftsreform. In Langewiesche, Dieter, Dowe, Dieter, and Haupt, Heinz-Gerhard (eds), *Europa 1848: Revolution und Reform*. Bonn, 1998, 167–95.

Langewiesche, Dieter, Föderativer Nationalismus als Erbe der deutschen Reichsnation: Über Föderalismus und Zentralismus in der deutschen Nationalgeschichte. In Langewiesche, Dieter, and Schmidt, Georg (eds), *Föderative Nation: Deutschlandkonzepte von der Reformation bis zum Ersten Weltkrieg*. Munich, 2000, 215–42.

Langewiesche, Dieter, 'Nation', 'Nationalismus', 'Nationalstaat' in der europäischen Geschichte seit dem Mittelalter: Versuch einer Bilanz. In Langewiesche, Dieter, and Schmidt, Georg (eds), *Föderative Nation: Deutschlandkonzepte von der Reformation bis zum Ersten Weltkrieg*. Munich, 2000, 8–30.

Langewiesche, Dieter, *Reich, Nation, Föderation: Deutschland und Europa*. Munich, 2008.

Langewiesche, Dieter, Historische Reflexionen zum Föderalismus in Deutschland: Wandel und Kontinuität seit dem 19. Jahrhundert. In Härtel, Ines (ed.), *Handbuch des Föderalismus*. Vol. 1: *Grundlagen des Föderalismus und der deutsche Bundesstaat*. Berlin, 2012, 129–43.

Langewiesche, Dieter, *Die Monarchie im Jahrhundert Europas: Selbstbehauptung durch Wandel im 19. Jahrhundert*. Heidelberg, 2013.

Lászlo, Péter, Die Verfassungsentwicklung in Ungarn. In Rumpler, Helmut, and Urbanitsch, Peter (eds), *Die Habsburgermonarchie 1848–1918*. Vol. 7: *Verfassung und Parlamentarismus*. Subvol. 1: *Verfassungsrecht, Verfassungswirklichkeit, zentrale Repräsentativkörperschaften*. Vienna, 2000, 239–540.

Laux, Stephan, Dem König eine 'ergetzlichkhait': Die Vertreibung der Juden aus der Steiermark (1496/1497). In Lamprecht, Gerald (ed.), *Jüdisches Leben in der Steiermark: Marginalisierung—Auslöschung—Annäherung*. Innsbruck, 2004, 33–57.

Laven, David, and Parker, Laura, Foreign Rule? Transnational, National, and Local Perspectives on Venice and Venetia within the 'Multinational' Empire. *Modern Italy*, 19/1 (2014), 5–19.

Lehmbruch, Gerhard, Der unitarische Bundesstaat in Deutschland: Pfadabhängigkeit und Wandel. In Lehmbruch, Gerhard, and Benz, Arthur (ed.), *Föderalismus: Analysen in entwicklungsgeschichtlicher und vergleichender Perspektive*. Wiesbaden, 2002, 53–110.

Lehning, Percy (ed.), *Theories of Secession*. London and New York, 1998.

Lein, Richard, Das Thronwechselprogramm der Militärkanzlei Erzherzog Franz Ferdinands aus dem Jahr 1911. *Prague Papers on the History of International Relations*, 2 (2011), 86–109.

Leiße, Olaf, *Der Untergang des österreichischen Imperiums: Otto Bauer und die Nationalitätenfrage in der Habsburger Monarchie*. Marburg, 2012.

Lemke, Björn, Zwischen zentrifugalen und zentripetalen Kräften: Ökonomische Integration in der Habsburgermonarchie. In Ambrosius, Gerold, Henrich-Franke, Christian, and Neutsch, Cornelius (eds), *Föderalismus in historisch vergleichender Perspektive*. Vol. 2: *Föderale Systeme: Kaiserreich—Donaumonarchie—Europäische Union*. Baden-Baden, 2015, 169–95.

Lengyel, György, Die ungarische Wirtschaftselite im 19. und zum Anfang des 20. Jahrhunderts: Lebensbahnen der Generationen. In Bácskai, Vera (ed.), *Bürgertum und bürgerliche Entwicklung in Mittel- und Osteuropa*. Vol. 2. Budapest, 1986, 591–694.

Lengyel, Zsolt K., Zum Problem der Landesvertretung im neoabsolutistischen Ungarn. In Brandt, Harm-Hinrich (ed.), *Der österreichische Neoabsolutismus als Verfassungs- und Verwaltungsproblem: Diskussionen über einen strittigen Epochenbegriff*. Vienna, 2014, 383–412.

Lentze, Hans, Die Problematik der Föderalisierung in Österreich. In Holotík, Ľudovít (ed.), *Der österreichisch-ungarische Ausgleich 1867*. Bratislava, 1971, 925–43.

Leonhard, Jörn, *Pandora's Box: A History of the First World War*. Cambridge, 2018.

Leonhard, Jörg, Hirschhausen, Ulrike von (eds), Multiethnic Empires and the Military: Conscription in Europe between Integration and Desintegration, 1860–1918. *Journal of Modern European History*, 5/2 (2007).

Leonhard, Jörg, Hirschhausen, Ulrike von, *Empires und Nationalstaaten im 19. Jahrhundert*. Göttingen, 2009.

Leonhard, Jörg, Hirschhausen, Ulrike von, Zwischen Historisierung und Globalisierung: Titel, Themen und Trends der neueren Empire-Forschung. *Neue Politische Literatur*, 56 (2011), 389–404.

Leser, Norbert, *Zwischen Reformismus und Bolschewismus: Der Austromarxismus als Theorie und Praxis*. 2nd edn. Vienna, 1985.

Leslie, John, Der Ausgleich in der Bukowina von 1910: Zur österreichischen Nationalitätenpolitik vor dem Ersten Weltkrieg. In Brix, Emil, Fröschl, Thomas, and Leidenfrost, Josef (eds), *Geschichte zwischen Freiheit und Ordnung: Gerald Stourzh zum 60. Geburtstag*. Graz, 1991, 113–44.

Lester, Alan, *Imperial Networks. Creating Identities in Nineteenth-Century South Africa and Britain*. London, 2001.

Lieven, Dominic, *The Russian Empire and its Rivals*. New Haven, 2000.

Lindström, Fredrik, Ernest von Koerber and the Austrian State Idea: A Reinterpretation of the Koerber Plan 1900–1904. *Austrian History Yearbook*, 35 (2004), 143–84.

Lindström, Fredrik, *Empire and Identity: Biographies of the Austrian State Problem in the Late Habsburg Empire*. West Lafayette, IN, 2008.

Lingg, Emil, Die staatsrechtliche Stellung Bosniens und der Herzegowina. *Archiv für öffentliches Recht*, 5 (1890), 480–528.

Liszt, Franz, *Das Völkerrecht systematisch dargestellt*. 5th edn. Berlin, 1907.

Löw, Raimund, *Der Zerfall der Kleinen Internationale: Nationalitätenkonflikte in d. Arbeiterbewegung d. alten Österreich 1889–1914*. Vienna, 1984.

Loewenfeld, Walter, Die Finanzen der Österreichischen Kronländer. *Finanzarchiv*, 25/2 (1908), 176–81.

Lorant, André, *Le compromis austro-hongrois et l'opinion publique française en 1867*. Geneva, 1971.

Lorenz, Reinhold, *Kaiser Karl und der Untergang der Donaumonarchie*. Graz, 1959.

Lotz, Walther, *Finanzwissenschaft*. 2nd rev. edn. Munich, 1931.

Löwenthal, Josef von, Die rechtliche Natur von Österreich-Ungarn: Eine Analyse der gemeinsamen Angelegenheiten. *Österreichische Zeitschrift für öffentliches Recht*, 3/6 (1918), 611–55.

Loy, Luigi, *Relatione e documenti della commissione sanitaria centrale di Trieste sul cholera morbus nel 1866*. Trieste, 1867.

Luca, Ignaz de, *Vorlesungen über die Oestreichische Staatsverfassung*. Vol. 1. Vienna, 1791.

Lučić, Iva, *Im Name der Nation. Der politische Aufwertungsprozess der Muslime im sozialistischen Jugoslawien 1956–1971*. Wiesbaden, 2018.

Luft, Robert, Nationale Utraquisten in Böhmen: Zur Problematik 'nationaler Zwischenstellungen' am Ende des 19. Jahrhunderts. In Godé, Maurice (ed.), *Allemands, Juifs et Tchèques à Prague 1890–1924/Deutsche, Juden und Tschechen in Prag*. Montpellier, 1996, 37–51.

Luft, Robert, Machtansprüche und kulturelle Muster nichtperipherer Regionen: Die Kernlande Böhmen, Mähren und Schlesien in der späten Habsburgermonarchie. In Feichtinger, Johannes, Csáky, Moritz, and Prutsch, Ursula (eds), *Habsburg Postcolonial. Machtstrukturen und kollektives Gedächtnis*. Innsbruck, 2003, 165–88.

Luft, Robert, Zivilgesellschaft im cisleithanischen Teil der Habsburgermonarchie bis 1914. In Hackmann, Jörg, and Roth, Klaus (eds), *Zivilgesellschaft im östlichen und südöstlichen Europa in Geschichte und Gegenwart*. Munich, 2011, 189–215.

Lustkandl, Wenzel, *Das ungarisch-österreichische Staatsrecht: Zur Lösung der Verfassungsfrage*. Vienna, 1863.

Lütge, Friedrich, Die Grundentlastung (Bauernbefreiung) in der Steiermark. In Lütge, Friedrich, *Beiträge zur Sozial- und Wirtschaftsgeschichte. Gesammelte Abhandlungen*. Ed. Eckart Schremmer. Stuttgart, 1970, 255–73.

Lutz, Heinrich, *Zwischen Habsburg und Preußen. Deutschland 1815–1866*. Berlin, 1985.

Lyotard, Jean François, *Das postmoderne Wissen: Ein Bericht*. Vienna, 1999.

Lyttelton, Adrian, Between Piccola Patria and Grande Patria: National Identity and Nation-Building in Nineteenth-Century Italy. In Hirschhausen, Ulrike von, and Leonhard, Jörn (eds), *Nationalismen in Europa: West- und Osteuropa im Vergleich*. Göttingen, 2001, 154–77.

Macmillan, Margaret, *Peacemakers: The Paris Conference of 1919 and its Attempt to End War*. London, 2001.

Macura, Vladimír, *Znamení zrodu a české sny*. Prague, 2015.

Maderthaner, Wolfgang, Das Entstehen einer demokratischen Massenpartei. Sozialdemokratische Organisation von 1889–1918. In Maderthaner, Wolfgang, and Müller, Wolfgang C. (eds), *Die Organisation der österreichischen Sozialdemokratie 1889–1995*. Vienna, 1996, 21–92.

Magocsi, Paul R., *The Roots of Ukrainian Nationalism: Galicia as Ukraine's Piedmont*. Toronto, 2002.

Magris, Claudio, *Donau: Die Biographie eines Flusses*. 11th edn. Munich, 2018.

Maier, Charles S., Transformations of Territoriality 1600–2000. In Budde, Gunilla, Conrad, Sebastian, and Janz, Oliver (eds), *Transnationale Geschichte. Themen, Tendenzen und Theorien*. Göttingen, 2006, 32–55.

Makowski, Krzysztof, Das Großherzogtum Posen im Revolutionsjahr 1848. In Jaworski, Rudolf, and Luft, Robert (eds), *1848/49 Revolutionen in Ostmitteleuropa*. Munich, 1996, 149–72.

Malfér, Stefan, Einleitung. In Malfér, Stefan (ed.), *Protokolle des Österreichischen Ministerrates*. Vol. 5/3: *Die Ministerien Erzherzog Rainer und Mensdorff (5. November 1861–6. Mai 1862)*. Vienna, 1985, pp. xix–xv.

Malfér, Stefan (ed.), *Protokolle des Österreichischen Ministerrates*. Vol. 5/3: *Die Ministerien Erzherzog Rainer und Mensdorff (5. November 1861–6. Mai 1862)*. Vienna, 1985.

Malfér, Stefan, Der gescheiterte Ausgleichsversuch vom März 1863. *Österreichische Osthefte*, 32 (1990), 405–26.

Malfér, Stefan, Una costituzione per il regno lombardo-veneto: Speranze e fallimenti 1848–50. In Zanolo, Alba Lazzaretto (ed.), *La 'primavera liberale' nella terraferma veneta 1848–49*. Venice, 2000, 113–27.

Malfér, Stefan Einleitung. In Malfér, Stefan (ed.), *Protokolle des Österreichischen Ministerrates*. Vol. 4/1: *Das Ministerium Rechberg (19. Mai 1859–3. März 1860)*. Vienna, 2003, pp. ix–lxx.

Malfér, Stefan (ed.), *Protokolle des Österreichischen Ministerrates*. Vol. 4/1: *Das Ministerium Rechberg (19. Mai 1859–3. März 1860)*. Vienna, 2003.

Malfér, Stefan (ed.), *Protokolle des Österreichischen Ministerrates*. Vol. 4/2: *Das Ministerium Rechberg (6. März 1860–16. Oktober 1860)*. Vienna, 2007.

Malfér, Stefan, Einleitung. In Malfér, Stefan (ed.), *Protokolle des Österreichischen Ministerrates. Vol. 4/3: Das Ministerium Rechberg (21. Oktober 1860–2. Februar 1861)*. Vienna, 2009, pp. ix–lxvii.

Malfér, Stefan (ed.), *Protokolle des Österreichischen Ministerrates.* Vol. 4/3: *Das Ministerium Rechberg (21. Oktober 1860–2. Februar 1861)*. Vienna, 2009.

Malíř, Jiří, Die Teilnahme von Frauen an den Ergänzungswahlen in den Mährischen Landtag 1865. In Svatoš, Michal, Velek, Luboš, and Velková, Alice (eds), *Magister noster: Festschrift in memoriam Prof. PhDr. Jan Havránek, CSc.* Prague, 2005.

Malíř, Jiří, Mähren und die Frage der Einführung des allgemeinen Wahlrechts 1848–1907. In Simon, Thomas (ed.), *Hundert Jahre allgemeines und gleiches Wahlrecht in Österreich. Modernes Wahlrecht unter den Bedingungen eines Vielvölkerstaates*. Frankfurt am Main, 2010, 255–75.

Maner, Hans-Christian, *Galizien: Eine Grenzregion im Kalkül der Donaumonarchie im 18. und 19. Jahrhundert*. Munich, 2007.

Maner, Hans-Christian, Zwischen 'Kompensationsobjekt', 'Musterland' und 'Glacis': Vienna er politische und militärische Vorstellungen von Galizien von 1772 bis zur Autonomieära. In Maner, Hans-Christian (ed.), *Grenzregionen der Habsburgermonarchie im 18. und 19. Jahrhundert: Ihre Bedeutung und Funktion aus der Perspektive Wiens*. Münster, 2005, 103–22.

Mann, Michael, The Autonomous Power of the State: Its Origins, Mechanisms and Results. *European Journal of Sociology/Archives Européennes de Sociologie/Europäisches Archiv für Soziologie*, 25/2 (1984), 185–213.

Mann, Michael, *The Sources of Social Power*. Vol. 2: *The Rise of Classes and Nation-States 1760–1914*. Cambridge, 2012.

Mannheim, Karl, *Konservatismus: Ein Beitrag zur Soziologie des Wissens*. Frankfurt am Main, 1984.

Mannová, Elena, Das Vereinswesen in der Slowakei im 19. und 20. Jahrhundert im Spannungsfeld von Zivilgesellschaft und Nation. In Hackmann, Jörg, and Roth, Klaus (ed.), *Zivilgesellschaft im östlichen und südöstlichen Europa in Geschichte und Gegenwart*. Munich, 2011, 217–28.

Manor, James, Center–State Relations. In Kohli, Atul (ed.), *The Success of India's Democracy*. Cambridge, 2001, 78–102.

Marczali, Heinrich, *Ungarische Verfassungsgeschichte*. Tübingen, 1910.

Marczali, Heinrich, *Ungarisches Verfassungsrecht*. Tübingen, 1911.

Mark, Rudolf A., *Galizien unter österreichischer Herrschaft. Verwaltung-Kirche-Bevölkerung*. Marburg, 1994.

Marshall, Thomas H., *Citizenship and Social Class: And Other Essays*. Cambridge, 1950.

Martin, Manfred, *Das Bankwesen in Tirol bis 1945*. Innsbruck, 1970.

Marung, Steffi, Middell, Matthias, and Müller, Uwe, Territorialisierung in Ostmitteleuropa bis zum Ersten Weltkrieg. In Hadler, Frank, and Middell, Matthias (eds), *Handbuch einer transnationalen Geschichte Ostmitteleuropas*. Vol. 1: *Von der Mitte des 19. Jahrhunderts bis um Ersten Weltkrieg*. Göttingen, 2017, 37–130.

Marung, Steffi, and Naumann, Katja, Einleitung. In Marung, Steffi, and Naumann, Katja (eds), *Vergessene Vielfalt: Territorialität und Internationalisierung in Ostmitteleuropa seit der Mitte des 19. Jahrhunderts*. Göttingen, 2014, 9–44.

Maťa, Petr, Die Habsburgermonarchie. In Maťa, Petr, Hochedlinger, Michael, and Winkelbauer, Thomas (eds), *Verwaltungsgeschichte der Habsburgermonarchie in der Frühen Neuzeit*. Vol. 1/1: *Hof und Dynastie, Kaiser und Reich, Zentralverwaltungen, Kriegswesen und landesfürstliches Finanzwesen*. Vienna, 2019, 29–62.

Maťa, Petr, and Winkelbauer, Thomas (eds), *Die Habsburgermonarchie 1620 bis 1740: Leistungen und Grenzen des Absolutismusparadigmas*. Stuttgart, 2006.

Mathieu, Jon, Statebuilding from Below: Towards a Balanced View. In Blockmans, Wim, Holenstein, André, and Mathieu, Jon (eds), *Empowering Interactions: Political Cultures and the Emergence of the State in Europe 1300–1900*. Abingdon and New York, 2009, 305–11.

Matis, Herbert, *Österreichs Wirtschaft 1848–1913: Konjunkturelle Dynamik und gesellschaftlicher Wandel im Zeitalter Franz Josephs I.* Berlin, 1972.

Matlekovits, Alexander (Sándor) von, *Das Königreich Ungarn: Volkswirtschaftlich u. statistisch dargestellt*. 2 vols. Leipzig, 1900.

Mayr, Josef Karl, Danelons Kurierreise 1813. *Mitteilungen des Instituts für österreichische Geschichtsforschung*, 52 (1938), 313–28.

Maxwell, Alexander, Walerjan Krasiński's Panslavism and Germanism (1848): Polish Goals in a Panslav Context. *New Zealand Slavonic Journal*, 42/1 (2008), 101–20.

Mazohl, Brigitte, *Österreichischer Verwaltungsstaat und administrative Eliten im Königreich Lombardo-Venetien 1815–1859*. Mainz, 1993.

Mazohl, Brigitte, Vom Tod Karls VI. bis zum Wiener Kongress 1740–1815. In Winkelbauer, Thomas (ed.), *Geschichte Österreichs*. Stuttgart, 2015, 290–358.

Mazohl-Wallnig, Brigitte, Männer Macht Geschichte. *L'Homme*, 7/1 (1996), 6–33.

Mazohl-Wallnig, Brigitte, Il governo austriaco durante il biennio rivoluzionario. In Zanolo, Alba Lazzaretto (ed.), *La 'primavera liberale' nella terraferma veneta 1848–49*. Venice, 2000, 21–34.

Mazohl-Wallnig, Brigitte, and Meriggi, Marco, *Österreichisches Italien—Italienisches Österreich? Interkulturelle Gemeinsamkeiten und nationale Differenzen vom 18. Jahrhundert bis zum Ende des Ersten Weltkriegs*. Vienna, 1999.

Mažuranić, Ivan, *Izabrani politički spisi. Ed. von Dragotin Pavličević*. Zagreb, 1999.

Medved, Mladen, Trotsky or Wallerstein? Approaching the Habsburg Monarchy in the Nineteenth Century. *East Central Europe*, 45 (2018), 39–62.

Megner, Karl, *Beamte: Wirtschafts- und sozialgeschichtliche Aspekte des k. k. Beamtentums*. Vienna, 1985.

Melichar, Peter, and Mejstrik, Alexander, Die bewaffnete Macht. In Rumpler, Helmut, and Urbanitsch, Peter (eds), *Die Habsburgermonarchie 1848–1918*. Vol. 9: *Soziale Strukturen*. Part 1: *Von der Feudal-Agrarischen zur Bürgerlich-industriellen Gesellschaft*. Subvol. 2: *Von der Stände- zur Klassengesellschaft*. Vienna, 2010, 1263–1326.

Melik, Vasilij, Das Jahr 1848. In Krahwinkler, Harald (ed.), *Staat-Land-Nation-Region: Gesellschaftliches Bewußtsein in den österreichischen Ländern Kärnten, Krain, Steiermark und Küstenland 1740–1918*. Klagenfurt, 2002, 229–37.

Melinz, Gerhard, and Zimmermann, Susan, *Über die Grenzen der Armenhilfe: Kommunale und staatliche Sozialpolitik in Wien und Budapest in der Doppelmonarchie*. Vienna and Zürich, 1991.

Meliorační svaz v markrabství moravském (ed.), *Meliorační rádce: Pro podniky meliorační, regulační a hospodářské vodovody*. Brno, 1912.

Melville, Ralph, Von der Patrimonialverwaltung zur Gemeindeselbstverwaltung in Böhmen und Österreich um 1848. *Documenta Pragensia*, 14 (1997), 51–64.

Melville, Ralph, *Adel und Revolution in Böhmen: Strukturwandel von Herrschaft und Gesellschaft in Österreich um die Mitte des 19. Jahrhunderts*. Mainz, 1998.

Meriggi, Marco, *Il Regno Lombardo-Veneto*. Turin, 1986.

Meriggi, Marco, Der lombardo-venezianische Adel im Vormärz. In Reden-Dohna, Armgard von, and Melville, Ralph (eds), *Der Adel an der Schwelle des bürgerlichen Zeitalters 1780–1860*. Stuttgart, 1988, 225–36.

Merki, Christoph Maria, Zucker. In Merki, Christoph Maria, and Hengartner, Christoph (eds), *Genussmittel: Ein kulturgeschichtliches Handbuch*. Frankfurt am Main and New York, 1999, 231–56.

Metcalf, Thomas R., *Imperial Connections: India in the Indian Ocean Arena 1860–1920*. Berkeley, CA, 2007.

Metternich-Winneburg, Richard (ed.), *Aus Metternich's nachgelassenen Papieren*. Vol. 3. Vienna, 1881.

Metternich-Winneburg, Richard (ed.), *Aus Metternich's nachgelassenen Papieren*. Vol. 7. Vienna, 1883.

Metternich-Winneburg, Richard (ed.), *Aus Metternich's nachgelassenen Papieren*. Vol. 8. Vienna, 1884.

Metzler, Gabriele, *Der deutsche Sozialstaat: Vom bismarckschen Erfolgsmodell zum Pflegefall*. Stuttgart, 2003.

Miaso, Jozef, Educational Policy and Educational Development in the Polish Territories under Austrian, Russian and German Rule 1850–1918. In Tomiak, Janusz J. (ed.), *Schooling, Educational Policy and Ethnic Identity*. Vol. 1: *Comparative Studies on Governments and Non-Dominant Ethnic Groups in Europe 1850–1940*. New York, 1991, 163–83.

Middell, Matthias, and Naumann, Katja, Global History and the Spatial Turn: From the Impact of Area Studies to the Study of Critical Junctures of Globalization. *Journal of Global History*, 5/1 (2010), 149–70.

Miller, Alexei, National Identities and the Forging of Political Loyalties: Little Russians versus Ukrainians during the 19th and 20th Centuries. In Osterkamp, Jana, and Schulze Wessel, Martin (eds), *Exploring Loyalty*. Göttingen, 2017, 61–72.

Miller, Michael L., Die Nationalgarde 1848: Grenzen der Emanzipation. In Kordiovský, Emil, Starek, Jana, and Teufel, Helmut (eds), *Moravští Židé v rakousko-uherské monarchii 1780–1918/Mährische Juden in der österreichisch-ungarischen Monarchie 1780–1918*. Mikulov, 2003, 151–9.

Miller, Michael L., *Rabbis and Revolution: The Jews of Moravia in the Age of Emancipation*. Stanford, CA, 2011.

Mischler, Ernst, *Der öffentliche Haushalt in Böhmen: Ein Beitrag zur Kenntnis und Beurteilung des Finanzwesens der Selbstverwaltung in Österreich*. Leipzig and Vienna, 1887.

Mischler, Ernst, Übersicht über die öffentliche Armenpflege und die private Wohltätigkeit in Österreich. In *Österreichs Wohlfahrts-Einrichtungen 1848–1898*. Vol. 1: *Armenpflege und Wohltätigkeit in Österreich*. Vienna, 1899, pp. vii–xlii.

Modráček, František, Zur nationalen Frage/K národnostní otázce [1899]. In Löw, Raimund, *Der Zerfall der Kleinen Internationale: Nationalitätenkonflikte in d. Arbeiterbewegung d. alten Österreich 1889–1914*. Vienna, 1984, Anhang I.

Möllers, Christoph, Skizzen zur Aktualität Georg Jellineks: Vier theoretische Probleme aus Jellineks Staatslehre in Verfassungsrecht und Staatstheorie der Gegenwart. In Paulson, Stanley L., and Schulte, Martin (eds), *Georg Jellinek: Beiträge zu Leben und Werk*. Tübingen, 2000, 155–71.

Möllers, Christoph, *Gewaltengliederung: Legitimation und Dogmatik im nationalen und internationalen Rechtsvergleich*. Tübingen, 2005.

Möllers, Christoph, *Staat als Argument*. 2nd edn. Tübingen, 2011.

Möllers, Christoph, *Die drei Gewalten: Legitimation der Gewaltengliederung in Verfassungsstaat, Europäischer Integration und Internationalisierung*. 2nd edn. Weilerswist, 2015.

Mommsen, Hans, *Die Sozialdemokratie und die Nationalitätenfrage im habsburgischen Vielvölkerstaat*. Vol. 1: *Das Ringen um die supranationale Integration der zisleithanischen Arbeiterbewegung 1867–1907*. Vienna, 1963.

Mommsen, Hans, Die Rückwirkungen des Ausgleichs mit Ungarn auf die zisleithanische Verfassungsfrage. In Holotík, L'udovít (ed.), *Der österreichisch-ungarische Ausgleich 1867*. Bratislava, 1971, 353–79.

Mommsen, Hans, Otto Bauer, Karl Renner und die sozialdemokratische Nationalitätenpolitik in Österreich von 1905 bis 1914. In Hitchins, Keith (ed.), *Studies in East European Social History*. Leiden, 1977, 3–32.

Mommsen, Hans, 1897: Die Badeni-Krise als Wendepunkt in den deutsch-tschechischen Beziehungen. In Brandes, Detlef (ed.), *Wendepunkte in den Beziehungen zwischen Deutschen, Tschechen und Slowaken 1848–1989*. Essen, 2007, 111–18.

Mommsen, Wolfgang J., *1848: Die ungewollte Revolution. Die revolutionären Bewegungen in Europa 1830–1849*. Frankfurt am Main, 1998.

Monzali, Luciano, Pokus o chorvatsko-srbsko-italské vyrování v Dalmácii 1903–1907. In Fasora, Lukáš, Hanuš, Jiří, and Malíř, Jiří (ed.), *Moravské vyrovnání z roku 1905: Možnosti a limity národnostního smíru ve střední Evropě*. Brno, 2006, 221–37.

Monzali, Luciano, *The Italians of Dalmatia: From Italian Unification to World War I*. Toronto, 2009.

Moraczewski, Jędrzej, O Kongresie słowiańskim w Pradze zebranym 31. maja 1848. In Žáček, Václav (ed.), *Slovanský sjezd v Praze roku 1848: Sbírka dokumentů*. Prague, 1958, 513–33.

Moravcová, Mirjam, Die tschechischen Frauen im revolutionären Prag 1848/1849. In Jaworski, Rudolf, and Luft, Robert (eds), *1848/49 Revolutionen in Ostmitteleuropa*. Munich, 1996, 75–96.

Moritsch, Andreas, Der Franziszeische Kataster und die dazugehörigen Steuerschätzungsoperate als wirtschafts- und sozialhistorische Quellen. *East European Quarterly*, 3/4 (1970), 438–48.

Moritsch, Andreas (ed.), *Der Austroslavismus: Ein verfrühtes Konzept zur politischen Neugestaltung Mitteleuropas*. Vienna, 1996.

Moritsch, Andreas Revolution 1848: Österreichs Slawen wohin? In Moritsch, Andreas (ed.), *Der Prager Slavenkongress 1848*. Vienna, 2000, 5–18.

Moritsch, Andreas (ed.), *Alpen-Adria: Zur Geschichte einer Region*. Klagenfurt, 2001.

Moser, Michael, Das Ukrainische ('Ruthenische') der galizischen Polen und Polonophilen zwischen 1830 und 1848/1849. *Zeitschrift für Slavische Philologie*, 62/2 (2003), 311–58.

Motyl, Alexander J., Thinking about Empire. In Barkey, Karen, and Von Hagen, Mark (eds), *After Empire: Multiethnic Societies and Nation-Building. The Soviet Union and the Russian, Ottoman, and Habsburg Empires*. Boulder, CO, 1997, 19–29.

Motyl, Alexander J., *Imperial Ends: The Decay, Collapse and Revival of Empires*. New York, 2001.

Mudry'i, Mar'ian, Rus'ky'j Sobor 1848 roku: Organizaciya ta chleny. In Yaroslav Isayevych (ed.), *Yuvilejny'j zbirny'k na poshanu Ivana Patera*. Lviv, 2008, 107–26.

Mueller, Christine, *The Styrian Estates 1740–1848: A Century of Transition*. New York, 1987.

Müller, Adam H., *Elemente der Staatskunst*. 2 vols. Ed. Jakob Baxa. Jena, 1922.

Müller, Uwe, Regionale Wirtschafts- und Nationalitätenpolitik in Ostmitteleuropa 1867–1939. In Müller, Uwe (ed.), *Ausgebeutet oder alimentiert? Regionale Wirtschaftspolitik und nationale Minderheiten in Ostmitteleuropa 1867–1939*. Berlin, 2006, 9–50.

Müller, Uwe, Transnationale Verflechtungen der Wirtschaft in Ostmitteleuropa während der ersten Globalisierung. In Hadler, Frank, and Middell, Matthias (eds), *Handbuch einer transnationalen Geschichte Ostmitteleuropas*. Vol. 1: *Von der Mitte des 19. Jahrhunderts bis zum Ersten Weltkrieg*. Göttingen, 2017, 257–323.

Münkler, Herfried, Fürstenbund und Bundesstaat: Der Erste Weltkrieg als (letzter) Reichseinigungskrieg. In Hausteiner, Eva Marlene (ed.), *Föderalismen: Modelle jenseits des Staates*. Baden-Baden, 2016, 181–206.

Myrbach-Rheinfeld, Franz von, *Grundriß des Finanzrechts*. Leipzig, 1906.

Myška, Milan, Der Adel der böhmischen Länder: Seine wirtschaftliche Basis und ihre Entwicklung. In Reden-Dohna, Armgard von (ed.), *Der Adel an der Schwelle des bürgerlichen Zeitalters 1780–1860*. Stuttgart, 1988, 169–89.

Nachbaur, Ulrich, 1918. Selbständiges Land Vorarlberg. In Bußjäger, Peter (ed.), *3. November 1918: Die Länder und der neue Staat*. Vienna, 2019, 57–139.

Nellen, Stefan, and Stockinger, Thomas, Staat, Verwaltung und Raum im langen 19. Jahrhundert. Einleitung. Administory, 2/1 (2017), 3–28.

Neschwara, Christian, Wege zur Umgehung der Unauflösbarkeit des Ehebandes von Katholiken. In Brauneder, Wilhelm, and Hlavačka, Milan (eds), *Bürgerliche Gesellschaft auf dem Papier: Konstruktion, Kodifikation und Realisation der Zivilgesellschaft in der Habsburgermonarchie*. Berlin, 2014, 145–59.

Nesemann, Frank, *Ein Staat, kein Gouvernement: Die Entstehung und Entwicklung der Autonomie Finnlands im russischen Zarenreich 1808–1826*. Frankfurt am Main, 2003.

Neudeck, Werner, Der Unterricht der Wirtschaftswissenschaften an der Akademie. Ein geschichtlicher Überblick. In Rathkolb, Oliver (ed.), *250 Jahre. Von der Orientalischen zur Diplomatischen Akademie in Wien*. Innsbruck, 2004, 339–53.

Neumann, Christoph K., Bad Times and Better Self: Definitions of Identity and Strategies for Development in Late Ottoman Historiography 1850–1900. In Adanir, Fikret, and Faroqhi, Suraiya (ed.), *The Ottomans and the Balkans: A Discussion of Historiography*. Leiden, 2002, 57–78.

Neumann, Dieter, Der Villacher Kreis in französisch-illyrischer Zeit. In Fräss-Ehrfeld, Claudia (ed.), *Napoleon und seine Zeit*. Klagenfurt, 2009, 199–208.

Neumann, Franz Xaver, *Volkswirtschaftslehre mit besonderer Anwendung auf Heerwesen und Militärverwaltung*. Vienna, 1873.
Neumann-Spallart, Franz Xaver von, *Österreichs maritime Entwicklung und die Hebung von Triest: Eine volkswirthschaftliche Studie. Mit 6 Karten und 2 Tafeln*. Stuttgart, 1882.
Newerkla, Stefan Michael, Wie toleranzintendierte Sprachengesetze zur nationalen Segregation führten: Die Aushöhlung des deutschen Schulwesens in Plzeň/Pilsen im langen 19. Jahrhundert. In Philipp, Hannes, Ströbl, Andrea, Weber, Bernadette, and Wellner, Johann (eds), *Deutsch in Mittel-, Ost- und Südosteuropa*. Regensburg, 2018, 372–97.
Niederösterreichischer Landesausschuss (ed.), *Die Entwicklung und Förderung der technischen Bodenmelioration und der ländlichen Wasserversorgung im Erzherzogtume Österreich unter der Enns in den Jahren 1857–1917*. Vienna, 1918.
Niedhammer, Martina, *Nur eine 'Geld-Emancipation'? Loyalitäten und Lebenswelten des Prager jüdischen Großbürgertums 1800–1867*. Göttingen, 2013.
Niedhammer, Martina, Loyalty as a Tool of Analysis for the Self-Image of Minorities: Prague's Jewish Upper Middle Class in the First Half of the Nineteenth Century. In Osterkamp, Jana, and Schulze Wessel, Martin (ed.), *Exploring Loyalty*. Munich, 2017, 157–65.
Nork, Friedrich [Pseudonym Friedrich Korn], *Die Ansprüche der Slawen in den österreichischen und preußischen Staaten, namentlich in Galizien, Posen und Prag*. Weimar, 1848.
Novotný, Jiří, and Šouša, Jiří, Wirtschaftsnationalismus und nationale Eliten im tschechischen Bankwesen. In Kubů, Eduard, and Schultz, Helga (eds), *Wirtschaftsnationalismus als Entwicklungsstrategie ostmitteleuropäischer Eliten*. Prague and Berlin, 2004, 49–70.
Nowak, Joanna, *Władysław Zamoyski: O sprawę polską w Europie 1848–1868*. Poznan, 2002.
Oates, Wallace E., An Essay on Fiscal Federalism. *Journal of Economic Literature*, 37/3 (1999), 1120–49.
Oberc, Michał, *Wizyty cesarza Franciszka Józefa I w Galicji*. Rzeszów, 2016.
Oeter, Stefan, 'Föderation' oder 'Bund' als Oberbegriff: Erscheinungsformen des Föderalen jenseits von Bundesstaat und Staatenbund. In Hausteiner, Eva Marlene (ed.), *Föderalismen: Modelle jenseits des Staates*. Baden-Baden, 2016, 235–66.
Oettinger, Józef, *Cholera Nagminna w Krakowie r. 1866*. Kraków, 1867.
Okáč, Antonín, *Český sněm a vláda před březnem 1848: Kapitoly o jejich ústavních sporech*. Prague, 1947.
Okey, Robin, *The Habsburg Monarchy: From Enlightenment to Eclipse*. New York, 2001.
Okey, Robin, *Taming Balkan Nationalism: The Habsburg 'Civilizing Mission' in Bosnia 1878–1914*. New York, 2007.
Olechowski-Hrdlicka, Karin, *Die gemeinsamen Angelegenheiten der Österreichisch-Ungarischen Monarchie. Vorgeschichte. Ausgleich 1867. Staatsrechtliche Kontroversen*. Frankfurt am Main, 2001.
Onciul, Aurel Constantin, *Aurel Ritter von Onciul und der nationale Ausgleich in der Bukowina*. Nuremberg, 1999.
Onojescu, Alexandru, Iudean, Ovidiu, and Popovici, Vlad, Parliamentary Representation in Eastern Hungary 1861–1918: Preliminary Results of a Prosopographic Inquiry. In Pál, Judit, and Popovici, Vlad (eds), *Elites and Politics in Central and Eastern Europe 1848–1918*. Frankfurt am Main, 2014, 211–24.
Orosz, Anton, *Worte eines eifrigen und uneigennützigen Staatsdieners, die bei Regulierung der neuen Verhältnisse des Constitutionellen Dalmatien beachtet werden mögen*. Zara, 1848.
Oser, Leopold, *Bericht über die Cholera-Abtheilung im k.k. allgemeinen Krankenhause während der Epidemie im Jahre 1866*. Vienna, 1867.
Osterhammel, Jürgen, *The Transformation of the World: A Global History of the Nineteenth Century*. Princeton, 2014.
Osterkamp, Jana, Cooperative Empires: Provincial Initiatives in Imperial Austria. *Austrian History Yearbook*, 47 (2016), 128–46.
Osterkamp, Jana, Geschichte als Argument: Das Böhmische Staatsrecht als politischer Leitbegriff im 19. Jahrhundert. *Střed/Centre*, 8/1 (2016), 9–27.
Osterkamp, Jana, Imperial Diversity in the Village: Petitions for and against the Division of Galicia in 1848. *Nationalities Papers*, 44/5 (2016), 731–50.

Osterkamp, Jana, 'Kooperatives Imperium': Loyalitätsgefüge und Reich-Länder-Finanzausgleich in der späten Habsburgermonarchie. *Geschichte und Gesellschaft*, 42/4 (2016), 592–620.

Osterkamp, Jana, Wasser, Erde, Imperium: Eine kleine Politikgeschichte der Meliorationen in der Habsburgermonarchie. In Ganzenmüller, Jörg, and Tönsmeyer, Tatjana (eds), *Vom Vorrücken des Staates in die Fläche: Ein europäisches Phänomen des langen 19. Jahrhunderts*. Vienna, 2016, 179–98.

Osterkamp, Jana, Ein Reich ohne Eigenschaften? Das Erbe föderaler Ideen in den 'Nachfolgestaaten' der Habsburgermonarchie. In Rumpler, Helmut, and Harmat, Ulrike (eds), *Die Habsburgermonarchie 1848–1918*. Vol. 12: *Bewältigte Vergangenheit? Die nationale und internationale Historiographie zum Untergang der Habsburgermonarchie als ideelle Grundlage für die Neuordnung Europas*. Vienna, 2018, 431–57.

Osterkamp, Jana, Gefühlshaushalt in Mähren: Leistungsverwaltung, Landesschulden und Loyalitäten nach 1905. *Administory. Zeitschrift für Verwaltungsgeschichte*, 3 (2018), 183–98.

Osterkamp, Jana, Kooperatives Imperium: Eine neue Perspektive auf Anspruch und Wirklichkeit imperialer Herrschaft. In Osterkamp, Jana (ed.), *Kooperatives Imperium: Politische Zusammenarbeit in der späten Habsburgermonarchie*. Göttingen, 2018, 1–21.

Osterkamp, Jana, Länderautonomie, Länderlobby, Ländergemeinschaft: Regionaler Eigensinn in Salzburg und Böhmen in der späten Habsburgermonarchie. In Ambrosius, Gerold, Franke, Christian, and Neutsch, Cornelius (eds), *Föderalismus in historisch vergleichender Perspektive*. Vol. 6: *Integrieren durch Regieren*. Baden-Baden, 2018, 369–88.

Osterkamp, Jana, and Schulze Wessel, Martin (eds), *Exploring Loyalty*. Göttingen, 2016.

Osterkamp, Jana, and Schulze Wessel, Martin, Texturen von Loyalität: Überlegungen zu einem analytischen Begriff. *Geschichte und Gesellschaft*, 42/4 (2016), 553–73.

Österreichische Erklärung über die zum Deutschen Bund gehörenden Provinzen und Gebiete der österreichischen Monarchie vom 6.4.1818. In Treichel, Eckhardt (ed.), *Quellen zur Geschichte des Deutschen Bundes*. Vol. 2: *Organisation und innere Ausgestaltung des Deutschen Bundes 1815–1819*. Munich, 2016, Nr. 51.

Ostrožinski, Ognjeslav, Programm zur Konstituierung des österreichischen Kaiserstaates nach dem Prinzipe der konstitutionellen Freiheit und der nationalen Gleichberechtigung. In Pejaković, Stjepan (ed.), *Aktenstücke zur Geschichte des kroatisch-slavonischen Landtages und der nationalen Bewegung vom Jahre 1848*. Vienna, 1861, Beilage II, 13–24.

Özkirimli, Umut, *Theories of Nationalism: A Critical Introduction*. 3rd edn. London, 2017.

Pacák, Bedřich, *Skizzen zur Regelung der Sprachenverhältnisse im Königreiche Böhmen*. Kuttenberg, 1896.

Pacholkiv, Svjatoslav, *Emanzipation durch Bildung: Entwicklung und gesellschaftliche Rolle der ukrainischen Intelligenz im habsburgischen Galizien 1890–1914*. Vienna, 2002.

Pál, Judit, Representation of the Transylvanian Towns in the Hungarian Parliament and Town MPs after the Austro-Hungarian Compromise 1866–1875. In Pál, Judit, and Popovici, Vlad (eds), *Elites and Politics in Central and Eastern Europe 1848–1918*. Frankfurt am Main, 2014, 225–47.

Palacký, František, *Oesterreichs Staatsidee*. Prague, 1866.

Palacký, František, *Gedenkblätter: Auswahl von Denkschriften, Aufsätzen und Briefen aus den letzten fünfzig Jahren. Als Beitrag zur Zeitgeschichte*. Prague, 1874.

Palacký, František, Druhý návrh říšské ústavy (leden 1849). In Bohuš Rieger (ed.), *Spisy drobné I: Spisy a řeči z oboru politiky*. Prague, 1898, 69–74.

Palacký, František, *Idea státu rakouského*. Prague, 1907.

Paleczek, Raimund, *Die Modernisierung des Großgrundbesitzes des Fürsten Johann Adolph II. zu Schwarzenberg: Beispiel einer deutsch-tschechischen Symbiose in Südböhmen im Neoabsolutismus 1848–1860*. Marburg, 2009.

Pammer, Michael, *Entwicklung und Ungleichheit: Österreich im 19. Jahrhundert*. Wiesbaden, 2002.

Pammer, Michael, Public Finance in Austria-Hungary, 1820–1913. In Cardoso, José Luís, and Lains, Pedro, *Paying for the Liberal State: The Rise of Public Finance in Nineteenth-Century Europe*. Cambridge, 2010, 132–61.

Pánek, Jaroslav, Ferdinand I. Der Schöpfer des politischen Programms der österreichischen Habsburger? In Maťa, Petr, and Winkelbauer, Thomas (eds), *Die Habsburgermonarchie 1620 bis 1740: Leistungen und Grenzen des Absolutismusparadigmas*. Stuttgart, 2006, 63–72.

Pap, József, Problems in the Career Analysis of Hungarian Representatives in the Age of Dualism. In Pál, Judit, and Popovici, Vlad (eds), *Elites and Politics in Central and Eastern Europe 1848–1918*. Frankfurt am Main, 2014, 177–90.

Pappenheim, Bertha, and Rabinowitsch, Sara, *Zur Lage der jüdischen Bevölkerung in Galizien: Reise-Eindrücke und Vorschläge zur Besserung der Verhältnisse*. Frankfurt am Main, 1904.

Părăianu, Răzvan, Von der kulturellen zur politischen Einheit der Rumänen. In Rumpler, Helmut (ed.), *Die Habsburgermonarchie 1848–1918*. Vol. 11: *Die Habsburgermonarchie und der Erste Weltkrieg*. Subvol. 1: *Der Kampf um die Neuordnung Mitteleuropas*. Part 2: *Vom Vielvölkerstaat Österreich-Ungarn zum neuen Europa der Nationalstaaten*. Vienna, 2016, 767–812.

Pascu, Stefan, and Göllner, Carol, La Lutte des Roumains de la Monarchie des Habsbourg contre le Dualisme. In Holotík, Ľudovít (ed.), *Der österreichisch-ungarische Ausgleich 1867*. Bratislava, 1971, 897–913.

Patočka, Jaromír, *Zemská správní komise pro Království české v letech 1913 a 1914*. Prague, 2006.

Patzauer, Hans, *Österreichs und Ungarns Staatswirthschaften*. Vienna, 1916.

Paulinyi, Ákos, Die Industriepolitik in Ungarn und in Österreich und das Problem der ökonomischen Integration 1880–1914. *Zeitschrift für Wirtschafts- und Sozialwissenschaften* 97/2 (1977), 131–66.

Paulmann, Johannes, Europäische Monarchen in der Revolution von 1848/1849: 'Die erste wahrhafte Internationale?' In Langewiesche, Dieter (ed.), *Demokratiebewegung und Revolution 1847–1849: Internationale Aspekte und europäische Verbindungen*. Karlsruhe, 1998, 109–39.

Paulmann, Johannes, *Pomp und Politik: Monarchenbegegnungen in Europa zwischen Ancien Régime und Erstem Weltkrieg*. Paderborn, 2000.

Pavlenko, Olga V., Die 'slavische Frage': Im Kontext der russisch-österreichischen Beziehungen während der Revolution 1848/49. In Moritsch, Andreas (ed.), *Der Prager Slavenkongress 1848*. Vienna, 2000, 19–38.

Pavlíček, Stanislav, *Naše lokálky: Místní dráhy v Čechách, na Moravě a ve Slezsku*. Prague, 2002.

Pavlíčková, Tereza, *Die Entwicklung des Nationalitätenkonflikts in der Znaimer deutschen Presse 1850–1938*. Olomouc, 2013.

Pearson, Sevan, *Wem gehört Bosnien? Die Nationalitätenpolitik der Kommunisten in Bosnien und Herzegowina, 1943–1974*. Stuttgart, 2019.

Pech, Stanley Z., Passive Resistance of the Czechs 1863–1879. *Slavonic and East European Review*, 36/87 (1958), 434–52.

Pekař, Josef, *Z duchovních dějin českých*. Prague, 1941.

Pellar, Brigitte, *'...mit sozialpolitischen Erwägungen': Staatliche Arbeitsstatistik und Gewerkschaftsmitsprache im Handelsministerium der Habsburgermonarchie*. Vienna, 2013.

Perić, Ivo, *Dalmatinski sabor*. Zadar, 1978.

Perić, Ivo, *Hrvatski državni sabor 1848–2000*. Vol. 2: *1868–1918*. Zagreb, 2000.

Peričić, Šime, *Gospodarska povijest Dalmacije od 18. do 20. stoljeća*. Zadar, 1998.

Pešek, Jiří, Zur räumlichen Struktur großstädtischer Dienstleistungen im Gesundheitsbereich in Prag und Wien um 1900. In Melinz, Gerhard, and Zimmermann, Susan (eds), *Wien, Prag, Budapest: Blütezeit der Habsburgermetropolen. Urbanisierung, Kommunalpolitik, gesellschaftliche Konflikte 1867–1918*. Vienna, 1996, 177–84.

Pešelj, Branko, Der ungarisch-kroatische Ausgleich vom Jahre 1868: Verfassungsrechtlicher Überblick. In Berger, Peter (ed.), *Der österreichisch-ungarische Ausgleich von 1867: Vorgeschichte und Wirkungen*. Vienna and Munich, 1967, 169–85.

Péter, László, *Hungary's Long Nineteenth Century: Constitutional and Democratic Traditions in a European Perspective*. Leiden, 2012.

Pfaff, Ivan, Tschechische Politik und die Reichsgründung. Jahrbücher für Geschichte Osteuropas, 20/4 (1972) 492–515.

Pfaundler, Richard, *Der Finanzausgleich in Österreich: Ein Beitrag zur Entwicklungsgeschichte der finanziellen Beziehungen zwischen Staat, Ländern und Gemeinden in den Jahren 1896 bis 1927*. Vienna, 1927.

Pfaundler, Richard, *Der Finanzausgleich in Österreich: Das System, seine Begründung und Durchführung*. Vienna, 1931.

Pfusterschmid-Hardtenstein, Heinrich, Die Orientalische- und später Konsularakademie 1848–1918: Eine frühe Fachhochschule im Zeitalter der Industrialisierung. In Rathkolb, Oliver (ed.), *250 Jahre: Von der Orientalischen zur Diplomatischen Akademie in Wien*. Innsbruck, 2004, 77–103.

Pichler, Rupert, *Die Wirtschaft der Lombardei als Teil Österreichs: Wirtschaftspolitik, Außenhandel und industrielle Interessen 1815–1859*. Berlin, 1997.

Pijaj, Stanisław, *Między polskim patriotyzmem a habsburskim lojalizmem. Polacy wobec przemian ustrojowych monarchii habsburskiej 1866–1871*. Kraków, 2004.

Pijaj, Stanisław, Pokusy o polsko-ukrajinskou dohodu v Haliči. In Fasora, Lukáš, Hanuš, Jiří, and Malíř, Jiří (eds), *Moravské vyrovnání z roku 1905: Možnosti a limity národnostního smíru ve střední Evropě*. Brno, 2006, 267–77.

Pillersdorf, Franz Xaver von, *Handschriftlicher Nachlaß des Freiherrn von Pillersdorff*. Vienna, 1863.

Plaschka, Richard Georg (ed.), *Mitteleuropa-Konzeptionen in der ersten Hälfte des 20. Jahrhunderts*. Vienna, 1995.

Plattner, Irmgard, Josephinismus und Bürokratie. In Reinalter, Helmut (ed.), *Josephinismus als aufgeklärter Absolutismus*. Vienna, 2008, 53–96.

Pleterski, Janko, Der Trialismus bei den Slowenen und die jugoslawische Einigung. In Plaschka, Richard G., and Mack, Karlheinz (eds), *Die Auflösung des Habsburgerreiches: Zusammenbruch und Neuorientierung im Donauraum*. Vienna, 1970, 195–202.

Pleterski, Janko, The Southern Slav Question. In Cornwall, Mark (ed.), *The Last Years of Austria-Hungary: A Multinational Experiment in Early Twentieth Century Europe*. Exeter, 2002, 119–48.

Pliveric, Josef, *Beiträge zum ungarisch-kroatischen Bundesrechte: Rechtliche und politische Erörterungen*. Agram, 1886.

Podrimavský, Milan, Die nationale Identität der Slowaken und das Bestreben um ihre staatsrechtliche Realisierung in den sechziger Jahren des 19. Jahrhunderts. In Kováč, Dušan, Suppan, Arnold, and Hrabovec, Emilia (eds), *Die Habsburgermonarchie und die Slowaken 1849–1867*. Bratislava, 2001.

Pogány, Ágnes, Wirtschaftsnationalismus in Ungarn im 19. und 20. Jahrhundert. In Pogány, Ágnes, Kubů, Eduard, and Kofman, Jan (eds), *Für eine nationale Wirtschaft: Ungarn, die Tschechoslowakei und Polen vom Ausgang des 19. Jahrhunderts bis zum Zweiten Weltkrieg*. Berlin, 2006, 11–71.

Pogány, Ágnes, Finanzgebarung, Kriegskosten und Kriegsschulden. In Rumpler, Helmut (ed.), *Die Habsburgermonarchie 1848–1918*. Vol. 11: *Die Habsburgermonarchie und der Erste Weltkrieg*. Subvol.1: *Vom Balkankonflikt zum Weltkrieg*. Vienna, 2016, 543–96.

Pók, Attila, Neue Staatsstruktur des Habsburgerreiches: Neues Verwaltungssystem nach dem Ausgleich mit Ungarn. In Glatz, Ferenc, and Melville, Ralph (eds), *Gesellschaft, Politik und Verwaltung in der Habsburgermonarchie 1830–1918*. Budapest, 1987, 189–202.

Pokludová, Andrea, and Kladiwa, Pavel, *Hans Kudlich (1823–1917): Cesta života a mýtu*. Ostrava, 2012.

Pokorný, Jiří, Ingenieure in Böhmen und der Tschechoslowakei 1890–1939. In McClelland, Charles E., Merl, Stephan, and Siegrist, Hannes (eds), *Professionen im modernen Osteuropa/Professions in Modern Eastern Europe*. Berlin, 1995, 367–81.

Pokorný, Jiří, Der Prager Slavenkongress und die Tschechen. In Moritsch, Andreas (ed.), *Der Prager Slavenkongress 1848*. Vienna, 2000, 63–70.

Polonsky, Antony, The Revolutionary Crisis of 1846–1849 and its Place in the Development of Nineteenth-Century Galicia. *Harvard Ukrainian Studies*, 22 (1998), 443–69.

Polzer-Hoditz, Arthur, *Kaiser Karl: Aus der Geheimmappe seines Kabinettschefs*. Zürich, 1929.

Popovici, Aurel C., *Die Vereinigten Staaten von Groß-Österreich: Politische Studien zur Lösung der nationalen Fragen und staatsrechtlichen Krisen in Österreich-Ungarn*. Leipzig, 1906.

Pöschl, Magdalena, *Gleichheit vor dem Gesetz*. Vienna, 2009.

Pravilova, Ekaterina A., *Finansy imperii: Den'gi i vlast' v politike Rossii na nacional'nych okrainach 1801–1917*. Moscow, 2006.

Prelog, Milan, *Pout' Slovanů do Moskvy roku 1867*. Prague, 1931.

Press, Volker, Landstände des 18. und Parlamente des 19. Jahrhunderts. In Berding, Helmut, and Ullmann, Hans-Peter (eds), *Deutschland zwischen Revolution und Restauration*. Königstein/Taunus, 1981, 133–57.

Press, Volker, Adel im 19. Jahrhundert: Die Führungsschichten Alteuropas im bürgerlich-bürokratischen Zeitalter. In Reden-Dohna, Armgard von, and Melville, Ralph (eds), *Der Adel an der Schwelle des bürgerlichen Zeitalters 1780–1860*. Stuttgart, 1988, 1–19.

Probst, Friedrich, Naturalverpflegsstationen in Österreich. *Statistische Monatsschrift*, 20 (1894), 65–76.

Prunk, J., and Rozman, F., Austromarxistische Konzeptionen der JSDS bei der Lösung der slowenischen Nationalitätenfrage. In Hitchins, Keith (ed.), *Studies in East European Social History*. Leiden, 1977, 33–42.

Putna, Martin C., *Obrazy z kulturních dějin Střední Evropy*. Prague, 2018.

Puttkamer, Ellinor von, *Föderative Elemente im deutschen Staatsrecht seit 1648*. Göttingen, 1955.

Puttkamer, Joachim von, *Schulalltag und nationale Integration in Ungarn: Slowaken, Rumänen und Siebenbürger Sachsen in der Auseinandersetzung mit der ungarischen Staatsidee 1867–1914*. Munich, 2003.

Puttkamer, Joachim von, *Ostmitteleuropa im 19. und 20. Jahrhundert*. Munich, 2010.

Radvany, Egon, *Metternich's Projects for Reform in Austria*. The Hague, 1971.

Radzyner, Joanna, *Stanisław Madeyski 1841–1910: Ein austro-polnischer Staatsmann im Spannungsfeld der Nationalitätenfrage in der Habsburgermonarchie*. Vienna, 1983.

Raeff, Marc, *Michael Speransky: Statesman of Imperial Russia 1772–1839*. 2nd edn. The Hague, 1969.

Rahten, Andrej, Der Krainer Landtag. In Rumpler, Helmut, and Urbanitsch, Peter (eds), *Die Habsburgermonarchie 1848–1918*. Vol. 7: *Verfassung und Parlamentarismus*. Subvol. 2: *Die regionalen Repräsentativkörperschaften*. Vienna, 2000, 1739–68.

Rahten, Andrej, *Ivan Šusteršič, der ungekrönte Herzog von Krain die slowenische katholische Bewegung zwischen trialistischem Reformkonzept und jugoslawischer Staatsidee*. Vienna, 2012.

Rak, Jiří, *Zachovej nám, Hospodine: Češi v Rakouském císařství 1804–1918*. Prague, 2013.

Raphael, Lutz, *Recht und Ordnung: Herrschaft durch Verwaltung im 19. Jahrhundert*. Frankfurt am Main, 2000.

Rath, John Reuben, *The Provisional Austrian Regime in Lombardo-Venetia, 1814–1815*. Austin, TX, and London, 1969.

Rauchensteiner, Manfried, '... nicht ohne ein glänzendes Vorbild abzugeben': Kärnten 1809. In Fräss-Ehrfeld, Claudia (ed.), *Napoleon und seine Zeit: Kärnten-Innerösterreich-Illyrien*. Klagenfurt, 2009, 111–48.

Rechter, David, *Jews of Vienna and the First World War*. London, 2001.

Rechter, David, Nationalism at the Edge: The Jüdische Volksrat of Habsburg Bukovina. *Aschkenas*, 18–19/1 (2009), 59–89.

Redlich, Josef, *Das Wesen der österreichischen Kommunalverfassung*. Leipzig, 1910.

Redlich, Josef, *Das österreichische Staats- und Reichsproblem: Geschichtliche Darstellung der inneren Politik der habsburgischen Monarchie von 1848 bis zum Untergang des Reiches*. Vol. I. Part 2. Leipzig, 1920.

Redlich, Josef, *Österreichische Regierung und Verwaltung im Weltkriege*. Vienna, 1929.

Redlich, Josef, *Schicksalsjahre Österreichs: Die Erinnerungen und Tagebücher Josef Redlichs 1869–1936*. 3 vols. Vienna, 2011.

Redžić, Enver, Die österreichische Sozialdemokratie und die Frage Bosniens und der Herzegowina. In Hitchins, Keith (ed.), *Studies in East European Social History*. Leiden, 1977, 94–117.

Reichsschatzamt (ed.), *Denkschriftenband.* Part 1: *Das Finanzwesen der öffentlichen Körperschaften Deutschlands.* Berlin, 1908.

Reichsschatzamt (ed.), *Denkschriftenband.* Part 3: *Die Finanzen von Frankreich, Großbritannien und Irland, Italien, Japan, Österreich-Ungarn, Rußland, der Schweiz, den Vereinigten Staaten von Amerika.* Berlin, 1908.

Reichsschatzamt (ed.), Österreich und Ungarn. In *Denkschriftenband.* Teil 3: *Die Finanzen von Frankreich, Großbritannien und Irland, Italien, Japan, Österreich-Ungarn, Rußland, der Schweiz, den Vereinigten Staaten von Amerika.* Berlin, 1908, 239–304.

Reifowitz, Ian, 'Threads Intertwined': German National Egoism and Liberalism in Adolf Fischhof's Vision for Austria. *Nationalities Papers,* 29/3 (2001), 441–58.

Reifowitz, Ian, *Imagining an Austrian Nation: Joseph Samuel Bloch and the Search for a Supraethnic Austrian Identity 1846–1918.* New York, 2003.

Reill, Dominique K., *Nationalists who Feared the Nation: Adriatic Multi-Nationalism in Habsburg Dalmatia, Trieste, and Venice.* Stanford, CA, 2012.

Reimer, Hans H., *Lutherisch in Südtirol: Die Geschichte der Evangelischen Gemeinde Meran. Eine Spurensuche zum Protestantismus in Südtirol und im Trentino.* Bozen, 2009.

Reinerman, Alan, *Austria and the Papacy in the Age of Metternich.* 2 vols. Washington, DC, 1979, 1989.

Reinhard, Wolfgang, *Geschichte der Staatsgewalt: Eine vergleichende Verfassungsgeschichte Europas von den Anfängen bis zur Gegenwart.* 2nd edn. Munich, 2000.

Reinhard, Wolfgang, *Geschichte des modernen Staates.* Munich, 2007.

Reinhard, Wolfgang, No Statebuilding from Below! A Critical Commentary. In Blockmans, Wim, Holenstein, André, and Mathieu, Jon (eds), *Empowering Interactions: Political Cultures and the Emergence of the State in Europe 1300–1900.* Abingdon and New York, 2009, 299–304.

Reinhard, Wolfgang, *Staatsmacht und Staatskredit: Kulturelle Tradition und politische Moderne.* Heidelberg, 2017.

Reiter, Ilse, 'Das Wahlrecht gebt uns frei!' Kampf der Sozialdemokratie für das allgemeine und gleiche Reichsratswahlrecht. In Simon, Thomas (ed.), *Hundert Jahre allgemeines und gleiches Wahlrecht in Österreich.* Frankfurt am Main, 2010, 167–212.

Renner, Karl [Pseudonym Rudolf Springer*], Der Kampf der Österreichischen Nationen um den Staat.* Part 1: *Das nationale Problem als Verfassungs- und Verwaltungsfrage.* Leipzig and Vienna, 1902.

Renner, Karl, *Die Nation als Rechtsidee und die Internationale.* Vienna, 1914.

Renner, Karl, *Das Selbstbestimmungsrecht der Nationen in besonderer Anwendung auf Österreich.* Vol. 1: *Nation und Staat.* Leipzig and Vienna, 1918.

Renzsch, Wolfgang, Föderale Finanzverfassungen: Ein Vergleich Australiens, Deutschlands, Kanadas, der Schweiz und der USA aus institutioneller Perspektive. *Jahrbuch des Föderalismus* (2000), 42–54.

Ress, Imre, The Hungarian-Croat Compromise of 1868. In Romsics, Ignác, and Király, Béla K. (eds), *Geopolitics in the Danube Region: Hungarian Reconciliation Efforts 1848–1998.* Budapest, 1999, 177–98.

Retegan, Simion, Die Siebenbürgischen Landtage 1848–1865. In Rumpler, Helmut, and Urbanitsch, Peter (eds), *Die Habsburgermonarchie 1848–1918.* Vol. 7: *Verfassung und Parlamentarismus.* Subvol. 2: *Die regionalen Repräsentativkörperschaften.* Vienna, 2000, 2317–43.

Řezník, Miloš, Der galizische Adel. In Rumpler, Helmut, and Urbanitsch, Peter (ed.), *Die Habsburgermonarchie 1848–1918.* Vol. 9: *Soziale Strukturen.* Part 1: *Von der Feudal-Agrarischen zur Bürgerlich-industriellen Gesellschaft.* Subvol. 2: *Von der Stände- zur Klassengesellschaft.* Vienna, 2010, 1015–42.

Rhode, Gotthold, Stände und Königtum in Polen/Litauen und Böhmen/Mähren: Bemerkungen zur Entwicklung ihres Verhältnisses vom 16. bis ins 18. Jahrhundert. *Jahrbücher für Geschichte Osteuropas,* 12/2 (1964), 221–46.

Richers, Julia, *Jüdisches Budapest: Kulturelle Topographien einer Stadtgemeinde im 19. Jahrhundert.* Cologne, 2009.

Rieber, Alfred J., The Comparative Ecology of Complex Frontiers. In Rieber, Alfred J., and Miller, Alexei (eds), *Imperial Rule*. Budapest and New York, 2004, 177–207.

Rieber, Alfred J., *The Struggle for the Eurasian Borderlands: From the Rise of Early Modern Empires to the End of the First World War*. Cambridge, 2015.

Rieger, Bohuš, *Ústava dle Frant. Palackého v l. 1848–49: In Památník na oslavu stých narozenin Františka Palackého*. Prague, 1898, 602–45.

Riker, William H., *Federalism. Origin—Operation—Significance*. Boston and Toronto, 1964.

Ritter, Gerhard A., *Der Sozialstaat: Entstehung und Entwicklung im internationalen Vergleich*. Munich, 2010.

Robert, Cyprien, *Le monde slave: Son passé, son état présent et son avenir*. Paris, 1852.

Robinson, Ronald E., Introduction: Railway Imperialism. In Davis, Clarence B., Wilburn, Kenneth E. Jr., and Robinson, Ronald E. (eds), *Railway Imperialism*. New York, 1991, 1–6.

Roksandić, Drago, Austroslavische Tendenzen bei den Serben. In Moritsch, Andreas (ed.), *Der Austroslavismus. Ein verfrühtes Konzept zur politischen Neugestaltung Mitteleuropas*. Vienna, 1996, 138–46.

Rosdolsky, Roman, *Untertan und Staat in Galizien. Die Reformen unter Maria Theresia und Joseph II*. Ed. Ralph Melville. Mainz, 1992.

Rosenmann, Stephan [Pseudonym Josef von Ürményi], *Staatsrecht des Königreichs Ungarn: Nach der heutigen Verfassung dieses Reichs bearbeitet*. Vienna, 1791.

Röskau-Rydel, Isabel, *Zwischen Akkulturation und Assimilation: Karrieren und Lebenswelten deutsch-österreichischer Beamtenfamilien in Galizien 1772–1918*. Berlin, 2015.

Rossová, Marcela (ed.), *Integration und Desintegration in Mitteleuropa: Pläne und Realität*. Munich, 2009.

Rotteck, Carl von, and Welcker, Carl (eds), *Staats-Lexikon oder Encyklopädie der Staatswissenschaften*. Vol. 12. Altona, 1841.

Rottenbacher, Bernd, *Das Februarpatent in der Praxis: Wahlpolitik, Wahlkämpfe und Wahlentscheidungen in den böhmischen Ländern der Habsburgermonarchie 1861–1871*. Frankfurt am Main, 2001.

Roubík, František, Doslov. In Roubík, František (ed.), *Petice venkovského lidu z Čech k Národnímu výboru z roku 1848*. Prague, 1954, 511–25.

Rozenblit, Marsha, Sustaining Austrian 'National Identity' in Crisis: The Dilemma of the Jews in Habsburg Austria 1914–1919. In Rozenblit, Marsha, and Judson, Pieter (eds), *Constructing Nationalities in East Central Europe*. New York and Oxford, 2005, 178–91.

Rozenblit, Marsha L., Die sozialen Grundlagen des Antisemitismus in der Habsburgermonarchie 1848–1918. In Rumpler, Helmut, and Urbanitsch, Peter (eds), *Die Habsburgermonarchie 1848–1918*. Vol. 9: *Soziale Strukturen*. Part 1: *Von der Feudal-Agrarischen zur Bürgerlich-industriellen Gesellschaft*. Subvol. 2: *Von der Stände- zur Klassengesellschaft*. Vienna, 2010, 1369–1418.

Rozman, Franc, Etbin Kristan und seine Idee der Personalautonomie. In Konrad, Helmut (ed.), *Arbeiterbewegung und nationale Frage in den Nachfolgestaaten der Habsburgermonarchie*. Vienna and Zürich, 1993, 97–109.

Rudnytsky, Ivan L., The Ukrainians in Galicia under Austrian Rule. In Markovits, Andrei S., and Sysyn, Frank E. (eds), *Nationbuilding and the Politics of Nationalism: Essays on Austrian Galicia*. Cambridge, 1982, 23–67.

Rudolph, Richard L., *Banking and Industrialization in Austria-Hungary: The Role of Banks in the Industrialization of the Czech Crownlands 1873–1914*. Cambridge, MA, 1976.

Rumpler, Helmut, *Das Völkermanifest Kaiser Karls vom 16. Oktober 1918: Letzter Versuch zur Rettung des Habsburgerreiches*. Munich, 1966.

Rumpler, Helmut, 'Es ist ein Kampf auf Leben und Tod, der noch lange nicht aus ist': Bismarcks Erfolgspolitik und das deutsch-österreichische Problem. *Mitteilungen des Instituts für österreichische Geschichtsforschung*, 101 (1993), 37–67.

Rumpler, Helmut, *Eine Chance für Mitteleuropa: Bürgerliche Emanzipation und Staatsverfall in der Habsburgermonarchie*. Vienna, 1997.

Rumpler, Helmut, 'Dass neu und kräftig möge Österreichs Ruhm erstehen!': Der Thronwechsel vom 2. Dezember 1848 und die Wende zur Reaktion. In Bruckmüller, Ernst, and Häusler, Wolfgang (eds), *1848: Revolution in Österreich*. Vienna, 1999, 139–54.

Rumpler, Helmut, Der österreichische Neoabsolutismus als Herrschafts- und Modernisierungssystem. In Kováč, Dušan, Suppan, Arnold, and Hrabovec, Emilia (eds), *Die Habsburgermonarchie und die Slowaken 1849–1867*. Bratislava, 2001, 9–21.

Rumpler, Helmut, Kaiser Karl, die Friedensprojekte und das deutsch-österreichische Bündnis. In Gottsmann, Andreas (ed.), *Karl I. (IV.), der Erste Weltkrieg und das Ende der Donaumonarchie*. Vienna, 2007, 13–22.

Rumpler, Helmut (ed.), Die Habsburgermonarchie 1848–1918. In Rumpler, Helmut, and Seger, Martin (eds), *Die Habsburgermonarchie 1848–1918*. Vol. 9: *Soziale Strukturen*. Part 2: *Die Gesellschaft der Habsburgermonarchie im Kartenbild: Verwaltungs-, Sozial- und Infrastrukturen. Nach dem Zensus von 1910*. Vienna, 2010.

Rumpler, Helmut, Vorwort. In Rumpler, Helmut, Scharr, Kurt, and Ungureanu, Constantin (eds), *Der Franziszeische Kataster im Kronland Bukowina/Czernowitzer Kreis (1817–1865): Statistik und Katastralmappen*. Vienna, 2015, 13–16.

Rumpler, Helmut, Die Todeskrise Cisleithaniens 1911–1918: Vom Primat der Innenpolitik zum Primat der Kriegsentscheidung. In Rumpler, Helmut (ed.), *Die Habsburgermonarchie 1848–1918*. Vol. 11: *Die Habsburgermonarchie und der Erste Weltkrieg*. Subvol. 1: *Der Kampf um die Neuordnung Mitteleuropas*. Part 2: *Vom Vielvölkerstaat Österreich-Ungarn zum neuen Europa der Nationalstaaten*. Vienna, 2016, 1165–1256.

Rumpler, Helmut, Scharr, Kurt, and Ungureanu, Constantin (eds), *Der Franziszeische Kataster im Kronland Bukowina/Czernowitzer Kreis 1817–1865: Statistik und Katastralmappen*. Vienna, 2015.

Ruthner, Clemens, Introduction: Bosnia-Herzegovina, Post/Colonial? In Ruthner, Clemens (ed.), *Wechselwirkungen: Austria-Hungary, Bosnia-Herzegovina, and the Western Balkans 1878–1918*. New York, 2015, 1–20.

Rychlík, Jan, Uhersko-chorvatské vyrovnání roku 1868 a národnostní konflikty v Chorvatsku. In Fasora, Lukáš, Hanuš, Jiří, and Malíř, Jiří (eds), *Moravské vyrovnání z roku 1905: Možnosti a limity národnostního smíru ve střední Evropě*. Brno, 2006, 175–87.

Sack, Robert David, *Human Territoriality: Its Theory and History*. Cambridge, 1986.

Sandgruber, Roman, *Ökonomie und Politik: Österreichische Wirtschaftsgeschichte vom Mittelalter bis zur Gegenwart*. 2nd edn. Vienna, 2005.

Sandonà, Augusto, *Il Regno Lombardo-Veneto 1814–1859: La costituzione e l'amministrazione*. Milan, 1912.

Sashegyi, Oszkár, *Ungarns politische Verwaltung in der Ära Bach*. Graz, 1979.

Sax, Emil, *Grundlegung der theoretischen Staatswirthschaft*. Vienna, 1887.

Scharf, Christian, *Ausgleichspolitik und Pressekampf in der Ära Hohenwart: Die Fundamentalartikel von 1871 und der deutsch-tschechische Konflikt in Böhmen*. Munich, 1996.

Scharpf, Fritz W., Reissert, Bernd, and Schnabel, Fritz, *Politikverflechtung: Theorie und Empirie des kooperativen Föderalismus in der Bundesrepublik*. Kronberg im Taunus, 1976.

Scharr, Kurt, *'Die Landschaft Bukowina': Das Werden einer Region an der Peripherie*. Vienna, 2010.

Scharr, Kurt, Der griechisch-orientalische Bukowinaer Religionsfonds 1783–1949: Einfluss und Bedeutung einer Institution. In Winkler, Markus (ed.), *Partizipation und Exklusion: Zur Habsburger Prägung von Sprache und Bildung in der Bukowina 1848–1918–1940*. Regensburg, 2015, 229–48.

Scheer, Tamara, K. u. k. Regimentssprachen: Institutionalisierung der Sprachenvielfalt in der Habsburgermonarchie in den Jahren 1867/8–1914. In Ehlers, Klaas-Hinrich, Nekula, Marek, Niedhammer, Martina, and Scheuringer, Hermann (eds), *Sprache, Gesellschaft und Nation in Ostmitteleuropa: Institutionalisierung und Alltagspraxis*. Göttingen, 2014, 75–92.

Scheer, Tamara, and Stergar, Rok, Ethnic Boxes: The Unintended Consequences of Habsburg Bureaucratic Classification. *Nationalities Paper*, 46/4 (2018), 575–91.

Schefbeck, Günther, Die Gewählten: Auf dem Weg zu einer Kollektivbiographie der österreichischen Parlamentsmitglieder. In Simon, Thomas (ed.), *Hundert Jahre allgemeines und gleiches Wahlrecht in Österreich*. Frankfurt am Main, 2010, 89–153.

Schennach, Martin P., Der wehrhafte Tiroler: Zu Entstehung, Wandlung und Funktion eines Mythos. *Geschichte und Region/Storia e regione*, 14/2 (2005), 81–112.

Schennach, Martin P., *Revolte in der Region: Zur Tiroler Erhebung von 1809*. Innsbruck, 2009.

Schennach, Martin P., Das Provisorische Gemeindegesetz 1849 und das Reichsgemeindegesetz 1862 als Zäsur? Reflexionen zum österreichischen Gemeindebegriff im 19. Jahrhundert. *Mitteilungen des Instituts für österreichische Geschichtsforschung*, 120 (2012), 369–90.

Schennach, Martin P., Die 'österreichische Gesamtstaatsidee': Das Verhältnis von Gesamtstaat und Ländern als Gegenstand rechtshistorischer Forschung. In Schennach, Martin P. (ed.), *Rechtshistorische Aspekte des österreichischen Föderalismus: Beiträge zur Tagung an der Universität Innsbruck am 28. und 29. November 2013*. Vienna, 2015, 1–29.

Schennach, Martin P. (ed.), *Rechtshistorische Aspekte des österreichischen Föderalismus: Beiträge zur Tagung an der Universität Innsbruck am 28. und 29. November 2013*. Vienna, 2015.

Schennach, Martin P., Gliedstaaten oder 'Kommunalverbände höchster Ordnung'? Länder und Landesverfassungen in der österreichischen Staatsrechtslehre bis zum Ende der Monarchie. In Ambrosius, Gerold, Henrich-Franke, Christian, and Neutsch, Cornelius (eds), *Föderalismus in historisch vergleichender Perspektive*. Vol. 6: *Integrieren durch Regieren*. Baden-Baden, 2018, 389–420.

Schermaier, Josef, *Wirtschaftsförderung durch zentralstaatliche Bildungsmaßnahmen im Vielvölkerstaat Österreich: Zentralanstalten und Staatsgewerbeschulen. Ein Beitrag zur Geschichte des höheren technischen, gewerblichen und kunstgewerblichen Unterrichts in Österreich*. Frankfurt am Main, 1999.

Scheuner, Ulrich, Das Bundesverfassungsgericht und die Bindungskraft seiner Entscheidungen. *Die Öffentliche Verwaltung*, 15 (1962), 641–7.

Scheuner, Ulrich, Kooperation und Konflikt: Das Verhältnis von Bund und Ländern im Wandel. In Scheuner, Ulrich, *Staatstheorie und Staatsrecht: Gesammelte Schriften*. Berlin, 1978, 399–415.

Schiera, Pierangelo, Zentralismus und Föderalismus: Strukturen und Kulturen im deutsch-italienischen Vergleich. Einleitende Bemerkungen. In Schiera, Pierangelo, Janz, Oliver, and Siegrist, Hannes (eds), *Zentralismus und Föderalismus im 19. und 20. Jahrhundert: Deutschland und Italien im Vergleich*. Berlin, 2000, 19–37.

Schima, Stefan, Die Revolution von 1848 und die Rechtsstellung der Juden. *Mitteilungen des Instituts für österreichische Geschichtsforschung*, 118 (2010), 415–49.

Schlachta, Astrid von, Die 'Verfassung' des Landes: Ein Erinnerungsort in der politischen Kommunikation in Tirol. In Mazohl, Brigitte, and Mertelseder, Bernhard (eds), *Abschied vom Freiheitskampf? Tirol und '1809' zwischen politischer Realität und Verklärung*. Innsbruck, 1809, 129–51.

Schlegel, Herbert, *Die Tirolische Landes-Hypothekenanstalt: Werden, Wirken und wirtschaftliche Entwicklung 1865–1965*. Innsbruck, 1966.

Schlesinger, Rudolf, *Federalism in Central and Eastern Europe*. New York, 2001 (reprint of 1945 edn).

Schlitter, Hanns, *Aus Österreichs Vormärz*. 3 vols. Vienna, 1920.

Schmerling, Anton von, *Der Vater der Verfassung: Aus der Sicht des Staatsministers Anton v. Schmerlings*. Ed. Lothar Höbelt. Frankfurt am Main, 1994.

Schmetterer, Christoph, *Kaiser Franz Joseph I*. Vienna, 2016.

Schmid, Ferdinand, *Bosnien und die Herzegovina unter der Verwaltung Österreich-Ungarns*. Leipzig, 1914.

Schmid, Josef, Sozialpolitik und Wohlfahrtsstaat in Bundesstaaten. In Lehmbruch, Gerhard, and Benz, Arthur (eds), *Föderalismus: Analysen in entwicklungsgeschichtlicher und vergleichender Perspektive*. Wiesbaden, 2002, 279–305.

Schmidt, Tim Mathias, *Sprachnationale Konflikte, Staatsreformdiskurs und Sozialdemokratie: Ein Vergleich zwischen den böhmischen Ländern und Belgien 1894–1938*. University dissertation, Munich, 2014.

Schmidt-Brentano, Antonio, *Die Armee in Österreich: Militär, Staat und Gesellschaft, 1848–1867*. Boppard am Rhein, 1975.

Schmied-Kowarzik, Anatol, *Unteilbar und untrennbar? Die Verhandlungen zwischen Cisleithanien und Ungarn zum gescheiterten Wirtschaftsausgleich 1897*. Innsbruck, 2010.

Schmied-Kowarzik, Anatol, Einleitung. In *Die Protokolle des gemeinsamen Ministerrates der österreichisch-ungarischen Monarchie 1867–1918*. Vol. 4: *1908–1914*. Budapest, 2011.

Schmitt, Carl, *Verfassungslehre*. Berlin, 1928.

Schmitz, Georg, *Die Anfänge des Parlamentarismus in Niederösterreich: Landesordnung und Selbstregierung 1861–1873*. Vienna, 1985.

Schmitz, Georg, Organe und Arbeitsweise, Strukturen und Leistungen der Landesvertretungen. In Rumpler, Helmut, and Urbanitsch, Peter (eds), *Die Habsburgermonarchie 1848–1918*. Vol. 7: *Verfassung und Parlamentarismus*. Subvol. 2: *Die regionalen Repräsentativkörperschaften*. Vienna, 2000, 1353–1544.

Schneider, Karin, Zwischen 'Monarchischer Union von Ständestaaten' und Gesamtstaat: Die Habsburgermonarchie im 18. und 19. Jahrhundert. In Schennach, Martin P. (ed.), *Rechtshistorische Aspekte des österreichischen Föderalismus*. Vienna, 2015, 31–49.

Schneller, Hans, *Die staatsrechtliche Stellung von Bosnien und Herzogowina*. Leipzig, 1892.

Schober, Richard, *La lotta sul progetto d'autonomie per il Trentino degli anni 1900–1902, secondo le fonti austriache*. Trento, 1978.

Schober, Richard, *Geschichte des Tiroler Landtages im 19. und 20. Jahrhundert*. Innsbruck, 1984.

Schober, Richard (ed.), *Theodor Freiherr von Kathrein 1841–1916: Landeshauptmann von Tirol. Briefe und Dokumente zur katholisch-konservativen Politik um die Jahrhundertwende*. Innsbruck, 1992.

Schönberger, Christoph, Die Europäische Union als Bund: Zugleich ein Beitrag zur Verabschiedung des Staatenbund—Bundesstaat-Schemas. *Archiv des öffentlichen Rechts*, 129 (2004), 81–120.

Schönberger, Christoph, *Unionsbürger: Europas föderales Bürgerrecht in vergleichender Sicht*. Tübingen, 2005.

Schopf, Franz Joseph, *Wahre und ausführliche Darstellung der am 11. März 1848 zur Erlangung einer constitutionellen Regierungs-Verfassung in der königlichen Hauptstadt* Prag *begonnenen Volks-Bewegung*. Leitmeritz, 1848.

Schopf, Franz Joseph, *Die organische Verwaltung des österreichischen Kaiserstaates in ihren seit einem Jahrhundert erfolgten Reformen und in ihrer gegenwärtigen Verfassung mit einer tabellarischen Übersicht der Ober- und Unterbehörden*. 2nd edn. Pest, 1859.

Schremmer, Eckart, *Steuern und Staatsfinanzen während der Industrialisierung Europas: England, Frankreich, Preußen und das Deutsche Reich 1800 bis 1914*. Berlin and Heidelberg, 1994.

Schubert, Anton, *Die Ämtervertschechung in Deutschböhmen. Deutschböhmen als Wirtschaftsgroßmacht*. Reichenberg, 1903.

Schubert, Anton, *Das Deutschtum im Wirtschaftshaushalte Österreichs: Ein Ausbauversuch der Schrift 'Deutschböhmen als Wirtschaftsgrossmacht' für ganz Österreich*. Vol. 1: *Der Besitzstand der Deutschen in Österreich*. Reichenberg, 1905.

Schüler, Isabella, *Franz Anton Graf von Kolowrat-Liebsteinsky (1778–1861): Der Prager Oberstburggraf und Wiener Staats- und Konferenzminister*. Munich, 2016.

Schüller, Richard, *Schutzzoll und Freihandel: Die Voraussetzungen und Grenzen ihrer Berechtigung*. Vienna and Leipzig, 1905.

Schullern-Schrattenhofen, Hermann, *Das Kolonat in Görz und Gradisca, in Istrien, in Dalmatien und in Tirol*. Vienna, 1908.

Schulz, Jan Pieter, *Finanzwissenschaft im deutschsprachigen Raum und in den Vereinigten Staaten 1865–1917: Ursprung, Inhalt und Wissenschaftstransfer*. Marburg, 2013.

Schulz, Matthias, Macht, internationale Politik und Normenwandel im Staatensystem des 19. Jahrhunderts. In Lappenküper, Ulrich, and Marcowitz, Reiner (eds), *Macht und Recht. Völkerrecht in den internationalen Beziehungen*. Paderborn, 2010, 113–34.

Schulze Wessel, Martin, *Russlands Blick auf Preußen: Die polnische Frage in der Diplomatie und der politischen Öffentlichkeit des Zarenreiches und des Sowjetstaates 1697–1947*. Stuttgart, 1995.

Schulze Wessel, Martin, Die Konfessionalisierung der tschechischen Nation. In Haupt, Heinz-Gerhard, and Langewiesche, Dieter (ed.), *Nation und Religion in Europa: Mehrkonfessionelle Gesellschaften im 19. und 20. Jahrhundert*. Frankfurt am Main and New York, 2004, 135–50.

Schulze Wessel, Martin, 'Loyalität' als geschichtlicher Grundbegriff und Forschungskonzept. In Schulze Wessel, Martin (ed.), *Loyalitäten in der Tschechoslowakischen Republik: Politische, nationale und kulturelle Zugehörigkeiten*. Munich, 2004, 1–22.

Schulze Wessel, Martin (ed.), *Nationalisierung der Religion und Sakralisierung der Nation im östlichen Europa*. Stuttgart, 2006.

Schulze Wessel, Martin, Frühneuzeitliche Glaubensflucht: Grenzüberschreitende Zugehörigkeiten und die Mythen von Toleranz und Vertreibung. In Thadden, Rudolf von, Kaudelka, Steffen, and Serrier, Thomas (eds), *Europa der Zugehörigkeiten: Integrationswege zwischen Ein- und Auswanderung*. Göttingen, 2007, 17–32.

Schulze Wessel, Martin, Religion, Politics and the Limits of Imperial Integration: Comparing the Habsburg Monarchy and the Russian Empire. In Hirschhausen, Ulrike von, and Leonhard, Jörn (eds), *Comparing Empires: Encounters and Transfers in the Long Nineteenth Century*. Göttingen, 2011, 337–58.

Schulze Wessel, Martin, *Revolution und religiöser Dissens: Der römisch-katholische und russisch-orthodoxe Klerus als Träger religiösen Wandels in den böhmischen Ländern und in Russland 1848–1922*. Munich, 2011.

Schulze Wessel, Martin, Identitäten und Loyalitäten im Zeitalter (neo-) imperialer Politik: Die Tschechoslowakei 1938 und die Ukraine heute im Vergleich. In Kleinmann, Yvonne, Heyde, Jürgen, Holste, Karsten, Hüchtker, Dietlind, and Katrin Steffen (eds), *Dekonstruieren und doch erzählen. Polnische und andere Geschichten*. Göttingen, 2015, 39–45.

Schumpeter, Joseph, Die Krise des Steuerstaats. In Schumpeter, Joseph, and Goldscheid, Rudolf, *Die Finanzkrise des Steuerstaats: Beiträge zur politischen Ökonomie der Staatsfinanzen*. Frankfurt am Main, 1976, 329–80.

Schumpeter, Joseph, and Goldscheid, Rudolf, *Die Finanzkrise des Steuerstaats: Beiträge zur politischen Ökonomie der Staatsfinanzen*. Frankfurt am Main, 1976.

Schuselka, Franz, *Ist Österreich deutsch?* Leipzig, 1843.

Schüßler, Wilhelm, *Die nationale Politik der österreichischen Abgeordneten im Frankfurter Parlament*. Berlin and Leipzig, 1913.

Schüßler, Wilhelm, Österreich und das deutsche Schicksal: Eine historisch-politische Skizze. Leipzig, 1925.

Schuster, Peter, *Henry Wickham Steed und die Habsburgermonarchie*. Vienna, 1970.

Schütz, Waltraud, Hilfe für Abgebrannte, ländliche Feste und medizinische Versorgung: Wohltätiges Engagement von Frauen im Niederösterreich des 19. Jahrhunderts. In Loinig, Elisabeth, Kühschelm, Oliver, Rosner, Willibal d, and Eminger, Stefan (eds), *Niederösterreich im 19. Jahrhundert*. St. Pölten, 2021, 381–412.

Schwartz, Michael, *Ethnische 'Säuberungen' in der Moderne: Globale Wechselwirkungen nationalistischer und rassistischer Gewaltpolitik im 19. und 20. Jahrhundert*. Munich, 2013.

Schwarz, Karl, Der Protestantismus in der Ära des Neoabsolutismus: Zum Projekt einer protestantischen Reichskirche in der Habsburgermonarchie. In Hrabovec, Emilia, Kováč, Dušan, and Suppan, Arnold (eds), *Die Habsburgermonarchie und die Slowaken 1849–1867*. Bratislava, 2001, 117–32.

Seewann, Gerhard, Rechberg, Bernhard Johann Graf. In Bernath, Mathias, and Nehring, Karl (eds), *Biographisches Lexikon zur Geschichte Südosteuropas*. Vol. 4. Munich, 1981.

Seewann, Gerhard, *Geschichte der Deutschen in Ungarn*. Vol. 2: *1860–2006*. Marburg, 2012.

Seibel, Wolfgang, *Verwaltung verstehen: Eine theoriegeschichtliche Einführung*. Berlin, 2016.

Seiderer, Georg, *Österreichs Neugestaltung: Verfassungspolitik und Verwaltungsreform im österreichischen Neoabsolutismus unter Alexander Bach 1849–1859*. Vienna, 2015.

Senghaas, Monika, *Die Territorialisierung sozialer Sicherung: Raum, Identität und Sozialpolitik in der Habsburgermonarchie*. Wiesbaden, 2015.

Senghaas, Monika, Föderalismus und Sozialpolitik in der Habsburgermonarchie. In Ambrosius, Gerold, Henrich-Franke, Christian, and Neutsch, Cornelius (eds), *Föderalismus in historisch vergleichender Perspektive*. Vol. 2: *Föderale Systeme. Kaiserreich, Donaumonarchie, Europäische Union*. Baden-Baden, 2015, 221–45.

Šesták, Miroslav, Jihoslovanské slovanství v habsburské monarchii v letech revoluce 1848–1849. In Veber, Václav (ed.), *150 let Slovanského sjezdu (1848). Historie a současnost*. Prague, 2000, 127–43.

Seydel, Max von, Der Bundesstaatsbegriff: Eine staatsrechtliche Untersuchung. In Seydel, Max von, *Staatsrechtliche und politische Abhandlungen*. Freiburg and Leipzig, 1893, 1–74.

Shedel, James, Emperor, Church, and People: Religion and Dynastic Loyality during the Golden Jubilee of Franz Joseph. *Catholic Historical Review*, 76/1 (1990), 71–92.

Sieber, Ernst Karl, *Ludwig von Löhner: Ein Vorkämpfer des Deutschtums in Böhmen, Mähren und Schlesien im Jahre 1848/1849*. Munich, 1965.

Sieghart, Rudolf, *Zolltrennung und Zolleinheit: Die Geschichte der österreichisch-ungarischen Zwischenzolllinie nach den Akten dargestellt*. Vienna, 1915.

Siegl, Gerhard, and Steiner, Guenther, *Ja, jetzt geht es mir gut…Entwicklung der bäuerlichen Sozialversicherung in Österreich*. Vienna, 2010.

Siemann, Wolfram, *Die Frankfurter Nationalversammlung 1848/49 zwischen demokratischem Liberalismus und konservativer Reform. Die Bedeutung der Juristendominanz in den Verfassungsverhandlungen des Paulskirchenparlaments*. Bern, 1976.

Siemann, Wolfram, *Vom Staatenbund zum Nationalstaat: Deutschland 1806–1871*. Frankfurt am Main and Vienna, 1995.

Siemann, Wolfram, *Metternich: Staatsmann zwischen Restauration und Moderne*. Munich, 2010.

Siemann, Wolfram *Metternich: Strategist and Visionary*. Cambridge, MA, 2019.

Simon, Thomas (ed.), *Hundert Jahre allgemeines und gleiches Wahlrecht in Österreich: Modernes Wahlrecht unter den Bedingungen eines Vielvölkerstaates*. Frankfurt am Main, 2010.

Simon, Thomas, Zur Stellung der Länder in der österreichischen und deutschen Staatsrechtslehre von 1867/71 und 1918. In Schennach, Martin P. (ed.), *Rechtshistorische Aspekte des österreichischen Föderalismus: Beiträge zur Tagung an der Universität Innsbruck am 28. und 29. November 2013*. Vienna, 2015, 63–86.

Singer, Kerstin, *Konstitutionalismus auf Italienisch. Italiens politische und soziale Führungsschichten und die oktroyierten Verfassungen von 1848*. Tübingen, 2008.

Sirka, Ann, *The Nationality Question in Austrian Education: The Case of Ukrainians in Galicia 1867–1914*. Frankfurt am Main, 1980.

Sked, Alan, Metternich and the Ficquelmont Mission of 1847–48: The Decision against Reform in Lombardy-Venetia. *Central Europe*, 2/1 (2004), 15–46.

Sked, Alan, *Metternich and Austria: An Evaluation*. Basingstoke, 2008.

Skedl, Arthur (ed.), *Der politische Nachlaß des Grafen Eduard Taaffe*. Vienna, 1922.

Skene, Alfred, *Der nationale Ausgleich in Mähren 1905*. Vienna, 1910.

Škvarna, Dušan, Die Slovaken und der Prager Slavenkongress. In Moritsch, Andreas (ed.), *Der Prager Slavenkongress 1848*. Vienna, 2000, 71–80.

Slapnicka, Harry, *Oberösterreich: Die politische Führungsschicht 1861–1918*. Linz, 1983.

Sluga, Glenda, *Internationalism in the Age of Nationalism*. Philadelphia, 2013.

Smith, Anthony, *Nationalism and Modernism: A Critical Survey of Recent Theories of Nations and Nationalism*. London and New York, 1998.

Smith, David J., and Hiden, Joe (eds), *Ethnic Diversity and the Nation State: National Cultural Autonomy Revisited*. Abingdon, 2012.

Smolka, Stanisław, *Die reussische Welt: Historisch-politische Studien. Vergangenheit u. Gegenwart*. Vienna, 1916.

Soboń, Marcin, *Polacy wobec Żydów w Galicji doby autonomicznej w latach 1868–1914*. Kraków, 2011.

Soldani, Simonetta, Annäherung an Europa im Namen der Nation: Die italienische Revolution 1846–1849. In Dowe, Dieter, Haupt, Heinz-Gerhard, and Langewiesche, Dieter (eds), *Europa 1848: Revolution und Reform*. Bonn, 1998, 125–65.

Sommaruga, Franz von, *Österreichs Zukunft und dessen Stellung in Deutschland*. Stuttgart, 1848.

Somogyi, Éva, *Vom Zentralismus zum Dualismus: Der Weg der deutschösterreichischen Liberalen zum Ausgleich von 1867*. Wiesbaden, 1983.

Somogyi, Éva, *Der gemeinsame Ministerrat der österreichisch-ungarischen Monarchie 1867–1906*. Vienna, 1996.

Somogyi, Éva, Die staatsrechtlichen Ansichten von Lajos Thallóczy. In Juzbašić, Dževad, and Ress, Imre (eds), *Lajos Thallóczy, der Historiker und Politiker: Die Entdeckung der Vergangenheit von Bosnien-Herzegowina und die moderne Geschichtswissenschaft*. Sarajevo and Budapest, 2010, 115–27.

Somoyi, Éva (ed.), *Protokolle des gemeinsamen Ministerrates der österrreichisch-ungarischen Monarchie 1867–1918*. Vol. VI. Budapest, 2011.

Sosnosky, Theodor von, *Die Balkanpolitik Österreich-Ungarns seit 1866*. Vol. 2. Stuttgart, 1914.

Sosnosky, Theodor von, *Erzherzog Franz Ferdinand*. Munich, 1929.

Spatzenegger, Hans, Die Katholische Kirche von der Säkularisation (1803) bis zur Gegenwart. In Dopsch, Heinz, and Spatzenegger, Hans (eds), *Geschichte Salzburgs: Stadt und Land*. Vol. 2/3. Salzburg, 1991, 1429–1520.

Speich, Daniel, *Helvetische Meliorationen. Die Neuordnung der gesellschaftlichen Naturverhältnisse an der Linth (1783–1823)*. Zürich, 2003.

Sperber, Jonathan, Kirchen, Gläubige und Religionspolitik in der Revolution von 1848. In Dowe, Dieter, Haupt, Heinz-Gerhard, and Langewiesche, Dieter (eds), *Europa 1848: Revolution und Reform*. Bonn, 1998, 933–59.

Sperber, Jonathan, *The European Revolutions 1848–1851*. 2nd edn. Cambridge, 2005.

Spiegel, Ludwig, Länder, Atutonomie und Selbstverwaltung in der Gegenwart. In Mischler, Ernst, and Ulbrich, Josef (eds), *Österreichisches Staatswörterbuch. Handbuch des gesamten österreichischen öffentlichen Rechtes*. Vol. 3. 2nd edn. Vienna, 1907, 395–430.

Spoerer, Mark, *Steuerlast, Steuerinzidenz und Steuerwettbewerb: Verteilungswirkungen der Besteuerung in Preußen und Württemberg 1815–1913*. Berlin, 2004.

Springer, Johann, Oeffentliches Recht des deutschen Bundes und der Bundesstaaten, von Johann Ludwig Klüber. *Zeitschrift für österreichische Rechtsgelehrsamkeit und politische Gesetzkunde*, 3 (1831), 421–3.

Springer, Johann, *Statistik des österreichischen Kaiserstaates*. 2 vols. Vienna, 1840.

Springer, Anton, *Protokolle des Verfassungsausschusses im Österreichischen Reichstage 1848–1849*. Leipzig, 1885.

Štaif, Jiří, Palacký, der Slavenkongress und die Zeitung 'Die Grenzboten': Bilder des 'Anderen' in der revolutionären Gesellschaft. In Moritsch, Andreas (ed.), *Der Prager Slavenkongress 1848*. Vienna, 2000, 47–61.

Štaif, Jiří, *Revoluční léta 1848–1849 a české země*. Prague, 1990.

Štaif, Jiří, *Obezřetná elita: Česká společnost mezi tradicí a revolucí 1830–1851*. Prague, 2005.

Stanislawski, Michael, *A Murder in Lemberg: Politics, Religion, and Violence in Modern Jewish History*. Princeton, 2007.

Šťastný, Vladislav (ed.), *Slovanství v národním životě Čechů a Slováků*. Prague, 1968.

Statistisches Departement der Landesregierung für Bosnien und die Hercegovina, *Die Ergebnisse der Volkszählung in Bosnien und der Hercegovina vom 10. Oktober 1910*. Sarajevo, 1912.

Stauber, Reinhard, *Der Zentralstaat an seinen Grenzen: Administrative Integration, Herrschaftswechsel und politische Kultur im südlichen Alpenraum 1750–1820*. Göttingen, 2001.

Stauber, Reinhard, Politische und soziale Integration in 'Illyrien' in der ersten Hälfte des 19. Jahrhunderts. In Bellabarba, Marco, et al. (eds), *Eliten in Tirol zwischen Ancien Régime und Vormärz*. Innsbruck, 2010, 61–82.

Stauber, Reinhard, *Der Wiener Kongress*. Vienna, 2014.

Stauber, Reinhard, Föderative Staatlichkeit in der Mitte Europas: Zur Entstehung des Deutschen Bundes. In Willoweit, Dietmar (ed.), *Föderalismus in Deutschland: Zu seiner wechselvollen Geschichte vom ostfränkischen Königtum bis zur Bundesrepublik*. Vienna, 2019, 215–35.

Stauter-Halsted, Keely, *The Nation in the Village: The Genesis of Peasant National Identity in Austrian Poland, 1848–1914*. Ithaca, NY, 2004.

Steed, Henry Wickham, *The Hapsburg Monarchy*. 3rd edn. London, 1914.

Stefanovski, Mirjana, *Ideja hrvatskog državnog prava i stvaranje Jugoslavije*. 2nd edn. Belgrade, 2008.

Stein, Lorenz von, *Lehrbuch der Finanzwissenschaft: Als Grundlage für Vorlesungen und Selbststudium mit Vergleichung der Finanzsysteme und Finanzgesetze von England, Frankreich, Deutschland, Oesterreich und Rußland*. 3rd edn. Leipzig, 1875.

Stein, Lorenz von, *Lehrbuch der Finanzwissenschaft*. Part 1: *Die Finanzverfassung Europas mit specieller Vergleichung Englands, Frankreichs, Deutschlands, Österreichs, Italiens, Rußlands und anderer Länder*. 5th edn. Leipzig, 1885.

Steinbach, Gustav, Die bosnische Verfassung. *Jahrbuch des öffentlichen Rechts der Gegenwart*, 4 (1910), 479–95.

Stekl, Hannes, Zwischen Machtverlust und Selbstbehauptung: Österreichs Hocharistokratie vom 18. bis ins 20. Jahrhundert. In Geschichte und Gesellschaft. Sonderheft Vol. 13, Europäischer Adel 1750–1950 (1990), 144–165.

Stenographischer Bericht über die Verhandlungen der am 28. August 1848 in Teplitz im Namen deutscher Städte, Gemeinden und konstitutioneller Vereine Böhmens zusammengekommenen Vertrauensmänner. Leitmeritz, 1848.

Stenographisches Protokoll der Enquete über die Landesfinanzen 7. bis 12. März 1908. Vienna, 1908.

Stenographisches Protokoll der Enquete über die Reform der Gebäudesteuer. Vienna, 1904.

Stenographisches Protokoll über die am 16., 17. und 18. Februar 1905 im niederösterreichischen Landhause zu Wien abgehaltene Konferenz der Landesausschüsse der im Reichsrate vertretenen Königreiche und Länder betreffend die Regelung der Landesfinanzen. Vienna, 1905.

Stenographisches Protokoll über die am 27. Februar 1909 im Herrensaal des niederösterreichischen Landhauses stattgefundene Konferenz der Landesausschüsse in Angelegenheit der Landes-Bierauflage. Vienna, 1909.

Stenographisches Protokoll über die am 9. Juni 1907 im niederösterreichischen Landhause zu Wien abgehaltene Konferenz der Landesausschüsse der im Reichsrate vertretenen Königreiche und Länder betreffend die Regelung der Landesfinanzen. Vienna, 1907.

Stenographische Protokolle des Abgeordnetenhauses, Eröffnungssitzung der XXII. Session am 30.05.1917. Vienna, 1917.

Stępień, Stanisław, Borderland City: Przemyśl and the Ruthenian National Awakening in Galicia. In Hann, Christopher, and Magocsi, Paul (eds), *Galicia: A Multicultured Land*. Toronto, 2005, 55–60.

Stimmer, Gernot, Die Konsularakademie im Spannungsfeld zwischen Leistungs- und Gesinnungselite. In Rathkolb, Oliver (ed.), *250 Jahre: Von der Orientalischen zur Diplomatischen Akademie in Wien*. Innsbruck, 2004, 105–39.

Stockinger, Thomas, *Dörfer und Deputierte. Die Wahlen zu den konstituierenden Parlamenten von 1848 in Niederösterreich und im Pariser Umland (Seine-et-Oise)*. Vienna, 2012.

Stockwell, Sarah (ed.), *The Rise and Fall of Modern Empires*. Vol. 3: *Economics and Politics*. Farnham, 2013.

Stöger, Otto, Die Unfallversicherung der Arbeiter. In *Österreichs Wohlfahrts-Einrichtungen 1848–1898*. Vol. 4: *Sociale Hilfspflege*. Vienna, 1900, 8–62.

Stolarczyk, Marian, *Działalność Lwowskiej Centralnej Rady Narodowej: W świetle źródeł polskich*. Rzeszów, 1994.

Stoler, Ann Laura, Imperial Formations and the Opacities of Rule. In Calhoun, Craig, Cooper, Frederick, and Moore, Kevin W. (eds), *Lessons of Empire: Imperial Histories and American Power*. New York, 2006, 48–60.

Stollberg-Rilinger, Barbara, *Der Staat als Maschine: Zur politischen Metaphorik des absoluten Fürstenstaats*. Berlin, 1986.

Stollberg-Rilinger, Barbara, *Das Heilige Römische Reich Deutscher Nation: Vom Ende des Mittelalters bis 1806*. Munich, 2006.

Stollberg-Rilinger, Barbara, The Impact of Communication Theory on the Analysis of the Early Modern Statebuilding Processes. In Holenstein, André, Blockmans, Wim, and Mathieu, Jon (eds), *Empowering Interactions: Political Cultures and the Emergence of the State in Europe 1300–1900*. Abingdon and New York, 2009, 313–18.

Stollberg-Rilinger, Barbara, *Maria Theresia: The Habsburg Empress in her Time*. Princeton, 2021.

Stolleis, Michael, *Geschichte des öffentlichen Rechts in Deutschland*. Vol. 2: *Staatsrechtslehre und Verwaltungswissenschaft 1800–1914*. Munich, 1992.

Stolz, Otto, *Geschichte der Verwaltung Tirols. Teilstück des 2. Bandes der Geschichte des Landes Tirol*. Innsbruck, 1998.

Stölzl, Christoph, *Die Ära Bach in Böhmen: Sozialgeschichtliche Studien zum Neoabsolutismus 1849–1859*. Munich, 1971.

Stourzh, Gerald, Galten die Juden als Nationalität Altösterreichs? Ein Beitrag zur Geschichte des cisleithanischen Nationalitätenrechts. *Studia Judaica Austriaca*, 10 (1984), 73–117.

Stourzh, Gerald, *Die Gleichberechtigung der Nationalitäten in der Verfassung und Verwaltung Österreichs 1848–1918*. Vienna, 1985.

Stourzh, Gerald, Verfassung und Verfassungswirklichkeit Altösterreichs in den Schriften Georg Jellineks. In Paulson, Stanley L., and Schulte, Martin (eds), *Georg Jellinek: Beiträge zu Leben und Werk*. Tübingen, 2000, 247–60.

Stourzh, Gerald, Max Diamant and Jewish Diaspora Nationalism in the Bukovina. In Stourzh, Gerald, *From Vienna to Chicago and Back: Essays on Intellectual History and Political Thought in Europe and America*. Chicago, 2007, 190–203.

Stourzh, Gerald, The National Compromise in the Bukovina. In Stourzh, Gerald, *From Vienna to Chicago and Back: Essays on Intellectual History and Political Thought in Europe and America*. Chicago, 2007, 177–89.

Stourzh, Gerald, Die dualistische Reichsstruktur, Österreichbegriff und Österreichbewusstsein 1867–1918. In Stourzh, Gerald, *Der Umfang der österreichischen Geschichte: Ausgewählte Studien 1990–2010*. Vienna, 2011, 105–24.

Stourzh, Gerald, Länderautonomie und Gesamtstaat in Österreich 1848–1918. In Stourzh, Gerald, *Der Umfang der österreichischen Geschichte. Ausgewählte Studien 1990–2010*. Vienna, 2011, 37–67.

Stourzh, Gerald, The Ethnicizing of Politics and 'National Indifference' in Late Imperial Austria. In Stourzh, Gerald, *Der Umfang der österreichischen Geschichte. Ausgewählte Studien 1990–2010*. Vienna, 2011, 283–323.

Stourzh, Gerald, Verfassungsbruch im Königreich Böhmen: Ein unbekanntes Kapitel zur Geschichte des richterlichen Prüfungsrechts im alten Österreich (1992). In Stourzh, Gerald, *Der Umfang der österreichischen Geschichte: Ausgewählte Studien 1990–2010*. Vienna, 2011, 139–56.

Strachan, Hew, Das europäische Mächtesystem und das Habsburgerreich in der Julikrise 1914. In Rumpler, Helmut (ed.), *Die Habsburgermonarchie 1848–1918*. Vol. 11: *Die Habsburgermonarchie und der Erste Weltkrieg*. Subvol. 1: *Der Kampf um die Neuordnung Mitteleuropas*. Part 1: *Vom Balkankonflikt zum Weltkrieg*. Vienna, 2016, 133–70.

Strakosch-Grassmann, Gustav, *Geschichte des österreichischen Unterrichtswesens*. Vienna, 1905.

Strakosch-Grassmann, Gustav, *Das allgemeine Wahlrecht in Österreich seit 1848*. Leipzig and Vienna, 1906.

Strobach, Vít, *Židé—národ, rasa, třída. Sociální hnutí a 'židovská otázka' v českých zemích 1861–1921*. Prague, 2015.

Struve, Kai, *Bauern und Nation in Galizien: Über Zugehörigkeit und soziale Emanzipation im 19. Jahrhundert*. Göttingen, 2005.

Stumpp, Hans, *Die Entwicklung des Finanzausgleichs in Deutschland von 1871 bis zur Gegenwart*. University dissertation, Würzburg, 1964.

Sturm, Roland, *Föderalismus: Eine Einführung*. 2nd edn. Baden-Baden, 2010.

Sturmberger, Hans, *Der Weg zum Verfassungsstaat: Die politische Entwicklung in Oberösterreich von 1792–1861*. Munich, 1962.

Šumrada, Janez, Les principaux traits de la politique napoléonienne dans les Provinces illyriennes. In Šumrada, Janez (ed.), *Napoleon na Jadranu/Napoléon dans l'Adriatique*. Koper and Zadar, 2006, 43–58.

Sundhaussen, Holm, *Der Einfluß der Herderschen Ideen auf die Nationsbildung bei den Völkern der Habsburger Monarchie*. Munich, 1973.

Suppan, Arnold, Die Untersteiermark, Krain und das Küstenland zwischen Maria Theresia und Franz Joseph (1740–1918). In Suppan, Arnold (ed.), *Zwischen Adria und Karawanken*. Berlin, 1998, 264–350.

Świątek, Adam, *Gente Rutheni, natione Poloni: Z dziejów Rusinów narodowości polskiej w Galicji*. Kraków, 2014.

Szabad, György, Lajos Kossuth's Role in the Conceptualization of a Danubian Federation. In Romsics, Ignác, and Király, Béla K. (eds), *Geopolitics in the Danube Region: Hungarian Reconciliation Efforts 1848–1998*. Budapest, 1999, 61–97.

Szabó, István, Das ungarische Wahlrecht am Anfang des 20. Jahrhunderts. In Simon, Thomas (ed.), *Hundert Jahre allgemeines und gleiches Wahlrecht in Österreich: Modernes Wahlrecht unter den Bedingungen eines Vielvölkerstaates*. Frankfurt am Main, 2010, 277–85.

Szász, Zoltán, Banking and Nationality in Hungary 1867–1914. In Teichova, Alice, Gourvish, Terry, and Pogány, Agnes (ed.), *Universal Banking in the Twentieth Century: Finance, Industry and the State in North and Central Europe*. Aldershot, 1994, 32–43.

Szász, Zoltán, The Nation-State in a Multinational Empire. In Gerö, András (ed.), *The Austro-Hungarian Monarchy Revisited*. New York, 2009, 169–92.

Szécsen, Anton, *Drei Jahre Verfassungsstreit: Beiträge zur jüngsten Geschichte Österreichs. Von einem Ungar*. Leipzig, 1864.

Szende, Paul, Der Staatshaushalt und das Finanzsystem Österreichs und Ungarns. In Gerloff, Wilhelm, and Meisel, Franz (eds), *Handbuch der Finanzwissenschaft*. Tübingen, 1929, 191–235.

Szlanta, Piotr, Der lange Abschied der Polen von Österreich. In Rumpler, Helmut (ed.), *Die Habsburgermonarchie 1848–1918*. Vol. 11: *Die Habsburgermonarchie und der Erste Weltkrieg*. Subvol. 1: *Der Kampf um die Neuordnung Mitteleuropas*. Part 2: *Vom Vielvölkerstaat Österreich-Ungarn zum neuen Europa der Nationalstaaten*. Vienna, 2016, 813–51.

Szymczak, Damian, *Między Habsburgami a Hohenzollernami: Rywalizacja niemiecko—austro-węgierska w okresie I wojny światowej a odbudowa państwa polskiego*. Kraków, 2009.

Szymczak, Damian, *Galicyjska 'ambasada' w Wiedniu: Dzieje ministerstwa dla Galicji 1871–1918*. Poznan, 2013.

Szymczak, Damian, Österreichisches rechtspolitisches System und die Bildung der Zivilgesellschaft in Galizien in der Autonomieära 1871–1914. In Brauneder, Wilhelm, and Hlavačka, Milan (eds), *Bürgerliche Gesellschaft auf dem Papier: Konstruktion, Kodifikation und Realisation der Zivilgesellschaft in der Habsburgermonarchie*. Berlin, 2014, 281–94.

Tafeln zur Statistik der österreichischen Monarchie für das Jahr 1843. Vienna, 1847.

Tafeln zur Statistik der österreichischen Monarchie für die Jahre 1847 und 1848. Vienna, 1853.

Talos, Emmerich, *Staatliche Sozialpolitik in Österreich: Rekonstruktion und Analyse*. Vienna, 1981.

Tänzer, Aron, *Die Geschichte der Juden in Tirol und Vorarlberg*. Vols. 1–2: *Geschichte der Juden in Hohenems und im übrigen Vorarlberg*. Meran, 1905.

Taylor, Miles, The British Empire in the Age of Nationalism 1815–1871. In Hirschhausen, Ulrike von, and Leonhard, Jörn (eds), *Nationalismen in Europa. West- und Osteuropa im Vergleich*. Göttingen, 2001, 117–32.

Techet, Peter, Gewaltmomente unter ländlichen Katholiken in der späten Habsburgermonarchie: Kirchenstreit in Ricmanje bei Triest. In Bouwers, Evelyn (ed.), *Glaubenskämpfe: Katholiken und Gewalt im 19. Jahrhundert*. Göttingen, 2019, 117–40.

Telesko, Werner, *Geschichtsraum Österreich: Die Habsburger und ihre Geschichte in der bildenden Kunst des 19. Jahrhunderts*. Vienna, 2006.

Telesko, Werner, *Kulturraum Österreich: Die Identität der Regionen in der bildenden Kunst des 19. Jahrhunderts*. Vienna, 2008.

Telle, Hans Günter, *Das österreichische Problem im Frankfurter Parlament im Sommer und Herbst 1848*. Marburg, 1933.

Teslaru-Born, Alina, *Ideen und Projekte zur Föderalisierung des Habsburgischen Reiches mit besonderer Berücksichtigung Siebenbürgens 1848–1918*. University dissertation, Frankfurt am Main, 2006.

Tezner, Friedrich, *Der österreichische Kaisertitel, das ungarische Staatsrecht und die ungarische Publicistik*. Vienna, 1899.

Tezner, Friedrich, *Die Wandlungen der österreichisch-ungarischen Reichsidee. Ihr Inhalt und ihre politische Notwendigkeit*. Vienna, 1905.

Tezner, Friedrich, *Österreichisches Staatsrecht*. Vol. 2: *Die Volksvertretung*. Vienna, 1912.

Thadden, Rudolf von, Kaudelka, Steffen, and Serrier, Thomas (eds), *Europa der Zugehörigkeiten: Integrationswege zwischen Ein- und Auswanderung*. Göttingen, 2007.

Thronrede vom 19. Juni 1907. Beilage 1 zu den Stenographischen Protokollen des Abgeordnetenhauses der 18. Session, 1–4. Vienna.

Ther, Philip, Die Grenzen des Nationalismus: Der Wandel von Identitäten in Oberschlesien von der Mitte des 19. Jahrhunderts bis 1939. In Hirschhausen, Ulrike von, and Leonhard, Jörn (eds), *Nationalismen in Europa: West- und Osteuropa im Vergleich*. Göttingen, 2001, 323–46.

Thun, Leo, *Die Stellung der Slowaken in Ungarn*. Prague, 1843.

Tiebout, Charles M., A Pure Theory of Local Expenditures. *Journal of Political Economy*, 64/5 (1956), 416–24.

Timon, Ákos von, *Ungarische Verfassungs- und Rechtsgeschichte mit Bezug auf die Rechtsentwicklung der westlichen Staaten*. Berlin, 1904.

Tomac, Elza, Die sozialdemokratische Partei in Kroatien und die Krise des Dualismus Österreich-Ungarns vom Jahre 1903 bis zum 1. Weltkrieg. In Hitchins, Keith (ed.), *Studies in East European Social History*. Leiden, 1977, 43–65.

Toman, Hugo, *Das böhmische Staatsrecht und die Entwickelung der österreichischen Reichsidee vom Jahre 1527 bis 1848: Eine rechtsgeschichtliche Studie*. Prague, 1872.

Tombs, Robert, The Political Trajectory of Nationalism in France. In Hirschhausen, Ulrike von, and Leonhard, Jörn (eds), *Nationalismen in Europa: West- und Osteuropa im Vergleich*. Göttingen, 2001, 133–53.

Tönsmeyer, Tatjana, *Adelige Moderne. Großgrundbesitz und ländliche Gesellschaft in England und Böhmen 1848–1918*. Vienna, 2012.

Tortella, Gabriel, Education and Economic Development since the Industrial Revolution: A Summary Report (The Less Developed Countries). In Tortella, Gabriel (ed.), *Education and Economic Development since the Industrial Revolution*. València, 1990, 3–45.

Traugott, Mark, *The Insurgent Barricade*. Berkeley, CA, 2010.

Treichel, Eckhardt, Einleitung. In *Quellen zur Geschichte des Deutschen Bundes*. Vol. 2: *Organisation und innere Ausgestaltung des Deutschen Bundes 1815–1819*. Munich, 2016, pp. lxv–lxxv.

Troebst, Stefan, 'Hochverehrter Meister und Genosse!': Karl Kautsky und die sozialistische Bewegung in Bulgarien (1887–1934). In Troebst, Stefan, *Zwischen Arktis, Adria und Armenien: Das östliche Europa und seine Ränder. Aufsätze, Essays und Vorträge 1983–2016*. Cologne, 2017, 89–99.

Turczynski, Emanuel, *Konfession und Nation: Zur Frühgeschichte der serbischen und rumänischen Nationsbildung*. Düsseldorf, 1976.

Turij, Oleh, Ukraińsko-polskie pogranicze i problem podziału Galicji w połowie XIX wieku. In Półćwiartek, Józef (ed.), *Sąsiedztwo. Osadnictwo na pograniczu etnicznym polsko-ukraińskim w czasach nowożytnych*. Rzeszów, 1997, 111–20.

Turij, Oleh, *Holovna Rus'ka Rada 1848–1851: Protokoly zasidan' i knyha korespondencii̇̈*. Lviv, 2002.

Ucakar, Karl, *Demokratie und Wahlrecht in Österreich: Zur Entwicklung von politischer Partizipation und staatlicher Legitimationspolitik*. Vienna, 1985.

Ulbrich, Josef, *Die rechtliche Natur der österreichisch-ungarischen Monarchie*. Vienna, 1879.

Ulbrich, Josef, *Lehrbuch des österreichischen Staatsrechts*. Vienna, 1883.

Ulbrich, Josef, *Das österreichische Staatsrecht*. 3rd edn. Tübingen, 1909.

Ullmann, Anton, Die Krankenanstalten Österreichs diesseits der Leitha in den Jahren 1848–1898. In *Österreichs Wohlfahrts-Einrichtungen*. Vol. 3: *Gesundheitspflege*. Vienna, 1900, 249–62.

Ullmann, Hans-Peter, *Der deutsche Steuerstaat: Geschichte der öffentlichen Finanzen vom 18. Jahrhundert bis heute*. Munich, 2005.

Umbach, Maiken (ed.), *German Federalism: Past, Present, Future.* Basingstoke, 2002.

Ungureanu, Constantin, Mittelschulen und höhere Lehranstalten in der Bukowina vor 1918: Nationen, Sprachen und Geschlechter. Ein statistischer Überblick. In Winkler, Markus (ed.), *Partizipation und Exklusion: Zur Habsburger Prägung von Sprache und Bildung in der Bukowina 1848–1918–1940.* Regensburg, 2015, 115–28.

Unowsky, Daniel, Reasserting Empire: Habsburg Imperial Celebrations after the Revolutions of 1848–1849. In Bucur, Maria, and Wingfield, Nancy M. (eds), *Staging the Past: The Politics of Commemoration in Habsburg Central Europe 1848 to the Present.* West Lafayette, IN, 2001, 12–45.

Unowsky, Daniel, Dynastic Symbolism and Popular Patriotism: Monarchy and Dynasty in Late Imperial Austria. In Leonhard, Jörn, and Hirschhausen, Ulrike von (eds), *Comparing Empires.* Göttingen, 2011, 237–65.

Urban, Karl, *Die Finanzen der territorialen Selbstverwaltungskörper in Österreich mit besonderer Berücksichtigung Böhmens.* Vienna, 1904.

Urban, Otto, *Die tschechische Gesellschaft 1848–1918.* 2 vols. Vienna, 1994.

Urban, Otto, *Kroměřížský sněm 1848–1849.* Prague, 1998.

Urbanitsch, Peter, Bürgerliche Eliten, Modernisierung und Wertewandel in Klein- und Mittelstädten Cisleithaniens. In Fasora, Lukáš, Hanuš, Jiří, and Malíř, Jiří (eds), *Občanské elity a obecní samospráva 1848–1948.* Brno, 2005, 49–65.

Urbanitsch, Peter, Die nationalen Ausgleichsversuche in den Ländern Cisleithaniens in den Jahren vor dem Ersten Weltkrieg: Gemeinsamkeiten und Unterschiede. In Fasora, Lukáš, Hanuš, Jiří, and Malíř, Jiří (eds), *Moravské vyrovnání z roku 1905: Možnosti a limity národnostního smíru ve střední Evropě.* Brno, 2006, 43–58.

Urbanitsch, Peter, The High Civil Service Corps in the Last Period of the Multi-Ethnic Empire between National and Imperial Loyalties. *Historische Sozialforschung/Historical Social Research,* 33/2 (2008), 193–213.

Urbanitsch, Peter, Das Schulwesen in Cisleithanien—Element eines kooperativen Imperiums? In Osterkamp, Jana (ed.), *Kooperatives Imperium: Politische Zusammenarbeit in der späten Habsburgermonarchie.* Göttingen, 2018, 95–115.

Urfus, Valentin, Die Ausprägung der Idee des historischen böhmischen Staatsrechtes in den sechziger Jahren des 19. Jahrhunderts und der österreichisch-ungarische Dualismus. In Holotík, L'udovít (ed.), *Der österreichisch-ungarische Ausgleich 1867.* Bratislava, 1971, 545–54.

Valentić, Mirko, Das Eisenbahnnetz in der Militärgrenze: Pläne und Verwirklichung. In Plaschka, Richard G., Drabek, Anna M., and Zaar, Birgitta (eds), *Eisenbahnbau und Kapitalinteressen in den Beziehungen der österreichischen mit den südslawischen Ländern.* Vienna, 1993, 99–131.

Valentin, Veit, *Geschichte der deutschen Revolution von 1848–49.* 2 vols. Berlin, 1930.

Varga, Bálint, The Making and Unmaking of an Austrian Space of Historical Scholarship 1848–1914. *East Central Europe,* 44/2–3 (2017), 341–66.

Varga, Bálint, Writing Imperial History in the Age of High Nationalism: Imperial Historians on the Fringes of the Habsburg Monarchy. *European Review of History/Revue européenne d'histoire,* 24/1 (2017), 80–95.

Vári, András, *Herren und Landwirte: Ungarische Aristokraten und Agrarier auf dem Weg in die Moderne 1821–1910.* Wiesbaden, 2008.

Vec, Miloš, From the Congress of Vienna to the Paris Peace Treaties of 1919. In Fassbender, Bardo, and Peters, Anne (eds), *The Oxford Handbook of the History of International Law.* Oxford, 2012, 654–78.

Vego, Milan N., *Austro-Hungarian Naval Policy 1904–14.* London, 1996.

Velek, Luboš, Národnostní vyrovnání jako cesta k soužití dvou národů v jedné země? Několik otázek souvisejících s pokusy o vyrovnání v Čechách 1870–1918. In Fasora, Lukáš, Hanuš, Jiří, and Malíř, Jiří (eds), *Moravské vyrovnání z roku 1905: Možnosti a limity národnostního smíru ve střední Evropě.* Brno, 2006, 309–18.

Velek, Luboš, Böhmisches Staatsrecht auf 'weichem Papier': Tatsache, Mythos und ihre symbolische Bedeutung in der tschechischen politischen Kultur. Bohemia, 47/1 (2007), 103–18.

Velek, Luboš, Úvod. Projekt česko-německého národnostního vyrovnání v Čechách v letech 1890–1915 a jeho geneze. In Drašarová, Eva, Horský, Roman, Šouša, Jiří, and Velek, Luboš (eds), *Promarněná šance: Edice dokumentů k česko-německému vyrovnání před první světovou válkou. Korespondence a protokoly 1911–1912.* Vol. 1. Prague, 2008, 3–42, 43–91.

Velek, Luboš, Die Idee des allgemeinen Wahlrechts im politischen Lager der tschechischen Liberalen 1861–1914. In Simon, Thomas (ed.), *Hundert Jahre allgemeines und gleiches Wahlrecht in Österreich.* Frankfurt am Main, 2010, 213–54.

Velek, Luboš, Die tschechischen bürgerlichen Parteien im Weltkrieg 1914–1918. In Heeresgeschichtlichen Museum Wien (ed.), *Der Erste Weltkrieg und der Vielvölkerstaat.* Vienna, 2012, 165–78.

Velková, Alice, and Velek, Luboš, Vnímání národnostní identity u venkovského obyvatelstva v Čechách na začátku 19. století. In Velková, Alice, Velek, Luboš, and Pokorný, Jiří (eds), *Nacionalismus, společnost a kultura ve střední Evropě 19. a 20. století. Pocta Jiřímu Kořalkovi k 75. narozeninám/Nationalismus, Gesellschaft und Kultur in Mitteleuropa im 19. und 20. Jahrhundert. Festschrift für Jiří Kořalka zum 75. Geburtstag.* Prague, 2007, 39–51.

Vencovský, František (ed.), *Dějiny bankovnictví v českých zemích.* Prague, 1999.

Verhandlungen der Enquete betreffend die Förderung des Blindenfürsorgewesens. Vienna, 1909.

Verosta, Stephan, *Theorie und Realität von Bündnissen: Heinrich Lammasch, Karl Renner und der Zweibund 1897–1914.* Vienna, 1971.

Verosta, Stephan, and Seidl-Hohenveldern, Ignaz (eds), *Die völkerrechtliche Praxis der Donaumonarchie von 1859 bis 1918: Eine Auswahl von Dokumenten.* Vol. 1. Vienna, 1996.

Vick, Brian E., *Defining Germany: The 1848 Frankfurt Parliamentarians and National Identity.* Cambridge, MA, 2002.

Vietor, Martin, Die Stellung der ungarischen Komitate in den Jahren 1860–1867. In Kovács, Kálmán (ed.), *Entwicklung der städtischen und regionalen Verwaltung in den letzten 100 Jahren in Mittel- und Osteuropa.* Vol. 2. Budapest, 1979, 375–408.

Viroszil, Anton, *Jus publicum regni Hungariae a primordiis hujus regni usque ad recentissima tempora ordine scientifico deductum.* 6 vols. Buda, 1850–4.

Viroszil, Anton, *Das Staatsrecht des Königreichs Ungarn: Vom Standpunkte der Geschichte und der vom Beginn des Reiches bis zum Jahre 1848 bestandenen Landes-Verfassung.* 3 vols. Pest, 1865–6.

Vocelka, Karl, *Glanz und Untergang der höfischen Welt: Repräsentation, Reform und Reaktion im habsburgischen Vielvölkerstaat.* Vienna, 2001.

Vodopiviec, Peter, Sympathisanten und Gegner der französischen Regierung in Krain. In Fräss-Ehrfeld, Claudia (ed.), *Napoleon und seine Zeit.* Klagenfurt, 2009, 209–24.

Von Hagen, Mark, The Russian Empire. In Von Hagen, Mark, and Barkey, Karen (eds), *After Empire: Multiethnic Societies and Nation-Building. The Soviet Union and the Russian, Ottoman, and Habsburg Empires.* Boulder, CO, 1997, 58–72.

Von Hagen, Mark, Federalisms and Pan-Movements: Re-Imagining Empire. In Von Hagen, Mark, Burbank, Jane, and Remnev, Anatolij V. (eds), *Russian Empire: Space, People, Power 1700–1930.* Bloomington, IN, 2007, 494–510.

Von Hagen, Mark, The Entangled Eastern Front and the Making of the Ukrainian State: A Forgotten Peace—A Forgotten War and Nation-Building. In Rumpler, Helmut, and Harmat, Ulrike (eds), *Die Habsburgermonarchie 1848–1918.* Vol. 12: *Bewältigte Vergangenheit? Die nationale und internationale Historiographie zum Untergang der Habsburgermonarchie als ideelle Grundlage für die Neuordnung Europas.* Vienna, 2018, 283–319.

Von Hagen, Mark, and Barkey, Karen (eds), *After Empire: Multiethnic Societies and Nation-Building. The Soviet Union and the Russian, Ottoman, and Habsburg Empires.* Boulder, CO, 1997.

Vrankić, Petar, *Religion und Politik in Bosnien und der Herzegowina 1878–1918.* Paderborn, 1998.

Vushko, Iryna, *The Politics of Cultural Retreat: Imperial Bureaucracy in Austrian Galicia 1772–1867.* New Haven, 2015.

Wadl, Wilhelm, *Liberalismus und soziale Frage in Österreich: Deutschliberale Reaktionen und Einflüsse auf die frühe österreichische Arbeiterbewegung 1867–1879.* Vienna, 1987.

Wagner, Adolph, *Finanzwissenschaft*. Vol. 1: *Einleitung, Ordnung der Finanzwirthschaft, Finanzbedarf, Privaterwerb*. 2nd edn. Leipzig and Heidelberg, 1877.

Wahl, Rainer, Die Entwicklung des deutschen Verfassungsstaats bis 1866. In Wahl, Rainer, *Verfassungsstaat, Europäisierung, Internationalisierung*. Frankfurt am Main, 2003, 277–319.

Waitz, Georg, *Grundzüge der Politik nebst einzelnen Ausführungen*. Kiel, 1862.

Wallas, Armin A., *Stände und Staat in Innerösterreich im 18. Jahrhundert: Die Auseinandersetzung um die Gerichts- und Verwaltungsorganisation zwischen den Kärntner Landständen und der zentralistischen Reformpolitik Wiens*. Klagenfurt, 1989.

Wank, Solomon, Zwei Dokumente Aehrenthals aus den Jahren 1898/99 zur Lösung der inneren Krise in Österreich-Ungarn. *Mitteilungen des Österreichischen Staatsarchivs*, 19 (1966), 339–62.

Wank, Solomon (ed.), *Aus dem Nachlaß Aehrenthal. Briefe und Dokumente zur österreichisch-ungarischen Innen- und Außenpolitik 1885–1912*. Part 2: *1907–1912*. Graz, 1994.

Wank, Solomon, The Habsburg Empire. In Barkey, Karen, and Von Hagen, Mark (eds), *After Empire: Multiethnic Societies and Nation-Building. The Soviet Union and the Russian, Ottoman, and Habsburg Empires*. Boulder, CO, 1997, 45–57.

Weber, Johann Philipp, Über die Gränzen des Landes Österreich unter der Enns. *Beiträge zur Landeskunde Oesterreichs unter der Enns*, 1 (1832), 169–204.

Wehler, Hans-Ulrich, *Modernisierungstheorie und Geschichte*. Göttingen, 1975.

Weinzierl, Erika, Revolution und Demokratisierung in Österreich. In Ableitinger, Alfred (ed.), *Demokratisierung und Verfassung in den Ländern 1918–1920*. Vienna, 1983, 18–28.

Welan, Manfried, and Ebner, Paulus, Die k.k. Hochschule für Bodencultur 1872–1918. In Welan, Manfried (ed.), *Die Universität für Bodenkultur Wien: Von der Gründung in die Zukunft 1872–1997*. Vienna, 1997, 21–64.

Wendelin, Harald, Schub und Heimatrecht. In Heindl-Langer, Waltraud, and Saurer, Edith (eds), *Grenze und Staat: Paßwesen, Staatsbürgerschaft, Heimatrecht und Fremdengesetzgebung in der österreichischen Monarchie 1750–1867*. Vienna, 2000, 173–346.

Wendland, Anna Veronika, *Die Russophilen in Galizien: Ukrainische Konservative zwischen Österreich und Rußland 1848–1915*. Vienna, 2001.

Wenzlhuemer, Roland, The Development of Telegraphy, 1870–1900: A European Perspective on a World History Challenge. *History Compass*, 5 (2007), 1720–42.

Wenzlhuemer, Roland, *Connecting the Nineteenth-Century World: The Telegraph and Globalization*. Cambridge, 2013.

Werth, Paul W., Imperiology and Religion: Some Thoughts on a Recent Agenda. In Matsuzato, Kimitako (ed.), *Towards Imperiology: From Empirical Knowledge to Discussing the Russian Empire*. Sapporo, 2007, 51–67.

Wertheimer, Eduard von, *Graf Julius Andrássy: Sein Leben und seine Zeit*. Vol. 1: *Bis zur Ernennung zum Minister des Äusseren*. Stuttgart, 1910.

Wesselényi, Nicolaus, *Eine Stimme über die ungarische und slavische Nationalität*. Leipzig, 1844.

Wettengel, Michael, Parteibildung in Deutschland: Das politische Vereinswesen in der Revolution von 1848. In Dowe, Dieter, Haupt, Heinz-Gerhard, and Langewiesche, Dieter (eds), *Europa 1848. Revolution und Reform*. Bonn, 1998, 701–37.

Wheatley, Natasha, The Life and Death of States: Central Europe and the Transformation of Modern Sovereignty. Princeton, 2023.

Wiederin, Ewald, *Bundesrecht und Landesrecht: Zugleich ein Beitrag zu Strukturproblemen der bundesstaatlichen Kompetenzverteilung in Österreich und in Deutschland*. Vienna, 1995.

Wienfort, Monika, Ländliche Rechtsverfassung und bürgerliche Gesellschaft: Patrimonialgerichtsbarkeit in den deutschen Staaten 1800–1855. *Der Staat*, 33/2 (1994), 207–39.

Wierer, Rudolf, *Der Föderalismus in Donauraum*. Graz, 1960.

Wigard, Franz (ed.), *Stenographischer Bericht über die Verhandlungen der Deutschen Constituirenden Nationalversammlung zu Frankfurt am Main*. Vol. 4. Frankfurt am Main, 1848.

Wigard, Franz (ed.), *Stenographischer Bericht über die Verhandlungen der Deutschen Constituirenden Nationalversammlung zu Frankfurt am Main*. Vol. 6. Frankfurt am Main, 1849.

Wigard, Franz (ed.), *Stenographischer Bericht über die Verhandlungen der Deutschen Constituirenden Nationalversammlung zu Frankfurt am Main*. Vol. 8. Frankfurt am Main, 1849.

Wiggermann, Frank, *K. u. k. Kriegsmarine und Politik: Ein Beitrag zur Geschichte der italienischen Nationalbewegung in Istrien*. Vienna, 2004.

Wilson, Kathleen (ed.), *A New Imperial History: Culture, Identity, and Modernity in Britain and the Empire, 1660–1840*. Cambridge, 2004.

Windler, Christian, *La diplomatie comme expérience de l'autre: Consuls français au Maghreb 1700–1840*. Geneva, 2002.

Wippermann, Wolfgang, 'Gesunder Volksegoismus': Vorgeschichte, Verlauf und Folgen der Polendebatte in der Paulskirche. In Timmermann, Heiner (ed.), *1848: Revolution in Europa. Verlauf, politische Programme, Folgen und Wirkungen*. Berlin, 1999, 351–65.

Wistrich, Robert S., *Socialism and the Jews*. London and Toronto, 1982.

Wistrich, Robert S., *The Jews of Vienna in the Age of Franz Joseph*. Oxford, 2006.

Witt, Peter-Christian, *Die Finanzpolitik des Deutschen Reiches von 1903 bis 1913: Eine Studie zur Innenpolitik des Wilhelminischen Deutschland*. Hamburg, 1970.

Witt, Peter-Christian, Reichfinanzen und Rüstungspolitik 1898–1914. In Schottelius, Herbert, and Deist, Wilhelm (eds), *Marine und Marinepolitik im kaiserlichen Deutschland 1871–1914*. Düsseldorf, 1981, 146–75.

Wodička, Wilhelm, *Die Bodenmeliorationen: Ihre Durchführungsorganisation und Finanzirung*. Vienna, 1898.

Wolf, Christiane, Representing Constitutional Monarchy in Late 19th and Early 20th-Century Britain, Germany, and Austria. In Cole, Laurence, and Unowsky, Daniel L. (eds), *The Limits of Loyalty: Imperial Symbolism, Popular Allegiances, and State Patriotism in the Late Habsburg Monarchy*. New York, 2007, 199–222.

Wolf, Franz, *Die Tulpenbewegung in Ungarn: Wirtschaftliche und politische Auseinandersetzungen zwischen Österreich und Ungarn*. Vienna, 1979.

Wolff, Larry, *The Idea of Galicia: History and Fantasy in Habsburg Political Culture*. Stanford, CA, 2010.

Wollstein, Günter, *Das 'Großdeutschland' der Paulskirche: Nationale Ziele in der bürgerlichen Revolution 1848/49*. Düsseldorf, 1977.

Wollstein, Günter, Die Oktoberdebatte der Paulskirche. In Jaworski, Rudolf, and Luft, Robert (eds), *1848/49 Revolutionen in Ostmitteleuropa*. Munich, 1996, 279–302.

Worte eines Lombarden an die Deutschen. Frankfurt am Main, 1848.

Wozniak, Peter, Professionalisation and Nationalism in a Career Group: Secondary School Teachers in Galicia 1849–1914. In McClelland, Charles E., Merl, Stephan, and Siegrist, Hannes (eds), *Professionen im modernen Osteuropa/Professions in modern Eastern Europe*. Berlin, 1995, 235–61.

Wullschleger, Marion, 'Gut österreichische Gesinnung': Imperiale Identitäten und Reichsbilder der letzten österreichischen Statthalter in Triest (1904–1918). In Buchen, Tim, and Rolf, Malte (eds), *Eliten im Vielvölkerreich: Imperiale Biographien in Russland und Österreich-Ungarn (1850–1918)*. Oldenbourg, 2015, 90–106.

Wysocki, Josef, *Infrastruktur und wachsende Staatsausgaben: Das Fallbeispiel Österreich 1868–1913*. Stuttgart, 1975.

Wysocki, Josef, Die Wirtschaft Salzburgs im 19. Jahrhundert. In Dopsch, Heinz, and Spatzenegger, Hans (eds), *Geschichte Salzburgs: Stadt und Land*. Vol. 2/4. Salzburg, 1991, 2713–42.

Zacek, Joseph F., Palacký and the Austro-Hungarian Compromise of 1867. In Holotík, L'udovít (ed.), *Der österreichisch-ungarische Ausgleich 1867*. Bratislava, 1971, 555–73.

Žáček, Václav, *Čechové a poláci roku 1848: Studie k novodobým politickým stykům česko-polským*. 2 vols. Prague, 1947, 1948.

Žáček, Václav, *Slovanský sjezd v Praze roku 1848: Sbírka dokumentů*. Prague, 1958.

Zahra, Tara, *Kidnapped Souls. National Indifference and the Battle for Children in the Bohemian Lands, 1900–1948*. Ithaca, NY, and London, 2008.

Zahra, Tara, Imagined Noncommunities: National Indifference as a Category of Analysis. *Slavic Review*, 69/1 (2010), 93–119.

Zeithammer, Antonín Otakar, *Zur Geschichte der böhmischen Ausgleichsversuche 1865–1871*. 2 vols. Prague, 1912, 1913.

Zerback, Ralf, Einleitung. In *Quellen zur Geschichte des Deutschen Bundes*. Vol. 1: *Reformpläne und Repressionspolitik 1830–1834*. Munich, 2003, pp. xi–xlix.

Ziblatt, Daniel, *Structuring the State: The Formation of Italy and Germany and the Puzzle of Federalism*. Princeton, 2006.

Zimmer, Oliver, *Nationalism in Europe 1890–1940*. Basingstoke, 2003.

Zimmermann, Susan, Das Geschlecht der Fürsorge: Kommunale Armen- und Wohlfahrtspolitik in Budapest und Wien 1870–1914. *L'Homme*, 5/2 (1994), 19–40.

Zimmermann, Susan, Armen- und Sozialpolitik in Ungarn im Vergleich zu Österreich. In Rumpler, Helmut, and Urbanitsch, Peter (eds), *Die Habsburgermonarchie 1848–1918*. Vol. 9: *Soziale Strukturen*. Part 1: *Von der Feudal-Agrarischen zur Bürgerlich-industriellen Gesellschaft*. Subvol. 2: *Von der Stände- zur Klassengesellschaft*. Vienna, 2010, 1465–1535.

Žolger, Ivan, *Der staatsrechtliche Ausgleich zwischen Österreich und Ungarn*. Leipzig, 1911.

Žolger, Ivan, Die staatsrechtlichen Grundlagen der Wehrmacht Österreich-Ungarns. *Österreichische Zeitschrift für öffentliches Recht*, 2/5–6 (1915/16), 525–615.

Zückert, Martin, Imperial War in the Age of Nationalism: The Habsburg Monarchy and the First World War. In Leonhard, Jörn, and Hirschhausen, Ulrike von (eds), *Comparing Empires: Encounters and Transfers in the Long Nineteenth Century*. Göttingen, 2012, 500–17.

Županič, Jan, Horčička, Václav, and Králová, Hana, *Na rozcestí: Rakousko-uherská zahraniční služba v posledních letech existence monarchie*. Prague, 2009.

Index of Names

For the benefit of digital users, indexed terms that span two pages (e.g., 52–53) may, on occasion, appear on only one of those pages.

Index of Places

For the benefit of digital users, indexed terms that span two pages (e.g., 52–53) may, on occasion, appear on only one of those pages.

The manufacturer's authorised representative in the EU for product
safety is Oxford University Press España S.A. of El Parque Empresarial
San Fernando de Henares, Avenida de Castilla, 2 - 28830 Madrid
(www.oup.es/en or product.safety@oup.com). OUP España S.A. also acts
as importer into Spain of products made by the manufacturer.
Printed and bound by CPI Group (UK) Ltd, Croydon, CR0 4YY
29/09/2026
02224922-0011